HANDBOOK
OF ORAL HISTORY

Handbook of Oral History

EDITED BY
THOMAS L. CHARLTON, LOIS E. MYERS, AND REBECCA SHARPLESS

ALTAMIRA
PRESS

A Division of
ROWMAN & LITTLEFIELD PUBLISHERS, INC.
Lanham • New York • Toronto • Plymouth, UK

ALTAMIRA PRESS
A division of Rowman & Littlefield Publishers, Inc.
A wholly owned subsidary of The Rowman & Littlefield Publishing Group, Inc.
4501 Forbes Boulevard, Suite 200
Lanham, MD 20706
www.altamirapress.com

Estover Road
Plymouth PL6 7PY
United Kingdom

British Library Cataloguing in Publication Information Available

Library of Congress Cataloguing-in-Publication Data

Handbook of oral history / edited by Thomas L. Charlton, Lois E.
  Myers, and Rebecca Sharpless.
    p. cm.
  Includes bibliographical references and index.
  1. Oral history.   I. Charlton, Thomas L. (Thomas Lee) II. Myers,
Lois E., 1946– . III. Sharpless, Rebecca.
  D16.14.H36 2006 2008
  907'.2—dc22   2005025536

    ISBN-13: 978-0-7591-0229-3 (cloth : alk. paper)
    ISBN-10: 0-7591-0229-5 (cloth : alk. paper)
    ISBN-13: 978-0-7591-1192-9 (pbk. : alk. paper)
    ISBN-10: 0-7591-1192-8 (pbk. : alk. paper)

Printed in the United States of America

⊖™ The paper used in this publication meets the minimum requirements of American
National Standard for Information Sciences—Permanence of Paper for Printed Library
Materials, ANSI/NISO Z39.48–1992.

Contents

Acknowledgments

Early in the planning stage for this project, we brought into the discussion some of the most authoritative scholars in the field of oral history. These individuals assisted us in the choice of topics to cover and the appropriate authors to seek for each topic. Furthermore, they lent the prestige of their names to our work, identifying with our handbook as its Editorial Board. Our appreciation, then, is twofold to these, our advisors and our friends: Albert S. Broussard, Texas A&M University; James E. Fogerty, Minnesota Historical Society; Ronald J. Grele, Columbia University; Robert Perks, British Library; Linda Shopes, Pennsylvania Historical and Museum Commission; Richard Cándida Smith, University of California at Berkeley; and Valerie Raleigh Yow, Chapel Hill, North Carolina.

The reader will recognize among our Editorial Board several of our authors, so our debt to them multiplies. Information about our authors' unique contributions to the field of oral history appears in the back of this book. Among our authors are people so closely associated in the minds of oral historians with their specific topic that our handbook would fail without their participation. To our authors, then, we express appreciation for their collective willingness to participate in this project, often at great sacrifice to their own overflowing work schedules. We thank them for putting down on paper their knowledge and experience with oral history and for patiently cooperating with us from start to finish. We are pleased that their expertise will continue to inspire best oral history practice through their contributions to this book.

All three editors are faculty members at Baylor University, Waco, Texas, with strong ties to the university's Institute for Oral History. The Institute is a freestanding program in the division of Academic Affairs, a position that allows us a broad interdisciplinary perspective. We report directly to a vice provost who is a scholar and teacher as well as administrator. In the years that we have worked on the handbook, three people have successively filled that office, granting us encouragement and resources to complete the task. We owe much to these administrators–scholars–friends: Dianna M. Vitanza, Department of English; Michael D. Beaty, Department of Philosophy; and James M. Bennighof, School of Music.

One of our greatest fortunes in the Institute for Oral History is the collegiality of our staff, whose faithful, consistent partnership allows us to pile special projects like this handbook on top of plates already overfilled. We are grateful to all of them. Becky Shulda, administrative associate, served as coordinator, handling correspondence with authors and filing articles and contracts as they arrived, always professionally, always sweetly, always quickly. Elinor Mazé, senior editor, not only provided significant editorial advice, but also willingly tackled the handbook's article on the controversial but necessary topic of transcribing. Former senior editor Kathryn Blakeman contributed editorial advice and encouragement from the start. Although she now lives hundreds of miles north of Texas, Kathryn remains one of our team in spirit and continues to help us with occasional editing and indexing projects. Leslie Roy Ballard, a doctoral candidate in philosophy at Boston College and editor at the Institute for Oral History, devoted months of his time over the past year to keeping the handbook's notes and references in conformity to the style manual. He earned well the title of editorial assistant for this handbook. Graduate students Shawn Moser, of the Department of History, and Sarah Chism Carbajal, of the School of Social Work, assisted him in tracking down and verifying notes and references. Shawn also created the first draft of the full reference list from the individual articles. The Institute's other graduate assistants and our undergraduate editorial assistants played their parts, too, particularly by keeping up with the transcribing, auditing, and editing processes so vital to our program. Several of them took time from their usual projects to re-type one of the articles for an author who has yet to surrender to the computer age. The staff members at the Baylor University Libraries, particularly Interlibrary Services, provided invaluable aid in making materials available to us.

We have learned much from our work on the handbook, and we have AltaMira Press to thank for the invitation to participate as its editors. Former editors Mitch Allen and Susan C. Walters responded to all our inquiries with patience and kindness. We are honored to have our names associated with theirs.

We believe in oral history, in its long-term significance as a means to transfer the past to the future through the voices of the present. We also believe in its immediate capacity to transform lives through the simple yet complex experience of people talking and listening to one another. Gathering these articles and making them accessible to a new generation of oral historians has been a pleasure for us, and we return now to our own oral history work better equipped to understand why we do what we do the way we do it and why that is a good thing.

Introduction

Looking for a Vade Mecum

Thomas L. Charlton

Vade mecum: "book or manual . . . for ready reference . . . commonly carried about by a person as being of some service."[1]

Awareness to Adoption

Reflecting today on my introduction to oral history as a graduate student four decades ago, I realize that the professional objectives of young historians of that generation seemed rather clear to me. We were taught to differentiate between primary and secondary sources in a dynamic discipline that was urging its followers to find consensus and common ground. At the same time, several important movements that questioned the adequacy of the discipline as a way to understand the world were stimulating historians. With an undergraduate degree in history and sociology, I was comfortable with the notion that the humanities and the social sciences could inform and strengthen each other, even intersect and blend in interdisciplinary ways. When two of my graduate mentors—the highly eclectic historians Walter Prescott Webb and Joe B. Frantz—introduced us to "history as high adventure," as Webb characterized the study of history,[2] many of my own initial thoughts about oral history became directly associated with his imperative that we cast our

1

nets widely for sources. That, in turn, led me to include a number of tape-recorded, personal interviews as integral parts of the documentation for seminar papers and a small portion of my M.A. thesis research. (I should add that our graduate professors were not hesitant to direct us to the Federal Writers' Project, and especially to the narrative interviews with former slaves in that important body of Works Progress Administration–era research and documentation.)

My next close contact with oral history as a research method came indirectly during the late '60s, when with some professional envy I watched Frantz and a group of my peers at the University of Texas at Austin organize and launch the vast, exciting oral history project on the life and times of Lyndon Baines Johnson, a far-flung research endeavor whose results would later attract so many scholars to the LBJ Library's archival collections. The earlier Franklin Roosevelt, Truman, Eisenhower, and Kennedy presidential libraries had made oral history a staple, but the Johnson library set a new, higher standard for both historians and archivists, while concurrently establishing a new university-connected model for subsequent libraries focusing on White House administrations. This new oral history project also enabled me to learn about the work of the National Archives and Records Administration (NARA), which was quite progressive in supporting oral history research and encouraging these specialized libraries and museums to reach beyond traditional archival practice.

Barely two years later, when the opportunity arose for me to collaborate with an ad hoc, interdisciplinary faculty group to establish a small, ambitious oral history "program," as we called it for a decade, at Baylor University, my time to enter oral history on a serious, ongoing basis was at hand. I eagerly joined the growing ranks of those who were ready to consider the contributions of oral historians in influencing scholarship in the United States and North America generally. (Our consideration of the needs and contributions of scholars in other parts of the world, as Ron Grele points out in his essay for this handbook, would come several years later.) Early during the 1970s, I began to allow myself to use the added, self-styled job title of "oral historian" in explaining my growing professional interests. As time permitted, more as pro bono activity than anything else at first, I also began assisting my state's historic preservation office as it adopted and explored oral history as a vital source for historic documentation and preservation related to its work under the 1966 National Historic Preservation Act. Disappointment came when oral history did not find widespread or quick acceptance among some traditional scholars in that generation and especially among some of my heroes in the historical profession.[3] Yet few of my mentor generation denied that something important was happening in many sectors of the discipline of history, in addition to a long-overdue acceptance of social history, ethnic studies, and environmental studies. Example after example of oral history provided credible scholarly evidence and broke the bounds of folklore and ethnography/cultural anthropology to become mainstream documentary sources. Those were stimulating times for me and my colleagues at Baylor and many other colleges and universities.

Democratization

Since Allan Nevins's bold call in the late 1930s for Americans to document and preserve their past through tape-recorded interviews with leaders in society,[4] the concept of oral history has grown (and spread) enormously. The practice not only invigorated huge archival holdings of NARA-related presidential libraries, stimulated higher education, and supported local and community history projects with eyewitness accounts, but it also spanned the arts and revised classroom pedagogy in secondary education. Oral history activity enriched large and small museums focused on largely under- or even undocumented peoples and cultivated documentary filmmaking that opened new understanding of important eras such as the civil rights movement and addressed important cultural themes such as American baseball. Even more important, the term *oral history* has become so "democratized," embraced, and used so freely in everyday parlance that the problem we experienced four decades ago—when but a tiny fraction of the American public could define oral history beyond that of an oral-health record taken when a person changed dentists—has largely disappeared. Today, the term *oral history* belongs to all people everywhere, and they freely exercise their right to use it in various ways, some easily understood and others somewhat vague and imprecise. Any proprietary notion that oral history belongs principally to an identifiable set of bona fide scholars who record memories of participants from selected historical events or to the trained archivists who administer tapes and transcripts and intellectual property agreements signed by interviewees misses an extremely important point: oral history, as an expression, has become ubiquitous, and moreover, it has been accepted as a normal, essential part of people's histories. It has cut across academic disciplines so many times that its *historical* research value may be exceeded at times by its enhanced, generalized research and public programming value in a dozen or more *nonhistorical* disciplines, making it now possible to argue that oral history may soon qualify as one of the most inter- or cross-disciplinary research movements (and much more!) to emerge, permeate, and shape modern cultures.

As a case in point, I now think back upon the eleven years (1975–1986) that it was my honor to edit the quarterly *Oral History Association Newsletter* very much as a halcyon time. In each issue of the newsletter, we gathered news and announced the creation of every emerging oral history project in the U.S. that we could identify, and we excitedly proclaimed the births of such projects by the hundreds in hopes of enlisting new Oral History Association members and inspiring readers to join an interdisciplinary movement that we believed needed support from enthusiastic true believers. Those were years of great interest in launching field interviewing projects for long-term archival processing and preservation. Sponsors of this innovative type of historic preservation ranged from large institutions to government agencies to corporations to secondary schools to local libraries and museums. Credit should go to the National Endowment for the Humanities for its grants and strong encouragement to fledgling oral history projects in those early years, as well as to the several dozen college faculty members who were so bold as to design and teach graduate seminars on oral history methodology. Perhaps it should be noted that those days of wild, bumptious enthusiasm appear to be over for the U.S.-based Oral History Association, which has matured into an international body that regularly publishes a scholarly journal and topical booklets for practitioners and whose standing in the historical profession in the U.S. has reached a very high level of respect.

A Vade Mecum

The task at hand is both pleasant and challenging: to provide a useful overview to the new *Handbook of Oral History*, a reference work aimed at scholars but also helpful to members of the general public with special interests in the subject. Herein both serious newcomers to oral history and veteran researchers interested in critical thinking will find answers to questions in the form of provocative essays written by a chosen body of oral historians whose careers have led them down many interesting yet somewhat divergent paths. While encompassing the breadth and scope of established oral history scholarship, the essay authors also stretch our minds to greater heights of analysis and creativity in application. As a "handbook," this compendium of essays is a fresh approach to producing a portable vade mecum (translated literally from Latin as "go with me") to travel alongside us, at elbow's length, into the research office, into graduate seminar rooms and other academic settings to stimulate discussion and shed practical knowledge, into government agencies where field historians or editors need occasional reference help, or even into the hands of community activists whose oral history pursuits seek to empower local citizen groups. So our hope is that this *Handbook of Oral History* will quickly become one of the most useful, helpful guidebooks ever published about the exciting field of oral history—a handy, highly mobile vade mecum that provides ready reference assistance and that travels conveniently alongside us for a long time.

Handbook of Oral History provides a new opportunity to bring together an interesting "faculty" of expert oral historians with readers who are in important ways both contributing to and benefiting from oral history. This book endeavors to satisfy the need for an updated history of oral history for those who wish to reconstruct a serious paper trail of scholarly writing about oral history. Of equal importance, this handbook strives to meet another need: an overarching, theoretical explication about oral history as evidence. Also, the handbook addresses both the theoretical implications and practical methodological matters involved in oral history "best practices" regarding research design, ethical and legal considerations, interviewing techniques, preservation and archival issues, and the ever-tantalizing questions raised concerning transcribing and editing oral history tapes. More direct theoretical discussions, some of which unapologetically cut across and overlap disciplinary boundaries, take the reader into current memory theory, life-stage theory, communication analysis, gender-related concepts, and broad narrative theory. Not to be overlooked is the section on applied oral history, this handbook's lagniappe, or bonus, that stimulates the reader with ideas about publishing oral history in print and other forms. This book also strives to address the needs of those who seek creative ideas about the use of oral history as artistic outcomes or artful productions and those who need new information about using oral history in sound and visual documentaries.

Like all organic projects, this reference book has evolved into something slightly different—and the editors hope much better—than originally proposed or intended. Conceptually, the handbook was supposed to have included both theoretical and practical topics pertaining to about two dozen topics deemed important to oral practitioners. Our board of editorial advisors was very helpful in identifying able and willing contributors of the essays herein presented. Together, we sought the most forward-looking oral historians and appreciators of oral history, who constantly seek new ways to understand the human condition. Some of the essays (and a few of the essayists!) proved elusive and, for a variety of reasons or circumstances, did not make it into the final collection. Thus the observant reader will note the absence of discrete essays on recording technology, including the latest, ever-changing innovations in digitization; on adaptations of oral history in the fields of education and public history; and on oral history's applications in family and community research, in social advocacy and empowerment, and in museum exhibits—all topics originally on our "must do" list.

Undaunted, the editors decided to brave criticism about these gaps and move forward, albeit with regret, when appropriate authors did not emerge for these and other important topics. Readers seeking the conceptual bases for the missing discussions, however, will find introductions to their specialized interests in the following essays and especially in the extensive reference list. Perhaps, in the true spirit of the oral history movement, such readers will then share their findings in their own essays in a future oral history vade mecum.

The Handbook at Hand

The first section of this work is called "Foundations" and features essays by two widely respected oral historians with long-time experience as directors of university oral history research centers and as active participants in U.S. and international oral history organizations. Rebecca Sharpless, the first essayist, brings to the table broad interdisciplinary research and publication in American studies, women's history, and the history of the American South. Firsthand knowledge qualifies and equips her to produce the essay tracing the history of oral history and thus providing the context for the essays to follow. Her survey of the significant literature that has defined and refined oral history thought and practice adds greatly to the important historiographical literature on oral history begun during the early 1970s by Manfred J. Waserman of the U.S. National Library of Medicine.[5] The second essay is from one of oral history's brightest theoreticians and critical (sometimes controversial) thinkers. Ronald J. Grele is a cultural historian trained at Rutgers University by Warren Susman. A veteran scholar with broad experience in both the public and private sectors, Grele is an activist who has long sought to enlarge the possibilities for oral history in serving nonelite people. His path-breaking book, *Envelopes of Sound*, oft quoted in its various editions by our *Handbook* authors, challenged practitioners to reconsider and examine anew the fundamental nature of oral history as a body of evidence evoked from human memory and sound and articulated in a reconstructive manner for later use. In the present essay, Grele organizes the theoretical foundations of oral history around two major themes in the genre's development—oral history as a source of information about the past (and therefore an archival artifact) and oral history as a means of exposing conflict (and therefore an active agent for social change)—and demonstrates ways these themes have come to coexist in recent oral history practice. He observes a transformation in the oral history literature beginning in the 1970s, with attention shifting from social history to cultural studies. Complicating the creation and interpretation of oral history evidence today, Grele contends, are considerations of such factors as interviewee–interviewer relationships, memory, myth, narrative, intersubjectivity, consciousness, ideology, and—since the subject is *oral* history—the properties of sound versus sight.

The second major section of the book, "Methodology," brings together a collection of essays on matters soon addressed by almost all new oral historians, as well as some obvious, practical subjects that continue to challenge veteran oral historians long after their "wet feet" have dried. In logical progression—from the conceptualization of a new oral history project and consideration of its legal and ethical requirements through its execution in one or more recorded interviews, the preservation and archiving of the recordings, and the extremely complex procedure of producing transcribed and edited oral memoirs—the essays chosen for this section raise issues and provide important advice for all practitioners, especially novices eager to learn from the experiences, both good and bad, of their predecessors.

The first two methodological essays highlight the all-important preparation phase of oral history interviewing. In her essay on "Research Design and Strategies," Mary A. Larson presupposes that planned oral history interviews and projects are preferable to those that are serendipitous or spontaneous. Holder of two graduate degrees in anthropology and a specialist in ethnohistory, Larson provides ample examples of some of the theoretical approaches—elite/nonelite, critical theory, grounded theory—that might direct oral history research. With more illustrations from the literature, she guides readers in ways to plan the structure of their research—topical, life history, community history, or family history—to choose interviewees and interviewers; to determine their project's scope; to research their topics and prepare early on for desirable end products and out-comes. The next essay, "Legal and Ethical Issues in Oral History," by Linda Shopes, covers two extremely important, linked areas that deserve special attention in every instance of oral history practice. Shopes, who thinks critically about both macro and micro oral history projects, upholds the promulgated, generally adopted standards of the Oral History Association, which she helped write, while also admitting that in some instances oral historians must rely on their own best judgments. Shopes demonstrates the legal necessities of informed consent, release forms, and copyright assignment, issues long recognized by oral historians but recently complicated by the availability of global publication on the World Wide Web. An authority on federal regulations governing human subjects in research, a topic particularly pertinent to university-based researchers, Shopes provides an up-to-date assessment of the matter as it relates to oral history. Ethical concerns arising out of the democratic stance of oral historians, Shopes explains, include power relationships and what she terms "overidentification" with the interviewee. In much the same vein as Grele, Shopes recognizes the "turn" of oral history to interpretive complexity, a development raising ethical issues of audience and authority.

The central methodological essay hones in on the heart of oral history research: the interview. It is impossible to summarize concisely the extent to which its author, Charles T. Morrissey, and his career have shaped the larger arena of oral history research, especially in the U.S. As archivist, author, and educator, Morrissey has shared his interviewing technique with a multitude of oral historians—both professional and amateur. In his essay, titled "Oral History Interviews: From Inception to Closure," with characteristic energy, Morrissey guides readers step by step through the interview process, using examples from his personal experiences. Having influenced the general tenets of interview practice through his prodigious research, writing, and teaching, Morrissey is extremely well qualified to speak in this volume for all who strive to become more than merely competent field interviewers.

Rounding out the methodological section of the *Handbook* are two articles answering the question: What do I do with the tape once I've recorded the interview? The essay on "Oral History and Archives: Documenting Context," by historian and archivist James E. Fogerty, reminds the reader that an oral history is first created, then archived, and at every step along the way, contextualization is part of the creation. Fogerty speaks to the creator of the oral history rather than the curator when he stresses the long-term value of documenting the full context of the interview from the outset of a project. As with any archival document, Fogerty claims, the value of an oral history tape or transcript grows with the amount of associated material also available to the researcher, from all related project files and the donor contract to photographs and various versions of the transcript indicating editorial changes. This chapter also addresses the positive and negative sides of videotaping interviews, supplies technical advice on the preservation of various formats of audio- and videotapes, outlines methods of developing finding aids for archived oral memoirs, and confronts questions raised in making oral history recordings and/or transcripts available on the World Wide Web. With expertise based on more than three decades of national-level activity in major professional associations for both archivists and oral historians, Fogerty elevates oral history to the level of important documentation that warrants our best efforts at preservation for future scholarly use. The final essay in the second section, "The Uneasy Page: Transcribing and Editing Oral History," by Elinor Mazé, complements the previous essay on preservation and archiving but, with sharp focus and a bold and prescriptive argument, brings together the body of knowledge on transcribing and editing oral history as integral parts of the internal processing of oral memoirs. Mazé's role as one of the editors for the oral historians' online discussion forum, H-Oralhist, places her in touch with inquirers from institution-based oral history projects with facilities to transcribe, edit, and index their oral history tapes, as well as persons who seek guidance in achieving high editorial standards for their personal, family, or community-level projects. For this handbook, Mazé summarizes many of the oral history transcription concepts and practices that have dotted the landscape of U.S. oral history since World War II. The question, to transcribe or not to transcribe, is serious and the intent of this essay is to help new scholars in oral history sort out some thorny issues and reach informed editorial decisions.

In the third major section of *Handbook of Oral History*—five essays on "Theories"—the reader will find both deeper consideration of issues raised in earlier essays in this reference book and important new contributions that add significantly to the literature about oral history and its cognate disciplines. Although the authors in this section come from both the humanities and social sciences, all of them are proud to be associated with oral history. Our authors apply the theories they consider mainly to the interpretation and analysis of oral history, but the ideas they raise provide insight for the entire oral history process.

In "Memory Theory: Personal and Social," labor historian Alice M. Hoffman and social psychologist Howard S. Hoffman update their earlier studies on the question of human memory and its impact on the reliability and validity of oral history interviews. Following an overview of literature on the psychology of memory as related to interviews and a brief description of lessons learned in the authors' own well-documented exercises in memory research, the Hoffmans review recent literature on the psychology of memory and make application to oral history. Thus readers consider, perhaps for the first time, the effects of time, absentmindedness, blocking, misattribution, suggestibility, bias, and persistence on the recollection and reconstruction of past events. Closely related to studies of memory in the U.S. in recent years are the forays into human development over the life span by scholars interested, either directly or tangentially, in oral history. Applying concepts and methods drawn from such research, historian Kim Lacy Rogers presents a case study based on oral history research in "Aging, the Life Course, and Oral History: African American Narratives of Struggle, Social Change, and Decline." Rogers examines ways in which life-course studies and social gerontology may help explain the recurrent themes of community deterioration and loss exposed in interviews she and colleagues conducted with African American community leaders in Mississippi Delta towns. This essay illustrates how some methods of quantification can be useful for interpreting the qualitative outcomes of oral history. Rogers provides appropriate highlights from the life histories of four of the interviewees for the Delta Oral History Project and introduces into the oral history lexicon such terms as *cohort, trajectories, transitions, careers, social stress, convoys of relationships,* and *linked lives.* The third essay on provocative theories is "A Conversation Analytic Approach to Oral History Interviewing," by interpersonal communication authority Eva M. McMahan. McMahan examines the literature on communication process and oral history, a scant body of work consisting entirely of scholarship produced by McMahan herself and a few of her close colleagues. In spite of the obvious fact that oral history is a communicative act, little discussion of communication dynamics appears in manuals on oral history interviewing. McMahan counters this lack by formulating a conversation analytic (CA) framework for interpreting oral history. From CA to oral history come concepts of the sequential order of talk and turn taking, contextualization and the question–answer complex—probing, countering, pursuing, answer and evasion, reformulation, and resistance. Researchable, transactional, two-way communication occurs in almost every instance of oral history interviewing, and McMahan draws attention to the need for more research and greater understanding of the topic among serious oral historians.

Sherna Berger Gluck is the author of the fourth theoretical essay, "Women's Oral History: Is It So Special?" The title reverses that of Gluck's highly influential, widely quoted, and often reprinted article, "What's So Special about Women? Women's Oral History." First published in 1977, that article revealed the depth of thought Gluck brings to the study of oral history by women and to the study of women through oral history. Gluck's main objective in the 1970s was to sensitize readers to the nuances of gender as they apply to the gathering and studying of oral histories generated by female scholars and to the careful study of women's history that exists in the form of oral history. In the current essay, Gluck traces contributions over the past three and a half decades to the literature on women's oral history. From the desire to give women visibility in history, the conversation on women's oral history, paralleling changes in larger philosophical arenas, deepened to include orality, intersubjectivity, and reflexivity and broadened to include contextual analysis, shared interpretation, gender, memory, and speech. In its fourth decade, women's oral history faces strong challenges, Gluck points out, including continuing concerns for advocacy and ethics as well as innovations in recording and publishing technology. Therefore, she predicts a continuing debate on the question provoked by her title.

In an effort to keep the *Handbook* on the cutting edge of oral history scholarship, the editors reached across the Atlantic to bring to the table an essay on narrative theory. In the final essay in the theoretical section, Mary Chamberlain, professor of modern history in Great Britain and authority on the life-story method, delineates the reasons behind and main spokespersons for the recent "narrative turn" in the social sciences and humanities, and its spillover into oral history methodology. She explains how the elements of time, language, and identity influence the way interviewees structure, recall, and speak about their lives. Aspects of her own cross-cultural research among peoples of the Caribbean strengthen her argument for the cultural specificity of narrative. Chamberlain proposes several methodological responses for oral historians to the "turn" to narrative theory.

The third and final major subdivision—"Applications"— explores a few representative examples of the possible outcomes of oral history research. With limitless imagination, oral historians find outlets for expressing the oral history experience and sharing it with the communities from which they sprang. As oral historians sow their work far and wide, however, they may encounter ethical and legal, methodological, and technological challenges. In the first essay in this section, "Publishing Oral History: Oral Exchange and Print Culture," cultural historian Richard Cándida Smith transports the reader into the realm of the printed word to address several important questions that have long challenged oral historians interested in seeing their work that began as either aural or video or film studies converted to print form. Smith validates the importance of oral history publications, even if print cannot convey the full meaning of the oral exchange. Following Smith's article, independent scholar and psychotherapist Valerie Raleigh Yow, author of the acclaimed text *Recording Oral History*, now in its second edition, brings the discussion of print publication to focus on biography. Yow points out the major developments in biographical and autobiographical studies in various disciplines of the humanities and social sciences. Using examples from her own work in researching and writing the biographies of novelists Betty Smith and Bernice Kelly Harris, Yow argues for the particular utility of oral history methods for biographical research. Among other things, she warns oral historians to be aware of personal and social agendas that influence biographical study and suggests inclusion of a range of narrators and a knowledge of the individual's cultural and temporal context.

The *Handbook*'s final essays carry oral history beyond the printed page to the creative realms of performance and sound and visual documentaries. In "Fractious Action: Oral History–Based Performance," dancer/choreographer/educator Jeff Friedman introduces the reader to the intersection where oral history meets and becomes art. His extensive review of literature on the theoretical foundations of performance culminates in writings on oral narrative as performance. Then Friedman provides a series of case studies or reviews illustrating a virtual explosion of diverse examples within dance, theater, and music performance genres. Friedman's essay pushes the boundaries of oral history beyond the tape and the printed page and raises important points about oral history as a visual as well as aural experience. Also thought-provoking is the final essay, "Oral History in Sound and Moving Image Documentaries," by cultural historian/oral historian/documentarian Charles Hardy III and archivist/oral historian Pamela Dean. Hardy and Dean show the progression of documentaries using sound recordings from radio to television and film to the World Wide Web. Implications arise in their discussion for collaboration between oral historians, who in their preference for the transcript over the tape often fail to achieve broadcast-quality recordings, and documentarians, who in their quest for the perfect "sound bite" often discard the full recordings. Like Friedman, Hardy and Dean review examples of sound and moving image documentaries, with particular attention to ways oral historians can conceptualize, capture, and express sound to convey information of historical and social import.

Something for almost everybody? The editors wish that were possible and true, but that would require the authors of the essays contained herein to be able to see around corners, to anticipate the questions of graduate students a decade or more into the future, to predict future "turns" in philosophical approaches to historical study, and to imagine the unimaginable in recording and publishing technology. This dilemma has encouraged the authors and the editors to produce a reference handbook that has both immediacy and some far-reaching characteristics—fully realizing that the shelf life of this or any other handbook may be much like the proof found in a pudding, unknowable until it is tasted and digested.

Notes

1. *Oxford English Dictionary Online*, s.v. "Vade mecum," http://dictionary.oed.com/entrance.dtl (accessed March 18, 2005).
2. Webb, "History as High Adventure."
3. See, for example, Tuchman, "Distinguishing the Insignificant."
4. Nevins, *Gateway to History.*
5. See Waserman, *Bibliography.*

I

FOUNDATIONS

1

The History of Oral History

Rebecca Sharpless

Oral history has its own history and as a modern movement has its roots in many locations, over many centuries. In the twentieth century, the methodology rose from several directions. Since the 1940s, however, the practice of oral history has been relatively unified in the Western academic world, with a high level of agreement on basic matters. This essay traces the historiography of oral history.

Practitioners of the modern oral history movement enjoy contemplating its ancient origins, sometimes pointing out with glee that all history was oral before the advent of writing. From the Greek side come the historians Herodotus, who employed first-person interviews in gathering information for his account of the Persian Wars in the fifth century BCE, as well as Thucydides, who interrogated his witnesses to the Peloponnesian War "by the most severe and detailed tests possible." In the Zhou dynasty of China (1122–256 BCE), the emperor appointed scribes to record the sayings of the people for the benefit of court historians. Africanists point to the *griot* tradition in recording history, in which oral traditions have been handed down from generation to generation. Historian and anthropologist Jan Vansina highlighted the Akan (Ghanaian) proverb *Tete ke asom ene Kakyere*: "Ancient things remain in the ear." In the Western hemisphere, observers point to Bernardino de Sahagùn, a sixteenth-century

Franciscan missionary to New Spain who brought together about "a dozen old Indians reputed to be especially well informed on Aztec lore so that he and his research assistants might interrogate them." Sahagùn and his colleagues produced a text and 1,850 illustrations.[1]

Despite the traditional prevalence of orally transmitted historical sources, such traditions fell into disfavor in the scientific movement of the late nineteenth century, and there arose a prejudice against oral history that remained strong for more than fifty years. Nineteenth-century German historian Leopold von Ranke, protesting moralization in history, said that the task of the historian was "simply to show how it really was (*wie es eigentlich gewesen*)," and other historians enthusiastically took up his cause.[2] Some historians, however, were never won over by the scientific approach. Californian Hubert Howe Bancroft, for example, recognized that missing from his vast collection of books, journals, maps, and manuscripts on western North America were the living memories of many of the participants in the development of California and the West. Beginning in the 1860s, Bancroft hired assistants to interview and create autobiographies of a diverse group of people living in the western part of the U.S. The resulting volumes of "Dictations" ranged from a few pages to a full five-volume memoir. Bancroft eventually entrusted his collection to the University of California at Berkeley, and it became the core of the library that bears his name.[3]

During the first third of the twentieth century, other historians began to see oral history accounts as valid. The Federal Writers' Project, part of the Works Progress Administration during the New Deal, emerged from the project administrators' democratic impulses to portray America in its cultural diversity.[4] W. T. Couch of the University of North Carolina Press decided to expand the Federal Writers' Project to collect life stories. Taking notes, the writers collected from ordinary Americans more than ten thousand first-person narratives, most of which were deposited in the Library of Congress. From this body of interviews, Couch published in 1939 a selection of interviews with ordinary Southerners as *These Are Our Lives*. Explaining his purpose, Couch wrote, "The idea is to get life histories which are readable and faithful representations of living persons, and which, taken together, will give a fair picture of the structure and working of society. So far as I know, this method of portraying the quality of life of a people, of revealing the real workings of institutions, customs, habits, has never before been used for the people of any region or country. . . . With all our talk about democracy it seems not inappropriate to let the people speak for themselves."[5] Folklorist B. A. Botkin focused on the Former Slave Narratives portion of the project in his 1945 work, *Lay My Burden Down: A Folk History of Slavery*. In his introduction, Botkin wrote: "From the memories and the lips of former slaves have come the answers which only they can give to questions which Americans still ask: What does it mean to be a slave? What does it mean to be free? And, even more, how does it *feel?*" The first-person narratives in the Federal Writers' Project answered at least in part such intimate questions.[6]

At the same time, but from a completely different vantage point, Columbia University historian Allan Nevins, formerly a "newspaperman," in 1938 decried a historical field that lacked life and energy. In his influential work *The Gateway to History*, Nevins called for a popularization of history and the creation of an organization that would make "a systematic attempt to obtain, from the lips and papers of living Americans who have led significant lives, a fuller record of their participation in the political, economic and cultural life of the last sixty years." Nevins cherished the idea of "the immense mass of information about the more recent American past . . . which might come fresh and direct from men once prominent in politics, in business, in the professions, and in other fields; information that every obituary column shows to be perishing."[7] He kept his idea and his dream alive for more than a decade during the difficult years of World War II.

American military historians used oral history extensively to gain contemporary accounts of World War II. The U.S. Army brought professionally trained historians into each theater to collect sources and write studies. A historian assigned to cover the Pacific theater, Lieutenant Colonel (later Brigadier General) S. L. A. Marshall, pioneered the army's oral history effort as he brought together participants shortly after the fighting (often within a few hours) and conducted group interviews. After the Allied invasion of Normandy in June 1944, Marshall traveled to

France to interview combatants from the 82nd and 101st Airborne Divisions. He then traveled throughout Europe collecting firsthand accounts of recent battlefield experiences. Hundreds of historians conducted similar interviews, the majority of which took place a week to ten days after the action or sometimes even later. The best-known field historian, Forrest C. Pogue, spent D-Day aboard a landing ship interviewing wounded soldiers who had participated in the assault. Historians assigned to the European theater alone collected more than two thousand interviews by the end of the war. The notes and transcripts from these endeavors eventually came to the National Archives.[8]

After World War II, Allan Nevins continued to pursue his interest in oral history research. He persuaded his friend Frederic Bancroft, a librarian with a family fortune, to leave Columbia University $1.5 million for the "advancement of historical studies." With a portion of the Bancroft funds, Nevins launched "the oral history project" at Columbia in 1948.[9]

A graduate student took notes in longhand for the first interviews, conducted by Nevins. The Columbia colleagues soon learned of a recent invention, the wire recorder, and lost no time in acquiring one. The process then moved much faster, and they began transcribing the interviews as a convenience to researchers. The first American-made tape recorders (as opposed to wire), modeled on a captured German Magnetophon, were launched in 1948, but tape recorders did not become widely available until several years later.[10]

Nevins selected the first oral history projects at Columbia because of their potential for external funding. The earliest projects included oil wildcatting, the Book-of-the-Month Club, the Ford Motor Company, and the timber industry, all chosen because of their potential to bring in payment from the corporations or individuals interviewed for the small department. The project focused on elite subjects, resulting in a group of biographies of powerful white males.[11]

As the Columbia project picked up speed, others in the United States began to employ the new recording equipment. At the University of Texas in 1952, archivist Winnie Allen organized and supervised a project to record stories of pioneers of the oil industry. Noted folklorists William Owens and Mody Boatright served as interviewers and project directors.[12] In the 1940s, the Forest History Society began taking notes on the reminiscences of veterans of the forest products industry. The society started tape recording in the early 1950s and gradually expanded its interviewee pool to include forestry educators, government employees, and conservationists.[13]

The University of California at Berkeley created its Regional Oral History Office in 1954. In the mid-1940s, George Stewart at Berkeley conceived the idea of continuing Hubert Howe Bancroft's interviews. In 1952, James D. Hart, director of the Bancroft Library, decided to interview author Alice B. Toklas, then living in Paris. After the next interviews, with the founder of the bohemian community of Carmel, California, the Berkeley program formally received funding in 1954. Willa Baum became its head in 1958 and remained so until 2000.[14] In 1959, the regents of the University of California at Los Angeles (UCLA) established the UCLA Oral History Program, upon the urging of historians, librarians, and other members of the UCLA community. Appropriately for its southern California location, the project focused strongly on the arts.[15] The first university-based oral history programs in the United States were well under way by 1960.

The National Archives of the United States began formal oral history work through the presidential libraries, starting in 1961 with the Harry S. Truman Library, in Independence, Missouri, and expanding rapidly with the John F. Kennedy Library in 1964, the Herbert Hoover Oral History Program in 1965, and the Lyndon B. Johnson and Dwight D. Eisenhower projects beginning in 1967. The presidential projects were monumental in scope and size. By 1969, the year after Lyndon Johnson left office, his oral history project already had 275 tapes.[16] The presidential projects played a crucial role in once again bringing the federal government into the oral history movement, and they also broadened the definition of political history, featuring interviews with ordinary people as well as the movers and shakers from the various White House administrations.

Throughout the 1960s, oral history research expanded dramatically. Part of this expansion was due to the availability of portable cassette recorders, first invented by the Philips Company in 1963. The philosophical underpinnings of the oral history movement, however, lay with the democratic impulses of the social history movement. The civil rights movement, protests against the Vietnam War, and the feminist movement all raised questions about American history based on the deeds of elite white men. Contesting the status quo, social historians began to explore the interests of a multiracial, multiethnic population with an emphasis on class relationships. As they sought to understand the experiences of ordinary people, historians turned to new ways of discovering the pluralistic "mind of the nation," in the words of historian Alice Kessler-Harris. Oral history, easily accessible and useful for talking with almost any type of person, became a primary tool for documenting the lives of ordinary people.[17] As Ronald Grele notes elsewhere in this volume, historians in England led the way in documenting lives of ordinary people, as Americans tended to focus their interviews on elites, but clearly a sea change was under way. Historians of the left hoped that, by giving voice to the voiceless, they could foster social change.

By 1965, the oral history movement had reached a critical mass. *Oral History in the United States*, a report published in that year by the Columbia University Oral History Research Office, identified eighty-nine oral history projects nationwide. Practitioners realized a need for standardization of practices and procedures, which Gould Colman, an archivist and oral historian at Cornell University, articulated in an article in the *American Archivist*.[18] The time seemed appropriate to call a gathering of people calling themselves "oral historians."

With the urging of Allan Nevins, James V. Mink, university archivist and director of oral history at UCLA, convened a nationwide meeting at Lake Arrowhead, California, in September 1966. Seventy-seven people came for the three-day "National Colloquium on Oral History," a lively gathering of archivists, librarians, historians, members of the medical profession, and psychiatrists from across the United States and including international participants from Lebanon. The colloquium consisted of panel discussions aimed at gaining consensus on definitions of oral history, the uses of oral history, directions for future work, techniques for interviewing, and professional objectives and standards.[19] The debates were prescient, highlighting some of the issues that would remain under discussion in oral history circles almost forty years later. In other areas, the attendees at Lake Arrowhead were able to reach consensus quickly.

The first area of consensus was on keeping the cumbersome term *oral history*. Louis Starr, the director of the Columbia oral history program, observed the phrase had "gone generic. The *New York Times* and even the *New York Daily News*, that ultimate authority, use it in lower case now."[20]

The discussions at the first meeting were lively and wide ranging. The opening discussions centered on exactly what constituted oral history—was it the tape? The transcription? Did it have to be recorded? Philip Brooks of the Truman Library argued that it did: "Now I think that a tape recorder is important enough to oral history to constitute almost a part of the definition. . . . I think I can take pretty good notes, and I could recreate pretty well what they said, but my notes do not constitute actually what they said, a record of their oral statements."[21] Brooks and like-minded colleagues carried the argument, and recording became a standard part of the definition of oral history in the U.S.

Some early programs, notably the Truman Library and Columbia University, recorded their interviews but did not believe in saving the tapes, making transcription crucial.[22] There was great worry about how to represent the memoirist in the final product: Should ungrammatical utterings be edited? What about material that the interviewee deleted from the transcript? Elizabeth Dixon of UCLA argued for destroying the tapes: "One thing is economy. You keep buying tape, and we're back to the budget again! We can't afford it. Another thing, as Dr. Brooks has said, is that many people would not give you such candid tapes, if they thought you were going to keep them forever because they may not like the way they sound on tape."[23] Louis Shores, dean of the library school at Florida State University, countered by pleading for "more serious consideration of the tape itself as a primary source. Strongly I urge that all of us who are developing oral history collections protect the master of the original tape for replaying by later researchers, and for the possibility that some new truth may be discovered from the oral original not revealed by the typescript."[24] Most programs assumed early on the right of the interviewee to close their memoirs, putting a time seal on interview materials to be made public at some future date. Some returned transcripts to the interviewees for their editing, while others wanted to let the first transcription stand in its original form. Still others destroyed their first drafts.[25] Programs varied on methods of dissemination. While some kept their transcripts as tightly controlled, rare items, the University of California at Berkeley distributed its completed transcripts to a number of selected depositories.

Underlying the arguments about the conduct of oral history programs was a deep concern with the ethics of oral history interviewing. To that end, attendees at the first oral history colloquium in 1966 vigorously debated a list of possible objectives and standards. The standards included issues over recording fidelity, verbatim transcriptions, the right of interviewees to review and change their transcripts, appropriate training of interviewers, and related materials to accompany the transcript.

The discussion of the need for a code of ethics began as early as 1967, stirred in part by William Manchester's controversial use of intimate interviews with the Kennedy family in his book *The Death of a President*. At its third meeting, in 1968, the Oral History Association adopted its first set of standards, labeled "Goals and Guidelines." The final document included three guidelines each for the interviewee and interviewer and one for sponsoring institutions. The first clearly stated the right of the interviewee: "His wishes must govern the conduct of the interview." Others stressed the mutual understanding between interviewer and interviewee regarding the conduct and outcome of the interviewing process. The "Goals and Guidelines" indicated a spirit of compromise regarding arguments about the retention of tape recordings and the need for transcription.[26] These guidelines stood unchanged for more than a decade.

As oral historians crystallized a common set of goals and standards, they worked to disseminate scholarship on oral history. The new Oral History Association, chartered in 1967, published the proceedings of its first meetings, then broadened the publication to an annual journal, titled the *Oral History Review*, in 1973.[27] Practitioners also realized the importance of spreading the gospel of high-quality oral history, and they began actively teaching others how to conduct projects according to the new standards. With funding from the Higher Education Act, for example, UCLA offered an eleven-day oral history institute in July 1968.[28] Beginning in 1970, the Oral History Association Colloquium (as the annual meetings were first called) also featured a workshop component.[29] Willa Baum, director of the Regional Oral History Office at the University of California at Berkeley, published *Oral History for the Local Historical Society*, the first how-to manual on oral history, in 1969. Numerous others soon followed.[30]

During the late 1960s and 1970s, oral history projects rode the crest of increasing grant funding for such work and fed directly into the social history movement in the United States. The National Endowment for the Humanities (NEH) and state humanities councils, founded at almost the same time as the Oral History Association (OHA), generously funded oral history projects through the early 1980s. A 1981 issue of the *Oral History Association Newsletter* listed thirty-two NEH grant awards, ranging from $400,000 to a local historical society in Nebraska to $2,500 to a youth center in Rochester, New York.[31] Funding from humanities organizations on both the national and state levels enabled academics and local communities alike to engage in oral history activities.

Oral history research reflected the social changes of the 1960s and 1970s. The growing acknowledgment of the importance of various ethnic groups in American society fueled an interest in their histories. One of the earliest such oral history endeavors was the Doris Duke project on Native American history. Between 1966 and 1972, tobacco heiress Duke gave a total of $5 million to the universities of Arizona, Florida, Illinois, South Dakota, New Mexico, Utah, and Oklahoma. The funding established multiple oral history centers to document the diversity among Native Americans, making possible interviews, for example, with members of every Native American tribe in Oklahoma. Portions of the South Dakota interviews were published in 1971 in a volume titled *To Be an Indian*.[32]

The civil rights movement gave impetus to numerous oral history projects on African American history. Noted author Alex Haley conducted numerous interviews with Malcolm X for his *Autobiography of Malcolm X*, published shortly after Malcolm X's assassination.[33] Between 1967 and 1973, Howard University gathered more than seven hundred interviews as part of its Civil Rights Documentation Project.[34] With funding from the Rockefeller Foundation, Duke University historians William Chafe and Lawrence Goodwyn between 1972 and 1982 specifically trained doctoral students as oral historians. Their interviews then created source material with which to rewrite the history of the U.S. in its multiracial complexity.[35]

Two of the most celebrated uses of oral history in African American history gained national recognition in the mid-1970s. Historian Theodore Rosengarten, conducting field research on the Alabama Sharecroppers Union, found in Ned Cobb an ideal interviewee. He conducted 120 hours of interviews with Cobb, which he published, to great critical acclaim, as *All God's Dangers: The Life of Nate Shaw*.[36] And Alex Haley traced his family's stories back to Gambia, publishing the results of his quest as *Roots: The Saga of an American Family*, which won the Pulitzer Prize. The ensuing television miniseries based on Haley's book set industry records for numbers of viewers when it aired in January 1977.

The women's movement also found oral history to be congenial to its aims. Some of the earliest work in that movement concentrated on women who had been active in the woman suffrage movement. The University of California at Berkeley interviewed leaders such as Alice Paul, while the Feminist Oral History Project, led by Sherna Gluck, focused on rank-and-file suffragists.[37] Radcliffe College launched its Black Women Oral History Project in 1976, interviewing seventy-two women of remarkable achievement.[38] Oral history proved to be a tool uniquely suited for uncovering women's daily experiences. In 1977, Gluck wrote, "Refusing to be rendered historically voiceless any longer, women are creating a new history—using our own voices and experiences. We are challenging the traditional concepts of history, of what is 'historically important,' and we are affirming that our everyday lives *are* history."[39]

Historians of labor and working-class people also realized early the potential for oral history. Between 1959 and 1963, Jack W. Skeels of the University of Michigan and the Wayne State University Institute of Labor and Industrial Relations interviewed fifty-four people to document the creation of the United

Auto Workers.[40] Labor activists Alice Lynd and Staughton Lynd interviewed rank-and-file workers about their experiences in the labor actions of the 1930s and 1940s, demonstrating that workers organized themselves rather than waiting for union officials to act.[41] Peter Friedlander relied on the memories of Edmund Kord, president of Local 229 of the United Automobile Workers in Detroit to produce an in-depth study of the founding and emergence of one union local.[42] Tamara Hareven employed numerous oral history interviews to portray life in a New Hampshire mill village in *Amoskeag: Life and Work in an American Factory-City.*[43] Across the U.S., significant archives arose containing oral histories of labor activists.

Community historians also soon realized the value of interviewing in documenting local history. With community history came attempts to "give back" history to the people. The idea also flourished that helping people record their local history would give those people efficacy in their lives, or empower them. In many locations in the United States, oral historians interviewed community members and created public programming from the interviews. Books, pamphlets, slide-tape shows, and readers theaters abounded. A typical project described in the *Oral History Association Newsletter* in 1981 was the Neighborhood Oral History Project in Lincoln, Nebraska. The project employed student interns to record the histories of Lincoln neighborhoods. Each neighborhood had a history committee that created a slide–tape presentation, and an oral historian–storyteller created stories to present to children. Director Barbara Hager expressed her hope that "through sharing cultural heritages while working on the project, participants will transfer their energies to revitalization and preservation of their neighborhoods."[44] One particularly creative, sophisticated application of oral history to community history was Project Jukebox, initiated in 1988 by the University of Alaska Fairbanks (UAF). UAF staff members conducted oral history interviews and loaded the transcripts, along with other materials, onto interactive "jukebox" players accessible to interviewees.[45]

Oral historians and folklorists also made common cause, discussing oral tradition as historical evidence. Folklorist Lynwood Montell used oral history to study a former community of mixed-blood people settling amid the white farmers in the Cumberland hills of southern Kentucky after the Civil War. In his introduction to *The Saga of Coe Ridge*, Montell makes a passionate argument for the use of oral tradition, where no written documentation exists, to produce "folk history."[46]

Such broad applications of interviewing methods unnerved traditional historians, many of whom were already uncomfortable with social history. As researchers began taking to oral history interviewing with great enthusiasm, traditionalist historians leveled criticisms at the methodology. Most notable was renowned historian Barbara Tuchman, who feared the type of history that oral sources buttressed. She compared the tape recorder to "a monster with the appetite of a tapeworm," and argued that it facilitated "an artificial survival of trivia of appalling proportions." "We are drowning ourselves in unneeded information," Tuchman said.[47]

Yet criticism of oral history also came from those who wished for more radical uses of interviewing. Historian Nathan Reingold critiqued established programs in his talk at the Oral History Association colloquium in 1969: "It would be very useful if people got away from these great men and deliberately looked for people, trends, and events that *are* largely bereft of conventional documentation." Reingold was responding to the uses of oral history in the biographies primarily of powerful white males, such as Forrest Pogue's four-volume work on General George Marshall and T. Harry Williams's study of Huey Long, which won both the Pulitzer Prize and the National Book Award.[48]

Reingold also raised the issue of validity, a concept that has continued to concern oral historians for many years: "I think you all know that if there is a contemporary letter saying one thing and an oral history saying the opposite and there are no other evidences whatsoever on this point, nine out of ten historians will take the contemporary letter."[49] Critiques such as Reingold's set up a continual challenge for oral historians: defending the reliability (the consistency with which an individual will tell the same story repeatedly) and validity (the agreement between the interview and other types of historical sources) of interviews.[50]

The expense of oral history worried some early critics. In 1967, Philip A. Crowl defended the expense of the John Foster

Dulles Oral History Project. He observed that 280 interviews, conducted over a period of three years at an expense of almost $67,000, were well worth the cost: "Oral history . . . is not meant to serve as a substitute for the documentary record. It does in fact supplement the record by producing some information not hitherto documented. But more important, it can provide guidelines to assist the historian through the jungle of data that confronts him."[51]

By the late 1960s, oral history was gaining popularity with the general public and academics alike. Chicago radio talk-show host Studs Terkel first used taped interviews in book form in *Division Street: America*, a study of seventy ordinary people in Chicago. He followed this with *Hard Times: An Oral History of the Great Depression* and *Working: People Talk about What They Do All Day and How They Feel about What They Do*. Terkel's work garnered widespread acclaim in the popular press. Terkel's methods remained in tension with the "Goals and Guidelines" of the Oral History Association, for he edited heavily and rearranged his interviews and made no provisions for archiving them.[52] Terkel nonetheless epitomized oral history for many Americans.

Another variety of oral history began when a desperate young school teacher enlisted students in his English class to gather the folklore around their home in Appalachian Georgia. The students and teacher, Eliot Wigginton, created a magazine known as *Foxfire*, which became wildly popular upon its initial publication in 1966. Doubleday published the first compilation in 1972, and it was followed by ten subsequent editions.[53] Foxfire created an intersection between oral history and pedagogy, as Wigginton used the project to teach numerous language-arts topics. The success of Foxfire gave rise to numerous other similar projects, several of which persisted into the twenty-first century.[54] It also created an industry of its own, including a 1982 Broadway play for which Jessica Tandy won a Tony Award for her portrayal of Aunt Arie Carpenter.

In 1975, the Oral History Association published a revised *Bibliography on Oral History*, enumerating ongoing work in the United States. The compiler, Manfred Waserman, observed that in 1965 there were 89 reported projects. By 1975, the number had risen to 230, with an additional 93 planned. Waserman commented, "In

1972 it was estimated that there were some 700 oral history centers in 47 states and several foreign countries. The literature on oral history, consisting of about 80 articles in 1967, more than doubled by 1971, and increased to around 300 through 1974. Publications incorporating oral history material have multiplied to the point where the presence of 'oral history' in a title is no longer uncommon." Waserman observed that the items in the bibliography were "products of oral history broadly defined and were produced by a wide spectrum of oral history practitioners extending, in the particular instance of academe, from scholars to high school students." The material varied greatly in quality and included "social, political, and cultural subject matter" as well as folklore and oral tradition. Waserman concluded, "While the merit of these works must be judged on an individual basis, this extension of the oral history phenomenon, with its publications, programs, and related literature has, nevertheless, blurred rather than defined and delineated the origins and scope of the subject."[55] As an acknowledgment of the growing appeal of the practice, the *Journal of Library History*, beginning in 1967, and *History News* (published by the American Association for State and Local History), beginning in 1973, featured regular articles on oral history.[56]

As a field of critical inquiry, oral history began to mature in the 1970s, influenced by cultural studies scholars such as Clifford Geertz. Postmodernism and oral history were well suited for one another, as oral texts easily moved away from positivism.[57] One of the first thoughtful responses to the interviewing phenomenon was "Oral History and *Hard Times*: A Review Essay," in which Michael Frisch used Studs Terkel's work to examine the nature of memory and the significance of recollecting an earlier time amid the turmoil of the 1970s. Frisch observed, "To the extent that *Hard Times* is any example, the interviews are nearly unanimous in showing the selective, synthetic, and generalizing nature of historical memory itself. . . . These capacities are shown to be not only present, but central in the way we all order our experience and understand the meaning of our lives."[58]

Ronald J. Grele edited *Envelopes of Sound: The Art of Oral History*, published in 1975. The outcome of a session at the 1973 Organization of American Historians meeting, *Envelopes of Sound* featured two major papers. One, by Grele himself, examined an interview through linguistic analysis, studied the interaction between the interview participants, and considered the cultural "problematic" brought into the interview by the subject. The second, by Dennis Tedlock, explored rendering narrative as poetry. An interview with Studs Terkel and dialogue between him and the OAH panelists, including chair Alice Kessler-Harris and commentators Jan Vansina and Saul Benison, further broadened the discussion.[59] Conversations about oral history began to move away from the literal process and the content to the theory behind the interview.

Intellectual cross-fertilization with trends in Europe, particularly England, increased in the 1970s as well. In his studies of East Anglia, George Ewart Evans argued for the relevance of oral tradition in supplementing written records.[60] Paul Thompson, oral historian at the University of Essex, published *The Voice of the Past: Oral History* in 1978, demonstrating how oral evidence can change the standard historical narrative. The development of the Oral History Society in England, which published its first journal in 1971, paralleled that of the Oral History Association in the U.S.

Even as it took on international dimensions, oral history became increasingly accessible to local and family historians. Many projects, often limited in scope, flourished in local historical societies, voluntary associations, and so on. Such projects often escaped the attention of academic historians but held deep significance for their communities of origin. As the number of practitioners grew at the grassroots level, regional and state-level oral history groups sprang up across the United States. The first, the New England Association for Oral History, began in 1974, while Oral History in the Middle Atlantic Region formed in 1976. The Michigan Oral History Council was founded in 1979. The Southwest Oral History Association was created in 1981, the Texas Oral History Association in 1982, the Northwest Oral History Association in 1983, and the Oral History Association of Minnesota in 1985. Each of these organizations fostered local history research while promulgating the highest standards of oral history practice, offering workshops, and giving awards for exemplary research.

Discussions over the nature and practice of oral history continued apace. While some issues easily coalesced into agreement, others remained contentious. In 1979, a selected group of Oral History Association members came together at the Wingspread Conference Center in Wisconsin to build upon the original "Goals and Guidelines" and to formulate a set of guidelines to "impart standards to oral history projects that were just beginning and to provide critical appraisal to established projects that wished review and advice from professional peers."[61] The resulting *Evaluation Guidelines*, an official publication of the Oral History Association, promulgated basic criteria for programs and projects. The guidelines included analyses of purposes and objectives; selections of interviewers and interviewees; availability of materials; finding aids; management, qualifications, and training; ethical and legal guidelines; tape and transcript processing guidelines; interview content guidelines; and interview conduct guidelines. The guidelines proved an invaluable touchstone for practitioners seeking to conduct interviews of the highest quality and provided a common ground for discussion.

Recording technology expanded beyond audio equipment with the appearance and spread of video recording, which appeared in professional discussions as early as 1970. Once again, oral historians debated over the nature of the product and how it changed when visual images were added to the verbal record.[62] The debate over videotaping continued into the 1980s, when the Alfred P. Sloan Foundation awarded the Smithsonian Institution funds to examine videohistory's effectiveness. By 1991, Smithsonian historians had completed more than 250 hours of tape in several different projects. Evaluator Stanley Goldberg expressed reservations about the increased administrative costs and the expense of high-quality recording, while Carlene Stephens commented on video's usefulness for documenting material objects and processes. Producer Brien Williams declared that preliminary audio interviews were critical to success. Their conclusions seemed to point to a limited but valuable role for video in oral history interviewing.[63]

Scholarship in oral history continued to mature. In 1984, Willa Baum and David Dunaway compiled and edited *Oral History:*

An Interdisciplinary Anthology. The reader brought together thirty-four germinal articles in the field, beginning with early writings by Allan Nevins and Louis Starr, and continuing with articles on interpreting and designing projects, applied oral history, the relationships with other disciplines, education, and libraries.[64] Writings on oral history became increasingly sophisticated. In 1986, Linda Shopes analyzed book reviews on oral history and concluded that a sustained critical voice was emerging.[65] Bibliographer David Henige's *Oral Historiography* (1982) investigated how oral historians shape "the past they reconstruct," looking at the role of the historian in selecting, recording, and interpreting sources.[66] In the field of communication studies, Eva McMahan and her colleagues pioneered studies in oral history as a rhetorical device, examining the interview as a communicative event and speech act.[67] Michael Frisch in 1990 published his collected essays in a volume evocatively titled *A Shared Authority: Essays on the Craft and Meaning of Oral and Public History.* Frisch's essays included thoughtful discussion of the collaboration between interviewee and interviewer.[68] In 1987, the *Journal of American History*, the quarterly publication of the Organization of American Historians, began an annual section on oral history, which was edited by Linda Shopes and Michael Frisch for ten years and then by Michael Gordon and Lu Ann Jones. The oral history section served as part of the journal's examination of resources available to historians. Over the next sixteen years, oral historians provided a mixture of topical and reflective essays designed not to be theoretical or methodological, but to "foster a more thoughtful evaluation of oral history source materials and a more self-conscious historical practice."[69]

Increasingly, American oral historians came to be influenced by scholars outside the U.S. The *International Journal of Oral History*, edited by American Ronald J. Grele, began publication in 1980, focusing on comparative approaches, cross-disciplinary or interdisciplinary approaches, and theoretical and methodological discussions, all within an international context. In 1992, the journal merged with *Life Stories* from the British Oral History Society to become the *International Yearbook of Oral History and Life Stories*, which published several thematic issues of mostly European and American scholarship in the mid-1990s.[70] The work of scholars such as Elena Poniatowska and Luisa Passerini began influencing American readers with their nuanced readings of oral interview data.[71] A group of oral historians from around the world met in Essex, England, in 1979, sharing their common interests. The group organized formally at its 1996 meeting in Göteborg, Sweden, as the International Oral History Association, held biennial meetings, and published a bilingual journal titled *Words and Silences/Palabras y Silencios*.

Historian Alessandro Portelli, whose research included Americans in Appalachia as well as his fellow Italians, published his important work *The Death of Luigi Trastulli and Other Stories* in 1991. Portelli's study of the versions of the death of steelworker Luigi Trastulli brought new questions to bear on the issues of validity and reliability in oral history. Portelli posited that the way that people remember is as important as what they remember: "Oral history has made us uncomfortably aware of the elusive quality of historical truth itself."[72] Trained in the field of literary studies, Portelli was keenly attuned to analysis of texts, and he significantly influenced the ways in which historians interpreted their sources. In the same year, Sherna Gluck and Daphne Patai edited *Women's Words: The Feminist Practice of Oral History*, a collection of thirteen essays by women in several academic disciplines. The authors reflect on personal politics, power dynamics, and race and ethnicity as well as gender. Elizabeth Tonkin's *Narrating Our Pasts: The Social Construction of Oral History* (1992) investigated the question of oral history and narrative, as Tonkin argued that narratives are both social constructions and individual performances.[73]

The breadth of oral history research continued to be one of its prime strengths. In 1988, Twayne Publishers, acknowledging the wide appeal of oral history, started its Oral History Series, edited by Donald A. Ritchie. Twenty-six books, on an expansive array of topics, appeared between 1990 and 1998, testimony to the span of the usefulness and applicability of oral history. The Twayne volumes centered around interview transcripts, carefully contextualized.[74] As gay and lesbian studies emerged in the U.S. academy, oral history again became a prime tool for documenting people and movements. Among the earliest titles in the field were Allan Berube's work on World War II soldiers, Lillian Faderman's general study of lesbians, and Elizabeth Kennedy and Madeline Davis's research on working-class lesbians.[75]

Two major manuals for oral history research appeared in the mid-1990s: *Doing Oral History*, by Donald Ritchie, and *Recording Oral History*, by Valerie Yow. Both books, each excellent in its own way, demonstrate the consensus that oral historians shared regarding standards and methods, the differences in approaches, and the vast possibilities for applications.[76] In 1998, British historians Robert Perks and Alistair Thomson pulled together much of the best scholarship of the late twentieth century into *The Oral History Reader*, considering critical developments, interviewing, advocacy and empowerment, interpretation, and "making histories."[77]

In the mid-1990s, technological issues took center stage as digital recording raised anew issues of representation of the interviewee's voice.[78] The issue of accessibility, widely discussed since the late 1960s, became even more pressing as the World Wide Web made possible unlimited distribution of oral history transcripts and sound files.[79] The Internet and e-mail also made possible digital exchanges between oral historians. Terry Birdwhistell of the University of Kentucky launched an Internet discussion list, OHA-L in 1993. It became affiliated with the rapidly growing organization known as H-Net in 1997 under the name H-Oralhist. Almost two thousand subscribers worldwide can communicate electronically about issues of mutual interest. The Internet has also facilitated a massive oral history initiative by the Library of Congress: the Veterans History Project. Spurred by the loss of World War II veterans, the project enlists volunteers nationwide to conduct interviews and deposit them in the Library of Congress. By May 2003, more than seven thousand interviews had been submitted to the project.[80]

Oral historians have long been concerned with issues of memory, particularly how people remember and what shapes their memories. Early works by Michael Kammen and John Bodnar raised the questions of public participation in the formulation of historical memory, opening the floodgate of later scholarship.[81] By the turn of the twenty-first century, discussions of memory pertained to the physical process not of a given individual but rather of society at large—what a society remembers and what that means.

Writing using oral history has continued to grow in sophistication. The Palgrave Studies in Oral History published its first volume in 2003. Edited by Linda Shopes and Bruce Stave, the Palgrave books are designed to look at oral history interviews in depth, to place them "in broad historical context and engage issues of historical memory and narrative construction."[82]

In 2005, oral history methodology continues to flourish. Both the Oral History Association and the International Oral History Association are thriving, and their publications continue to increase in quality. The methodology continues to prove itself useful in a broad array of topics, and applications continue to become more creative. As the World Wide Web grows in scope and influence, it undoubtedly will have an impact on the dissemination of oral history. But the basic dynamic, two people sitting and talking about the past, has remained largely unchanged. Despite the sophistication of analysis and interpretation, a middle-school student can still do a legitimate oral history interview. Where individuals communicate, oral history will continue to be useful.

Notes

I thank Bruce Stave and Thomas Charlton for their careful reading of and suggestions for this chapter.

1. Starr, "Oral History," 4; Moss, "What Is It," 5; Strassler, *Landmark Thucydides*, 15; Vansina, *Oral Tradition*, xi (originally published as *Oral Tradition: A Study in Historical Methodology*); Haley, "Black History," 12, 14–17; Hanke, "American Historians," 6–7. For an overview of historiography in Europe and Africa, see Henige, *Oral Historiography*, 7–22.

2. Carr, *What Is History?* 3.

3. Hart, *Catalogue*, vii–viii.

4. Hirsch, *Portrait of America*, 6. Hirsch provides an elegant discussion of the intellectual impulses behind the Federal Writers' Project.

5. Couch, preface to *These Are Our Lives*, ix, x–xi.

6. Botkin, *Lay My Burden Down*, ix. Ann Banks discusses the history of WPA project anthologies in her 1980 collection of eighty previously unpublished

interviews in *First Person America*, xi, xiii, xv. Later, in 1993, Theda Perdue published *Nations Remembered*, a selection of WPA interviews with Native Americans. An extended debate over the veracity of the slave narratives took place in the *Oral History Review*. See Soapes, "Federal Writers' Project"; Rapport, "Life Stories"; and Terrill and Hirsch, "Replies."

7. Nevins, *Gateway to History*, iv. See Hirsch, *Portrait of America*, 141–47, for a contrast between the Federal Writers' Project and Nevins's approach to collecting personal narratives.

8. Everett, *Oral History Techniques*, 4–7; Pogue, *Pogue's War*, 99.

9. Nevins, "How and Why," 31–32.

10. Starr, "Oral History," 8–9, 22.

11. Nevins, "How and Why," 32; Starr, "Oral History," 10–11.

12. Boatright and Owens, *Derrick Floor*, ix–x.

13. Annotations of the Forest History Society interview collection first appeared in Holman, *Oral History Collection*, and are now available online at Forest History Society Oral History Program, Understanding the Past for Its Impact on the Future, http://www.lib.duke.edu/forest/Research/ohiguide.html (accessed January 31, 2005).

14. Hart, *Catalogue*, vii–viii.

15. Grele, introduction to *UCLA Oral History Program*, 1. See also UCLA Oral History Program, History and Description, University of California at Los Angeles, http://www.library.ucla.edu/libraries/special/ohp/ohphist.htm (accessed January 31, 2005).

16. Starr, "Oral History," 12; Herbert Hoover Presidential Library and Museum, Research Collections: Historical Materials, Oral History Transcripts, http://www.ecommcode2.com/hoover/research/historicalmaterials/oral.html (accessed January 26, 2005); Truman Presidential Museum and Library, Oral History Interviews, http://www.trumanlibrary.org/oralhist/oral_his.htm (accessed January 26, 2005); Eisenhower Presidential Library Information Archives, Eisenhower Library Information Resources: Oral Histories, http://www.ibiblio.org/lia/president/EisenhowerLibrary/oral_histories/Oral.html (accessed January 26, 2005); John F. Kennedy Library and Museum, Historical Materials in the John F. Kennedy Library: Oral History Interviews, http://www.cs.umb.edu/~serl/jfk/oralhist.htm (accessed January 31, 2005); Lyndon Baines Johnson Library and Museum, Oral History Collection, http://www.lbjlib.utexas.edu/johnson/archives.hom/biopage.asp (accessed January 26, 2005).

17. Kessler-Harris, "Social History," 233–34, 237.

18. Colman, "Oral History," 79–83.

19. Dixon and Mink, *Oral History at Arrowhead*.

20. Dixon, "Definitions," 14.

21. Ibid., 6.

22. Ibid., 5. By the mid-1970s, 70 percent of U.S. programs were transcribing their interviews, opposed to British and Canadian programs, which left theirs in recorded form only. Louis Starr concluded, "This is not so much because those who favor the transcript have the better of the argument on theoretical grounds as because of practical convenience." Starr, "Oral History," 7.

23. Dixon, "Definitions," 22.

24. Nevins, "Uses," 40.

25. Dixon, "Definitions," 19; Dixon and Colman, "Objectives and Standards," 78, 80.

26. "Oral History Association Adopts Statement about Goals and Guidelines during Nebraska Colloquium," *Oral History Association Newsletter* 3, no. 1 (January 1969), 4. The "Goals and Guidelines" were subsequently revised in 1975.

27. Editors to date are Samuel Hand, 1973–1978; Richard Sweterlitsch, 1978–1980; Arthur A. Hansen, 1981–1987; Michael Frisch, 1987–1996; Bruce M. Stave, 1996–1999; and Andrew J. Dunar, 2000–2005. *Oral History Review* began publishing twice yearly with volume 15 in 1987.

28. *Oral History Association Newsletter* 2, no. 2 (April 1968): 1.

29. *Oral History Association Newsletter* 4, no. 3 (July 1970): 6.

30. Other significant manuals prior to the 1990s included Moss, *Program Manual*; Davis, Back, and MacLean, *Tape to Type*; Ives, *Tape-Recorded Interview* (1980); Charlton, *Oral History for Texans* (1981); and Sitton, Mehaffy, and Davis, *Guide for Teachers*.

31. *Oral History Association Newsletter* 15, no. 1 (1981): 6–7.

32. Cash and Hoover, *To Be an Indian*.

33. Haley, "Black History," 7–8; X, *Autobiography*.

34. Browne, "Civil Rights," 90–95.

35. Jefferson, "Echoes from the South," 43–62.

36. Rosengarten, *All God's Dangers*, xiii–xxv.

37. Bancroft Library Regional Oral History Office, Oral History Online: Suffragists Oral History Project, University of California at Berkeley Library, http://bancroft.berkeley.edu/ROHO/projects/suffragist/ (accessed January 31, 2005); Gluck, *Parlor to Prison*.

38. Hill, *Women of Courage*, 3–4.

39. Gluck, "What's So Special" (1984), 222.

40. Starr, "Oral History," 12; Walter P. Reuther Library, Oral History Collections: UAW Oral Histories, Wayne State University College of Urban Labor and Metropolitan Affairs, http://www.reuther.wayne.edu/use/ohistory.html#uaw (accessed January 26, 2005).

41. Lynd and Lynd, *Rank and File*, 3.

42. Friedlander, *UAW Local*.

43. Hareven and Langenbach, *Amoskeag*.

44. "Neighborhood OH Changes Lives," *Oral History Association Newsletter* 15, no. 2 (1981): 6.

45. University of Alaska Fairbanks Oral History Program, Project Jukebox, Elmer E. Rasmuson Library, University of Alaska Fairbanks, http://uaf-db.uaf.edu/Jukebox/PJWeb/pjhome.htm (accessed January 26, 2005). Following Baum's early community history guide, *Oral History for the Local Historical Society*, the Oral History Association produced its own guide by Mercier and Buckendorf, *Using Oral History in Community History Projects*. For a particularly good example of a community history, see Fee, Shopes, and Zeidman, *Baltimore Book*.

46. Montell, *Coe Ridge*, ix–xxvii.

47. Tuchman, "Distinguishing the Significant" (1984), 76.

48. Reingold, "Critic Looks at Oral History," 219. Pogue, *George C. Marshall*; Williams, *Huey Long*.

49. Reingold, "Critic Looks at Oral History," 217.

50. Hoffman, "Reliability and Validity." Hoffman has continued her work for several decades, particularly with her husband Howard Hoffman's memories of his service during World War II. See Hoffman and Hoffman, *Archives of Memory*.

51. Philip A. Crowl, "The Dulles Oral History Project: Mission Accomplished," *American Historical Association Newsletter*, February 1967.

52. For Terkel's discussion of his editing, see Grele, "Riffs and Improvisations," 31–39.

53. Wigginton, *Foxfire Book*. For a description of how the Foxfire movement began, see Wigginton, *Shining Moment*.

54. Two of the most successful projects include Loblolly, Gary, Texas, and The Long, Long Ago Oral History Project, Suva Intermediate School, Bell Gardens, California. See Sitton, *Loblolly Book*, and Brooks, "Long, Long Ago." High school students in Lebanon, Missouri, published *Bittersweet: The Ozark Quarterly* from 1973 to 1983. See Massey, *Bittersweet Country*.

55. Waserman, *Bibliography*, rev. ed., iii–iv.

56. The *Journal of Library History* articles ran twice yearly from 1967 (Volume 2) to 1973 (Volume 8) and were often descriptions of oral history projects and activities. *History News* articles appeared occasionally through 1976.

57. Bonnell and Hunt, introduction to *Beyond the Cultural Turn*, 2–3, 4.

58. Frisch, "Oral History and *Hard Times*" (1990), 13.

59. Grele, *Envelopes of Sound* (1975).

60. Evans, *Where Beards Wag All*.

61. Oral History Association, *Evaluation Guidelines*, 1. The guidelines were updated in 1989 and again in 2000.

62. Frantz, "Video-Taping"; Colman, "Where to Now?" 2; Charlton, "Videotaped Oral Histories."

63. Goldberg, "Manhattan Project Series," 98; Stephens, "Videohistory," 107; Williams, "Recording Videohistory," 143–44.

64. Dunaway and Baum, *Oral History* (1984).

65. Shopes, "Critical Dialogue."

66. Henige, *Oral Historiography*, 128.

67. McMahan, *Elite Oral History Discourse*.

68. *Oral History Review* 30, no. 1 (Winter/Spring 2003) featured essays by seven authors commenting on the collaborative process.

69. Frisch and Shopes, "Introduction," 593. The annual oral history sections of the *Journal of American History* began in 1987 (Volume 74) and continued through 2002 (Volume 89). The editors were Michael Frisch and Linda Shopes (1986–1996) and Lu Ann Jones and Michael Gordon (1997–2002).

70. Grele, "Editorial," 2. The first *International Yearbook* was Passerini, *Memory and Totalitarianism*.

71. Poniatowska, *Nothing, Nobody*; Passerini, *Fascism in Popular Memory*.

72. Portelli, *Death of Luigi Trastulli*, viii–ix. Portelli followed with the equally engaging *Battle of Valle Giulia* and *Order Has Been Carried Out*.

73. Tonkin, *Narrating Our Pasts*.

74. Donald A. Ritchie, e-mail message to author, January 26, 2004. The first Twayne volume was Lewin, *Witnesses to the Holocaust*.

75. Berube, *Coming Out*; Faderman, *Odd Girls*; Kennedy and Davis, *Boots of Leather*.

76. Ritchie, *Doing Oral History* (1995); Yow, *Recording Oral History* (1994). The 2003 revised edition of Ritchie, *Doing Oral History*, contains a significant bibliography. The second edition of Yow's manual, updated and enlarged, appeared in 2005.

77. Perks and Thomson, *Oral History Reader*.

78. Gluck, Ritchie, and Eynon, "New Millennium."

79. Large oral history programs produced printed guides to their collections. In the mid-1980s, the Southwestern Oral History Association produced a unified database of interviews in the region. See Gallacher and Treleven, "Online Database." The importance of this issue is demonstrated by the heated arguments in late 2003 on H-Oralhist, the Internet discussion list, regarding plans for a database by the Alexander Street Press.

80. Veterans History Project News and Events, Veterans' Stories Online for Memorial Day, Library of Congress American Folklife Center Veterans History Project, http://www.loc.gov/folklife/vets//news-courage.html (accessed January 26, 2005).

81. Kammen, *Mystic Chords of Memory*; Bodnar, *Remaking America*.

82. The first volume is Polishuk, *Sticking to the Union*. The call for manuscripts is located online at Palgrave Global Publishing at St. Martin's Press, Palgrave Studies in Oral History, University of Connecticut Center for Oral History, http://www.oralhistory.uconn.edu/palgrave.html (accessed January 31, 2005).

2

Oral History as Evidence

Ronald J. Grele

The question of evidence is as good a one as any, and probably better than most, around which to organize a few thoughts about oral history. What follows is a series of short discussions about the history and some of the unique characteristics of oral history, organized to highlight some interesting ways to discuss the context of the evidence produced by the oral history interview.

When asked to give a brief definition of evidence, a cynical lawyer friend claimed it was whatever the judge allowed. Now, the issue is much more complex, but it is useful to be reminded that a good deal of what is admissible (accepted) depends upon the gatekeepers, those who sanction the evidentiary value of whatever statements of fact or interpretation are offered in support of an argument or proposition. But those gatekeepers; their values, attitudes, and power; and the institutions they inhabit and structure change over time. Thus what historians consider evidence changes as well. To understand the ways in which oral history has been used as evidence it is necessary to sketch the larger and more complicated milieu of its history, a history now recognized as both international and interdisciplinary.

There are two themes to that history: the transformation of oral history from a source of information (data) to the production and interpretation of texts, and the alteration of the view of the oral historian/interviewer from objective and contemplative observer to active participant in the process. These two changes, which took place within a set of attitudes and traditions that structured the work of historians in general, and oral historians in particular, define our project. As the practice emerged after World War II, the attitudes and traditions within which it did so reflected the tension between those who saw oral history as archival practice and those who envisioned oral history as the handmaiden of social history.

From early reports and brief descriptions of oral history at particular institutions and in various parts of the world, the tension between archival projects and efforts in social history emerges clearly.[1] While there are distinctions to be made, complications to be noted, and silences to be explored, the general consensus is that the origin of oral history in the United States lay in archival practice, while in Europe the origin was the work of social historians. Therefore, those who followed the North American model established archival projects, and those following the European model accented the importance of social history.[2] Even a cursory examination indicates, however, that in the U.S. there was a good deal of oral history interviewing as part of the thrust of the new social history and that in most European countries many oral history projects did, indeed, spring from archival concerns. Although oral history efforts in various parts of the world responded to unique local traditions and particularistic pressures,[3] the archives–social history distinction seems to have been the general case, and it is still a useful way to categorize oral history in order to understand the evolution of its uses as evidence.

Oral History as Archival Practice

In the U.S. and those areas of the world affected by trends or institutions in the U.S., those who articulated, or tried to articulate, a definition of oral history linked that definition to archival practice. Worried that in the age of the telephone and an era when men of affairs no longer kept diaries or wrote memoirs, the founders of oral history in the U.S., those who gathered in California in 1967 to found the Oral History Association, argued that personal interviews, properly researched and processed, on file in manuscript collections and archives, would provide the basis for historical research and for the publications of historians and others in the future. The goal of this effort was to complement the existing written record with information gleaned from interviews and fill in the gaps in that record in the same manner that letters, journals, and diaries had done since the dawn of widespread literacy. According to Allan Nevins, the founder of the Columbia University Oral History Research Office, this effort sought to "hold in view the publishable book."[4] The implication was twofold: oral history interviews were to be collected to become the basis of the publication of more history books by people other than the people who gathered the interviews, and the individual oral history itself was to be treated as a book.[5] The oral history was to be transcribed, indexed, and edited as if it were a publication. In some cases this transcript was called a memoir, and it was often edited just as a publishable manuscript would be edited. For example, in the project Nevins led at Columbia University, where editing by project staff was minimal, the date of submission (completion of the process), not the date of the conduct of the interview, was the officially cataloged date of the interview, mimicking the world of publishing.[6] In all of this it was clear that the final product was to be offered to the historical profession as a document upon which, when complemented with written materials, books could be based. In line with this modest goal, Arthur M. Schlesinger Jr. spoke for many of his colleagues in seeing the value of oral history as "essentially supplementary evidence. What it is good at is to give a sense of the relations among people—who worked with whom, who liked whom, who influenced whom. . . . The recollected material cannot pretend to the exactitude of, say, the White House tapes of the Nixon years."[7] Many other members of the profession, however, thought the end result was minimally useful, providing only color or anecdote.[8]

Thus it was not extraordinary that most of the earliest American oral history projects were situated in archives, libraries, or manuscript collections, either academic or governmental, rather than within history departments at major universities, and that a great deal of attention was spent on

questions of access, copyright, processing, and cataloging. Obviously, one of the major reasons for such a concern was to
make the information contained in the interviews easily available. Scholars would not have to spend hours in a laborious effort to listen to the original tapes, and since tapes were not to
be listened to, in some cases they were destroyed. Transcripts
could much more easily be indexed, and in addition, transcribing imposed a standard for citation and quotation. It was also
a way to enable archivists to apply all of the traditional standards that had been applied to written sources to these new
sound recordings.[9] A secondary concern, but an important one,
was to protect the interviewee from any embarrassments that
the spontaneous interviewing technique might engender. Thus
the transcripts were returned to the interviewees for their correction. While a case could be made that this produced a much
more reliable document and therefore more reliable evidence
because it included a second, more measured consideration on
the part of the person interviewed, the major consideration
seems to have been the feelings of unease on the part of
archivists about the collection of potentially embarrassing, if
not slanderous, material. Oral history evidence, since it was to
be publicly available through the auspices of an institution,
was to be evidence that would pass muster in line with the
canons of the respectable publishing world. In addition, the
concern with the rights of authors, in this case those interviewed, meant that the evidence produced by oral histories
was to be subject to the ethics and legalities of the traditions of
Anglo-American publishing.[10] The positive side of this practice
was the fact that the document was to be made widely available, thus encouraging multiple interpretations and countering
any tendency toward source monopoly.

The most striking characteristic of this effort was the concentration upon movers and shakers, those who ordinarily
would have amassed a written record of their activities through
saving of correspondence or in the minutes of meetings or other
documents. This was certainly the case in various governmental projects, such as those at the presidential libraries, but was
also true of those at the major universities. Even projects in labor history were more than likely to center their activities on

union leaders rather than rank-and-file members of those same unions. In terms of who was to be interviewed, most projects were elitist to the core.

The experience and prestige of American oral history institutions, especially those connected to the federal government or located at major universities, such as Columbia, the University of California at Berkeley, and the University of California at Los Angeles, acted as a spur to oral history efforts in other nations. In some cases, such as Israel, the connection was direct. Elsewhere, such as in Malaysia, the connection was a U.S.-trained archivist who established the first organized government project. In other countries, such as Brazil and Indonesia, early efforts were funded by American foundations and purposely modeled on American practice.[11] In Mexico, France, and Canada, all areas with deep traditions of social history, many early projects were nonetheless located in archives, and archival concerns were an important part of the debates over the usefulness of oral history. In Singapore, David Lance, one of the few in the British oral history movement at the time concerned with archives and a recent arrival in the republic, was instrumental in assisting in establishing the first governmental archival projects. In other nations, such as Spain, Germany, the Philippines, and New Zealand, contacts between scholars using oral history and American archival projects were much more informal, but instrumental.[12] All of this activity meant that by the mid-1970s there was a flourishing of the collection of oral history recordings to be placed in archives or other depositories.

Oral History and Social History

If in the U.S. the original impetus for the development of the field was a concern for creating documents to fill a perceived vacuum in the existing record, elsewhere oral history emerged from the traditional practices of historians who had long used interviews as part of their effort to research the past. While the actual practice was nothing new, the name was, as was the mission, which as formulated for the most part by New Left historians was double edged: to create a history of the everyday lives of those who had heretofore been ignored by historians and thereby produce a "better" history, and to radicalize the practice of history by contesting a "hegemonic" view of agency and power.

The most thoroughly articulated description of the conjoined evolution of oral history and the "new" social history is *The Voice of the Past* by Paul Thompson.[13] In Thompson's view, oral history was the latest stage of a long tradition in the use of "oral evidence" to uncover the history of everyday life, in the fullest sense of "everyday," from the minutest aspects of the interior world of the family to the largest propositions of oppositional culture. Starting with Herodotus, including Jules Michelet's study of the French Revolution, and moving through folklore studies, the traditions of social reportage, such as Henry Mayhew and Beatrice and Sidney Webb, the work of the Chicago school of sociology, and the Works Progress Administration's American slave narratives, Thompson traced a long lineage for oral history.[14] If archival oral history came into its own as something new with the invention of the tape recorder, oral history in social history had always been a part of historical studies. Its patrimony was social history with a small *s*. No longer the story of Lady Millicent and Lord Gotrocks and their comings and goings on their estates or in their town houses, this was the history of the ordinary and everyday life of the working class and its constituent components, such as women, children, and racial and ethnic minorities, those whose stories had been ignored in the traditional tale of political and economic power. Oral history was, thus, to play a vital role in the culturalist formations of social history being articulated by British and American social historians, most notably E. P. Thompson, Eric Hobsbawm, Herbert Gutman, and Eugene Genovese.[15] It was to be a part of the struggle to produce a history from below.[16]

Practitioners believed that not only would this use of oral history produce a better history, one more attuned to the real tensions of the social order, but it would also provide the base for a reorientation of the discipline of history. At a minimum, oral history would aid in the transformation of history from a discipline to an activity.[17] At its most ambitious, the claim was that the study of history would become a tool for the reconstruction of the social order, a method of consciousness raising, and that the oral history interview would be both another moment in that consciousness raising and the basis for the articulation of a radical vision among activists.[18] Those studied would be radicalized by the process of recalling their pasts and its oppressions, and those studying would become part of the ongoing struggle against oppression. Radical and dissenting traditions would be revived and become a part of current social movements. This double vision was an integral part of the thrust of oral history not only in Great Britain and Scandinavia but also in many parts of the world where historians were attempting to understand the legacy of oppression, such as with fascism and Nazism or Stalinism in continental Europe, apartheid in South Africa, locally repressive regimes such as those then existing in various parts of Latin America, or the lasting effects of a brutal colonialism.[19] Unsurprisingly, the *History Workshop Journal*, one of the loci of oral history in Great Britain, was founded by, and titled itself a journal for, socialist historians.

The differences in the two approaches to the collection of oral history interviews were clear. There seemed to be little consensus on such questions as who was to be interviewed, who was to do the interviewing, and what should be done with the interview. Broadly speaking, in one view, those who left a record as a research base were to be the subjects of an interview while in the other the exact opposite was the goal. Archival projects separated the creation of the interview from the end use, while social historians argued that those who did the interviews should also be responsible for their use and interpretation, thereby introducing one of the most crucial distinctions between oral history and other forms of historical research: the fact that in this case historians themselves were creating the very documents that they were called upon to interpret. Although the claim may bring a smile today, the charge made by Philip C. Brooks of the Truman Library at the founding meeting of the U.S. Oral History Association, that "the person who is collecting a stock of evidence for other researchers to use is almost by definition to be doing a more objective job than the one who is writing his own book, especially the one who has a case to prove," clearly demonstrated that there is a fundamental, unresolved theoretical and methodological issue involved in the practice.[20]

There was also dispute as to the final disposition of the interview. While archivists and manuscript librarians were deeply concerned with the ways in which the interview was to be processed and made available to the public, this was not a major concern for practicing historians. Nor, did it seem, was source monopoly a particular issue.

It might be easy to draw too sharp a geographical line between these two forms of oral history. As noted above, there were any number of archival projects in various European and Latin American nations, Australia, and South Africa and, likewise, many U.S. projects in social history, particularly at the University of North Carolina and Duke University.[21] The arguments, however, could become personal and heated.[22] In time, interest in these distinctions, which once seemed so important, waned. As more researchers working in archives began to make use of their interviews for various purposes, sometimes even publishing monographs using the interviews, as more projects in social history were founded as both archives and publishing ventures, and as more historians sought to locate their interviews in various repositories, the controversy faded.[23] But the division between the two forms of oral history persisted, and rightly so, for they do define real differences in approach, use, and audience.[24] Interviews collected in an archive are used by historians several steps removed from the process of creation, and historians who deposit their interviews find that they are used and interpreted by others in ways sharply at odds with their creation. These differences are important considerations in the resolution of the debates over all aspects of the oral history process. In time, however, even with these concerns in mind, one was able to discern, from a different perspective, ways in which both oral history as archival practice and oral history as social history shared a set of assumptions about historical practice.

A Common World

Looking back at the ways in which the practice of oral history emerged in the 1960s and 1970s, it now seems clear that—whatever the forms—the thought and actual work were based upon a set of common interests and assumptions. Chief among these were a concern with local history, a view of the relation of oral history to the historical profession, and a common set of epistemological assumptions. Each of these commonalities contained its own unique problems and possibilities.

For differing but complementary reasons, both strands of thinking in oral history had a great interest and effect upon efforts at local history. Those who sought to build archives of oral documents often encouraged local libraries, historical societies, or voluntary agencies to initiate projects to collect interviews with local leaders. Building upon long traditions of local history, it was quite natural that oral history would become a part of the surge to know one's local history and to create a documentary basis for that history. So, too, the thrust of social history to move beyond the history of the political center or the capital gave a political urgency to local efforts to document daily life. If, for example, the new agricultural history was to move beyond parliamentary debates or national markets to a study of daily farming practices, it was to the local that one would have to turn for evidence; so, too, with all the other subfields of social history. In the long run, it may be that the greatest glory of oral history was its role in the revivification of local history. But this was also a new local history, one that sought to inculcate pride and identity as well as political agency in the local.[25] In this sense, community historians introduced a new concept of evidence into the discussions of oral history and revealed the tension within social history between some academic professionals and community historians.

A corollary of this interest in local and community history was the use of oral history as a teaching tool on the elementary and high school levels. Especially in the Anglo-Saxon world, teachers received encouragement to send their students into the community to conduct interviews and found welcome within the major national and regional associations, most of which very early established separate education committees to promote such a use for oral history.[26]

Both the new social historians and archivists building collections also shared the assumption that the evidence produced by oral history interviewing was similar to other evidence used by historians and thus could be tested and analyzed in the same manner as historians had done in the past. For many local historians this was also the case. But community historians saw the world somewhat differently, as the term *community* indicates. Community implied that there was some emotional or symbolic (subjective) relationship between people in a local area, and between the historian who was working in that area collecting interviews and the people he or she was interviewing. Oral history evidence was therefore evidence of those connections. Despite the fact that it proved very difficult to come to any general or theoretical understanding of or definition of "community," advocates claimed that oral history was to have uses far beyond the creation of historical texts, and those uses were many and varied, ranging from political mobilization to forms of therapy.[27]

The overlap between social historians and archivists was also, and most importantly for the issues of this essay, apparent in their shared vision of what kind of historical work was to be privileged, what a historical document was, and how it was to be read. While it is important to recognize the differences in attitude between the archival view of oral history and the social history view, ironically enough, spokespeople for both shared a basic assumption that the end result to be privileged, even among some local and community projects, was the published monograph. The leaders in the field recognized the vitality of oral history collection for purposes of museum exhibits, radio programming, or community programs, but when assessing the value and achievements of oral history, it was the listing of monographs published from interviewing that remained the focus. A close look at Thompson's chapter on the achievement of oral history and at the footnotes to that chapter, and an equally close look at the various annual reports written by Louis Starr and published by the Columbia University Oral History Research Office, will immediately reveal the similarity.[28] In both cases, there is a defensive posture that seeks, since oral history was then still seen as a marginal practice, a certain respectability by reference to its usefulness to the profession's traditional heart.

This defensiveness speaks to the marginality of oral history at that time, which in turn helps to explain the traditionalism of the description of what an oral history interview was, how it was created, and how it was to be read.[29] Oral history interviews were seen as documents similar to all other documents, to be treated by the historian in the same manner as he or she would treat any other source. Thus, theorists argued, there was an understandable gap between the historian and the source (the person interviewed). The historian as interviewer and interpreter was a distanced and contemplative observer in the same manner as someone examining a manuscript. The source was what was to be observed. The knowledgeable and "objective" historian was to use the tools of a traditional historiography to discover the "truth" that resided in the sources in the guise of facts that were to be extracted. These facts were transparent in their meaning and could be tested for their accuracy, verifiability, and representativeness by the historian, whose role was unquestioned and whose cultural position in a world of production was invisible. Knowledge lay in the accumulation of the facts, the interconnectedness of which was assumed to be discoverable by the properly trained outside observer, and the problems of those using oral history were the same for those using all sources and were matters of technique. The goal was the production of information, which could be weighed by the traditional methods of historical inquiry for its reliability and verifiability.

It is not unusual that the fullest description of a discourse rests with the critique of that discourse. In this case, the clearest exposition of the view of interviews as data can be found in two critical analyses of *The Voice of the Past*: one by the Birmingham Centre for Contemporary Cultural Studies Popular Memory Group and the other by John Murphy for the Australian journal *Historical Studies*.[30] Both critiques were deeply skeptical of what they saw as the empiricism and positivism of Thompson's view of oral history, especially his emphasis on accuracy and his unwillingness to see the oral history as a cultural artifact. It must be noted, however, that Thompson was hardly alone in this view. Therefore, it is somewhat unfair to single him out for criticism. Brooks, as noted earlier, articulated the same vision in the U.S. in the early deliberations of the Oral History Association, as did Nevins, who went even further than Thompson in claiming that interviewers must settle for no "evasions," and that it was their "duty" to get "clear and veracious answers" through a "rigid" and "severe" "cross-examination."[31] Essays by Alice Hoffman, William Cutler, and William Moss made the same points, although a bit more subtly. The same assumptions could be found in most reports from the field in any number of national publications.[32] They informed most of the handbooks and primers published during these years, either explicitly with reference to works in the social sciences or implicitly, as if such a view was to be beyond question.[33]

The general lack of theoretical introspection about such issues resulted in endless discussion of the techniques of interviewing. There was, to be sure, a naïve realization that the oral history interview was somehow different because it exhibited certain unique characteristics in its reliance upon memory and the social relations of the interview, which involved the historian directly in the face-to-face creation of the documents that he or she would later use or that would be used by others at some later date. But the discourse focused on how the interview situation could be manipulated to overcome this relationship or how it could be used to obtain the most valid document. The problems presented by the interview were solvable within the traditions of common sense that historians applied to all sources. Such an articulation of the task was the common discourse among oral historians.

Despite these theoretical limitations and despite the seeming cogency of the criticism that the narrow view of the practice resulted in the failure by those who collected and used oral history interviews to realize the full potential of oral history to challenge the traditional strictures of the historical profession or to realize its radical promise, it was clear by the early 1970s that both oral history approaches—archival and social history—had attained a popularity and respectability beyond question. Even looking with a skeptical eye over the various bibliographies touting the practice, it was a remarkable product. More and more historians, especially former 1960s activists who had entered the academy and were creating the subfields of working-class, women's, African American, and ethnic history were using oral history collections or conducting interviews for their monographs. Oral history had, indeed, creatively expanded the horizons of the new social history by producing new evidence or new ways to read old evidence. Colleges and universities in large numbers were offering courses in the technique, and increasing numbers of foundations were willing to fund work in oral history. It took no one by surprise when the Oral History Association in the U.S. titled its 1974 annual meeting "Oral History Comes of Age." It was simply one echo of the self-congratulatory tone that was creeping into discussions among oral historians.

Academics and Activists

The hesitancy to join in this chorus of praise for the academic uses of oral history came, for the most part, not from traditional historians, although there were some holdouts to this euphoria, but from community historians and especially those with a New Left political agenda, who argued that the increasing use of oral history for academic purposes had put the practice out of reach for ordinary people. In addition, the increasingly abstract nature of the language used and the high prices of academic publications posed a barrier to effective politics. Such charges reflected the tensions between academic and activist historians.[34]

As noted above, community historians and political activists had long recognized that the intimate relationship engendered in the interview situation was as important as the reading of the texts it produced, and many had come to argue that that relationship now made it possible to gather history "pure." If the academy had failed to produce a history of the heretofore excluded, one reason was that academicians had not been willing to listen to them. Now it was possible to get a history from, as some said, "the horse's mouth," directly from the people without the intervening ideology of the professional caste of historians and sociologists. The radicalism of oral history lay in the fact that it gave a voice to the people themselves. This became a very potent argument in the world of oral history.[35]

Because there was, with few exceptions, no deeper dialogue, the discussion of the interview relation devolved into the debate over, on the one hand, the practice of "professional" historians and archivists seeking to produce works that neutralized the relationship between the parties to an interview while retaining the right of interpretation for the historian versus, on the other, the reification of the experience in the name of consciousness raising. The contrast between these two attitudes was brilliantly dissected by Michael Frisch. Reviewing Studs Terkel's *Hard Times*, Frisch raised fundamental questions about the nature of oral history as it had emerged from the 1960s as a source for information and insight to be used in traditional ways and as a way of bypassing historical interpretation. Frisch found in the enthusiasm surrounding oral history a contradictory set of attitudes toward history, neither of them very historical and both deeply conservative in their implications. The first was the view that oral history was more history, simply piling on more and more data. The second was the populist drive to escape history embedded in the articulated mission to somehow go beyond professional historians and get a purer history from the voices of the folk. Neither posture, he argued, spoke to the potentials of oral history or to the issues of the ways in which memory and historical construction guided the ways in which people made their histories and lived their lives in history. The real issue for Frisch was how readers are "to understand the variable weave of pure recall and reflective synthesis—historical statements as well as historical information—that characterize almost all of the interviews" in Terkel's work.[36] Neither more history nor no history speaks to the larger issues of the understanding of consciousness. Instead, Frisch saw a much more complex task for oral history:

> By studying how experience, memory, and history become combined in and digested by people who are the bearers of their own history and that of their culture, oral history opens up a powerful perspective; it encourages us to stand somewhat aside of cultural forms in order to observe their workings. Thus it permits us to track the elusive beasts of consciousness and culture in a way impossible to do from within. . . . Although it is so tempting to take historical testimony to be history itself . . . the very documents of oral history really suggest a different lesson.[37]

It was clear that oral historians were being called upon to rethink the practice in ways that would move the theory of evidence beyond the search for data about events and force a consideration of the dynamic and dialectic relationship of interviewer and interviewee in the creation of what could only be called a text.

The Transformation

The approach that Frisch took toward reading an oral history interview was one of a number of new ways of understanding and speculating upon the practice that emerged in the mid- to late 1970s that would transform the field: the transformation, already noted, from the search for information to a search for a method of reading the text as more than simply a document. This in turn was a part of a much wider and deeper shift in historical studies from social history to cultural studies.[38]

From the earliest days, there had always been voices urging a more complex reading of oral histories. In England, Elizabeth Tonkin in her concern with "oracy" sought to combine social anthropology, ethnomethodology, and literary analysis to understand the sense of history underlying oral testimony, while in the U.S., Corinne Gilb urged archivists collecting oral history interviews to use those interviews for insights into cultural construction. In another example, Saul Benison talked about the interview as a first interpretation and noted that the mutual creation of the interview is both the strength and the weakness of the document.[39]

One of the most interesting early examples of the changing nature of the discourse about oral history is the work of Martin Duberman in *Black Mountain*, a study of an experimental college in North Carolina that flourished in the 1930s and 1940s. Elsewhere, I have gone into some detail about *Black Mountain*.[40] My reading of the book is that Duberman found himself caught between the traditional expectations of the historical profession as to how evidence should be mobilized and the creative possibilities of oral history fieldwork, a tension so severe that he himself admits he had to put the work aside for a number of years because he had to break through the boundaries of the discipline. His problem was how he could explore and represent the reactions of those he interviewed to their own historical experiences and his own at the same time. The following excerpt catches his dilemma:

> My journal, Monday, August 3, 1970: The data is taking over again. Or rather, my compulsiveness about being totally accurate and inclusive. I start letting myself go . . . [but] get deflected into incorporating . . . material into earlier sections; mostly additional citations to footnotes rather than changing interpretations—just the kind of silly "iceberg" scholarship . . . that I rhetorically scorn. By the time I come back to the question that had started to excite me, I am leaden with repetitive information to other people's reactions to other issues. How can I explore theirs and mine simultaneously? I don't want to evade and distort their views, but I don't want fidelity to theirs to take over, to obliterate mine. . . . It's an example of how destructive so-called "professional training" can be: it initiates you into and confirms the rightness of techniques previously used by others. Yet . . . there aren't any techniques, only personalities.[41]

Today this tension is termed the quest to understand intersubjectivity. That Duberman could not fully resolve the contradictions is not surprising, but the effort is a wonderful example of a moment in the history of oral history. Harshly criticized when first published,[42] the book has become one of the classic texts in oral history.

By the mid- to late 1970s, the questions that captured Duberman's attention were being asked by more and more historians using oral history or doing oral history interviews. If oral history interviews were evidence of the ways in which one understood the past, they were unique documents. The intervention of the historian in the very document he or she was called upon to interpret was something new. In addition, it was clear that oral histories were documents of the here and now about the then and there, fusing past and present in a complex web of interpretation. Also, with the fascination with "reconstituting the small details of everyday life" and "the shift from 'places to faces,' from topographical peculiarities to the quality of life,"[43] in the words of Raphael Samuel, oral history ran into all of the problems of the individualizing tendencies of biography. The oral history interview also brought subjectivity, the subject's view of himself or herself as a cultural actor, to the fore. In their dialogical creation, layers of interpretation, and varied uses, oral history interviews raised fundamental historiographical questions.[44]

It was clear that the interview did uncover what happened in the past and that oral history did expand the realm of what was studied, but it was also clear that the interview was evidence of the ways in which history lived on in the present and the ways in which the present informed a view of the past. In the words of Alessandro Portelli, "The unique and precious element which oral sources force upon the historian and which no other sources possess in equal measure (unless it be literary ones) is the speaker's subjectivity; and therefore if the research is broad and articulated enough, a cross-section of the subjectivity of a social group or class. They tell us not what people did, but what they wanted to do, what they believed they were doing, what they now think they did. . . . Subjectivity is as much the business of history as the more visible facts."[45] In accepting this view, however, it was necessary to accept the view that those interviewed were more than just repositories of facts to be gathered by the historians. It was necessary to see interviewees, if not as direct voices from the past, as in some manner their own historians, capable of elaborate and sometimes confusing methods of constructing and narrating their own histories.

What then was the nature of the relationship between the past as expressed in the interview and the present in which the interview was being conducted, and in what ways did the interaction of the interviewer and interviewee influence or determine these relationships? Also, how is the interviewer to understand the testimony given when it was clearly more than a simple recitation of what happened in the past, but also articulated complicated mental reconstructions? While the arguments over these questions have a very convoluted and complex history, in brief, these issues merged with a New Left concern with questions of subjectivity—not only the subjective areas of mental life, such as ideology, memory, consciousness, and myth expressed by both interviewer and interviewee in the interview, but also the question of how the subject is formed in history, the structured and structuring of consciousness. In Italy, Luisa Passerini merged the fieldwork she undertook interviewing working-class Italians in Turin with the questions of subjectivity as asked by George Lukács and Antonio Gramsci in order to understand the complicated interweaving of the work ethic and silences about the fascist period in Italy. This allowed her to talk about those silences as a deep wound in worker consciousness of their acceptance of fascism and, in the process, raise fundamental questions about the ability of the traditional categories of social history to deal with such subjectivity. In those same years, Portelli began to apply the concerns of narrative theory to the oral history interview in order to see the telling of a story as a cultural practice with consequences for an understanding of consciousness.[46]

In England, the Birmingham Popular Memory Group in its critique of Thompson called for a new and more radical way of thinking about oral history in order to understand the struggles over popular memory. The manifesto of that group was the most explicit in denying the epistemological basis of both the traditional methods of the profession and the new social history, in particular.[47] In *Envelopes of Sound*, I tried to merge a concern with the structure of the interview and the work of Louis Althusser to understand the social, linguistic, and ideological structure of the historical text, which I termed a conversational narrative. The goal was to capture the two dimensions of our interest: the nature of the story and its creation through the interaction of the two parties to the interview.[48] Work with a similar concern with text, work that significantly enlarged the boundaries of the discussion about oral history, was done by Tonkin in Great Britain, Lutz Neithammer in Germany, and Phillipe Joutard in France.[49] By 1979, the *History Workshop Journal* could editorialize: "Recent developments in the methodology [of oral history] suggest that the potential exists for a more speculative and analytic approach to the evidence. For Marxists [the particular audience for the *Journal*], conversely, they show that theoretical categories and questions can be transformed in light of a critical interpretation of the evidence."[50]

All of this produced a very lively and complicated mix. Recognizing the potential of oral history to radically alter the ways in which history was understood led some scholars to ask new questions about memory and consciousness, while others began to think of new ways to teach history and new ways to mobilize sound and the new media in that teaching. Others saw in oral history the potential for historical drama or therapy. The inherent interdisciplinarity of the practice was evident.[51]

While it would take the rest of this volume to list the various sources of this new view of the possibilities of oral history, a few publications should be noted. The work of Passerini and Portelli, already mentioned, is crucial for an understanding of the explorations of subjectivity as well as the relationship between interviewer and interviewee. Portelli's chapter in *The Death of Luigi Trastulli*, on oral history as an experiment in equality, Michael Frisch's *A Shared Authority*, and the various essays in *Interactive Oral History Interviewing*, edited by Eva McMahan and Kim Lacy Rogers, explore in different ways the problems of the fieldwork relationship that so vexed Duberman.[52] Again, Portelli's various volumes have been instrumental in developing our thinking on the role of narrative in oral history, collective and individual memory, and the politics of history. Peter Friedlander, Virginia Yans-McLaughlin, and Samuel, concentrating on the relationship between individual biography and collective consciousness as expressed in the interview, contributed to a much more complex understanding of the nature of autobiography and political militancy. *Amoskeag*, by Tamara Hareven, explored the interstices of industrial and labor history. The essays compiled by Sherna Gluck and Daphne Patai in *Women's Words*, as well as the essays by Sally Alexander, Anna Davin, and other feminists writing in *History Workshop* and other journals, explored the crucial and variegated relations between feminist theory, subjectivity, narrativity, and oral history. All of this work has been predicated upon the proposition that oral history, while it does tell us about how people lived in the past, also, and maybe more importantly, tells us how that past lives on into and informs the present.[53]

One area in which oral historians were confronted with questions about the ways in which this tension between past and present expresses itself is trauma studies, a genre in itself. Centered at first among those who were interviewing Holocaust survivors, the concerns with issues of trauma were quite naturally extended to interviews with survivors of political torture, experiences such as rape, or other horrendous events. On such projects it was clear that the historian could not remain a contemplative presence, that the interview process itself as an experience became a moment in the resolution of the conflicts over the past, or a moment in the revivification of the original emotions of powerlessness and victimization and all the attendant consequences of that re-emergence. While these issues cannot be explored here in any great detail, it is important to keep them in mind in any discussion of what kinds of evidentiary uses of oral history are possible, any discussion of subjectivity in the interview, and our later discussion of memory. As stated by Jay Winter and Emmanuel Sivan, "Under specific conditions and occasionally long after the initial set of 'traumatic events,' . . . extrinsic contexts can produce overwhelming recall. At this point memory crowds out everything else; it is potentially paralytic."[54] Dominick LaCapra has been particularly insightful about the consequences for the oral historian (and, by implication, the challenges for historical reconstruction and dialogic exchange) of the ways that the past is reworked in Holocaust testimonies.[55] Many of these issues will be noted again in the discussion of the uses of oral history in the post–Cold War era.

The collective effect of work in oral history in the 1970s and 1980s that sought to move from issues in social history to cultural studies, as previously noted, was summed up in 1990 by Samuel and Thompson in their introduction to *The Myths We Live By*, a compilation of papers delivered at the Sixth International Oral History Conference held at Oxford, England, in 1987. "This volume," the authors argued,

> suggests how far the concerns of oral historians have shifted over the last decade. When we listen now to a life story, the manner of its telling seems to us as important as what is told. We find ourselves exploring interdisciplinary territory alongside others for whom the nature of narrative is a primary issue: among the anthropologists, psychoanalysts, historians . . . who recognize history itself as a narrative construction, literary critics who read metaphors as clues to social consciousness. This new sensitivity can strengthen some of the earlier purposes of oral historians. . . . As soon as we recognize the value of the subjective in individual testimonies, we challenge the accepted categories of history.[56]

When one examines the content of that volume, there is no disputing the claims of the editors. For anyone interested in the ways in which oral history interviewing, when creatively conceived and used, can open new avenues of thought about historical processes, many of the essays in the volume provide the starting point. The essays excite the reader with how myth, memory, narrative, and history are interwoven with an insight into how biography and testimony, in both manner and mode, can penetrate into the ways in which language becomes history. Certainly, there are questions to be asked about some of the points raised by the particular uses of myth in these essays, but gone are the tentativeness and apologetics that governed much of the early work with oral history interviews. Present is a comfort with subjective evidence and the ways in which it can be conceived theoretically.[57]

This transformation of oral history was, of course, part of a much larger transformation, one that has come to be called the "linguistic turn," "the historical turn," or the turn to cultural studies.[58] To detail these changes in any depth is beyond the charge of this essay. Essentially what was involved was the acceptance of a set of assumptions about the study of history, many of which had a period of long gestation. Grounding all else was the concept that history (knowledge about the past) was not something to be discovered in the facts or in the events of the past. It was, rather, a historically and culturally specific construction, and the ways in which it was constructed had to be comprehended for it to be understood and analyzed. Foremost, history, as all knowledge, was constructed through the agency of language and discourse. Historical narratives were not evinced in the ways in which events related to one another in a system of causality, but in the ways the imagination of the historian used words to create a symbolic world. It was through language that one discerned what Clifford Geertz called the "ensemble of texts" that composed a culture.[59] Language was structured and structuring. Thus, social history, with its accent upon what was now seen to be a narrow, class-based sociology, was to be invigorated with a new cultural vision. In part, this was a reaction to the trends of the 1960s arguing that historical studies must make way for issues of race, gender, and sexuality, which could not be explained within the traditional categories of social history.

In this view it was not the facts of experience but the "experience of experience" that was of interest. There was no master narrative but only stories and ambiguities. In a world where the personal was the political, one was concerned with the interrogation of such categories as nation, race, and gender to capture how understanding was revealed in practice. Thus data was interpretation. Gone was the objective observer, and politics was to be understood as the process by which plays of power and knowledge constitute identity and experience.

Oral historians, increasingly concerned with issues of narrative and subjectivity, found a comfortable milieu in cultural studies and a new sense of security about what it is they were studying and how they wished to study it: thus the optimism of the *History Workshop Journal* 1990 introduction. This optimism was confirmed by the privileged place given oral history in a special 1989 edition of the *Journal of American History* devoted to the analysis of memory. In that issue, David Thelen, the journal's editor, stressed the importance of oral history in studying memory and encouraged the profession to examine the rich literature then emerging.[60] To a large degree it was obvious that if the historical profession had gatekeepers who determined what was and what was not evidence, oral history had been admitted to the bar.

Thus, in the mid-1980s, three new critiques of the practice of oral history went almost totally ignored, despite the fact that they were offered by three major figures in the profession who under ordinary circumstances would have been considered gatekeepers. In the first case, Dominique Aron-Schnapper, in her comments at the Fourth International Conference on Oral History in Aix-en-Provence, France, argued that oral historians should not concern themselves with elaborate constructions to understand subjectivity but should return to and concentrate upon the archival task of filling in the gaps in the written record. In the second case, Louise Tilly, then president of the Social Science History Association in the U.S., speaking from the perspective of quantification and social history, criticized both oral history and people's history. And Patrick O'Farrell, in Australia, argued that the whole mission, either of social history or community history, was a waste of the historian's time for little gain:

a feckless effort to fill the pages of history with the history of "ordinary" people, whose history, basically, is uninteresting.[61]

The most cogent of these critiques was that of Tilly because it stated the case so clearly. The task of social science history, she argued, is "research that attempts generalizations of some breadth verified by . . . quantitative analysis when appropriate."[62] The concern with subjectivity and the claims made by oral historians and people's historians rested upon a "radical passivity" mixed with a concept of "subjectivity" and would never produce a valid historiography. In particular, she argued, the emphasis upon the individual testimony as an insight into collective representations and cultural identities is "ahistorical and unsystematic."[63] The responses from a number of oral historians, and then Tilly's response to those comments, all of which were published in the *International Journal of Oral History*, offer a wonderful insight into the then current debates over the nature of the evidence produced by oral historians and its uses.[64]

While these critiques are now of some historical interest, they did little to alter the direction of oral history. That direction was clear: oral history was becoming increasingly interdisciplinary, increasingly international, increasingly focused upon issues of subjectivity, and increasingly interested in how to use the potential of the interview and the language of the interview to understand that subjectivity, whether it was memory, ideology, myth, consciousness, identity, desire, or any other such attributes. One caution from that time, however, must be noted and is addressed below. In his review of the English version of Passerini's *Fascism in Popular Memory*, Richard Cándida Smith warned that in viewing the oral history interview as a cultural form that merges subjectivity and the narrative mode, "further thought needs to be given to how oral history can be read for evidence of the interaction of culture and political action."[65]

Narrative

Because it has always been first and foremost a fieldwork practice, oral history had always looked to other disciplines for guidance, if not standards. Its early practitioners were particularly interested in similar work in sociology, behavioral psychology, law, applied anthropology, or journalism.[66] This was a natural crossover for those concerned with gathering and using evidence that for the most part was to be transposed into written form or into measurable or statistical relationships and therefore could meet the judgment of verifiability, reliability, validity, and representation as defined by the dominant intellectual strictures of the time. Even when one recognized the natural affinity for biographical and autobiographical studies, as Nevins obviously did, the basic approach mirrored the empiricism of these disciplines. A clear example of this connection is Thompson's first major work, *The Edwardians*, in which he tried to meld his oral history interviewing with a selection of interviewees based upon a properly drawn sample derived from early twentieth-century censuses.[67] By the mid-1980s, however, attention was directed toward disciplines such as cultural anthropology, linguistics, literary studies, philosophy, folklore, and cultural studies, which were more likely to attract students of language and culture broadly defined.[68] To be sure, many, if not most, studies using oral history were still concerned with the ways in which individual recitations of experience could be related to collective behavior, but such studies would now also note the importance of language and story in the formation of the connection. This resulted, among other things, in a new fieldwork stance. Whereas in the search for a "scientific" procedure for interviewing the traditional advice was to urge the interviewer into a contemplative and distanced relation with the person interviewed, oral historians now argued for a closer and more interactive response. In the language of the time, the shift was from transactional to intersubjective.[69] In this shift the role of the conception of narrative was fundamental.

When I talked about a conversational narrative in *Envelopes of Sound*, I had in mind a very unsophisticated idea of what was meant by narrative. Essentially, I defined it simply as the telling of a tale of change over time. If any theory was involved, it was quite simple. The story, however conceived, began with a description of a state of stasis, then some disruptive event or experience was introduced to upset that stasis, and finally some resolution that restored stasis was forthcoming. Even a brief examination of the use of narrative by oral historians today, such as Passerini, Portelli, Daniel James, and especially Tonkin, reveals how naïve that earlier insight was, especially its implication of the unity of action and meaning.[70]

Passerini describes her interviews in various places as oral narratives, but the actual relationship between those interviews and narrative theory is embedded in the detailed discussion of particular interviews and the forms that they take. The interview, she says, is "a semi-structured conversation, which is . . . more concerned with drawing out forms of cultural identity and shared traditions than with the factual aspects of social history."[71] The most concise statement of Passerini's idea of a narrative can be found in the Smith review already noted, in which he pulls together the discussion of narrative inherent in Passerini's treatment of fascism. In that review, Smith notes how "the ideas, images and linguistic strategies found in oral narratives constitute what Passerini calls 'the symbolic order of everyday life.'"[72] This view allows Passerini to open her investigation to the ways in which traditional oral sources provided a repertoire for and merged into the new telling of the story for the historian, the ways in which silences become a part of the narrative, and the possibilities of understanding collective memory and thought through the oral narrative.

Portelli is equally concerned with the search for the subjective in oral narratives, but his use of narrative theory is much more, by his own admission, ad hoc and inductive, seeking to find in the stories themselves the structures of form. He uses, he says, "literature, folklore, and linguistics to develop a method for the study of subjectivity by focusing on the implications of the verbal strategies used by the narrators. . . . Oral historical sources are *narrative* sources. Therefore the analysis of oral history materials must avail itself of some of the general categories developed by narrative theory in literature and folklore. This is as true of testimony given in free interviews as of the more formally organized materials of folklore."[73] Some of the elements of narrative Portelli suggests one look for are shifts in velocity, distance, perspective, folk elements, digressions, anecdotes, and other recurring structures.

Portelli is also intrigued with the dialogic nature of the interview, his own role in the process, and the ways in which narratives emerge through this dialogue.[74] Because his use of narrative is ad hoc, it appears throughout his by now fairly large corpus, but a casual glance at any number of essays will reveal to the reader the constant and steady negotiations between oral expressions and literary works and traditions, and how those works and traditions help explain and, in turn, are explained by the dialogic nature of the oral history interview.[75]

It should be clear that narrative in an oral history interview does not mean a clearly articulated story that runs in precise chronological pattern. In fact, the request for that kind of narrative might be precisely the wrong kind of question for an interviewer to ask.[76] Rather, the oral historian must follow the patterns set by the people interviewed, which is not that difficult to do since it is the form of every conversation—to follow the gist. The more complex story is usually reconstructed at a later time. In other words, the narrative is constructed syntagmatically.[77]

Drawing upon the oral history work of Passerini and Portelli and the writings on narrative of a wide range of scholars from various disciplines, James succinctly states the case in his life history of an Argentine working-class militant, with reference to David Carr's *Time, Narrative, and History*: "The 'recent blurring of the genres' has induced an increased sensitivity among historians— perhaps most intensively among oral historians—to the importance of narrative as an ordering, sense-making device at both the collective and individual level. As Carr argues, 'At the individual level, people make sense of their lives through stories that are available to them, and they attempt to fit their lives into the available stories. People live by stories.'" James adds, "At a more general level, communities, too, adopt narratives that inculcate and confirm their integrity and coherence over time."[78] In this view, narrative has become the central characteristic and organizing principle for the oral history interview. In essence, the narrative itself becomes a fact of historical interest.

The most complex and nuanced recent treatment of oral history and narrative form is Tonkin's work in *Narrating Our Pasts*, wherein she sets for herself the difficult task of understanding "the mode or genre in which temporal accounts occur in order to grasp the character of the interlocutors' social action and to evaluate the information that the account conveys."[79] Quoting Karin Barber, Tonkin outlines the paradoxical complexity of the task:

"To grasp their historical intent we need to view [representations of pastness] as literature; to grasp their literary mode we need to view them as part of social action; to grasp their role in social action we need to see their historical intent."[80] Assuming that the historian who uses the recollections of others cannot just seek facts, "like currants from a cake," because those facts are embedded in interpretations and therefore can only be understood by understanding the representation, its ordering, its plotting, and its metaphors, Tonkin raises most of the basic issues of narrative analysis of oral accounts—their structuring, the ways in which they relate to social conditions, the performative nature of orality (or oracity, as she calls it), which distinguish oral from literary accounts—and explores questions of memory ("the dialectical interlocking of recall and social nexus") and time.[81] All of this is done within a keen grasp of the interwoven aims and ambitions and social conditions of both parties to the fieldwork experience. *Narrating Our Pasts* must now be the starting point for any discussion of the role of narrative in the understanding of the meaning of the evidence produced in an oral history interview.

In his 1984 critique of Thompson, John Murphy calls for an interpretative reading of oral history texts. In particular, he argues for attention to the problems of the interaction between language and memory and for the centrality of metaphor, since "metaphor is the dominant mode in which oral history functions . . . and a key to a cultural reading on how the past is remembered."[82] Just how far in that direction oral history work has come can be seen in the essays in *Narrative and Genre*, edited by Mary Chamberlain and Paul Thompson, that examine narrative from a variety of perspectives, including literary studies, anthropology, philosophy, folklore, and communications theory, and that, in most cases, begin their analysis with references to Tonkin. The editors' introduction is an excellent posing of the problems and potentials of genre studies of oral autobiography.[83] These and other such studies, almost by necessity, point us to other much more fundamental considerations of narrative, such as those posed by Carr, Jerome Bruner, Donald Spence, and Donald Polkinghorne.[84]

Narrative was a vital part of the so-called cultural turn, and issues raised by narrative, genre, storytelling, and autobiography became an important part of the discourse across disciplinary boundaries.[85] It is far from the task of this essay to parse the subtle similarities and differences between these authors, particularly as to the issue of the discontinuity or continuity between narrative and everyday life, but a few general points should be noted. Narrative means more than simply the mode of the telling of a story that can be studied in a manner abstracted from the life of the person telling the story. Narrative has come to be described as an act of mind, one that, as Carr stated, "arises out of and is prefigured in certain features of life, action, and communication."[86] Karen Halttunen explains, "For Carr, our narratives reflect a fundamental property of human consciousness; they are part of the fabric of human life."[87] In this sense, it is narrative that lends structure to the experience of experience and unites the individual to the collective practically, cognitively, and aesthetically, and therefore encompasses a social relationship and identity. Integral to the construction of memory, narrative is the "organizing principal of human experience," according to Polkinghorne.[88] In the transformation of oral history from a concern with data to a concern with narrative, what one considers evidence also shifted. The question now is, how are metaphor, emplotment, sequence, and all the other attributes of narrative understood as evidence, and of what are they evidence? The issue has moved from historiography to historical cognition. As Bruner says, "Eventually the culturally shaped cognitive and linguistic processes that guide the self telling of life narratives achieve the power to structure perceptual experience, to organize memory, to segment and purpose-build the very 'events' of a life. In the end we *become* the autobiographical narratives by which we 'tell about' our lives."[89]

In *Envelopes of Sound*, I traced out some of the tactical and epistemological consequences of the concern with narrative among oral historians.[90] In brief, I noted that the telling of the story being recorded is not, in most cases, the first time the story was told,[91] that each time it was told it was told within the linguistic, logical, and factual limits of the time of the telling as well as the limits of public and private memory, and thus each time it was told it changed. It is the oral historian's task, through research, to understand the history of these tellings and then to explore the contradictions within the story, contextualize the telling, and thereby help the narrators create the fullest narrative possible at this moment of time. This will allow the researcher to, in the words of Paul Ricoeur, "appropriate the text." "What has to be appropriated," Ricoeur argues, "is the meaning of the text itself, conceived in a dynamic way as the direction of thought opened by the text. In other words, what has to be appropriated is nothing other than the power of disclosing a world that constitutes the reference of the text, . . . the disclosure of a possible way of looking at things, which is the genuine referential power of the text."[92]

In this appropriation one can begin to plumb all the contradictions inherent in ideology, memory, and language. The most obvious explorations of the errors, elisions, and evasions (inaccuracies) that are a part of the different ways of looking at things are the essays that form *The Death of Luigi Trastulli*, by Portelli. The key essay noted in any discussion of the book explores the meaning of the misdating of the death of worker militant Trastulli and why, despite the fact that evidence of the correct date is right at hand, narrators insist Trastulli died on a different date. For Portelli, this insistence becomes a key to understanding the consciousness of his narrators and the ways in which they make sense of their own history.[93]

Of course, common sense tells us, errors, elisions, and evasions can only be understood and be given meaning within some context the reader or listener has constructed. Thus a consciousness of the historicity of the historian as well as the interviewee is vital in making such judgments. Far from being absolved of the sometimes onerous tasks of research and interpretation, oral historians must, in order to realize the potential richness of the oral history document, extend themselves even further into that study.

Documenting International Human Rights

No mention of the growth of oral history in the last decades of the twentieth century can ignore the consequences of the politics of the post–Cold War world and new uses for oral evidence in documenting human rights abuses. Oral historians, especially in

Europe and Latin America, had been, from the start of the practice, interested in documenting political oppression, in particular the history of fascism, Nazism, and colonialism. Oral histories of Holocaust survivors, as already noted, made up a large portion of the organized oral history projects throughout the world long before the recent interest of the Shoah Foundation. The late 1980s and 1990s, however, saw an efflorescence of projects interviewing those whose histories had been stripped from them by repressive regimes. With the collapse of the Communist governments of the Soviet Union and Eastern Europe and other dictatorships, such as those in Latin America, projects were organized almost immediately to rescue the memory of daily life. Sometimes organized with the assistance of Western oral historians, many times rising spontaneously in community groups or university history or sociology departments, there was a rapid expansion of the global reach of oral history. In addition, with the collapse of the apartheid regime in South Africa, oral history came to play a new role as part of the effort to document the history of Africans long denied a history and to assist in efforts at truth and reconciliation. Then, with a new outbreak of general slaughter of populations in areas such as Cambodia and the former Yugoslavia, oral history projects were mounted to document war crimes and other traumatic experiences, such as genocide, torture, and rape, and to provide firsthand testimony of oppression to be offered as evidence at international tribunals or in order to gain reparations.[94]

Many of these projects resonated with issues raised by Holocaust interviews. First and foremost was the necessity and primacy of oral testimonies, given the distorted or nonexistent written record, which if it did exist, by definition lacked any evidence of the extent and detail of the apparatus of oppression and its effects upon ordinary citizens, that is, the subjectivity of oppression. Second, such interviewing narrowed the gap between history and therapy as it documented the trauma of severe dislocations, such as torture or the disappearance of loved ones, and gave a new life to traumatic memories. As noted earlier, such questions were new for oral historians, and the consequences for the definition of the practice remain controversial to this day.

An equally new and sometimes uncomfortable role for oral historians involved questions of human rights and reparations. Long committed to a politics against oppression, their work was now to be used as evidence in trials or tribunals of varying power and potency. Oral history interviews conducted in the 1960s and 1970s on the history of Nazism and fascism were, by and large, conducted at a time long enough removed from the terrors of World War II to provide some space for reflection. In addition, the war crimes tribunals following that war had seemingly settled the case for juridical punishments and, in many cases, reparations. The currency of events at the close of the twentieth century, new calls for reparations, and the revival of old claims such as Native American land rights, however, posed new definitions of oral evidence and therefore new problems for the oral historian.

The growing internationalization of the oral history movement brought to the fore other major theoretical and methodological issues. Was it possible to maintain European and North American notions of narrative and subjectivity, given the development of the field in Latin America, Africa, and Asia, with their own historiographical traditions and modes of oral transmission of the memories of the past? And how were the tools and interpretations developed in the past twenty years to be used in understanding the violence of a new era? In the first case, the debates over the relationship of oral history to the study of oral traditions in Africa indicate how complicated the issues are, and those debates are the debates of Western scholars, for the most part.[95] In the second case, could the telling of one's history aid in the break from a "rigid and limiting constellation of violence"?[96]

Intersubjectivity

In her analysis of the oral history interview as a hermeneutic act, McMahan argues for the centrality of intersubjectivity, which, following Alfred Schutz, she describes as a "precondition for human symbol-using activity." Quoting Schutz, she notes, "The world 'is intersubjective because we live in it as men among other men, bound to them through common influence and work, understanding others and being understood by them.'"[97] The concept, used in this way to describe communication in the oral history interview as a search for understanding, is the logical extension of the concern with issues of subjectivity and narrative, encompassing both. Building upon the work of Hans-George Gadamer, McMahan lists three suppositions upon which a "hermeneutic" conversation (Gadamer's term) is based. First, interpretation is "always performed within the universe of linguistic possibilities and . . . these linguistic possibilities as performed mark out the historicality of human experience."[98] Or, in the words of Martin Jay, "Our finitude as human beings is encompassed by the infinity of language."[99] Second, McMahan says, "Interpretation . . . always is guided by the biases that an interpreter has at a specific moment in time." Jay agrees, stating, "It is only through prejudices that our horizons are open to the past."[100] Third, McMahan claims, "'An act of interpretation must always be concerned directly with the historical phenomen[on] itself, e.g., not with an interviewee's intended meaning but what the intended meaning is about.'"[101] At any one moment, intersubjectivity is limited by language, bias, and the nature of the object of investigation. As Jay says, "Understanding is not a reproductive procedure, but rather always a productive one."[102] In this manner the interactive nature of the oral history interview becomes a cooperative effort to interpret the past through the recognition of the role of the historicity of both parties to that interview.

In his usual perceptive manner, Portelli, noting the consequences of this subjectivity, describes the interview situation as "an exchange between *two* subjects; literally a mutual sighting. One party cannot really *see* the other unless the other can see him or her in turn. The two interacting subjects cannot act together unless some mutuality is established. The field researcher, therefore, has an objective stake in equality, as a condition for a less distorted communication and a less biased collection of data."[103] This, he argues, is the basis for the view of oral history as an "experiment in equality," an equality that is based upon the recognition of difference, since equality and sameness are not interchangeable. Thus, intersubjectivity in the interview rests upon two pillars: difference and equality. The various ways oral historians have described and worked with this tension tells us much about how evidence is dialectically and dialogically produced in the interview and for what purposes.

The most popular and easily understood description of this process is Michael Frisch's, given at length and with many wonderful examples in *A Shared Authority*. The idea of shared authority is the means whereby Frisch resolves the tension he earlier describes between more history and the populist attempt to bypass history. Noting the dual meaning of authority encompassing both authorship and power, the idea of shared authority allows Frisch both to note the creative role of the interviewee as well as the interviewer and to make the political point for the necessity of the sharing of interpretative power in the process. Frisch, however, leaves the issue open as to exactly how that sharing will work out in the interview.[104]

The basic assumption of both McMahan and Frisch is that there is a set of differences between interviewees and interviewers that must in some form be negotiated in order for the interview to be conducted and to continue once begun. As Portelli argues, this "joint venture" is an experiment in equality.[105] Far from erasing the gulf between interviewer and interviewee, however, the actual procedure, despite the search for the "reciprocity of perspectives," McMahan explains, is a "tension-laden" one. The interview is therefore a situation of "contrariety."[106]

In this view, because of the wide differences in social power between the parties to the interview, fieldwork equality, as Portelli notes, is difficult to achieve. But these differences are more than simply social power. They include all the cultural assumptions and biases that march in the wake of that power. Thus the historian and the person being interviewed must, on even the most rudimentary level, recognize the rights of the other in the dialogue.[107] At the least, the interviewee must agree that the aims and ambitions of the historian in his or her project are worthy and in some manner even useful to pursue, while the historian must recognize the autonomy of the view of the interviewee. The complexity and the depth of the difficulty of achieving this understanding I have tried to spell out elsewhere by examining the different languages and attitudes that both parties bring to the interview: the historian's professional language of analysis, which in turn reflects his or her professional identity and politics, and the interviewee's historically located language of narrative in which the experience is embedded. Thus the quality of an interview, rather than being the result of the resolution of the basic tension in the process, is determined by the ability or inability of each participant to enter the world of the other.[108]

James, in his life history of Doña María, shows in practice how difficult this is. Other examples of the tension abound. Essays in a recent issue of the *Oral History Review* devoted to the exploration of the idea of shared authority, now defined to encompass much more than simply authorship, reveal the complexities of the relationship in community history projects, ranging from a situation of sympathetic and cooperative political involvement and consensus between historians and members of the community to a situation of near total breakdown of the interview relationship because of the inability to overcome the tension between historian and interviewee.[109] In another study, Glen Adler in his interviews with South African union members under apartheid has documented the enormity of the gulf between even the most well-meaning historian and the interviewees in situations of political repression.[110] A more recent, interesting example of the negotiations between the parties to the interview involved in the search for the winding path of the skein of a life through the various modes of self presentation, evasion, and even lies of a narrator can be found in Sandy Polishuk's introduction to *Sticking to the Union*.[111] If one is to engage in any fieldwork, he or she must agree with Henry Glassie that people, when they tell their stories, do attempt to get the facts of their lives and communities as correct as they can.[112] One must also, however, recognize that the idea of what is accurate and what history should know is not an easily agreed upon conclusion. Very often what is involved is the deep, sharp, and conflicted view of the relationship of self and society on the part of each party to the interview. This is the case, I would argue, even in situations where the relationship comes perilously close to resembling a psychoanalytic session of transference and countertransference.[113]

Enrica Capussotti expresses a more optimistic view of understanding the disruptions of intersubjectivity, based upon the ways in which these contradictions emerge. In summing up her fieldwork experiences interviewing Kosovar Albanians and Kosovar Romany, she states:

> One could say that throughout the 1970s, oral history was written from within a movement which would have liked "to give words" to the subaltern (the working class, for example) and women. In our times, however, oral history is capable of prefiguring the relationships between different subjectivities and cultures and revealing the contradictions between the individual and the community. Oral history can therefore be used to criticize the mechanism of inclusion or exclusion, and the process of identity construction based upon national values. The tensions between the voice of the individual and the dominant discourses of the public sphere, which legitimize the declaration and self position, emerge in every one of the testimonies, and might serve as a powerful "weapon" with which to enter the critical debate on public memory and the political use of the past.[114]

As Passerini notes in her comments on Capussotti's essay, it is optimistic and legitimate "precisely because it presupposes a heterogeneity of subjectivities."[115]

Sound

The direct relationship of interviewer and interviewee is not the only unique trait of the oral history interview. The oral history interview is also unique because it exists as sound. This fact has been noted and commented upon, again, since the early days of oral history. Much of that discussion centered upon four distinct but interrelated problems: modes of presentation, recording practices, preservation, and the distinctions between literacy and orality. In the first case, the question was how to present in an accessible form the essential aural content of the interview. This discussion had two components: the question of transcribing and radio uses of oral history. In the first case, it was obvious, despite the pressures and need for transcription in order to make the interview easily accessible to the widest number of researchers, that the transcript could not catch the fullness of the conversation.[116] It was, recalling Samuel, a mutilation of the word. Transcription leveled the language, put everything in place, could not indicate the tone, volume, range of sound, and rhythms of speech, and as Portelli claimed, denied the orality of oral sources.[117] Arguing for the saving of tapes, Benison noted that "the physical voice helps give a rounded psychological portrait of the man or woman being interviewed and contributes a truth to the oral history account that the typed page can never convey."[118] In addition, the expense of transcription led many to seek new ways of preparing the recordings for listening, such as the TAPE system developed at the Wisconsin Historical Society or, later, various digital indexing systems.[119] These systems for the most part concentrated upon what were seen as traditional users of oral histories, for the most part academic professionals.

Radio was seen as the most compatible medium for the use of oral histories as sound material to reach larger audiences, and many oral historians and projects naturally gravitated to various kinds of radio production, a form of activity that has generated a fairly extensive literature.[120] But it should be noted that even with radio productions, as Peter Read has pointed out, problems of presentation came to the fore. Production for the media meant that silences had to vanish, whole minutes of talk would be transposed, certain speaking styles did not lend themselves to reproduction or interest, and there was no way to convey the intimacy of the interview in a mass medium.[121] Recording practices and preservation are in large part determined by the particular equipment one uses and the particular recording media, factors covered in many manuals and guidebooks.[122]

The topic of orality of oral sources spawned a rich and complex literature on the differences between spoken and written narratives, in particular the work of Walter Ong and Deborah Tannen.[123] Giving primacy to the spoken word, and in some cases to the tape over the transcript, the literature set about to understand the rules of rendition in oral transmission, or the "communicative repertoire." The goal was to understand what was spoken and its performative context and to draw a distinction between spoken and written genres of storytelling.[124] If scholars paid attention to listening, it was to urge historians to pay attention to what was said and how it was said.[125] One of the most interesting comments about the role of sound in the oral history interview was Dennis Tedlock's argument that the dialogue could best be understood as poetry and his experimentation with ways to transcribe an interview in order to catch the cadences and rhythms of a poem.[126] Here again, the goal was to better understand the oral performance.

There is no doubt that some of the most interesting, important, and insightful debates in oral history have addressed themselves to the complicated dialectic between oral and literate cultures, or more centrally to the dialectic between orality and literacy within both literate and oral cultures.[127] But such issues do not exhaust our concern with the phenomenon of sound in the oral history interview, especially in the so-called digital age.[128] To extend these concerns, one must shift attention to sound itself and then speculate on the ways in which the intersubjectivity of the interview is constructed through listening.

What unites the discussion of sound thus far is the focus on speech. It is speech that must be understood, either in spoken or written form; it is speech that must be presented to a larger audience; it is speech that must be recorded properly in order to be understood; and it is spoken genres that define orality. It is the focus on speaking that has led oral historians to be so unconcerned with sound itself.

Listening is to hearing as reading is to sight.[129] Our first object of interest is the sense of sound—hearing. But we have to be clear as to what we are listening. The point that the critics of transcribing seem to be making is that in the concentration upon speech we are missing the full range of voice. It is those aspects of voice that are not speech that we lose in the application of a written orthography. It is also clear, although the point does not seem to have been made, that in the concentration on speech we have ignored the ways in which communication by other aspects of voice is often based upon class, race, and gender differences.[130] Even with the best of intentions in transcribing or in various modes of aural presentation, however, a selection process takes place in which it is somehow determined that certain vocalisms are not to be included in the document and others are. A conversation is full of burps, groans, laughs, sighs, beeps, whistles, and other sounds. Oftentimes in a transcript a laugh or a pause or a sob might be noted (as long as it is not considered embarrassing), while in radio production, in the name of efficiency, only a few of these characteristics are retained. But, it must be noted, each time such editing takes place it is an interpretative act. We must also be aware that the first selection has come in the very act of recording, for the technology itself has selected, out of the total range of sound, both of the voice and the audio world of the voice, only that which can be heard by the microphone. Therefore, even listening to the tapes rather than reading a transcript, although it may get one closer to the phenomenon of the interview, does not replicate the interview fully.[131] In the present age, one must remember, most of what one hears and listens to is media produced and thus edited.

Charles Hardy has been particularly inventive in imagining ways in which oral historians can mobilize the digital media in order to create what he calls "aural art," or sound montages of oral histories, archival recordings, and sound elements, to create a "soundscape." Soundscape here has two dimensions: the recording of the world of sound in which the interview takes place and the presentation of the recorded interview within the context of other sounds from the period under discussion or of the events being discussed. Hardy lists a number of radio presentations that have attempted to merge these two dimensions and points to the possibilities for creative uses of future three-dimensional sound recording. He also notes the limits to such work posed by our print biases, the marginality of radio, and the lack of exposure to high-quality sound recording. There is also a limit in the ways in which we have imagined the world of sound.[132]

Bruce R. Smith, in his study of the acoustical world of early modern England, summarizes recent work on the phenomenology of sound as a sensory experience. He notes four ways to think about sound: as a physical act, as a sensory experience, as an act of communication, and as a political performance.[133] For the most part, oral historians have said little about the first two and focused upon the last two. As a physical act, the sound of a voice arises from within the speaker and surrounds the listener. We have two voices: one we hear and one others hear. We hear ourselves within ourselves and others from without; there is a hereness and thereness. While we cannot go into the kind of detail that Smith recounts, it is important to note three characteristics of an auditory field: surroundability, directionality, and continuity.[134] All of this is posed in direct opposition to sight and reading. Visualized objects stay outside of one. Sound penetrates the body; sound is inescapable. We close our eyes, and we do not see. If we bore of a book, we simply shift focus and look elsewhere. We cannot escape the voice of an interviewee droning on. We may not listen, but we always hear. Sight knowledge is presented to exist quite apart from the body of the knower; in sound one is immersed. Reading is ontological; listening, phenomenological.[135]

Several points follow for the oral historian. As noted, a recording, however faithful, cannot reconstruct the sound world of the interview. It, too, captures only a part of that world. Second, shifting our focus to the ways in which the physical fact of sound becomes a psychological experience reveals an added fullness to the intersubjectivity of the interview, for the aural world is also culturally and historically situated. The project now is to see in which ways we can manipulate new ways of recording in line with new ways of envisioning the world of sound in order to redefine the evidence of the interview. How can we understand evidence derived from a sense other than sight?

Memory, Myth, Ideology, Consciousness

Writing in 1992, James Fentress and Chris Wickham, in one of the few works devoted to memory that directed specific attention to oral history, took oral historians to task for their emphasis upon the analysis of their documents that accented "more or less true statements about the lived past" rather than explaining "how social identities are actually constructed by this or that version of the past" or searching "memories for their social meaning." While noting that a "sea change" was taking place in oral history, work on memory, they claimed, was only theoretical. They saw the reluctance of oral historians to accent memory as a desire on their part to establish a pedigree for the practice and as contentment with a narrow textual view of memory. What was needed, they continued, were concrete examples of the ways in which memory became history.[136] Whether or not that charge stood up at the time, we will evaluate below. It certainly does not now. Even a swift glance at Portelli's latest work, *The Order Has Been Carried Out*, reveals the depth and insight that oral history interviews, carefully conducted and interpreted, can bring to our understanding of the complicated set of relationships involved in the dialectical tension between memory and history. Frisch, in comments printed on the book's dust jacket, states, "Analytically, meditatively, passionately, and poetically, Portelli explores and documents, as fact and as memory, an episode critical to the history of Italy and World War II and to the postwar world down to the present. . . . [The book] reminds us that oral history matters because it demonstrates how the past and present necessarily, if not comfortably, live together within all of us."[137] In many ways, Portelli's work stands as the culmination of a generation's thinking about the role of memory in oral history and the transformation in ways in which we have conceived our tasks.

Questions of memory have been a part of the discourse on oral history from the early origins of the practice.[138] Definitions and conceptions of memory within that discourse, however, have changed dramatically. Initially, the concern was with the accuracy and reliability of memory or the distinctions between long-term and short-term memory, while memory was seen as a repository from which recollections were brought to consciousness in response to various types of stimuli. One's interest was in the processes and structural coding of memory rather than the convoluted relationship of memory and history, which were seen to be locked in opposition to one another. As insightful as some of this work was, in particular Thompson's discussion in the first edition of *The Voice of the Past* or the speculations of John Neuenschwander in the U.S., it was a world away from later considerations, brought on by a transformation, interestingly enough, traced out by Thompson in a 1994 essay. Ten years earlier, he had noted, oral historians, "saw the main problem as being whether that information within the informant was distorted or contaminated by the passage of time, by remembering, or by reevaluating earlier memories. They were not, in other words, concerned with what we now see as essential mental processes of thinking about experience, of conceiving it in order to express it."[139] Samuel noted that "Memory, so far from being merely a passive receptacle or storage system, an image bank of the past, is rather an active, shaping force: it is dynamic—what it contrives symptomatically to forget is as important as what it remembers—and that is dialectically related to historical thought, rather than being some kind of negative order to it."[140]

Of course, oral historians were not alone in either an interest in memory or in the changing view of the issues and controversies involved in the historical study of memory and their meaning for our understanding of past experience. The literature on the topic is now quite extensive and points to a view of memory as a process dynamically related to history, not as a timeless tradition but as being progressively altered from generation to generation. In this view, memory, narrative, personal and collective identity, and past experience are interwoven in a finely textured and complicated process of historical reconstruction.[141] This has obvious implications for oral historians. The call for concrete examples by Fentress and Wickham, noted above, resonated with a similar but earlier call by Ulrich Neisser for a concentration on the everyday uses of memory.[142]

These critiques of oral history were, however, a bit off base. As far back as the late 1970s and early 1980s, oral historians had presented abundant examples of the role of memory in concrete situations. Passerini had explored issues of memory and political and gender identity in her study of Turin autoworkers. Portelli also had explored social memory in a local and concrete situation in Tierni, Italy. John Bodnar, writing in 1989, had stated explicitly his interest in using oral histories with Studebaker automotive workers in the U.S. for insight into social memories. Joutard in an extended work had documented the social memories of French Protestants. Since that time, Karen Fields, Alistair Thomson, Samuel Schrager, as well as Rogers, Tonkin, and James, just to mention some North American and European writers, have had very interesting and important things to say about social memory. Indeed, a full tally encompassing work in other areas of the world, noting studies by Elizabeth Jelin, Antonio Montenegro, José Carlos Sebe Bom Meihy, and others, as well as a full listing of publications in the U.S. and Europe, would uncover an enormous contribution of oral history to views of social memory in concrete situations, much of which has been ignored by mainstream historiography on memory.[143]

One of the more interesting attempts to understand memory in the oral history process is the work of Howard and Alice Hoffman, described in their essay in this volume. The Hoffmans' work is remarkable for three unrelated reasons: it is one of the few efforts by oral historians to speculate about the process of memory rather than its cultural meaning; it raises the question as to whether it is possible to purposely not remember something, or at least hold memories in abeyance; and it accents the role of research by the interviewee and interviewer prior to the interview.[144]

In his masterly compilation of essays about the relationship between history and memory, Pierre Nora mentions oral history only once, and very briefly in passing, as far as I have been able to determine. Noting the enormous amount of time it takes to process just one hour of tape-recorded conversation, the incredible growth of the number of holdings of interviews, and the fact that these recordings make sense only if listened to in their entirety, Nora wonders what possible purpose they would serve: "Whose will to remember do they ultimately reflect, that of the interviewer or that of the interviewee?" Oral history is, he argues, "a deliberate and calculated compilation of a vanished memory. It adds a secondary and prosthetic memory to actual experience, which is altered by the very fact of being recorded." It is, he concludes, "the clearest expression yet of the 'terroristic' effect of historical memory."[145]

The question of use is incidental to us since our experience has been that interviews are widely used. It is the idea of "secondary" that intrigues. In some sense, all memory is secondary since it is really impossible for us to isolate ourselves from daily reminders and memory jogs about our past experiences. As LaCapra notes, no memory is purely primary.[146] Memory may be selective, but when we tell our stories to others, intervening events and what we have experienced, read, or discussed since the time of the original event under investigation (which, with oral history, may stretch to years) all influence that articulation. In fact, the enhanced story is the one that we as historians now want to tell. Because as oral historians we do not usually go into the field to test memory, we often, especially in archival projects, bring along memory jogs, such as photographs, correspondence, or other documents, or we ask those we interview to review their experiences, consult scrapbooks if available, confer with others, or tour sites. Therefore the memories we collect are refreshed. For these reasons oral history may not have much to tell us about the processes of memory, but it has a great deal to tell us about the dialectical relationship between memory and history, how memory becomes history, and how history becomes memory. For us, memory is not psychology; it is historiography.

In a finely textured and insightful essay on the interplay of history and memory in the creation of the history of the American South and the importance of politics and the poetics of agency and critique, Jacquelyn Dowd Hall makes an interesting point: "We bring to our writing the unfinished business of our own lives and times; moreover, the experience of traveling so long in the country of research *becomes* our past, for our stories grow from a process of remembering and forgetting our encounters with the relics, fragments, whispers of an always already-recollected time. In all these ways, we live both the history we have learned through reading and research and the history we have experienced and inherited, passed down through the groups with which we identify, sedimented in the body, and created through talk."[147]

For the oral historian, that point is central to a discussion of memory because it brings us back to our own historicity. If we accept the proposition that the interview is a joint creation, a shared authority, then we must interrogate the ways in which the memories of the historian/interviewer—our memories—find expression in the interplay of the participants. Every aspect of memory that we attribute to those whom we interview must also be explored in ourselves: the social determinants, such as class, region, background; our professional and research memories; the "relics, fragments, whispers" Hall so eloquently describes. Only in this manner will we be able to assess in what ways memory becomes evidence in the oral history interview.

Assessing the tension between memory and history begins with an examination of the role played by myth. The category of memory in this problematic is collective, social, or popular memory, but what is the definition of myth within this context?[148] Too often *myth* has been used to connote something that is in error, often intentionally so. At other times, such as in Fentress and Wickham, the reference is to legends or deeds of heroes. When I use the term here I am referring to a much broader conception: myth as a narrative that is felt by large numbers of people to be "relatively immune to the distortions of untrustworthy and interested individual reporting"; that is "valued as the most generalized *topos* of socially significant space-time"; and that "sets out the ways in which human activity can be given meaning as episodes in living narrative, as parts of a larger and more encompassing story, a universally salient history."[149] Viewing myth in this sense, it is striking how often the discussion of the tension between memory and history introduces a discussion of myth.

Alistair Thomson notes the clear connection in what he sees as the search for composure in memory and the ways in which myth grants socially acceptable memories, in particular the myths of the nation.[150] Indeed that may be the connection. Many collective memories focus on the ethno and national construction of identity as the universally salient history and thus, as Anthony Smith explores in detail, become open to myths of a special people with a special mission.[151] Thus, like collective, social, or popular memory, myth is by definition a process that subsumes individual insights and explanations of experience. Both memory and myth refer to collectivity, even in the construction of "myth-biographies." In this sense the relationship between myth and history is far more complex than the tension between a correct and an incorrect view of the past.[152] Myths are organizing principles of memory and are crucial to the construction of a collective vision of a past—a history. This dialectic relationship between myth and history has been aptly described by Samuel in *Island Stories*: "Myth and history are not mutually incompatible, but coexist as complementary and sometimes intersecting modes of representing the past. Myth, so far from being timeless, is subject to a constant process of change. [Myths] accrete their own history, introducing fresh episodes and adding new characters. [Further], historians, however wedded to empirical inquiry, will take on, without knowing it, the deep structures of mythic thought."[153]

In a similar manner, Jonathan Hill notes in an extended essay on the complementarity of mythic and historical consciousness:

> Although not phenomenally separable, myth and history can be analytically distinguished as modes of social consciousness according to the different weightings each gives to the relations between structure and agency. Mythic consciousness gives priority to structure and overriding, transformational principles that can crosscut, contradict, and even negate the sets of relations established through social classifications. . . . If human actors are perceived as having any power to change their conditions, it is because they possess some form of controlled access to the hierarchical structuring of mythic power of liminal, neither-here-nor-there beings [priests/God, communicants/saints—my notes]. Historical consciousness gives greater weighting to agency and social action in the present, which is informed by knowledge of past times that are qualitatively the same as the present. Like the present, the historical past is seen as inhabited by fully human, cultural beings who, although perhaps living in different conditions from those of the present time, had essentially the same powers for making changes as do people living in the present.[154]

The distinction drawn between structure and agency is a fruitful one to keep in mind, as is the fact of complementarity. But it is also important that we not conceive of mythic or historic consciousness as categories of mind but as ways of interpreting social and historical processes. There are several other features of myth that should be noted. First, myths do not rely for their validity upon an appeal to empirical evidence but rather upon the emotive and cognitive participation of the believer in the rites and rituals defining the mythic experience, the ways in which one gains admission into and finds one's place within the hierarchical world of the myth. In some sense, they rely upon the creation of what Passerini in another context has termed a "mythbiography."[155] Rites and rituals are important in the formation of memory, as Paul Connerton reminds us, but they also carry with them access to some form of sacerdotal meaning for their effectiveness.[156] Marching in a commemorative parade not only refreshes the memory of the event being commemorated and the mythic heroes at the center of that event, but it also reaffirms one's position in the hierarchical world in which that commemoration and those heroes have meaning. Often, too, myths point to the special relationship between the collective people and the past by the constructions of narratives of origin.

Comparison of the essays in *The Myths We Live By*, according to James a seminal publication in oral history,[157] with the publications noted above, especially the works of Portelli and James, demonstrates that oral historians have rather consistently submitted the mythic structures of consciousness, as defined above, to the exigencies of concrete instances of human agency. Altogether, these works document through the memories of interviewees the constant creation and reformulation of myths, both personal and communitarian, especially myths surrounding the nation-state, formed sometimes in the face of a contentious history and sometimes, such as in the cases of concentration camps and oppressive regimes, when agency and historical consciousness are impossible. In many of the examples, myths articulated a history that on examination proved to be particularly fraught with violence or, for any number of reasons, great failure. In others, they rationalized the successes of certain types of personalities, ethnic groupings, or classes of people while relegating others to silence or irrelevance. In all cases, they seemed to promise a future of possibility. If, in the words of Alistair Thomson, "memory is a battleground,"[158] the battle is not necessarily between private and public memories but between myth and some form of historical consciousness in both. The key is the particular ways in which the myths dialectically relate to the concrete histories in which they are centered. Something happens to myth on its way to becoming history. It either loses its sacerdotal garment or it becomes its own form of historical consciousness, replacing history with dream and desire.

A problem arises, however, with the conception of historical consciousness. If myth is a fundamental feature of all historical thought, and I think Samuel is correct in that claim, then the analytic categories lose some of their distinctiveness, and historical consciousness seems to simply float, despite disclaimers, beyond the historical processes themselves. History has a history, and when we place historical consciousness within a history—

that is, historicize history—and contextualize what Hill means by historical consciousness, the difference becomes clearer. Without reducing the cultural to the political, I would argue that this historicizing is what sets apart an ideology. And it is the tension between myth and ideology, not between myth and historical consciousness, that distinguishes the construction of the historical narrative created in an oral history interview.[159] As Warren Susman used to tell his students, myth sets the stage; ideology gets the show on the road.

Ideology, as James Scully notes, is a debased term.[160] Historically, the word has been used to describe something that is in error, antiscientific, wrong, full of bias and prejudice, or beyond reasonableness. Also, it has been used to connote a set of ideas that has a strong resonance with a Marxist conception of false consciousness and, furthermore, has been described as a weapon in the class struggle, a symbolic action, a specific type of belief, or the atmosphere indispensable to social respiration.[161] Noting the difficulty of speaking of a politics of interpretation without a working notion of ideology, Gayatri Chakravorty Spivak describes ideology in action as "what a group, as a group, takes to be natural and self-evident" and the subject of ideology as "freely willing and consciously choosing in a world that is seen as battleground."[162] In *Japan's Modern Myths*, Carol Gluck summarizes important works on ideology: "For the anthropologist Clifford Geertz, ideology renders social life significant for those who must live it; . . . [it] provides 'maps of problematic social reality' without which the societal arrangement would seem meaningless. . . . Ideologies . . . reflect and interpret the social realities that sustain them. . . . [They are] what Althusser calls 'the "lived" relation between men and their world.' . . . Since different people construe their world differently, there is always a multiplicity of ideological formations within a society."[163]

If we take the term *historical consciousness* as it appears in the Hill essay quoted above and substitute the term *ideology*, we have an excellent description of the tension between myth and ideology in historical construction. But keep in mind that ideologies are formed in struggle and always exist in tension, if not conflict, alongside other ideologies. While myths promote cohesion and promise the elimination of struggle, ideologies promote division and promise the joy of struggle. Ideologies are also imperial because the classes for which and to whom they speak are imperial. They try to co-opt whatever forms of understanding reality are available to a given group of people at a given time, including scientific categories or myths themselves. Something happens to myths as their adherents attempt to mobilize them in history. Their categories no longer make cohesive sense. They must compete with other myths and other forms of categorization. In short, by putting myths into an ongoing process of change over time they become ideologies.

Ideologies in action exhibit the following characteristics. They contain some more or less empirical description of present social reality and some more or less logical explanation of the origins of (the history of) those social relations. In many cases, given the potency of the myth of scientific explanation in Western culture, often these descriptions will be given in terms open to measurement, such as the percentage of people living in poverty/prosperity or the numbers of slum dwellers. The logical explanations of social conditions will contain a view of the past and also the future. This is how we came to be who we are, and this is what must be done if we are to become who we want to be.

Ideologies are thus always historical narratives, and they always pose some form of future, often stealing visions of utopia as well as rituals and rites from mythic sources. When examined, these narratives inevitably pose the necessity of one group of people and one group alone that has the necessary virtue, intelligence, relation to the world of production, or public trust to carry the mission of the culture, of history, be they the Puritan elect, the proletariat, men of property, men or women, the young or the sages. If one participates in a myth by transcending the present chaos and finding one's place through a transformative experience in a hierarchy (being born again), one participates in an ideology by placing oneself in history through the understanding of the history of one's collectively identified agency.[164] If personal identity is structured collectively through myth it is given agency through ideology.

All of this may seem far afield from our original concern with the evidentiary value of oral history, but the complex understanding of the relationship between myth, memory, ideology, and consciousness provides us with the mediation between culture and politics that was at the center of Richard Cándida Smith's critique and provides the connectedness between individual and collective memory. Through the oral history interview we can marshal the evidence to begin to explore how history is constructed, not through self-conscious literary efforts but through the experience of broad swaths of the people as they struggle to situate themselves in their world and demand their rights to their own understanding of that world. Also, through a careful analysis of interviews, the oral historian is able to marshal evidence of the processes and personal and collective consequences of the active attempts to erase memory—to move beyond a passive conceptualization of forgetting to an analysis of the concerted efforts to obliterate from our past our history of that past.

As Michael Denning notes, "Our moment is not the moment where liberation and culture are the key words. But we have much to learn from a left for whom they were the key words, and as we try to build a newer left, a global left whose symbolic antagonists have been the IMF and the WTO, and the new enclosures that are privatizing the commons . . . we would do well to keep alive the promises and problems of a half century of radical cultural analysis."[165] In the long run, this is what oral history has been and what it continues to promise, with the addendum that oral historians, alone among their peers, by the very fact of what they do, ask a wide variety of people to participate with them in that journey.

Notes

1. Hartewig and Halbach, "History of Oral History." International reports in the 1976 *Oral History Review* included Campbell, "Australia"; Browne, "Brazil"; Meyer, "Mexico and Latin America"; and Lance, "Update from Great Britain."

2. Thompson, "North America"; Grele, "Development, Cultural Peculiarities"; Lance, "Update from Great Britain."

3. A sense of this complexity is evident in the "News from Abroad" section of *Oral History: Journal of the Oral History Society* (hereinafter *Oral History*). See also Meyer, "Recovering, Remembering"; Meihy, "Radicalization"; Passerini, "Oral History in Italy."

4. See Dixon and Mink, *Oral History at Arrowhead*. See also the series of interviews with the association founders published in *Oral History Review*: Treleven, "Jim Mink"; Polsky, "Elizabeth Mason"; Hardy, "Alice Hoffman"; and K'Meyer, "Willa K. Baum." Nevins, "Uses," 27.

5. Treleven, "Jim Mink," 125–27.

6. Polsky, "Elizabeth Mason," 164.

7. Bonfield, "Conversation," 466, quoted in Schlesinger, *Robert Kennedy*, 1: xv.

8. See the commentary of various notable historians in Starr, *Second National Colloquium*.

9. Starr, "Oral History," 7. That this standard has survived until the age of sound archives is seen in Wallot and Fortier, "Archival Science."

10. A typical statement of oral history procedures is Oral History Research Office, Interviewing and Interview Processing, Columbia University, http:// www.Columbia.edu/cu/lweb/indiv/oral/interviewing.html (accessed January 31, 2005). For an example of the concern over embarrassing interviewees, see the comments of Philip C. Brooks in Dixon, "Definitions," 7.

11. See Hebrew University of Jerusalem, *Catalogue* 1: 1; Shariff, "Narrating History," 40; Meihy, "Radicalization"; Browne, "Brazil." In 1972, the Ford Foundation sent Charles T. Morrissey, then Oral History Association president, to Indonesia to consult with archivists, particularly at the National Archives of Indonesia, on methods of establishing projects.

12. See the report on the Singapore Oral History Unit under "News and Notes," *International Journal of Oral History* 1, no. 3 (November 1980): 213. Mercedes Vilanova, of Spain, noted her visits to both the Columbia and University of California at Berkeley oral history offices in Vilanova, "Struggle for a History." Likewise, see Neithammer, "United States," and Foronda, "Philippines." A fuller description of the movement in the Philippines is found in Foronda, *Kaysaysayan*.

13. See Thompson, *Voice of the Past*, 2nd ed. A more nuanced description is Samuel, "Local History."

14. Thompson, *Voice of the Past*, 2nd ed., 27–59.

15. See Oral History Society (UK), "Interview in Social History," for reports on a conference on the topic held by the Social Science Research Council, University of Leicester, March 23–25, 1972; La Hausse, "South African Historians"; Popular Memory Group, "Popular Memory"; Lance, "Oral History in Britain." On the concept of "culturalism" in the new social history, see Johnson, "Socialist Humanist History," and Sewell, "Concept(s) of Culture."

16. See special issues of *Oral History*: Vigne, "Family History," and Bornat et al., "Women's History"; also see the journal's "News from Abroad" reports on oral history in Germany, available in Oral History Society (UK), "Europe," and in Australia, available in Oral History Society (UK), "Australasia." See also the various international reports in "Oral History and Regional Studies," Part 5, Dunaway and Baum, *Oral History*, 2nd ed., 341–424.

17. Samuel, "Unofficial Knowledge."

18. The most obvious locus for this view is in the pages of *History Workshop Journal*, but the editors of that journal were not alone in these hopes.

19. See the essays in Thompson and Burchart, *Our Common History*; Lindqvist, "Dig Where You Stand"; Oral History Society (UK), "Finland"; Contini, "Italy"; Meyer, "Recovering, Remembering"; and Andrade, "Mexico." Bozzoli and Delius, "Radical History," and La Hausse, "South African Historians," note oral history's role in keeping alive an oral tradition of resistance to apartheid. A brief bibliography on oral history activism is found in Perks and Thomson, introduction to "Advocacy and Empowerment."

20. Dixon, "Definitions," 6.

21. Thompson, "North America"; Jefferson, "Echoes from the South."

22. Thompson, "North America," was particularly sharp about the expensive processing practices and elitism of the Columbia University Oral History Research Office. Louis Starr, Columbia director, returned the favor in his review of Thompson's work: "In sum, parts of *The Voice of the Past* are more mellifluous than the whole, an exercise in which the right minded are held up to us, and the hell with everyone else." Starr, review of *Voice of the Past*, 68. Delivered in many venues, none published, the most thoroughgoing critique of archival projects belongs to Lawrence Goodwyn, who argued that it was foolish to hire someone else to do one's interviewing, that interviewing should always be done with a definite research agenda in mind, transcribing was a waste of time since no one should be expected to use anyone else's interviews, and the relationship between archivists and their subjects was too close to ever promote a proper adversarial stand between the two.

23. Thompson, "Sharing and Reshaping," describes this process in Great Britain. An excellent example of a publication from an archival project merging the research and interviewing of several authors is Hall et al., *Like a Family*. Community history projects had long blended the collection of interviews and the publication of research results. As examples, see Fee, Shopes, and Zeidman, *Baltimore Book*; National Archives (Singapore), *Kampong Days*; Brecher, Lombardi, and Stackhouse, *Brass Valley*.

24. Grele, "Why Call It Oral History."

25. Sources for the relationship of oral history and community history are too voluminous to reproduce here. The various issues of *Oral History, Oral History Review, History Workshop Journal, Oral History Association of Australia Journal, Canadian Journal of Oral History*, and the *International Journal of Oral History* contain any number of articles or notices of such efforts. In addition, the programs of annual meetings of various national associations and of international meetings are rife with such descriptions. For a discussion of the differences between local and community history and insight into some of the problems with the terms, see Samuel, "Local History."

26. See, for instance, Wood, *Projects in Your Classroom*.

27. See Thompson, "Projects." Jamieson, "Some Aspects," reports on a number of local projects, many long-standing, devoted to various forms of social service and therapy.

28. Thompson, "Achievement." See publications reported in Oral History Research Office, *Oral History: Columbia University* (New York: Oral History Research Office, 1974), 13–15, (1975), 12–15, (1980) 11–14, and (1981), 14–18.

29. See the critique in Fentress and Wickham, *Social Memory*, 89–90.

30. Thompson, "Evidence"; Popular Memory Group, "Popular Memory"; Murphy, "Voice of Memory."

31. Dixon, "Definitions," 7, 8. Brooks, in fact, called interviewees "victims"; ibid., 18. Nevins, "Uses," 28.

32. Hoffman and Hoffman, "Reliability and Validity"; Cutler, "Accuracy"; Moss, "Appreciation." For an indication of the international scope of the empirical view of oral history, see Oral History Association of Australia, "Local History." See also Bozzoli, "Women of Phokeng," 147, which recognizes other uses of the interview but gives primacy to "sources of information."

33. See Nathan, *Critical Choices*; Langlois, *Aural Research*; Moss, *Program Manual*. For an early example of the references to social science literature, see Musto and Benison, "Accuracy." See also Thompson, "Evidence." Lummis, "Structure and Validity," provides a sophisticated version of the argument. The paradoxes of interviewing as a method and the contradiction between the need for rapport in the interview and for an interviewer who is a "passive tool" is brilliantly explored in Merton, Fiske, and Kendall, *Focused Interview*, a work that, interestingly, does not appear in most of the commentary on oral history interviewing.

34. Popular Memory Group, "Popular Memory," 215–16.

35. Yeo, "Community Publications"; Lowenstein, *Weevils in the Flour*; Lynd, "Guerrilla History"; Lynd, "Personal Histories"; Rosen and Rosengarten, "Shoot-Out at Reeltown," 67. But see also J. Green, review of *Rank and File*, which questions the editors' lack of any reference to their editing and selection techniques. Similar are the assumptions, sometimes overt, often unstated, behind the myriad publications of seemingly unedited oral history interviews, ranging from the work of popular historians such as Studs Terkel to Latin American testimonials, to the 1930s U.S. slave narratives, to any number of as-told-to autobiographies. In many ways this was, and remains, the popular view of oral history.

36. Frisch, "Oral History and *Hard Times*" (1979), 76.

37. Ibid., 78.

38. For description and analysis of the complexities of this shift, see La-Capra, "Rethinking Intellectual History."

39. Tonkin, "Implications of Oracy"; Gilb, "Tape Recorded Interviewing"; Benison, "Reflections." Benison was one of the very few American oral historians concerned with the larger questions of sound documentation, and also the mutual creation of the document, which he saw as both the strength and weakness of oral history.

40. Duberman, *Black Mountain*; Grele, "Languages of History."

41. Duberman, *Black Mountain*, 89–90.

42. Conkin, review of *Black Mountain*, 512, called the work "embarrassing," "pretentious," and "the very epitome of bad taste."

43. Samuel, "People's History."

44. Grele, "Anyone over Thirty."

45. Portelli, "Peculiarities," 99–100.

46. Passerini, "Work Ideology and Consensus"; Portelli, "Peculiarities." I cite these two articles instead of the authors' better-known books—Passerini, *Fascism in Popular Memory*, and Portelli, *Death of Luigi Trastulli*—to highlight the fact that both first appeared in *History Workshop Journal*, which was often accused of empiricism and positivism. Also, the time lapse before publication of the English versions of the books obscures the earlier date of the work.

47. Popular Memory Group, "Popular Memory."

48. Grele, "Movement without Aim."

49. Tonkin, "Boundaries of History." Again, the reader is directed to Tonkin's early 1980s articles, which reveal the cumulative thinking behind her later book, *Narrating Our Pasts*. Neithammer and von Plato, *Lebensgeschichte und Sozialkultur.* See Freddy Raphaël's review of these volumes in Raphaël and Breckner, "German Working Class," 201–203. Joutard, *La Legende des Camisards*.

50. *History Workshop Journal*, "Editorial," iii.

51. Both editions of Ritchie, *Doing Oral History*, have extensive discussions of the various ways in which oral history has been and can be used.

52. Passerini, *Fascism in Popular Memory*; Portelli, "What Makes Oral History Different." In Frisch, *Shared Authority*, see particularly "Part II: Interpretative Authority in Oral History: Headnotes," 55–58; "Oral History and the Presentation of Class Consciousness," 59–80; and "Oral History, Documentary, and the Mystification of Power," 159–78. In McMahan and Rogers, *Interactive Oral History Interviewing*, see, in particular, Grele, "Languages of History"; Chase and Bell, "Women's Subjectivity"; and Futrell and Willard, "Intersubjectivity."

53. Portelli, *Battle of Valle Giulia*; Friedlander, *UAW Local*; Yans-McLaughlin, "Metaphors of Self"; Samuel, *East End Underworld*; Hareven and Langenback, *Amoskeag*; Gluck and Patai, *Women's Words*; Alexander, "Women, Class"; Bravo, "Solidarity and Loneliness"; Rocha Lima, "Women in Exile"; Meyer, "Recovering, Remembering"; Benmayor et al., "Stories to Live By."

54. Winter and Sivan, "Setting the Framework," 15.

55. LaCapra, "Holocaust Testimonies." See also Rogers, "Trauma Redeemed," and her longer study, *Righteous Lives*.

56. Samuel and Thompson, introduction to *Myths We Live By*, 2.

57. James, "'Case of María Roldán,'" 122.

58. Essays in Bonnell and Hunt, *Beyond the Cultural Turn*, explore in some detail the varieties and complexity of these shifts. See, in particular, Bonnell and Hunt's introduction; Biernacki, "Method and Metaphor"; and Sewell, "Concept(s) of Culture." Eley, "Is All the World a Text?" outlines the close relationship of the 1960s generation to the cultural turn. Bonnell and Hunt's claim that this turn represented the decline of interest in Marxism is contested by the essays in Nelson and Grossberg, *Marxism*. Denning, *Culture,* is an extraordinarily provocative interpretation of the cultural turn. All three anthologies include little or no mention of oral history despite the obvious complementary nature of the questions asked. Consideration of oral history theory and method would have avoided some embarrassing statements, such as Biernacki, "Method and Metaphor," 78, which claims, "Historical researchers by and large have as evidence of the past only what has been inscribed in static texts or in material

artifacts appropriated as texts." Sadly, this represents the continuing marginality of oral history as much as the myopia of the academy.

59. Geertz, *Interpretation of Cultures*, 452.

60. Thelen, "Memory and American History," 1118–19.

61. Dominique Aron-Schnapper, comments at the Fourth International Conference on Oral History, Aix-en-Provence, France, September 26, 1982. Ironically enough, this was the first international meeting where issues of memory and subjectivity had been broached openly from the perspective of narrative. See also Passerini, "Memory"; Tilly, "People's History"; O'Farrell, "Facts and Fiction," 5–6. I first noted these criticisms in 1985. See Grele, *Envelopes of Sound*, 2nd ed., 282n56.

62. Tilly, "People's History," 7.

63. Tilly, "Tilly's Response," 41, and Grele, "Concluding Comment." I have purposely used quotations from Portelli and Samuel also used by Tilly in her critique so that the reader can see them in two distinctly different contexts.

64. See Thompson et al., "Between Social Scientists," and Tilly, "Tilly's Response."

65. R. C. Smith, "Popular Memory," 106.

66. See, for instance, essays in Dexter, *Specialized Interviewing*. The connection was continued to be viewed as natural, as seen in the currently most useful American oral history handbook, Yow, *Recording Oral History* (1994).

67. Thompson, *Edwardians*.

68. Compare essays in Grele, *International Annual 1990*, to those in Dexter, *Specialized Interviewing*. See also Samuel and Thompson, introduction to *Myths We Live By*, 9–20; Grele, "Surmisable Variety."

69. See the final footnote in Adler, "Politics of Research," 245, wherein Adler answers the argument that "researchers . . . [should] be somewhat aloof from the individuals and organizations they examine, to be freed from the political demands of competing political movements that approve of some categories and not others in their definitions of legitimate politics," by noting, "It's unclear exactly how such distancing can be accomplished, and if it is achieved, whether it provides the interviewer with any better vantage point for addressing these concerns."

70. For a discussion of the complexity of the uses of the concept of "narrative," see Martin, *Recent Theories*.

71. Passerini, *Fascism in Popular Memory*, 8.

72. R. C. Smith, "Popular Memory," 98.

73. Portelli, *Death of Luigi Trastulli*, 48–49.

74. Ibid., ix–xii.

75. See, for example, Portelli, "*Absalom, Absalom!*"; Portelli, "Philosophy and the Facts"; and Portelli, "Oral History as Genre."

76. Connerton, *How Societies Remember*, 19–20.

77. See Grele, "Listen to Their Voices."

78. James, *Doña María's Story*, 228.

79. Tonkin, *Narrating Our Pasts*, 3.

80. Barber, "Interpreting *Oriki*," 15, quoted in Tonkin, *Narrating Our Pasts*, 3.

81. Tonkin, *Narrating Our Pasts*, 6, 109.

82. Murphy, "Voice of Memory," 164.

83. Chamberlain and Thompson, "Genre and Narrative." See also essays in McMahan and Rogers, *Interactive Oral History Interviewing*, in particular, Rogers, "Trauma Redeemed."

84. See Carr, *Time, Narrative, and History*; Bruner, "Narrative Construction of Reality"; Bruner, *Actual Minds, Possible Worlds*; Spence, *Narrative Truth*; Polkinghorne, *Narrative Knowing*.

85. Bonnell and Hunt, *Beyond the Cultural Turn*. See also Nash, *Narrative in Culture*.

86. Carr, *Time, Narrative, and History*, 16.

87. Halttunen, "Cultural History," 171.

88. Polkinghorne, *Narrative Knowing*, 15–17.

89. Bruner, "Life as Narrative," 15.

90. Grele, *Envelopes of Sound*, 2nd ed., 261–68.

91. There are obvious exceptions, especially the telling of narratives of terror, rape, and genocide. For instance, in the case of the Japanese American internment, for many years there was an unwillingness among former internees, out of shame, to discuss the experience. Of course, the fact that a story has been told before does not negate the fact that it can be told anew even to the surprise of the person interviewed: "I never thought of it that way until just now."

92. Ricoeur, *Interpretation Theory*, 92.

93. Portelli, "Death of Luigi Trastulli."

94. Thompson and Burchart, *Our Common History*; Passerini, *Fascism in Popular Memory*; Contini, *La Memoria Divisa*; Talsma and Leydesdorff, "Netherlands"; Botz, "Austria." Literature on oral histories of the Holocaust is quite extensive, but a brief listing of early works is found in Thompson, *Voice of the Past*, 2nd ed., 277. Miller and Miller, "Armenian Survivors"; Sherbakova, "Gulag in Memory"; Kamp, "Three Lives of Saodat"; Kamp, "Restructuring Our Lives"; Schendler, "Post-Communist Discourse"; Bennett, "Forced Settlement"; Dhupelia-Mesthrie, "Dispossession and Memory"; Losi, Passerini, and Salvatici, "Archives of Memory"; Jelin and Kaufman, "Layers of Memory"; Maguire, *Facing Death*; Gluck, "Women's Mass Organizations"; Lutz, Phoenix, and Yuva-Davis, *Crossfires*. For some indication of the complexity of the issues involved, see Torpey, *Politics and the Past*.

95. Tonkin, "Subjective or Objective?" has a particularly useful explanation of these tensions with a focus mostly on the work of Vansina, *Oral Tradition*. See also essays on oral history in *Social Analysis* 4 (Spring 1980), including Rosaldo, "Doing Oral History," which, although not addressed to African studies but to fieldwork in the Philippines, speaks directly to the point. For a description of "oral literature" and its similarity to oral history practice, see Okpewho, *African Oral Literature*, 328–59. Larger issues are explored in Halttunen, "Cultural History"; Meihy, "Radicalization"; and Feierman, "Colonizers." Carr, *Time, Narrative, and History*, 179–85, addresses these issues. See also Faseke, "Nigeria", and Kwang, "China."

96. The term is from Losi, "Beyond the Archives," 6.

97. Schutz, "Common-Sense," 10, quoted in McMahan, *Elite Oral History Discourse*, 97–98.

98. See Gadamer, *Truth and Method*. Jay, "Intellectual History," provides an insightful discussion of the major points of Gadamer's theory of hermeneutics. Clark, Hyde, and McMahan, "Communication" (1980), 30, quoted in McMahan, *Elite Oral History Discourse*, 3.

99. Jay, "Intellectual History," 94.

100. McMahan, *Elite Oral History Discourse*, 3; Jay, "Intellectual History," 97.

101. Clark, Hyde, and McMahan, "Communication" (1980), 30, quoted in McMahan, *Elite Oral History Discourse*, 4.

102. Gadamer, *Truth and Method*, 264, quoted in Jay, "Intellectual History," 95.

103. Portelli, *Death of Luigi Trastulli*, 31.

104. Frisch, *Shared Authority*.

105. Portelli, *Death of Luigi Trastulli*, 31–32.

106. McMahan, *Elite Oral History Discourse*, 98–99, 56.

107. Ibid., 43–44.

108. Grele, "Languages of History."

109. James, "'Case of María Roldán'"; Thomson, "Sharing Authority"; Kerr, "'What the Problem Is'"; Sitzia, "Shared Authority."

110. Adler, "Politics of Research."

111. Polishuk, *Sticking to the Union*, 1–16.

112. Glassie, *Passing the Time*, 620.

113. See LaCapra, "Holocaust Testimonies," 223–25; Roper, "Analysing the Analysed."

114. Capussotti, "Memory," 214.

115. Passerini, "Afterthought," 220.

116. Shores, "Directions," 42; Dixon and Colman, "Objectives and Standards," 78–81.

117. Samuel, "Perils of the Transcript" (1998), 389; Portelli, "What Makes Oral History Different," 46–47.

118. Benison, "Reflections," 76.

119. Treleven, "TAPE System." For one example of digital indexing of recordings, see the work of the Randforce Associates, Amherst, NY, at http://www.randforce.com (accessed January 26, 2005).

120. See, for example, Dunaway, "Radio"; Read, "Different Media."

121. Read, "Different Media," 415–16.

122. The only two noted here are Jackson, *Fieldwork*, and Ward, *Sound Archive Administration*. Both editions of Yow, *Recording Oral History*, and Ritchie, *Doing Oral History*, have fairly extensive bibliographies on these issues.

123. Ong, *Orality and Literacy*; Tannen, *Spoken and Written Language*.

124. Tonkin, *Narrating Our Pasts*, 50–65; Finnegan, *Oral Literature in Africa*.

125. Slim et al., "Ways of Listening"; Anderson and Jack, "Learning to Listen."

126. Tedlock, "Learning to Listen"; Tedlock, *Finding the Center*.

127. See, for instance, Hofmeyr, "Nterata."

128. Read, "Different Media," 416.

129. Reading in this context is more than examining a book. It is reading in the sense of reading a landscape, or a painting, or a city street, or a face.

130. See Applebaum, *Voice*.

131. A point made by Ihde, *Listening and Voice*, 4–5, while discussing the transformation of listening as a result of the electronic communications revolution.

132. Charles Hardy III, "Authoring in Sound: An Eccentric Essay on Aural History, Radio, and Media Convergence" (1999), State University of New York at Albany, spring 2004 course syllabus of Gerald Zahavi, "Producing Historical Documentaries and Features for Radio," http://www.albany.edu/faculty/ gz580/documentaryproduction/authoring_in_sound.html (accessed January 31, 2005). On the idea of "soundscape," see Schafer, *Tuning of the World*. An interesting example of an aural essay available online is the collaborative work of Hardy and Portelli, "I Can Almost See the Lights of Home: A Field Trip to Harlan County, Kentucky," http:// www.albany.edu/jmmh/vol2no1/ lightssoundessay.html.

133. B. R. Smith, *Acoustic World*, 3.

134. Ihde, *Listening and Voice*, 76–81. Much of Bruce Smith's theoretical presentation is drawn from Ihde's work but, to my mind, is far more comprehensible.

135. B. R. Smith, *Acoustic World*, 9–10; Ihde, *Listening and Voice*, 3–16. For an interesting exploration of the ways in which vision has been privileged and has assumed a totalitarian hold on the Western imagination (all the fault of Descartes), see Levin, *Listening Self*, 29–65.

136. Fentress and Wickham, *Social Memory*, 89. In this essay I follow Fentress and Wickham and use the term *social memory* instead of *collective memory*, partly because I think *social memory* does not carry the baggage of racial or ethnic "spirit" and other dubious constructions. But it must be recognized that *social memory* is subject to reductionism and the argument that memory is the articulation of social position and therefore subject to all the criticisms leveled at social history from a culturalist position.

137. Portelli, *Order Has Been Carried Out*.

138. Almost all the initial reports of the Oral History Association, in the U.S., and the Oral History Society, in Great Britain, were replete with discussions of memory or articles speculating about memory. For the more interesting, see Musto and Benison, "Accuracy"; Storm-Clark, "Miners"; and Thompson, "Problems of Method."

139. Thompson, *Voice of the Past* (1978), 100–108. Neuenschwander, "Remembrance"; Thompson, "Believe It or Not," 3.

140. Samuel, *Theatres of Memory*, 1: x.

141. Some idea of the extent of memory literature is evident in citations in Crane, "Collective Memory." On changing definitions, see Connerton, *How Societies Remember*. On narrative and memory, see Fentress and Wickham, *Social Memory*, 49–59, and Tonkin, *Narrating Our Pasts*, 97–112. The generational image is from Samuel, *Theatres of Memory*, 1: I–xi. Hutton, *Art of Memory*, 1–26. Winter and Sivan, "Setting the Framework." For a less optimistic view, see Maier, "Surfeit of Memory."

142. Neisser, "Important Questions," 12.

143. Passerini, *Fascism in Popular Memory*. Passerini continued exploring memory in *Autobiography of a Generation*. Portelli, *Death of Luigi Trastulli, Battle of Valle Giulia*, and *Order Has Been Carried Out*; Bodnar, "Power and Memory"; Joutard, *La Legende des Camisards*; Fields, "Cannot Remember Mistakenly"; Thomson, *Anzac Memories*, and the earlier Thomson, "Anzac Memories"; Schrager, "What Is Social"; Rogers, *Righteous Lives*; James, "Meatpackers"; Araújo, *Eu Não Sou Cachorro*; Montenegro, *História Oral e Memória*.

144. Hoffman and Hoffman, *Archives of Memory*; a shorter version is Hoffman and Hoffman, "Reliability and Validity."

145. Nora, "Between Memory and History," 1: 10.

146. LaCapra, *History and Memory*, 20–21.

147. Hall, "'Remember This,'" 441.

148. While distinctions between collective, social, and popular memory and the consequences of the use of each of these terms must be recognized, for my purposes here I use the terms indiscriminately.

149. Abercrombie, *Pathways of Memory*, 321. See also Samuel and Thompson, introduction to *Myths We Live By*; Connerton, *How Societies Remember*, 53–61; Maier, "Surfeit of Memory"; Mayer, *Final Solution*, 15–21; A. Smith, *Myths and Memories*.

150. Thomson, "Anzac Legend," 76–78.

151. A. Smith, *Myths and Memories*, 57–123. Bodnar, "Pierre Nora," has much of interest to say about the complementarity of memory studies and the nation-state.

152. This view is at odds with Kammen, *Mystic Chords of Memory*, although Kammen's discussion of the relation between myth and tradition is a vital consideration in the argument for the inherent collectivity of myth.

153. Samuel et al., *Island Stories*, 14. See also Susman, "American Intellectual"; Bidney, "Myth, Symbolism"; Hill, "Myth and History."

154. Hill, "Myth and History," 6. See also the discussion of the transformation of Christ as savior into a historical person in Susman, "American Intellectual," 247.

155. Passerini, "Mythbiography," 59.

156. Connerton, *How Societies Remember*, 41–71; Kirk, *Myth*. See also essays in Dundes, *Sacred Narrative*.

157. James, "'Case of María Roldán,'" 122.

158. Thomson, "Anzac Legend," 73.

159. As early as 1975, I argued that an oral history interview could be understood as a conversational narrative structured linguistically, socially, and cognitively and that the cognitive structure was to be understood through an examination of the tension between myth and ideology revealed in the construction of the history being articulated. See Grele, *Envelopes of Sound* (1975), 139–43. I see no reason to change my mind, and the essays in Samuel and Thompson, *Myths We Live By*, and additional recent works illustrate that tension.

160. Scully, "Defense of Ideology," 9.

161. In Marxist tradition *ideology* has been used in a variety of ways in addition to error. See Eagleton, *Ideology*, and S. B. Smith, *Reading Althusser*, 29–70. Authors who discuss these distinctions are outlined in Boudon, *Analysis of Ideology*, 17–33.

162. Spivak, "Politics of Interpretation," 347.

163. Geertz, "Ideology," 220, and Althusser, *For Marx*, 252, quoted in C. Gluck, *Japan's Modern Myths*, 6–7. See also Burger and Luckman, *Social Construction of Reality*; Eagleton, *Ideology*, 1–31; Althusser, "On Ideology"; and Therborn, *Power of Ideology*.

164. The tension between myth and ideology resonates with similar distinctions made between mythos and logos in Bruner, "Myth and Identity," and between ideology and utopia as used by Jamieson and Hall and described in Denning, *Culture*, 97–104.

165. Denning, *Culture*, 150–51.

II

METHODOLOGY

3

Research Design and Strategies

Mary A. Larson

> A sense of humor is as much a necessity as the flexi-
> bility that allows one to face apparent disaster several
> times a day and somehow keep going.
>
> —Ramon Harris et al., *Practice of Oral History*

Oral historians must have an innate ability to adapt and, as noted above, flexibility and a sense of humor. To help them maintain said flexibility and humor, however, a prerequisite is a good research design. The concept of research design almost by definition encompasses most aspects of an oral history project, since it guides work on a project from its inception to its completion. This chapter will of necessity discuss topics that are treated in more detail in other areas of this reference work. Because of the overarching nature of research design, these issues must still be addressed under this heading, but the discussion is primarily limited to how these subjects impact the overall design and planning of a project.

When researchers begin to think about developing an oral history project, they almost always have a subject in mind. This chapter aims to guide researchers through the process of clearly defining their topic and deciding on the type of oral history they will be conducting, with whom they will be conducting it, and which theoretical bases will be guiding it. Once these particulars have been determined, there are also practical concerns that must be addressed relative to project design, and these are discussed as well.

Structure of the Project

> Every project should be started by determining its objectives.
>
> —Donald Ritchie, *Doing Oral History* (1995)

Genres

One of the first decisions to be made in a project is the type or genre of oral history interview that will be conducted, as that will determine many of the other aspects of the research design. The different genres of oral history could be grouped in many ways (see, for example, Sherna Gluck's division into topical, biographical, and autobiographical).[1] For the purposes of this chapter, however, we will be considering oral histories as categorized into four basic types: subject-oriented histories, life histories, community history, and family history. These divisions have been chosen for this discussion because of the ways in which they point up various aspects of research design. Please note that these groupings are not meant to be mutually exclusive, and some overlap will almost always occur.

Subject-Oriented Oral Histories

The topically based oral history is one of the most common, as this is the type that researchers often turn to when trying to explicate specific questions rather than entering the broader realms defined by life, community, or family histories. Subject-oriented research from the beginning is more focused, with a more clearly conceived agenda and perhaps a stated hypothesis. Even so, at the beginning of the process, investigators need to ask themselves the following questions posed by David Henige: "Is the problem really a significant one whose study will contribute not only to informing its own context but also to illuminating other problems? Has the work been done before? If it has, why does it need to be done again?"[2] It is not enough to just have a topic of interest. There must be a need for the subject to be addressed, or if it has already been addressed, a need for it to be approached differently. The responses to Henige's questions are important, as they will in part guide other considerations of the research design. For example, if previous work has been done and there is not enough information already, then the project must be structured to target the gaps. If earlier attempts at the topic have ignored the voices and experiences of important groups, then these people must be incorporated in the new research.

Oral histories focusing on a specific topic have wide latitude in the choice of research issues.[3] A review of the literature, however, shows that most questions pursued in this manner are based somewhere in the not-so-recent past. This is, of course, partly due to the historical nature of oral history inquiry, even when it is being utilized by anthropologists, sociologists, political scientists, or others. It should be kept in mind, however, that this need not be the case. Growing numbers of projects have been collecting the impressions of interviewees immediately following events of local and national importance. One of the better-known efforts in this vein is the September 11, 2001 Oral History Narrative and Memory Project at Columbia University. Interviewing for that project has taken place across the United States in an attempt to record people's reactions to that day's terrorist attacks in New York City.[4]

Similar research has targeted the documentation of a 1972 flood in Rapid City, South Dakota, and the assassination of Martin Luther King Jr.[5] Work in Mexico City by Elena Poniatowska investigated the immediate aftermath of that city's 1985 earthquake, and the next year, follow-up interviews were begun by the Archivo de la Palabra of the Instituto de Investigaciones to gauge how people's reactions had changed during the intervening time.[6] As Poniatowska noted regarding the immediacy of the first phase of the work, "Documenting our country means writing chronicles and essays about the immediate happenings; writing its real history of the moment. It is important to write down, to rescue; later will come others who will give the interpretation."[7] Following rare campus dissent and demonstrations at the

University of Nevada on Governor's Day 1970 (immediately following the shootings at Kent State), Mary Ellen Glass and her associates conducted interviews with a number of participants on
both sides of the dispute. Almost three decades after the fact,
Brad Lucas interviewed some of the same individuals to determine how their interpretations of the day's events had evolved.[8]

Projects on the recent past, then, can be seen to be equally
valuable as those concerning the more distant past, as they will
provide material for researchers in the future. Both types of subject-oriented project will contribute to the array of resources offered by oral history collections.

On a practical note, subject-oriented oral histories can also
benefit greatly by having advisory boards composed of individuals who are well versed in a particular topic or who were participants in an event under study. Such boards can help with the
identification of possible interviewees and with other advice on
how to proceed,[9] and as Ritchie notes, they are often looked
upon favorably by funding agencies.[10]

Life History

The life history is also a popular type of oral history because
of the possibilities inherent in the genre. It can give us insight into
the lives of the famous or can provide a view of a less-celebrated
life that could contextualize history. As William Schneider has
observed, "The two most common reasons for writing life histories are to portray the events and experiences of an extraordinary
person and to emphasize a person whose life illustrates the experiences and history of others in the region."[11]

There are a number of approaches that can be taken when
considering the final product of a life history interview, and the
choice of which path to take may impact the collection of information. To the extent that this is the case, decisions must be
made early in the process. David Dunaway describes three types
of life history. The first is similar to a standard biography but includes oral history interviews; the second consists of interviews
with a range of people who discuss the subject of the life history;
and the third is the "oral memoir," "which features the subject
telling his or her own story, with the writer adding explanation

and footnotes."[12] (The second and third categories parallel Gluck's biographical and autobiographical categories.)[13] The final form of an oral history, therefore, will influence not only who will need to be interviewed but also how much context building and analysis will be required of the researcher.

Different preparation for life histories should also be considered in research design. As Alessandro Portelli notes, "The life story as a full, coherent oral narrative does not exist in nature; it is a synthetic product of social science—but no less precious for that."[14] But while complete, ordered explications may not spring full blown from the mouths of interviewees, that does not mean that the concept of the life history is necessarily foreign. Margaret Blackman, in discussing her work with Florence Edenshaw Davidson, a Haida woman, observed that whether or not life history per se is an indigenous Haida genre, it is certainly compatible with the Haida emphasis on the individual.[15] This may not always be the case, however, and individuals' comfort with conceptualizing the process of life history documentation, and the ability to do so, may well vary depending upon cultural background or other factors such as gender, race, age, and class. Researchers should remember this while planning their work and be aware that they may need to discuss their understanding of a life history with their interviewee in order for everyone to be on the same page when work begins.

Various groups of individuals may also respond to life history not only in different ways but also with different information, a factor that could be important to the goals of a project. As Nancy Grey Osterud and Lu Ann Jones note, for example, "Some feminist literary critics maintain that women adopt distinctive forms of autobiography. Women often describe themselves in relational terms, constituting themselves through their relationships with significant others; they also tend to construct a fluid self."[16]

Community History

The pursuit of community history is well documented, with such notable works as Laurie Mercier and Madeline Buckendorf's *Using Oral History in Community History Projects*, Willa

Baum's *Oral History for the Local Historical Society*, and Barbara Allen and Lynwood Montell's *From Memory to History*. Although this type of project has been around for some time, there have been spikes of interest in the genre as the result of various events. The *Foxfire* movement of the mid-1960s, for example, spurred many communities to start recording their own pasts from within, while the United States bicentennial in 1976 (and associated available funds) triggered another rush to documentation in the mid-1970s.[17] And while there has in the past been some disdain toward those researchers focusing on the community level, there seems to be an increasing trend toward such work.[18] The focus of these projects can be on a geographical community (as was the case with the project on Agincourt, Ontario, winner of an Oral History Association award in 2002) or on less physically bounded communities defined by factors such as race, gender, age, class, occupation, or avocation.

From the standpoint of research design, perhaps the most important aspect to emphasize regarding community history is its potential for collaborative work, whether the work is being done by insiders, outsiders, or a combination of both. It is imperative for researchers to meet with the community in question from the very beginning. As Schneider observes, "Without the cooperation, interest, and collaboration of the people, there is no chance to understand what they know and no right to use their information."[19] Schneider's work with Project Jukebox, a series of interactive computer databases of oral history, exemplifies the collaborative approach to this type of research. Most Project Jukebox programs are community based, and from the outset of work, residents are involved in meetings and local liaisons are enlisted to help guide progress and provide input into what is important to them.[20]

Foxfire projects evolved in much the same way (albeit years earlier), with students and teachers presenting their gathered information to interested audiences. At the same time, community members reciprocated with suggestions of interviewees and topics and additional material.[21] As will be discussed later in this chapter, such meetings are often not just courtesy acts demonstrating a cooperative spirit; they may also be required with the community or with local leaders.[22]

Family History

To many, the notion of family history connotes only geneal-ogy or perhaps oral tradition, but serious oral history research can and has been done in this area. It does not even have to be the study of one's own family (although that is most common), but family dynamics, experiences, and interactions can be stud-ied in groups that are not constituted by one's relatives.[23]

Just as there have been catalysts to the study of community history, so too have there been with family history. In the United States, groups such as the Daughters of the American Revolution popularized family history for genealogical purposes around the turn of the twentieth century, particularly in a reaction to the in-flux of new immigrants.[24] The 1960s, with their emphasis on identity as well as on the lives of average people, also boosted family history's popularity, albeit for different reasons. Linda Shopes has observed that historians "have paid particular atten-tion to the history of the family since it is so fundamental a social institution and shapes so much of people's daily lives."[25] Then in the 1970s, although there has since been controversy over the na-ture of the material collected by Alex Haley for his *Roots* saga, the book and associated television miniseries opened popular imag-ination to the possibilities of such investigations. What seemed to capture people's attention was not even so much the actual history presented but rather the research process.[26]

With some exceptions—such as Alex Haley's novel and tele-vision miniseries, *Roots: The Saga of an American Family*, and Pe-ter Farquhar's multimedia CD, *The Marjory B. Farquhar Family History*—family history is often not presented in any sort of pub-lic form, but research design for such projects is still important. A collection of family anecdotes will rarely yield any sort of his-tory that can be interpreted within a larger social or cultural con-text, so to get beyond that, planning is necessary. A number of approaches to structuring the projects are available. Linda Shopes suggests three possible categories of inquiry: "The im-pact of major historical events and trends; . . . the relationship of various aspects of social life . . . to individuals within the family; and the structure and dynamics of family life itself."[27] James Hoopes, in contrast, discusses investigating the internal versus external aspects of family life as a way to trace the connections within a family as well as its ties to the outside world.[28]

Theoretical Approaches

Once a researcher has settled on the genre of oral history to be conducted, the next step is deciding upon or becoming aware of the theoretical base informing the interview process for his or her project. Although oral historians make use of multiple theoretical perspectives in their work, a review of the literature indicates that there are three perspectives that stand out in publications: the elite/nonelite dichotomy, critical theory, and grounded theory. Again, as with a number of categories discussed in this chapter, they are not necessarily mutually exclusive, nor should this list be considered exhaustive.

Elite/Nonelite

The debate concerning elite versus nonelite oral histories is, from a theoretical standpoint, mainly one of coverage and who deserves it. Perhaps more ink has been spilt over this topic than almost any other in theoretical and methodological discussions of oral history. Eva McMahan, in detailing James Wilkie's definition of elites and nonelites, describes his view as follows: "The elites . . . are those persons who develop a lore that justifies their attempts to control society. The nonelites, on the other hand, are those persons who create a lore to explain their lack of control."[29] Elite oral history is often considered to be part of the "great white men" school of oral history that was represented by Allan Nevins at Columbia University. It consisted of, as Michael Frisch notes, "the debriefing of the Great Men before they passed on," and began with the inception of the Columbia oral history program in 1948.[30]

Set in opposition to this approach was the interviewing of nonelites—that is, ordinary people—most often described as history "from the bottom up." Early proponents of this idea were British oral historians in the 1950s and 1960s, while researchers in the United States became more heavily invested in this approach in the 1960s (although there were, of course, earlier exceptions).[31]

Both schools have their advocates. In what has become perhaps the most famous (or infamous) defense of elite oral history, Barbara Tuchman once stated that:

> With all sorts of people being invited merely to open their mouths, and ramble effortlessly and endlessly into a tape recorder, prodded daily by acolytes of oral history, a few veins of gold and a vast mass of trash are being preserved which would otherwise have gone to dust. . . . I should hastily add here that among the most useful and scintillating sources I found were two verbal interviews with General Marshall. . . . Marshall, however, was a summit figure worth recording, which is more than can be said for all those shelves and stacks of oral transcripts piling up in recent years.[32]

Similarly, Patrick O'Farrell critiqued the social history being done by Paul Thompson by saying that it only supplied the history of "ordinary" people—something he viewed as inherently uninteresting.[33] And Henige notes the argument of those who believe that, "In their attempt to enshrine the ordinary and the obscure, . . . those who practise oral history are really turning the role of historian on its head. They are modern-day antiquarians, unable to distinguish the fascinating but unimportant aspects of the past from those that really mattered."[34]

Unlike some of these views, however, most of those currently practicing elite oral history do not feel that it needs to be done to the exclusion of nonelite oral history, and they recognize that there is room for both types of interviewing. Alice Hoffman has noted that even Louis Starr, who trained under Nevins and was later director of the Columbia program, thought that both approaches were necessary.[35] It should also be pointed out that elite oral history does not always pertain just to "great white men," but is now seen as relating to those in power, no matter what their racial, ethnic, or gender affiliations. To this end, Blackman in 1982 discussed the fact that most Native American life histories done to that point had been conducted with Native American elites (notably men), although a change in that trend seemed to be occurring.[36] So even underrepresented groups can lay claim to elite/nonelite debates.

On the other end of the continuum (and a gradual continuum is really what it is) are those who strongly advocate for
nonelite oral history and its benefits. Some proponents, such as
Gary Okihiro, see a nonelite approach as crucial to the identity
of oral history, noting that, "Oral history is not only a tool or
method for recovering history; it is also a theory of history which
maintains that the common folk and the dispossessed have a history and that this history must be written."[37] Echoing this senti-
ment is Poniatowska, who asserted in 1988 that "in the strictest
sense, oral history is almost always related to the vanquished,
the defeated, the earth's forsaken ones, that is, the people. Oral
history walks side by side with defeat, not victory. Victory is the
space of biography."[38] During the revolutions of the 1960s, oral
historians around the world became more and more drawn to
the idea of capturing the everyday lives of everyday people, or
the "inarticulate" and those "hidden from history," as the literature sometimes refers to them.[39] They disappeared from (or really never initially appeared in) the historical record, because
they left behind no autobiographies or archived records or were
not identifiable by their paper trails.[40]

Much oral history since the 1960s has tried to render these
groups visible. In truth, the work of many oral history programs
attempts, above all, to record representatively the views of eyewitnesses to history. This work is a combination of interviews
with both elites and nonelites as the topics require, and its primary theoretical underpinnings are of appropriate coverage. Despite the merits purported by both camps, the fact that the
debate has been ongoing and will probably continue for some
time is highlighted by Charles Crawford in his 1974 presidential
article in the *Oral History Review*. He stated that while he thought
it overly optimistic to assume that there would be a quick settlement to the controversy, "it has certainly made intelligent comparison more feasible by accumulating extensive quantities of
both kinds of data for historical analysis."[41]

The last word on this subject, at least as far as this chapter is
concerned, is reserved for Edward "Sandy" Ives, who summed
up his perspective on the discussion most succinctly: "Elit-
ism/non-elitism is a ridiculous polarity to begin with. Between
the two there is no great gulf fixed. No one is common, and
'great men' are a dime a dozen, and getting cheaper."[42]

Critical Theory

> Reality is complex and many-sided, and it is a primary
> merit of oral history that to a much greater extent than
> most sources it allows the original multiplicity of
> standpoints to be covered.

> —Paul Thompson, *Voice of the Past*, 3rd ed.

Critical theory derives initially from the field of literary criticism
but has since become part of many of the humanities and social
sciences within which oral history is practiced. Although there
are many proponents of critical theory in the United States, it
would be fair to say that its effect has been even greater in Europe, particularly in Great Britain and Italy, where at least published material would indicate that class concerns (a focus of
critical theory) dominate the work of oral historians. Critical theory revolves around the concept of representing the underrepresented and giving voice to their views, particularly as regards
gender, class, race, and ethnicity. It is also informed by the theoretical tenets associated with studies of those factors, so each
subset may have a slightly different theoretical stance (which
will, in turn, bear on the research design of oral history projects).

To some extent, because of its focus on the disenfranchised,
critical theory is concerned with the issues of elite versus
nonelite coverage, but it can also represent both elite and
nonelite members of these communities (per Blackman's discussion on elite interviewing among Native Americans). Also, although members on either side of the elite/nonelite dichotomy
can be politically motivated (as with almost any theoretical
stance), they are not necessarily so, while most practitioners of
critical theory are overt about their politicization. There is also a
tendency toward nonbelief in the possibility of (or necessity for)
objectivity, and advocacy and empowerment movements have
sprung to a large degree from these theoretical underpinnings.

Feminism. Looking primarily at the study (or re-study) of
women through oral history, feminist theory has important beliefs
relative to a project's research design. On the part of many scholars, there is a repudiation of hierarchy (both in the research and
between the interviewer and interviewee), a rejection of the desir-
ability of objectivity, and an embrace of the collaborative effort.[43]

It is seen as juxtaposed not only to elite history but even to the very dichotomy of elite versus nonelite. As Gluck observed: "Not only is the political base of women's oral history different from the Nevins model, but also, and, just as important, the content is special. No matter what women we choose to interview, regardless of how typical or atypical their life experiences have been, there are certain common threads which link all women."[44]

In regaining the voice of women, scholars see a number of benefits for history and other disciplines as well as for women themselves. History derives an advantage not only from the increase in perspectives but also from acquiring the viewpoint of less-practiced respondents. Hoopes described Jean Stein's experience while interviewing individuals for *American Journey: The Times of Robert Kennedy*. Stein noted that "the freshest, most informative material seemed to come less from the public figures than from those for whom being interviewed must have been a novelty, the women particularly."[45] While the husbands, being in the public eye, had pat-and-practiced answers for most questions, their wives had the benefit of knowing the same information and having seen many of the same things, but they were responding to many of these queries for the first time and were not, Hoopes noted, "jaded."[46]

The perceived benefit to women is empowerment on a number of levels. First, and perhaps most basically, a person's self-esteem is increased by the fact that a researcher wants to hear about her life.[47] But second, as projects are completed and results disseminated, the research also allows women to understand the challenges faced by other women and how they coped with their particular situations.[48]

A final cautionary note regards the assumption of homogeneity among women. Although there will be, as Gluck observed, shared experiences between women, Osterud and Jones warn against a belief that there are no distinctions within groups of women: "We must explore the commonalities and differences among women as well as between women and men that flow from class position, race, and ethno-cultural identification."[49]

Class. To a degree, class more than any other critical theory subset is related to the discussion of representation of the nonelite, since so often the "non-elite" and the "working class" are inextricably linked by researchers.[50] The rules of participation, as Staughton Lynd outlined them, are much the same as with feminist theory, with a focus on equality between interviewer and interviewee, collaborative work with a meaningful output for the community, and an assumption of personal involvement on the part of the interviewer (and hence a lack of objectivity).[51]

There is also an explicit emphasis on empowerment, particularly by increasing the awareness of the interviewee through the oral history process. Thompson notes this as a requirement of this theoretical base when he states: "For the historian who wishes to work and write as a socialist, the task must be not simply to celebrate the working class as it is, but to raise its consciousness. There is no point in replacing a conservative myth of upper-class wisdom with a lower-class one. A history is required which leads to action; not to confirm, but to change the world."[52]

Although the degree to which individual projects and researchers reflect such politicization obviously varies, the emphasis on class in oral history research has become commonplace. Henige observed that work done to represent the views of the disenfranchised in Britain, France, and the United States, "has closely reflected this interest, with studies of farmers, miners, and members of the urban working class being featured prominently."[53]

Beyond the empowerment sought through the raising of consciousness and through increasing self-esteem by showing interest in workers' views,[54] there is also another perceived benefit to both the interviewee and his or her community. Alice Hoffman, who spent many years working with steelworkers and unions through oral history and other educational programs, explained the value simply: "Oral history can make it possible for a person to recover, preserve, and interpret his own past, and not have it interpreted for him or imposed upon him."[55]

Race/Ethnicity. Perhaps even more than critical theory, the civil rights movement of the 1960s and the interest in ethnic identity in the 1970s helped to first inform this approach to oral history. Although the projects supported during the United States bicentennial may have celebrated the blending together of ethnic groups and races into an anonymous whole, Tamara

Hareven noted, "The current search for ethnic roots is in itself a rebellion against the concept of the melting pot; it is an effort to salvage what has survived homogenization."[56]

In some regard, many of the studies undertaken under this banner are community histories, although these communities may be culturally rather than geographically bounded. In fact, while many viewed *Foxfire* as a community history endeavor, one of its proponents, Brian Beun, saw it as ethnic studies, "a powerful formula for helping 'cultural minority students' at home and abroad."[57]

As with many underdocumented groups, a lack of available information was a barrier to creating accurate histories for racial and ethnic communities. Alphine Jefferson observed that, "In order to write a balanced multiracial history, it was felt, new sources had to be located."[58] Oral history interviews supplied that new resource, as projects throughout the United States and elsewhere began to focus their efforts on ethnic–racial topics.[59]

Duke University's oral history program, which existed from 1972 to 1982, was founded specifically for the stated purpose of "training a generation of scholars conversant with oral history methodology as an essential tool in preserving the history of the inarticulate," particularly as it related to blacks and other groups. The program was founded with the support of a Rockefeller Foundation grant, and for ten years it focused primarily on the collection of civil rights material (although other topics were also addressed).[60]

One of the goals of racial and ethnic studies, as noted above, was the balancing of history. As with other critical theory subsets, however, empowerment was also a goal for some adherents to the approach. Gary Okihiro saw such projects as "the first step toward ultimate emancipation," with ethnic groups finally having the ability to break free from colonized history.[61]

Again, there is a caution offered regarding assumptions of homogenization within these types of studies. Arthur Hansen, who has for many years worked with Japanese Americans in southern California, notes the diversity within that community and the way it has impacted his work: "Those of us studying such [racial–ethnic] communities would have to attend to age, generational, class, gender, and ideological divisions within them if we wanted to gain a more complex sense of past reality and avoid the charge of racism."[62]

Grounded Theory

A school of thought first arising out of the discipline of sociology, grounded theory was outlined by Barney Glaser and Anselm Strauss.[63] In its original form, it is an insistence that researchers come to a chosen topic without a hypothesis or preconceived notions. As research continues with a person or group, scholars can form their conclusions or hypotheses by analyzing the data as they gather them and reinterrogating their information to see what insights they can gain. As Strauss and Juliet Corbin note: "A researcher does not begin a project with a preconceived theory in mind (unless his or her purpose is to elaborate and extend existing theory). Rather the researcher begins with an area of study and allows the theory to emerge from the data."[64] Hence the theory derived is *grounded* in the data.

In oral history, this theory has manifested itself in a number of features that have a bearing on research design. Perhaps the most important is that some grounded theorists in oral history believe that the emphasis on a lack of preconceived notions requires that the researcher have no prepared questions or defined problem.[65] Regarding the former, Thompson observes: "The strongest argument for a completely free-flowing interview is when its main purpose is less to seek information than to record a 'narrative interview,' a 'subjective' record of how one man or woman looks back on their life as a whole, or part of it. Just how they speak about it, what they miss out, how they order it, what they emphasize, the words they choose, are important in understanding any interview; but for this purpose they become the essential text which will need to be examined."[66]

Others do not take as extreme a view of the process. Portelli, for example, sees "thick dialogue" as requiring a flexible interview approach, but not to the point of noninterference. His perspective is still in keeping with the revelatory nature of grounded theory in that, as he states, "In thick dialogue, questions arise dialectically from the answers."[67]

Another emphasis of grounded theory that has translated to oral history is the focus not only on the words being spoken by an interviewee but also on awareness of their body language and physical response, although it could be said that oral historians of many theoretical bents try to be cognizant of such things. A final characteristic to note regarding research design is that some oral historians whose work is informed by grounded theory also believe that research into a topic should not be done as a first step in the process since other sources might contaminate their understanding of the issue. Interviews should be begun first, and as themes and potential problems are identified for further investigation, then documentary research can take place.[68]

The project most often referenced as a successful example of what grounded theory can produce is Thompson and Thea Vigne's study *The Edwardians*. They chose a representative sample of British residents that compared occupationally to a 1911 census, and they amassed a daunting number of oral histories, which they then analyzed in order to be able to make observations about Edwardian society. The "thick description" of everyday life by such a large number of individuals provided the data for their analysis.[69]

Planning

While the theoretical and methodological decisions made during the process of structuring the project will have an important impact on the more pragmatic features addressed in this section, it should also be noted that resource availability will also be a decisive factor in the implementation of the research design. By remaining flexible and being constantly aware of the project plan and available resources, however, a balance can be achieved.

Selecting Interviewers

> The key to oral history, be it individual or project, is personnel. The right people must be found to do the interviewing, and the right informants have to be identified.
>
> —Ramon Harris et al., *The Practice of Oral History*

The first step in putting decisions into practice is to select interviewers. The choice of interviewers will be guided partially by the theory informing the process and partially by more practical concerns, including whether or not interviewers should be topical or methodological specialists, insiders or outsiders.

A topical specialist may be particularly appealing to those engaged in subject-oriented projects. An expert in the field under consideration brings to the research a level of background experience that time and resources probably would not permit someone unfamiliar with a topic to develop, so there is that advantage. The ideal situation would be to acquire someone with both subject knowledge and interviewing experience, but as that is not always possible, topical experts can be enlisted to do the work if properly trained in oral history methodology.[70]

Another option would be to find interviewers who are specialists in either interviewing or the historical method more generally. Just as inexperienced interviewers with topical knowledge need to hone interviewing skills, so do experienced interviewers need to acquire a good working knowledge of the subject involved.

Some researchers believe that an interviewer should be a specialist in one of the two above areas.[71] Other oral historians, however, feel differently. For example, *Foxfire* projects have recovered vast amounts of information for community history projects, but the project has been derided by individual scholars for being the moral equivalent of "pothunting," because research was being done by schoolteachers and students (and not by academics). Along the same line, Gluck asserts that, "Oral history is not, nor should it be, the province of experts. On the contrary, some of the best work today is being done by individuals and groups outside 'the groves of academe.'" She goes on to acknowledge, however, that some reading about the process of interviewing is useful in those cases.[72]

One of the most discussed issues regarding interviewer selection is whether interviewers should be insiders or outsiders relative to the group or individual under consideration. There are both advantages and disadvantages to either choice.

The general sense, at least as reflected in the oral history literature, is that insiders have the benefit of an existing rapport with interviewees, they know much of the necessary back-ground material (or at least where it is located), and they may have access to privileged information. However, there is also the perception that insiders are not seen as neutral (not necessarily a problem at least as regards critical theory); they may overlook obvious questions because they take certain things for granted; and, knowing the rules of engagement in a community, the in-sider may not want to ask the difficult question. An outsider, however, may be viewed by interviewees as being more objec-tive, and since the interviewer will not be staying in the com-munity, he or she may be given information that someone remaining in the community would not be able to elicit.[73]

Researchers have also noted a difference in not only the amount but also the basic nature of information they have re-ceived when they have been an insider versus an outsider. Alessandro Portelli was an outsider in his work with Kentucky coal miners, but an insider doing research within his university in Rome. He observed that, because of his status, "one conse-quence is that the Kentucky interviews emphasize storytelling and history-telling, with a great deal of straight information and narrative, while the Rome interviews read like tentative essays replete with commentary evaluation and analysis. . . . Narrators will assume that a 'native' historian already knows the facts, and will furnish explanations, theories, and judgments, instead."[74]

A simple view of the insider/outsider dichotomy, however, would be misleading. First, as Schneider notes, there is the question not only of having an interviewer be an outsider, but also of the envisioned audience. Whenever an oral history takes place, there is the immediate audience of the interviewer, but depending on the intended purpose of the materials, there is also a second, anticipated audience in those who will be viewing the final product. Whether that audience is perceived as being insiders (e.g., for material placed in a local library) or outsiders (e.g., for a documentary produced for public televi-sion) may also make a difference in the types and nature of the information divulged.[75]

Second, there is the issue of how an insider versus an out-sider is defined in a particular community or for a specific indi-vidual. This returns to the ongoing discussion of the assumption of homogeneity that has been raised by Hansen, Osterud and Jones, and others.[76] For example, an interviewer may be a member of a geographical community being studied (as in the case of a neighborhood), but if that person's gender or age are significantly different from that of the interviewees, is that person an insider or an outsider? As Allen and Montell observe, "The researcher's sex and ethnic background can also pose methodological problems and can serve as both an aid and hindrance to local history research."[77] The same might be true of other possible characteristics, including class, race, occupation, and religious affiliation. The point is that even within physically or culturally bounded communities, there is diversity that needs to be considered when planning research.

Selecting Interviewees

> "How do you find these wonderful people?" That is a question I have often been asked, and it implies that "interviewees" are a special kind of animal and that finding them is something like catching night-crawlers: "You gotta be quick!"
>
> —Edward Ives, *The Tape-Recorded Interview*, 2nd ed.

Finding good interviewees can be a daunting task, but it must be done with care, as it will greatly affect the nature and quality of the information gathered. Perhaps more than anything else, the choices made in this regard will be inextricably tied to the theoretical decisions made earlier.

First, information must be disseminated about a project, and interviewees must be generally recruited. There are a number of ways to accomplish that task. Some researchers advertise on television, radio, or in newspapers, through organizations or newsletters, while others find names through research in local records or in discussions with advisory boards or other interviewees.[78] Ives suggests writing letters to the editor of local papers with an explanation of the project, as that affords one a known identity when first visiting a new location.[79]

There is a danger, however, in mass recruitments for projects, especially if the scope of work will be limited by either resource availability or theoretical concerns. Eliciting more respondents than one can ultimately use may end up causing hard feelings or ill will toward the work, so Ritchie suggests that, "Rather than disappoint people by not interviewing them, projects can limit their initial appeals to informal networks before going public through the media."[80] That approach ultimately gives researchers more control over the process.

Once there is a potential pool of interviewees, selection needs to be done in some manner, usually with an eye toward representative coverage of the groups involved. As Thompson notes, self-selected groups derived from media publicity are rarely representative of the whole, so researchers will probably need to look beyond any initial draws in that regard.[81]

A common way of ensuring adequate coverage for a project is using a matrix. During the research design phase, the topics under consideration can be listed down one axis, while the groups related to those topics can be listed across the top axis. For example, a community oral history project might list as potential topics the Depression, World War II, the 1966 closing of a local mine, the Vietnam War, and the local flood of 1978. Groups needing to be represented could be delineated by occupation (e.g., ranchers, miners, schoolteachers), ethnic or racial groups, or gender, age, or class considerations, in part depending upon the theoretical underpinnings of the research. A grid is then formed that, ideally, would be filled with the names of chroniclers who could address topics from the particular perspectives desired. A similar matrix, called a control chart, is suggested by David Lance, although he mentions it as a way to track what progress has been made in the course of a project rather than utilizing it as a planning tool.[82]

Other means of selecting interviewers include specific types of sampling to ensure proper representation (although this approach can also be used in conjunction with a matrix). Snowball sampling is less statistically based and really refers more to a recruiting tactic. It consists of obtaining suggestions for interviewees from those already interviewed and continuing on in that manner as work progresses. Stratified sampling entails interviewing at all levels of a community or group in order to get equal representation, and purposive sampling is essentially stratified sampling with the additional goal of having all sides represented on controversial or sensitive issues.[83]

Quota sampling reflects an attempt to match the population of a certain place and time with a closely correlated group of interviewees. For example, in Thompson and Vigne's study on Edwardian England noted earlier, they chose a group of interviewees that closely mirrored the demographic proportions listed in the 1911 national census.[84] The various quota categories for sampling—for example, age, gender, race, education, occupation, religion—may vary depending upon the question under study.[85]

And a note in regard to sampling as it pertains to grounded theory: at least as the guidelines for this theory were originally envisioned for sociology, quantitative sampling (i.e., sampling other than that of the snowball variety mentioned above) was seen as unnecessary and perhaps inappropriate to the theoretical goals. Strauss and Corbin noted that, "Researchers are not trying to control variables; rather they are trying to discover them. They are not looking for representativeness or distribution of populations; rather they are looking for how concepts vary dimensionally along their properties. So, although random sampling is possible, it might be detrimental because it could prevent analysts from discovering the variations that they are looking for."[86]

This does not necessarily have to be the case with oral history projects informed by grounded theory, however. One of the most commonly cited examples of successfully implemented grounded theory is Thompson and Vigne's Edwardian study, which is also referenced above as an effective utilization of quota sampling.

When representationally ideal interviewees have been located (however one's theory defines that), there are a few practical considerations that should be addressed as part of the selection process. First, the interviewees must actually be able to participate in the oral history process by being able to communicate their firsthand recollections.[87] That is, not only must they have eyewitness accounts, but their memory must be good enough and they must be sufficiently articulate about their remembrances to be involved in an interview. Second, keep in mind that interviewees do not need to be elderly to have pertinent memories. This is particularly true when projects are addressing current events, but the tendency to work with older chroniclers is so embedded that younger interviewees may be overlooked.[88]

Last, but certainly not least, is the possibility that monetary donations and grants will drive the interviewee selection process. Simply put, this should not happen. As Ritchie asserts, "Economic realities may be inescapable, but oral history projects should include as wide a range of interviews as possible and not be limited to those who can pay for it. Care must be taken not to allow funding sources to inhibit the choice of topics or interviewees."[89]

Determining Scope

The matter of determining the scope of a project will in large part be decided by resources and the availability of interviewees as much as by the research design, and much of this will occur well into the project's progress. To the extent, however, that various aspects are planned for in advance (particularly for proposals to granting agencies or for institutional review board presentations), the following suggestions are presented.

First, the matrix and the control chart discussed earlier are convenient guides both for planning the scope of a project at its outset and for understanding how well the material gathered is meeting the research goals as far as coverage is concerned. These charts are not meant to be carved in stone but can (and should) be adapted as the project evolves.

Second, an interview guide is generally considered a necessity by most oral historians (although not by all grounded theorists). Such a guide can consist of anything from a basic list of topics to a detailed, ordered list of questions, and they are especially useful for projects where there is more than one interviewer, as everyone then goes into the interview with the same goals. Lance suggests making an initial list of subjects to be discussed, then delineating more specific queries under each heading (keeping in mind, of course, what information will be available based on the age and experience of interviewees).[90]

And while this list can be as vague or as detailed as desired, Hoopes cautions against writing out every question verbatim, as that tends to make the conversation seem less spontaneous and detracts from the interactive nature of the interview.[91]

However researchers choose to use interview guides, it should be remembered that they are *just* guides. As Valerie Yow notes, "The guide contains the topics the interviewer will pursue but does not limit the interview to those topics because the narrator will have the freedom to suggest others"[92] (as will the interviewer). Oral history sessions are discussions between two individuals (generally), and they should retain that dialogic nature if they are to be considered oral histories.

Background Preparations

Research

Although there is some disagreement regarding when background research should be done (see the earlier discussion on grounded theory), there is almost complete consensus that scholars should, at some point, conduct extensive research into the subject they are studying.[93] Not only does the advance preparation show proper respect for the interviewee, but it also allows the interviewer to identify inconsistencies in responses and use time with the interviewee to best advantage, for as Hoopes observes, "Having a limited amount of time with the interviewee, you do not want to spend it learning information that you can acquire elsewhere, before the interview."[94]

It is also important to note that background research does not include only investigations of literature on the subject or historical period in question, but should also include research into oral history methodology. Field guides, anthologies, and theoretical works are good places to start.[95]

While most researchers will be able to visit libraries and archives or access materials online, useful sources will not always be available in those locations depending upon the nature of the project. Prominent individuals may be represented by a conspicuous paper trail, but nonelites or those from underdocumented groups may not. In these instances, Gluck suggests consulting sources on the historical era and general living conditions, and Hoopes recommends being creative and using local newspapers (if birth or marriage dates are available) or sources such as high school yearbooks. He further notes that such research is not only possible, but also important, "because one justification usually cited for resistance to studying the history of the poor and minority groups is that the bottom ranks of society supposedly do not leave useful records."[96]

Family histories can also pose a problem in this regard, but if one is researching one's own family, helpful artifacts and documents are often available. Family Bibles and photographs are good resources, and if important dates are known (which is more common within families), public records and newspapers can be valuable sources for information. Shopes suggests that, in doing background research, family historians should compile individual information forms for each family member, adding details as they are uncovered, which provides an easy way to organize material as it is gathered.[97]

Meetings and Clearances

Although community meetings were mentioned earlier as a means of encouraging collaboration, there are also meetings that will be mandatory rather than voluntary and clearances that must be obtained. When entering some communities for research—most notably Native American reservations and other sovereign entities—the approval of certain leadership groups often must be acquired before research can begin. In some instances it will be a tribal or elders' council, while in other cases it will be a different sort of local or regional governmental body, but bear in mind that approval must be obtained before work in some communities can commence.[98] During these meetings, release forms should also be reviewed to ensure that there is no misunderstanding about the nature of the releases or the disposition of materials. If these issues need to be negotiated, it is much easier to do so at the beginning of a project than after a portion of the work has been completed.

Another clearance that must often be obtained, at least in many academic and governmental contexts, is that of the institutional review board (IRB). IRBs and their origins are discussed in more detail in Shopes's chapter elsewhere in this volume, but suffice it to say that one reason for having a clearly defined research design and resolved release form and representation issues is so that a researcher can present his or her plan to an IRB committee with no loose ends. If an IRB review is required at a given institution, a scholar must satisfy the IRB that the project will be conducted in an ethical manner and in accordance with the *Evaluation Guidelines* set forth by the Oral History Association.[99] (Note that following the guidelines and behaving in an ethical fashion are, of course, expected of all oral historians and not just those going before IRB committees, but this is simply mentioned in the context of the IRB review.)

End Products and Availability

These topics are discussed in depth elsewhere in this book, but brief mention will be made of them here to the extent that they impact or are impacted by the research design. For a number of reasons, the planning for all projects needs to take final products into consideration. The first are practical. If the goal of the research is to produce an illustrated book, then photographs should be gathered in the course of work. If a multimedia program is planned, the necessary materials must be collected and the audio must be of a quality so as to be usable. Also, release forms should reflect the possible uses to which the materials can be put.

On a more theoretical level, however, there are other considerations. If interviewees (either on an individual or community scale) trust researchers with their memories and opinions, what do oral historians provide them with in return? What is a researcher's responsibility to interviewees? To a degree, certainly, interviewees may experience an increase in self-esteem or local status because their recollections are viewed as interesting and important, and as mentioned previously, many projects advocate for the empowerment of their participants. But as far as the end products of the oral history go, what do interviewees receive, and if they receive anything, is it of use to them? On this question of restitution, Portelli inquires, "Does the intended audience [for an oral history's final product] include the social circle of the narrators, and what responsibility does the text take on their behalf?"[100]

Oral historians have become more conscious of the need to give something back to interviewees. Many programs provide copies of tapes or transcripts to chroniclers. On a larger, community-wide scale, end products have been designed with local audiences and their needs and wants in mind. Examples include the Web site, "From Here: A Century of Voices from Ohio," produced by The Wallpaper Project, of Auglaize County, Ohio; the museum exhibition, "Agincourt: A Community History," developed by the Multicultural History Society of Ontario at the Scarborough Historical Museum, in Scarborough, Ontario; the video documentaries on Washoe culture, *Rabbit Boss* and *Tah Gum*, produced by the University of Nevada Oral History Program, Reno, Nevada; and various community publishing projects popular in Great Britain.[101] Researchers should take these concerns under consideration when compiling their research design, especially to ensure congruity between the theoretical aims of a project and its final products, as a project that claims empowerment as one of its goals and then returns nothing to the community is contradictory at best and hypocritical at worst.

One way that oral historians attempt to make materials useful to communities is through their placement in local and regional libraries, cultural centers, and museums. This also fulfills researchers' obligations to the academic sphere, by making tapes and transcripts available to other scholars.[102] Perhaps Alice Hoffman best summarized the contribution of such a placement to both researchers and interviewees with the following story: "I remember thanking profusely a steelworker for his time in giving me his memories and his answer was very good. He said, 'Oh hell, Alice, it's better than a tombstone.' He had a better sense than I did that his angle of vision was going to be at Penn State, in the archives for a long time."[103]

This anecdote also highlights the reason that oral historians need to take their research designs and their work seriously. Through the projects they plan, researchers are entrusted with recording and preserving people's memories and ensuring that they will be available and useful "for a long time." That, in itself, is a weighty task.

Notes

1. Gluck, "What's So Special" (1996), 217.

2. Henige, *Oral Historiography*, 23; on selecting previously undocumented topics, see also, Ritchie, *Doing Oral History* (1995), 23.

3. Ritchie, *Doing Oral History* (1995), 24.

4. Oral History Office, September 11, 2001 Oral History Narrative and Memory Project, Columbia University, http://www.columbia.edu/cu/lweb/indiv/oral/sept11.html (accessed January 31, 2005). For a discussion of oral history on current topics, using this project as the focus, see "Images of Sept. 11 Fill Half-Day Session at OHA Conference: 'History Hot' Reveals Complexities Masked in Media Accounts," *Oral History Association Newsletter* 36, no. 3 (Winter 2002): 8–10.

5. Harris et al., *Practice of Oral History*, 51; Crawford, "State of the Profession," 4.

6. Meyer, "Elena Poniatowska," 4; Andrade, "One Year Later," 22.

7. Poniatowska, "Earthquake," 16–17.

8. Governor's Day oral history collection, University of Nevada Oral History Program, Reno.

9. Hardy, "Alice Hoffman," 111.

10. Ritchie, *Doing Oral History* (1995), 30.

11. Schneider, *So They Understand*, 118.

12. Dunaway, "Oral Biography," 257, quoted in Schneider, *So They Understand*, 112.

13. Gluck, "What's So Special" (1996), 217–18.

14. Portelli, *Battle of Valle Giulia*, 4.

15. Blackman, *During My Time*, 14.

16. Osterud and Jones, "'I Must Say So,'" 4.

17. Sitton, "Descendants of *Foxfire*," 20; Hareven, "Generational Memory," 246.

18. Allen and Montell, *Memory to History*, vii–viii, 5.

19. Schneider, *So They Understand*, 20.

20. University of Alaska Fairbanks Oral History Program, Project Jukebox, Elmer E. Rasmuson Library, University of Alaska Fairbanks, http://uafdb.uaf.edu/Jukebox/PJWeb/pjhome.htm (accessed January 26, 2005).

21. Sitton, "Descendants of *Foxfire*," 29–30.

22. Harris et al., *Practice of Oral History*, 18; Henige, *Oral Historiography*, 25.

23. Hoopes, *Oral History*, 57.

24. Hareven, "Generational Memory," 243.

25. Shopes, "Using Oral History," 232.

26. Hareven, "Generational Memory," 243–44.

27. Shopes, "Using Oral History," 234.

28. Hoopes, *Oral History*, 58.

29. McMahan, *Elite Oral History*, xiv.

30. Frisch, "Oral History and *Hard Times*" (1998), 32; Perks and Thomson, "Critical Developments," 1; Henige, *Oral Historiography*, 107; Hardy, "Alice Hoffman," 109.

31. Perks and Thomson, "Critical Developments," 1; Yow, *Recording Oral History* (1994), 3; Dunaway, "Interdisciplinarity," 8; Shopes, "Using Oral History," 232.

32. Tuchman, "Distinguishing the Significant" (1996), 96.

33. O'Farrell, "Facts and Fiction," 5–6, cited in Grele, *Envelopes of Sound*, 2nd ed., 282n56.

34. Henige, *Oral Historiography*, 109.

35. Hoffman, "Who Are the Elite?" 3–4.

36. Blackman, *During My Time*, 5.

37. Okihiro, "Ethnic History," 42.

38. Poniatowska, "Earthquake," 15.

39. Jefferson, "Echoes from the South," 43–44; Lynd, "Oral History from Below," 1; Perks and Thomson, *Oral History Reader*, ix.

40. Harris et al., *Practice of Oral History*, 4; Perks and Thomson, *Oral History Reader*, ix; Henige, *Oral Historiography*, 17; Jefferson, "Echoes from the South," 46.

41. Crawford, "State of the Profession," 3.

42. Ives, *Tape-Recorded Interview*, 2nd ed., 11.

43. Thompson, *Voice of the Past*, 225; Stacey, "Feminist Ethnography," 112; Osterud and Jones, "'I Must Say So,'" 2.

44. Gluck, "What's So Special" (1996), 217.

45. Stein, *American Journey*, x, quoted in Hoopes, *Oral History*, 26–27.

46. Hoopes, *Oral History*, 27.

47. Gluck, "What's So Special" (1996), 217.

48. Osterud and Jones, "'I Must Say So,'" 3.

49. Ibid.

50. Moss, "Future of Oral History," 14–15; Perks and Thomson, *Oral History Reader*, ix; Perks and Thomson, "Critical Developments," 1; Hardy, "Alice Hoffman," 109.

51. Lynd, "Oral History from Below," 2–5; Portelli, *Battle of Valle Giulia*, xvi–xvii.

52. Thompson, *Voice of the Past*, 3rd ed., 22.

53. Henige, *Oral Historiography*, 107.

54. Perks and Thomson, *Oral History Reader*, ix; Lynd, "Oral History from Below," 1–2.

55. Hoffman, "Who Are the Elite?" 5.

56. Hareven, "Generational Memory," 254.

57. Brian Beun, quoted in Sitton, "Descendents of *Foxfire*," 22–23.

58. Jefferson, "Echoes from the South," 46.

59. For example, the civil rights collections housed at the University of Southern Mississippi's Center for Oral History and Cultural Heritage, Hattiesburg, Mississippi, and at the archives of Tougaloo College, Tougaloo, Mississippi.

60. Jefferson, "Echoes from the South," 43–44.

61. Okihiro, "Ethnic History," 43.

62. Hansen, "Riot of Voices," 136.

63. See Glaser and Strauss, *Grounded Theory*.

64. Strauss and Corbin, *Qualitative Research*, 12.

65. Yow, *Recording Oral History* (1994), 8; Sima Belmar, "For the Record: The Legacy Oral History Project Gets It in Writing," *San Francisco Bay Guardian*, April 30, 2003.

66. Thompson, *Voice of the Past*, 3rd ed., 227.

67. Portelli, *Battle of Valle Giulia*, 11; see also Yow, *Recording Oral History* (1994), 8; Thompson, *Voice of the Past*, 3rd ed., 227.

68. Henige, *Oral Historiography*, 33.

69. Thompson, *Edwardians*, 7; Thompson, *Voice of the Past*, 3rd ed., 146–48; Yow, *Recording Oral History* (1994), 17; Jensen, "Quantification," 15.

70. Ritchie, *Doing Oral History* (1995), 31; Harris et al., *Practice of Oral History*, 10.

71. Harris et al., *Practice of Oral History*, 45.

72. Gluck, "What's So Special" (1996), 219–20.

73. Ritchie, *Doing Oral History* (1995), 31; Allen and Montell, *Memory to History*, 11–12; Gluck, "What's So Special" (1996), 221; Schneider, *So They Understand*, 21; Harris et al., *Practice of Oral History*, 24–25.

74. Portelli, *Battle of Valle Giulia*, 11; Gluck, "What's So Special" (1996), 221.

75. Schneider, *So They Understand*, 21.

76. Hansen, "Riot of Voices," 136; Osterud and Jones, "'I Must Say So,'" 3; Kikumura, "Family Life Histories," 2–3.

77. Allen and Montell, *Memory to History*, 13–14.

78. Ritchie, *Doing Oral History* (1995), 30–31; Green, "Returning History," 54; Yow, *Recording Oral History* (1994), 45; Gluck, "What's So Special" (1996), 220–21.

79. Ives, *Tape-Recorded Interview*, 2nd ed., 26–27.

80. Ritchie, *Doing Oral History* (1995), 30–31.

81. Thompson, *Voice of the Past*, 3rd ed., 22.

82. Lance, "Project Design," 140.

83. Yow, *Recording Oral History* (1994), 45–47; Strauss and Corbin, *Qualitative Research*, 281; Hardy, "Alice Hoffman," 116.

84. Thompson, *Edwardians*, 7; Thompson, *Voice of the Past*, 3rd ed., 146–48; Yow, *Recording Oral History* (1994), 47.

85. Jensen, "Quantification," 19.

86. Strauss and Corbin, *Qualitative Research*, 281.

87. Thompson, *Voice of the Past*, 3rd ed., 212–13.

88. Hoopes, *Oral History*, 28.

89. Ritchie, *Doing Oral History* (1995), 28.

90. Lance, "Project Design," 138.

91. Hoopes, *Oral History*, 80.

92. Yow, *Recording Oral History* (1994), 36.

93. Grele, *Envelopes of Sound*, 2nd ed., 164; Thompson, *Voice of the Past*, 3rd ed., 222; Harris et al., *Practice of Oral History*, 15; Henige, *Oral Historiography*, 24; Jefferson, "Echoes from the South," 52; Yow, *Recording Oral History* (1994), 33; Lance, "Project Design," 136; Hoopes, *Oral History*, 72–73; Okihiro, "Ethnic History," 38.

94. Hoopes, *Oral History*, 72.

95. Grele, *Envelopes of Sound*, 2nd ed., 141; Gluck, "What's So Special" (1996), 220; Okihiro, "Ethnic History," 38.

96. Gluck, "What's So Special" (1996), 223; Hoopes, *Oral History*, 75–76.

97. Shopes, "Using Oral History," 233.

98. Harris et al., *Practice of Oral History*, 18; Henige, *Oral Historiography*, 25.

99. Oral History Association, *Evaluation Guidelines*.

100. Portelli, *Battle of Valle Giulia*, 18–19; see also Lynd, "Oral History from Below," 2.

101. See The Wallpaper Project, From Here: A Century of Voices from Ohio, Ohio Humanities Council, http://www.ohiohumanities.org/current_int/ wallpaper/support.htm (accessed January 26, 2005), and University of Nevada Oral History Program, Publications, University of Nevada, http://www.unr .edu/cla/oralhist/ohweb/bestsel.htm (accessed January 26, 2005). On British community history publications, see Bornat, "Two Oral Histories," 78.

102. Ives, *Tape-Recorded Interview*, 2nd ed., 85–86; Ritchie, *Doing Oral History* (1995), 54–55; Thompson, *Voice of the Past*, 3rd ed., 214.

103. Hardy, "Alice Hoffman," 133.

4

Legal and Ethical Issues in Oral History

Linda Shopes

Legal and ethical issues are often discussed sequentially within oral history, with the law understood as defining state-sanctioned rules for specific elements of practice and ethics as setting a higher standard for the right conduct of relationships within the broad context of an interview or project. Although this distinction is not entirely inaccurate, it unnecessarily segregates the two, obscuring their relationship within the overall development of oral history as a mode of historical practice. Thus, in this essay, I will discuss legal and ethical issues within an overall historical framework. I identify three stages in oral history's evolution: its origins as an archival practice, its expansion as a means of democratizing both the historical record and the act of doing history, and its maturation as a complex intellectual and social practice.[1] While these stages have occurred somewhat in succession over the past half century, they also overlap chronologically and conceptually. Discussion of the first stage is heavily weighted toward fundamental legal issues, for they are closely related to oral history's archival origins; discussion of the second and third stages extends to broader ethical concerns.

Oral historians living and working in different nations have codified principles to guide their work according to the legal codes and historical conditions of their various countries. In the United States, the governing document is *Oral History Evaluation*

Guidelines, initially developed by the U.S. Oral History Association (OHA) as "Goals and Guidelines" in 1968, amplified as a checklist of "Evaluation Guidelines" in 1979, and then revised in 1989 and again in 2000 to take into account new issues and concerns.[2] The OHA guidelines, as well as other associations' codes, conceptualize legal and ethical principles as a series of rights and responsibilities governing relationships between interviewers and narrators; among interviewers, their various professions and disciplines, and the broader public; and between sponsoring institutions and interviewees, interviewers, the professions, and the public. The challenge for oral historians occurs when responsibilities to one party collide with responsibilities to another, when ethical considerations thus pull in opposite directions. I will discuss some of these conflicts in the body of the essay.

While *Evaluation Guidelines* is a touchstone for any discussion of legal and ethical issues in the U.S. and considerably informs this essay, it is also a historical document, grounded in assumptions about individual and property rights deeply embedded in U.S. laws and culture as well as standards of professional practice that are by definition both exclusionary and protectionist. Recognizing this, Alessandro Portelli has written: "Ultimately, in fact ethical and legal guidelines only make sense if they are the outward manifestation of a broader and deeper sense of personal and political commitment to honesty and to truth. . . . Sticking close to the letter of professional guidelines may not be incompatible with subtler strategies of manipulation and falsification. Ethical guidelines may be, in this case, less a protection of the interviewee from the manipulation of the interviewer than a protection of the interviewer from the claims of the interviewee."[3]

It is important to remember, therefore, that legal and especially ethical issues are at bottom judgment calls. Certainly legal transgressions can have serious consequences for individual researchers and their sponsoring institutions. Ethical lapses not only can harm narrators and burden a researcher, but they can also discredit the work of others. Nonetheless, in my view, individual oral historians need to understand where they stand vis-à-vis accepted practice, act according to their own best judgment, and accept the consequences of their actions.

Law, Ethics, and Oral History as an Archival Practice

Oral history in the U.S. generally dates its origins to the 1940s, with the work of Allan Nevins at Columbia University. Although there were numerous earlier efforts to record firsthand accounts of the past, most notably the life histories gathered by the Great Depression–era Federal Writers' Project, it was Nevins who first initiated a systematic and disciplined effort to record on tape, preserve, and make available for future research recollections deemed of historical significance.[4] Two fundamental ethical issues in oral history are linked to its origins as an archival practice: obtaining the narrator's informed consent for the interview and securing legal release of the interview tape and transcript. The former is linked to the goal of creating as full and accurate account as possible for the permanent record, the latter to issues of copyright and, more broadly, concerns about making interviews both physically and intellectually accessible to potential users.[5] This last point deserves elaboration. Although oral history interviews are by definition intended for permanent preservation, ad hoc projects without the institutional capacity to archive completed interviews and individual scholars conducting interviews for their own work at times neglect to make interviews accessible to others after they have served their immediate purpose. Professional standards enjoin the group or individual to place interviews in a permanent repository where others may have access to them, and in the case of interviews used for scholarly work, so others may interrogate and build upon the work.[6]

Informed Consent

Because a primary goal of oral history is to enhance the extant historical record, good interviewers work with narrators to "speak to history," that is, to create a record worthy of preservation, one that is accurate, expansive, and thoughtful and hence of value not only to scholars but also to society's collective understanding of the past. There are many ways for an interviewer to cultivate a good interview, as discussed elsewhere in this volume. Fundamental, however, is a respect for the person whose story one seeks. Respect, too, can be demonstrated in many ways. Of importance here, however, is the process of informed consent, whereby the interviewer tells the potential narrator everything that person needs to know in order to decide whether or not to participate in an interview and to continue participation once interviewing has begun. Thus potential narrators need to be informed about the purpose, scope, and value of the interview, how it will proceed, and the interviewer's expectations for the interview. Interviewees need to know the intended use of the interview as well as possible future uses; that they will have the opportunity to review and emend the transcript, if project protocols include transcription; and where the interviewer or project intends to place tapes and transcripts for permanent preservation. Narrators must also be informed that they will be asked to sign a copyright release form at the conclusion of the interview, by which they will define the terms according to which the interview can be used, and that the interviewer and the project cannot entirely control the uses to which the interview will be put once it has been made publicly available nor protect it against subpoena. It is also appropriate to discuss any relevant financial considerations, including payment to narrators and disbursement of royalties resulting from publication of the interview. Finally, interviewees need to know that they can refuse to answer any given question during the interview and can terminate the interview at any time with no adverse consequences.

These terms and conditions need thorough review prior to the interview. Unless specific circumstances dictate otherwise, it is also advisable that they be codified in a consent form or memorandum of agreement written in language appropriate to the interviewee and signed by both interviewee and interviewer. Though it can be argued that undue attention to interview protocols and narrator rights prior to the interview can have a chilling effect on the interview itself, in fact quite the opposite can be true. Insofar as securing the narrator's informed consent is approached as more than a pro forma exercise, it can be a means of educating the narrator about the nature and purpose of oral history and can generate enthusiasm for the interview, which in turn helps cultivate a good interview as the narrator is oriented to the interview situation, understands his or her role, and presumably is motivated to create a record of historical value. Moreover, securing informed consent does not end once the form is signed and the tape recorder is turned on. Respect grows—or not—over time, and so consent is negotiated throughout the entire interview as narrators are given the opportunity to tell their story in their own way, as unexpected openings are pursued, as the interviewer both accedes to and presses against constraints imposed by the narrator, as developing trust results in an increasingly frank account or growing mistrust to conversation that is guarded, responses that are perfunctory. In my own interviewing, I have found that once I have assured narrators that they do *not* have to answer questions on any given subject—family finances is often one of these "nervous subjects"—they frequently proceed to talk about precisely that subject in great detail. The point, it seems to me, is that I have demonstrated a respect for the narrators' right to control what they say; and in so doing, I have gained trust and hence the right of access to information not shared casually.

Attention to the process of informed consent also guards against defamation, a particular concern of those conducting interviews for archival purposes. John Neuenschwander, whose *Oral History and the Law* is the single best guide to legal issues in oral history, defines defamation as "a false statement of fact printed or broadcast about a person which tends to injure that person's interest." He goes on to say that "the accepted rule is that anyone who repeats, republishes, or redistributes a defamatory statement made by another can be held liable as well."[7] Thus any interview for the record, that is, any interview made available to others in a public repository and/or reproduced for others in any medium, is potentially liable for defamation. Defamation is a serious charge; it is also one that is not easy to prove. Neuenschwander defines five specific elements that must be present for a statement to be deemed defamatory: the statement itself must be false; it must specifically identify the person claiming injury; it must be communicated to a third person, for example, a researcher listening to the offending interview; the injured party's reputation must have been damaged; and the perpetrator must be at fault, that is, responsible for the injury claimed.[8] Additional constraints also obtain: most states have imposed a statute of limitation on the time between first publication of the offending material and the charge of defamation; the courts have established a much higher bar for proving defamation of public figures as opposed to private individuals; and statements construed as opinion, "nothing more than conjecture and rumor," in the words of one court case, are not considered defamatory—though the line between opinion and fact admittedly can be blurred.[9] Finally, and of particular interest to oral historians, the party claiming injury must be alive—the dead, in other words, cannot be defamed.

This final constraint suggests that the easiest course of action for an oral historian confronted with a potentially defamatory statement is to counsel the narrator to seal that portion of the interview until such time as the person under discussion can reasonably be assumed to be deceased.[10] In addition to this practice, Neuenschwander suggests as alternatives either excising the questionable material from the tape and transcript or deleting the identity of the person in question. Both of these actions, while reasonable, assume that the questionable statements are, in fact, defamatory. But on whose judgment? Perhaps they are accurate. Perhaps the narrator knows something others do not. Hence, an equally reasonable approach may be to try to ascertain the truth or falsity of the statement in question by consulting other sources. If it is true, it is not defamatory.[11]

The larger point in this discussion, however, is that a respectful process of informed consent before and during an interview, by which both interviewer and narrator agree that they are "speaking to history" and not chatting or gossiping informally, can guard against defamatory statements. An interviewee who understands the purpose of the interview, who knows he or she is speaking for the record, can measure comments about another person. A conscientious interviewer can avoid setting up too intimate an exchange, one that nurtures imprudent confidences. If the interviewer/interviewee relationship is trusting enough, they can also engage in a metaconversation about the interview itself while it is going on, that is, decide together within the context of an interview whether or not to pursue a particular line of talk.

The above discussion suggests that informed consent is both universally desirable and possible. Yet a question arises about how much to reveal about the purpose of an interview to a potential narrator, "who," as Jeremy Brecher phrased it some years ago, "if they really understood what we were going to do with the material, would probably not cooperate?"[12] Kathleen Blee further complicates the matter by suggesting that the men and women she interviewed about their participation in the 1920s Ku Klux Klan in Indiana could not give true informed consent to the interviews because they "found it impossible to imagine that I— a native of Indiana and a white person—would not agree, at least secretly, with their racist and bigoted world views."[13] Here, then, is a place where ethical judgments are in order. Typically, oral historians counsel telling a narrator the truth about the subject, purpose, and disposition of an interview but argue that they are under no obligation to inform the narrator of the interpretation they will bring to bear upon an individual's story. But again Brecher raises a provocative question: "What is the nature of our implied contract with our informants, and what limits should that contract place on the way we present them?"[14] In general, too, outright deception is quite rightly considered beyond the bounds of ethical practice. Yet there is the example of filmmaker Claude Lanzmann, who exposed perpetrators of the Nazi Holocaust by filming them with a hidden camera and then included their testimony in his epic film *Shoah*.[15] Does the public's right to hold war criminals accountable trump Lanzmann's failure to secure their consent to the interview? Or not?[16] Standard professional practice, which privileges the rights of narrators, would claim that Lanzmann acted unethically; broader civic and or moral claims would suggest otherwise.

Release Forms and Copyright

Because oral history originated as an archival practice, early practitioners were especially concerned with gaining ownership of completed interviews and transcripts, for without this, they would not have the right to grant others access to this material. This remains an important concern, for put simply, an interview is understood as a creative work owned by the interviewee and hence is subject to the laws of copyright. (The status of the interviewer is less certain, as discussed below.) For an interview to be used by anyone other than the interviewee, the interviewer or the project or institution for which he is working must secure a legal release agreement once the interview is complete, assigning rights to the interview to either the interviewer or to the repository where it will be permanently housed. As Neuenschwander writes, *"Without a legal release, the possessor of the tape or transcript of an oral history interview cannot legally utilize, loan, publish, or make it available to researchers without infringing upon the rights of the interviewee and possibly the interviewer"* (emphasis in original).[17] Rights can be assigned by means of a deed of gift or contract. Both will allow others access to the interview; they will also allow those who retain ownership the rights to use, reproduce, and disseminate the interview, as well as to protect them from its illegal use by others. Both include specific elements, generally phrased in commonly accepted, legally sanctioned language. Although template forms are available, one size does not fit all, and interviewers, projects, and repositories are advised to consult legal counsel to develop a deed of gift or contract appropriate to their project.[18]

Oral historians generally agree that the most important right to secure by means of a legal release is copyright; that is, they seek the transfer of ownership of the creative work that constitutes the interview from the interviewee to the interviewer, project, or repository. Whoever owns the copyright can then reproduce, publish, distribute, and sell the interview and legally prevent others from doing so without explicit permission. However, a narrator does not have to sign over copyright to the interview in order to make it available to others; the narrator can retain the copyright, placing physical custody of the tape and transcript with an individual or archives and permitting limited use or requiring potential users other than the interviewer to secure the narrator's permission if they wish more extensive use. While some oral history programs and archives will thus allow a narrator to retain the copyright to the interview, they usually require that it revert to the institution upon the narrator's death and not transfer to heirs, for repositories cannot track heirs over time. Copyright protection, however, is not maintained in perpetuity. According to the terms of the Copyright Act of 1976, copyright protection for works created on or after January 1, 1978, extends seventy years beyond the life of the author (i.e., interviewee), after which the work enters the public domain. Interviews can also be placed in the public domain at the time of their creation, thereby avoiding the issue of copyright altogether, but this too must be done by means of a legal release.[19]

The status of the interviewer as cocreator and hence joint owner of the copyright to the interview is unclear at this time; it is also related to the interview's position vis-à-vis the sponsoring project or organization. Although the courts have not ruled on the issue, the U.S. Copyright Office recognizes the interviewer as a joint author, "in the absence of an agreement to the contrary."[20] It is generally advised, therefore, that interviewers also sign over copyright when interviews are retained by a project or archives. The one clear exception is an interview conducted by a full-time employee of a given entity as part of his job duties; under such circumstances, termed "work made for hire," the interviewer/employee's rights to the interview are automatically ceded to the employer.[21] However, many interviewers are not full-time employees of the organization or institution sponsoring an oral history project; they are temporary or part-time employees, independent contractors, or volunteers who are not therefore covered by the terms of "work made for hire." Under these circumstances, the sponsoring institution would be wise to secure rights to the interviews at the outset of the project by means of a work for hire or assignment of copyright agreement with the interviewer. Yet it may be appropriate to tailor arrangements to individual circumstances: if, for example, a contract interviewer is interviewing on a subject related to his own research interests or a scholar is conducting interviews without official institutional sponsorship but nonetheless plans to permanently archive the interviews within the institution, he may wish to secure the right to exclusive use of the interviews for a specified period of time.[22]

In addition to addressing the issue of copyright, the legal release also allows the narrator to define the terms according to which the interview can—and cannot—be accessed and used by others. While historians generally prefer releases with no restrictions, an interviewee can protect sensitive material by closing all or portions of the interview for a given number of years. Such a restriction, however, is not inviolate; it can be overruled by court order if the interview is deemed of potential value to a legal proceeding. An interviewee can also forbid users to quote directly from the interview and can require anonymity for a period of time or in perpetuity. This latter situation is especially discouraged by historians, for whom anonymous sources are suspect, but sometimes is requested by a narrator to protect personal safety or privacy.

Regrettably, numerous interviews exist, some of them in public archives, for which no legal release has been obtained. Making these interviews available to others before the expiration of copyright is both illegal and unethical. In these cases, narrators should be recontacted and signed releases for the interviews secured. If a narrator is deceased, efforts should be made to contact heirs to whom copyright has passed and to secure their release of the material. Because the Copyright Office recognizes the interviewer as a joint author, and because copyright law allows a joint author to convey rights to a third party without the approval of the other author, another alternative, if the narrator and his heirs are deceased or cannot be located, is for the interviewer to sign over rights to the interview. Publishers of works that incorporate oral history materials for which no release exists will sometimes accept the institution where the interviews are permanently archived as the de facto owner, who must then indemnify the publisher from any adverse consequences resulting from publication of the interviews.

Explaining release forms and copyright issues to a narrator before an interview can admittedly seem a sterile exercise, one not conducive to the informal collegiality desirable in an interview. Like securing informed consent, however, done in the right spirit, these explanations can affirm the seriousness of the inquiry and the value of the narrator's story. Moreover, while the release and underlying concern about copyright are primarily legal issues, they also confirm a fundamental ethical principle in oral history: that the interviewee is deemed to have a certain authority over what he or she has said in an interview. Some researchers are uncomfortable giving narrators so much control over their stories; journalists, they argue, do not secure releases from their sources, allowing them to define the terms according to which the interview can be used. Historians, however, are not journalists; oral history interviews, unlike most conducted for journalistic purposes, are intended for permanent preservation. Historians also have a higher standard for evidence than journalists; they are enjoined by the canons of the profession to make their sources available to others so they can both interrogate and build upon one another's work. And, unless there is an outstanding reason not to, oral historians simply owe it to their narrators to make their stories known, to include them in the permanent record of the culture. Thus, because oral history interviews are preserved for the record, they are subject to laws of copyright; and the narrator, as original owner of the interview, has the right to define the terms of use.

Other questions arise over issues of confidentiality, that is, the status of information given in an interview that, if revealed, could put the narrator or others at risk of legal sanctions, public embarrassment, or other adverse consequences. Again, a conscientious process of informed consent should alert a narrator to the need for caution in revealing potentially incriminating information, but if the interviewer is about to broach a potentially damaging topic, for example, the narrator's possible involvement in a crime, should he again alert the narrator to the fact that the interview is for the record? Or suppose the narrator, consciously or not, reveals his participation in a crime but fails to request that the material be sealed for a period of time or excised from the interview. Should the interviewer suggest that he do so? Or what if the narrator reveals participation in a crime and requests that the incriminating evidence be closed, but the interviewer, weighing personal protection against the claims of justice or the public's right to know, wonders about the ethics of concealing knowledge of a crime? Should revelations of especially disturbing crimes or crimes with broad social consequences—war crimes or embezzlement of public moneys or domestic violence, for example—enjoy the protection of confidentiality? Or what if the issue is not a crime but behavior one might consider socially reprehensible, for example, prejudicial actions against minorities or women that are not illegal but could, if revealed, prove embarrassing or worse to the narrator? Should the interviewer always retain a neutral stance, refusing to judge—or reveal—an interviewee's incriminating past action?[23]

Evaluation Guidelines states that "interviews should remain confidential until interviewees have given permission for their use" and further affirms narrator privilege to restrict access to the interview.[24] The American Anthropological Association's *Statements on Ethics* emphatically privileges the research subject's right to privacy over other claims: "In research, anthropologists' paramount responsibility is to those they study. When there is a conflict of interest, these individuals must come first. Anthropologists must do everything in their power to protect the physical, social, and psychological welfare and to honor the dignity and privacy of those studied."[25] The American Sociological Association's *Code of Ethics*, however, recognizes that certain circumstances may compromise the protection of confidentiality afforded to research subjects, although its guidelines suggest that the conflict lies not with revealing past actions but with disclosing intended future actions that may be harmful to others: "Sociologists may confront unanticipated circumstances where they become aware of information that is clearly health- or life-threatening to research participants, students, employees, clients, or others. In these cases, sociologists balance the importance of guarantees of confidentiality with other principles in this *Code of Ethics*, standards of conduct, and applicable law."[26]

There are clearly no easy answers to questions about the claims of confidentiality. Neuenschwander notes that while historians, unlike attorneys, clergy, and psychiatrists, do not enjoy client privilege, in fact, few legal sanctions obtain for failure to report knowledge of a crime. He also urges caution in reporting a crime, based on careful consideration of statutes of limitation, potential defamation or claims of defamation, and legal sanctions for breach of confidentiality. In the end, however, professional ethics may conflict with a researcher's perceived civic duty or moral sensibility; researchers must live with themselves and thus decide for themselves how to handle such conflicts.

Oral History and the World Wide Web

The increasing use of the World Wide Web as a means of disseminating oral history interviews has raised additional issues of informed consent and access. If future use of an interview may include posting all or part of it on the Web, an interviewer obviously needs to discuss this with a potential narrator as part of the informed consent process. But the question arises: How can someone unfamiliar with the Web, particularly its potential for making the interview available to millions of people within seconds and permitting little or no control over how it will be used, give informed consent to posting their interview on the Web? At minimum, the interviewer facing this situation should demonstrate the Web and explain its capacities to the interviewee.

Release forms should also include language that allows for—or restricts, if the narrator chooses—placement of interviews and transcripts on the Web. Even if there is no immediate plan to do so, inclusion of such language will allow Web publication in the future. But what about uploading an interview collected in the pre-Web era? If the release includes language governing the future use of the interview that can be interpreted broadly to include dissemination via the Web, project managers can probably do so with impunity. But is this ethical, if the narrator had no knowledge of the Web's capacities when he signed the release? And what about interviews for which the releases include no language that can be construed as supporting Web publication? These issues were much debated in the late 1990s within the Oral History Association. Many felt that if Web publication was desired and an interview release did not include specific language permitting it, the copyright holder was obliged to contact the narrator or his heirs and secure specific permission to do so. Archivists, however, upon whom the burden of this task would fall, understandably balked, arguing that recontacting narrators or their heirs would simply place too great a burden on them. So, the compromise adopted by the association and included in the 2000 iteration of its *Evaluation Guidelines* states, "Good faith efforts should be made to ensure that the uses of recordings and transcripts comply with both the letter and spirit of the interviewee's agreements," implying the need for prudent judgment on the elasticity of existing future use agreements and the advisability of recontacting narrators whose release forms are ambiguous on the issue of Web posting.[27]

The issue is not solely one of narrator agreement, however. Certainly, posting interviews on the Web enhances access enormously. Powerful search engines enable students and other researchers to learn about source material they otherwise would not know existed; and if that material is itself online, the Internet brings it to their computer screen within seconds. But is this sort of uncontrolled and anonymous access always desirable? Opportunities for copyright violation and for misuse of a narrator's words are multiplied a thousandfold, with few of the checks imposed by archives when dealing with patrons face to face.[28] For these reasons, as well as technical and financial considerations, many oral history programs do not post full interviews on their Web sites. Others choose to post audiotapes or transcripts but impose certain constraints, including notifying users of copyright restrictions; requiring permission to quote; and requiring submission of a registration form, stating the purpose for which the user wants to view or listen to the interviews, before access is granted. Yet others, seeking to help users make good sense of the interviews, present them along with contextualizing background information.[29]

Oral History and Federal Regulations Governing Research Involving Human Subjects

Increasingly throughout the 1990s and early 2000s, researchers affiliated with colleges and universities have been required to submit protocols for oral history interviewing projects to their campus Institutional Review Board (IRB) prior to conducting any interviews. IRBs, charged with insuring compliance with federal regulations for the protection of human subjects of research, have claimed authority over oral history because these regulations, codified as Title 45 Public Welfare, Part 46 Protection of Human Subjects (referred to as 45 CFR 46 or the Common Rule), included "interaction" with human subjects as one of the research modes subject to review.[30] However, 45 CFR 46, initially intended to protect research subjects from such unethical practices as those employed in the Tuskegee syphilis study or the Milgram experiments on obedience to authority, defined protection within a framework appropriate to biomedical and behavioral research. As a result, constraints appropriate to these forms of research have been inappropriately applied to oral history:

interviewers have been asked to submit detailed questionnaires in advance of any interview; to maintain narrator anonymity, despite an interviewee's willingness to be identified; and to destroy tapes and transcripts after the research project is completed. Clearly these practices violate fundamental principles of oral history.

Most troublesome, however, has been the concern expressed by some IRBs that interviewers not ask any questions for which, in the language of 45 CFR 46, "any disclosure of the human subjects' responses outside the research could reasonably place the subjects at risk of criminal or civil liability, or be damaging to the subjects' financial standing, employability, or reputation"[31]; or questions that might prove psychologically harmful. While the regulations themselves don't prohibit this sort of research, requiring only that efforts be made to "minimize" risk or harm, some IRBs have interpreted them as constraining challenging or difficult lines of inquiry in an interview. Historians thus have become increasingly concerned that IRB review of oral history is having a chilling effect on legitimate inquiry and indeed impinging upon their academic freedom.[32]

Recognizing these concerns, in 1998 the American Historical Association (AHA) and the Oral History Association initiated contact with what was then the Office for Protection from Research Risks, which was renamed in 2000 the Office of Human Research Protections (OHRP) in the Department of Health and Human Services (HHS), which is the federal office responsible for implementing human subjects regulations, to raise questions about the legitimacy of IRB review of oral history within the existing regulatory framework or, failing that, to secure agreement about a form of review that conforms to the ethical principles of the field. After five years of discussion, in 2003, OHRP concurred with a policy statement developed by the AHA and OHA that "most oral history interviewing projects are not subject to . . . regulations for the protection of human subjects . . . and can be excluded from institutional review board . . . oversight because they do not involve research as defined by HHS regulations." The basis for exclusion hinges on the regulatory definition of research as contributing to "generalizable knowledge." To quote further from the policy statement: "While historians reach for meaning that goes beyond the specific subject of their inquiry, unlike researchers in the biomedical and behavioral sciences they do not reach for generalizable principles of historical or social development, nor do they seek underlying principles or laws of nature that have predictive value and can be applied to other circumstances for the purpose of controlling outcomes."[33] The policy does not imply that oral history is not a legitimate form of research, only that it is not *the type of research* the regulations were designed to cover. Nor does it signal an erosion of concern about high ethical standards for oral history by the AHA or OHA, only that oral historians are free to act in accordance with ethical and legal standards appropriate to oral history, not biomedical or behavioral research.[34]

Local IRBs, however, which enjoy considerable autonomy in interpreting the Common Rule, have generally not accepted the policy of excluding oral history from review; and OHRP itself, subsequent to its concurrence with the AHA/OHA policy statement and in response to queries from local IRBs, issued contrary—and conflicting—guidance, identifying some forms of oral history as in fact subject to review. Challenged by the AHA and OHA on this guidance, OHRP reaffirmed the original policy excluding oral history from review. As of this writing in late 2005, therefore, the matter of IRB review of oral history remains unresolved and indeed quite muddled: IRBs generally claim the authority to review interview protocols; OHRP maintains conflicting points of view; oral historians are obliged to conform to regulatory oversight that, at best, fits awkwardly with the work they do, at worst, constrains it; and professional societies' concerns remain unheeded at the federal level.[35]

Ethics and the Democratic Practice of Oral History

If oral history began as an archival practice in the 1940s, it exploded as a social practice in the 1970s, largely in response to the social and political movements of that era. Social history, that is, the history of social relationships among generally unequal and often competing groups, became the dominant historiographic paradigm, reflecting—and at times attempting to influence—the issues and tensions of contemporary public life. People and groups previously absent or underrepresented in our collective history became the subject of historical inquiry, and these new histories became the occasion for a fundamental rethinking of what properly constitutes historical knowledge. Grassroots groups, frequently in collaboration with local scholars, began to engage with their own history, often motivated by a belief that knowledge of one's past can be empowering in the present. Oral history, as a source of information about the past not available elsewhere, and as a reasonably accessible way of learning about that past for those without advanced training in history, was—and remains—intrinsic to this move to democratize both the content and the practice of history. While oral history in this democratic mode certainly didn't begin in the 1970s—one thinks, for example, of George Ewart Evans's pioneering work in England in the 1950s recording the lifeways of rural people with roots in the nineteenth century—its great efflorescence in the last decades of the twentieth arguably found its impetus in 1970s activism. Yet, for all its value in opening up new areas of inquiry and as a tool for grassroots history, oral history's focus on documenting what have sometimes been termed "the nonelite" also has raised a number of broadly ethical questions. Here I focus on two of the most important: power relationships in oral history and what might be termed the "overidentification" of interviewer with interviewee.

Power Relations in Oral History

As oral historians came to focus interviewing projects on members of various ethnic and racial groups, labor activists and blue-collar workers, and a variety of communities, they became acutely aware that the oral history process, from designing the project to interviewing to using the interviews, often involves a relationship between social unequals, with the oral historian in the dominant position. An interviewer's questions, driven by a particular intellectual agenda, could, it was argued, constrain a narrator from giving a full account of himself, on his own terms; his manner of speech and self-presentation could inhibit a narrator unfamiliar with the codes of middle-class, academic culture; subtle cues, verbal and nonverbal, could unwittingly communicate negative judgments of the narrator's experience; the book or other product resulting from the interviews could objectify complicated individuals as one-dimensional characters, with their words cut and pasted into the work in ways that simply confirm the author's views. Questions were raised about appropriating for personal gain the life stories of those not likely to reap much benefit from having told those stories and about returning something to narrators and their communities in exchange for having extracted their stories.

These questions were not confined to oral history, for the social conditions that gave rise to them reverberated throughout the culture, affecting most intellectual work and having an impact on all field-based research. Anthropologists, for example, considered the implications of their tendency to "study down," and as colonial empires crumbled, questioned their own social role in emerging states. The questions took on a particular urgency for feminists, who, interviewing and writing about women less privileged than they, could all too easily find themselves in the compromised position of reproducing precisely the unequal social relationships they criticized. It's no surprise, then, that issues of power within oral history were raised most pointedly within a feminist frame, most notably in four issues devoted to women's oral history of *Frontiers: A Journal of Women Studies* (appearing in 1977, 1983, and 1998) and in Sherna Berger Gluck and Daphne Patai's 1991 volume, *Women's Words: The Feminist Practice of Oral History*.[36] Collectively, essays in these works argue for both the value of oral history as a means of documenting women's experiences and the need for rigorous self-consciousness about method and modes of presentation.

At times, it must be said, this discussion of power relations has been overwrought and marked by its own kind of hubris. It certainly has underestimated the narrator's power over the interviewer—the power to refuse to talk, to withhold information, even to lie; the power to use an interview to say what the narrator wants to say, whatever the interviewer's questions. It similarly has failed to recognize that narrators too can "get" something from an interview—an opportunity to talk with a sympathetic listener, to gain insight into one's life trajectory, to achieve status within one's own community, and most especially, the satisfaction of having an account of one's experiences included in the collective record of the past. Taken to its extreme, concerns about power inequalities can lead to a paralyzing inaction or the misdirection of attention away from the narrator's story and onto the oral historian's own ethical dilemmas. Yet the dilemmas remain real, and the conscientious oral historian has good reason for an occasional case of the "moral jitters," as Robert Coles has termed the disquiet that arises from an acute sense of one's own privilege in relation to those one is interviewing.[37] How does one negotiate a nonexploitative or nonpatronizing relationship in a situation of social inequality? What do we owe narrators, financially, intellectually, personally? What obligation do we have to return the fruits of our interviewing to the individuals with whom or community with which we have worked?

Once again, *Evaluation Guidelines* defines some general principles and standards to help address these questions. The document cautions interviewers to recognize the effect of social differences on an interview and to keep their own conceptual grid in check: "Interviewers should work to achieve a balance between the objectives of the project and the perspectives of interviewees. They should be sensitive to the diversity of social and cultural experiences and to the implications of race, gender, class, ethnicity, age, religion, and sexual orientation. They should encourage interviewees to respond in their own style and language and to address issues that reflect their concerns." It recognizes the need to treat communities respectfully and to make one's work available to them: "Interviewers should be sensitive to the communities from which they have collected oral histories, taking care not to reinforce thoughtless stereotypes nor to bring undue notoriety to them. Interviewers should take every effort to make the interviews accessible to the communities." And it suggests that narrators are entitled to some return for participating in an oral history project: "Interviewers and oral history programs should conscientiously consider how they might share with interviewees and their communities the rewards and recognition that might result from their work."[38]

Yet these are only guidelines, general statements of principles that must always be worked out in actual practice with *this* interviewee, in *this* community. Nonetheless, it may be helpful to consider good interviewing practice as itself a form of ethical behavior. Taking time to get to know something about who a narrator is before doing the interview; listening carefully to figure out what the narrator is getting at during the interview and then asking the questions that will draw out the narrator; being less concerned with the number of interviews one amasses and more concerned about the quality of relationships that undergird them, whether for an afternoon or a decade—such behavior demonstrates a kind of respect that doesn't obliterate social inequalities but does mitigate them within the fairly bounded social space of an interview. Likewise, establishing a presence in a community before undertaking any interviewing, involving community consultants in the project design, paying attention to diverse social experiences and varying points of view within a single community, recognizing that trust builds over time as trustworthiness is demonstrated can all help establish a respectful relationship between oral historians and the communities in which they work, neutralizing some of the ill effects of a still-present inequality.

Once the interview is over, every interviewee should certainly be given a copy of the interview tape and transcript. Likewise, it is appropriate to place a community-based interview collection in a public repository accessible to community members. In addition, some who have earned royalties for works based on interviews share them with narrators or use a portion of them in ways that benefit narrators' families or communities; others believe their obligation is solely to present narrators' words without misrepresentation. Some oral historians share the fruits of their interviewing in a public forum, allowing narrators, their families, and neighbors the pleasure of hearing their stories, enlarging on them, perhaps correcting the historian's presentation of them, perhaps learning how their individual experiences fit into a broader picture. Others work with local institutions to develop public programs—exhibits, radio shows, increasingly Web sites—to present interviews to broader audiences. All are reasonable responses to questions of equity. Yet as Portelli has reminded oral historians, "returning" to communities what they already know or "giving voice"—as it is sometimes phrased—to people who have no trouble speaking, however well intentioned, can nonetheless be subtly patronizing. He suggests instead that the task is to use the very skills that accompany privilege to bring what one has learned about narrators and their communities into public discourse, to "amplify" narrators' voices so that their experiences and views extend outward to others who otherwise would not hear what they have to say.[39] Acting responsibly in the context of inequality thus has less to do with adherence to professional guidelines than with, on the one hand, poise in negotiating complex social exchanges across lines of difference and, on the other, an understanding of the role of knowledge in society. The issue then becomes how one uses knowledge gained from narrators to advance broadly social goals.

Nonetheless, inequality persists, despite our good intentions and best efforts. Ultimately, as Patai notes, "in an unethical world, we cannot do truly ethical research."[40] Yet some oral historians have begun to press against this "unethical world" in an effort to subvert existing inequalities in generating and interpreting knowledge. They are reimagining their own roles as researchers and scholars and self-consciously cultivating a collaborative relationship with narrators and their communities. Rose T. Diaz and Andrew B. Russell have termed this the "cooperative ideal" and lay out a framework by which oral historians, "functioning as advocates, mediators, and intermediaries," can "bridge existing gaps between academe, public history, and the 'real world.'"[41] Some have expanded upon Michael Frisch's influential notion of "a shared authority" in the interview exchange to work toward "sharing authority" with narrators throughout the entire oral history process.[42] Others, operating within a framework of community development and empowerment, have similarly attempted to adopt a radically democratic practice in doing community history. While much fine work has resulted, all have found that enacting any "ideal" is inevitably messy: tensions and conflicts arise; successes are tempered by breakdowns in communication and failures to complete work as planned; old patterns of professional authority and local deference emerge. In this unethical world, we can expect it to be no different and can only do the best we can.[43]

Overidentification with the Narrator

Many oral historians involved in the effort to democratize the historical record do so from a position of broad sympathy with those whom they interview. They recognize the injustice and indignities narrators and their communities have experienced and respect, often support, narrators' efforts to cope with and change the circumstances of their lives. Some also see their own work as part of a larger cultural project to maintain or restore these lives and struggles in popular memory, to cultivate public appreciation for them, and to present narrators in positive ways. These are worthy sentiments and indeed are frequently sharpened by the particular intimacy that can develop within the interview exchange. Yet they can also veer, with several troubling consequences, toward "liking narrators too much," to paraphrase Valerie Yow.[44] Profoundly painful memories are unwittingly dismissed with ameliorative words because the interviewer cannot bear the dreadful story the narrator is recounting. Cues to information that might shake the interviewer's positive view of a narrator are not heard or are ignored. Hard questions are not asked out of deference or to avoid an awkward conversation.

Coles, reflecting on his years of talking with both black and white families in the American South as he studied the effect of school desegregation on their children, describes with vivid honesty how this "liking too much" affected his own work:

> In the black homes, I went out of my way to give everyone the benefit of the doubt, to notice hospitality, generosity, warmth, liveliness, humility, spirituality—and there was plenty of all that to notice in certain homes. But in other black homes there was a cold distrust and irritability, and even a frank unfriendliness that I also went out of my way to understand, to explain to myself, but not to stress for others, for I was, meanwhile, expressing again and again my unstinting admiration for the obvious bravery of every one of the black children I had met. . . .
>
> I am not saying that I refused any mention of certain unattractive traits in certain families. Rather, I emphasized the attractive and appealing qualities in the families I liked best—to the extent that my descriptive writing, both in professional

journals and for the so-called lay public, drew heavily from my notes taken while working with the children of those families. . . . More and more I downplayed the troubles I encountered in favor of the resiliency I also encountered. . . .

On the white side of the tracks, however, I had considerably less trouble acknowledging the less attractive side of human nature as I spotted it in the families whose children were the first to attend school with black classmates. With those families, I could be relentlessly observant, especially when I heard nasty comments directed at black people. When I heard such comments directed by black people at black people, sometimes within a family, and sometimes with devastating meanness and seriousness, I could only turn my head away, or shake that head with a kind of sad resignation and understanding that I did not feel among my white informants.[45]

As Coles goes on to explain, his sympathies, in fact, had shaped the way he had defined his research problem in the first place, that is, as the way black and white children managed the stresses of school desegregation in the face of massive white racism. Defining the problem as such thus allowed a "'research methodology' that concentrated on certain kinds of 'evidence'" which not incidentally supported Coles's personal abhorrence of racism and concern for its victims.[46]

What a researcher values will always inflect his work; the alternative to "liking too much" is not a naïve neutrality or denial of the fact that an interviewer's posture invariably inflects the interview. Nonetheless, for historians and others engaged in documentary work, there is the ethical problem of, on the one hand, maintaining regard for the people one is interviewing and, on the other, adhering to the disciplinary imperative to tell the truth, not in some essentializing, positivist sense, but by trying to get the whole story, even if following the evidence where it leads undercuts one's sympathies; by probing hesitations, contradictions, and silences in a narrator's account; by getting underneath polite glosses; by asking the hard questions; and by resisting the tendency to create one-dimensional heroes out of the people interviewed, for romanticization is its own form of patronization.

Again, *Evaluation Guidelines* offers a helpful, albeit general ethical principle, stating that "oral history should be conducted in the spirit of critical inquiry" and that "oral historians have a responsibility to maintain the highest professional standards in the conduct of their work, . . . to uphold the standards of the various disciplines and professions with which they are affiliated, . . . [and to] strive to prompt informative dialogue through challenging and perceptive inquiry."[47] And again, the challenge is working this principle out in actual practice. Rapport, after all, can be a fragile thread, easily broken by a mistimed question or insensitive probe. As a way of managing the problems of overidentification with the narrator, Yow suggests a critical reflexivity when interviewing, monitoring one's own emotional reactions to the narrator, challenging one's interests and ideological biases, thinking beyond the questions one intends to ask to consider alternative lines of inquiry.[48] Also important is recognizing that, however highly one regards a narrator, interviewing is always done across lines of difference—otherwise, why interview? And this difference, acting as a counterweight to the very real engagement that can occur in an interview, serves to distance interviewer from narrator, thereby opening up a social space that allows the interviewer to assess and question. Just how much one does so in a given interview is, like much else in oral history, very much a judgment call, one that depends on the specific goals and circumstances of the interviewing project as well, perhaps, as on the temperaments of both interviewer and narrator. Finally, consciously defining the interview as a critical exchange when first discussing protocols with a potential narrator, alerting him or her to the seriousness of historical inquiry, may also pave the way for, in the words of the *Evaluation Guidelines*, "critical inquiry."[49]

Ethics and Oral History's Move to Interpretive Complexity

As oral history matured through the 1980s, its practitioners became increasingly aware that an interview is not a transparent document conveying "new facts" about the past that must simply be assessed as empirically true or false. Rather, an interview came to be understood as a narrative account, an artifact of memory, ideology, language, and the social interaction between interviewee and interviewer, to be interpreted as a text. Certainly the influence of cultural studies upon scholarship during the 1980s and 1990s partially accounts for this growing recognition of the inherent subjectivity of oral narratives. Of equal importance among oral historians was the theoretically inclined *International Journal of Oral History*, published from 1980 to 1990, which routinely included articles that reflected on the unique nature of oral evidence. Perhaps the single most important articulation of a textual approach to oral history is Portelli's often-cited essay, "The Death of Luigi Trastulli: Memory and the Event," in which he writes: "Errors, inventions, and myths [in oral narratives] lead us through and beyond facts to their meanings. . . . They allow us to recognize the interests of the tellers, and the dreams and desires beneath them."[50] The task of the oral historian and others who use interviews for scholarly and creative work thus becomes an interpretive one; the effect is work that moves further and further away from the narratives themselves toward an explication of their meaning. This in turn raises a number of formal concerns about the presentation of narratives that have broadly ethical implications; here I address two: the audience for work in oral history and questions about interpretive authority.

Audience

Oral history narratives can be presented in a variety of media—books, films and videos, radio broadcasts, exhibitions, dramatic presentations, and most recently, Web sites. Whatever the medium, the author or creator must decide how to structure the presentation of narratives within the context of the medium. A book, for example, can take the form of an oral (auto)biography, with minimal commentary by the interviewer/author; it can be a compilation of multiple narratives, organized either thematically or as a succession of individual stories, with editorial commentary to connect and contextualize them; it can integrate quotations from interviews, along with other sources, as part of a broader line of argument developed by the author. Similarly, a film can be structured solely around oral testimony, or it can combine testimony with varying proportions of contemporary accounts and scholarly "talking heads." The approach taken depends on the purpose of work itself; the point here is not to argue one as superior to another or to discuss the relative merits of different modes of presentation.

Whatever the medium, but especially in printed works, as oral historians pursue a more theoretically informed agenda, the interview text tends to be subsumed by its explication, and the work itself is less and less accessible to the kinds of people one has interviewed and about whom one is writing. While *Evaluation Guidelines* focuses on making interviews accessible to others, it also recommends that "all works created from [oral history materials] . . . be available and accessible to the community that participated in the project."[51] Indeed, there is something incongruous about adopting the forms of academic culture to present people's lives when one has learned about those lives through rather ordinary face-to-face interaction with individuals who might reasonably be expected to read what one has to say about them. This incongruity is rooted in a recognition of oral history's value for democratizing the audience for history, as much as the content and the "doing" of history. For while many dismiss formal or scholarly history as "boring," they are nonetheless engaged by personal stories of the past. At their best, works of oral history can be a means of negotiating this paradox, drawing in the reader (or listener or viewer) with a good story, creating sympathy and interest, and then using that to open the reader/listener/viewer to experiences very different from his own, or to help him understand the relationship between personal experience and social life, or to perceive an underlying coherence in a cacophony of voices—to think like a historian, in other words.

Questions of audience are at bottom ethical questions, for by asking for whom one is producing a work, one is ultimately asking why one does what one does. And like all ethical questions, they require judgments—in this case, how to reach the intended audience. The point is not to abandon theoretical explorations, for they enrich oral historians' work enormously; and even work that is ostensibly nontheoretical, that presents interviews without much commentary, nonetheless rests on a substratum of broadly theoretical ideas about the significance of the story being told and appropriate editorial intervention. In fact, some oral historians, ignoring or rejecting the claims of democratic access, choose to produce highly interpretive work for largely academic audiences. However, some choose not to interpret interviews explicitly at all nor to deeply contextualize them, in an effort at broad accessibility, letting the reader/viewer/listener appreciate the story and make of it what he or she will. Others, recognizing the claims of multiple audiences, present their work in different media or write in different voices for different audiences. And yet others, unwilling to segregate interviews from theoretical assessments, and perhaps recognizing that general readers can understand complex ideas if they are presented in clear language, attempt to integrate the two. This last is perhaps the most creative of oral history work, as it seeks new forms of presentation, alternating narrative and analytic chapters in a book, for example; or playing theoretical speculations off of concrete examples quoted from interviews; or moving seamlessly between author's voice and narrator's voice, interlacing one with the other. This work is also perhaps the most respectful of its audience, recognizing the reader/viewer/listener's desire for stories as well as for understanding the meaning of these stories.[52]

Interpretive Authority

As oral history has become more theoretically informed, those who conduct and use interviews have also come to understand more fully how these narratives are social documents, reflecting not only a narrator's individual creativity but also his particular historical position and his relationship with the interviewer, who also participates in the interview from a particular social position. As a result, those who draw upon interviews in a creative work are less likely to let narrators simply have their say; they too claim a voice as interpreter of the interview text. This claim also raises a set of formal questions with broadly ethical implications: Whose voice dominates in such work, the narrator's or the work's putative "creator"? Where does the balance of interpretive authority lie?

While these questions are likely to remain in the background when narrator and creator share the same perspective on the topic at hand, they emerge with particular sharpness when there is a conflict of voices. What does an author do, for example, when he disagrees with a narrator on a given point? Or when his understanding of a matter is fundamentally different from that of the narrator's? Or when he finds out that a narrator is simply wrong, willfully or not? Karen Fields confronted these issues repeatedly as she worked with her grandmother, Mamie Garvin Fields (1888–1987), to produce her oral memoir, *Lemon Swamp and Other Places*, which describes the elder Fields's life as an educated, middle-class black woman in Charleston, South Carolina, through most of the twentieth century. In some places in her story, Mamie Fields wanted to include local details that Karen Fields felt would be meaningless, indeed "tedious," to readers beyond Charleston. At times, Mamie Fields, for whom "matters of race and color are a permanent presence without being [the] principal subject" of her life, criticized Karen Fields for her "angry" preoccupation with them. Like most authors confronting these problems, Karen Fields attempted compromise, but not without battles with her grandmother and not without a residual unease.[53] Sandy Polishuk, writing an oral biography of labor activist Julia Ruutilla based upon interviews she had conducted with her some years earlier, discovered that Ruutilla had falsified certain details of her background, including her racial identity; had obscured other elements of her life; and had overstated her role in various political events. Because Ruutilla had died in the intervening years, Polishuk was unable to ask her to explain discrepancies between her account and the written record, so she appropriately pointed them out to readers, attempted to explain them, and ultimately let most of them remain in the finished work, stating, "Julia must be allowed to speak for herself, but at the same time I had to tell what I knew and believed."[54]

Questions about interpretive authority—or who gets to say what—are especially challenging in community projects and in public history when multiple stakeholders lay claim to a given work: the subjects of the work wish to present a positive view of themselves, the producers wish to adhere to professional standards and maintain a certain intellectual dispassion, the audience wants a good story. Barbara Franco describes the play of these voices in the development of an exhibit about the Winnebago Indian community at the Minnesota Historical Society, a process that echoed the dynamics of many community-based oral history projects: "The exhibit team's curators wanted to examine the history of the Winnebago in Minnesota as a case study that focused on their recent history as an urban Indian community without a reservation land base in the state. The Winnebago [advisory] board, however, was more interested in connecting the current Winnebago community to traditional Winnebago life and in educating outsiders about the early history of the Winnebago and their long connection to Minnesota. . . . Most contemporary issues of urban living were off limits." As the planning process continued, curators muted their voices out of respect for their Winnebago collaborators and in the interests of a continuing relationship with them. "The exhibit that resulted," Franco continued, "was not as interesting to visitors as it might have been. It was very traditional in its approach and didn't connect visitors to the more dynamic contemporary issues in Winnebago culture such as conflicts between urbanization and traditional religion." At issue, she concludes, were "two sets of ethics operating in this exhibit development process—people ethics and historian ethics," or one might reframe it, the ethics of narration and the ethics of interpretation.[55]

For those seeking to present interviews in ways that respect both their own and the narrator's authority, it is perhaps useful to consider negotiating a midcourse between what Frisch has termed the "anti history" approach to oral history, that is, the "view [of] oral historical evidence, because of its immediacy and emotional resonance, as something almost beyond interpretation or accountability, as a direct window on the feelings and, in some senses, on the meaning of past experience," and what Frisch called the "more history" approach, that is, "reducing oral history to simply another kind of evidence to be pushed through the historian's controlling mill."[56] Just *how* to strike a proper balance, of course, remains the challenge. *Evaluation Guidelines* articulates the most fundamental principle for anyone drawing upon interviews in a scholarly or creative work: "Users have a responsibility to retain the integrity of the interviewee's voice, neither misrepresenting the interviewee's words nor taking them out of context."[57] Beyond that, however, *Evaluation Guidelines* remains silent. Nonetheless, just as questions of audience are leading oral historians to seek new forms of presentation, so too is the issue of interpretive authority, resulting in work that explicitly plays with the tension of different, often competing voices. Katherine Borland suggests that we extend "the conversation we initiate while collecting oral narratives to the later stage of interpretation," opening up the possibility of a multilayered account, in which interpretive conflict between interviewee and interviewer, "subject" and author, is presented directly, without an authoritative resolution.[58] In her biography of activist Anne Braden, Catherine Fosl rendered Braden's words in italics, "to retain her voice as clearly distinct from mine, . . . [in order to] allow me a free hand at interpretation without creating a power differential in which [Braden] felt suppressed, particularly at points when our perspectives on her life diverged."[59] Alicia Rouverol, recognizing that interviewees can provide more than a "direct window" on feelings, asked explicitly analytic questions in her interviews with Maine poultry worker Linda Lord. She writes also about restraining her own urges to maintain analytic control over the interview in her published work; of "surrendering to the text" as Lord's words "fought back" against her own interpretive biases about unions and deindustrialization; and of her own efforts to resist imposing a false coherence on Lord's apparently contradictory views on many matters.[60] In these and other ways, oral historians are seeking to represent the dialogue—the open-ended back and forthing—that lies at the heart of the oral history enterprise and to recognize that work resulting from this dialogue is a cocreation of interviewer and narrator.

Conclusion

Legal and ethical considerations permeate the practice of oral history, from initial contact with a potential narrator to final disposition and use of an interview. They are so central because oral history is fundamentally grounded in a relationship between two people, and like all relationships, it is framed by rules, norms, and standards of behavior. It is also a relationship that extends outward to include others—individuals and communities discussed in an interview, users of the interview, the audience for work based on oral history—and they too are included in the web of relationships governed by oral history's legal and ethical standards.

While the legal framework for oral history is rather straightforward—the law permits this, disallows that—ethical concerns, which can sometimes arise in a legal context, are more subjective, requiring, as I have emphasized throughout, judgment on the part of project managers and interviewers. Both, however, as I have also attempted to emphasize, are social constructs, arising in relation to the particular historical circumstances within which oral history has been practiced. They are, accordingly, not fixed, but require the continuing attention of both the field and its individual practitioners. This essay is not, therefore, the last word.

Notes

1. Gluck, "First Generation," 1–9, suggests a similar chronological development.
2. Oral History Association, *Evaluation Guidelines*. In 1967, Dixon and Colman, "Objectives and Standards," became the first record of discussion of professional guidelines in oral history. In 1975, Fry, "Reflections on Ethics," raised the ethical conundrums in the original guidelines. Oral History Association, "Evaluation Guidelines: Wingspread Conference," reported on the development of the evaluation guidelines in 1979. Ethical guidelines from other national oral history organizations include, from the United Kingdom, Alan Ward, "Copyright and Oral History: Is Your Oral History Legal and Ethical?" (Colchester: Oral History Society, 2003), http://www.oralhistory.org.uk/ethics/ (accessed January 26, 2005); National Oral History Association of New Zealand, "Code of Ethical and Technical Practice" (Wellington: National Oral History Association of New Zealand, 2001), http://www.oralhistory.org.nz/Code.htm (accessed January 26, 2005); and Oral History Association of Australia, "OHAA Guidelines of Ethical Practice" (Sydney: Oral History Association of Australia, n.d.), http://cwpp.slq.qld.gov.au/ohaa/Guidelines%20of%20ethical%20practice.htm (accessed January 26, 2005).
3. Portelli, "Tryin' to Gather," 55–56.
4. Starr, "Oral History," describes the origins of the Columbia Oral History Research Office.
5. See Eustis, "Get It in Writing"; Hamilton, "Law of Libel"; Romney, "Legal Considerations"; and Welch, "Lawyer."

6. Oral History Association, *Evaluation Guidelines*, 6, states: "With the permission of interviewees, interviewers should arrange to deposit their interviews in an archival repository that is capable of both preserving the interviews and eventually making them available for general use." The American Historical Association's guideline for interviewing for historical documentation is almost word for word the same as OHA's: "Interviewers should arrange to deposit their interviews in an archival repository that is capable of both preserving the interviews and making them available for general research." American Historical Association, "Statement on Interviewing for Historical Documentation," *Standards of Professional Conduct* (Washington, DC: American Historical Association, 2003), http://www.historians.org/pubs/Free/ProfessionalStandards.htm (accessed January 26, 2005).

7. Neuenschwander, *Oral History and the Law*, 18.

8. Ibid., 19.

9. Ibid., 23.

10. Of course, the question arises: What if the interviewee does not agree to close the statement in question? Elizabeth Millwood described the response of the Southern Oral History Program when this situation arose. The program decided to "bury" the offending interview in its collection by not including it in any finding aids, on the assumption that when someone finally did discover the interview, the offended party would be dead. Millwood herself does not recommend this approach, and in fact, it would seem that a repository, assuming it had legal title to the interview, could act in its own self-interest and close the offending material without the narrator's consent. Millwood, "Oral History Offices."

11. Neuenschwander, *Oral History and the Law*, 18, 23.

12. Brecher, review of *Brothers*, 196.

13. Blee, "Evidence, Empathy, and Ethics," 604.

14. Brecher, review of *Brothers*, 196.

15. Lanzmann, *Shoah: Complete Text*. See also Lanzmann, *Shoah*, DVD.

16. Brecher, review of *Brothers*, 196; Blee, "Evidence, Empathy, and Ethics," 604.

17. Neuenschwander, *Oral History and the Law*, 5.

18. Typically, a narrator assigns rights to both the tape and the intended transcript of it, that is, signs the release form, at the conclusion of the actual interview, before the transcript has been created. Reviewing the transcript or significantly emending it, the narrator could subsequently decide he wishes to change the terms of access to the tape, the transcript, or both, in which case a new release form would need to be negotiated. Assigning rights to the transcript before it is actually produced is somewhat questionable, yet it is standard practice because there is often a considerable time lag between the conduct of the interview and the production of its transcript, during which the narrator may have died or otherwise become unavailable. The narrator may also be disinclined to assign rights to an interview long past or simply be negligent in returning the form. Rights to the tape and to the transcript may be uncoupled, but that would create administrative complexities that are largely unnecessary, insofar as the vast majority of narrators neither question the terms

of their release upon reviewing the transcript nor significantly alter the transcript itself. Project administrators seem to agree that the best practice is to handle specific concerns on a case-by-case basis.

19. U.S. Copyright Office, "Copyright Law of the United States" (Washington, DC: U.S. Copyright Office, 2002), http://www.copyright.gov/title17/ (accessed January 31, 2005).

20. U.S. Copyright Office, Compendium II, Copyright Office Practices, Sec. 317, quoted in Neuenschwander, *Oral History and the Law*, 31.

21. Neuenschwander, *Oral History and the Law*, 32.

22. It should also be noted that colleges and universities are increasingly claiming rights to the intellectual property produced by faculty and staff working within the institution. Scholars working in an academic setting, conducting interviews for their own research, should thus clarify their campus policies regarding ownership of their intellectual work, including interviews.

23. Hall, "Confidentially Speaking," raises many of these and additional questions about confidentiality and suggests—without resolving—several ethically challenging situations.

24. Oral History Association, *Evaluation Guidelines*, 4.

25. Council of the American Anthropological Association, "Relations with Those Studied," *Statements on Ethics: Principles of Professional Responsibility* (Arlington, VA: American Anthropological Association, 1971), http://www.aaanet.org/stmts/ethstmnt.htm (accessed January 26, 2005).

26. American Sociological Association, *Code of Ethics and Policies and Procedures of the ASA Committee on Professional Ethics* (Washington, DC: American Sociological Association, 1999), 10, http://www.asanet.org/members/coe.pdf (accessed January 26, 2005). On reporting a crime, see Neuenschwander, *Oral History and the Law*, 55–57.

27. Oral History Association, *Evaluation Guidelines*, 5; Neuenschwander, *Oral History and the Law*, 43.

28. The decision of the U.S. Supreme Court in *New York Times v. Tasini*, in 2001, has raised particular concerns about transferring copyrighted material from one medium to another without prior permission from the author. The Court ruled that freelance writers who did not explicitly agree to electronic distribution of their work previously published in the *Times* could claim that their copyright agreement was violated, that electronic publication, in other words, constituted a different form of publication. Neuenschwander, *Oral History and the Law*, 43, states that "this decision would seem to strongly support the right of an interviewee to cry foul if and when a program or archive places his or her interview on the Internet without clear or reasonably implied authorization to do so." For further discussion of the copyright issues of Web publication, see Neuenschwander, *Oral History and the Law*, 44–45.

29. For further discussion of the ethics of oral history on the Web, see Mary Ann Larson, "Guarding against Cyberpirates," *Oral History Association Newsletter* 33, no. 3 (Fall 1999): 4–5, and Larson, "Potential, Potential, Potential."

30. Department of Health and Human Services, Office of Human Research Protections, Code of Federal Regulations, Title 45 Public Welfare, Part 46

Protection of Human Subjects, Subpart A, Basic HHS Policy for Protection of Human Research Subjects, http://www.hhs.gov/ohrp/humansubjects/guidance/45cfr46.htm (accessed December 12, 2005). Paragraph 46.102 (f)(1) defines a "human subject" as a "living individual about whom an investigator . . . conducting research obtains data through intervention or *interaction* [emphasis added] with the individual." Interaction is further defined as "includ[ing] communication or interpersonal contact between investigator and subject."

31. Ibid., Paragraph 46.101 (b)(2)(ii).

32. American Association of University Professors, "Protecting Human Beings," offers a thorough discussion of the difficulties of applying regulations developed within a biomedical frame to nonbiomedical research. See also Church, Shopes, and Blanchard, "Common Rule?"; Van den Hoonaard, *Walking the Tightrope*; and Nelson, "Can E. T. Phone Home?"

33. The full text of the policy statement is available from the American Historical Association, Press Releases, http://www.historians.org/PRESS/IRBLetter.pdf (accessed December 12, 2005).

34. Further explication of the policy is available from American Historical Association, Questions Regarding the Policy Statement, http://www.historians.org/PRESS/2003-11-10IRB.htm (accessed December 12, 2005); and American Historical Association, Linda Shopes, Historians and Institutional Review Boards: A Brief Bibliography, http://www.historians.org/PRESS/2003-11-10-IRB-Bib.htm (accessed December 12, 2005).

35. OHRP's reaffirmation of its original policy statement is available from Oral History Association, Linda Shopes and Donald Ritchie, An Update on the Exclusion of Oral History from IRB Review, http://www.dickinson.edu/oha/org_irbupdate.html (accessed December 12, 2005). For a summary of the current state of affairs regarding IRB review of oral history, see Robert Townsend and Meriam Belli, Oral History and IRBs: Caution Urged as Rule Interpretations Vary Widely, *AHA Perspectives Online*, 42, no. 9 (December 2004), http://www.historians.org/perspectives/issues/2004/0412/0412new4.cfm (accessed December 12, 2005). In November 2005, the American Historical Association contacted OHRP, outlining conflicting statements from that office, critiquing its misapprehension of the methods of oral history, and seeking—again—a generalized exclusion of oral history from IRB review; as of this writing, no response had been received. Meanwhile, the AHA's Research Division has developed a guide to the issues for historians: American Historical Association, *Oral History and Institutional Review Boards*. A generalized critique of the ever expansive embrace of IRBs is also developing; see, for example, Hamburger, "New Censorship"; and Center for Advanced Study, University of Illinois, The Illinois White Paper: Improving the System for Protecting Human Subjects: Counteracting IRB "Mission Creep" (November 2005), available at http://www.law.uiuc.edu/conferences/whitepaper/whitepaper.pdf (accessed December 12, 2005). This latter document argues that "most journalism and oral history cannot be appropriately reviewed under the Common Rule" (page 22).

36. *Frontiers* 2, no. 2 (1977); 7, no. 1 (1983); 19, no. 2 (1998); and 19, no. 3 (1998); Gluck and Patai, *Women's Words*. On the issues of power in anthropology, see Clifford and Marcus, *Writing Culture*, and more recently, Jaarsma, *Handle with Care*.

37. Coles, *Doing Documentary Work*, 85.

38. Oral History Association, *Evaluation Guidelines*, 5, 6.

39. Portelli, "Tryin' to Gather," 67–71.

40. Patai, "U.S. Academics," 150.

41. Diaz and Russell, "Oral Historians," 214.

42. Frisch, *Shared Authority*, xxii.

43. Patai, "U.S. Academics," 150; Diaz and Russell, "Oral Historians," 214; Frisch, *Shared Authority*, xx–xxii. For discussions of collaborative oral history work, see Kerr, "What the Problem Is"; Rickard, "Collaborating with Sex Workers"; Rouverol, "Collaborative Oral History"; Sitzia, "Shared Authority"; Shopes, "Commentary"; Frisch, "Commentary, Sharing Authority." For an especially frank discussion of the challenges of community documentation projects, see Hinsdale, Lewis, and Waller, *Comes from the People*.

44. Yow, "Do I Like Them."

45. Coles, *Doing Documentary Work*, 57–58.

46. Ibid., 57–59.

47. Oral History Association, *Evaluation Guidelines*, 4–6.

48. Yow, "Do I Like Them," 79.

49. Oral History Association, *Evaluation Guidelines*, 4.

50. Portelli, "Death of Luigi Trastulli," 2. I am indebted to Ronald J. Grele for formulating the distinction between oral history as document and oral history as text.

51. Oral History Association, *Evaluation Guidelines*, 10.

52. See, for example, Hall et al., *Like a Family*; Nasstrom, *Everybody's Grandmother*; Portelli, *Order Has Been Carried Out*; and Rogers, *Righteous Lives*.

53. Fields, with Fields, *Lemon Swamp*; Fields, "Cannot Remember Mistakenly," 93, 98–99.

54. Polishuk, *Sticking to the Union*, 13.

55. Franco, "Doing History in Public," 8. See also Franco, "Raising the Issues."

56. Frisch, *Shared Authority*, 160.

57. Oral History Association, *Evaluation Guidelines*, 6.

58. Borland, "Not What I Said," 73.

59. Fosl, "When Subjects Talk Back," 7.

60. Chatterley, Rouverol, and Cole, "*I Was Content*," 124.

5

Oral History Interviews: From Inception to Closure

Charles T. Morrissey

When oral historians assembled at Lake Arrowhead in California in 1966 for their first national meeting, my presentation—outdoors on a gorgeous September morning—was an informal talk about oral history interviewing skills. Since 1962, as oral historian for the Harry S. Truman Library and John F. Kennedy Library Oral History Project, I had been evolving some interviewing "do's and don'ts." In my talk that day, I remarked in an offhand way, "Let me say that very little has been written about techniques of oral history."[1] That gentle comment understated the meagerness of bibliography about the interviewer's role in oral history relationships with memoirists.

Allan Nevins, founder and director of Columbia University's Oral History Research Office (OHRO), showed little interest in question-making processes. As a professor, author, and administrator, his primary quest was to address neglected topics in American history.[2] For us today, it is incredible that the Columbia OHRO did not include an interviewer's questions in preparing the transcripts of its early interviews. Questions were discarded as unimportant.[3]

Moreover, oral history in the U.S. grew from antecedents in the archival profession. As a novice in oral history, from 1962 to 1966, I was instructed by an excellent archivist, James R. Fuchs of the Truman Library, and both of us were employees of the National Archives and Records Service, forerunner of today's National Archives and Records Administration. Now I am astounded to encounter myself giving this tight scope to oral history while speaking to an audience of professional historians in 1964: "Since oral history is usually defined as an effort to fill gaps in written records, it is necessary for an oral historian to know where the gaps are."[4] True, but such constricted vision! Such an obsession with paper! Clearly, I was an anal oral historian. Dare I further admit that I went to Lake Arrowhead advocating that oral historians not organize a separate Oral History Association but instead align with the Society of American Archivists?

The "gaps" have grown, but Ronald J. Grele has ably summarized the broadening of the scope of oral history from the 1966 Lake Arrowhead colloquium to the present: "Originating in many areas as a way to fill in the gaps in the written record, either as archival practice or because that written record simply ignored so much of the daily life of so many people, oral history has outgrown its roots in the search for data and has become an activity seeking to understand all forms of subjectivity: memory, ideology, myth, discourse systems, speech acts, silences, perceptions, and consciousness in all its multiple meanings."[5]

My thinking about oral history, almost forty years after James V. Mink of the University of California at Los Angeles brought us together at Lake Arrowhead, continues to evolve. As you read this personalized assortment of "do's and don'ts," please ponder shrewd advice from William Warner Moss, one of my successors as head of the Kennedy Library Oral History Project. Moss points out, wisely, "Just as no two interviewees are alike, so no two interviewers are alike, and success depends to a great extent on the capability and interest of the people involved rather than a structured application of designed questions."[6] Question-asking in oral history interviews is an art, individualized, and even intuitive. The oral history bibliography still lacks a volume titled "The Historian as Interviewer," but here is one person's approach, grounded in practical experience, to asking informants to share their memories.

I

First, ask questions of yourself before asking questions of the memoirists you hope to interview. By answering your own questions thoughtfully before your interviews are scheduled, you raise the likelihood that your questions in actual interviews will stimulate informative answers.

Before each interview, I think carefully about how each prospective interviewee in an oral history project should be invited to participate. Should the initiative come from me? Or is it wiser for the chief officer of the institution whose history I am documenting by recording oral history interviews to extend the invitation? The latter has the imprimatur of authority.

Usually, you are seeking collaboration from strangers you hope will agree to cocreate a historical document consisting of their answers to your questions. Building rapport with these persons is crucial because oral history is a mutual endeavor.[7] Moreover, it is a voluntary activity. Prospective memoirists are free to demur from being interviewed. The invitation is not a subpoena to testify by court order in a legal dispute. They may lament that time has eroded their memories of names, dates, and details of events. They may view a historian's queries as irrelevant in today's workaday world with its frenetic pace of decision making. Oral historians in the United States must bear in mind that they function in a media-dominated culture that is present minded and future oriented, where historical amnesia is a national flaw. They may recall unpleasantly the boring history courses they endured as students and the mind-numbing textbooks they had to memorize. Colloquially, they may echo Carl Sandburg's disdainful "The past is a bucket of ashes" ("Prairie," *Cornhuskers*, 1918) or Henry Wadsworth Longfellow's "Let the dead Past bury its dead!" ("A Psalm of Life," *Knickerbocker Magazine*, 1838). They may even view you, the oral historian, as the next-to-last person they will encounter in their lifetimes, the final one being the mortician who will come to fetch the corpse. To you they may insist they never did anything of historical importance, and you will have to convince them, tactfully, that indeed they did.

Oral historians are exactly that—historians—and they interview about the past. Specialists from other disciplines function as historians when doing oral history. Accordingly, most oral sources are older rather than younger occupants of the demographic life charts. It is best to contact these sources initially by mail, with the invitation coming directly from the person most appropriate to issue it. Letterheads and job titles signify the official auspices of the sponsoring institution. But think carefully about stationery that lists trustees or other supporters in a vertical column along the left-hand or right-hand margins. If these names represent a cohort of like-minded advocates uniformly positioned on the political spectrum, they will not engender cooperation with your project from their political opponents. Their endorsement will also raise concerns about your professional objectivity; you may be dismissed contemptuously as merely a court historian, a hired gun, not an open-minded inquirer. If your sponsors are all rich white men who live in one section of town, their names will not induce cooperation from laboring African American women who live in a different part of town.

Ideally, this initial mailing should ask and answer six basic questions; below you will read how every oral history interview is configured by asking the same six basic questions. Limiting your letter to two pages at most, explain *who* (you) will do *what* (record an oral history interview), *where* and *when* (a place and time convenient for the recipient), and *how* (by recording the exchange of questions and answers, transcribing the conversation, allowing the respondent to edit the transcript, depositing the finalized transcript in a suitable archive, and devising a legal agreement governing ownership, access, and dissemination). All of this is difficult to communicate and may raise apprehensions among people who are skittish about having their voices recorded if they fear they will expose to posterity their truncated educations or halting use of English as a second language (or even as a first language, despite an elite education at Andover, Yale, and the Harvard Business School). Or they may be fearful of any interaction entailing legal commitments in a litigious society overpopulated with lawyers. (In more ways than one are lawyers the enemies of historians; see below.) And you still need to answer the most important and most difficult of the six basic questions: the *why* question. The recipient of this letter will ask, Why does this oral history project want to interview me? Your answer: because the prospective respondent has memories of historical significance worth preserving.

Each letter concludes by explaining that the oral historian—you—will telephone a few days after the prospective memoirist has received this mailing to explore any concerns about the "basic six" and discuss the *when* and *where* questions so scheduling can be arranged. In this phone conversation, I review the procedures outlined succinctly in the letter, often emphasizing that this collaboration will not be a media interview for tonight's newscast or tomorrow's newspaper; instead it will be a history interview for archival deposit. Journalists rank near lawyers as hazards if prospects view oral historians as similar practitioners; many have woeful tales of journalists distorting what they were told.[8] I routinely refer to the respondent's opportunity for editorial review so that the ultimate transcript will convey the memoirist's intended narrative. But I assure all that minimal editing is preferred to retain the oral character of our session together, and I may pointedly assure academics they won't be expected to revise their transcripts into the stilted formal language of professional publications in their specialties. As graduate students, many scholars were taught never to use the first-person singular in professional papers, but in oral history narratives the first-person singular is unavoidable. I repeat assurances about devising a legal agreement as a safeguard against abuse of the interview's content, but do so gently to avoid rousing the specter of legal complications. If a memoirist is willing to exchange candor for confidentiality by agreeing to give an interview with the proviso it be legally closed for a stipulated length of time, I concede to this preference. Ideally, in the world of oral history it is best that as much as possible of oral history reminiscences be opened to public access as soon as possible, but the arguments for temporary restrictions have compelling logic, too. It is better to obtain oral history memoirs and have to wait to use them than never to procure those memories at all.

In this phone conversation, I ask the respondent if he/she can recommend any materials I should consult in order to prepare myself as interviewer. As examples, I mention scrapbooks, diaries, letters, annual reports, yearbooks, class reunion books, press coverage, even photo albums. Every active physician in academic medicine has an up-to-date curriculum vitae, and grant applications to funding agencies are informative depictions of their past achievements and clear aspirations when their grant proposals were submitted. I tell them a truism about oral history: the more the interviewer—you—knows *before* an interview, the more you will learn *in* the interview. Preparation is essential. When prospective interviewees suggest sources I should consult as preparation, I assiduously do homework in these materials.

Before asking interviewees about sources I should consult, I have tried to learn all I can in other independent sources. In libraries, I read all I can find about my interviewees—written by them, about them, and about their locales, work, lifestyles, and the like. Usually, I forge working relationships with archivists who can provide me with institutional records—minutes of trustees' meetings, official correspondence, in-house newspapers or employee bulletins, files of press releases, accreditation reports, and so forth. Oral history can be defined as recorded interviews that preserve historically significant memories for future use, but an oral historian can be defined as a person who uses all kinds of materials, in addition to recording spoken memories, to document and explain the past. Bear in mind the sage advice of Leopold von Ranke, the nineteenth-century German historian at the University of Berlin, who proclaimed that the best historical sources are those created contemporaneously with events.[9] Closer is better. Memory can be distant and is continually reconfigured over time, causing some memories to fade into disappearance, others to balloon into exaggeration, and still others to get constantly revised. Oral historians cannot deny the fragility of memory and must acknowledge it is supple and pliant. Nor can oral historians deny that von Ranke got it right. Oral history is best done in conjunction with traditional archival research. My former students have heard me preach this gospel, and one of them, John A. Kayser of the Graduate School of Social Work at the University of Denver, is fond of quoting my stricture: "Paper trail first, memory trail second."[10]

Rewards for doing prior research are numerous.[11] Consider these:

- Following the paper trail first helps you to determine who was where when and thus should be interviewed about specific topics. Some people have dropped out of historical consciousness but can be retrieved by studying the paper trail and then interviewed on the memory trail. Others have mythic reputations for accomplishments falsely attributed to them, and you can deduce that early.[12] Although Americans deny that they live in a class-segmented society, and anonymous people who were decisive role players are obscured in popular memory by prominent people claiming more credit than justifiably warranted, you can identify those who are historically knowledgeable and select them as interviewees, deflating the bloviators.
- Research on the paper trail can identify those gaps that your interviewees can fill by speaking their memories. Decisions made by long-distance telephone negotiations may leave no paper trails beyond monthly bills for numbers called on specific dates and lengths of conversations. E-mail messages can be erased. Jet aircraft speed conference participants to a central meeting place, and after returning them swiftly home leave no paper trail remnants except for airline ticket receipts. Lawyers advise businessmen not to make records of meetings that federal regulators could subpoena in search of antitrust or other violations. In academe, tenure review committees are cautioned not to keep minutes of their deliberations; disgruntled candidates refused promotions can get access to them if litigation ensues. Presidential selection committees are told to camouflage candidates with code names and confer orally among themselves; minutes and memoranda may get leaked to the curious media. Forthright letters in which professors are asked to evaluate their students are no longer written. Diaries get destroyed, journals get junked, files get filched. While researching the paper trail, you can deduce what is absent from the array before you ask about the missing links.

If this litany of transgressions—the defilement of files—is disturbing to you, bear in mind that photocopying machines often restoreth to knowledge what other forms of electronic communication and aircraft taketh away. Perusing more than one paper trail can provide you with data missing from the first one you examined.

- Researching archival collections for questions to ask prospective interviewees is much quicker and simpler than researching paper-trail sources to answer historical questions. Issues in American history through the nineteenth century must be answered solely by archival research; no Civil War soldiers still survive as veterans to interview. But researching for questions to ask, as distinct from answers to give, can move rapidly. Applying the basic six, the paper trail often divulges who (the poet you will interview), did what (won a Pulitzer Prize), when (year of award, reported in newspapers), how (by writing praised verses), where (in a cabin in the woods), but not why (the motivation that spurred her creativity). Your research can isolate the *why* question, important to ask in your interview. You may learn that creativity sprang from angst in the personal life of the poet in unresolved mother–daughter tensions and other psychological issues, revealed through psychotherapy. How to ask about such intimate probings? Read on!

- If you wonder if your respondents will lie to you or slyly try to mislead you, the answer is "no" as soon as they realize you have thoroughly done your homework. They wouldn't dare distort the factuality of a situation lest they get caught as deceivers. Occasionally, a respondent mumbles, "You probably know more about this than I do." Smile; you're being complimented for your preparation. But don't gloat. Rapport does not thrive on one-upmanship.

- Thorough preparation will impress your interviewee that you are seriously committed to good interviewing and will encourage full, detailed answers to your questions, not short, casual responses that barely scratch the surface of the memoirist's deeper knowledge.

- At the outset of every oral history project, the questions you are asked about it are entirely quantitative: How many people are you going to interview? How many tapes or pages of transcript will you obtain? (Be wary of these queries; tapes vary in length and pages can be single-spaced or double-spaced.) How long will your project continue? How much will it cost? When the project is completed, however, the questions shift from quantitative to qualitative: Just how good is all that stuff you taped? Ask the qualitative question at the outset, because it will be the ultimate criterion by which your project will be measured for its value. Preparation germinates quality.
- Preparation can help you to decide what sequence is best for scheduling your interviews. I plot my prospective memoirists onto an oval diagram, much like the round target Vermont hunters might emplace on a tree when shooting their guns during rifle practice before deer season begins. Into the bull's eye go the handful of names of most important memoirists. In concentric circles go the other names, with importance declining within each band farther from the center. On the outer rim go the names of the least important prospects. Sequentially, I start interviewing people named on the outer rim, moving in a circular route toward the prime occupants of the bull's eye. My theory is that you want to be best prepared—at the top of your game—when you aim for the bull's eye, and interviewing others on outer peripheries will heighten your marksmanship. You want to do your best with your best. Moreover, if the denizens of your bull's eye are busy people who might give you one session but not two, you need to do your best within the single opportunity afforded to you. Planning interviews sequentially also allows you to link your preparation with the experiences of your prospects. You can proceed colleague by colleague, thereby isolating reluctant interviewees by pointing out, diplomatically, that they are the last holdouts and that others may question their stubborn resistance.
- During your preparation, you can identify and photocopy particular documents you can carry to the interview and

share with respondents. This can prompt memories evoked by looking at photographs or reading texts. This can clarify items with muddled meanings. Be sure to key your "props" so that the words spoken on tape are directly linked to the items being discussed.[13]

Before each interview, I sit quietly and cogitate on questions such as these:

- How can I make this interview useful for others? For instance, what questions could I ask this person to help a genealogist, a local historian of the town where this person came of age, an architectural historian interested in the spaces this person has inhabited, a historian of this person's religious sect, a public historian wanting to incorporate spoken recollections into the audio interpretation of museum artifacts, or someone such as Jeff Friedman, interested in artistic outcomes?
- I visualize a college campus and ask myself what a political scientist, a sociologist, a folklorist, or students of public administration or educational practices and policies would ask in an interview like this one. Academe divides the world of learning into discreet compartments called departments, but real life in the real world is not arranged like a university. Oral history is multidisciplinary; this is one of its glories. Oral historians have to think outside the boxes.
- I mull on what divides me from my interviewee in terms of numerous social factors: age, gender, race, class, ethnicity, education, regional dialects, political outlook. The list goes on and on: I am a New Englander in Texas, a humanist among physicians, a flatlander (born out of state) among woodchucks (native-born Vermonters), a technophobe interviewing computer nerds in biomedical informatics. I try to identify each difference between me and my interviewee and formulate verbal strategies for surmounting those differences. The good news is that differences often contribute to dispassionate clinical relationships that make interviews flourish. A stranger interacting

with a stranger can produce candid answers to probing questions.[14] Clinical relationships are professional encounters. With forethought, I try to capitalize on differences to clasp clinical relationships.[15]

- I also mull on what unites me with my interviewee in ways that may help cultivate rapport, but likewise may pose problems in terms of professional competition, or shared family myths, or professional courtesies, or reluctance to speak critically of our common alma mater or other "home institutions." The bad news is that similarities often contribute to emotionally laden relationships that make interviews awkward. An intimate interacting with another intimate—members of the same family, say—can produce squeamish answers to resented questions. Intimate relationships are not clinical and not professional. Grandchildren hoping to interview grandparents may think insider status is an advantage, and surely they may be right, especially when it comes to gaining access, but being an insider poses its own set of problems.[16] This oral historian prefers clinical relationships.
- Reviewing my interviewee's life, probable knowledge, and hopefully retentive memory, I ask myself beforehand: What can he/she speak from experience that could possibly be most helpful for enlarging understanding, providing explanations, resolving perplexities, and in other ways contributing to my project?
- What might be the most surprising disclosures I might hear from my interviewee?
- What sensitivities should I anticipate? This is not easy to foresee because some people will surprise you by being skittish about questions you assume innocently are free of tension and by not being uncomfortable when asked questions you figure will touch raw nerves. Sensitivities are subjective; they vary from person to person.
- If the time allotted for my interview is unexpectedly shortened, what are the most important questions I need to ask? My scheduled forty-five minutes with U.S. Senator Jacob Javitz, longtime Republican from New York, evaporated to fifteen minutes as he talked on his office phone,

his back turned to me seated across his desk. Concluding his conversation and placing the phone on its cradle, he whirled in his chair to face me and tersely said, narrowing his eyes, "You have fifteen minutes." Revising my agenda, I asked the most important questions, realizing that the delay had stolen most of those I had prepared.

- I don't memorize questions before an interview, but I do choose carefully the wording for questions that may be viewed as sensitive or difficult to answer. The most sensitive questions in America today are not about sex but about money. Instead of querying a politician about how he/she funded a campaign by bluntly asking, "Where did you get the money?"—which might prompt a defiant "None of your business!"—I use milder words for money, such as *wherewithal* or *support*. I anticipate which questions may need to be objectified or framed in a two-sentence format (see below).

- This sounds elementary, but be sure to know mundane logistics about getting to your interviewees: route directions, ample driving time, parking perplexities. You don't want to interrupt an interview to feed a parking meter and find your pockets don't contain enough coins. If you need to cool your heels before an interview, you can productively use these moments to review your notes one final time. Be prepared for hassles; the security officers at the Hughes Aircraft Company in southern California would not let me pass the reception desk carrying a tape recorder, even though my interviewee was in charge of security for the company and earlier had handled security for Howard Hughes.

- Dress? I adhere to what I foresee to be prevailing practices in the place I will enter: no neckties for union carpenters in Vermont. Once, however, dressed like an executive when I went to interview DuPont's retired chief executive officer, Irving Shapiro, in Wilmington, Delaware, I was surprised to find him sporting golf clothes. "I've got a golf game after we get done," he explained. For the second interview session the next morning I arrived at his office dressed casually, but he was attired in a blue business suit.

"I've got an important business lunch when we get done," he explained.

- With respect to equipment, I put in my briefcase more cassette tapes than I expect to need, each one capable of recording sixty minutes (thirty minutes on two tracks, or sides). I carry an extension cord. My microphone and power cords are already inserted into the recorder. Likewise, on a cassette already inserted into the recorder, I first dub identifying information: the interviewee's name, the date and place of the upcoming interview, the project's title, and my name. That cassette is ready to record as soon as the recorder is activated at the place of the interview. I carry batteries if I'm uncertain about plug-in power, which I strongly prefer. Batteries run down.[17]

Now I'm ready to head toward the interview site, my rendezvous with destiny, feeling prepared, but knowing each interview is different from every other interview. The British diplomatic historian H. A. L. Fisher was right when he said that a historian "should recognize in the development of human destinies the play of the contingent and the unforeseen."[18] Oral historians know that each oral history interview also entails of "the play of the contingent and the unforeseen."

II

Before you interview, think long and hard about logistical situations. To augment rapport, I readily agree to interview people where they are most comfortable. This means I go to their homes, which in turn means, if I have not been there before, I must find the route and get there early. It also means I am entering an unfamiliar place with unanticipated recording hazards. Train your eyes to look for power outlets you can use for plugs. Avoid kitchens—ice-making refrigerators can be surprisingly noisy, and even shake floors. Avoid woodstoves—logs crackle. In your mind's eye, try to visualize how you can shift furniture quickly and easily to put two chairs near an outlet, with a table for positioning your tape recorder. Try to place the microphone on a separate surface and on a plastic holder or a soft cushion such as a pocket-size package of facial tissues. Be prudent; if you, as a stranger who is invited inside a domicile as a guest, try to rearrange the furniture brashly and abruptly, your rapport may plummet.

I glance at the dining room and often suggest we sit across the corner of the table, using a third chair for placing the tape recorder where I can see it easily, but my respondent cannot. For interviewees, this follows the time-worn adage "Out of sight, out of mind." Respondents are less likely to be nervous about a tape recorder in the room if they can't see it. But never tape surreptitiously. That is unethical. You can signal casually with your fingers as you calmly say, "I'll turn this on now, if you're ready."

In office environments, I ask beforehand if there is a conference room we can use, with telephones rendered mute so incoming calls won't tinkle. Beware of heating pipes that can bang noisily in winter and air conditioning ducts that drone in the summer. Tape recorders do not distinguish between human voices and other sounds; they record what is dominant. If your respondent agrees to come to your home turf for the interview, you have a great advantage that eases your stress. In the huge Texas Medical Center in Houston, I identified several conference rooms with excellent acoustic qualities, and thanks to helpful office managers, I have reserved these for interviewing, set up my tape recorder and microphone beforehand, walked to the office of my interviewee and walked him or her back to the interview site. (Even old-timers can be confused by veering hospital corridors heading toward *terra incognita*.) I sit my companion in the designated chair for the interviewee and seat myself in the chair designated for me, with notepad and pen already at hand. Still, in the best of circumstances noise will intrude. Doctors practice near hospitals, to which emergency vehicles rush the ill and injured, sirens screaming. Neighbors mow their lawns, and evangelists seeking souls to save—yours and mine—do come knocking at the door, causing interruptions. Trash collectors in trucks that repeatedly blare beep-beep warnings will know that you are inside, trying to record an interview. This is not paranoia; flight controllers at nearby airports will alter landing and takeoff patterns so noisy airplanes will bedevil you. Once, while

I was recording an interview in Monument, Colorado, two Siamese cats discovered I had invaded their living room. One climbed the draperies, demonstrating it could outdo monkeys in the zoo. The other saw my plug-in cord flex slightly and leaped at it, hoping to swing from it, exhibiting agility worthy of stardom with a traveling circus, but instead this nimble but naughty feline caused—pardon the pun—catastrophe.

You will have a logistical problem if you set out to interview one person but find two, or more, are ready to greet you when you arrive. In general, I advocate one-on-one, that is, one interviewer and one respondent, alone together in a quiet room, as best. Group interviewing has undeniable advantages: economically, you accomplish more by interviewing several people at one sitting, and one person's recollections can spark otherwise forgotten memories in another person's mind. But a hierarchy of deference may quickly emerge, with the person with senior status (due to age, wealth, authority, or accomplishments) dominating the discussion, and others reluctant to diverge from the consensus being established. Males may dominate, or a single blowhard may declaim, and the timid may be mum.[19] Respondents lined up like panelists on a talk show may start conversations among themselves while one is answering a question, creating a cacophonic array of voices layered like a thick deli sandwich for the transcriber to spend tedious and protracted time trying to decipher. Economy doesn't serve to fulfill the qualitative aims for your project, and with careful preparation, an interviewer can stimulate the memory prompts that might have occurred in a group interview. Mature historical judgments recognize the nuances of analysis, and group interviews don't cultivate nuances. Before an interview, you may have to stipulate that one-on-one is the practice of your project and do so diplomatically to avoid jeopardizing rapport. Nonetheless, you may find one mate hovering to protect the other. In San Leandro, California, I found the second husband kibitzing on how his spouse and her first husband raised their children during the "hard times" of the Depression of the 1930s and the war years that followed, even though he was not part of that domestic scene. I was asking her to document the household dynamics before he later entered her life as her second husband. His comments lacked historicity, but I could not get him out of the room. (By speaking during the interview, he became part of it, and accordingly a party to the legal agreement.)

You and other oral historians may decide you will together interview a single respondent. Two on one is acceptable if you both have specialized knowledge you can bring to interviewing persons with the same types of knowledge. But before the interview, you and your partner need to agree on three matters: who will solely be in charge of the recording machine, who will pursue which lines of questioning, and that neither will interrupt the other. In the interview itself, you should sit so the respondent can see you sitting together, chair by chair. Don't put the respondent between you, forcing him or her to turn left and right, trying to involve you both as conversationalists and fearing maybe one is being neglected due to unintended discourtesy.

III

Across the doorstep, into my interviewee's home, I do not unclasp my briefcase. Instead, I try to make cordial conversation with my host/hostess, showing that an oral historian can be an affable Irish American, disarming any trepidation about the reason I am there: to conduct the upcoming interview. My immediate task is to solidify rapport. Gently, I try to locate ourselves physically where the interview can be conducted. I review again the procedures of the oral history project, mentioning safeguards. When the person starts to reminisce about a topic relevant to my mission, I say perkily, "This is exactly what I am hoping you will share with me today, and to spare you the trouble of repeating yourself let me turn on this tape recorder." Swiftly into the outlet goes the power cord, in front of the memoirist goes the microphone, onto a separate surface (but visible to me) goes the recorder. With spools spinning, I say, "You were just saying about—," identifying the topic, and the respondent joins on cue by saying, "Yes—," and the recorded interview is underway.

When I explain this procedure to students during oral history workshops, they often express surprise. You don't start at the beginning? they ask. No, I don't start with, What is your name? What is your birth date? I don't want interviewees to sense this is a legal deposition or a visit by a census taker or inquisitive, government-employed gumshoe investigating fraud. Nor do I dictate that preliminary information on the tape in their presence. Nor do I want them to stiffen uncomfortably when the technology brought across their doorstep is made to function. I am not a dentist with a drill making house calls. I want to swing into the interview as smoothly as possible. Starting by recording a story the respondent has offered to tell means we're starting in an upbeat, voluntary way. Rapport is the keystone of every oral history interview you will ever conduct.[20]

Now that you have surmounted that huge hurdle of getting the actual interview underway:

- Ask one question at a time. If you bunch several questions together, your respondent will choose one in preference to the others, and the others—all worth asking—may get neglected.
- Make your questions open ended, inviting your interviewee to speak his/her story in self-chosen words, constituting an autobiographical narrative. Don't ask respondents to verify your preconceptions; your version may be wrong. Don't pose either/or alternatives, forcing your respondent to fit remembered life experiences to your imposed framework. Instead of asking, "Why did you locate your business in Springfield instead of Pittsfield?" ask "How did you decide where to locate your business?" There may have been alternatives beyond the two you juxtaposed from your pre-interview research.[21]
- Express your questions in lay language. Professional jargon does not cross the doorstep. Make your questions so crystal clear there can be no doubt about understanding them. Some answers I've read in transcripts, I fear, are actually responses of puzzlement about the essence of the question.
- Speak up and speak slowly in the presence of elderly folks. Ears age more rapidly than other body parts. When you have asked a question, you can remind yourself to

shut your mouth and bite your tongue. Learn to live with silences that seem like eternities; actually they are surprisingly short.[22] Wordless vacuums are awkward in social conversations, but in oral history interviews they provide interviewees with unfettered moments to organize their thoughts, possibly about topics they haven't contemplated for decades. Pauses induce quality responses. If you feel impelled to fill a verbal vacuum by attaching an example to the question you just asked, your respondent may address your example, not your question. Don't complicate questions. Emulate Henry David Thoreau, the hermit of Walden Pond: "Simplify! Simplify!" ("Where I Lived and What I Lived For," *Walden, Or a Life in the Woods,* 1854.)

- Listen carefully to what you hear. Don't tune out. Time after time, your next question will most likely emerge from what your respondent is saying. Remember your question to be sure your memoirist is dealing with it. Remember your question also in case your companion asks you to repeat it. If you bungle this reasonable request, you are admitting you are not paying minimal attention to the interview you are conducting. Your rapport will sink.

- Don't argue, for the same reason: you don't want to lose your rapport. Ask for elaborations, clarifications, explanations. Be a student in the presence of a teacher, not a lawyer cross-examining a witness for the opposition.

- Go with the flow. If your interviewee makes abrupt transitions, from chronology to topics to players, from past to present and back to disjointed segments of the past, follow the course as set for you. Dr. Sigmund Freud alerted us more than a century ago to the idea that free association reveals a person's patterns of thought and emotion even if a verbalized stream of consciousness seems random.[23] Make notes about points you want to return to. Transcripts of my interviews often show I am passive during the first one quarter or one third of an interview, gradually becoming more active, concluding aggressively in the last quarter. If good rapport is persistently maintained, this shift can occur seamlessly.

Proceeding on the assumption that some topics are likely to be sensitive and might threaten the rapport carefully cultivated, I deliberately defer these difficult questions until the interview is well beyond its onset. Moreover, I try not to ask about sensitive matters in immediate or close succession. Instead, I try to intersperse them among queries I assume the respondent will enjoy addressing. However, if a respondent voluntarily alludes to an issue deemed sensitive by my previous reckoning, I use that allusion to pursue the subject he/she has helpfully introduced into our dialogue. William Emerson Brock III, as an example, was elected in 1970 in Tennessee to the U.S. Senate as a Republican, a remarkable political achievement in an era when Tennessee was still predominantly a Democratic state in its voting behavior. But as the incumbent senator running for a second term in 1976, he lost his seat to James Sasser, his Democratic opponent. Pre-interview research in an obvious and widely available resource, *The New York Times Index*, alerted me that in October 1976, shortly before election day, Sasser was criticizing Brock for raising campaign funds illegally. Thus I had two sensitivities regarding Brock's senatorial career: the money issue and the fact that he lost his bid to stay in the Senate. No politician is happy talking about defeats. Indeed, some even delete lost campaigns from their self-authored entries in *Who's Who in America*, thus demonstrating how paper trails can contain deliberate omissions. All politicians enjoy talking about victories. My interview with William E. Brock started with his 1970 success, and his cool blue eyes sparkled with evident pleasure as he told the story. Casually, he mentioned he faced some charges of fiscal malfeasance in that campaign similar to accusations he had confronted six years later. His allusion allowed me, in my next question, to pursue the 1976 allegations. Using the same simple words he had just spoken, I framed my question this way: "You say you faced some charges in 1970 that you faced again in 1976." With an affirmative head nod he agreed. "With respect to the 1976 campaign, how did you deal with those charges?"

Notice how this question to Brock consists of two sentences. The first is a confirmation that he had just said something of historical interest. The second, based on the first, pursues the historical significance of what he has said.

Regularly, I deploy this two-sentence format whenever I sense an interviewee needs to hear why I think a forthcoming question requires a justification as part of our interview.[24] The first sentence establishes the relevance of a line of upcoming questions, attempts to defuse the topic emotionally, or suggests why it merits our attention. The second sentence is the question, rationalized by its predecessor, and always ends with a question mark. In effect, the first sentence says, I need to ask you this, and the second sentence says, Here is what I need to ask you.

Sometimes I rationalize questions I need to ask by citing major figures in the scholarly professions, past and present. Frederick Jackson Turner, the famous progenitor of the Frontier Thesis about the development of America's democratic ethos, emphatically urged his students at the University of Wisconsin, and later at Harvard University, when they were doing research in primary sources to ask an epistemological question about the creator of the documents they were analyzing: What was "the opportunity of a witness to know?"[25] I borrow Turner's advice and apply it when respondents make statements, and I wonder how they know what they claim to know. This is especially worrisome when from prior research I know they were not in the room when a particular decision was made by others. Evidentially, how much historicity lies in their assertions? How much weight can a future researcher give to their testimony? The first sentence of my two-sentence format would be: "The famous historian of the American frontier, Frederick Jackson Turner, urged his students, when they studied the papers of a historically significant figure, to ask, What was his opportunity to know this?" The second sentence, always a question, would be, "What was *your* opportunity to know this?" The answer would clarify for you the historicity of his claim to knowledge. Consider the possibilities (but don't verbalize them): he could hear voices through a transom; a secretary in the room taking stenographic notes told him about the decision-making process a few minutes after the meeting ended; he heard gossip about it two days later in the faculty lounge; he read about it in the newspaper (possibly reported by a journalist also not in the room). If I blurted out, "How do you know this?" my respondent might interpret my bluntly worded probe as imprudently suggesting I doubted his/her veracity. Implying your interviewee is a liar or deceiver doesn't enhance rapport.

In similar fashion, I sometimes escort an invisible colleague to my interviews and involve him in the question-asking process. His name is Harvey, so named after the six-foot invisible rabbit also named Harvey in the 1944 play and the 1950 movie titled *Harvey*. Jimmy Stewart was the star actor in the Hollywood version—not that I fantasize myself as the Jimmy Stewart of the oral history profession. Harvey is a future historian, and I mobilize him as an ally. "Imagine if a future historian sat here in this room with us now, participating in this interview," I say to a reluctant interviewee (phrasing my question in the two-sentence format). "This future historian would likely speak up now and say he needs to ask the obvious question: How did you deal with that issue?" Or, varying the language while tangling with the same problem: "A future historian would be grateful to you for hearing how this difficulty was confronted." Or: "A future historian reading the transcript of this interview would at this point expect me to ask you—." Or: "A future historian would rank me as remiss for not now giving you the opportunity to answer this important question." Then I pop the tough one. Harvey smiles—invisibly, of course.[26]

A longtime chemist at Procter and Gamble (P&G) in Cincinnati, Ohio, remarked casually in his interview that when he was a young employee in the 1920s it was company policy not to hire Roman Catholics on the management side of that large producer of household products. Inwardly, I bristled at this comment—my Irish was stirred—but outwardly I tried to sustain an unflinching professional composure. I did not interrupt him; I did not quarrel with this revelation (to me) of bigotry. But when the time quickly arrived for my next question, I said: "A future historian would fault me for not asking you to elaborate about the company employment policies you just mentioned were practiced in the 1920s." Sentence two: "Why were Catholics not hired on the management side of the company?" He had raised this topic; I tried to validate its pursuit by appealing to the needs of the future. This strategy worked. I sat quietly, not volunteering possible explanations I could conjure in my imagination, such as the Ku Klux Klan threatened a consumers' boycott if P&G hired

Catholics. His answer? The company's blue-collar workforce was heavily unionized. Many workers were Roman Catholics of German ancestry, since Cincinnati was ethnically a heavily German city. Corporate leaders feared Catholics on the management side would be spies for the union's leaders. After hearing this explanation, Harvey figuratively reached over and patted my shoulder, murmuring in my ear, "It's a good thing you didn't accuse him of being in cahoots with the Ku Klux Klan. He would have tossed both of us out of this room."

While every oral history interview asks six basic questions, the most important of the six is the *why* question. Here you are asking for motivation, inspiration, aspiration, objectives, ideals, maybe visceral stimuli that might not be known unless you ask respondents to articulate them. Likewise, paper trail records may answer five of the basic six and neglect the why explanation. Consider an example similar to the one you read above, about our Pulitzer Prize–winning poet. In this instance, four of the basic six are known, the fifth is partly known, and the sixth is totally unknown. Or in a different instance: who (a board of trustees), did what (authorized a new policy), when and where (the date and place specified in the minutes of the meeting), how (by approving a resolution), why (reasons unstated). The minutes may simply read: "It was moved, seconded, and voted to—." By interviewing a trustee who attended the meeting, you can ask if there is more information that answers the *why* question. Did the passing vote follow intensive premeeting negotiations that were off the record and involved trade-offs, such as, "I'll vote for your resolution if you vote for mine"? From this trustee, you can get answers from a witness for the unaddressed *why* question in the minutes. Always assume people are motivated by more than one reason, so ask for reasons. Also assume that many decisions are close calls and that people cogitated gravely over what course to follow. As discussed below, "the art of contrary interviewing" may impel you to reverse the *why* question and ask *why not*, revealing why a different course of action did not ensue.

Be mindful that the *why* question can threaten rapport because it presumes people are dispassionate about rational decisions. Some people may squirm uncomfortably if unable to rationalize intuitive compulsions. Some may fear you are a psychiatrist in the guise of an oral historian. Some may feel you are trespassing across an invisible line separating a person's public life from personal life, and you may find it wise to preface your *why* question with an explanation of why you're asking it. Remember our Pulitzer Prize–winning poet whose verses were rooted in mother–daughter tensions and other psychological hang-ups? When interviewing her, you need to justify your *why* question about the emotional seedbed from which her verses flowered. Feminist scholars emphasize that the personal is political in the lives of women, but this generalization applies to males as well as females, although males may be reluctant to concede this point is valid.

Generalizations are the curse of oral history memoirs, and specifics are often the nuggets that make them glitter. Asking the basic six questions may spawn generalized answers, throwing the burden on you to ask follow-up questions. This burden is obligatory. Welcome it; follow-up questions can transform a mediocre interview about generalities into a superior interview that is meaty. Go from generalities to specifics, asking for as many particulars as you can possibly glean. Invite each respondent to give an example of each point he/she makes. After listening to the example to be sure it is drawn from your respondent's experiences, ask for a second example. Hearing two, ask for three. This is called postholing. Your mantra is alliterative: Dig for details, probe for particulars, scour for specifics.[27] Liberate yourself from the orthodoxy of America's mass media, where reportage surveys huge subjects in brief overviews and miniscule sound bytes are candy capsules for the public mind. Delving for details helps us to deal with a reality of all historical subjects: they are more complex than they initially appear.

Just as *why* questions may trouble some respondents, so your probe for particulars may strike them as irksome because they cannot recall the details you request. If respondents say with visible frustration, "I can't remember the date of that meeting," you can say, "Don't worry; just tell me what happened at that meeting." Or you hear, "I can't remember the address of that house on Spruce Street in Berkeley where my landlady was

Mrs. Rinne from Finland." I say, "Don't let that bother you; I can look it up in an old city directory or phone directory." If the search for particulars is difficult for respondents (undeniably, the aging process does thin the chemical synapses in human minds), I simply ask, "What is foremost in your memory when you were a graduate student renting a room in Mrs. Rinne's house on Spruce Street?"

Oral history interviews are superb opportunities for documenting matters of historical significance that are not documented elsewhere. Whenever you sense your respondent is knowledgeable about something for which you suspect little or no independent paper trails or other sources exist, ask eagerly about these holes your interviewee can fill. Childhood is one such area in every lifespan; for many families, the only surviving documents are photographs, the snapshots having already been weeded by fond parents to show their little darlings as bright and charming progeny. Courtship is another, if the amorous couple lived within easy distance of each other and did not write letters, as soldiers and sweethearts did during World War II. Unlawful activities are secretive to avoid the creation of incriminating evidence, and if your informant has childhood memories of the bootlegging of illegal liquor in the Prohibition Era of 1920–1933, you can obtain those verbalized recollections to fill that void. Whenever a respondent refers to the unwritten rules of a workplace, I am immediately alerted that I confront an inviting opportunity to hear documentation of guidelines not formalized in any paper trail record. How gay culture operated in the era before gays could publicly affirm their sexual orientations can be documented through spoken memories. Whenever people tell me how they beat the system—by hiding Holocaust survivors, or circumventing government rationing during World War II or the military draft during the Vietnam War, or smashing the glass ceiling restraining talented women—I ask how they beat the system.

When paper trails presumably do exist but for privacy reasons are not available to you, lack of access can be at least partly skirted by asking informants to speak about the unattainable data. For example, unless you are an official federal investigator, librarians cannot ethically or legally disclose to you which patrons borrowed which books. So if you are not a government gumshoe but are doing an individual's oral biography, you can ask your interviewee what books he or she found useful at libraries.

Just as oral history interviews can document the otherwise undocumented, so these interviews are opportunities to ask about and obtain documents that can be filed with the tapes of your interview or appended to the transcript. Even when people tell me during my pre-interview preparation phase that they were not diary keepers, I will ask, after they have recounted an interesting episode, if they made a record of that occasion. A letter the Peace Corps volunteer wrote home? A report to superiors, or a memo for the file? Did the campus newspaper publish a report of that campus unrest? Did someone with a camera snap photographs? Conducting oral history interviews and acquiring manuscript materials are tandem activities.

Furthermore, in oral history interviews you can ask informants to evaluate the scope and reliability of independent sources bearing on your respondent's recollections. Did the student newspaper accurately reflect student opinion? Did the letters home omit unsavory details? Did the office files mask realities instead of exposing them? Did institutional culture discourage any negative comments in written communications? Oral history interviews allow the interplay of memory and other materials as you and others confront a basic research question about all documents of all kinds: How can you believe your sources are credible?

Like *credibility*, another important word in my oral history lexicon is *evocations*. I invite respondents to evoke past occasions and personalities that had great personal meaning for them. Questions as examples: "Would you evoke for me what it was like for you when you first learned the Supreme Court had outlawed segregated schools in *Brown v. Board of Education*?" "—when you heard John F. Kennedy had been shot in Dallas?" "—when you heard the doctor say your child had polio?" Or, if a person has just explained how a particular teacher was a tremendously important life-shaping model, I will ask, "Please evoke for me how this teacher was for you a powerful presence?" (Don't add "in the classroom" but leave your question open-ended in case the influence was exerted outside the classroom.) Evocations can provide insightful descriptions of the personal chemistry between individuals or the drama of tense situations or the humor of ludicrous situations. Ask about the cultural texture of times and places. Evocations are word pictures arising from invitations to provide the type of material that novelists skillfully compose about their fictional figures, but oral historians don't fictionalize. In oral history, we can hear genuine tales of real people in real situations. Paper trail accounts of emotive occurrences are often dry-as-dust documents, but oral histories can convey affective meanings. Encourage these evocations of the span of human feelings, from horror to elation.

Some interviewees are so present minded that their answers convey their current thinking about your history-centered questions, not their verbalized memories of what you asked about. Grele warns oral historians to consider "how the now informs the discussion of the then."[28] Try to persuade your respondents to depict themselves in the context of the times you are asking about. Here again I mobilize the two-sentence format as my technique. Suppose you are interviewing a person, such as Senator John F. Kerry, who was a critic of America's war in Vietnam, 1965–1975. To establish the relevance of my questions, I start with today's first draft of history, the daily newspaper, and move to yesterday's concern, which is the historical issue I want spoken memories to document. The first sentence is: "There is much discussion today about America's military presence abroad." The second sentence is: "Going back to the 1960s, at that time how did you view the escalation of America's presence in Vietnam?" History textbooks narrate the American story from past to present, but oral historians reverse this sequence and justify questions by going from the present to the past.

Outcome determines recollection: this is another problem confronting historians who solicit spoken memories and reckon their validity. Electoral campaigns are remembered through victories or defeats; a marriage that ends in divorce is not warmly remembered in images of the gaiety of the wedding reception but is remembered as tribulations that led to divorce court. You can encourage respondents to avoid filtering their memories through outcomes by using the two-sentence format to position them in the context existing before outcomes were known. When people recount their lives as a series of sequences that in retrospect seem natural, even inevitable, I might ask, "Go back to your senior year in high school." Sentence two: "At that time, how did you view your future choices?" This invites them to slow down a narrative that leaps from high school to a particular college to a particular graduate school with a particular career in mind. Life as lived is a constant process of making choices among alternatives; life as remembered in oral history interviews allows respondents to explain choice-making in their lives, thus enriching the texture of how they traveled from past to present. Paper trails tend to document choices that were made. Oral history can retrieve choices that were pondered.

Oral historians also practice "the art of contrary interviewing." While listening carefully to what respondents say, they also listen for what is unsaid, and later ask about the omissions. If, when reminiscing about childhood on a family farm, a respondent gives only warm weather examples of rural life, I'll subsequently ask about the farm in winter. If memories of influential figures in adolescence center on the father, I'll ask about the mother. If memories of schooling are classroom scenes, I'll ask about the playground, getting to school, and after-school activities. When I ask about childhood in a particular town and hear about stores, schools, and churches, I'll ask about unmentioned institutions, such as the library, the movie theater, and disreputable places such as pool halls or the hobo jungle near the railroad tracks. If accounts feature rich people who lived in spacious houses on the hill, I'll ask about poor people who lived below in rookeries in the flats. If the town is portrayed as the abode of white people, I'll ask about the town's African American population, and how in the age of virulent Jim Crow segregation race was managed in the social system.

While oral historians are listening, they also are visualizing how life was lived by the person giving a first-person account of it. The ability to imagine how others have lived is a valuable resource for oral historians. The spoken memories we hear spark visual images on the movie screen I argue exist in everybody's mind. (Admittedly, my biomedical colleagues at Baylor College of Medicine in Houston disputed this neurological claim about brain components.) Onto this movie screen, we project images that translate into our own lived experiences what others are saying, and herein lies a danger. Hearing a respondent tell about elementary school experiences causes me to visualize him/her walking inside the red brick walls of the Pierce Grammar School on Chestnut Street in West Newton, Massachusetts, where I started kindergarten in 1938 and continued through sixth grade. When my informant talks about an influential sixth-grade teacher, I see *my* sixth-grade teacher, Miss Ruth O'Donnell, encouraging my aspirations to be a writer and lamenting my doltish ineptness with arithmetic. The lesson for oral historians is clear: don't suppose you understand another person's story without hearing it spoken. Ask, don't assume. One of the worst blunders we can make is to blurt out a sudden, "I know exactly what you mean!" Restraint, careful listening, and interrogation may produce a narrative different from your own but nonetheless authentic in terms of representing genuinely the life as lived by the person reminiscing about it.

When an informant tells a story that clearly holds strong emotional content—you can tell by tone of voice, facial grimness, and similar body language—but I don't hear explanations of why this episode is vividly recalled, I often ask the *meanings* question. Specifically: "What meanings has that experience carried for you since it happened?" Or if a person laughs lightly now about an experience that could have been painful when it happened, I'll ask, "Has the meaning of that episode varied over time during your life?" Whenever I'm uncertain about the meanings people apply to the memories they recount, I ask them to express the meanings themselves. I don't want to guess about them afterward or force users of my transcripts to conjecture about them.

If you sense your informant is rambling, be tolerant of the ramble. You may be discrediting a monologue as irrelevant to the purposes of your interview, only to learn your interviewee is taking a circuitous discursive approach to the essence of your question. Relevance and rambling are subjective judgments on our parts, and we may be wrong about their pertinence to memories of historical significance. One person's dismissal of a commentary as blather unhitched to the focus of the interview may be another person's arrow to the heart of a researcher's topic. For linguists, the research value of oral history memoirs is how words are pronounced and linked, not exclusively how they convey meaning. Oral historians in Idaho recorded an interview they subsequently lamented had no likely usefulness for any researcher who might visit their library. But an architectural historian was delighted to learn, from reading the transcript, how the interviewee described her childhood home as an adobe structure on the Idaho High Desert, the farthest north this particular style had migrated from the American Southwest. The researcher was ecstatic on discovering the location of this migratory specimen of the architectural style she was studying.

An interviewee may respond to one of your keen questions by saying something such as: "That is an interesting question. Would you please turn off your tape recorder?" When this happens, try earnestly *not* to turn off your tape recorder. Once it is off, you may have difficulty getting it back on. Hearing a respondent off tape poses a problem: if you define the interview as what you both say on tape, what do you do with this unrecorded information? If you and the interviewee discuss the relevance or sensitivity of the answer to your question and agree it belongs on the tape, the second telling, after the tape recorder is activated, will always be a shortened paraphrase of the off-tape version you just heard. Try to keep the tape recorder functioning by saying, "I'll save you time; if you decide it doesn't belong on tape, you won't have to repeat it." Or: "You'll be getting a transcript of this interview to edit, and maybe that is the suitable time for deciding if it should be part of the interview." Or: "We find in oral history interviewing that people tend to abbreviate their stories when they repeat them." But you may lose these valiant battles to get the bothersome story initially on tape, and to maintain rapport you may resort to the diplomatic alternative: reluctantly, you turn off your recording machine.

During an interview, your partner may casually ask you what you think about challenges and choices in his/her life that you hear in the narrative being recorded. Beware of suddenly but subtly being asked to answer questions instead of asking them. Once the roles are reversed and you are being queried by the person you came to interview, it may be difficult to get the relationship back on its bearings. Try gently but firmly to avoid the pitfalls of becoming a respondent instead of an interrogator by saying, "It is better that I hear you express your knowledge of these topics than we hear my ignorance of them," or, "You were there; I was not." "You're my teacher; I'm your student," or, "Let's defer my opinions of these matters to our postinterview conversation rather than clutter the interview with them now."

Some people want me to concur with their judgments in controversial issues. "It was okay," says a Caucasian Californian, expectantly, "to relocate those Japanese American spies soon after the Pearl Harbor bombing, right?" I avoid swallowing the bait and getting hooked on their line. Rapport is threatened if I blurt out my own personal belief: "Wrong; internment of Japanese Americans was totally unwarranted for security reasons and unjust for constitutional reasons." Diplomatic alternatives? "I was a youngster eight years old and three thousand miles east of the Pacific Coast when internment happened; you were here and saw it happen." To this, in a second sentence, I add a question, or I add a tactic that worked perfectly for me in an interview recorded high in the Berkeley hills: "I've never understood why Japanese Americans were interned but Italian Americans were not, and in World War II we were fighting Italy as well as Japan." That unleashed a panegyric about Italian Americans in the San Francisco region, ranging fondly from Joe DiMaggio's upbringing in the North Beach neighborhood to iconic Napa Valley wine makers. Oral history interviewing is one of the very few activities in life in which you can mobilize your ignorance as an asset.

Be prepared also for a respondent to ask, either innocently or deviously, what another participant in your project has said about the controversies being recounted. All oral history memoirs are considered confidential until signed legal agreements make them open. They continue to be confidential if legal agreements stipulate closure of all or segments of transcripts. To refuse to answer your respondent's inquiry, "What did Harry say about this when you interviewed him?" may fracture your rapport. You can respond by saying, "In oral history we treat all materials being processed as confidential until legal agreements make them open." You might add that your role is akin to a doctor's professional ethic requiring protection of patients' records. If my respondent looks skeptical, I might add, "I can't tell you what Harry said because I won't tell Harry what you're saying now." Most nod their heads affirmatively when hearing this assurance.

When your interviewee voices an interpretation about a past event that you (silently) sense does not fit the consensus of opinion about what actually happened, ask your informant to mention other people who were present as participants or witnesses. If you need to obtain further testimonies about this particular occasion, you will now know whom to approach.

Oral historians are listening and watching intently during interviews, but their tape recorders are only listening.[29] Humans have eyes and ears; tape recorders have only ears. I watch the nonverbal behavior of my interviewees attentively. Visually, I can detect clues to how they feel about my questions, varying from joyful welcome to derisive disdain to vexing discomfort. These clues help me decide the choice and wording of upcoming questions. Also, if memoirists communicate by nonverbal references, I can either make notes for the transcript or put into words what was conveyed but unsaid. "In spring that stream was about as wide as that lawn," says the interviewee, pointing through a glass window to her yard. "About fifty feet wide?" ask I. "Yes," says she, and thus the future knows what she signaled but did not speak.

Videotapes record more than audiotapes hear, of course, but before lugging lights and cameras across an interviewee's doorstep, think long and hard about technology as a menace to rapport between individuals. With some people, the simple act of turning on a tape recorder can be a thorny transition. From experience, I have learned to separate videotaping as a second step after audiotaping as a first step. The initial goal is to get the entire interview recorded on audiotape. Later, the second goal is to pose the informant where selected portions of the transcribed audiotape are best repeated for telling to a video camera.

Listeners to your tapes—your transcriber, especially—will be grateful to you if you keep your own voice hushed except to ask questions. Even though spontaneous vocal rejoinders such as "uh-huh" and "hmmmm" show you are listening attentively and buttress rapport, these so-called phatic sounds on tapes interfere with the much more important words your narrator is speaking. I try to clamp my mouth shut (not an easy task) and respond to what I hear with facial and other visual signs of comprehension. Interviews are not occasions to hear myself talk beyond asking questions. But even this self-imposed gag rule can have ironic consequences. Proud of myself for being a tight-lipped listener during an interview with a Baylor-trained physician, I didn't realize he was attentive to my nonverbal responses. After the interview concluded, he remarked, "You know, you dilate your eyes a lot."

One exception to this self-imposed gag rule does routinely occur when one side or track of a cassette is about to expire or a cassette is nearly full and needs to be replaced by a fresh one. When flipping a tape, I speak in order to prevent the memoirist from talking while the machine is not recording. I don't want to lose that unrecorded segment. With practice, you can flip a cassette or switch cassettes in about two seconds of deft handling while uttering words as trite as, "I'm certainly enjoying this interview and appreciate your contribution to our project." If your fingers fumble clumsily, you can add, "You're kind to share your memories, and others will appreciate your kindness, too." When starting with a fresh side or track or new cassette, you can repeat an abbreviated summation of your narrator's words just before the transition caused an interruption: "You were just saying—." These words also cover the blank tape at the outset of each reel. By the time your narrator affirms your brief reiteration, the transition is a smooth linkage. Then lean away from your recorder and even pivot toward your narrator, signaling that all is well with the third pair of ears in the interviewing room and the conversation can genially continue without attention to the electronic equipment.

IV

Every interview can be ended by asking two questions.

First, "Are there any questions I've failed to ask you which you would like to raise?" Respondents almost always reply with a hearty no, sometimes telling you they're surprised you had so many questions to ask. Sometimes you will be complimented for your preparation and knowledge of the interview subject. Hearing this, you now know how dead people feel when St. Peter invites them to step forward and enter heaven's pearly gates.

Second, "Are there any topics you would like to return to and say more about?" Maybe half of all respondents will pause, ponder, and say yes, elaborating on a point made earlier, or clarifying it, or emphasizing it.

Then I say, "Thank you." I want these words on tape because they deserve to be part of the official record. Back to basics: oral history doesn't happen if memory-rich respondents don't voluntarily allow us to make it happen.

Then I turn off the tape recorder. But I do not pull the cord from the outlet, nor do I move the microphone. Together we sit, and I usually mention something about the interview that is positive about its usefulness. For example, "What you said about college girls providing farm labor during World War II will be helpful to historians because there is nothing in the historical society's archives about that topic, except male farmers complaining about farmhands being drafted at harvest time." Or: "Your account of the library board's refusing to fire the librarian accused of being a pinko during the McCarthyism hysteria of the early 1950s is helpful because the library's records are silent on that issue." In a surprised voice you may hear, "Is that right?" Note how this second example enforces the value of speaking candidly about sensitive subjects in a community's history. The more I reckon a respondent is downcast about the interview— memories had faded, names and dates did not instantly come to mind—the more I cite remembered vignettes as beneficial testimony. If a person has summarized ninety years of life in ninety minutes of reminiscing, I don't want to leave her feeling glum about the worthiness of it. Our role is not to create depression in the mindsets of the elderly, but to leave them feeling good about how they have been good to us and others. Moreover, their willingness to edit the transcript you'll be sending will be higher if they share your upbeat outlook. Depressed people procrastinate.

The postinterview session is when you ask your respondent to spell proper names, explain obtuse professional nomenclature or shorthand, demystify place-names and acronyms, and the like. On my notepad I have jotted these phonetically during the interview. But rather than twirling and shoving my notepad toward the respondent, asking him/her to spell my guesses correctly, I do the asking and the writing because some people—physicians especially—have such poor handwriting you have to decipher their scrawl, which can be as perplexing as the words you heard when uttered in the interview. Be prepared for a truncated postinterview session. Doctors will rise telling you they have patients waiting. Befriend secretaries. Ask, "Does the doctor's daughter spell her name Leslie or Lesley?" "Is Kelly Boyd a son or daughter?" Ask if you can phone if you have questions to answer, in order to simplify the task upcoming for your transcriber. Ask if your transcriber can phone.

In the postinterview session, I ask the respondent if I may phone if, while reviewing the transcript, one or a handful of questions arise that I should have asked during the interview but failed to do so. Asking questions by phone and integrating them into the transcript, clearly identified and dated as to provenance, saves you the time and expense of scheduling another interview session. Don't tape a telephone conversation without first asking and receiving permission to do so.

More shoptalk can center on scheduling another session or outlining what lies ahead: transcription, editing, negotiating the legal agreement. I tell informants I will enclose a sample (i.e., boilerplate) legal form with the transcript mailed for review and phone a few days later to ask if they have any questions about either. This creates the risk of the interview being condemned to limbo if your interviewee should die before signing a release and you have to deal with the executor of his/her estate. But ethically I prefer not to discuss ownership issues and assignment of legal rights until the respondent knows fully and exactly what product our labors have mutually created.

After interviews have ended, I may ask for advice about who else might be considered for this project. If I sense a person who should be interviewed may be averse to being approached and I know my current interviewee was, or is, friendly with my reluctant prospect, I ask if I may mention to my prospect that we have recorded this memoir. "By all means," is what I hope to hear, with an added, "Tell her she should give you an interview. Your project won't be complete without her."

If at any time during this postinterview conversation a respondent suddenly exclaims, "Oh, I forgot to tell you about—," I promptly say, "We can remedy that easily. I'll just turn on the recorder again." Then, signaling with two fingers as I do so, I say, "You want to add about—." By not moving the microphone or pulling the plug, we have allowed an addendum to enrich the interview. Once again, I say, "Thank you." Once again, I don't tinker with the microphone or plug in case a second recollection abruptly occurs and we need to tape it.

The postinterview session is time for the social conversation you wanted to pursue in the interview, when instead you bit your tongue and deferred it. "You mentioned you went to Oberlin College; my daughter, Susan, is an Oberlin graduate." "Oh," comes the rejoinder, "when was she there?" Off you go bopping on the Oberlin odyssey. If you were offered a liquid libation before or during the interview and discreetly declined, you can now accept it and make as much noise as you like with spoons and crockery or cascading ice cubes in a tall glass. You can summon sullen family members you exiled to far corners of the house and engage them in friendly conversation so they no longer feel like social pariahs. You can laugh or chortle. You can talk about yourself. You can be the social animal you know you are. Oral historians are extroverts.

Finally, when I stand up to leave, I pull the plug and bundle all my equipment into my satchel, thanking everybody profusely while heading to the doorway and back across the doorstep. Yes, your plug has been pulled on your interview, but the plug has not been pulled on the interview process. Your rendezvous with destiny entails more work. Duplicating tapes and then transcription lie ahead. Other tasks will follow. Real work— dare I say reel work?—beckons you forward. You and Harvey chuckle at your pun—reel work—as the door clicks behind you.

Notes

1. Schippers, "Techniques," 54.
2. Fetner, *Immersed in Great Affairs*, 65.

3. Saul Benison, in charge of OHRO interviews on the history of medicine, 1955–1960, wrote, "I shall be plain; it has been my experience that many oral historians are less than meticulous in their research, that they do not include their questions in the memoirs, that they care little for the niceties of bibliography and care less for coping with historical problems." Benison, "Reflections," 73–74.

4. Morrissey, "Truman," 55. This article was given first as a paper during the annual meeting of the Mississippi Valley Historical Association (subsequently, the Organization of American Historians), in Cleveland, Ohio, on April 30, 1964.

5. Grele, "Oral History," 2: 881.

6. Moss, *Program Manual*, 45.

7. Mutual interviewer–interviewee responsibilities are detailed in Oral History Association, *Evaluation Guidelines*.

8. On the differences in interviewer–interviewee relationships between journalism and oral history, see Feldstein, "Kissing Cousins," 14–17.

9. Krieger, *Ranke*, 2.

10. Kayser and Morrissey, "Historically Significant Memories," 62.

11. See, for example, Ritchie, *Doing Oral History*, 2nd ed., 85–86.

12. On mythmaking, see Morrissey, "Mythmakers." On mythmaking by creation of paper-trail documents, see Morrissey, "Stories of Memory."

13. For more on use of props and other devices to aid memory recall, see Slim et al., "Ways of Listening," 119–25.

14. Ives, *Tape-Recorded Interview* (1980), 38, discusses "stranger value."

15. See also Yow's chapter on "Interpersonal Relations in the Interview," in *Recording Oral History* (1994), 116–42.

16. Ibid., 199–202, discusses family dynamics in historical research.

17. Concerning the purposes of the recorded introduction, see Sommer and Quinlan, *Oral History Manual*, 67. On the matter of avoiding batteries, Ritchie, *Doing Oral History*, 2nd ed., 58, agrees with me, but Yow, *Recording Oral History* (1994), 51, disagrees.

18. Fisher, *History of Europe*, v.

19. For more on group interviews, see Slim et al., "Ways of Listening," 118–19.

20. Yow, *Recording Oral History* (1994), 60–66, discusses behaviors that either build or hinder rapport.

21. For more on questioning technique, see McGuire, "'Existential' Interviewing," 58–69.

22. On listening, see Anderson and Jack, "Learning to Listen," 169–70, and on silences, see White, "Marking Absences," 173–78.

23. For a full definition of free association, see *The Freud Encyclopedia: Theory, Therapy, and Culture*, ed. Edward Erwin (New York: Routledge, 2002), s. v. "Free Association." Peter Gay recounts Freud's development of free association in *Freud*, 73, 297–98, but note that on 127 free association is misnamed because the spoken sequences "are invisibly but indissolubly welded together." The similarities and differences between oral history interviewing

and psychiatric interviewing are examined by James W. Lomax, a psychiatrist, and me in Lomax and Morrissey, "Interview as Inquiry." For more on oral history interviewing and the psychology of autobiographical memory, see my remarks in Morrissey, foreword, which appears in Hoffman and Hoffman, *Archives of Memory*.

24. I introduced the two-sentence format in 1966 at the first national meeting of oral historians. See Schippers, "Techniques," 53. Twenty years later, the practice was automatic for me. See Morrissey, "Two-Sentence Format," 44.

25. As recalled by Herbert Eugene Bolton in an undated letter in the fall of 1951 to Wilbur R. Jacobs, in Jacobs, *On Turner's Trail*, 265.

26. Charles T. Morrissey, "Asking Hard Questions: Harvey the Historian as Colleague," *Oral History Association Newsletter* 38, no. 2 (2004): 8.

27. Charlton, *Oral History for Texans*, 2nd ed., 27–28, lists seven specific probing techniques, including nonverbal ones.

28. Grele, "Anyone over Thirty," 43.

29. On the "aesthetics" of tape recording interviews, see Dunaway, "Field Recording," 32–36.

6

Oral History and Archives: Documenting Context

James E. Fogerty

Oral history is a unique form of documentation in that it does not exist in a defined form before it is created through the interaction of an interviewer with a narrator. Despite the occasional reference to "collecting" oral history, the interviews represented in any oral history collection had to be created before they could be deposited in a library or archives. The existing resources of the narrator's memory, drawn upon and undoubtedly formed in part by the interviewer's inquiry, are thus used to create a new resource.

It is the long and often laborious process of creation that we address in this chapter. Too often, oral historians, caught up in the pleasure and excitement of the interview and the personal interaction it offers, forget that the interview itself is neither the beginning nor the end of the process of creating oral history. It begins, in fact, with the conception of an interview or series of interviews and continues through research, narrator selection, and the interviews to transcription, editing, publication, and finally, public use in a variety of formats. At each stage of the process, context is created that becomes an important part of the interview and its meaning.

One of oral history's greatest benefits—the fact that nearly anyone, properly directed, can create it—has also proven one of its occasional drawbacks. The seeming ease with which oral history can be created—an interviewer appears to need only a recorder, some tape, and a narrator willing to talk—has fostered the illusion that oral history is a simple undertaking. This misunderstanding of the realities of oral history creation has spawned an abundance of poorly planned and executed interviews that have little residual value for research.

If lack of planning and poor execution often limit the uses for interviews, lack of attention to context is the greater problem, as pointed out by Canadian archivists Jean-Pierre Wallot and Normand Fortier. Even skilled oral historians may ignore the fact that "the circumstances surrounding the interview—the *context*—and the way the interview is conducted" are critical elements to the end users of oral history.[1] The reality of context, and its documentation, are not new to archives, though contextual reality has been applied infrequently in dealing with nontraditional archival materials such as oral history. Canadian theoretician and educator Hugh A. Taylor instructed archivists that this "contextual approach is concerned in the first instance with acquiring knowledge of the context in which information is recorded rather than knowledge of the information contents of records."[2]

Documenting Context

Few oral historians are archivists, however, and thus few of them begin the process of creating oral history with documentation of the process, as well as the narrator's memory, in mind. Archivists and curators of many different collections refer to the history of an item as its "provenance," referring to the what, when, where, how, and why of its creation. Insofar as possible, for instance, an art curator will want to document where, how, with what materials, and by whom a work of art was created, as well as the record of its ownership through the years. Other information will be sought as well, such as the inspiration for the work, the setting in which it was created, and the identity of the subject.

Such information is equally important for oral history interviews, for it establishes the context within which each interview was conceived and created, thus establishing an important frame of reference. Wallot and Fortier explain, "Oral sources depend on the relationship established between the interviewer and interviewee: a complete appreciation of the result therefore depends on a knowledge of the interview and its context (place, presence of third party, relationship between interviewer and subject, and so on)."[3] This information is critical to a user's ability to interpret the information contained in each oral history interview.

Since oral histories do not exist until created by an interviewer, the opportunity to create a record of provenance is clearly there. An interview should never become a "found object," stripped of the story of its creation and without any record of its context except that intuited by an eventual cataloger or user.

It is useful to note the confusion that can be engendered by terminology—especially when a widely used term is misapplied in some instances.

> With reference to oral history, the term "collect" is frequently employed—as in "We're collecting oral history." Still worse is the term "gather"—as in "We're gathering oral history to supplement our collections." Both terms, but particularly the often-used "collect," are inaccurate when applied to oral history. "Collect" implies that oral history, like a manuscript collection, exits and is only waiting to be found and acquired. While the data that becomes oral history is present in the minds of potential narrators, it does not exist in any organized, collectible form. It must, rather, be created—and not alone, but through the interaction of an interviewer with the narrator. Existing resources are thus used to create, not collect, a new resource.[4]

There are two main avenues by which oral history may enter an archives, library, or other repository. The most proactive is direct creation, through which the repository staff participates in every aspect of interview creation, from conception through narrator selection, interviewing, and preparation for research use. While this approach is increasingly common in many institutions, it may also be viewed as an expensive alternative to a more passive role.

The second avenue is to collect actively, or simply to accept, interviews created by others. This is the path followed by a great many institutions as they build collections and provide permanent housing and access for oral history created without direct linkage to a repository. While the acceptance of previously created oral history may spare a repository the expense of conception and creation, it is hardly without cost. Indeed the costs may be excessive if the interviews have been created without care and attention to context. Donation of interviews to a repository is often an afterthought on the part of the creator whose work is complete and who wishes simply to ensure a permanent home for the interview tapes. As Wallot and Fortier indicate, the act of "the depositing in archives of recordings without appropriate documentation makes evaluation of the recordings very costly, and, consequently, proper use of the recordings very difficult."[5]

Appraisal of potential accessions is a key component of collection building in any institution. Oral histories that lack such essentials as adequate documentation of the process of their creation, transcripts for each interview, narrator contracts, and other important elements can seldom be considered viable candidates for acquisition. The cost of acquiring such interviews is enormous, and the potential for their eventual use too uncertain to allow most institutions to consider adding them to existing collections. The expense of re-creating context where no record exists is far too great.

Individual Interviews versus the Project

While each oral history interview is indeed "individual" in that it deals with a single person, there are significant differences between what might be termed "solo" interviews and those created as part of a larger project. Both have context that must be documented, but the context for the project interviews will be much larger and more complex. Life histories, for instance, derive their value from the experiences of a single individual whose views are documented without reference to similar or competing views of others. Interviews created as part of a defined project, however, derive special value from their relationship to one another. If carefully selected, these narrators will both corroborate and differ from the views of others, thus providing highly valuable perspectives on the issues that are the subject of the project.

There are many examples of oral history projects; for illustration, I will refer to several that have been undertaken by the Minnesota Historical Society's Oral History Office. Projects on environmental issues, the farm economy, the resort industry, the controversial construction of a high-voltage power line across farmland, and a number of immigrant communities all exemplify the rationale for constructing a project with complementary interviews rather than a series of unrelated individual interviews.[6] The environmental issues project, for instance, allowed selection of narrators with widely differing views on public use of protected recreation areas and on levels of protection afforded shoreline set aside under the Wild and Scenic Rivers Act. The resort industry project included operators of large facilities with multiple entertainment options and mom-and-pop resorts that relied principally on fishing. It also included resort operators from two quite different areas of the state, allowing documentation of the contrast between the businesses and their guests. Protesters, supporters, and those caught in the middle were interviewed for the power-line construction project, and projects documenting new immigrants also draw on narrators whose perspectives display differences as well as similarities. The first project, dealing with Minnesota's Asian Indian community, for instance, was carefully structured to include Hindus, Sikhs, Muslims, Jains, and others, as well as people from many geographic areas of the vast Indian subcontinent. Subsequent projects in the India series include generational variety as well.

The reality of creating such oral history projects must be carefully documented as part of the process. The work of creating focus, selecting narrators, maintaining balance, and articulating issues for discussion during the interviews is critical to their understanding and interpretation. It is important for oral historians to understand that documentation of oral history begins with the conception of each interview, whether it is the life history of a single narrator or one of a series of interviews that form part of a project. The ways in which project goals are defined, topics for discussion chosen, and narrators selected should be reflected in documents created as the project progresses. It is also important to document who participated in those discussions, since they will have played major roles in shaping the project and its context.

These examples of the considerations necessary to the proper documentation of oral history lead us to discussion of the products of that creative process.

The Products of Oral History

The creation of even the simplest oral history interview, if it is to be of archival quality, requires the assembly or creation of a good many documents. I have chosen to list them by category below, with a discussion of each and specific examples of the documents that might become part of such a collection. The list is extensive, and competent oral historians will recognize that they already create or gather these documents as part of their work in creating interviews. The task at hand is simply to recognize that these documents are all critical components of each interview's context and establish its provenance and thus its credibility.

A key consideration in the building of background files is the reality that institutional memories are short and uncertain. The departure of project staff familiar with specific interviews may render materials difficult to use without adequate identification.

Research Files

The assembly of items to provide background information for an oral history project will begin before the project is even launched. The information gathered will help project development in such areas as the definition of scope, selection of narrators, and development of topics for discussion. Research files may become quite bulky and are usually maintained separately from the files of individual narrators. A distinction should be made between information gathered to be of use in overall project development and the narrator-specific, biographical information that may be placed in each narrator's file.

Projects will differ, of course, in the level and extent of documentation gathered as part of background research. The Minnesota Powerline Construction Oral History Project, for instance, came to include several large storage boxes of material gathered to document the complex issues and the individuals and organizations involved. Among the materials are reports on the conception, development, and construction of the power-generating plant and power line; reports detailing all aspects of health issues believed to be associated with the power line; press releases from the line's builders, the governor's office, and other organizations; flyers and broadsides announcing community meetings and other events; federal government reports on the line; maps, local news articles, newsletters issued by groups formed to protest construction; and photographs. Additional materials include an excellent paper on the controversy prepared by a graduate student at the University of Minnesota, Morris, and the procedures manual prepared to guide the oral history project's staff. This collection has become a key resource for researchers using the power line oral history interviews. The newsletters issued by local protest groups, for instance, were informally produced and ephemeral; those at the Minnesota Historical Society form the only comprehensive collection now in existence. And while some of the other documents may exist in other places, their inclusion in a single collection at a central location associated with the oral history collection is a major boon to research.

Unfortunately, many items of this sort do not survive the completion of oral history projects. While collected to aid research and facilitate the development of interview discussion topics, the project organizers frequently fail to recognize that the background documents are also valuable to researchers. Whenever practical, they should be brought together to form a collection, catalogued and made available for use. The electronic cataloging now in use in virtually every institution provides great ease in linking the oral history interviews to the associated collection of project research materials.

Project Files/Narrator Files

Every oral history project will generate communications common to more than one narrator or aimed at those who offer support for, or interest in, the project as a whole. Those items should be filed together for ease of access and to prevent the needless duplication of generating additional copies of these items for each narrator file. There is no need, for instance, to make copies for individual narrator files of project information sheets, invitations to project events, or project press releases. Those items need to be included in the project archives, and the creation of project-level files obviates the necessity to make multiple copies.

Communication with individual narrators should be separated into files dedicated to each person interviewed. In that file are placed copies of correspondence with that person, the person's photograph, a copy of the completed donor contract, and any background research material relating specifically to that individual.

By creating these separate series of files, information on the project is organized for rapid retrieval.

Correspondence/Communication

Copies of all correspondence with narrators should be filed with all of the material relating to that individual interview. *Include e-mail!* Print out relevant e-mail communications with narrators and others relating to the project or interview. Printing out the e-mail may seem like duplication of effort, but it ensures that a permanent record of all communication with that individual will be filed in one place and available for reference in the future. Retaining the e-mail as a computer file does not ensure its permanence and definitely does not ensure its availability for future reference. Since important issues regarding an interview may well be resolved through the exchange of e-mail, it is critical to retain this record as part of the permanent file.

Donor Contract

The contract concluded with each narrator, assigning rights for use, copyright, and ownership to the institution sponsoring the project, is perhaps the most important piece of paper in the project files. Without written transfer of interview ownership to the institution, the tapes cannot be transcribed or used in any way by anyone and are thus without value. The donor contract should be signed at the conclusion of the taped interview. If more than one interview session is held with a single narrator, the contract should be signed at the conclusion of the final taping session. It should clearly state the narrator's intent to transfer ownership and copyright to the institution. If any restrictions are imposed on use, they should also be spelled out clearly in the contract, with a specific date given for expiration of the restriction. Interviews should never be accepted with permanent restrictions on use, and the expiration of restriction should never be stated as the narrator's death. No institution possesses the resources to track hundreds of narrators throughout their lives in order to establish specific dates of death.

Oral history is created to be used. Restrictions on use should be discouraged and, when inevitable, kept to a minimum. There are certainly instances in which candor cannot be ensured without the imposition of restrictions on immediate use of the interview. But the number of interviews restricted should be minimized by attention to narrator concerns and by the interviewer's clear explanation of the influence of the passage of time on sensitive information. Restrictions of more than a decade after the date of the interview should be the exception, not the rule.

Contracts should be created in duplicate, with both copies signed by the narrator at the conclusion of the interview or interview series. If the contract covers a series of interviews, the dates of each interview must be listed in the contract. One copy of the signed contract remains with the narrator; the other returns to the institution where it is copied immediately. The copy is filed in the narrator file; the original is filed with others from that project in a secure location where its permanence can be assured.

Photographs

An important ingredient in many oral history interviews is a photograph of the narrator. Nearly all interview transcripts at the Minnesota Historical Society include a photograph of the narrator, since we have found that virtually all users enjoy seeing the narrators as well as reading their comments. Inclusion of a photograph also personalizes the interview transcript and increases its value to many narrators and their families.

A photograph of the narrator may be augmented by more photographs, depending on the project and its goals, funding, and the desires of its sponsors. Interviews documenting the history of a corporation, for instance, might include photographs of former officers, company products, company logos as they evolved through the years, and company facilities. The illustrations will usually depend upon the content of the interviews and on the availability of suitable images. An interview with a prominent churchman in Minneapolis, for instance, included not only a photograph of him taken near the time of the interview, but also an additional photograph of him as a younger man, as well as photographs of his church at various points in its history, previous pastors mentioned in the text, and even one of the city, locating the church within the wider context of its surroundings.

Copies of every photograph included should be retained in the narrator's file or in a file devoted to project photography. Since only a scanned image of the photograph is used in the final document, retention of the original or copy is a simple undertaking. Each photograph should be clearly identified on the reverse using a soft 6B drawing pencil that is available in art supply shops. Identification will obviously facilitate use of the files for research and also for future institutional use should the interviews be reprinted.

Interview Transcripts

Every interview should be transcribed. While transcription is a labor-intensive and protracted process, it is necessary to a main goal of creating oral history—its use. In this day of declining consumer patience and an Internet-fueled demand for instant gratification, production of interviews that cannot be accessed without listening to an audiotape is a waste of resources.

The availability of word processing has greatly decreased the expense of producing transcripts, but unless one has access to low-cost or volunteer transcribers and editors, it remains somewhat costly. The benefits, however, far outweigh the costs. With word processing, one creates a document that can be edited, updated, corrected, and reprinted with far less effort and expense than was true only fifteen years ago. And the electronic document thus created can allow a user to conduct word and subject searches across an entire project of related interviews, thus greatly increasing their potential utility to a wide variety of audiences.

All transcripts should be retained in both electronic and paper files. The electronic file will serve as the principal copy for generating replacement copies of the transcript as needed. Electronic copies of all of a project's interview transcripts can be gathered into a single file and presented to users as a unit, thus allowing the term searches noted above. Electronic files should be located on a secure server to prevent the unintended damage that can occur to documents stored on a computer's hard drive.

Editing of oral history transcripts is done to prepare them for public use, eliminating elements (such as repetitive false starts and misstatement of names and locations) that are part and parcel of any conversation. False starts, for instance, may be understandable when listening to the spoken word but confusing and misleading when reduced to a page of printed words. Editing is usually accomplished on paper copies of the transcript to allow the editor (usually the interviewer) to have a sense of the appearance of the printed document that will eventually become the published version available for public use. The edits are then transferred to the electronic record.

There will be several printed copies in existence by the time the editing process is complete, each bearing evidence of alterations that will define the interview's transformation from spoken to printed document. Several of those paper edit copies will become important components of the archival record of each interview's creation.

The archival record of the oral history project should be structured to include three copies of each interview transcript. They are:

- the initial edit—usually performed by the interviewer
- the narrator's edit
- the final edit, contained in a copy of the printed/ published transcript

Although the transcript may be subject to many other full and partial edits, the three listed above are the only ones necessary to retain in the permanent project file.

It is important to retain the initial edit because it records changes made in the original interview. This may include the removal of some false starts, repetitions, conversational idiosyncrasies ("you know"), and the insertion of a word here and there to clarify the narrator's intent. The record of the initial edit is thus a critical document, for it clearly delineates the ways in which the transcript has been altered for use.

The narrator's edit is equally important, for it reflects the interview subject's own clarifications, additions, spelling corrections, and other preferences. Retention of this document ensures that narrators' possible future concerns over transcript content can be matched directly with their written instructions.

Oral history project managers should bring some imagination to the work of producing finished transcripts, since they are often the most tangible, visible products of the interviews. Oral historians should never forget that, while they may be focused on gathering information and assembling it for use, each interview represents part of the narrator's life and experience. It thus becomes a highly personal document and one worthy of careful attention to its production.

At the Minnesota Historical Society, we regard transcripts as key products of each interview and every project. They are handsomely bound not only for permanence and to increase utility to users, but also as presentation copies to narrators and sponsors. The pleasure with which these are received on every occasion leaves no doubt of their importance in promoting the value of oral history and its significance. I well recall the family whose grandfather I interviewed about his experiences in business. Though the interview was no life history, it was a well-illustrated and articulate look at an aspect of his life less well known to family members. Shortly after he received a presentation copy, we received a request for one hundred additional copies for distribution to family members at Christmas. The scale of the order was a bit unusual, but not the intent. It was a reminder of the power of oral history to its subjects, a reality often overlooked by oral historians.

Video Log

If the project includes a video component, a video log should be compiled for all of the videotape footage. A video log is a scene-by-scene index to the videotape, without which its use is difficult. Video footage without a log is rather like audiotape without a transcript. It can only be accessed by those users willing to watch hours of tape in the hope of finding relevant images. If they do locate usable footage, they are then faced with the necessity of creating their own video logs to relocate footage they have already viewed.

Video footage will often have two components—an interview with a narrator and background footage filmed to illustrate or accompany the oral history interview. Options that should be considered in the creation of video oral history are covered in a separate section below.

The narrator's interview on video should be transcribed without editing. Users of the footage will need to know as closely as possible what is said. Even the dreaded "conversational idiosyncrasies" must be included, for this transcription is intended to facilitate use of videotape, not for research use.

The background footage will be logged scene by scene, with whatever detail is appropriate to guide users to the images they need. The log should briefly describe the scenes as they unfold but without overly involved description that will only confuse the users. A printout of the video log should be filed in the project file; the electronic copy should become part of the project documentation, stored safely on a central server.

Funding Proposal Text and Budget

If the oral history project received funding from outside the sponsoring institution, a copy of the funding proposal and budget should be retained in the project files. The proposal will include the project rationale, supporting data, a plan of work, time schedule, list of personnel, and information on the budget and its allocation. While the budget information may not be public, it and the proposal text are key documents that establish both purpose and procedure for the project. In doing so, they provide important evidence of the goals and objectives of the project interviews.

In addition to the funding proposal, periodic reports prepared as part of the project should also be included in the permanent files. These reports trace the realities of project operation, documenting plans that succeeded as well as those that were altered. The final report is of special importance, since it will summarize the work accomplished and evaluate, to some extent, success in achieving project goals.

Project Introduction

Every transcript in every project should include the same introduction, written to place that interview in the context of the project as a whole. It is critical that users understand that while project interviews stand as individual entities, they were created as part of a larger undertaking. That knowledge will help to explain the interview's focus on specific topics to the exclusion of others and the size and scope of the complete project. Regardless of which interview in a project is first accessed by a user, it should clearly communicate a sense of the project and its intent. A copy of the final introduction should be placed in the project file for future reference. Even though an electronic copy of the document will, of course, be retained on a secure server, the file copy will alert future users to its existence and provide against the possibility of damage to the electronic version.

Publicity

Many oral history projects will merit publicity on conclusion—and perhaps during their progress. Oral history is a popular form of documentation, and its immediate connection to real people creates numerous opportunities to present the project and its products to the public. Whether the publicity is a notice published in the scholarly press, a news article in a local newspaper, or a public event held to honor narrators and their families, all publicity should be retained for the project files. Such files would include the inevitable newspaper clippings, with the name of the publication and date carefully noted for posterity and hopefully copied to a medium more permanent than newsprint.

Promotional announcements, time schedules for public programs, news releases, and photographs will help to document events held to celebrate the completion of a project. At the Minnesota Historical Society, events held to celebrate the completion of projects are routinely photographed, with the images kept in the project files and used in reports, publicity, and public presentations.

Videotape as a Component of Oral History

The decision to include videotape in the production of oral history interviews brings additional considerations to the planning mix. From documentation of context to cataloging of both audio and videotapes to issues of preservation and use, video adds more than images to an oral history project.

The question of whether to videotape oral history interviews or not is debated during the planning stages of many oral history projects. The ubiquitous presence of video technology—and its rapid descent in both price and complexity—has made its relationship to oral history a major issue. Context is an especially important factor in the production of oral history with a video component, and preservation of an archival quality master tape is also a critical consideration.

Most oral history interviews do not contain a video component, despite the availability of equipment and the ease of its use. The majority of oral history interviews created today are recorded the old-fashioned way—on some tape medium, be it analog or digital. More about that debate a little later. Regardless of that fact, videotape has become the medium of choice for an increasing number of oral history interviews. Given that reality, it is useful to review the options available in its use.

Videotape is variously employed in oral history, sometimes to tape entire interviews as an adjunct to audiotaping, sometimes to incorporate illustration of a narrator's descriptions. Video provides significant opportunities and also has several drawbacks. Here is a brief discussion of both.

Pros

Video offers the viewer the opportunity to see the places or processes a narrator describes in an interview. For example, the use of video in the Minnesota Resort Industry Oral History Project allows users to virtually walk through the famous Bay Lake Lodge resort, admiring the panorama of water, trees, and wildlife as they go. When lodge owner Jack Ruttger describes the view of the lake and its effect on guests, researchers can see and admire it, too. And when another resort owner describes the new swimming pool that has become a major amenity, one can see and assess it through the medium of videotape. Video also offers increased opportunities for postinterview use of the visual images, which may be used alone or in concert with other images. Agricultural landscapes that form part of the Minnesota Farm Economy Oral History Project, for instance, have seen service in a variety of television productions.

Video also offers a tremendous advantage when interviewing craftspeople, for instance, whose work and the conditions under which it is produced are part of the story. Thomas L. Charlton explained: "Oral history interviewees who are, or have been, craftsmen find video recording to be far superior to audio recording when they are asked to tell of their life experiences."[7] Videotape is integral to an understanding of such Minnesota craftspeople as Ojibwe elder and beadworker Batiste Sam or the eminent carver of fish decoys John Jensen. It can also illuminate the work of such people as architects. The value of the Minnesota Historical Society's interview series with Vienna-born architect Elizabeth Close is greatly increased by video footage of some of the buildings designed by Close and her husband.

Cons

Video is expensive, both in terms of equipment and personnel. Moreover, videotape itself makes poor archival material because it is not permanent and it cannot be easily transcribed. Audiotapes must be dubbed from the videotape or recorded simultaneously and used for creating the transcript.

Video is also intrusive. Despite reduction in the size of video cameras, they remain much larger than audio recording equipment. And the presence of a videographer and a sound engineer, in addition to the interviewer, does not contribute a sense of intimacy to the interview. There is also the issue of quality. While handheld video cameras are readily available to consumers, few of them create images of the quality necessary to merit permanent preservation. Light and sound quality are key components of video oral history, and both require much more than the services of a single amateur armed with the best the local electronics outlet store has to offer. That best may be fine for recording family events, but it is seldom adequate for the permanent record oral history becomes. And it is almost never adequate to the multitude of uses to which oral history videotape may be put by future users. The major "cons" of videotaping may thus be summed up as expense and intrusion.

The legal realities of videotape must also be considered. As Charlton stated, "It may not be enough for oral historians to rest their cases on U.S. copyright law. Video recordings—with images that can be distorted, deliberately or inadvertently, and a potential for tape editing vastly more complex than that normally associated with audiotapes—may lead to legal proceedings fraught with danger for oral historians."[8] Quotation from an audiotape transcript is one thing; a narrator's video image, flashing across thousands of television screens in an instant, presents a distinctly different set of considerations.

Why Use Video in Oral History?

As with every other component of oral history, the use of video should be carefully reasoned and based upon the value it adds to the final product. Too often, video is adopted because it is there, rather than because it actually adds much information to the underlying oral history interviews.

Video is visual! That rather obvious fact is overlooked in the planning of many oral history projects that employ videotape. If the video footage offers little addition to the narrator's information, which can be captured perfectly well on audiotape, then video should not be employed. Endless footage of a narrator seated in a chair against a static background offers hardly any information or context that cannot be contained in several good photographs taken on the day of the interview.

Taking everything into account, the use of video should be undertaken only when it brings something unique to the project. The most thoughtful and appropriate process for creating video history is one I have dubbed the "Perlis Plan" in tribute to Vivian Perlis of Yale University. A pioneer in defining the use of video in oral history, Perlis discarded the idea of simply turning the camera on a seated narrator and letting the tape run. Instead, she correctly noted that what users wanted was to see the things the narrator described, or better still, to see the narrator doing something rather than talking about it. Video footage of a farmer using his land and showing the accommodations he has made to balance production and ecology, for example, offers a great deal of visual information to supplement the interview text.

A critical consideration in the production of video oral history is the fact that, especially with background or illustrative material, one is creating raw footage for possible future use. Unlike the details of audio- and videotape in which the narrator appears directly, background footage is created largely on the speculation that it will prove valuable to future users. It should be *informed* speculation, of course, based upon a genuine understanding of how such material is likely to be used in television and film production. If carefully produced, background footage may have residual value that outweighs that from the associated interviews. The Minnesota Historical Society has found that footage of dawn breaking over a northern lake, people settling in to campsites, and children playing in the headwaters of the Mississippi River have definite value to television production companies for whom the choice of sending a crew to create such images is far more expensive than licensing existing material.

These considerations are highly important when assessing both the value videotape may add to oral history and the archival and preservation realities that will be faced when the videotape—as well as the audiotape—finds its way into the permanent collection. Any video oral history program should be based upon a clearly defined statement of purpose, including principles such as:

1. To add a visual dimension to selected oral history interviews, with emphasis on providing visual information that enhances an audio interview with the same narrator.
2. To provide visual context for narrators and the subjects they discuss.
3. To build an archive of broadcast-quality videotape interviews and cover footage for research use.
4. To develop teaching aids from both interview and cover videotape footage that will provide instruction to participants in the society's oral history workshops and seminars.
5. To develop edited videotape segments that will heighten understanding of the oral history program by both the general public and potential funding agencies.

Before committing the resources necessary to produce high-quality video oral history, and the accompanying documentation, an oral history program director should answer the following questions:

1. What is the purpose of the video interview?
   a. Will it be part of a finished "program"?
   b. Will it mainly be for research and reference and typically viewed in its entirety?
   c. Why do you need moving images and visual elements?
   d. How does the purpose support the goals and objectives of your project or organization?
2. What is your budget? How can you make the most of it? Do you want to emphasize technical quality (best camera, best format) and good editing, or do you want to create the greatest number of interviews you can afford?
3. Who is the audience?
4. Where and how will the video be used? Where will the master be preserved?
5. Is video the correct medium (as opposed to slide/tape program or audio only interview)?

6. What visuals will add information and interest to the interview?
7. Where will the interview be taped (studio, home, office, outdoors)?
8. How will the video interview be made known and distributed?

Oral History and Preservation

No one wants to invest in oral history only to find that the chosen medium of the collection cannot be preserved for future use. An important goal of a project director is to ensure that the products of oral history, which represent the hard work of many people, are of archival quality, with both master and user copies stored suitably for long-term preservation and for public access. As Wallot and Fortier warn, "Over and above the requirements with respect to the environment and the handling of the tape . . . one must take into account the variety of recording formats, which are usually incompatible, and rapid technological change, particularly in the case of video recordings. Consequently, archives [may] have to constantly recopy documents in a common format, since it is hardly possible to maintain a complete inventory of playback and copying equipment."[9]

The permanent preservation of nearly any media presents a complex array of issues. The ways in which these issues are addressed are topics debated at great length among conservators, users, tape manufacturers, and those—like archivists—concerned with the realities of maintaining fragile media for the longest possible period of time.

Preservation of oral history media is also complicated by the continuing development of new and different recording media. Digital audiotape (DAT), recordable compact discs (CD-Rs), and minidiscs are only a few of the "new" media challenging oral historians and archivists. As always, newer is inevitably better to some, including to some oral historians whose greatest interest is in the immediate public use of tape recordings, rather than in long-term preservation. Since use can always be made of oral history interviews recorded on media suitable for preservation, that is the focus of the discussion in this chapter.

While the basics of tape preservation may be summarized for wide application, the nuances are complex, indeed, and subject to widely varying interpretations. This chapter cannot include an extended discussion of these nuances; it includes only a summary that will guide the producers and holders of oral history collections toward best practice.[10] Here, then, is a brief discussion of the basic considerations involved in the preservation of audio- and videotape.

Audiotape

Audiotape remains the most widely used medium for recording oral history interviews. Even when interviews are recorded on videotape, an audiotape recording of the interview should be made for preservation.

Format

Most oral history is recorded on analog audiotape. The taped interview represents the core product of every oral history interview. While the transcript, edited, bound, and attractively presented for public use, may be far more heavily used than the tape, it is the tape itself that represents the interview in its purest form. The master tapes must be carefully preserved, for they are the most faithful record of the interview as it happened.

That said, the interview must be conducted using the best audiotape available. As in many other aspects of real life, "best" does not always mean "most expensive." In fact, the more expensive high-bias audiotape developed for use in recording music does not offer any appreciable advantage over basic professional-grade audiotape.

The cassette tape with sixty minutes of recording time (thirty minutes on each side of the tape) is the standard recording and preservation medium. Master recordings on reel-to-reel tape should be retained in that format, with use copies provided on cassette tape.

The increasing popularity of DAT, CD-R, and other formats has created another challenge for oral historians and archivists. Despite the interest in these formats and their utility in certain instances, neither has supplanted professional-grade analog audiotape as the medium of choice for long-term preservation. And, given the reality that digital copies can easily be made from analog masters, there is no reason to gamble future preservation on formats without proven viability for the long term. Those charged with making the substantial investment necessary to create oral history interviews must take the safest route possible to ensure they exist in usable form in the future.

Storage

It does little good to use the best possible materials in the creation of oral history if the resulting tapes are stored in less than suitable conditions. Audiotape is susceptible to damage from such environmental problems as dirt, light, and excessive heat and humidity. Audiotape masters should be stored in a secure location, each standing upright on its edge and enclosed in an archival-quality box for safety and ease in shelving. Master storage should be in temperatures calibrated to a steady forty to fifty degrees Fahrenheit, with humidity maintained in the range of 20–30 percent. Audiotape copies intended for ready use should be stored on edge in containers, with temperatures of sixty-five to seventy degrees Fahrenheit and a humidity of 45–50 percent. Master copies should never be used except to strike further use copies if those are damaged.

Videotape

The attraction of videotape in the production of oral history has grown rapidly in recent years. As video recording equipment has become less awkward and space consuming, and as the image quality has improved, the opportunity to create moving images as part of oral history has been taken by many oral historians. While hardly appropriate for all interviews, videotape does offer downstream user values that may balance its considerable cost, storage requirements, and difficulties as a preservation medium.

Format

Most oral history videotape is created using analog tape in one of the variations of VHS or in Betacam-SP. VHS is by far the most widely utilized, though it is not appropriate for long-term preservation. If it must be used in creating the master tape, the S-VHS format is preferable to lower-quality VHS varieties. It should be kept in mind, however, that VHS was not developed with preservation in mind. It is a highly flexible and widely viewable format for dissemination of images for public use, but it is not designed for archival use.

The major investment in creating video oral history, however, is best made in the highest archival-quality videotape available. Betacam-SP continues to fill that place despite fears that it, like so many other formats, will be superseded by others. It remains widely available, though the recording equipment necessary to produce the finest product is both expensive and complex. The video history program of the Minnesota Historical Society's Oral History Office has used Betacam-SP since its inception in 1984. The use of contract videographers ensures that the recording equipment used is of very high quality, without the necessity of an institutional commitment to acquire and continually upgrade such equipment. In addition to its value as an important analog video format of archival quality, Betacam-SP has other advantages. Its excellent quality ensures that duplicate copies made for public use on VHS tape will have far greater visual quality than copies made from VHS masters. Commercial use of video oral history is also far more likely when users find they can edit from a duplicate Beta-SP master.

Digital videotape is also available, of course, and may be preferred by users who fear the obsolescence of analog tape or who believe a digital format offers them more production options. Not all digital videotape is of archival quality, however, and tape created using the process known as compression is never of archival quality for long-term preservation.

Storage

As with audiotape, videotape is susceptible to damage from dirt, light, and excessive heat and humidity. Long-term storage conditions should be stabilized at around fifty degrees Fahrenheit and 20–50 percent relative humidity. Tapes should be housed in protective casings (they are usually purchased in plastic or paper cases) and shelved on edge.

Preparing Oral History for Use

As has been stated many times, oral history is created for use. Whether and how it is uscd is in part dependent upon the way in which access to the interviews is created. For years, oral history has been catalogued as a library material, though without the guidelines that standardize access to books, serials, photographs, and other documents. The result is a perplexing variety of cataloging conventions, often jerry-built by librarians and archivists trying to fit oral history into classification systems ill suited to its particular needs.

The difficulties evident in finding and using oral history interviews have been noted for years. In part, this situation has been exacerbated by the fact, identified by Bruce Bruemmer, that "oral historians are producers, not curators. Most of their work is developed as a means to a final product, whether it be a book, an article, a motion picture, or a public-relations device. Understandably, when the final product is completed, there is little incentive to follow-up interviews with tedious editing, abstracting, and cataloging."[11] The problem was also deepened by the fact that to many of those archivists and librarians who control the cataloging—and thus the access—to material in their collections, oral history seemed, as Bruemmer states it, rather like "the occasional odd-sized document that is left on the accession shelf because it is difficult to catalog."[12]

For years, much oral history languished in limbo—uncataloged and thus unfindable, or forced into cataloging conventions that obscured its content and value. This reality attracted only sporadic attention from oral historians, who often seemed unaware of the problem and indifferent to its solution. In 1990, however, a concerted effort was mounted by a small group of oral historians, archivists, and librarians aware of the dangers of continued inattention to the issue of public access. The effort received further impetus at the 1991 annual meeting of the Society of American Archivists, when this group met and issued a public call for action. Shortly thereafter, led by former Oral History Association presidents Lila Goff, Dale Treleven, and Kim Lady Smith, they acquired a grant from the National Historical Publications and Records Commission to address the issue of access to oral history by creating a cataloging system anyone could use.

The result of this effort was the groundbreaking *Oral History Cataloging Manual*, published in 1995 by the Society of American Archivists. It has become the basic reference in the field and has instituted an oral history cataloging standard that has greatly increased the visibility and accessibility of oral history wherever it is used. The manual's principal author, Marion Matters, expressed quite clearly the thought behind the successful construction of a framework for the cataloging of oral history: "Because of the affinities between oral history materials and archival records, this manual is based heavily on the archival approach to cataloging. Archival cataloging is characterized by its focus on the context in which materials were created (their provenance) as much as on their content or physical characteristics. It is also characterized by collective description; that is, the description of groups of materials related by provenance. Archival (and oral history) descriptions are created by supplying information extracted from various sources, rather than transcribing information from a chief source of information such as a title page, label, or screen."[13]

While the *Oral History Cataloging Manual* has made it possible for oral histories to be presented for public use in a standardized fashion, the basics of preparing them for cataloging remain. Interviews must still be assigned accession and catalog numbers, labeled (both master tapes and public-use copies), and shelved. In addition, the transcripts must also be prepared and cataloged, since they are likely to receive far more use than the tapes ever will.

Oral History and the Internet

To anyone concerned about the use of oral history, the Internet offers a dazzling array of possibilities. Access is worldwide and virtually immediate, connecting users to resources with only a few clicks of a computer mouse or touch pad. The standardized cataloging formats provided by the *Oral History Cataloging Manual* are especially important in this environment, for they standardize the appearance and terminology so important to the search engines (such as Google and Yahoo) that deliver resources to users through the World Wide Web.

The increasing use of Web site access to the catalogs of libraries and archives has sealed the fate of published catalogs of oral history collections. While some may still be printed for the purpose of promoting a particular collection to its immediate community and supporters, published catalogs are virtually irrelevant to the Internet generation. Printed catalogs are usually out of date before they are printed, and the number of users they can deliver to library and archival resources is miniscule compared to the international audience available through the Internet.

Nothing Is Perfect: Internet Concerns for Oral Historians

While Internet access offers remarkable opportunities to increase the visibility and use of oral history interviews, those opportunities are not without parallel concerns. Chief among these are the twin issues of copyright and privacy.

Copyright

Copyright in most oral history interviews is held by the institution that sponsored them. As noted earlier, copyright is formally dealt with in the contract between the narrator and the institution that establishes the legal status of each interview.

While access to the information contained in oral histories is a key objective of their creators, absolute access cannot be created without assessing its consequences. Internet access to most oral history interviews consists of access to the catalog summary of interviews and projects created during the cataloging process. The summaries contain contextual information on projects and individual interviews, describing the objectives for which they were created and listing the narrators by name. Each interview may also be summarized to create another level of information.

The full text of oral history interview transcripts can easily be made available. Most interviews created in the last fifteen years have been transcribed using one or another word processing program (such as Microsoft Word or WordPerfect), and are thus already in electronic format. Despite this fact, most oral history transcripts are not available through Internet access to the catalog Web sites of libraries and archives. The admittedly great opportunity to create worldwide access to individual oral history transcripts has largely been rejected for reasons of control and copyright.

In subscribing to these concerns, the administrators of most oral history collections have adopted the stance of book publishers in refusing to make their products available without the certainty of copyright protection. While this concern is likely to be addressed in the future, reluctance to place the full text of interview transcripts on Web sites accessible to anyone at any time is likely to inhibit any such move by the institutions holding the largest and most important oral history collections. Control of a resource created at considerable expense and with painstaking care is not something relinquished with much ease.

Privacy

Linked to issues involving copyright are those concerning privacy. Oral history interviews represent close and personal relationships between interviewers, narrators, and sponsoring institutions. This relationship is taken seriously by all parties. Interviewers feel a sense of obligation to the people who have allowed them to create a record of their feelings and perspectives. Narrators feel an inevitable connection to stories that are very much their own. Institutions have a vested interest in ensuring the maintenance of good relations with those who trust them with the responsible management of the interviews they create.

The interlocking interests shared by interviewers, narrators, and institutions inevitably affect the use of oral history interviews. Many institutions do not allow unrestricted copying of either tapes or complete transcripts, and thus the uninhibited use of transcript text possible through the Internet is not always attractive. The concept of worldwide access to text is alluring; the reality offers pause for consideration. It is one thing to make transcripts available to researchers who must appear in a library or archives, or request interlibrary loan, to gain access. It is quite another thing to make full text of those same interviews available without restriction to distant, faceless users who may be anywhere, at any time.

Privacy concerns extend even to the personal information on narrators provided as part of the summary data in catalog records. Once limited to on-site use in controlled situations, the magic of the Internet makes this information available to a wide audience that may contain far more curiosity seekers and commercial users than traditional researchers. In an age beset by increasing concerns over identity theft and Internet snooping, institutions providing public access to their collections via the Internet must be aware of the realities they confront. These considerations have already led many institutions to limit the personal information provided in interview summaries. To be "Google-stalked," as one narrator phrased it, is not a pleasant experience, nor can an institution escape responsibility for providing personal information without carefully considering the risks involved.

Solution

The ability to use the Internet to make oral history transcripts (and sound and images) available worldwide is already at hand. Oral historians, archivists, and librarians continue to be frustrated by issues of copyright and privacy that remain obstacles to harnessing that potential. Sooner rather than later, it will surely be possible to make full text of oral history transcripts available through institutional Web sites without the risks of unauthorized use. Once these risks can be controlled, the remarkable reality of full-text word searching across a whole project of interview transcripts will be realized. Then the value of investments in oral history will be much more apparent as wide public use results from greatly increased access.

Conclusion

The lasting value of oral history interviews can be realized only if they are carefully preserved, made available for wide and easy use, and supported by records that faithfully document the context within which they were created. The costs of creating oral history have frequently been exaggerated, but they are real and considerable. Those costs can only be justified if the resulting product is treated with the same care and respect accorded other records of permanent value.

Treating oral history tapes and transcripts as documents with enduring value also ensures that the narrators—without whom there would be no oral history—are treated with similar respect. The power of oral history is often noted by proponents; that power is only evident in interviews that can be found and used.

The more widely oral history is known and used, the more important will be the record of its creation. Ensuring that such records are created and maintained is a key responsibility of every oral historian.

Notes

1. Wallot and Fortier, "Archival Science," 371.
2. Nesmith, "Taylor's Contextual Idea," 16.
3. Wallot and Fortier, "Archival Science," 372.
4. Fogerty, "Filling the Gap," 151.
5. Wallot and Fortier, "Archival Science," 371.
6. For more on these projects, see Minnesota Historical Society, Oral History Collection, http://www.mnhs.org/collections/oralhistory/oralhistory.htm (accessed January 30, 2005).
7. Charlton, "Videotaped Oral Histories," 232.
8. Ibid., 235.
9. Wallot and Fortier, "Archival Science," 373.
10. For more information on this topic, see, in addition to other references cited in this article, Child, *Information Sources*; Fogerty, "Oral History as a Tool"; Ritchie, *Doing Oral History*; and Van Bogart, *Magnetic Tape*. Several Web sites contain excellent summary information on audiotape and videotape preservation and provide links to other sources. See, for example, Association of Moving Image Archivists, http://www.amianet.org (accessed February 1, 2005);

Stanford University Libraries, Preservation Department, Cool: Conservation OnLine, Resources for Conservation Professionals, http://palimpsest.Stanford .edu (accessed February 1, 2005); and Library of Congress, "Cylinder, Disc and Tape Care in a Nutshell," http://www.lcweb.loc.gov/preserv/care/record .html (accessed February 1, 2005).

    11. Bruemmer, "Access," 495.

    12. Ibid.

    13. Matters, *Cataloging Manual*, 1.

7

The Uneasy Page: Transcribing and Editing Oral History

Elinor A. Mazé

> Speech is the best show man puts on.
>
> —Benjamin Whorf

> Speech is somatic, a bodily function, and it is accompanied by physical inflections—tone of voice, winks, smiles, raised eyebrows, hand gestures—that are not reproducible in writing. Spoken language is repetitive, fragmentary, contradictory, limited in vocabulary, loaded down with space holders. . . . And yet people can generally make themselves understood right away. As a medium, writing is a million times weaker than speech. It's a hieroglyph competing with a symphony.
>
> —Louis Menand, *New Yorker*

The transcript has been a part of oral history practice in the United States from the beginning. In the beginning, the transcript was the only record of an interview to survive, to be archived, preserved, and made accessible for study. Of Allan Nevins's inaugural program, launched in 1948 as the Oral History Research Office at Columbia University, Alice Kessler-Harris wrote, "Except for a small fragment of the original interview, intended to illustrate the subject's voice and style, tapes of the interviews

238 / Elinor A. Mazé

were erased. The written transcript was considered sufficient information."[1] Nevins's first interviews, in fact, were done without benefit of an electronic recording device, according to Louis Starr, Nevins's successor at Columbia; a graduate student sat by taking notes as Nevins and his interviewees conversed.[2] These transcripts, rough drafts typed from the student's handwritten notes, are what remains of what many consider to be the beginning of modern oral history.

Created before the advent of accessible recording technology, the antecedents of oral history were, necessarily, written transcripts. Among these early antecedents are the extensive interviews with former slaves conducted and transcribed by John B. Cade at Southern University and Prairie View State College and by Ophelia Settle at Fisk University, beginning in 1929.[3] The Federal Writers' Project continued this work during the 1930s, transcribing interviews with thousands of "ordinary" representatives of everyday America. This early work was not called oral history, but the transcribed interviews—deposited in the Library of Congress and now accessible via the World Wide Web[4]—are considered by many oral historians to be the most important twentieth-century antecedents of modern oral history.

Earlier examples of verbatim transcripts of interviews for historical purposes are the "Dictations" of Hubert Howe Bancroft. Transcriptions of hundreds of interviews with pioneers in the American West are now in the archives of the Bancroft Library at the University of California at Berkeley.[5] Bancroft—or members of his staff—conducted most of the interviews in the late 1880s. A few years earlier, Lyman Copeland Draper, secretary of the Wisconsin Historical Society, labored hard to transcribe his interviews with individuals he considered to be of historical importance, among them Daniel Boone's son, Nathan.[6] These early practitioners considered it worthwhile to record more or less verbatim, as best they could with pen, paper, and memory, the words of their informants. The choices they made as they created their transcripts, choices concerning transcription of idiolect and dialect, choices of omission and inclusion, choices of style and historical or contextual comment, were not yet matters of scholarly debate. When recording interviews for historiographic purposes became the discipline of oral history, whether and how to transcribe the recordings became matters of perennial concern.

Should oral history interviews be transcribed? From the practical point of view, for most historians, the argument is lopsidedly in favor of creating transcripts whenever possible. In 2001, Carl Wilmsen wrote, "Interview tapes are transcribed for three major reasons: to enhance the ease of use of the interview, to render it more readily accessible to a variety of audiences, and since paper has a longer shelf life than magnetic and digital media, to increase its longevity in an archive."[7] By 1977, Starr had already declared the debate to be nearly over, "because of the overwhelming preference of users for transcripts, calls for which exceed calls for tape in some of the larger oral history collections by ratios of a thousand to one and higher. . . . Tapes, no matter how carefully indexed, are awkward to use."[8] A year later, David Lance wrote, "Given that the average speed of reading is about three times as fast as the average rate of speaking . . . the value and importance of the transcript obviously lies in the convenience of access it permits."[9] In 1997, Tracy K'Meyer asked oral historian Willa K. Baum, "What would you say if someone asked the question, 'Why not just leave things in tape form?'" Baum replied, "It's an easy answer. Nobody would use them."[10] Donald Ritchie has reiterated the point in the 2003 edition of his comprehensive guide to oral history: "Given a choice, researchers invariably prefer transcripts over tapes. Eyes can read easier than ears can hear. . . . Archivists note that very few researchers ask to listen to the tapes if transcripts are available."[11]

Manuals of oral history practice have likewise generally advocated transcription whenever resources permit.[12] The convenience of the printed page and its relatively unmediated accessibility—for literate researchers, at least—are the reasons most often cited. There are other reasons, as well. David Henige wrote, "Whenever the historian transcribes oral materials the very act of transcription enhances his grasp of their content."[13] Dennis Tedlock also made this point, adding, "It should be done while the interview is still fresh in [the interviewer's] mind so that he can provide such details as might not be clear from the tape alone, such as gestures."[14] Henige and Tedlock both urged interviewers to do the transcription themselves, a practice that may actually be uncommon, at least in larger institutional oral history programs. Nonetheless, Henige's advice, if extended to include a careful reading of the transcript, is still sound in the opinion of many: "Whenever possible, and every effort should be made to render it possible, each interview or small group of interviews should be transcribed almost as soon as (and certainly within a few days [of when]) they have been conducted. The variable and dynamic aspects of oral research—the living sources—make this procedure absolutely imperative because it is really the only way the historian can detect new areas of discussion or different points of view, as well as anomalies, contradictions, and textual uncertainties that he will need to follow up."[15] Thad Sitton, George Mehaffy, and O. L. Davis wrote concerning oral history projects for young students that "the majority of projects require interviewers to transcribe their own tapes. Students who listen to their own interviews will naturally become more proficient interviewers; the evidence is clear on that." Further, they pointed out, the benefits of transcribing cut across the curriculum: "The student must transcribe the material and struggle with the problem of ordering the oral testimony by punctuation and paragraph. A better inquiry lesson into the practical usefulness of such formal structures can scarcely be devised!"[16] A recent posting to the H-Oralhist discussion echoed this point: "It always astounds me how much richer the interview is when listening to it piece by piece in the transcription process. It's impossible to 'hear' all the subtleties when doing the actual interview, when we interviewers are so focused on questions, keeping the process moving along, monitoring equipment, etc."[17] Separate, then, from the question of the value and meaning of the transcript as an archived text is the notion that the act of transcribing is valuable as it forces close, attentive listening to the recording. From such careful listening should come better scholarship and written or performed works more faithful in understanding and interpretation to the original oral dialogue.

Even when recordings remain the main object of study, the transcript can provide a very helpful guide to the audio record. On the Library of Congress Web site announcing the availability of recordings of interviews with former slaves, it is noted that "those recordings that suffer from poor audio quality have gaps in their transcriptions, but even in those cases, the transcriptions are a useful tool for following and understanding the interviews."[18]

Oral historians in the United States have insisted on transcription, and many consider the transcript to be a primary source, equal for research purposes to the audio recording from which it was made. Canadians, among others, have taken a different view. Writing about the source of differences between Canadian and U.S. practice in oral history, Richard Lochead cited the Canadian Broadcasting Company (CBC) as a major determining force. The CBC had, after World War II, a "cultural mandate to try to seek out and find the Canadian identity and express it wherever it was found."[19] The CBC collected untranscribed tapes and deposited them in Canada's national archives, and Lochead attributed Canadian oral historians' insistence on the primacy of the audio recording to that which became Canadian national archival practice. The Canadian Oral History Association states the matter on its Web site: "Oral history, therefore, refers to recorded interviews with individuals about the past, or first-person reminiscences. The primary form of the oral history document is the recorded human voice. This document, in turn, may be applied as informational source material or directly in sound or transcribed form."[20] Likewise, a browse through the online catalog of oral histories at the British Library Sound Archive[21] suggests that, in that collection at least, the sound recordings are preeminent. When they exist, transcripts are noted in the catalog records as "documentation," suggesting that the transcripts are considered to be guides to the primary audio source.

Oral history practice with respect to transcription thus varies around the world, and debate about it continues. The debate extends beyond practical matters of processing and managing oral histories. It engages historians in questions about the theoretical foundations of oral historiography, the ethics of accessibility, and standards of preservation.

The question at once most vexing and most interesting is, What becomes of the spoken word when it is written down? The question has been considered from several points of view and within various disciplines. Linguists, psychologists, ethnographers, and philosophers have all studied the consequences of literacy, and oral historians have used research from these fields as they formulated their own theories and practices. The relationship between the oral history interview—the interpersonal event itself—and the printed transcription of it has been scrutinized and debated in every decade since the 1940s. There has evolved no consensus that "the transcript is nothing more and nothing less than the whole truth of what was spoken during that interview."[22]

In a 1984 commentary in the *Oral History Review*, David Dunaway wrote, "What do we do when we transcribe? 'Turn tape into type' is one uncomplicated answer. But even verbatim transcription (if possible) and careful notes cannot re-create the history-telling interview. . . . The oral interview is a multilayered communicative event, which a transcript only palely reflects."[23] The point has been made by many oral historians. In *The Death of Luigi Trastulli and Other Stories*, Alessandro Portelli wrote, "Even if we tried to print interviews in their entirety, we would end up with lengthy and almost unreadable texts (in which the mechanical fidelity of transcriptions thinly veils the qualitative betrayal of turning beautiful speech into unreadable writing); and we would be turning oral into written discourse anyway, which is no minor interference."[24]

In his 1994 book, *The World on Paper: The Conceptual and Cognitive Implications of Writing and Reading*, David Olson put the matter this way:

> No writing system, including the alphabet, brings all aspects of what is said into awareness. . . . Even scripts such as the alphabet, which may be taken as representing the verbal form of an expression, fail to provide an explicit representation for the illocutionary force of an utterance. To the extent that they transcribe *what* was said, they fail to transcribe *how* it was said, and with it the indicators of how the speaker intended for the listener to take what was said. What is lost in the act of transcription is precisely what is so difficult to recover in the act of reading, namely, how the expression is to be taken. . . . Even modern readers and writers have difficulty recognizing that texts, no matter how well written, never provide more than an indication of a speaker's or writer's audience-directed intention. Alphabetic scripts represent verbal form, what was

said, not the attitude of the speaker to that verbal form, what was meant by it.[25]

Olson has been taken to task for his "unfalsifiable idealizing of spoken discourse" and his implicit assumption that there is "some magical nonspoken access" to a speaker's meanings.[26] It is certainly true that divining authorial intention is viewed as a murky and fruitless venture by many modern critics. Olson's point about the "illocutionary force" of spoken language is important, nonetheless. An interviewee's innermost intentions—certainly complex and perhaps at least partly nonverbal—may not be accessible to either listeners or readers, but the former have more to go on in their interpretive efforts. The oral history interview begins not as a composed text but as an interpersonal event, a conversation, a dual performance, created not only with spoken words but with gesture, silence, intonation, rhythm, volume, accent, and dozens of other elements of expression that convey meaning during the event but that are utterly lost—"locked out," in Dunaway's words[27]—in the transcript, and that even an audio recording is inadequate to preserve. Beyond the dozens of ways in which words can be said, each way conveying a different meaning, there are the interpersonal and situational currents that shape the speaking, currents that are palpable to those present, even to those seeing a video or hearing an audio recording, but completely missing from the printed page. "Spoken words," wrote Walter Ong, "are always modifications of a total situation which is more than verbal."[28] How much more, then, is the transcript a modification of the more-than-verbal "situation" of the oral history interview. Elizabeth Tonkin warned that researchers "have not been taught to consider that interviews are oral genres." Considering the many illocutionary aspects of speaking, Tonkin concluded, "Transcription of oral accounts . . . is not just a problem, it is, properly speaking, impossible."[29] The difficulty for oral historians lies in the fact that transcriptions of spoken words and texts that begin life as writing, deliberately composed and intended to be read, are fundamentally different genres, but the production of a printed text in the end in both cases blurs the distinction. Writing in 1970, Gould Colman was sanguine about the communicative power of the transcript when he argued, "What we are engaged in is the most valid form of historical documentation that exists. . . . What are we documenting? . . . Of course, what we are documenting is the interaction that occurs between interviewer and respondent. Our document is a record of that interaction. If we keep the tape recorder going, and if we don't mess it up by editing, we can turn out a verbatim transcript which is far more valid than other primary source material."[30] Such optimism about the transcript is probably shared by few oral historians today, even though transcribing is standard practice in most projects and reliance on transcripts for research is still widespread.

For methods of writing transcripts to preserve more of what is lost, oral historians have turned to scholars in other fields. Linguists, anthropologists, ethnographers, and others have invented orthographic systems to represent the nonverbal aspects of speech—the many kinds of laughter, facial expressions, and intonation, for example—that can make such a critical difference between what a speaker conveys as he or she speaks and what a reader understands. Workers in the field of discourse analysis have developed several schemes of notation to serve a wide range of research and therapeutic endeavors.[31] Reflecting on the possible usefulness of discourse analysis methods for transcribing oral history interviews, Michael Agar wrote, "Discourse analysis is a powerful analytic tool for the transcribed interview, as useful to oral historians and ethnographers as it is to any other group with an interest in texts."[32] The transcription methods used in discourse analysis include various symbols and coding systems to represent inflection, intonation, pauses, and other aspects of communication not represented by typing out spoken words alone. Oral historian Dennis Tedlock developed a simpler system of notation to convey more of the nonlexical, nonsyntactical aspects of speech, more of what he considered the poetical qualities of oral history. Tedlock's system used ordinary typographical features such as boldface fonts, capitalization, indentation, and line spacing to represent variations in volume, rhythm, and other aspects of speech.[33] Reviewing Tedlock's work, Tonkin noted that "even this visually suggestive transposition does not of itself render pronunciation features, such as the 'accent' which in Britain is such a socially significant part of speech performance."[34]

Tedlock and Agar may be right that using specialized orthographic systems would be useful to oral historians. But many oral historians have been wary of these systems. Portelli demonstrated the effect of typographic style on the meaning of a transcribed passage. Centered on the page, each line with an initial capital, his sample text "hesitates between historical statement, epic poem, and monument; the way readers understand it depends to a large extent on the historian's decision to transcribe it, respectively, as linear prose, verse, or epigraph."[35] The complexities and dangers of special transcription lead many oral historians to espouse a view expressed by Francis Good. "In the end," wrote Good, "those wishing to move over the border into disciplines involving such elements as conversational analysis would be wise to go back to the sound record. It is simply unrealistic to believe it is possible to capture much of the important information conveyed in speech mannerisms that is missing in conventional print transcripts."[36] Specialized orthographic systems are tools for research and analysis, not primary documents, mostly because they remove the transcription to a rarified realm accessible only to a very small number of specially trained researchers, among whom number few oral historians or interviewees. It would, in other words, do the opposite of what many oral historians intend to do, which is to make of oral history an account that belongs to the people, to the tellers and their peers, an account as accessible and meaningful to them as to scholars piecing together wider contexts.[37]

Another problem presented by transcription is that in some cultures—especially but not exclusively in literate and bureaucratic ones—the creation of a printed document can convey an authority upon a narrative that it does not possess in spoken form. In a passage often quoted by proponents of oral history transcription, Ong wrote, "Nothing is more evanescent than sound, which has its being only while it is in process of perishing. *Verba Volant, scripta manent.* If sound is metamorphosed or reduced to spatial equivalents by writing, the resulting product has, if not eternal duration, at least a repose which suggests imperishableness."[38] As Portelli put it, "Especially after being transcribed—thus acquiring the supposed objectivity of 'documents'—words can be detached from their context and used independently of the original intention."[39] Ong's comments about the permanence of writing overlook the importance of audio and video recording, of course, which can offer an equal illusion of imperishability to sound and sight. There is no doubt, however, that the oral history interview, metamorphosed into a written transcript, a printed text, bound, deposited in a library or archive, and cataloged, acquires an aura of imperishable authority that the extemporaneous interview event did not have.

One way of understanding the difference in significance between the spoken and printed words of an interview is viewing it as a matter not only of how the transcript is written, but also of how it is read. As Olson put it, "Conceptual implications arise from the *ways of reading*, for it is the art of reading which allows a text to be taken as a model for verbal form, that is, for 'what is said.' These models of what is said, whether as sounds, words or sentences, are always incomplete, giving rise to problems of interpretation."[40] It is important to remember, then, that transcripts are created for many kinds of readers. Oral historians, interviewees and their families and community members, and scholars from many academic disciplines, all differ in their interpretive sophistication and critical experience, their attitudes toward printed texts, and their ability and willingness, Olson argued, "to infer those aspects of meaning which are not represented graphically at all" in those texts.[41] Generalizing the implications of these differences is hazardous at best, and the hazards give rise to continuing debate about what oral history is and what form it should take.

Another of the important aspects of a written text is its authorship. As Michel Foucault pointed out, for Western literate culture, attribution of authorship is crucial to how texts are read; authorship imposes a "principle of thrift in the proliferation of meaning."[42] If transcription conveys permanence and authority upon an oral history memoir, the question of authorship acquires even greater importance. Whose name goes on the title page of an oral history transcript? Whose name is the main heading for the transcript in a library catalog? Kathryn Marie Dudley wrote, "The production of oral testimony is always a collaborative, dialogic, jointly orchestrated affair. Out of this social interaction emerges a document of which it can rightly be said that the author function is up for grabs. . . . What gives the author function its critical edge in oral history and ethnography is the fact that no one 'authors' the texts we produce, yet the truth conditions of our discourse require that *someone* step forward to claim that authorship, with all the legal, political and moral ramifications it entails."[43] If the interview is most productively understood as a dialogic event, formed by the narrative strategies of both the interviewer and the interviewee, then any archived representation of that event must somehow grant equal authorship to those on all sides of the microphone. A hardbound transcript, with author and title lettered on the spine and a set of entries in a library catalog, grants immutable stature to the version of the text between the covers and to the authorship attribution required for conventional archival handling.

The question is, therefore, how different is this acquired immutability—if not authority—for the transcriptions compared to the audio or video recordings? Hayden White wrote, summarizing Foucault, "Any given mode of discourse is identifiable, then, not by what it permits consciousness to *say* about the world, but by what it prohibits it from saying, the area of experience that the linguistic act itself cuts off from representation in language."[44] Is it possible that the immensely fuller record of the interview afforded by audio or video media, which capture so much more of the communicative gestures of body and voice that the transcript omits, preserves more of what Foucault claims the linguistic act represses? It might be argued that the linguistic act alone—the words alone, spoken or written—has repressive power that can be loosened to some extent by preservation of more of the performance features of that linguistic act through audio and visual media. If so, the transcript is not adequate. But the preference for it will persist, certainly as long as historical inquiry and the universe of scholarship exists primarily in print. There is no sign that this will soon change. Scholars may claim that the worlds of thought and culture themselves are radically changed by the ubiquity of audio and visual media; the cases for these claims are still made and critiqued in writing.

Explorers, missionaries, anthropologists, ethnographers, and folklorists have long been engaged in the documenting, preserving, and understanding of oral traditions and cultures of people whose most important narratives are not written. In recent decades, oral historians have been involved in these activities as well, and there have been many discussions about the appropriateness of oral history techniques—including transcription—for those tasks. Consideration of the survival of meaning in oral traditions—storytelling, ritual, narrative performances—when they are committed to written texts also informs the debate about the nature and validity of any transcription of speech, including that of the highly literate.

As Tonkin stated, "Features of delivery—voice quality, chanting or singing, accompanying music or dancing, the type of occasion on which a performance occurs and the place, the status of the performer and the nature of the audience itself—all these can be criterial features of an oral genre, as they prepare the audience to respond in certain ways. The oral conditions of performance mean too that oral genres are actively 'dialogic': they are social activities in real time."[45] Tonkin's work examines oral narratives and demonstrates how they blur distinctions between performance, ritual, art, history, and literature. They are oral, and they may recount a people's notion about the past, but the occasion of their telling is a complex matter, crucial to their meaning. These stories are bound to be misconstrued if they are not somehow transmitted inseparably with the facts of that occasion. William Schneider put the matter this way:

> Years ago, Alan Dundes (1964) pointed out that stories contain at least three elements: text—what the story is about; texture—the way the story is told; and context—the circumstances surrounding the telling. . . . These considerations have become basic to our understanding of oral literature and the verbal arts, terms which are often used interchangeably but carry slightly different emphases. . . . Taken together, the terms point to the hallmarks of oral tradition. It is creative and personal, but it is also structured and experienced by a group of people who share a basic understanding of the way stories are told and how to comprehend their meaning.
>
> This tension between structure, creativity, and meaning is easily lost in oral recordings, which are made at one point in time and passed on to an audience of people who don't know the speaker or his or her culture. This dilemma challenges us

to ask: What have we captured on tape and what eludes us on the machine but is integral to the telling?[46]

If, as Schneider contended, much that is crucial to understanding is missing from audio (or video) recordings, certainly much more is missing from the transcription. Can a transcription convey anything reliably meaningful about what happens in an oral performance? From studies among Alaskan and Yukon cultures, Schneider and fellow researcher Phyllis Morrow deduced, "Oral tradition is negotiated, performative, and interpretive. It cannot be captured." Furthermore, they concluded:

> Oral tradition is less about tellers and texts than about relationships. . . . It is people's relationships with each other and their experiences that prompt all telling, remembering, and hearing. Because oral traditions live when they are told, preserving texts on paper . . . does nothing to maintain the relationships through which the cultural processes we term traditions are enacted. Because oral traditions are only told when they live, as the relationships among the people that tell and hear them change, so do the symbolic forms with which they make meaning. . . . There are no meanings without meaning makers. . . . What we can reconstruct or infer from their structure at best lacks warmth and subtlety and at worst gives us a false sense of accomplishment.[47]

How to transmit occasion is the challenge for scholars—oral historians, among others—who wish to preserve these oral events for present and future study. In Schneider's view, "Oral history is both the act of recording and the record that is produced."[48] Concerning storytelling performance, anthropologist Ruth Finnegan wrote, "Oral literature is by definition dependent on a performer who formulates it in words on a specific occasion."[49] This can inform our understanding of present-day oral cultures, cultures where the meaning of stories told depends upon the familial or tribal relationships of tellers and listeners and the occasions of their telling. A story meant for ritual recounting, a performance by an authorized person in a traditional context, becomes a different thing when recorded by an outsider and even stranger a thing when it is transcribed and deposited in an archive. Oral historians must ask, then, what the transcript means to the story-teller and to readers removed in time and location from the telling. Can a scholar retrieve from it anything useful for an understanding of the people from whom it was taken?

Many have grappled with the problem of understanding the role of literacy in predominantly oral cultures. Even at the outset of such considerations, defining literacy is problematic. "On the most simple level," wrote Isabel Hofmeyr, "reading and writing . . . do not automatically go together and each can be disaggregated into a range of subsidiary skills and activities."[50] All varieties of literacy influence in various ways an interviewee's way of speaking and attitude toward the occasion and toward the transcript, the written record of that speaking. Echoing the opinion of Ruth Finnegan, Hofmeyr noted that "universal claims about the cognitive consequences of writing . . . rarely hold true for a variety of contexts. . . . Instead, . . . one should be as specific as possible by spelling out the effects of literacy on orality in particular situations."[51] Deborah Tannen argued for acknowledgment that "orality and literacy are not mutually exclusive. Rather, they are complex and intertwined dimensions, the understanding of which enriches and enables our understanding of language." Tannen based her view in part on a "close analysis of tape-recorded, transcribed casual conversations" among New York Jewish speakers, a group her study found to be both highly oral and highly literate.[52] Greg Sarris, reflecting on his experiences with American Indian storytellers, wrote, "In oral discourse the context of orality covers the personal territory of those involved in the exchange, and because the territory is so wide . . . no single party has access to the whole of the exchange. One party may write a story, but one party's story is no more the whole story than a cup of water is the river."[53] The context, the audience, and the occasion are everything in traditional oral recitations. In the role of archive creator, the oral historian faces the challenge to preserve the sources in their most original form and to place these on public deposit. The role of transcription, and often of translation, is important if the world beyond narrow borders is to know something of what has been gathered, but the possibilities of misinterpretation are many when the performance is committed to the printed page.

Another of the challenges of transcribing is how—or whether—to render speakers' dialect, idiolect, or both on the printed page. In a 1937 note to interviewers in the Federal Writers' Project, Sterling A. Brown, the project's editor for Negro affairs, instructed, "Simplicity in recording the dialect is to be desired in order to hold the interest and attention of the readers. It seems to me that readers are repelled by pages sprinkled with misspellings, commas and apostrophes. . . . Truth to idiom is more important, I believe, than truth to pronunciation. . . . In order to make this volume of slave narratives more appealing and less difficult for the average reader, I recommend that truth to idiom be paramount, and exact truth to pronunciation secondary."[54] Brown further suggested a number of specific spellings for what he judged to be common features of the "Negro dialect," and in so doing obviously made many assumptions about who would be reading and judging the transcripts and what uses they would be put to by his own and future generations. None of his assumptions would withstand scrutiny today. As noted on the Library of Congress's Born in Slavery Web site,

> The interviewers were writers, not professionals trained in the phonetic transcription of speech. And the instructions they received were not altogether clear. . . . [Brown] urged that "words that definitely have a notably different pronunciation from the usual should be recorded as heard," evidently assuming that "the usual" was self-evident.
>
> In fact, the situation was far more problematic than the instructions from project leaders recognized. All the informants were of course black, most interviewers were white, and by the 1930s, when the interviews took place, white representations of black speech already had an ugly history of entrenched stereotype dating back at least to the early nineteenth century. What most interviewers assumed to be "the usual" patterns of their informants' speech was unavoidably influenced by preconceptions and stereotypes.[55]

In her essay on the WPA slave narrative transcriptions, Lori Ann Garner wrote, "Because of the contextual change from a speaker and audience to a printed page and silent reader, it is important to recognize the issues that those attempting to make this shift must confront. . . . In the case of the WPA narratives, the new performance arena of the printed page is a context in which dialect features convey much more than objectively transcribed speech patterns and are charged with associative values."[56] Any transcription of dialect draws attention to itself, especially in a scholarly—printed and archived—context. The normative conventions of writing are pervasive, even among people whose dialect differs markedly from those conventions. As Keith Gilyard pointed out, "People don't read solely the way they speak. Nor do they write the way they speak unless they draw only upon native oral resources." Gilyard echoed the view of many linguists, maintaining that the dialects of ethnic minorities are "linguistically equal and . . . the fact that they are not equal in society is a matter of society, not linguistics."[57] This social inequality makes transcription of dialect a political issue that cannot be ignored. It is not a simple issue, however. Garner was critical of historian C. Van Woodward, who saw uniform racial bias in the WPA slave narratives and concluded that less attempt to transcribe dialect meant less racial bias. "First," wrote Garner, "this theory mistakenly equates transcription of 'thick dialect' unequivocally with implied racial slurs, denying the multiple associative meanings dialect can adopt in an author's or transcriber's work." Garner, citing cases in which dialect was transcribed by black interviewers and served various roles in the narratives when employed by both white and black transcribers, observed, "All seem to be employing selectively techniques of literary dialect to distinguish their own voices from those of their subjects."[58] As the discipline of oral history has evolved, most transcribers have eschewed renderings of the phonetic aspects of dialect in transcripts, while leaving intact the morphological, syntactical, and lexical variations that also distinguish most dialects. The extent to which this renders the transcript unreliable as a historical document is a matter still debated.

As noted above in the discussion of traditionally or predominantly oral cultures, many kinds of spoken language live uneasily at best on the printed page. This is true in some predominantly literate cultures as well. Russian Mat, the highly obscene street language firmly suppressed in imperial and Soviet Russia, is a particularly interesting example. Since the collapse of the Communist regime, Mat has partly emerged from suppression; it is no longer exclusively the language of working-class men, and it now appears in print in literary as well as popular genres. But there are still governmental efforts to suppress it, and it remains a language charged with political and cultural tensions.[59] Oral history must certainly deal with such popular oral forms of language; one of the challenges is conveying the context of its utterance in transcripts. Even interviewees who speak a "standard" variety of language, one that closely resembles standard written language, may utter obscenities in an interview but do so by mouthing the words soundlessly or accompanying them with gesture and expression that pull the punch in ways lost in the transcription. The recent brouhaha among H-Net discussion list editors over a conference announcement that included an obscenity further illustrates the great difficulty—not to say impossibility—of contextualizing some kinds of language in scholarly texts. In spite of a great deal of learned and reasoned writing by both those who were offended and those who were not, the offending gerund continued to appear peculiar and off register in the forum's postings and discussion logs.[60] A squeamishness about committing obscenity to written text forces us to face the incongruities of transferring the oral history interview from a spoken to a written genre. It is an expansion of the point made by Gilyard, cited above, that linguistically equal dialects are not socially or politically equal. The inequality is reflected in the unease that characterizes some forms of spoken language appearing in print.

Critical theorist Mikhail Bakhtin saw it as a matter of style: "Any style is inseparably related to the utterance and to typical forms of utterances, that is, speech genres."[61] Although Bakhtin's point of departure was the critical understanding of literary texts, his views are not irrelevant to the understanding of other narrative texts, including transcripts. As Sherna Gluck and Daphne Patai pointed out, "Contemporary literary theory—challenging the older historian's tendency to see oral history as a transparent representation of experience—made us aware that the typical product of an interview is a text, not a reproduction of reality, and that models of textual analysis were therefore needed."[62] Thus are Bakhtin's further observations relevant:

"Where there is style there is genre. The transfer of style from one genre to another not only alters the way a style sounds, under conditions of a genre unnatural to it, but also violates or renews the given genre."[63] There may indeed be a potential for renewal of the transcript genre—even, perhaps, for composed, literary genres—in each instance of transcribing speech that does not usually appear in print. It is perhaps this potential that continues to inspire oral historians to pursue their craft and create works of scholarship and performance based on their recordings and transcriptions. It is what Portelli termed the "creative complexity of oral narrative."[64]

Oral historians have been increasingly concerned with empowerment, especially of minorities and of those whose voices have not been heard or considered in mainstream scholarship. The transcript and its processing and uses are part of this concern. As Eric Peterson and Kristin Langellier stated, "Transcribing is a decontextualizing (from performance) and textualizing (to print) movement that locates cultural conventions and social structures of the personal and of narrative. Transcription is not simply a problem of representation, of choosing the 'best' technique among multiple models. Rather, transcription constitutes text and context in ways that are not just partial but political, implicating narrator, interviewee, and researcher(s) alike within a system of power relations."[65] Gluck and Patai, in their book about gender issues in oral history practice, made the point that "a story or statement that, in its oral form, is 'by' the speaker very often reaches the public in the form of a text 'by' the scholar, whether as a life history or as excerpts used by a scholar to illustrate a line of argument."[66] Many feel that this transfer of genre and authorship constitutes a betrayal of the democratizing and empowering potential of oral history, and the edited transcript is implicated in the process. As Staughton Lynd put the matter in 1993, "Transcription of the interview for use in the historian's written presentations to an academic audience is not the only purpose of an interview, and perhaps not the most important." Some years earlier, Lynd and co-author Alice Lynd had written in the preface to *Rank and File: Personal Histories by Working-Class Organizers*, "The purpose of the interviews . . . was emphatically not to provide raw material for conventional academic history by ourselves or anyone else. Instead, the idea was to get beyond a situation in which one group of people (workers) experience history and another group of people (professional historians) interprets the experiences for them." The Lynds intended the occasions of recounting—community forums, workshops, as well as interviews—to be opportunities in which "young people in the community could receive an oral tradition."[67] And yet recordings of the Lynds' oral history occasions—and transcripts as guides to the content of those recordings—surely have great value for succeeding generations of activists as well as historians. This does not run counter to the Lynds' activist motivation to generate occasions for oral recounting; it would seem rather to support it and to contribute to the longevity of their work.

Accessibility of the products of oral history interviews is also a matter of concern, a matter related to the issues of empowerment. In its statement of principles and standards for oral historians, the Oral History Association makes clear the importance of accessibility: "In recognition of the importance of oral history to an understanding of the past and of the cost and effort involved, interviewers and interviewees should mutually strive to record candid information of lasting value and to make that information accessible. . . . Interviewers should make every effort to make the interviews accessible to the communities."[68] But many questions have been raised on this point: Accessible in what form, and to whom, and on what terms, and in whose judgment? As Portelli wrote, "On the one hand, museums and archives are not always accessible and friendly to nonprofessional users; on the other, what do we do with the precious informant who does not know how to read the transcript or does not own a cassette player or VCR to play back the tapes?"[69] Decisions about the form, preservation, and availability of the transcript have far-reaching implications for what oral history is or should be. Printed text is accessible—to the literate—and relatively unmediated, but arrangements for preservation and access usually interpose barriers that, to some memoirists and their communities, can be formidable if not insurmountable. An oral history transcript handled as an archival manuscript, for example, available for reading only on formal request, is in no practical sense accessible to many of the people whose stories it is oral history's unique mission to collect. Access and archival practice are considered at length elsewhere in this volume; the point here is that those matters intersect with issues concerning the authenticity and appropriateness of transcripts.

Oral history transcripts always require editing of some sort, and there are many questions to consider regarding editorial practice for these documents. Important among these issues are, first, the right of the interviewee to review and edit the transcript and, second, oral historians' practices in preparing transcripts for preservation and access.

Oral historians remain divided on the question of whether interviewees should have the opportunity to review transcripts of their interviews. Some have argued that the transcript gains authenticity when the interviewee has had a chance to correct, amplify, even censor the written account of what he or she said. Writing for the *Oral History Review* in 2004, Rebecca Jones stated, "It is only at the time of the review, when the narrator sees a manuscript that might be published, that he or she considers the story as a public text. This encourages them to reflect on the story they have told and modify, add, or subtract information."[70] Others have argued that only the unedited, verbatim transcript is the true account. In this view, the value of the interview is its spontaneity, the opportunity it provides to catch the unguarded and uncensored comment, even in spite of the interviewee's intentions. This view is hard to defend, however, since as Thomas Charlton has pointed out, *The very act of transcribing . . . is a major editorial step*" (emphasis in original).[71] The current trend, sensitive to matters of empowerment, seems to be in favor of allowing interviewees to possess their texts, to review and edit them as they wish. This does not solve the problem of fairly representing in editable text the words of interviewees who do not feel at ease with reading and editing, who may not even recognize their speech in texts rendered in standard spelling and typographical conventions. According to Portelli, "The conventions of grammar, punctuation, and typographic style, unavoidable in the rendering of spoken narrative into printed text, impose an arbitrary and alien rhythm upon that narrative."[72] Nor is this discomfort with the transcript limited to the less literate. "Strange, isn't it, how less-than-literate a writer is when he only talks," lamented an interviewee in a letter that accompanied his heavily edited transcript, sent back to the oral history office—the Baylor University Institute for Oral History—for final processing. The institute's policy in preparing transcripts for the archives is to incorporate interviewees' editorial changes.[73] In this case, the changes will result in a document that is much more a written autobiographical memoir than a transcript of an interview, a nearly complete shift of genre. In the institute's view, it is interviewees' prerogative to do this. However, if interviewees in no way restrict access to the recordings of their interviews, a note in the front matter of the edited and deposited transcripts may inform readers that the transcript differs significantly from those recordings.

Many oral historians continue to make the case that transcribing itself, and certainly all editing, constitutes creation of a new text that cannot be viewed as merely a replica of the oral interview. Even the application of punctuation to the verbatim transcript can effect a powerful transformation—not to say deformation—of the original spoken narrative. "The function of most punctuation," wrote Louis Menand, "is to help organize the relationships among the parts of a sentence. Its role is semantic: to add precision and complexity to meaning."[74] Oral history transcribers and editors punctuating transcripts are thus adding precision and complexity and thereby creating meanings that are not those of the speaker. As Anthony Pym put it, "Writing may do far more than fail to represent nonwriting."[75] That the new text is not a replica of the oral interview does not necessarily invalidate it. Many have felt that the new text is more authentic as a record of the interviewee's intended meanings, if not of the words she or he spoke. Edward Ives wrote, "If what you do is to transcribe the interview and then send the transcription to the informant for correction or amplification, and if the informant does in fact make alterations—deleting passages, adding fuller explanations, correcting sentence structure and the like—then the resultant manuscript becomes the primary document, the tape and transcript merely rough drafts. In this situation, if you want to find out what the informant 'said' about something, you would not go to the tape but to the corrected transcript."[76] This is problematic because of the dialogic nature of the oral history process. Meanings, intentions, memories all change over time, even the relatively short time between interview and review. The interview itself, questioning and prompting by the interviewer, the time for reflection and reconsideration afterward, further research in memorabilia, an innumerable variety of events and influences can make one day's account of historical memories seem inaccurate, inappropriate, in need of revision. Interpersonal power dynamics may be at work, too. As Wilmsen pointed out, "The fact that narrators have varying experience with the written word, the world of publishing, research archives, libraries, et cetera, affects what editing decisions are made, who makes them, and why." He argued, "If the power differential is viewed as large, . . . narrators may be less inclined to challenge editing decisions of interviewers/editors, or may be more timid about making editorial decisions themselves. . . . On the other hand, narrators who are highly experienced with the written word may also defer to the interviewer/editor and the 'expert' in oral history as to how the interview should proceed and what editorial decisions should be made." Privileged narrators, he explained, "may be well versed in getting a point across in written text. . . . They will thus shape their responses to the questions in the interview for this audience as well as to achieve whatever other purpose they may have in consenting to the interview." In contrast, Wilmsen wrote, "in the case of non-privileged people . . . many have limited experience with the production of written texts for broad audiences. . . . They thus could be more candid. . . . On the other hand, such narrators may be quite skilled in the use of the spoken word. They may thus seek to control the interview itself rather than rely on the editing process to refine the text."[77]

Michael Frisch argued in favor of correcting the transcribed speech of "common people or the working class" as an attempt to redress the imbalance between them and "people of position or power," whose statements are "routinely printed with correct syntax and spelling," whose news media interviews are "selectively edited so that articles or reports always contain coherent statements."[78] These views make it clear that review by the interviewee, granting the interviewee editorial prerogative, does not settle the issue of the transcript's validity as a representation of the interviewee's story.[79] Perhaps the best one can say is that all versions of the recounted story are artifacts, useful to someone who wishes to scrutinize them and the circumstances of their creation. Arguments about what is the primary text and what is not are perhaps beside the point. What is called for simply is full and careful attention to the processes and circumstances that bring an oral history into existence.

Oral historians also remain deeply divided on how to handle the "ums" and "ers," the false starts and midsentence changes of direction, the constant repetitions of "like" and "you know" with which oral speech is often filled. In another recent case, an interviewer penciled across the top of a transcript, "Please take out all the 'you-knows.' [The interviewee] would want that; he is highly educated and articulate." More than one issue is raised by this example. First, of course, is the fact that the interviewer was asserting what the interviewee would want, a judgment that may be correct and perceptive, but may not. Secondly, it raises the issue of the editorial handling of the oral speech. Some advocate extensive editing. Frisch wrote, "To transcribe each pause or false start or tic would make an otherwise clear tape absolutely unreadable on paper, inevitably suggesting to readers an inarticulateness anything but characteristic of the speaker-as-heard. On the other hand, to eliminate them all arbitrarily might risk a distortion of a different kind. . . . When one knows an interview intimately, it is possible to sense how many 'you knows' are needed in print to give the feel of a speaker's rhythm and style without distorting how their voice 'reads.'" Frisch proclaimed, "The integrity of a transcript is best protected, in documentary use, by an aggressive editorial approach that does not shrink from substantial manipulation of the text."[80]

Others feel strongly that verbatim transcribing, including the "ums" and "ers," is the only way to make a faithful, reliable account of the interview. Allen claimed,

> Because of the nature of the oral history interview and its potential value as a spontaneous expression of a person's opinions or recollections, in oral history transcribing we retain the broken-off sentences, the stops and starts, even parts of words

> uttered and checked. These pieces of conversation form a ma-
> trix which may be clear to no one at the moment, but they may
> have a particular or a cumulative value for some researcher in
> the time to come. . . . Our care in the handling of the tape and
> the transcript is the only thing that the future researcher can
> trust if he is to trust in the validity of oral history at all.[81]

As Phaswane Mpe has pointed out, "'There is often such a stress
on getting to the point . . . that the point, expressed as it sometimes is in small details, gets missed altogether."[82] In a similar
vein, Jeff Friedman wrote, "Theoreticians have noted that a
'break-down' of the narrative is often a cue for the inability of an
asymmetrical power relation between narrator and interviewer
to continue. This is often a result of interview situations which
call for an 'official' narrative given in 'official language' which
suppresses a narrator's actual subject position. Once that stretch
between subject positions is too much to sustain, the narrative
breaks down into fragments and crutch words." Eliminating the
fragments and crutch words, Friedman contended, removes
crucial evidence of interpersonal power dynamics from the
transcript.[83] Thus the question again can be seen as a matter of
democratization—empowerment, in effect; editors must always
ask themselves whose ends they are serving by their editorial
decisions, whose version of the story they are crafting and preserving. Portelli summarized the matter this way: "There is no
all-purpose transcript. . . . The same applies to editing: Is it intended to reproduce as carefully as possible the actual sounds of
the spoken word or to make the spoken word accessible to readers through the written medium?"[84] Wilmsen concluded that
"transcribing and editing are integral parts of the interview
process and the same social forces which shape meaning in the
interview come to bear on the editing process."[85]

Most would agree, perhaps, that editing requires the utmost
sensitivity; the uses of the interview, the diverse interests of the
present and future audiences for it, cannot be foreseen, and as
few assumptions as possible should be made about how to serve
those interests. There may be few today who share Allen's optimism: "The comforting thing about editing a transcript is that
according to standard grammatical rules there does exist a logi-

cal and correct way to punctuate anything."[86] In 1971, Raphael Samuel called for transcription standards that are little closer to realization today than then when he wrote, "It would be helpful if historians could be dissuaded from transcribing speech according to the conventions and constrictions of written prose, if they could make some attempt to convey the cadences of speech as well as its content, even if they do not aim to be phonetically exact. There is no reason why sentences should make an orderly progression from beginning to end, with verbs and adjectives and nouns each in their grammatically allotted place."[87]

Many oral historians share with enthusiasm the view expressed by Linda Shopes and Bret Enyon, among others, concerning the potential of electronic media and the Internet "for restoring orality to oral history."[88] These advocates contend that the advantages of electronic publication extend to the transcript as well as to the audio recording. As Shopes put it on a Web site for teachers, "Electronic technologies are democratizing access to extant oral history collections by on-line publication of both actual interview recordings and written transcripts of them." Shopes continued, "Web publication of interviews has numerous advantages beyond mere access. Electronic search engines enable users to identify material relevant to their own interests easily and quickly, without listening to hours of tape or plowing through pages of transcript. Hypertext linkages of excerpted or footnoted interviews to full transcripts allow a reader to more fully contextualize a given quote or idea; to assess how carefully an author has retained the integrity of a narrator's voice in the material quoted; and to more fully evaluate an author's interpretive gloss on a narrator's account."[89] Furthermore, as Mary Larson pointed out, the capacity of the Web to bring together in a single point of access information in many media and from many physical sources can "give a researcher a much more solid background, . . . particularly important in cross-cultural settings where chroniclers are concerned that their words or images will be misinterpreted by people who know nothing about their community."[90]

Not all oral historians agree that hypertext Web forms contribute to the understanding of transcripts, however. The concerns of those who disagree are similar to concerns described earlier with regard to the significance of differences between oral and written genres. These theorists contend that as narrative is linear, hypertext markup of a transcript cannot accurately convey the process by which the narrative developed and its meanings were conveyed.[91] Jay David Bolter, however, cautioned against oversimplification in analyzing hypertext: "It is often said that a printed text is linear, whereas a hypertext is nonlinear, but this is not quite accurate. Our experience of reading takes place in time, and in that sense any particular instantiation of a hypertext, like any particular reading of a printed work, is linear. Hypertexts are not non linear, but rather multilinear." He goes on to point out that it is possible to make print media multilinear—newspapers, magazines, and dictionaries are examples—and to make hypertext linear, with the links serving merely to move the reader from the end of one section to the beginning of the next.[92] Indeed, even the simple index or table of contents appended to a transcript makes it possible to read—and hence interpret, wisely or not—in an order other than that in which the speech it records occurred. Transcribing is an editorial act and a transformation of genre; in some ways, use of a non-print medium is no more radical a transformation than the initial transcription. In any case, there is danger of both overestimating and oversimplifying the implications for meaning when a narrative is transported to different media.

Other writers have expressed concerns about the distracting and superficial qualities of electronic media. Advice to Web-page builders always emphasizes the importance of fast downloads, attention-grabbing design, and condensation of essential content to fit on a single screen. As Paul Thompson observed, "The fascination is in flicking from one sort of information to another, rather than in exploring anything in depth. . . . Hence, while multimedia can store life stories, it is designed for a form of use which is fundamentally inimical to any sustained narrative or authorial argument. In other words, it depends on what its users make of it."[93] But Thompson also recognized the great potential for preserving precisely those crucially meaningful aspects of oral histories that the written transcript jettisons and that audio and video recording can help preserve. He wrote, "In principle it would be possible to organize an archive so that you could read a transcript, and then at will switch over and hear the sound of the same passage, and see the expressions of the speaker: which would represent an enormous advance in the accuracy and potential interpretative insights of researchers using interviews."[94]

Democratization of access is another advantage claimed for Web versions of transcripts. The claim is valid for many researchers, readers, and communities, but it is not universally so. The so-called digital divide still exists; many people still do not have access to computers or networks, especially in rural and sparsely populated regions. For these people, the issue of accessibility—so-called repatriation—of the oral history is still unresolved.

Including transcription in oral history processing is expensive; in fact, the cost of transcription is perhaps chief among its practical drawbacks. That cost is chiefly labor cost. Many hours of skilled work are required to transcribe oral histories and to prepare the transcripts for access and preservation. The time required for creating and processing transcripts is always many times a multiple of the hours of interview recorded. Published estimates of how long it takes to transcribe, audit, correct, and edit an oral history interview vary from ten to twenty to over forty hours per hour of recording.[95] The higher estimates usually include time for indexing, abstracting, and preparing for archival deposit, and practices vary with respect to these final processes. In any case, transcription procedures and costs, practical matters of budget and management, bear directly upon the matter of access to the final product. On the issue of accessibility, practical and theoretical concerns converge. Again, notwithstanding these issues, transcribing continues.

The technology of transcribing has evolved with the media of audio recording, although the greatest hope—voice recognition software that can reliably, efficiently, and entirely automate the transcription process—remains unrealized. Systems now exist, however, for manual transcribing of both digital and analog audio recordings of interviews. The most convenient of the systems include headphones and foot pedals to facilitate close listening and replaying of short segments. Word processing software is obviously a great boon to easy and efficient production of transcripts, although the usual caveats apply: reliance on the autocorrection functions of such programs as Microsoft Word can produce highly undesirable results, especially when dealing with the idiosyncrasies of spoken language.

Many have recognized the value of the interviewer doing the transcribing. It is likely that this is relatively rare, however, at least in larger oral history organizations. Some interviewers do provide word lists or other background materials to help transcribers with names and terms peculiar to the interview. Editorial policies and practices vary concerning what becomes of the verbatim transcript before it is turned over to the archives or the public; many of the issues involved have been discussed at length above. But whatever editing is done, the beginning point is the verbatim transcript in which every word is committed to the page. The next step is usually a so-called audit check, best done by someone other than the transcriber. The audit checker listens to the recording while reading the verbatim transcript and notes any discrepancies between what was transcribed and what was spoken. Once any transcribing errors have been corrected, the editing process continues with corrections to spelling and punctuation and verification of proper names, unfamiliar terms, and such. Again, policies vary with respect to the extent of editorial changes allowable at this stage. It is best to adopt a set of reference guides for editors' use, including a style manual and dictionaries for general and specialized or regional vocabularies. Some oral history organizations have developed their own style guides that adapt standard ones to the specialized demands of oral history. The important thing in any case is to make editorial policies explicit and to apply them consistently.

Once the transcript has been created, audit-checked, and edited—usually very lightly—it is given sometimes to the interviewer to review, and almost always to the interviewee. Interviewees are usually invited to make whatever corrections, additions, clarifications, or other emendations they wish to the transcript; it is not uncommon, however, to send a cover letter urging the interviewee to accept the unpolished quality of transcribed speech and to concentrate instead on supplying missing names and clarifying anything poorly heard or wrongly transcribed. Instructions to interviewees usually also include a time limit, a statement that after a specified length of time the transcript will be considered complete, whether or not the interviewee's edited version has been received. Oral history organizations are usually generous in these terms and willing to extend deadlines on request. Deadlines, even flexible ones, are necessary to avoid having transcripts languish in processing limbo.

Transcripts prepared for deposit in archives or for other public uses usually include front matter of some kind that provides necessary and helpful additional information. In addition to the full names of interviewees, interviewers, the date and location of the interview, the sponsoring organization, and the copyright date—typical title page information—this front matter also often includes details about editorial policy, processing steps, legal status, names of people who worked on the volume, and a statement about the legal status of the volume. Many oral history programs also include other information to help contextualize the oral memoir. Biographical information about the participants in the interviews, a description of the project of which the interview was a part, its sources of funding, and its organizational context may be included. Statements about the relationship between the transcript and the audio or video recording can also be included. Oral history archivist Francis Good provides an example: "My transcripts bear a detailed 'Note to reader' which includes the warning that users should listen to the original sound recording, at least in part and particularly for any aspect that is critical for the reader; and I include a short attempt at explaining the principles used to interpret words from sound to print."[96]

Another common addition to oral history transcripts is an index. This may be simply an index of names and concepts in the transcript itself, or it may be a list of or include references to timed locations in the audio recordings. The latter sort of references are greatly enhanced in digital media, of course; digitization allows nearly instant linkage between transcript and audio, as well as access through the Web, on local networks, on compact disc, or through any number of other digital means.

The processing of oral history interviews for the archives and public access generates a sizeable number of documents— letters, deeds of gift or statements of copyright or other legal restrictions, and perhaps most significantly, versions of the

transcripts edited in the hands of the interviewees, the so-
called autograph copies of transcripts. These are often documents that researchers would find extremely interesting,
especially if the interviewee has restricted access to the recordings or transcripts or has heavily emended the transcripts.
Their great potential interest notwithstanding, these materials
must be kept in safety and in confidence; it devolves upon oral
history organizations or their archivists to ensure the preservation of these materials as well as adherence to the stated wishes
of interview participants.

The editing of transcripts, verifying proper names and terms
and indexing concepts, creates a large body of information that
some oral history organizations have attempted to preserve as a
research aid in itself, either for internal use by editors or for end
users of completed transcripts. This body of information, com-
prising indexes, word lists, abstracts, and other such matter, can
be stored in a data management system and made accessible
through a more or less sophisticated search engine, depending
on the resources available to build and maintain the system.[97]

"The historian creates history and makes sense of it," David
Faris wrote, stating simply a view with a long pedigree in philosophy and historiography. He continued, "Events themselves,
at least insofar as they can be considered historically, have meaning only as pasts of stories."[98] The transcriber and the editor, in
creating printed documents from what was itself an event of
more or less historical importance, create a new narrative; they
impose a new story line on the recounted human events. The
crucial question for oral history practice is how to represent the
genre accurately, how to capture it for present and future study.
The interview itself is a complicated social event, understood
differently by each participant. In the end, the possible scenarios
of interpretation are as varied and individual as the people who
participate. It may be that there is little value in trying to create
a comprehensive taxonomy of psychological, social, political,
and other forces and currents that shape the record—transcript
and recording—of a particular oral history interview. Analyzing
and interpreting the record insightfully simply requires the best
of a researcher—the widest knowledge, the deepest experience,

the greatest sensitivity, the most acute self-awareness. More than this, we ask that the record be accessible to the most diverse population of readers possible, that diverse wisdom be brought to bear in the analysis and interpretation, in the creation of historical meaning in diverse contexts.

The words of Raphael Samuel, first written in 1971 when oral history was a young discipline, remain relevant: "Research can never be a once-and-for-all affair, nor is there ever a single use to which evidence can be put. Historians in the future will bring fresh interests to bear upon the materials we collect; they will be asking different questions and seeking different answers."[99]

Notes

1. Kessler-Harris, introduction to *Envelopes of Sound* (1975), 2.
2. Starr, "Oral History," 8–9.
3. Norman R. Yetman, "An Introduction to the WPA Slave Narratives: Collections That Led the Way," Born in Slavery: Slave Narratives from the Federal Writers' Project, 1936–1938, American Memory Collections, Library of Congress, http://memory.loc.gov/ammem/snhtml/snintro06.html (accessed January 4, 2005).
4. "American Life Histories: Manuscripts from the Federal Writers' Project, 1936–1940," American Memory Collections, Library of Congress, http://lcweb2.loc.gov/ammem/wpaintro/wpahome.html (accessed January 4, 2005).
5. Bancroft Library, "Bancroft Collection of Western and Latin Americana," University of California at Berkeley, http://bancroft.berkeley.edu/collections/bancroft.html (accessed January 4, 2005).
6. See Conaway, "Lyman Copeland Draper."
7. Wilmsen, "For the Record," 69–70.
8. Starr, "Oral History," 7.
9. Lance, *Archive Approach*, 20.
10. K'Meyer, "Willa K. Baum," 101.
11. Ritchie, *Doing Oral History*, 2nd ed., 64.
12. See, for example, Sommer and Quinlan, *Oral History Manual*, 75; Davis, Back, and MacLean, *From Tape to Type*, 34; Deering and Pomeroy, *Transcribing without Tears*, 1; Yow, *Recording Oral History* (1994), 227; Hoopes, *Oral History*, 114; Baum, *Transcribing and Editing*, 14–15; Henige, *Oral Historiography*, 63; Ives, *Tape-Recorded Interview* (1980), 88; and Lance, *Archive Approach*, 20.
13. Henige, *Oral Historiography*, 63.
14. Tedlock, "Learning to Listen," 122–23.
15. Henige, *Oral Historiography*, 63.
16. Sitton, Mehaffy, and Davis, *Oral History*, 81, 18.

17. Millie Rahn, "Deed of Gift Issues," posting to H-Net: Humanities and Social Sciences Online, H-Oralhist Discussion Network, October 28, 2004, http://www.h-net.org (accessed January 4, 2005).

18. Library of Congress, American Memory Collections, "Voices from the Days of Slavery: Former Slaves Tell Their Stories," About This Collection, http://memory.loc.gov/ammem/collections/voices/vfsabout.html (accessed January 4, 2005).

19. Lochead, "Oral History in Canada," 5.

20. Canadian Oral History Association, "What Is Oral History," http://oral-history.ncf.ca/index.html (accessed January 4, 2005).

21. British Library, "British Library Sound Archive," http://www.bl.uk/collections/sound-archive/cat.html (accessed January 4, 2005).

22. Allen, "Editorial Ego," 36.

23. Dunaway, "Transcription," 115–16.

24. Portelli, *Death of Luigi Trastulli*, 76. Similarly, Michael Frisch wrote that "speech that sounds articulate and coherent to the ear tends to read, when too-literally transcribed in print, like inarticulate stage mumbling; such transcription becomes an obstacle to hearing what the person in the interview is trying to say." Frisch, *Shared Authority*, 45. Likewise, Paul Thompson noted, "We have already had to learn how different an interview is on audio tape from a typed transcript with words only. The typed form can never convey more than a hint of the tones, accents and emotions in the spoken word, and the irregular pauses of speech necessarily disappear behind the logical sequence of grammatical punctuation." Thompson, "Sharing and Reshaping," 178. Gould Colman put the matter this way: "Even with the most skilled and conscientious transcribers, part of the interview will be lost in transcription, the extent of the loss being related to the speaker's use of inflection and other untranscribable elements of language." Colman, "More Systematic Procedures," 82.

25. Olson, *World on Paper*, 260–61.

26. Pym, review, 134.

27. Dunaway, "Transcription," 116.

28. Ong, *Orality and Literacy*, 100.

29. Tonkin, *Narrating Our Pasts*, 54, 75.

30. See Reingold, "Critic Looks at Oral History," 223–24.

31. For a comprehensive review of these notational techniques, see Edwards and Lampert, *Talking Data*. A basic reference in the field of discourse analysis is Schiffrin, Tannen, and Hamilton, *Handbook of Discourse Analysis*.

32. Agar, "Transcript Handling," 219.

33. Tedlock, "Learning to Listen."

34. Tonkin, *Narrating Our Pasts*, 75.

35. Portelli, "Oral History As Genre," 40.

36. Good, "Voice, Ear and Text," 104.

37. See Oral History Association, *Evaluation Guidelines*, which explicitly promotes making oral history accessible.

38. Ong, "Grammar Today," 402.

39. Portelli, *Death of Luigi Trastulli*, 260.

40. Olson, *World on Paper*, 18–19.

41. Ibid., 272.

42. Foucault, "What Is an Author?" 159.

43. Dudley, "In the Archive," 165.

44. White, "Foucault Decoded," 32.

45. Tonkin, *Narrating Our Pasts*, 51–52.

46. Schneider, "Lessons from Alaska Natives," 186. Schneider refers to Dundes, "Texture, Text, and Context."

47. Morrow and Schneider, *When Our Words Return*, 224–25.

48. Schneider, *So They Understand*, 62.

49. Finnegan, *Oral Literature in Africa*, 2.

50. Hofmeyr, "Jonah," 640.

51. Ibid., 653.

52. Tannen, "Commingling of Orality and Literacy," 42.

53. Sarris, "Mabel McKay's Stories," 176.

54. Sterling A. Brown, "Notes by an Editor on Dialect Usage in Accounts by Interviews with Ex-slaves," Federal Writers' Project, 1936–1938, Work Projects Administration for the District of Columbia, *Slave Narratives: A Folk History of Slavery in the United States from Interviews with Former Slaves* (Washington, DC, 1941), xxviii, in Library of Congress, "Born in Slavery: Slave Narratives from the Federal Writers' Project, 1936–1938," American Memory Collections, http://memory.loc.gov/cgi-bin/ampage?collId=mesn&fileName=001/mesn001.db&recNum=26 (accessed February 9, 2005).

55. Library of Congress, "A Note on the Language of the Narratives," "Born in Slavery: Slave Narratives from the Federal Writers' Project, 1936–1938," American Memory Collections, http://memory.loc.gov/ammem/snhtml/snlang.html (accessed February 9, 2005).

56. Garner, "Representations of Speech," 216.

57. Gilyard, *Let's Flip the Script*, 70.

58. Garner, "Representations of Speech," 226, 228.

59. See Smith, S. A., "Social Meanings"; Erofeyev, "Dirty Words."

60. See the call for papers for "Performing Excess," special issue of *Women and Performance*, submitted to H-Announce on July 2, 2004, announcement ID no. 139498, http://www.h-net.msu.edu/announce/show.cgi?ID=139498 (accessed February 15, 2005). Discussion of the language of the announcement occurred on HNET-STAFF, the private, internal policy discussion list for H-Net editors and administrators.

61. Bakhtin, *Speech Genres*, 63.

62. Gluck and Patai, introduction to *Women's Words*, 3.

63. Bakhtin, *Speech Genres*, 66.

64. Portelli, "Oral History as Genre," 40.

65. Peterson and Langellier, "Personal Narrative Methodology," 144.

66. Gluck and Patai, introduction to *Women's Words*, 2.

67. Lynd, "Oral History from Below," 3.

68. Oral History Association, *Evaluation Guidelines*, 5–6.

69. Portelli, *Battle of Valle Giulia*, 68.

70. Jones, *"Blended Voices,"* 35.

71. Charlton, *Oral History for Texans,* 2nd ed., 51.

72. Portelli, *Death of Luigi Trastulli,* 47–48. Others who have made this point include Raphael Samuel, who wrote in 1971: "The imposition of grammatical forms, when it is attempted, creates its own rhythms and cadences, and they have little in common with those of the human tongue. People do not usually speak in paragraphs, and what they have to say does not usually follow an ordered sequence of comma, semi-colon, and full stop; yet very often this is the way in which their speech is reproduced." Samuel, "Perils of the Transcript" (1971): 19.

73. There are a few exceptions to this policy. Spelling and punctuation changes are not incorporated if they are inconsistent with the institute's adopted guides: the latest edition of the *Chicago Manual of Style,* an in-house style guide covering special and frequently encountered cases, and the most recent edition of *Merriam-Webster's Collegiate Dictionary.*

74. Menand, "Bad Comma."

75. Pym, review, 134.

76. Ives, *Tape-Recorded Interview* (1980), 87–88.

77. Wilmsen, "For the Record," 76.

78. Frisch, *Shared Authority,* 86.

79. Gluck and Patai, introduction to *Women's Words,* 2, expressed doubt that giving interviewees one single chance to review their transcripts makes them "true partners in the process."

80. Frisch, *Shared Authority,* 83, 45.

81. Allen, "Editorial Ego," 41.

82. Mpe, "Orality and Literacy," 83.

83. Jeff Friedman, "Re: Ums uhs ers etc. in Transcript," posting to H-Net: Humanities and Social Sciences Online, H-Oralhist Discussion Network, November 10, 2004, http://h-net.org (accessed November 18, 2004). Friedman refers readers to Rosenwald and Ochberg, *Storied Lives,* for more information.

84. Portelli, *Battle of Valle Giulia,* 15.

85. Wilmsen, "For the Record," 69.

86. Allen, "Editorial Ego," 45.

87. Samuel, "Perils of the Transcript" (1971): 21.

88. Linda Shopes, History Matters: Making Sense of Evidence, "Making Sense of Oral History," George Mason University, http://historymatters.gmu.edu/mse/oral/online.html (accessed December 3, 2004). See also Enyon, "New Century," 17.

89. Shopes, Oral History Online (see note 90).

90. Larson, "Keeping Our Words."

91. See, for example, the careful comparison of printed and Web text versions of oral interviews with Holocaust survivors in Schiffrin, "Linguistics and History."

92. Bolter, "Hypertext," 5.

93. Thompson, "Sharing and Reshaping," 179.

94. Ibid., 177.

95. Ives, *Tape-Recorded Interview* (1980), 88; Ritchie, *Doing Oral History* (1995), 42; Baum, *Transcribing and Editing*, 18–19.

96. Francis Good, "Editing Confusion," posting to H-Net: Humanities and Social Sciences Online, H-Oralhist Discussion Network, September 12, 2004, http://h-net.org (accessed January 5, 2005).

97. See, for example, the description of the research aids developed at the Northern Territories Archive Service in Darwin, Australia, in Francis Good, "Interview Summaries," posting to H-Net: Humanities and Social Sciences Online, H-Oralhist Discussion Network, September 16, 2004, http://h-net.org (accessed December 14, 2004).

98. Faris, "Narrative Form," 168–69.

99. Samuel, "Perils of the Transcript" (1971): 22.

III

THEORIES

8

Memory Theory: Personal and Social

Alice M. Hoffman and Howard S. Hoffman

Memory is the capacity to store experience and then to recall or retrieve it. It is obviously essential to our ability to function. There are three basic classifications of memory that are accepted by most cognitive psychologists: short-term memory, sensory memory, and long-term memory. Short-term memory is the system or systems that enable one to store and retrieve information for a short interval, for example, storing and retrieving a telephone number only for the length of time required to dial the number. Sensory memory is dependent upon visual, auditory, or tactile sensation, taste, and smell. These perceptions may find expression either in short-term or long-term memory. Furthermore, as stated by psychologist Alan Baddeley, "A person does not lose his memory in the sense of all these systems failing simultaneously; if they did, the person would be reduced to a vegetable."[1]

Historical Perspective

The investigation of memory has occupied the attention of scientists for more than a century. Some of the earliest insights were provided by Hermann Ebbinghaus. In order to establish appropriately controlled conditions for his investigations, Ebbinghaus devised the nonsense syllable, a consonant-vowel-consonant configuration that did not form a three-letter word. After constructing several thousand such syllables, Ebbinghaus made lists of varying lengths, and he measured the amount of time and the number of trials that were required before he himself could recite a given list without error. He realized that his experiments were primarily of individual significance; nevertheless, he hoped that his results would provide a set of relationships that might apply to all memory.[2]

That Ebbinghaus was successful in this endeavor is revealed by the fact that at a centennial symposium on memory at the twenty-sixth annual meeting of the Psychonomic Society, a group of memory theorists, in Boston in 1985 honored Ebbinghaus's contribution and agreed that his methodology and empirical results had provided an important guide to the proper conceptualization of memory. They noted, for example, that Ebbinghaus must be credited with the discovery of the memory trace. When previously learned material can neither be recalled nor even recognized as familiar, some trace of it must remain in the nervous system, as it can often be relearned more rapidly than new material. Ebbinghaus also found that recall is better if learning exposures are distributed in time rather than bunched together. Thus, it was Ebbinghaus who first demonstrated the superiority of spaced practice over massed practice. Ebbinghaus was also the first to demonstrate that while the loss of information from memory is most rapid at first, the rate of loss gradually declines over time and eventually levels off at some nonzero value. This almost universal effect, called Ebbinghaus's curve of forgetting, has proven to apply to most learning situations with all kinds of material.[3]

In 1932, while at Cambridge University, Frederic C. Bartlett published a landmark book titled *Remembering*. Bartlett criticized the use of nonsense syllables to study memory by noting that in most situations human subjects make innumerable associations to the material to be remembered. He reasoned that the use of nonsense syllables to try to avoid associations must necessarily neglect an important aspect of the memory process.[4] In one sequence of often-cited experiments, Bartlett presented his student subjects with a story that had been derived from an Eskimo folktale. In it, two young men went hunting for seals.

When his subjects were later asked to recall the story, they exhibited a clear tendency to shorten it, to reduce it to its gist, a structural organization that Bartlett called a "schemata." His subjects also tried to make the story fit their own experience and viewpoint. Thus "kayaks" in the story often became "boats," and "something black came out of his mouth" was frequently recalled as "foaming at the mouth." It was of special interest that once these changes had been made, they tended to remain stable whenever the story was recalled.[5]

Subsequent studies of "naturalistic memory" have corroborated Bartlett's findings. Michael Howe reported an experiment conducted by H. Kay in 1955 in which the researcher asked subjects to listen while he read two short passages. The subjects were then asked to try to write a verbatim version of what they had just heard. When they had done so, Kay read a correct version to the subjects. A week later, the subjects were asked to try to again reproduce what they had heard. This process continued for seven weeks. In each case, subjects remembered their own reproductions more accurately than the correct version, even though the correct version had been presented to them at the end of each of the seven sessions. It is noteworthy that Kay's findings may have resulted, in part, from the fact that subjects wrote out their own versions, whereas they merely listened to the correct version.[6] Howe replicated Kay's experiment with similar results. Many of Howe's subjects reported that they knew that they were reproducing their own versions, but they were unable to recall the original version. These studies point to the primacy of what is initially recalled, and it suggests that once material has been coded into memory, it may be relatively stable.[7]

In 1982, Ulric Neisser published an influential book titled *Memory Observed*, which consisted of a collection of naturalistic studies by a variety of investigators, each of whom studied one or another aspect of the memory process. In commenting on the motivations for his book, Neisser suggested that since memory is employed to define ourselves, to confirm and retain our impressions of what we have experienced, and to plan future activity, it would be important to document the study of memory as it is used in real-life situations.[8]

One of the contributions to Neisser's collection is particularly relevant to oral historians. It was an extensive study of her own memory by Marigold Linton. Each day, Linton selected two or three events and made notes about each on a separate card with its date. Once a month, she picked seventy-five pairs of cards at random from her increasingly large collection and tried to recognize the events and recall which of the pair had occurred first. When she was unable to recognize an event, the card was discarded. At the end of the first year, 1 percent of the cards had been discarded. In each of the next two years, 6 percent more of the cards were discarded. Linton drew several conclusions from this interesting investigation: (1) an event is likely to endure in memory if it is perceived as highly emotional at the time of its occurrence; (2) an event is likely to endure in memory if the subsequent course of events makes the event appear to have been a turning point of some sort; and (3) an event will endure in memory if it remains relatively unique (i.e., it has not been made indistinct by having occurred repeatedly).[9]

In 1974, one of the present authors published a paper that examined the concepts of reliability and validity as they apply to the oral history interview. For its purposes, the term *reliability* was employed to describe the degree to which an interviewee tended to tell the same story on separate occasions. The term *validity* was employed to describe the degree to which a given account could be corroborated by the other available resources that related to the event described. In short, *reliability* and *validity* were employed to describe the repeatability and accuracy of a given interviewee's memory claim. When used in this way, it was obvious that a memory claim might be reliable without being totally valid, but it could not be valid if it was not reliable.

In that paper, two interviews with steelworker John Mullen were cited. In them, Mullen described how, while he was employed by the Carnegie-Illinois Steel Company, an employers' organization tried to induce him to serve as a spy for management. In both interviews, he described the means used to recruit him and how he was to be paid for his services. One of the interviews had been conducted in 1966 as part of the Pennsylvania State University Oral History Project on the United Steel Workers of America; the other had been conducted thirty years earlier by the author Robert R. Brooks. A transcription of this earlier interview appeared in Brooks's 1940 book, *As Steel Goes.* Surprisingly, the published account in Brooks's study and the transcription of the interview conducted thirty years later are almost the same word for word. In short, the interviews were quite reliable. Their validity, however, was less than perfect. Discrepancies appeared between the interviewee's testimony and accounts of industrial espionage uncovered by the LaFollette Senate Committee to Investigate the Violation of Civil Liberties, as well as between Mullen's testimony and the statements of other respondents in the Penn State oral history project. Apparently, as suggested earlier, when tested against other evidence, an interview that had proven to be quite reliable was not totally valid.[10]

In 1990, the present authors published a book titled *Archives of Memory.* It documents a study in which we sought to combine the analytical methodologies of psychology and historiography to assess directly the reliability and validity of the kind of memory claims that most frequently are sought in the oral history interview. The plan for the study was quite straightforward: Howard Hoffman would be the subject of three sequences of interviews conducted by Alice Hoffman. In the first two sequences, each of which would occur over a period of several months, Howard was to recall everything that he could from his time as a young soldier in World War II. After basic training, he had experienced a year of combat that began at Casino in Italy and ended when his unit met the Russians at the Elbe River in Germany. He served first during this period as a mortar crewman and later, during and after the invasion of southern France, as a radio operator and forward observer. The first two sequences of oral interviews were to be of the free recall variety in that Howard was merely to describe everything he could remember from his time in the army. He was to begin on the day he entered the army and end on the day he was discharged.

The first recall sequence began forty years after the events to be recalled and produced 142 pages of written transcript. The second sequence began four years later and produced 146 pages of transcript. Because the methodology of the two interviews was virtually identical and because Howard avoided reading about or rehearsing his war memories during the intervening years, a comparison of the two transcripts would indicate the extent to which the same story was told on widely separated occasions. In short, it would enable us to determine something of the reliability of Howard's memory claims.

The third sequence of interviews was conducted in the years following the assessment of reliability. One of our goals in this series was to determine the degree to which the presentation of various recognition cues might enhance memory claims. The recognition cues included having exposure to photographs taken at the time of the events, locating and meeting with soldiers with whom Howard had fought, and visiting places where he had trained and European locations where he had fought.

Finally, Howard was presented with a variety of primary historical documents that Alice had located in the National Archives Federal Records Center. Because these documents included all of the daily combat reports of the fighting unit with which Howard had fought, they provided him with an extensive and most salient set of recognition cues. In addition to enabling us to assess the degree to which recognition cues facilitated memory, the availability of the daily reports written at the site and at the time of the events themselves made it possible to assess something of the validity of those memories.

The results of our study can be briefly summarized as follows:

1. The recall documents were quite reliable, though not word for word. The two recall documents included descriptions that were essentially the same, with no major discrepancies or omissions.
2. The presentation of recognition cues neither enhanced the reported memories nor produced any important new memories. This was a surprising finding and may be characteristic of the consolidation and intense rehearsal found in archival memories rather than being applicable to long-term memory in general. It is an area where further research is needed.
3. With a few exceptions, when the events described in the recall documents coincided with those described in the

historical material, the match was very close. Moreover, when the exceptions occurred it was unclear whether it was the recall document or the historical document that was the more accurate. Considered overall, it was concluded that to the extent that the assessment of validity was possible, the recall documents exhibited a reasonably high degree of validity.

4. This configuration of results implied that there is a form of long-term memory that seems best described as archival. More specifically, it implied a class of long-term memories that fit well with Linton's definitions of retention.[11] These are memories that are readily recalled, change little, if at all, with the passage of time, and are resistant to enhancement by the presentation of recognition cues. These are the memories of which we say, "I will never forget, so long as I live."

5. Our work also provided evidence that if a memory is to achieve an archival quality, it must be sufficiently unique that it is rehearsed, either consciously or unconsciously, during the week or so that follows the experience it documents. Without this rehearsal the memory might be evoked for months or even years later when one encounters an appropriate recognition cue, but eventually the memory will dim to the point where even the most salient of recognition cues produce either nothing or, at most, a vague sense of familiarity.[12]

Some Contemporary Views

In the ten years since we completed our study, there have been a number of scientific advances in the analysis of memory. One of our purposes here is to describe some of the insights into the nature of memory derived from that research and to suggest their relevance to an understanding of the work of the oral historian. In an informative book, *The Seven Sins of Memory*, published in 2001, Daniel L. Schacter provides a useful amalgam of the recent findings by describing the various ways that memory can become distorted or otherwise fail. According to Schacter, the seven sins of memory are transience, absentmindedness, blocking, misattribution, suggestibility, bias, and persistence.[13]

Before examining these so-called sins, it is important to recognize that memory is a complex personal experience and that, as with that other complex personal experience, perception, psychologists have found it profitable to study it under conditions that reveal its limits. Historically, the study of illusions has enabled psychologists to document the parameters of the various brain systems responsible for perception. In a similar fashion, the study of memory's distortions and failures (its sins) has enabled psychologists to document the parameters of the various brain systems that enable us to remember what has been experienced. As Schacter notes, we must examine "the dark sides of memory" in order to comprehend its "blessing."[14]

Despite the research focus on limitations, it is also important to keep in mind that unless fundamentally flawed, the brain systems responsible for memory, like those responsible for perception, are extraordinarily effective. Under the vast majority of circumstances, the probability exists that the information provided by memory, like that provided by most perceptions, is trustworthy.

Studies of localized brain activity using positron emission tomography reveal that neither perception nor memory is a unitary thing. During visual perception, for example, the color, shape, and motion of an object are processed in widely separated parts of the brain. Similarly, during the act of remembering, various widely separated parts of the brain light up (become active), depending on whether the memory is for a sound, a conversation, or an image. It should come as no surprise, therefore, that various kinds of brain injury produce quite specific effects on memory as well as on perception. Nor should it come as a surprise that there is an intimate relationship between perception and memory.[15]

It will be helpful to consider that if an experience is to be remembered for any reasonable length of time it must be perceived, encoded into appropriate neural activity, and placed in the long-term storage sites where it will reside, perhaps as changes in the protein structure of appropriate brain cells. Unless modified by subsequent events or by the passage of time it-self, these changes must remain available until they are called forth during the act of remembering. As will be seen, the seven sins of memory involve interferences with the normal activity in various stages of the sequence of events that begin with perception and end with the retrieval of whatever remains in storage.

1. The Sin of Transience

To illustrate transience, Schacter describes an investigation of the way in which episodic autobiographical memory changes with the passage of time. Every month for the first six months following Thanksgiving, a new group of about a hundred students was asked to recall whatever details they could remember of their previous Thanksgiving dinner. They were also asked to indicate the vividness of each detail. As might be expected, the vividness and number of unique details of the specific dinner (such as the clothes worn and the content of conversations) was high for the one-month group, but both declined rapidly in the groups tested at two and three months. This was followed by a slower decline in the groups tested at four, five, and six months. In essence, the standard curve of forgetting, first reported by Ebbinghaus, was reported here, but rather than reflecting forgotten nonsense syllables, this forgetting curve was exhibited by memories of what is usually a significant personal event. As would be expected, memory for some aspects of the dinner declined quite slowly. Thus the memory of what was eaten and of who attended the dinner showed little decline over the six months of testing. Of course, this outcome illustrates social or semantic memory, in which general knowledge of Thanksgiving traditions, including family gatherings and turkey dinners, enabled recall.[16]

Schacter further describes memory's transience as follows:

> At relatively early points on the forgetting curve—minutes, hours, and days, sometimes more—memory preserves a relatively detailed record, allowing us to reproduce the past with reasonable if not perfect accuracy. But with the passing of time, the particulars fade and opportunities multiply for

interference—generated by later, similar experiences—to blur our recollections. We thus rely ever more on our memories of the gist of what happened, or what usually happens, and attempt to reconstruct the rest by inference and even sheer guesswork. Transience involves a gradual switch from reproductive and specific recollections to reconstructive and more general descriptions.[17]

This so-called sin of transience is no more, it would seem, than a reasonably accurate description of the normal course of episodic autobiographical memory. It should be understood, however, that episodic autobiographical memory is one of the systems produced by evolution that enable us to maximize the utility of a storage system with limited capacity. Without the property of transience, it would be necessary that every sensory input processed by our nervous system throughout our lifetime be permanently stored and readily accessed (i.e., remembered). This is an obviously impossible requirement for the brain of any living individual. As William James said, "If we remembered everything, we should on most occasions be as ill off as if we remembered nothing."[18]

If the sin of transience is merely a description of the normal course of episodic autobiographical memory, then what of the other six so-called sins? We would argue that each is the product of some modifying factor that acts at one or another point in the normal course of either the creation, storage, or retrieval of an episodic autobiographical memory.

2. The Sin of Absentmindedness

This is a sin that most busy persons commit with some frequency. It is exemplified by the failure to readily locate one's keys. As noted by Schacter, in most cases the failure to recall the location of one's keys is a failure to properly attend to, encode, and store the memory of where the keys were discarded. Schacter suggests that this kind of failure usually occurs because one is busy initiating some other task at a time when he or she should be encoding and storing the memory of the keys' location.[19]

3. The Sin of Blocking

A common experience, especially as we age, is the inability to recall the name of a person whom we might know quite well. In the retirement community where we now live, two residents once met. One said to the other, "Old friend, I've known you for twenty years but I just can't remember your name." The friend replied, "How soon do you need to know?" The Oral History Association's *Evaluation Guidelines* call attention to this problem by indicating that oral history interviewers should take care to use "skills appropriate to: the interviewee's condition (health, memory, mental alertness, ability to communicate, time schedule, etc.)."[20]

A moment's thought reveals that while a name denotes an individual, it does not usually imply any attribute of that person. As it turns out, this is a major factor in the phenomenon of blocking. Schacter describes a study in which subjects were told to study a series of photographs of faces. They were also told that they would later be shown the same pictures and be asked to recall the word that was written below each picture. One group of subjects was told that the words denoted the occupation of the person in each picture, while another group of subjects was told that the words were the surnames of the persons in the photographs. By using words that could be either a surname or an occupation, for example, Farmer, Miller, Potter, Baker, it was possible to expose both groups to the identical series of photographs. The result, known as the Baker/baker paradox, was that the recall of the words was more accurate and extensive when subjects were told that the words denoted occupations than when told that the words were surnames.[21]

We now know that the sound of a word is recorded in a different part of the brain than the meaning of the word. It has been suggested that it is easier to associate words that are descriptive of images because we can attach many additional associations, for example, what bakers do, to the image of the face than to associate a single word, Baker, that bears no intrinsic relation to the image of the face. The fact that we can often pull forth the initial part of a name (I feel that it begins with a B) might be expected if the association is only for a sound with no additional associations.[22]

4. The Sin of Misattribution

Misattribution occurs when we fail to recall properly the source of our recollection or memory. There is a story that the great physicist Richard Feynman tells. He once received a phone call from a woman he had known at Los Alamos. She tearfully informed him that Herman had died and suggested that since Feynman and Herman had been such close friends, she was sure that Feynman would want to be a pallbearer. Feynman could not at the time remember any close friend named Herman, but assuming it was a fault of his own memory, he thanked her and proceeded to attend the funeral and help carry the casket. As it turned out, not only did Feynman fail to recall ever knowing Herman, but the recognition cues provided by viewing him in his open casket were of no help. The experience was quite disconcerting to Feynman until a year or so later when the same woman called him to apologize for her mistake. As it turned out, Herman had arrived at Los Alamos shortly after Feynman had left there. She and Feynman had been very close and because she and Herman also became close friends, she incorrectly remembered that Feynman and Herman were friends.[23]

Another rather common example of misattribution is manifested when, having seen pictures of oneself as a child, we may come to think that we remember the event being photographed. If pressed, however, we can provide no accurate information about the event other than what is visible in the picture.

5. The Sin of Suggestibility

It is well known that leading questions can color our memories and under some circumstances induce false memories. Elizabeth Loftus has done a number of informative experiments on the effect upon memory of providing false or misleading information. In these experiments, subjects were shown slides of automobile accidents. Loftus then tested their ability to remember and report what they had seen by asking them to respond to a series of questions. In some of the conditions of the experiment, false information was embedded in the questions. For instance, Loftus would ask where the green car was in relation to the damaged vehicle when, in fact, the car in question had been blue. She discovered that the false information had a powerful influence on the reports, and all the more so if the false information was supplied by an authority figure.[24] On one occasion, the present authors had the opportunity to discuss Loftus's research with her. We asked if there were individuals who resisted the effects of supplying misleading or false information. She said yes, there were people who insisted upon their original perception in their recall.[25] We think that persons of this sort provide a valuable resource in our society, since they would be equipped to resist propaganda and efforts to manipulate their political allegiances. It is our feeling that interviewees who are able to resist misleading external influence upon their memory claims are likely to be especially valuable participants in the shared authority provided by an oral interview.[26]

6. The Sin of Bias

According to Schacter, "The sin of bias refers to distorting influences of our present knowledge, beliefs, and feelings on new experiences or our later memories of them."[27] Just as what we are likely to see is determined by our interests and our biases, what we remember can be influenced by our interests and biases. The Oral History Association's *Evaluation Guidelines* urge interviewers to make an assessment of the possible effects of bias, particularly the bias of the interviewers themselves.[28]

An experiment that one of the co-authors, Howard, routinely conducted in the introductory psychology courses that he taught while on the faculty at the Pennsylvania State University casts light on the effects of bias. His classes were very large (three hundred or so students). Early in the semester, the students in the right half of a given class were asked to imagine what they would feel like if they had been called from class and told that their father was going blind, that the condition was hereditary, and that if treated early enough it could be prevented. The students on the left side of the same class were asked to imagine how they would feel if the instructor told them that he had access to their physical fitness scores, and that as a fanatic on physical fitness and as an independently wealthy man, he would give five thousand dollars to the student who, in the next seven days, showed the greatest improvement in physical strength. Next, after drawing on the board two side-by-side circles connected by a short line, the instructor asked the students to write down the name of what had been drawn. The great majority of the students on the right side of the class always wrote down "eyeglasses," whereas the great majority of the students on the left side of the class always wrote down "barbells."

While the Penn State experiment provides evidence of the effects of biasing information on perception, it does not directly address the issue of the effects of bias on memory. It seems reasonable to suppose, however, that if the question of what had been drawn was postponed for a week or so, the results would have been essentially the same. In this regard, it is relevant to note that in class discussion it was always pointed out that this experiment dealt with the biases of stereotyping and bigotry. It was also pointed out that if those obviously transparent stories could affect what students thought they had seen, they should consider seriously the effects on their perceptions of a lifetime of exposure to well-organized but potentially biasing input.

7. The Sin of Persistence

Schacter notes that some memories refuse to fade, and when this occurs the memory tends to involve regret or trauma or some other negative emotion. He suggests that all emotions tend to strengthen a memory but that negative emotions can strengthen the memory to the point where it is intrusive and interferes with normal activity. He further explains, "Although intrusive recollections of trauma can be disabling, it is critically important that emotionally arousing experiences, which sometimes occur in response to life-threatening dangers, persist over time. The amygdala (a brain center that becomes active during fear) and related structures contribute to the persistence of such experiences by modulating memory formation, sometimes resulting in memories we wish we could forget."[29]

In an analysis of the recall of momentous and sometimes life-threatening events, David B. Pillemer and his co-authors utilized the narrative in Hoffman and Hoffman's *Archives of Memory* to demonstrate the tendency to describe those events in the present tense. It is as if the narrator is reliving those experiences in the telling.[30]

We would suggest here that an important contributor to the persistence of the memory of a momentous event is the tendency to think about and thereby rehearse that memory in the days, weeks, and perhaps even months and years that follow the experience. In this respect, it would appear that the sin of persistence is not fundamentally different from what we have characterized as a key feature of an archival memory. For a long-term memory to achieve an archival quality, it must be sufficiently unique that it is rehearsed either consciously or unconsciously during the week or so that follows the experience it documents. There is a difference, however. Archival memories need not necessarily document an emotion-arousing experience. The important factors are that the experience is unique and salient and that the experience is relevant to the way one defines oneself.

Schacter ended his book with a chapter titled, "The Seven Sins: Vices or Virtues?" He concluded that chapter with the following statement: "The seven sins are not merely nuisances to minimize or avoid. They also illuminate how memory draws on the past to inform the present, preserves elements of present experience for future reference, and allows us to revisit the past at will. Memory's vices are also its virtues, elements of a bridge across time which allows us to link the mind with the world."[31]

Earlier it was suggested that under the vast majority of circumstances, such as our immediate perceptions of our experiences, our memories of our experiences are necessarily reasonably accurate. Were this not so, we would be severely handicapped and our very survival would be endangered. We normally trust our perceptions of our environment as we move from place to place throughout the day. When we subsequently recall those experiences, we trust our memories of where we have been and of what we did. It seems axiomatic that we would be especially likely to trust our memories of experiences that are unique and somehow salient to our self-images. As we recall such experiences, we engage in exactly the kind of rehearsal that ultimately endows those memories with an archival quality.

There is, of course, always the possibility that at some point in the interval between perception and recall, what gets stored can be distorted by bias. It seems reasonable to hypothesize that, in the absence of some other pathology, only the specific perceptions or memories that are relevant to the biasing factor would be distorted. There is no reason to expect that the vast majority of our other memories, including our archival ones, would depart from what anyone else who had the same or similar experiences (for example, corroborating witnesses) would be likely to report.

The psychologist Eugene Winograd has observed that while memory research by psychologists has focused on memory failures and distortions, that research should not be misunderstood. Overall, he notes that recall is usually reasonably accurate. Clearly our memory would be of little use to us if this were not so. Winograd cites, for example, Michael Ross's study on remembered earnings, in which recall errors occurred only 4 percent of the time. Ninety-six percent of the time the amount recalled was corroborated by the documentary evidence. Winograd concluded, "It is important to note that Ross provides a theory of how memory changes *when* it changes."[32]

No less than most scientists, most historians, we suggest, operate under the assumption that there is a reality to be approximated and that this can be best accomplished through the judicious application of the tools of one's trade. For the scientist, one of those tools is the carefully conducted experiment on an issue of some relevance. For the oral historian, one of those tools is an interview. Interviews, therefore, provide scholars with a primary source, albeit one that offers advantages over written documents and manuscripts in that it is produced with a knowledgeable interviewer under circumstances that leave no doubt about who created the document. Nevertheless, like all other primary sources, the oral history interview is best utilized by subjecting it to the usual canons of historical scholarship.

Social Memory

In 1972, the Canadian psychologist Endel Tulving classified long-term memory into two types: episodic memory, which is the ability to remember personal events over time, and semantic memory, which is the memory for learned material, for example, recalling that Paris is the capital of France.[33]

In 1994, Ulric Neisser further refined the taxonomy of long-term memory as follows: Reconstructions of personal experience "are examples of *episodic memory*. If the remembered event seems to have played a significant part in the life of the rememberer, it becomes an example of *autobiographical memory* and may form part of a *life narrative*."[34] Narrative construction forms the basis of social memory and indeed is dependent upon it. Social memory contains elements of what Tulving called semantic memory in that it draws upon the constructs embedded in the culture of the subject to communicate meaning to others. So, for example, in describing a trip to Paris, the narrator will utilize shared information that has been learned rather than experienced and that can be assumed also to be part of his listener's mental furniture, for instance, that most people in Paris speak French.

Almost from the inception of the oral history movement, practitioners have debated one or the other of two alternative views about memory functions and their effects upon the process and goals of conducting oral interviews. One school of thought argues that personal or autobiographical memory provides information from individuals who have experience, preferably direct, of events of historical significance.

Among examples of oral projects primarily focused on efforts to record and preserve historically significant events are the interviews connected to the administrations of each U.S. president since Franklin D. Roosevelt. A more specific example would be the interview, held in the John F. Kennedy Library, with the journalist Elie Abel that records only Abel's memories of the Cuban Missile Crisis.[35]

Another school of thought argues that independent of its scholarly value as a primary source of information, the value of an interview lies in its presentation of the views of a particular actor drawn from a particular community at a set time. It therefore has merit as it stands as a text that can be subjected to literary, anthropological, or social analysis and can provide insight into cultural or social experience. As stated by the principal editors of a series of studies on memory and narrative:

Unravelling the meanings and construction of narrative has long been a preoccupation of literary scholars. The richness and power of oral sources . . . has been well acknowledged. At the same time, a renewed interest in autobiography, as a literary form . . . has focused attention on the process and representation, as well as the content, of recall. With this has come an understanding that memories are rarely "raw" but shaped in and by social and historical narrative.

Disparate disciplines thus prove to be linked by common interests and preoccupations, so that historians as well as social and behavioural scientists now are concerned with searching for narrative structures which inform the memories they seek to analyse.[36]

The Archives of Folklore and Oral History at the University of Vermont provide examples of social history.[37] An important example of this type of interview may be found in *Archives of Memory: Supporting Traumatized Communities Through Narration and Remembrance*, edited by Natale Losi, Luisa Passerini, and Silvia Salvatici. This work, not to be confused with Hoffman and Hoffman's *Archives of Memory; A Soldier Recalls WWII*, was designed to provide psychosocial support, through oral history interviews, to victims of war and violence in Kosovo. The attempt was to provide some degree of healing via the "collective dimension" of the trauma through the process of shared stories that could provide "appropriate meaning."[38]

No oral history document is likely to be simply a reflection of a purely personal memory or a social memory. It will clearly contain both, in that it will draw from the narrator both episodic, purely personal descriptions of a unique perception of past experience and will also contain information that is grounded in the social, conversational, and cultural styles of the informants' backgrounds and memorial histories. Early in the study of memory, Bartlett made this point when he described the fact that his English subjects recalling an Eskimo story described kayaks as canoes.

In 1969, at the Fourth National Colloquium of the Oral History Association, David Musto presented a summary of research findings on the reliability over time of the information that parents gave with respect to the medical and training histories of their children. Although many facets of the reports were found to be quite reliable, especially the "hard facts" (for example, reports of the baby's birth weight), certain aspects of the reports, such as those dealing with the parents' attitudes and emotions, were less reliable.[39] Moreover, in one of the studies cited by Musto, a test of the validity of these kinds of oral reports was also made. At New York University, there was a large and long-term study of child rearing, so that it was possible to compare the parents' oral reports with clinical records over time. Again, certain factual information was quite accurate; but when there was distortion, it tended to be in the direction of recommendations by child-care experts.[40]

This tendency toward conformity with acceptable norms provides a clear example of social or semantic memory, and as with personal or episodic memory, it deserves special attention by the practitioners of oral history. The concept of semantic memory, it will be recalled, includes those memories that have been derived from what has been taught about the collective experience and the social structure of the members of various groups, including the members of one's own group. Because they are reflective of what has been taught, social memories can, on certain occasions, take on the character of legends or myths.

The collection of interviews at the Pennsylvania State University Labor Archives reflects a tendency to exhibit features best described as social (or semantic) memories.[41] These interviews were collected primarily in the 1970s and 1980s. Recurrent themes appear in the interviews. These are stories that are told in several interviews about a number of individuals so that they assume the character of old myths. One is the story of the effective labor organizer who emphasized the need for collective action by telling workers that you cannot hit an antagonist with one finger extended; you will only break your finger. Instead, you must put all your fingers together and make a fist. This story was repeated and told about many different organizers in a variety of settings. Another persistent story was told by workers who described being asked to become a foreman. When asked why they refused, the standard reply was, "Well, after all, I have to look in the mirror every morning when I shave, and I wouldn't want to have to see a foreman there." Stories of the rejection of the concept of rugged individualism and of support for class solidarity run through these interviews like a persistent melody. They combat the idea of individuals who rise by their own virtue and hard work and substitute for it the concept of a community effort that enables the individual to be a part of an effective group. The garment workers had another way of putting it: "I wanted to be a person; the union made it so."

No doubt as oral historians examine interviews reflecting a variety of groups and communities, similar social memories will become evident, and while they may not be true in the sense that they represent some particular episodic moment, they nevertheless reflect some important insights into the social dynamics of the group. In her study on oral history and reliability, Barbara Shircliffe commented,

> As [Selma] Leydesdorff argues, it is important to be critical of oral testimonies about the past. However, to dismiss nostalgia as false historical consciousness denies the opportunity to utilize the unique data oral history uncovers. As Alessandro Portelli argues, "the importance of oral testimony may lie not in its adherence to fact, but rather in its departure from it, as imagination, symbolism, and desire emerge." From this perspective, the study of nostalgia . . .—a yearning for something past that is no longer recoverable—allows historians to explore how individuals invest past experience with meaning and use historical memory as a starting point for social commentary.[42]

Conclusion

For some oral history practitioners, the primary purpose of an interview is to obtain information about an event of historical significance. For these practitioners, the issues of the reliability and the validity of personal memory would seem to be critical to their endeavor. Other practitioners conceive of the interview as a tool to document an interviewee's account of his or her experiences in a given setting at a given time. As was noted above, these kinds of interviews are often treated as text that can later be adapted to literary, anthropological, or social analysis. We have suggested that interviews of the latter sort rely heavily on what has been described as semantic memory, and the issues of reliability and validity are not ordinarily of central concern. It seems apparent, however, that regardless of how a practitioner conceptualizes the purpose of an interview, that interview is very likely to call forth an interplay of both personal (i.e., episodic) and social (i.e., semantic) memories.

Notes

This chapter is based, in part, on an invited paper presented by the authors at the annual meeting of the Oral History Association, St. Louis, Missouri, 2001.

1. Baddeley, *Your Memory*, 6.
2. Ebbinghaus, *Memory*, viii.
3. See Gorfein and Hoffman, *Memory and Learning*.
4. Bartlett, *Remembering*, 8.
5. Ibid., 64–66, 83, 87–88, 200.
6. Kay, "Retaining Verbal Material," 82, quoted in Howe, *Human Memory*, 81–82.
7. Howe, *Human Memory*, 82.
8. Neisser, "Memory," 13.
9. Linton, "Transformations of Memory," 89–90.
10. Hoffman, "Reliability and Validity" (1996), 89–90.
11. Linton, "Transformations of Memory," 89–90. Summarizing the results of studies on memory retention in older subjects in her study of the effects of aging on autobiographical memory, Gillian Cohen utilizes the term "archival memory" as cited and defined by Hoffman and Hoffman in *Archives of Memory*. Cohen, "Effects of Aging," 110–11.
12. Hoffman and Hoffman, *Archives of Memory*.
13. Schacter, *Seven Sins*, 4.
14. Ibid., 11.
15. Rubin, "Autobiographical Remembering," 57–62.
16. Friedman and deWinstanley, "Subjective Properties," cited in Schacter, *Seven Sins*, 12–14.
17. Schacter, *Seven Sins*, 15–16.
18. James, *Psychology*, 300.
19. Schacter, *Seven Sins*, 47.
20. Oral History Association, *Evaluation Guidelines*, 14.
21. Schacter, *Seven Sins*, 62–63.
22. Ibid., 63.
23. Feynman, *What Do You Care*, 69–71.
24. Loftus and Palmer, "Reconstruction," 109–15.
25. Elizabeth F. Loftus, personal conversation with authors, February 1989, Waco, Texas.

26. "Shared authority" in oral history projects includes mutuality in memory retrieval. For further discussion, see Frisch, *Shared Authority*.

27. Schacter, *Seven Sins*, 138.

28. Oral History Association, *Evaluation Guidelines*, 14.

29. Schacter, *Seven Sins*, 187.

30. Pillemer, Desrochers, and Ebanks, "Remembering the Past," 145–60. For additional discussion, see Pillemer, *Momentous Events*.

31. Schacter, *Seven Sins*, 206.

32. Winograd, "Authenticity and Utility," 246–47.

33. Baddeley, *Your Memory*, 13.

34. Neisser, "Self-Narratives," 1.

35. *Oral History Index*, 1.

36. Chamberlain et al., "Introduction to the Series," xiv.

37. *Oral History Index*, 407.

38. Losi, Passerini, and Salvatici, *Archives of Memory*, 13.

39. Musto and Benison, "Accuracy," 168.

40. Ibid., 171–72.

41. Labor History Collection, Historical Collections and Labor Archives, Special Collections Library, Pennsylvania State University, University Park.

42. Leydesdorff, "Screen of Nostalgia," 115, and Portelli, *Death of Luigi Trastulli*, 50, quoted in Shircliffe, "'We Got the Best,'" 62.

9

Aging, the Life Course, and Oral History: African American Narratives of Struggle, Social Change, and Decline

Kim Lacy Rogers

Social deterioration and a loss of community cohesion are recurring themes in many narratives of American history. Since the first European settlements in the New World, religious writers, political leaders, and ordinary citizens have frequently decried changes associated with population growth, perpetually deteriorating "family values," increasing cultural heterogeneity, and gains in individual rights and freedoms—to name only a few of the signs of decline.[1] While Americans have become accustomed to such laments from elite white academics, conservatives, and politicians, relatively few European Americans hear a parallel story of community decline and loss from local leaders and former civil rights activists within African American communities. Many of the oral history narratives recorded by researchers for the Delta Oral History Project, a collaborative effort of Tougaloo College, Mississippi, and Dickinson College, Pennsylvania, between 1995 and 1998, echo the stories purveyed by elite white authorities, but with a profound difference.[2]

Many of the one hundred African American community leaders we interviewed in small Mississippi towns and cities told stories of community deterioration and loss. They spoke of a loss of cohesion and discipline throughout their communities and a profound loss of ambition and industriousness among African American young people. They attributed these losses to developments that they had noticed at neighborhood levels: a lack of firm and consistent parenting, a growing materialism among younger generations, and a lack of respect for elders and authority figures. Many African American leaders believed that school desegregation and increased federal intervention in the forms of public housing, welfare expenditures, and unemployment benefits had caused or exacerbated the unraveling of their communities. As civil rights leaders, many narrators had taken considerable personal risks to bring political rights and federal programs to the impoverished African Americans of the Mississippi Delta. At midlife and late life, they often lamented the results of this intervention and attributed many of their community ills to integration or, more correctly, to the process of desegregation of public schools. A second source of decline was the increased utilization of federal transfer payments and public subsidies by the black poor.

The laments of age against the seeming fecklessness of youth are clichés in narratives of decline. But the tenor and vehemence—and the targeting of the sources of decline—among many Delta leaders beg for explanations beyond the usual complaints of old versus young. In this essay, readers are asked to consider evidence from four of the personal narratives that my colleagues and I recorded. The elders' statements of anger and loss are in fact the expressions of a sense of collective grief and despair that are the products of a history of profound social suffering and collective trauma.[3] Many narrators seemed to be mourning a history of personal and collective losses—their own and those of their communities. Their despair is, as therapist Miriam Greenspan has argued, a "complex emotion that contains core elements of grief, anger and helplessness. It is fundamentally related to social conditions and to how we make meaning of our suffering and pain. It has a distinctly moral and social dimension that cannot and should not be ignored."[4] Part of the elders' sense of loss stemmed from what they perceived to be the evaporation of the values that sustained their own survival and achievement: thrift, industry, and sexual virtue. Postmodern consumer culture, based on spending and debt, was a moral affront to many narrators. Consumerism had made the common virtues of the past seem irrelevant.

The collective suffering inflicted upon African Americans in the Mississippi Delta during the age of segregation forced families into rigorous patterns of personal and collective discipline in order to survive the hardships and dangers of rural life. Families that achieved some security and were able to educate their children for at least several years in rural schools internalized the values of uplift and striving. Their sense of collective hope was linked to personal and collective work, frugality, ceaseless improvement, and vigilance.[5] The civil rights movement of the 1960s raised the level of personal and collective hopes significantly, and these cherished hopes helped narrators to survive the risks and terrors of the movement years.

In the wake of the economic stagnation within poor black communities in the 1980s and 1990s, many narrators saw their personal and individual hopes realized in their own lives and in their children's successes. But the hopes that they nurtured for the larger African American community were undermined by what they saw as alarming changes within local neighborhoods and families. Narrators perceived a loss of collective discipline that they associated with the disappearance of the community-centered, all-black schools of the age of segregation and with the decline of the moral authority of churches and civic leaders. This led, they contended, to the spread of indolence, materialism, and violent behavior among young working-class African Americans and a too-ready acceptance of "handouts" such as subsidized housing and welfare payments.

Narrators had infused both personal and collective hopes for progress and betterment with the values of uplift, community service, and hard work. It is important here to distinguish personal hopes for success from social hopes. As psychologist Rudolph M. Nesse has maintained, "Hope at the individual level is fundamentally conservative, but hope at the social level deeply threatens those at the top."[6] Individual activists' hopes for the future were realized by their experience of improvement and by the achievements of those close to them. Such success stories validated the rigorous moralistic virtues of uplift ideology, which contained an implicit condemnation of individuals and groups who did not appear to practice the dictates of relentless striving, frugality, and sexual monogamy. The class-based civil rights "movement of the poor" in the Mississippi Delta directly threatened the interests of white elites and other groups who had profited from segregation. Yet the institutional successes of the movement—which had allowed considerable economic mobility to the African American middle class and to members of the striving working class—did not seem to significantly change either the status or the prospects of the black poor in Delta counties. Thus the social hopes of many activist leaders collapsed in the face of the seemingly intractable condition of the black poor. Unfortunately, the values of uplift, which had propelled activists into politics and community improvement efforts, included an explanation for neither the economic stagnation of the region nor the long-term effects of structural violence on the most vulnerable segments of the population. Indeed, as Kevin Gaines has indicated, one consequence of the internalization of the values of uplift has been the tendency among some African American elites to blame the poor for their own condition.[7]

Such collective grief and despair are in fact the products of the lifetime *costs* of social suffering, elevated collective hopes, and the risks and strains of the movement years.[8] Lives marked by economic deprivation, unending hard work, and considerable risks in the movement had been sustained by promises of personal and collective liberation and progress. Movement expectations, in turn, reinforced the values of frugality, striving, and virtue that were promoted in the African American ideology of uplift in the twentieth century. The narrators' adherence to the virtues of uplift as the mechanisms of community progress clouded their ability to assess the choices made by subsequent generations of African American poor people. Their vision of decline is a reflection of their own individual and collective life experiences rather than of seismic changes in the hopes and behaviors of the poor.

Several concepts from the literatures of the life course in sociology and social gerontology unpack the relationships between narrators' accounts of their personal and collective experiences and the sources of their visions of decline. The structures that support and constrain human agency provide a framework for understanding the impact of lifetime social change upon subjectivity in midlife and late life. Also, consideration is given to the American values of progress and improvement that helped shape the expectations—and hence the disappointments—of leaders of a successful social movement.

Concepts and methods drawn from life-course studies and social gerontology benefit oral historians in a number of ways. First, such concepts as the intersection of historical, social, and biological timing in individual lives can help explain sometimes troubling or counterintuitive narratives among different groups and individuals. Notions of individual agency expressed in specific choices of "institutional pathways, developmental trajectories, and [life] transitions" aid understanding of the grounding of individual lives in specific social contexts and constructs. Further, an emphasis on the "construction of lives [and] . . . linked or interdependent lives" and attention to the specific constraints inherent in particular historical times and places[9] contribute to an understanding of the sometimes complicated relationships that narrators negotiate between their own autobiographical narratives, the surrounding narratives propagated by local communities, and the national narratives produced by governments and the media. National narratives cohere as "official stories" of wars, social movements, and flush or hard times. These metanarratives often intersect with local knowledge in surprising and confounding ways.[10]

The Narratives

"My experience in school—Mama sent her children to school. I did graduate from Booker T. Washington in Memphis, Tennessee, and the business school. I had a degree at Coahoma Junior College and studies at Delta State University in library science." At fifty-four, Juanita Scott was an administrator in the Head Start program in Bolivar County, Mississippi. Her own success story included early work in the house where her mother raised ten children after her husband deserted the family. Scott and her siblings also labored on the sharecropping tract that her mother worked. All of the children went to segregated schools in Sunflower County.

From a life of early hardship and collective labor, Scott viewed with dismay the changes in the Mississippi Delta's schools and in their students in the 1990s:

> Students today are not taught discipline. They are not taught to follow authority, and they don't have any goals in life, especially the ones which is the majority. The parents are not training them. But out of my family, we were taught to reach for the stars, and we have PhD's in chemistry in my family, principals of schools, nurse anesthetists, computer programmers, environmental specialists, registered nurses, medical doctors, commercial arts and graphics. . . . All of us are making it for ourselves. Some of my mom's children felt she was too hard on us and allowed their children to do nothing, and that's exactly what they are doing. As a whole, our community seems to be regressing sometimes instead of progressing. There are not enough positive changes in the minds of people. They are not registering to vote, and that is the key to success in any community.

Scott linked the erosion of discipline in child-rearing practices in the African American communities of the Delta to other aspects of community decline—to an apathy toward voting, education, and self-improvement. Especially, she mourned the loss of the all-black segregated schools as a critical binding force in her community's life. The desegregation of the Delta's public schools, she believed, was a disaster for the African American community and for its young people:

> To me, integration was one of the worst things that happened to black people, when they went to school. They lost all of their identity. They lost all of their dignity. They just lost it, and now they are fat in the minds and they don't have no direction. [The all-black school] was very much important for those kids, very much important. We've got people over there [in the schools] who don't care what they do. And then our young parents don't care what they do. So that's when you lost the togetherness from the church, and the home, and the school, and when you lose that communication, you lose that child. You lose your community, and that's what has happened. Those three institutions are torn down: the house, the home, and the school. And that has caused our problem, I feel.

Scott was appalled by the dependence of the black poor on public entitlements such as welfare, which she saw as another manifestation of consumer culture. This materialism, when not tied to a strong work ethic and social discipline, made black communities less safe and healthy places than the neighborhoods of the past. Juanita Scott's mother, Mattie Scott Pace, had told her children, "If you don't work, you're going to steal." Scott likewise considered the widespread acceptance of public subsidies to be a form of stealing: "I would see all of these people on the corner, I say they're not working. I know they're stealing something. Even they're stealing from the government if they're getting a check. That's stealing, stealing from the government if you're not working."[11]

Like Scott, civil rights activist Cora Fleming was one of the founders of the local Head Start program in Sunflower County in 1965. Believing that War on Poverty funds would arrive to fund the early childhood education program for poor communities in the Delta, civil rights activists Fleming, Scott, and their peers recruited children, fed and clothed many of them, and eventually received funding from the federal agencies. Although Fleming's organization, the Associated Communities of Sunflower County, was later subsumed under the middle-class–led Community Action Programs, the early organizing experience was a pivotal turning point for many of the women who worked in the early centers. Through their employment in Head Start, many "improved" themselves through educational requirements that included high school equivalence degrees and college course work. They also saw substantial improvements in the lives of their young students, many of whom came from the most deprived families in the Delta. But at sixty-one years of age during her 1995 interview, Fleming expressed despair at the condition of the young people she saw in her community, stating, "They've lost the will to try to survive without getting in trouble." She traced this development to a lack of adequate discipline, instigated in part by laws that prohibited child abuse: "They tried to stop people from whipping their children and chastise them and discipline them like they should. I told them [black parents] back then, 'They're getting ready to put all of you in jail now. You'd better take a look at what's going on around you, because if you can't whip your child, he's going to get in trouble then.' It's your right to chastise them. . . . Now, they say everything you do is child abuse. It's child abuse, all right, so they can put them in jail later on. The jails are full right now."[12]

Like Fleming and Scott, Kermit Stanton of Shelby, Mississippi, attributed many of the social ills of his community to a lack of proper parenting and a lack of discipline among younger generations. Born in 1925, Stanton dropped out of high school to work on his family's farm in Deeson, Mississippi. Using the GI Bill after his navy service in World War II, Stanton became an auto mechanic for the largest car dealership in Shelby. In the 1960s, Stanton became involved with parents who demanded changes in the administration of Shelby's black public schools. This involvement and his welcoming of the young activists from the Student Non-Violent Coordinating Committee (SNCC) and the Council of Federated Organizations (COFO) led to leadership positions in the county's civil rights movement. In 1968, he was elected to the Bolivar County Board of Supervisors, the body that controlled the county's finances. As the first black county supervisor in Mississippi since Reconstruction, Stanton received death threats from the Ku Klux Klan, and nightriders shot into his house in Shelby shortly after his election.

Kermit Stanton served a number of terms on the Board of Supervisors and saw positive and negative changes in the African American communities of Bolivar County: "When I was elected supervisor, I said to myself, well, twenty years from now, you know, I predicted that things would be so much better in every standard as far as education and everything else. . . . [But] it didn't change. We have the same things now that we had forty, thirty years ago." He admitted that educational standards in local schools were not "what they should be," but continued: "It seems as if you've got to force education on young black people, because they have the opportunity and they won't accept it. They start dropping out of school, using crack, selling crack cocaine. It seems like they're getting more ignorant every day than they were thirty years ago. And they have educational opportunities and they won't accept it."

Stanton decried the number of poor families who lived in public housing and received welfare checks each month and other public subsidies if they had disabled children, but who also "use[d] these funds to buy crack with." He blamed this cycle of idleness and crime on the welfare system: "Seems that the federal government has got a mechanism out here to control the black people." He continued, "The welfare system is the worst system you ever saw. Now, all of this money that's being spent in our community is welfare system. We opened up some new apartments right up the street here a couple months ago, and a guy got killed up there Sunday before last, dealing with crack. And until the government changes the system, the way these things are here, I don't think it's going to get any better. It's going to get worse."

Stanton believed that improvidence and materialism were rampant among younger generations, leading even employed people to live beyond their means and to forgo savings for transitory pleasures. Young workers were "further in debt than they were thirty years ago. They're living better and everything but they don't own anything." Federal subsidies, he believed, had crippled the motivation of the African American poor:

> The values are all screwed up, you know. You can go up there [to downtown Shelby] and find fifteen on the street, and you ask them do they want to work, and, no, they won't work. They're going to wait till they get that check on that unemployment. They're not going to work. They won't work. I don't know what the trouble is. I think the federal government did this on purpose to people . . . by giving them too much. They get free housing, they get free food, they get a check every month. What you want to work for? You don't have to work. You're getting the same thing you're going to get if you work, for free.[13]

Mayor Robert Gray of Shelby voiced similar feelings of despair from his vantage point in city office. Born in Montgomery County, Tennessee, in 1941, Gray moved to Shelby as a school-teacher in the 1960s. With Stanton, he had been instrumental in establishing the first Head Start centers in the plantation town. He was elected to Shelby's City Council in 1968, and in 1996 he revived a dormant auto-parts firm as part of his larger mission of bringing new economic activity to Shelby. Although a civil rights leader in Shelby who had benefited from the political changes—the increased black vote in the county—Gray judged desegregation to have been a disaster for the black community. He believed that "there's been a breakdown in family structure, and a lot of it is because of integration." He explained:

> We [African Americans] had a way of disciplining our children that worked, and white people had their way—that our people can't relate to—but we had to take on their way because of [school] integration, rather than the way that we were doing it, which was successful. You know, Mama was gone, Mama next door looked after her children. Now, that don't take place in the white community. The only thing Johnny, who is black, re-lates to is a spanking from time to time. White people can dis-cipline their children, "I'm not going to carry you to London this summer. I'm not going to carry you to Egypt. I'm not go-ing to carry you to the coast over Easter break." That's the dis-cipline in the white community, but we had to take on that, because, you know, it has never been a true integration. When you talk about integrate, you meet.

In desegregated public schools, black teachers could not ad-minister corporal punishment to white children and so declined to administer it to African American children. Additionally, the new consolidated, desegregated public schools, although heavily black in student population, seemed remote and intimidating to many African American parents who had felt a degree of per-sonal and community involvement with the smaller all-black schools. This rift between parents, schools, and traditional meth-ods of child rearing and discipline was compounded by the dis-appearance of black businesses—another result of desegregation, according to Gray. "We lost all our businesses," he said. "We lost the schools, you know, control of the schools. . . . So while it might appear from the surface that we made progress, when you add up all the intangibles into the situation, we retrogressed."[14]

Gray, Stanton, Fleming, and Scott all saw several causes of the ills of their communities: lax parenting, school desegrega-tion, with an accompanying decline in student discipline and learning, and the enervating and ambition-sapping effects of the welfare system and other public benefits that came with federal intervention since the 1960s. Behind all of the policies, however, lurked local white elites and faceless state and national governments that seemed to be intent on further ruining the characters and life chances of poor African Americans. Thus these stories of decline were shadowed by the narrators' suspicions of white elite conspiracies to diminish black communities through policies that weakened the ambition and will of the lower class.

Lives and Social Change

Part of the background of this disillusionment is the magnitude of social changes that the Delta leaders had experienced over their lives. Gray, Stanton, Scott, and Fleming grew up within an almost preindustrial agricultural system that was based on the family economy as a primary unit of income production among tenant farmers and small independent farmers in the "Black Belt" South. While much of the rest of the country had thoroughly modernized agricultural practices, the Mississippi Delta still depended on an exploitative sharecropping system to plant, cultivate, and pick its cotton crops through much of the 1960s. Farmers plowed their rows in the rich Delta soil with mules. All-black segregated rural and small-town schools often ran "split shifts" that regulated schooling around the demands of cotton chopping and picking. Most of the state's black public schools were underfunded and poor, and many black Deltans received only two to four years of plantation schooling, sometimes under teachers whose only training was in similar black schools.[15]

The sharecropping system itself was based on planter control and gross economic exploitation. Federal government interventions during the Great Depression of the 1930s—innovations such as cultivation restriction and price supports for the cotton crop—provided funds primarily to the planters and large farmers. Pressed themselves by the agricultural disasters of the 1930s, these men had few qualms about dismissing their unneeded labor force, swelling the flow of dispossessed farmers and agricultural people to Northern and Western states during the decade.

Families who stayed on the land were those who survived the numerous stresses of agricultural labor, economic exploitation, and political oppression, as well as outbursts of white terrorism and violence from state authorities, organizations such as the Ku Klux Klan, or less formalized vigilante groups of local whites. Such families survived by a stringent thrift, collective labor, and a sometimes harsh social discipline. The family economy was based on a principle of "cooperate and survive," values that were instilled quite early in the families of Fleming, Scott, Stanton, and Gray. At midlife and late life, these leaders expressed a pride in their own industry and achievement, which were, in turn, part of larger stories of family motivation and progress.

How can concepts from life-course study help to make sense of the discrepancies between the narrators' personal, family, and social histories and those of other Americans who inhabited a parallel, but very different, historical time and setting? And how can life-course concepts help us to unpack the sources of the rage and disappointment that tinge their narratives with a sense of loss and collective victimization? Several concepts from life-course research help to untangle the relationships between social suffering, collective hope, and collective grief and despair that haunt many Delta narratives. Prominent life-course scholars suggest ways in which the Delta narrators' sense of a chaotic transformation of social and personal time is a product of very real differences between their experiences and those of a majority of Americans of the twentieth century.

African American women and men born to rural farm families in the first half of the twentieth century faced the coming of the twenty-first century with values and belief systems rooted in a preindustrial family culture and social system. The difficulties of collective survival forced family members to internalize an often harsh regime of discipline and work. The black Delta communities they inherited in the late twentieth century resembled in many ways postindustrial Third World landscapes. All four counties were majority African American in the late 1990s and were blighted by enormous social problems produced by a chronically impoverished infrastructure. Many depressed Delta communities had the abandoned look of industrial ghost towns, except that the region had been neither disciplined nor blessed by the ultimately beneficial process of industrialization and social modernization.[16]

Life-Course Studies

Life-course theory and studies have been developed since the 1960s and 1970s by a number of sociologists and demographers, and some historians. Among the most prolific scholars in the fields of life-course studies, aging, and human development are Glen H. Elder Jr., John Modell, Matilda White Riley, Gunhild O. Hagestad, Tamara Hareven, Jill Quadrango, and Peter Laslett.[17] The studies loosely grouped within the categories of human development and the life course have included investigations into the lifelong effects of the 1930s Depression on two groups of California children, changes in the timing of life events over the course of the twentieth century, and short-term and long-term effects of disruption and stress on the lives of specific populations. Many such studies have been made possible through technological developments that have fostered the ability of historical demographers to make significant advances in what we can know about individuals of past centuries through the examination and computer analysis of aggregate records of births, deaths, taxes, voting patterns, migration, and economic activities.

According to sociologist Martin Kohli, life-course theory developed as a response to an awareness that the demographic conditions of life had altered tremendously over the past three centuries of modernization in western Europe and the United States, areas that experienced industrialization, urbanization, and substantial growth in state bureaucracies and capacities for social control. With economies based increasingly on large-scale industrial production, states needed to regulate public social norms to conform to the changing demands of factory work requirements.[18]

Premodern—or at least preindustrial—European and American life had been based on a family economy as the primary "unit of production." In the agricultural family economy, work and family life were largely undifferentiated. Mortality rates were very high for infants, but death could—and did—strike at any time during one's life. For instance, historian Philip Greven found that in colonial Andover, Massachusetts, one-fifth of the inhabitants did not live to age twenty. Furthermore D. E. Stannard concluded that "with average birth rates on the order of

8 or 9, colonial families could expect that 2 or 3 of their children would die before reaching age 10."[19]

In developing industrial communities in western Europe and the United States, rural migrants to factory towns adapted the family economy to the demands of frequently dangerous and low-wage industrial work. The ethos of this family was "cooperate and survive," and all family members were expected— and sometimes even forced—to contribute to the family's income. High mortality rates among Americans and Europeans throughout the nineteenth century meant that death was a common experience, and families often memorialized their losses with funeral photographs of dead infants, children, and adults.

Although death remained a familiar presence for late nineteenth- and early twentieth-century families, the long-term impact of industrialization included an increasing life expectancy over the nineteenth century. According to Victor W. Marshall, "In most European countries, life expectancy at birth increased from 40 years in 1840 to 50 years in 1900."[20] Although families continued to suffer high mortality rates due to infant deaths, work injuries, and illness, life expectancy in American urban areas also reached fifty years of age at the turn of the century. By the 1990s, life expectancy had exceeded seventy years of age for Americans, and the "old old"—those over age eighty-five—constituted a growing percentage of the swelling numbers of the elderly. While only 5.4 percent of Americans were over sixty years of age in the 1880s, by the 1980s and 1990s, 15.9 percent of the American population was sixty years and older, leading demographer Peter Laslett to note that the increasing longevity and declining mortality rates of advanced countries have created a "novel . . . situation. . . . Average individual lifetimes last for very much longer than they ever have before anywhere or at any time, and these populations have among them quite unprecedented numbers of elderly people."[21]

The demographic transition of the last century has altered the age at death, as Kohli says, "from a pattern of randomness to a pattern of a predictable life-span." While death routinely ended the lives of infants, children, and adults in previous centuries, it has come to be concentrated "in the upper age brackets" in recent decades. This development has rendered the death of infants and young people as "unnatural" events in the families of late-twentieth-century Westerners. The greatly expanded life expectancy, Kohli continues, has also led to an increasingly state-regulated cycle of "normative life events" over the life span. States have actively promoted a widespread acceptance of a "normal biography" based on a predictable sequence of life experiences: preparation and training for work, followed by a lengthy period of work or employment activity, followed by a lengthening period of retirement. Since the late nineteenth century, states have stratified the timing of these life events through the mechanisms of compulsory education with age-graded standards for achievement and promotion, age-specific rights and public obligations and duties—such as military service, social security contributions, and driving—and specific ages at which workers can expect to receive pensions, social security payments, and entitlements to such benefits as Medicare. The industrial and postindustrial cultures that have mandated this normative life span and its predictable sequence of careers, Kohli says, have made this life plan "a primary source of identity" for contemporary Americans and Europeans. The predictable timing of life events, coupled with an increasing cultural emphasis on psychology and on the individual as the basic unit of social life, have engendered a "developmental conception" of the self that has flourished in nineteenth- and twentieth-century autobiographies. Among such writers, developmental trajectories mirror the wider culture's conceptions of progressive improvement. According to Kohli, "the individualized life course emerged as the basic code for constructing one's experiences and perspectives." While numerous social and economic changes have produced this predictable temporally and progressive construction of the self, it is the welfare state, he writes, that is most "responsible for the increasing age grading of life."[22]

Taking their cue from both aggregate population data and qualitative research methods, life-course scholars created a body of concepts and methods to study change in the lives of contemporary and vanished populations. These concepts attempt to place individual and collective human agency within the constraints imposed by time, place, social system, and relational context. This reflects life-course scholars' recognition that human life and decision making are constrained by history, economy, and interactively created perceptions of possibility. Some of the most creative works have included Laslett's study of seventeenth-century England, Greven's work on colonial Massachusetts, Modell's research into the changing age expectations and timing of life events among American youth of the twentieth century, and Hareven's work on nineteenth-century industrial labor and family life.

One of the most important scholars in this field is sociologist Glen Elder, whose pioneering *Children of the Great Depression*, first published in 1974, focused on longitudinal research on two cohorts of young people from Depression-era families in Oakland and Berkeley, California. A prominent researcher and theorist of the concept since his early work, Elder described the life course as "a sequence of socially defined, age-graded events and roles that the individual enacts over time." The timing and structuring of these roles has a great deal to do with the "social meanings of age" within the community the individual inhabits.[23] One example cited by life-course scholars is that the social meanings of age and work differ between working-class, middle-class, and professional men. Working-class men see an earlier end to their work lives than do men who are in the administrative and professional classes. For the former, their work is indeed often "written on the body" and produces physical injuries and stressors to an extent that white-collar work does not. Not surprisingly, men who choose to continue working past a retirement age of sixty-five are most often those in the executive or administrative/professional ranks.

Important aspects of life-course theories include the concepts of cohort, trajectories, transitions, and careers. These constructs interactively link individuals and their social roles to historical change. Life-course theorists prefer to see operative age units within populations in terms of cohorts rather than generations. Generations are understood to have genealogical or familial derivation, but cohorts are composed of individuals born within a generally limited number of years, say, intervals of five to ten years. Placement within a specific birth cohort determines one's experience of historical change. In *Children of the Great Depression*, Elder shows that the timing of Depression hardship upon families in Oakland and Berkeley, California, had varying effects on children of different birth cohorts, who were thus at different ages when economic loss struck the family. The younger the age of the children when severe economic loss occurred, the more severe were their psychological and social problems. This was especially true of young male children.[24]

Life-course theory also locates cohorts in specific developmental trajectories, which, according to Elder, encompass "social or psychological states over a substantial part of the life span." Within these long-term life patterns or trajectories, individuals experience and frequently choose life-changing experiences called transitions. The latter are changes of shorter duration and often refer to an alteration of "state or states, such as when children leave home or a mood changes from depressed feelings to happiness." According to Elder, since these short-term changes in relational life, roles, and feelings are "always elements of trajectories, a substantial change in direction during a transition may represent a *turning point* as well." Writes Elder: "Trajectories and transitions are elements of established pathways, individual life courses, and developmental patterns. Among individuals, social roles evolve over an extended span of time, as in trajectories of work or family; and they change over a short time span. . . . Each transition, combining a role exit and entry, is embedded in a trajectory that gives it specific form and meaning. Thus, work transitions are core elements of a work life trajectory; and births are key markers along a parental trajectory."[25]

Social roles within trajectories may cohere in individuals' lives as careers and career sets. Limited in duration over the life span, careers include individual roles within the domains of work, family, and social life. Indeed, an individual's career set may include multiple careers: spouse, parent, worker, church member, and political activist. The duration of careers and the transitions between roles and the careers in which they are embedded are given meaning by the timing of these changes in an individual's life. For individuals who inhabit multiple careers over their lives, the balancing and coordination of the various roles associated with work, parenthood, marriage(s), friendships, religion, and community life, necessitate, claims Elder (emphasis in original), "*strategies of coordination or synchronization.*"[26]

The sequence of roles that individuals occupy, the timing of these roles within the life course, and the institutional pathways, developmental trajectories, and transitions that define their life constructions, Elder says, are constrained by the perceived opportunities available in particular historical times and places. The individual's agency and her or his choices about work, the timing of transitions, and the meanings that he or she creates from these events are further filtered through relationships with parents, family members, friends, and coworkers. These individuals form networks or "convoys" of social supports and, indeed, collectively construct the meaning of individual and group experiences. Such convoys help individuals to interpret reality, and they function as the *"linked lives"* that both enable and constrain individual choices.[27]

Undergirding life-course theory and studies is a notion of human development across the life span, a process that results in a continuing interactive cocreation of an individual's personal biography, collective experience, and interpretation of history itself.[28] According to researchers Robert L. Kahn and Toni C. Antonucci, the life-course approach "emphasizes the importance of past experiences in explaining current behavior and predicting responses to future situations." Convoys of social support can provide needed assistance and affirmation to their members in times of personal stress. Such networks also help to shape individual perceptions of opportunities and dangers in particular historical and geographic environments.[29] Shared relational perceptions—what we could call collective definitions of reality—can prompt individuals to make life choices that are likely to result in cumulative advantage or disadvantage over a lifetime.[30]

Particularly important is the impact of social stress upon individuals and their convoys of relationships. The importance and effect of various stressors—from childhood abuse and poverty to war and natural disasters—differs with the age at which such crises are experienced and the individual's previous experience within his or her relational convoys. Elder has found that World War II service and the economic dislocations of the 1930s Great Depression and the 1980s agricultural crisis in northern Iowa farming communities served to reinforce and heighten individuals' habitual and temperamental responses to challenges. Confronted with the strains of joblessness and economic hard times, resourceful parents and children became even more resourceful, while individuals with explosive or violent temperaments became even more aggressive.[31]

According to Elder and others, the individual effects of various life transitions also vary according to the nature of the transition, which in turn promotes differing selection and transition effects. Selection effects occur after individuals have chosen a particular role and set of behavioral norms as a result of a transition, and individuals are then affected themselves by their transition to the new environment. An example that Elder has cited are risk takers in the military who are assigned to combat units.[32] Another example, drawn from my own work in African American communities, suggests that the most ambitious and leadership-oriented young people in segregated African American communities were those most frequently drawn into the often dangerous civil rights activism of the 1960s.[33] For both the young men who entered combat units as risk takers and the young people who joined movement efforts, the collective influence of the selection choice was sometimes a profound resocialization into the norms of the collectivity. According to Elder, "Transitions of this kind generally accentuate the behavioral effect of the selected dispositions, producing greater individual differences and heterogeneity between groups."[34]

An example of the cumulative effect of life transitions that tend to resocialize and at the same time reinforce individual beliefs and attitudes can again be drawn from the World War II veterans and 1960s civil rights activists. The experiences of wartime service and postwar educational achievements through the GI Bill gave millions of American veterans significant opportunities for social mobility during the postwar boom. These positive experiences infused them with the assurance that the war had been a "good" war, and that governmental policies during the Cold War were correct and prudent. Consequently, many veterans were baffled and angered by 1960s opposition to the Vietnam War, a response they often saw as an affront to their wartime sacrifices and political convictions. Similarly, African American Mississippians came to the civil rights movement with a profound distrust toward their state's government and white elites

in general. Activists who experienced movement-born disillusionment with the federal government's promises of protection
and assistance accordingly voiced an increasing skepticism and
distrust of the intended effect of federal policies between the
1970s and 1990s. Their suspicions were reinforced by continuing
recalcitrance on the part of local and state white conservative
leaders and from the burgeoning strength of the Republican
right in the 1980s and 1990s.

While the concepts of a normative life course—expressed
in terms of particular birth cohorts, with distinctive trajectories, transitions, linked lives, and cumulative advantages and
disadvantages—have special significance for the historical and
social experiences of a majority of twentieth-century Americans and Europeans, what relevance do these notions have for
the enormous transformations that many African American
community activists in the Mississippi Delta experienced between the 1920s and the 1990s? What can these constructs tell
us about the shaping of their notions of personal agency, survival, and community improvement? And how can these ideas
help explain their profound disappointment and anger at the
conditions of life within their communities in the 1990s?

The Life Course of African American
Mississippians under Segregation

Social movement leaders constitute a small minority in any population, and most of the African American community leaders
interviewed by the Delta Oral History Project's researchers recalled family and educational experiences that placed them in a
relative elite within their birth cohorts in their home communities. Our narrators told family and personal stories that stressed
resourcefulness, resilience in the face of hard times, and a
parental determination to educate their children. Our narrators'
parents seem to have shared the great hunger for education and
betterment frequently expressed by rural black Southerners in
the decades after emancipation.[35] This parental generation encouraged and supported their children's schooling, and in some
cases, in order to send their children to school, even defied

planters for whom they worked. Their children, in turn, recalled their own readiness to struggle for and utilize all educational advantages that were available to them throughout their lives. Women who became involved with Head Start projects in the 1960s eagerly attended classes and took whatever course work became available through Mississippi colleges and universities to "improve" themselves and to become better educated. They credited their own strength, ambition, and resourcefulness to the examples set by their parents and grandparents, who exercised strict self-discipline and parental discipline to feed and provide for their children. But these families were a minority within African American communities in the Delta. They had enough resources—personal, social, and economic—to withstand pressures exerted by planters, by hard times, and by scarcity to keep their children in the fields during school sessions, when many other black children labored year-round in the cotton fields and on farms.[36]

For example, Kermit Stanton, until he was drafted in 1944, worked on his family's 160-acre farm in Deeson, Mississippi, on land originally purchased for twenty-five cents an acre by his grandfather sometime in the years after Reconstruction (1866–1876). The seventh of nine children, Stanton completed eight years of education in a school held in a church at Deeson before he dropped out to work on the family farm. Remembering the Depression years as "tough," he also recalled, "My parents owning the farm and everything, we were still poor, but we survived, but it was hard. It was a little different from being on a plantation, but it was hard to survive." His memories of farming included a range of food and food production: "We grew all the vegetables and the meats, the corn. And we had a grist mill. We ground and made our own meal. And we also made meals for the people that lived on the plantation [the sharecroppers who worked on the nearby Delta Pine and Land plantation]. That's where I used to work at every Saturday, at the grist mill." The family also raised hogs, chickens, and cows for meat, eggs, and milk, and Stanton added, the boys hunted for "squirrels, rabbit, duck, if you could find the shells to hunt them with." Furthermore, he said, "Money was scarce, really scarce. You could take a nickel or fifteen cents and buy a meal with it. You know what I mean, but it was hard getting the nickel and fifteen cents."[37] Despite these privations, Stanton's family was fortunate in its independence and resources: only about 4 percent of African American farmers in the Delta owned their own land in the 1920s and 1930s.

Juanita Scott grew up on the Sunflower County sharecropping tracts worked by her mother, who raised and fed ten children after her husband walked out on the family when Juanita was five. Scott remembered Mattie Scott Pace's resourcefulness:

> From that time on, every move was made by my mother. She was the backbone of the family. I remember my mother with eight children, pregnant with the ninth, had to make all the decisions made. She would gather us together like a chicken with her chicks, sit us down, and explain to us what our chores were. We knew what we had to do, and we knew how to do it. We all had a CS and an FST degree at an early age: it was Common Sense and Fire Side Training.
>
> The oldest children were the girls. They had to cut wood, and when I say cut wood, we had to go in the woods, cut down trees the sizes they could handle, drag them outside of the brake, and hope that someone with a wagon would come along and help them get the wood to the house. . . . My job, along with my brother Joe, was to pick up chips in a number-three washtub. We would find the chips in the spots where men had cut down a large tree, which made large chips. After the wood was at home, my sisters would use a cross-cut saw to cut the wood to fit the stove, the heater, the fireplace. This type of work was done on Saturdays only.

On weekdays, the children all attended school or worked in the cotton fields. School was a five-mile walk each way, Scott recalled, "but none of Mama's children, the nine of us, had a chance to ride a school bus ever." On Sundays, the family attended church and the children had time to play in the afternoons. The two eldest girls did the family's housework, which included "cleaning the house, milking the cows, washing the clothes, and cooking dinner." Scott herself "had to cook for the whole family at the age of eight." Everyone in the family labored to produce the cash income from sharecropping. Scott said, "We would pick twenty or more bales of cotton a year, and, at the settlement, Mama would get eight- to nine-hundred dollars at the highest, but she did tell us that sometimes she didn't get anything that year. But when she did get a settlement—that's when she got her money—she would order our winter clothes, which included our shoes, our coats, socks, et cetera, and she would buy ten- to fifteen-cent-per-yard material, and any dress we would pick out of the Sears-Roebuck catalog, she would make it by using a newspaper pattern that she made."

Juanita Scott learned to sew from her mother and made her doll's clothing by copying the dresses her mother made for her daughters. The family lived in several sharecropper cabins on the plantation tracts where they lived. Generally, these were two- or three-room wooden structures, with the house and porch set on brick supports several feet above the ground. The houses lacked outhouses and were without running water or electricity. Scott remembered her childhood as happy, however, "because we were taught that we were very important, we were as good as anyone, and we would accomplish anything we wanted to do in life as long as we didn't steal or lie. [Mama] instilled in us that if you feel you were right, stand up for what you believe. As far as race relations, I was taught I was as good as anyone." Together, the family produced almost all of the food they needed. Mattie Scott Pace's gardens were filled with sweet potatoes, peanuts, corn, and peas, and she had a steer and a hog to butcher once a year, plus chickens for the family's consumption year-round. Scott recalled:

> Our beef was canned in jars, and our pork was salted down and put into a wooden box four-feet by four-feet, while the hams and shoulders of the hog were smoked in a cotton house. The fat of the hog was fried out and used for lard. The curing was done after harvesting of the cotton to be used for food in the winter and fall. We had canned vegetables in the winter and fresh vegetables in the spring and summer, which included the greens, beans, soup, okra, corn, beets, tomatoes, carrots, and the fruit consisted of peaches, pears, and blackberries.

Scott and her siblings harvested and shelled the corn and thrashed and stored the dried beans and peas. "Through these processes," she recalled, "we, as children, was taught survivor-hood." The self-sufficiency and dignity instilled in her children by Mattie Scott Pace led several of them to become active in Sunflower County's 1960s civil rights movement. Juanita Scott registered to vote in the 1960s, and in the rallies, marches, and meetings in Indianola, the county seat, she met "my idol, Mrs. Fannie Lou Hamer. She inspired me in so many ways. She was standing up for what she believed in, and I said, 'This is an-other Negro woman like me.' Instead of me being like her, she was like me."

Scott's determination and resourcefulness were evident in her efforts with the early Head Start program. Before federal funding arrived, local activists organized the first centers in any space available to them, including individual homes. Very few of the black ministers in Indianola would allow Head Start centers to operate from their churches, so Juanita Scott founded a center in her house where she kept fifty-three children. She remem-bered, "We fed each of them by the help of the community do-nating food, and the adults volunteered and took up money for milk. I think the milk was about two cents a box at that time. The children played games. They used newspaper for finger paint-ing. Paper toys was made by my mother. I still have a bear she made for the children to play with. . . . There was story-reading, word games, naps, and outdoor play, but most of all, those chil-dren was taught pride and dignity."[38]

Pride in family strength and dignity also resonated in Cora Fleming's narrative of her life. The sixth of ten children, Fleming grew up in the Mississippi hill country near Starkville, where her parents owned a small farm before later migrating to Sunflower County. Her father worked as a farmer and also as a blacksmith, and her mother, who had been a schoolteacher, worked as a housewife, taking care of her large family. At age sixteen, Flem-ing finished elementary school and entered high school. At age seventeen, however, she married and left school until the 1960s, when she began working for Head Start. Fleming proudly re-ferred to her family as "hill people," black Mississippians who were more outspoken and less fearful than were people who had lived for generations as sharecroppers on the Delta plantations. "In the hills, we had to be independent," she explained, "and down here [in the Delta] they're dependent on people, on the white folks. See, we had to work for our own up there. We had our own land, everything our own." Fleming's family experienced hard times during the Depression years of the 1930s, when the early months of spring were times of deprivation:

> My mother generally raised a garden. We had vegetables, peas, butterbeans, corn, okra, all that kind of stuff. And they raised cows. They raised chickens. They raised hogs. So the hardest time was like in March and April, the worst time in our lives. The winter food was gone. We had come through winter fine, but then in March and April, everything had run out. You had to get other things to grow then, the vegetables to grow in the garden. So that was the worst time of our lives, I think, when I was growing up. We never went hungry, but just a shortage of food.

After her marriage, Cora Fleming and her husband moved north for higher wages and better jobs. She worked in Chicago for years but returned home to Indianola in 1961 to care for her mother, who had suffered a stroke. In the early 1960s, she became involved in the local civil rights movement, as did several of her siblings. She attributed their actions to the attitudes of her own parents. "I guess we came along when things began to change, I reckon, want to be a change in the minds of the elderly people, want to change and see better things for their children. And they had [that desire]. I guess they couldn't act on it, but they had it in their minds, I believe," said Fleming. In 1964, a racially mixed team of young organizers for the COFO came to Indianola. When Fleming and her mother saw the "different races all of them mixed up together coming down the street," they knew that the sight was "unusual around here." When the organizers canvassed the black neighborhood, asking residents to come to a meeting at a church that evening, Fleming recalled, "My mother looked at them, she said, 'You know, I've lived all my life, worked all my life for nothing.' And she said, 'You go to church. When you get sick and get down, they don't know you.' She said, 'It's time now for a change to come about, and it's time for y'all to take an active role in it.' I said, 'You mean that?' She said, 'Yes, I do.'"

Cora Fleming went to the church meeting that night and spoke publicly to the crowd, which included a number of share-croppers from the plantations that surrounded Indianola. She remembered:

> I said, "You've been working in the fields all your days. Now you're suffering for fifteen dollars a week. I'm working for the same thing. I made a hundred and some dollars a week in Chicago, and now you're making fifteen dollars a week. And what can you do with fifteen dollars? Nothing." Children in bare feet, hungry half the time, but that was the best they could do at that time. And a lot of people who were going to that meeting didn't even realize what was going on, the changes that were taking place. A lot of them was scared, but they went anyway. Lost their jobs. My sister lost her job.

Fleming's resilience was tested during the years of Sunflower County's civil rights struggle. One night, the driver of an eighteen-wheel truck tried to run her car down on one of the Delta's dark two-lane highways, and another night, nightriders shot into her house. Subsequently, she developed a "bad case of nerves" from her years of living in fear. Throughout the 1960s, Sunflower County nurtured a particularly violent white resistance to African American voting rights, freedom schools, and Head Start initiatives. In 1965, the Baptist school, a site of local movement meetings, was firebombed and burned, as was the house of activist Irene McGruder and the store and home of Alice Giles and her husband. Local planters had organized the first chapter of the White Citizens' Council, a virulently segregationist organization, after the *Brown v. Board* decision of 1954, and the county was the home of the notorious racist senator James O. Eastland, whose family owned a large plantation there. White terrorists targeted movement activists such as Fleming, Fannie Lou Hamer, and Kermit Stanton. Threats, drive-by shootings, the terrorizing of leaders' family members became part of the price of movement participation. For Fleming, the terror "took its toll on me in later years. A lot of personal fear, I guess, kind of balled up in me. In the long run, it kind of got the best of me."

The terrorism led Cora Fleming to hate whites "with a passion" for some time, she admitted, "but I learned later on that everybody wasn't the same. . . . You've got to meet on a common ground somewhere." But Fleming was also deeply disappointed by the takeover of the local Head Start programs pioneered by the grassroots-led Associated Communities of Sunflower County. The federal government's ceding control of statewide Head Start programs to the federally controlled Community Action Programs led her to leave Head Start and to return to work at the local cotton compress. At a local level, the dominance of Community Action Program guidelines meant that War on Poverty programs were to be controlled by boards of white moderates and middle-class African Americans. This leadership effectively replaced more radical grassroots leaders such as Fleming in the decision-making positions in the programs. Fleming appreciated the education she received through Head Start, but she expressed anger at the change in the program's leadership structure: "It was educating all of us because we all began to be trained. We trained through Mary Holmes College and different sources. But the federal government just wasted money when they trained us to do the job. They just threw away money. . . . Wasted a lot of money training a whole lot of people for the power structure and the so-called educated blacks to take over. Why did they use that money to train us for if they weren't going to need us later on, millions of dollars?"[39]

For all of the harshness of her life, Cora Fleming had some advantages when compared with many other black Deltans. Her family had nursed a spirit of independence and resilience, she had attended school through at least the beginning of high school, and she had the comparative advantage of having worked in Chicago for many years before she returned to Sunflower County. She knew that conditions could be different, and better, for the black people of the Delta, and she was not afraid to take a leadership role in pushing and promoting change.

Robert Gray's family was also relatively advantaged. The third of six children, he grew up in a rural Tennessee community in which his family had long been landowners and small business people. This background, he said, "gave me some inclination to want to be a business person. [My relatives] never worked for anybody." After finishing high school, he received a basketball scholarship from a black junior college in Natchez,

Mississippi, and completed his degree at Mississippi Valley State University before moving to Shelby as a schoolteacher in the mid-1960s. The sheer numbers of African Americans in Mississippi and the relatively high numbers of black property owners in places such as Bolivar County persuaded Gray that the civil rights movement could create massive political and economic development among black populations in the Delta.[40]

Although these four narrators experienced significant social mobility over their lives, they all remained frustrated and angry over the nature of change in their communities. Cora Fleming had significant health problems at the time of her interview in 1995 and died within the next two years. Kermit Stanton, who lived in a modest home in Shelby and had a secure retirement income, likewise died within two years of our 1996 interview. Juanita Scott had a secure administrative position with Head Start in Cleveland, Mississippi, and continued to live in Indianola with her mother in the small house where she had once held Head Start classes. Robert Gray served as mayor of Shelby and worked to build his parts company, and his wife still worked as a schoolteacher in Shelby. These leaders had achieved modest but significant economic and educational gains since their childhoods. Each had taken part in a major social movement and had experienced tremendous growth and personal development as a result of those experiences. Why, then, were all of them so angry and disappointed? Why the sense of betrayal by the federal government and other white elites and an enraged disappointment at the lack of progress by the African American poor?

For much of its black population, the Delta of the last decade of the twentieth century was indeed an impoverished region. Historian James Cobb cited findings of the Lower Mississippi Delta Development Commission, created in 1988 by the U.S. Congress, which described "overwhelming evidence of hard-core unemployment, severe educational deficiencies, and the utter absence of local capital or entrepreneurial expertise."[41] Cobb further noted that federal transfer payments supported both rich and poor Deltans but with marked differences in effect: large farmers and planters received generous agricultural subsidies for their production of staple crops, and the white and black poor received supplemental supports in terms of welfare payments, food stamps, public housing, and programs such as Head Start and school lunches.[42] Statistical surveys and census reports confirm a dismal life for all too many African American Delta residents in the 1990s. More of them were poor and undereducated, experienced health problems and lack of health care, and faced higher infant mortality and, indeed, increased adult mortality rates than the state or national averages.[43] Compounding these problems was the nature of the few jobs available to poorly educated residents. While regional elites and mayors sought to lure manufacturing businesses into their communities with a number of enticements, employment for unskilled workers remained insecure and at low-wage levels. Catfish and poultry processing, which employed thousands of African American women and men in the Delta, were both minimum-wage jobs, and in the 1990s, even a full-time worker was unable to support herself and three children on her wages.

While the enduring poverty of many of the region's African Americans was a source of continuing frustration and anger for many former activists, the numerical indicators that tell a story of poor schools, low educational levels, massive poverty, and poor health care do not reveal the worst fact of all: the numbers recorded in the 1990s represent a significant improvement over the conditions of the past. African American life chances in earlier decades of the twentieth century in Mississippi had been even more dismal.[44] Demographers have estimated that a "baby born in 1900 could expect to live about fifty-one years if white and roughly forty years if black." By 1940, life expectancies for both groups had risen by about ten years—whites "born in the rural South in 1939 could expect to live about sixty-four years if they were male and more than sixty-seven years if they were female," whereas "black males born in 1939 could expect to live an average of fifty-six years, with black females enjoying only two more"—but adult death rates remained high among rural blacks: "Nearly 18 percent of all twenty-year-old blacks (male or female) . . . could expect to die before turning forty-five. The comparable risk of death was substantially lower for southern whites—9 percent for males, and 7 percent for females."[45] Maternal mortality due to death in childbirth, linked to the widespread absence of affordable prenatal and obstetric care for African Americans, composed a large part of the adult mortality figures for black women.

Higher mortality rates in Mississippi and in the Delta counties, particularly, were a consequence of the poor diet on which many plantation workers subsisted. African American home economics agent Dorothy Dickins researched the diets of black tenant farmers and sharecroppers in 1926 and found evidence of severe deficiencies in terms of calories, protein, calcium, phosphorous, and iron. Tenant families consumed less meat and milk than they needed, which contributed to the high incidence of pellagra in the Delta counties. Blacks' diets were also deficient in essential vitamins, which diminished their resistance to infectious diseases, such as tuberculosis. Vitamin and mineral deficiencies, especially calcium and phosphorous, also made children prone to developing rickets. Dickins found that the nutritional deficiencies, which resulted from a lack of quality and variety of foods, related to the "high death rate[s], the frequent illnesses, and the lack of energy of negroes as compared to whites." Black tenants consumed high amounts of fat and insufficient amounts of protein, vegetables, and fruits. A combination of factors explained the poor diets: lack of incentives (or even opportunities) to grow supplemental gardens on some plantations, lack of education about nutrition and diet, and perhaps most importantly, the "inadequate income" upon which many tenants were forced to survive.[46]

Delta diets were not much improved during the Depression years of the 1930s, when, Howard Odom and other researchers discovered, half of all schoolchildren in the Black Belt counties of the cotton South had poor teeth, and "50 percent of all Southern children in large areas receive inadequate diets for any normal health standard." This situation resulted in the high incidence of tuberculosis, rickets, pellagra, and anemia among Mississippi Delta tenant farming families, among whom 95 percent were African Americans.[47] Similar conditions prevailed into the 1960s, when health and poverty researchers found that many of the children of poor and sharecropping African American families still suffered from rickets, anemia, malnutrition, and infectious diseases that could have been easily prevented by adequate nutrition and health care.[48]

Like mortality, health, and diet, the educational advancements made by white and black Deltans in the 1990s were significant when compared with the past. Neil R. McMillen listed illiteracy rates of 8.2 percent for whites and 49.1 percent for African Americans in 1900, which unfortunately declined to 2.7 percent and 23.2 percent by 1930. However, the paltry opportunities for high school education for blacks through the 1950s demonstrated the state government's unwillingness to educate its African American citizens. In 1930–1931, for example, 46 percent of whites between fifteen and nineteen years of age were enrolled in grades 9–12; the corresponding figure for black Mississippians was 4 percent. By 1950, the numbers had climbed to 62 percent and 25 percent, but in that year, only 13 percent of black students were enrolled in the twelfth grades of their schools. According to McMillen, in 1950, 75 percent of the African American population of high-school–aged students were not attending high schools.[49] The differentials in educational opportunities had predictable results: in 1960, white Mississippians had a median school completion number of eleven years; the corresponding figure for African Americans was six years.[50]

This history of high mortality rates, poor diet and nutrition, extreme poverty, and scarce educational opportunities were products of the system of racial oppression and exploitation controlled for much of Mississippi's history by the planter elite and the state government. The poverty and powerlessness of many poor blacks were perpetuated by an oppressive legal and social system and by the hovering threat of social violence that was a frequent fact of African American life through the 1960s. Police harassment, high incarceration rates of accused black males, and random violence from white authorities in the forms of lynching and terrorism were experiences that nearly every African American in the Delta could expect to face or to know about. These conditions of social suffering and chronic collective trauma bred a widespread and constant fear among Delta blacks, which according to physician Paul Farmer were manifestations of structural violence, a process through which "large-scale social forces come to be translated into personal distress and disease."[51]

Farmer's analysis of the structural violence of extreme poverty and brutality was based on his work in 1980s and 1990s Haiti, a country ravaged by a brutal military dictatorship that condemned most poor rural Haitians to lives of terrible poverty, ill health, and early death. Ironically, the vital statistics Farmer cites as evidence in Haiti of extreme social suffering due to structural violence and exploitation are similar to those shared by many rural black Mississippians between 1900 and the 1960s. These conditions led many black Deltans to endure what some scholars have referred to as the "violences of everyday life."[52]

Medical anthropologist Arthur Kleinman considered the multiple and interlocking forms of oppression that many of the poor in contemporary Third World societies share as conditions of social suffering. Such suffering is the result of the "devastating injuries that social force inflicts on human experience." Results of the "social violence" that governments and political systems inflict upon people are seen in "diseases and premature death" and in forcing many people into a condition in which "everyday life . . . does violence to the body and to moral experience." Although the social consequences of this violence are numerous, Kleinman found a particular example among survivors of Maoist terrorism in China. Among a number of Chinese citizens he interviewed from the 1970s through the 1990s, "the ordinary ethos was fear—pervasive, unappeased, based in terrible realities, yet amplified from a relatively small number of events into an emotion close to terror that was present every day. And terror experienced, not far below the surface of the ordinary, on a daily basis created cowardice, betrayal, and abiding rage." While overt terror and violence punctuated daily life on a sometimes infrequent basis, "in its aftermath, the response of a community, or a neighborhood, or a family to short-term horror is inseparable from that humdrum background of violence as usual."[53] These responses replicate those described by numerous narrators in Delta communities in their memories of childhood, youth, and adult leadership in the civil rights movement. Delta leaders frequently expressed their resentment at compliant and cowardly middle-class African Americans, as well as against overtly hostile whites.

Interpretations

Given the extreme poverty and other forms of social violence to which many African Americans in the Delta were subjected in the past, how might we understand the anger and disappointment expressed in oral history interviews by a number of former activists? How might we comprehend their reverence for the strength obtained by enduring and prevailing over past difficulties and their clear sorrow at conditions in the 1990s?

The effects of age, cohort, and life-course trajectory help to piece together some parts of the puzzle. Gray, Fleming, Scott, and Stanton came from a preindustrial family ethos and work environment, motivated by their parents' relentless desire for their betterment. At midlife and late life, they seemed to possess a faith that achievements such as their own would follow hard work, diligence, and social discipline. These values and beliefs are rooted in nineteenth- and early-twentieth-century America and in the African American ideology of racial uplift that flourished during the first half of the twentieth century. These values found obvious expression in the narrators' descriptions of those in their families who are doing better, moving up, succeeding. Thus the individual hopes of the narrators were realized through intimate examples of industry and progress.

Their beliefs were shared by colleagues from their convoys of movement relationships—by the women and men who worked in voter registration projects, in early Head Start centers, and in public office. Those to whom they were linked through family, friendship, and work shared their values and worldview. They also shared a reverence for parents, grandparents, and communities that had made their progress possible. Convoys of personal relationships and activist networks promoted a redundancy of the values of uplift and of the movement-based optimism about the opportunities for achievement and progress. But if individual hopes had been fulfilled by work, activism, and family ambition, their social or collective hopes were disappointed.

Several scholars of aging and the life course provide some clues to activists' emotional ties to a past of hardship and survival.

Focusing on the role that emotionality plays in the creation of a self and biography, researcher Wilhelm Mader suggested connections between the functions of emotionality and continuity in structuring a life story. He claimed that "patterns of emotional sensitivities" are created at early ages and become "self-maintaining self-referential systems" that seem to solidify with age. As individuals age, a sense of continuity with the values and achievements of the past becomes increasingly important, and people then tend to project a desired future in terms of those early values.[54] Of great importance are those periods in life that can be described as instrumental to the "love and learning process,"[55] that is, to those periods in which the narrator can see and recall great personal growth and development. Moreover, Mader contended, "the older one grows, the more continuity itself becomes a value of its own."[56] The valued past then, becomes the model of a desirable future: dedicated teachers, ambitious and hard-working young people, frugal and self-sacrificing parents. Thus the communities of those childhood and adult years of growth and movement participation become the model of the good cohesive society.

The segregated community and the movement community were, however, exceptional places in a number of ways. First, the cohesion was maintained due to the very real threats from white authorities, landlords, police, and ordinary citizens. Both communities were embattled and had the edgy solidarity developed by citizens who had to survive a prolonged state of siege. And these communities could only nurture and promote a limited number of individuals in this course of development. Families had to have sufficient social and economic capital to be able to keep children in school, and individuals as adults had to be independent enough to be able to risk being fired from employment, or being blacklisted by banks, creditors, and other authorities. Activists also needed the resilience to be able to face the real possibility of terrorism, violence, and harassment from hostile whites and disapproval from more conservative members in their own communities. Not everyone felt that they could take these risks. Many simply could not. So the perspective of activist narrators is one shaped by extraordinary circumstances and shared by a rather small cohort of extremely re-silient individuals.[57]

The desired qualities of the good old/bad old days is a cliché in life-history and oral history research. Scholars are beginning to document the reverence with which many middle-class African Americans now regard the segregated black community and the all-black schools. Some have suggested that this nostalgia might function as a critique of the more anonymous and less-connected schools and communities in a desegregated, but by no means egalitarian, American society. And certainly this seems to hold true for Delta narrators. The embattled communities that nurtured them often lavished praise and rewards on ambitious and hard-working young people and expressed an admiration for schooling and knowledge through a veneration of and tremendous respect for schoolteachers and other educated community leaders.[58]

But still another life-course effect could be operative among our oral history narrators. Each of them, while describing the positive aspects of the families and communities of their youth, nevertheless knew the conditions in which the majority of poor farmers and sharecroppers lived. Indeed, the recitation of the family's provision of rural plenty was ritualistic among our Delta narrators and often became a statement of bounteous nurturing and plenty. But I think that the chronicling of meats, vegetables, breads, jellies, fruit, and food had another function. By this listing, narrators were in fact celebrating their relative plenty and privilege in a world in which they knew all too well that many people suffered from malnutrition and disease. The recitation of foods became, in effect, a form of self-nurturing: a statement of the high value they held as family members and children within a dominant society that denigrated African American efforts to achieve.

These differences were brought home to many of our narrators when they worked for Head Start programs and recruited children from the most destitute sharecropping families: children with bulging stomachs and bowed legs, who had never tasted milk or fruit, who had never seen a doctor, who had never visited a dentist, and who were painfully terrified to leave their mothers' sides. Visits to the homes of these early Head Start registrants shocked many Delta leaders and must have driven home the relative bounty that their own parents and families had provided.[59]

Our narrators, then, speak with the voice of survivors—survivors of structural violence, social suffering, and a collective trauma that still stunts the life chances of many poor African Americans in Delta counties. They all knew that their survival was contingent upon many pieces of good fortune: strong-willed parents, good health, a relative freedom from the worst violence of the segregated system. Their rage at both elites and the poor can be read, I believe, as an angry acknowledgment of the *costs* of their survival, a cost that has been extracted through years of hard work, frustration, and much disappointment. At midlife and in late life, their gratitude to the past has become a gratitude at a number of simple and complicated survivals. And their motto, as with other survivors of human disasters, has become "Never Forget." And yet that memory has generated a corrosive politics of anger, directed at both the young people who do not seem to know the costs of their survival and at the elites whose policies seem to dampen the ambition and agency of the poor. Behind this anger we can find a lingering and costly residue of fear and distrust. Our narrators fear that the young will not learn their lessons of survival and resilience, and they fear that, without this knowledge, such young people will again become victimized by political and economic exploitation by elites. Anger, fear, and distrust are then the consequences of social suffering and collective trauma and are shared by many women and men who created and led the most important American social movement of the twentieth century.

The anger and fear are also expressions of grief and despair. Grief is the narrators' response to the too-real hardships and dangers of the past. Despair is an expression of blasted social hopes. After the hard work and risks of social suffering and activism, the expected regeneration of the community had not occurred. Although more young people become educated, many leave for opportunities elsewhere. And the social problems that had plagued segregated communities appeared to be intractable in the late 1990s. Grief and despair were the consequences of social suffering, the buoyant hopes of a social movement, and a resilient faith in individual and collective progress.

Notes

I would like to thank Andrea Hinding, John Lankford, Susan Rose, George Lipsitz, and Dan Schubert for their comments and suggestions for this essay. The faults, of course, are mine alone.

1. Several examples of this genre include Lasch, *Culture of Narcissism*; Berman, *Twilight of American Culture*; and Schlesinger, *Disuniting of America*.

2. The Delta Oral History Project produced life-history interviews with more than a hundred community activists and citizens from four contiguous Mississippi Delta counties—Bolivar, Coahoma, Sunflower, and Washington—with funding from a National Endowment for the Humanities collaborative projects grant. Principal interviewers were Owen Brooks of the Delta Ministry, Kim Lacy Rogers of Dickinson College, and Jerry Washington Ward Jr., formerly of Tougaloo College and now on the faculty of Dillard University in Louisiana.

3. See Farmer, "Suffering and Structural Violence," 261; Kleinman, "Violences of Everyday Life."

4. Greenspan, *Healing*, 125.

5. See Gaines, *Uplifting the Race*.

6. Nesse, "Hope and Despair," 470. See also Lazarus, "Hope."

7. Gaines, *Uplifting the Race*, 9–13.

8. See Greenspan, *Healing*; Lazarus, "Hope."

9. Elder, "Life Course and Human Development," 942.

10. See, for example, Rogers, "Trauma Redeemed."

11. Juanita Scott, interview by Owen Brooks and Kim Lacy Rogers, September 15, 1995, transcript, Delta Oral History Project (hereinafter DOHP), Tougaloo College Archives, Tougaloo, MS, and Dickinson College Community Studies Center Archives, Carlisle, PA.

12. Cora Fleming, interview by Owen Brooks and Kim Lacy Rogers, August 16, 1995, transcript, DOHP.

13. Kermit Stanton, interview by Owen Brooks and Kim Lacy Rogers, April 8, 1996, transcript, DOHP.

14. Robert Gray, interview by Owen Brooks and Kim Lacy Rogers, March 28, 1996, transcript, DOHP.

15. See Woodruff, *American Congo*; Cobb, *"Most Southern Place"*; McMillen, *Dark Journey*; Woods, *Development Arrested*; and Tolnay, *Bottom Rung*.

16. See Woodruff, *American Congo*; Cobb, *"Most Southern Place."*

17. See Elder, *Children of the Great Depression*; Elder, *Life Course Dynamics*; Elder, "Time, Human Agency"; Riley and Foner, *Aging and Society*; Riley, "Age Stratification"; Hagestad, "Social Perspectives"; Hareven and Plakans, *Family History*; Hareven, *Aging*; Quadrango, *Color of Welfare*; Laslett, *World We Have Lost*; Greven, *Four Generations*; Modell, *Into One's Own*.

18. Kohli, "World We Forgot."

19. Greven, *Four Generations*, 22; Stannard, "Puritan Child," 18, quoted in Marshall, "Aging and Dying," 132.

20. Marshall, "Aging and Dying," 132.

21. Laslett, "Necessary Knowledge," 3, 13.

22. Kohli, "World We Forgot," 284, 286.

23. Elder, "Life Course and Human Development," 941.

24. See the 1999 enlarged edition of Elder, *Children of the Great Depression*.

25. Elder, "Life Course and Human Development," 955–56.

26. Ibid., 956.

27. Ibid., 960. See also Kahn and Antonucci, "Convoys."

28. See McMahan and Rogers, *Interactive Oral History Interviewing*.

29. Kahn and Antonucci, "Convoys," 384.

30. Elder, "Life Course and Human Development," 964–66.

31. Ibid., 969–75.

32. Ibid., 957–58.

33. Rogers, *Righteous Lives*, 110.

34. Elder, "Life Course and Human Development," 958.

35. See McMillen, *Dark Journey*.

36. See McMillen, *Dark Journey*; Cobb, *"Most Southern Place"*; Curry, *Silver Rights*.

37. Stanton, interview (see note 13).

38. Scott, interview (see note 11).

39. Fleming, interview (see note 12). For events in Sunflower County, see Dittmer, *Local People*; Moye, "Black Freedom Struggle."

40. Gray, interview (see note 14).

41. Cobb, *"Most Southern Place,"* 331.

42. Ibid., 329–33.

43. For example, in the mid-1990s Bolivar County's black population was almost twice its white population, and only a little more than half the county's inhabitants over 25 years old had graduated from high school, with less than 16 percent holding college degrees. In 1993, 40.1 percent of Bolivar's population lived below the poverty line. See U.S. Census Bureau, U.S.A. Counties General Profile 1998: State and County Quick Facts: Bolivar County, Mississippi, http://www.census.gov/statab/USA98/28/011.txt (accessed January 26, 2005). Likewise, a 1989–1990 Bolivar County Consolidated School District survey found 59.93 percent of persons in poverty, compared to 24.52 percent for Mississippi total, and 12.76 percent for the U.S. The problem fell mostly on African Americans, for of all students surveyed, 81.16 percent of whom were enrolled in public schools, 82.63 percent were black. See Bolivar County Consolidated School District profiles in National Center for Education Statistics, Census 1990 School District Demographics Data Files, http://nces.ed.gov/surveys/sdds/tablemain90.asp (accessed February 2, 2005). Mississippi's children in poverty outranked the national average by 14 percent in 1990 and 5 percent in 1998. Compared to the national average in 1998, 2 percent more Mississippi children lived in extreme poverty, in families whose income fell 50 percent below the poverty level. See Mississippi profiles at Annie E. Casey Foundation, Kids Count: Census Data Online, http://aecf.org/kidscount/census (accessed January 26, 2005). Furthermore, the Lower Mississippi Delta

Development Commission reported in 1990 that "death rates in the Delta were higher across all age, ethnic, and gender groups, and for all causes of mortality. Death rates for Blacks in the rural areas of the region were higher than those of rural non whites in other parts of the USA from age one to age forty-four." Woods, *Development Arrested*, 249–50.

44. Mississippi infant mortality rates illustrate the trend. In 1990, the state's infant mortality rates were an average of 2.5 percent higher than the national rate. Thirty years earlier, in 1960, 54.4 out of 1,000 black infants born died under one year of age, compared with 26.3 white infants; and 29.6 black infants died before reaching one month, with the corresponding rate for white infants being 20.2. In the Delta, mortality rates for infants under one year were even worse: in Bolivar County, for black infants, 45.2, compared to 26.2 for white infants; in Coahoma County, 62.2, compared to 16.0; in Sunflower County, 55.0, compared to 16.3. Earlier, reports for 1939–1940 indicated Mississippi had infant death rates of 60.9 for blacks and 46.3 for whites, and in 1922, rates of 78.4 for blacks and 50.1 for whites. Annie E. Casey Foundation, Kids Count: Census Data Online, http://aecf.org/kidscount/census (accessed January 26, 2005). Additional statistics from Mississippi State Department of Health, "Births, Fetal Deaths, Deaths under 1 Year and Deaths from Certain Selected Causes, 1960" and "Infant and Maternal Death Rates by Counties, 1939–1940" (Jackson, MS: Bureau of Public Health).

45. Preston and Haines, *Fatal Years*, 70, quoted in Tolnay, *Bottom Rung*, 96. U.S. Bureau of the Census, United States Abridged Life Tables, 1939, Urban and Rural by Regions, Color and Sex (Washington, DC: Government Printing Office, 1943), cited in Tolnay, *Bottom Rung*, 97.

46. Dickins, "Nutrition Investigation."

47. Odom, *Southern Regions*, 51–59.

48. Cobb, *"Most Southern Place,"* 262–64.

49. McMillen, *Dark Journey*, 88–90.

50. Lee, *For Freedom's Sake*, 6.

51. Farmer, "Suffering and Structural Violence," 261.

52. Kleinman, "Violences of Everyday Life."

53. Ibid., 226, 234, 239.

54. Mader, "Emotionality and Continuity," 40.

55. Elias, "Human Beings," 105, quoted in Mader, "Emotionality and Continuity," 50.

56. Mader, "Emotionality and Continuity," 51.

57. See Rogers, *Life and Death*.

58. See Shircliffe, "'We Got the Best'"; and Harris, *Deep Souths*, 180–83.

59. See Rogers, "Crisis of Opportunity."

10

A Conversation Analytic Approach to Oral History Interviewing

Eva M. McMahan

> Given the active participation of the historian-interviewer . . . and given the logical form imposed by all verbal communication, the interview can only be described as a conversational narrative: conversational because of the relationship of interviewer and interviewee, and narrative because of the form of exposition—the telling of the tale.
>
> —Ronald J. Grele, *Envelopes of Sound*

Prior to the publication of the first edition (1975) of *Envelopes of Sound*, Ronald Grele discovered that "there had been little theoretical or methodological debate over the use of and nature of oral history."[1] In that volume and its later revisions, Grele called attention to the interactive processes that constitute an oral interview. He suggested that the oral history interview is a conversational narrative that contains a set of interrelated structures that must be understood if the historical account, or product of oral history, is to be interpreted and understood. The first set of relationships identified by Grele refers to the "linguistic, grammatical, and literary structure of the interview." The second set refers to the "interaction of the interviewer and interviewee." Grele explains that "contained within this relationship are those aspects of the interview which can be classified as performance.

Since the interview is not created as a literary product is created, alone and as a result of reflective action, it cannot be divorced from the circumstances of its creation, which of necessity is one of audience participation and face to face confrontation."[2] The third set of relationships deals with the idea that the interviewee as respondent speaks to the historian and also speaks through the historian to the larger community.

While each of these relationships spurred interest and debate over the next two decades, contributing to what oral historian Valerie Yow calls a "shift in the paradigm" in oral history, the concept of the oral history interview as a jointly created conversational narrative performance is most pertinent for this essay.[3] My contention is that principles of conversation analysis can inform the interpretation of oral history as a conversational narrative performance. In order to support that contention, I trace efforts to theorize interactive oral history interviewing, and I provide a conversation analytic framework for investigating the oral history interview.

Theorizing Interactive Oral History Interviewing

Grele's concern with the nature and use of oral history interviewing drew attention from many quarters. Most of the interest focused on issues that hit closest to home for historians; these included, but were not limited to, the role of the oral historian in creating a historical document that becomes documentary evidence to be interpreted within a sociohistorical space and tradition; the relationship among language, authority, and narrative; memory and history; and the impact of the interview on the interviewees and on the interviewer.[4] During that same time period, although not inspired directly by Grele's works, myriad works also were devoted to the theory and practice of research interviewing.[5] These works contributed greatly to the advancement of thinking about the oral interview as a research tool. Only a few scholars, however, were concerned specifically with the communication processes constituting oral history.

Inspired by Grele's interest in the performance elements of oral history, communication studies professors E. Culpepper

Clark, Michael J. Hyde, and Eva McMahan theorized the conversational narrative of oral history as a hermeneutic act. They argued that hermeneutics (the science of interpretation) is "the vital nexus" linking communication theorists and historians.[6] They defined oral history as "the process whereby an historian seeks to create historical evidence through conversation with a person whose life experience is deemed memorable. The process involves the understanding and interpreting of a past event in such a way as to sediment its meaning at a given point in time."[7] Moreover, only by understanding the nature of the communicative processes constituting the interview can the historical evidence be understood and interpreted.

Hermeneutics provides a foundation for conceptualizing the interview as a "synchronic communication event in which the construction of meaning emerges or unfolds through the interaction of interviewer and interviewee. . . . The meaning thus constructed and its relationship to future understanding ultimately will depend on the 'communicative performance' of *both* interviewer and interviewee."[8] This synchronic communication event constitutes a hermeneutical situation that itself has four interdependent relationships: the relationships between the interviewer and the interviewee; the relationship between the interviewer and the historical event to be interpreted; the relationship between the interviewee and the historical event; and the interdependent relationships among the interviewer, the interviewee, and the historical event.[9] Clark, Hyde, and McMahan theorized that the meaning that emerges out of oral history interviewing is dependent on "how *both* the interviewer and the interviewee achieve 'hermeneutical conversation.'"[10] As conceived by the German philosopher Hans Georg Gadamer, "To conduct a [hermeneutical] conversation means to allow oneself to be conducted by the object to which the parties in the conversation are directed. It requires that one does not try to outargue the other person, but that one really considers the weight of the other's opinion."[11] Based on Gadamer's framework, Hyde described a dialectical logic that could be applied to the oral history interview.[12] He argued that two relationships can emerge through the communicative performance. Which relationship emerges will depend upon how the conflict inherent in the different perspectives of the participants is managed. These relationships are contradiction and contrariety: "Contradiction occurs when interviewer and interviewee reify their separate understandings, interpretations, and meanings of the historical event. . . . Contrariety occurs when both interviewer and interviewee maintain their separate understandings, interpretations, and meanings of any feature of the historical event while acknowledging the potential validity of the other's world-view."[13] The relationship of contrariety generates hermeneutical conversation.

Subsequently, McMahan focused attention on the actual conduct of elite oral history interviews. She extended the hermeneutical foundation established earlier, and she introduced conversation analysis and discourse analysis as tools for unpacking the complex communicative performances of historians and respondents. Using audiotapes and written transcripts of interviews conducted by historians, she analyzed the "speech and counterspeech" of the oral interviews as they unfolded into contradiction or contrariety. The significance of understanding such processes, she argued, "is found in the relationship between the process of oral interviewing and its product(s). The discourse itself displays the unfolding thought processes. Rather than showing the last thing one thinks as in writing, conversation shows the first, second, third, etc., transformations of thought as the interaction evolves. . . . In other words, the dialogue between the participants displays the 'question-and-answer complex' that underlies the explication of the historical event."[14]

One of the most frequent relationships that emerged during the analyses was the interviewer in the role of "information elicitor" (relationship of contradiction) as contrasted with "information assessor" (relationship of contrariety).[15] In this situation, certain characteristics of topic management were revealed: (1) the interviewer's role as questioner legitimizes her or his overall topic control; (2) any utterance by the interviewer or interviewee may be heard as containing or implying a relevant topic and is fair game for further discussion; (3) topic talk is "retroactive and locally managed," that is, implicit topics can become explicit topics in future turns; (4) the actual topic can become extended, depending upon the interviewer's "third-turn response"; (5) "Although the adjacency pair (question-answer) is the fundamental structural unit of an interview, the three-unit question-answer-response is the necessary structure for extended topic management"; (6) "As a neutral elicitor of information," the interviewer's "possible third-turn responses are limited."[16] In addition, a parallel between topic management in news interviews and in oral history where the historian is simply an elicitor of information is identified. Finally, in this situation, the class of illocutionary acts known as requests comprise the majority of such acts initiated by the interviewer. Unsurprisingly, the most common form is the request for information. Others include requests for clarification and confirmation, to name a few.

Putting off requests is a topic management tactic used by interviewees who do not want to answer but also want to display cooperation with the interviewer. One common form of indirect refusal is illustrated below:

(01) E: Newspapers in reporting this said that our word was they were going to kidnap Leibowitz and Brodsky and while we were concerned with them that they would mob lynch the Blacks, Crowe told me there was never a word mentioned about the Blacks. Didn't consider them. Well, I left a Sergeant in charge.

(02) R: Did you talk to reporters about this incident? [Request]

(03) E: I'll tell you **about that** as I come to it. I'd left one of my best sergeants at the jail in charge. [Indirect Refusal][17]

While relationships of contrariety (hermeneutical conversation) are less common in the interviews examined, some instances are identified. The common factors contributing to the emergence of hermeneutical conversation are "the interviewer's use of requests for confirmation, disputable assertions, and mitigated challenges."[18] The following excerpt illustrates the use of a disputable assertion in the interviewer's third-turn response as well as the resulting hermeneutical conversation (emphasis in original).[19]

(01) R: All right. Now how did things change over the course of the time that you were there? What were some of the

significant developments as you saw them? [Request for Information]

(02) E: Overall the most significant one, I suppose, was the increase in size of the U.S. contingent out there! Equally, the steadily increasing *interest* by the United States *government* in Vietnam, which of course was just a follow-on to the decisions that the President had made as the effort gained momentum. This is almost true from the very beginning although the momentum built up as time went on! As to the organization in *country*, the major significant one of course was the establishment of the Military Assistance Command, MACV, in February of 1962. . . . Although COMUSMACV was officially established in February of '62, it seemed to me that no effect of MACV was felt until the following year, actually I would say about the latter part of 1962. . . . [Grant/Assertion]

(03) R: MACV's a sort of *curious breed of cat*, isn't it? You've got a four-star rank running the show, and yet he's subordinate to CINCPAC, and yet he *really has* his line going all the way back to Washington! How difficult was this command relationship? [Request for Confirmation/Disputable Assertion]

(04) E: It did not cause any difficulty as far as **I** was concerned. If there were any difficulty I would say it transpired because with a senior commander on scene, related especially to one service, it made it a little stickier to get my problems heard at the highest level! As to the idea that you bring up, I think that in *my mind* it amounted to something like this, CINCPAC was back in Honolulu. He had many other responsibilities around the Pacific area, and so in essence in my mind anyway it was something like *that part of the CINCPAC* organization that was focusing entirely on Vietnam had moved out to Saigon, and that was sort of the way I rationalized MACV. There's no *question* it was a one-over-one *command* situation which always seems to be a peculiarity. [Grant/Affirm][20]

Analyses such as those above demonstrate *language-in-use* as a part of the communicative work of the historians and respondents. Focus on these communicative performances underscored the need to attend to the creative processes involved during the interview itself. Clearly, concern with attention to only the product— a long tradition in oral history—no longer would suffice.

In 1994, McMahan and history professor Kim Lacy Rogers edited a volume containing essays that discussed the multidimensional and interactive nature of oral history interviewing. In that work, for example, Grele explored further the nature of oral history interview conversation and its effects on both historians and respondents. In an afterword, he also questioned the long-held view that democratic assumptions about fieldwork relations should prevail. Other authors addressed issues such as intersubjectivity in the interview, racial and ethnic variables in the interview, social psychological features of the interview, and the narrative construction of violence. The center that holds the essays together is the view that the oral history interview is both a form of and a product of communication and that multidisciplinary perspectives are necessary to probe the complexity of the interview.[21]

Despite the fact, as pointed out by McMahan and Rogers, that the oral history interview has been shown to be "a unique documentary form in which the evidence originates in the act of oral face-to-face communication,"[22] no other works focusing specifically on the communication dynamics of oral history have been produced. Moreover, discussion of the oral history interview is usually given short shrift in research handbooks, thereby neglecting many important elements, including the communicative dynamics.[23] In the following section, I propose a partial remedy for such neglect by providing a conversation analytic (CA) framework for interpreting and understanding oral history interviews.

A Conversation Analytic Framework

The proposed CA framework draws, first, on the general approach of conversation analysts[24] and, second, on the work of conversation analysts who focus on interaction in "institutional contexts."

Conversation analysis is a highly technical, microscopic approach to language-in-use. Although, as pointed out by sociologist Don H. Zimmerman, CA was "developed primarily within the discipline of sociology,"[25] it has no disciplinary boundaries. Practitioners of CA come from many disciplines and, as Zimmerman explained, "view conversation as a describable domain of interactional activity exhibiting stable, orderly properties that are *the specific and analyzable achievements of speakers and hearers.* Discovering the organization of this domain is the overriding concern of conversation analysis" (emphasis added).[26]

"The course of conversational interaction," according to Zimmerman, "is managed on a turn-by-turn basis, with the sequential environment providing the primary context for participants' understanding, appreciation, and use of what is being done and said in talk." *Sequential organization*, thus, is a primary interactional form, and it forms the foundation for the work of CA. Zimmerman continues:

> The critical point is that for sequentially organized actions, a speaker's present turn displays a particular understanding of the prior turn. In this fashion, a speaker can look to the next turn to find an analysis of what has just been said through the recipient's response to that talk. If the understanding does not align with that of the first speaker's, the opportunity to address that issue would be afforded in the next turn after, which would permit the recipient to discover the discrepancy. It is worth reiterating in this regard that the notion of adjacency and other sequential forms as templates of both action and interpretation provides not only a basic organizational form for interaction but also, as we have seen, a methodological resource for inquiry.[27]

CA's textual focus is on the language-in-use at a given moment in time. Interaction is analyzed, in Emanuel Schegloff's words, "as the primordial site of the social—the immediate and proximate arena in which sociality is embodied and enacted, whatever else may be going on at so-called 'macrosociological levels.'"[28] The features of interaction that are considered to be shapers of social interaction include adjacency pairs, turn taking, membership categorization devices, preference structure, openings, closings, sequential organization, person reference, and lexical choice. Identity management is also of concern, but it is treated as emerging out of the interaction; that is, identity is constituted and displayed in the give and take of the interaction. Meaning, as explained by anthropologist Michael Moerman, is generally thought to lie "neither in an apparent object nor a privately experienced subject, but in a world composed by the interaction and interpenetration of the seeming two."[29] In addition, structure is viewed as a feature of situated social interaction. Interactants orient to the structure as they manage the interaction. CA seeks to show how the participants orient to the structure, hence, to the design of the talk. As Ian Hutchby and Robin Wooffitt note, "What do we do when we talk? Talk is a central activity in social life. But how is ordinary talk organized, how do people coordinate their talk in interaction, and what is the role of talk in wider social processes? Conversation analysis has developed over the past thirty years to address these questions."[30]

In answering these questions, conversation analysts have studied the sequential order of talk and how persons accomplish orderly turn taking; turn taking in the display of understanding and in the response to prior turns; the inferential nature of talk; conversational sequences such as adjacency pairs, preferences and dispreferences, overlapping talk, repairs of talk, the asymmetrical nature of talk, storytelling, the management of interaction, how power is produced through talk-in-interaction, and the organization of factual accounts of events; and membership categorization devices. While the breadth and depth of the above is too vast for this essay, the work of conversation analysts who focus on interaction in institutional contexts will inform the remainder of this essay. Those analysts draw from the general work in CA, but focus their interest on a particular type of language-in-use: talk in institutional settings.

Talk in institutional settings refers to task-related interactions that, as defined by sociologists Paul Drew and John Heritage, "involve at least one participant who represents a formal organization of some kind."[31] Some of the contexts for such interactions include news interviews, court proceedings, job interviews, medical interviews, and psychiatric consultations.[32] It is useful to acknowledge that oral history interviewing falls under the rubric of institutional interaction. Clearly, oral history is task related; an interviewer sets out to obtain a respondent's story *for the record*. And, although the oral historian/interviewer might not represent a formal organization, the historian, nevertheless, represents her/his professional identity as a historian. As Drew and Heritage note, "The institutionality of an interaction is not determined by its setting. Rather, interaction is institutional insofar as participants' institutional or professional identities are somehow made relevant to the work activities in which they are engaged."[33] Anyone who has conducted an oral history interview knows that such identities permeate the process from beginning to end. Whenever oral history interviewing is viewed as institutional interaction, a common goal for conversation analysts is to elucidate how the conduct of an oral history interview is shaped or constrained by the way interactants orient themselves to each other and as representatives of social institutions. Such orientation has an important bearing on understanding the nature of the historical record produced via oral interaction. As Moerman puts it, "Those who use talk in order to discover what people think must try to find out how the organization of talk influences what people say."[34] Discovering the organization of the institutional interaction that comprises the conversational narrative of oral history is a worthy goal. What follows, then, is an incipient framework for such a project.

Sequential Organization

Clearly, the "speech and counterspeech" of the oral history interview is grounded in the sequential forms of adjacency pairs (question-answer) and third-turn responses (question–answer–follow-up question).[35] In fact, interviews are governed more strictly by this type of question-answer complex than are routine conversations; that is, by definition, interviews are question driven. Hence, the management and achievement of questions and of answers is central to the interactional form.[36] It follows, therefore, that the communication practices of the interviewers and of the respondents as they are governed by sequential organization and by the question-driven form of the interview should be of primary importance.

Graham Button, for example, demonstrates two sequential practices used in job interviews. One is the practice of not correcting a problematic understanding of the answer. The second refers to the questioner controlling the talk in order to prevent the respondent from returning to an answer. Button argues that these practices enable the interviewers to distance themselves from the answers, thereby giving the appearance of neutrality or objectivity.[37] Attention to such issues in the context of oral history would be helpful in assessing the influence of the oral historian upon the historical record. In earlier work, McMahan refers to interviewers as information elicitors (versus information assessors), a practice similar to that described by Button.[38] Since her research is based on a limited study of oral history interviews with elite respondents, many questions about sequential practices by interviewers remain.

Work that has been conducted on news interviews also can be useful because those interviews are created in order to produce some kind of record. Broadcast news interviews are somewhat unique in that they are produced for an "overhearing audience." More often in oral history, the third party to the interaction is the "imagined audience" or imagined recipient who will, sometime later, be privy to the interview record, either in its entirety, or more likely, in an edited form. Regardless of the degree of immediacy of the audience, we see the potential for the institutional elements of the interaction, including identity management, as well as the sequential organization of talk to influence the interview itself. Steven Clayman, for example, describes three procedures used by interviewers to display neutrality in television news interviews: "embedding statements within questions, attributing statements to third parties, and mitigating."[39] Such interactional work is at the heart of interview discourse, and it signals collaboration among all parties for task achievement. In a later study, Clayman describes how footing shifts in the question-answer complex of a news interview enable the questioner to achieve neutrality.[40] The footing shift is accomplished by attributing a potentially controversial statement to a third party. The interviewee's response, which grants that neutrality, affirms the fact that the achievement of neutrality is locally managed via the sequential organization of the interview.[41] In addition, Clayman discusses how footing shifts can be used by interviewers to present another side, to generate disagreement between interviewees, and to defend themselves against criticism.[42]

Agenda shifting is the concern of David Greatbach in a study of topical organization in news interviews. Some of the procedures used by interviewees to shift the agenda include violation of the interviewer's topical agenda by introducing a new topic into the answer and by suggesting that after discussing the new topic, the earlier topic will be addressed. Greatbach calls this "pre-answer agenda shifting" and suggests that interviewees exert control over the interview by using such tactics. Greatbach concludes that "in the context of the modern news interview it is not only a matter of how far an interviewer will allow an interviewee to go in avoiding answering and shifting topic. For the issue also arises as to what extent an interviewee can engage in these types of behavior before the benefits to be gained from them are outweighed by the possibility of their creating a disadvantageous impression on the broadcast audience."[43] By examining turn-taking in medical interviews, Richard Frankel shows that "the medical interview is restricted with respect to turn types and speaker identity and that these restrictions amount to a dispreference for patient initiated questions and patient initiated utterances."[44]

Greatbach uses an investigation of turn-taking in news interviews to demonstrate the management of disagreement between news interviewees.[45] Thus the interview context is extended to include interviews with panelists. The research is grounded in the work by CA on preference organization. In other words, agreements and disagreements in conversation and news interviews are referred to by CA in terms of preference organization. It is generally true that disagreements are dispreferred actions. Interactants, therefore, utilize various tactics for delaying, mitigating, or passing over disagreements. Greatbach shows the management of disagreements within the structure of turn-taking in news interviews. Generally, such disagreements are managed by invoking a third party to which a disagreement can be attributed. In the case of panel interviews, the respondents have more choices for such disagreement management. They can wait for the interviewer to address a question to them, or they can wait for the initial response from the addressed person, then disagree, or they can preemptively disagree, prior to the copanelist's response. Greatbach argues, among other things, that the choices made by the interviewees signal the strength and urgency of their disagreements. Moreover, it is usually the interviewer who must disengage the interviewees from their disagreements once they have been produced.

Again, research projects that focus on turn organization and turn types, including footing shifts during turns and preference organization, have the potential for elucidating the conversational narrative of oral history. In addition, the focus of CA on the ways participants manage the interaction, as stated by Hutchby and Wooffitt, "demonstrates that institutional contexts are the ongoing accomplishment of the participants in their interactional conduct, rather than external constraints which cause certain forms of conduct to occur."[46] Such a perspective is consistent with the prevailing view of the research interview as a "construction site of knowledge."[47] It is likewise consistent with the view presented here that oral history interview interaction is constitutive and that CA can aid in understanding the constitutive features of such a process, thereby illuminating the historical record.

Context

Context also is significant for CA and oral history interviewing. The idea here is that "structural resources used in conversation are simultaneously context-sensitive and context-free."[48] To be context-free means that interviewers and interviewees can accomplish their work whether or not they are in an institutional context. Their management of the question-answer complex is, on the one hand, not very different across contexts. On the other hand, the interviews are context sensitive, hence the management of the talk will be influenced by current talk, and that talk will influence the nature of the future talk. As Hutchby and Wooffitt note, "On each specific occasion, *these* participants in particular are designing their talk in the light of what has happened before in *this* conversation, and possibly also in their relationship as a whole, among other contextual specifics."[49] The local management of context-sensitive resources is illustrated in the following selection from McMahan's *Elite Oral History Discourse*:

(01) R: Okay, let me ((uh)) ask you about the relationships with other agencies then. ((uh)) To what extent were you directly or indirectly part of the National Security Council? I'm particularly interested in whether there was a special relationship there, of course, with Bill Bundy and Mac Bundy.

(02) E: ((uh uh)) Well, of course, you couldn't avoid a direct relationship between Bill Bundy and Mac Bundy.

(03) R: Right.

(04) E: But I don't know that this really affected the way things were handled. We worked very closely with State and had representatives from State in the Pentagon, ((uh)) for various meetings, although more often I was over at State.

(05) R: [uh huh]

(06) E: In connection with these problems we got to know the ((uh)) AID people as well as the State Department people rather well because . . . always worked closely together ((uh)) the military assistance and the economic assistance groups. We tried to mesh them as closely as we could the ((uh)) objectives sometimes differed, country by country.

(07) R: In what way?

(08) E: Well ((uh)) I thought of that when I said it. Now I've got to come up with an example.[50]

Turns 07 and 08 explicitly illustrate the production and monitoring (local management) of talk. The interviewer asks a follow-up question, "In what way?" The interviewee says, "Well ((uh)) I thought of that when I said it. Now I've got to come up with an example." The above also demonstrates what Heritage and Roth call the "context renewing" quality of interaction; "the interactional context is continually being developed."[51]

The Question-Answer Complex

The most well-developed research on institutional interviews focuses on the dynamics of the question-answer complex. Peter Bull, for example, investigates the interactional production of equivocation in political interviews, finding that interviewees are adept at appearing to give full and complete answers without actually doing so. Among the techniques used are partial replies, half answers, and interrupted replies.[52]

Greatbach shows how interviewers use supplementary questions as means for following up on the topic of interest. For example, *probing* includes tactics such as requesting supportive details, asking for an account of the interviewee's reported actions or opinions, and asking hypothetical questions. *Countering*, another supplementary question, involves conveying doubt about the answer or challenging the answer. *Pursuing* is used when the interviewee does not answer.[53]

Clayman pursues a line of research he calls answers and evasions. In a study of news interviews and press conferences, he finds that reformulating the question is a device used by interviewees to "answer/not answer" the interviewer's question. The study focuses on interviews with political candidates, elected officials, and public figures in the United States. Clayman notes:

> The scrutiny continues when news writers select excerpts from interviews and press conferences to construct sound bites on the nightly news and quotation sequences in print; these excerpts frequently show the public official to be resistant to the course of questioning. . . . Political commentators are more explicit, often discussing at length the extent to which politicians are forthcoming or evasive under questioning. . . . And ordinary citizens, having been exposed to extensive professional commentary and analysis, are perhaps predisposed to closely monitor such conduct for themselves. Accordingly, this is an arena where significant political outcomes may be influenced by mundane interactional skills and practices.[54]

Even though oral history interviews are not exclusively concerned with such public figures, my contention is that since the interview is institutional talk *for the record*, there is an element of public notoriety attached. Hence, what can be learned about the interactional production of news interviews has potential to inform oral historians.

Clayman's study, therefore, focuses on a communicative practice he calls "reformulating the question." He demonstrates that interviewers have the ability "to recognize and counter evasive formulations when they occur, while respondents can in turn employ such reformulations in ways that resist detection."[55] Basically, reformulations "recast" the question "in a way that alters its character," thereby enabling the respondent to take control, albeit temporarily, of the interview discourse. According to Clayman,

> The vast majority of question-answer sequences do not contain question reformulations, but those that do share certain common properties; question reformulations thus crop up disproportionately in certain sequential environments. Specifically, reformulations appear in environments where the relationship between 1) what the question is seeking to obtain, and 2) what the response actually provides, is potentially problematic. The "fittedness" of a response can become problematic when the question is particularly complex, or when the response diverges in some manner from the topical agenda established by the question, or some combination of these.[56]

Clayman identifies two practices that are common: "managing a response trajectory and shifting the topical agenda." Managing a response trajectory occurs when the respondent refers back to something in the prior interaction as the object of concern. This is atypical because CA tells us that usually the most recent topic is the preferred one in the interaction sequence. Clayman argues that respondents use question reformulations "when they are about to depart from this pattern, and by doing so they provide advance warning that something other than a standard response trajectory will be followed." Less innocent reformulations, Clayman notes, involve agenda shifting. Here the question is not complex but simple. The reformulation, therefore, is used not to clarify, as might be the case in managing a response trajectory, but is used to initiate a new topical direction. Clayman argues that determining whether an answer is evasive or not depends on the "perceived distance between the topical agenda as framed by the original question and the agenda established by the reformulation."[57] What is relevant here is that Clayman demonstrates the locally managed, interactional work that constitutes interviews. Oral history interviewers can learn from such microanalyses when applied to the oral history interview context.

Clayman's more recent research continues to center on questions and evasions in journalistic interviews. Yet, as indicated above, the relevance for oral historians is similar. Oral history interviews are potentially created for public scrutiny, although a limited public may actually see the interview transcripts. Even so, historians interpret those transcripts and audiotapes into a history for the public eye. Just as is the case for public figures, respondents must be careful about what they say in their answers. In order to save face, maintain credibility, or cover their footprints, interviewees may be less than truthful in the face of a knowledgeable and potentially hostile interviewer. But, as Clayman notes, "Evasiveness has a downside. Answering questions is treated as a basic moral obligation, not only for public figures in journalistic interviews but also for interactional participants more generally. . . . But while interactants generally expect each other to be properly responsive to questions, the responsive conduct of politicians is perhaps more closely scrutinized, so that attempts to resist, sidestep, or evade can be costly in a variety of ways."[58] Clayman, therefore, focuses on "doing answering" in this 2001 study. The basic question is how the respondents accomplish the communicative practice of answering. Some of the findings are instructive for oral history interview analysis.

Clayman finds that "some answers take a roundabout trajectory; they begin with a unit of talk which cannot in itself be construed as a possible answer, but which is a part of a larger stretch of talk that can be seen in its entirety as answering." In part because of this roundabout trajectory, interviewers must evaluate the answers as they are built "incrementally." This incremental or evolving process is constitutive of conversational interactional. This is turn-by-turn management of the talk. Even if the audience knows that interviews occur on such a basis, roundabout answering can lead to the suspicion of evasion. Clayman finds that an answering practice that is less vulnerable to such suspicion is "minimal answer plus elaboration" because the respondent "begins with a first unit of talk in response that provides the information targeted by the question, albeit in a minimal way, followed by subsequent talk that clarifies and elaborates,"[59] as in a yes-or-no question that can prompt a minimal response prior to clarification.

Clayman also explores two dimensions of resistance as they pertain to answering questions. They are the negative and the positive. Negative resistance includes those instances wherein the respondent fails to provide an adequate answer to the question, including refusal to talk about the question or its issues. The positive dimension of resistance occurs when the respondent "moves beyond the parameters of the question, saying and doing things that were not specifically called for. . . . The most dramatic form of departure involves a substantial change of topic."[60]

The management of such resistant answering practices provides clues for analysis of oral history interviews. For example, the respondent might be "overt" by indicating to the interviewer a change of topic or shift of agenda is forthcoming. Clayman demonstrates that one such practice is to "request permission from the IR to shift the agenda." Or the respondent might offer a "token request for permission" in that the answer proceeds without actually requiring a response from the interviewer. The advantage to the respondent of using such tactics is to mitigate interpersonal damage to the interviewer/interviewee relationship, thereby influencing the nature of subsequent interaction during the interview, and perhaps the interviewer's interpretation of the event after the fact. Other evasion practices include "minimizing characterizations" that essentially indicate that only a minor agenda shift or digression is forthcoming. Other interviewees actually "explain and justify" their efforts to divert the discussion away from the interviewer's agenda. The most extreme evasion, of course, is a refusal to answer, which carries with it severe breaches of conversational and interview etiquette. When executing such a refusal, the common practice is to try to place the blame for the refusal elsewhere, in fact, anywhere but with the respondent. For example, the respondent might claim confidentiality or ignorance of the answer or lack of authority to divulge the information. According to Clayman, such refusals can also implicate the interviewer by suggesting implicitly that the question was inappropriate, hence deflecting the responsibility back on the interviewer. Clayman also points out that when refusing to answer, it is in the best interest of the respondent to depersonalize the process in order to effect damage control. He calls this the refusal to answer "as a matter of general policy."[61]

Covert practices of answering are also evident in the data examined by Clayman. The end result is once again evasion; the process is not to acknowledge that an evasion is in process. The answer itself appears to be cooperative, but the respondent through word choice and repetition of words used by the interviewer manages to change the meaning of the words and of the question and answer. A similar practice is to modify the question at the start of the answer. Such a reformulation enables the respondent to appear to be cooperative and to answer the question.

What Clayman and others show through their conversation analytical approaches to interviews is that the interview is a complex communication phenomenon. Moreover, interactants are knowledgeable and skillful managers of interview interaction. Clayman states, "It is now apparent that the interview, far from being a neutral conduit for the transmission of information and opinion, is in fact a strongly institutionalized genre of discourse that exerts a pervasive influence on the conduit of journalists and public figures, and on the manner in which they form their talk with one another."[62]

My contention is that the same can be said of oral history interviews and their participants. Yet efforts to analyze oral history interview data and to theorize the communicative dynamics of oral history interviewing are incomplete. This is due, in part, to the lack of attention on the part of researchers to the oral history context. Plus, the research that has been produced is limited in its scope. I proposed a conversation analytic framework to be applied to oral history. I presented some basic tenets and concepts of CA, demonstrated selected findings from talk in institutional settings that have relevance for oral history, and suggested that more work on oral history interviewing by conversation analysts is needed. Until that happens, the work that Grele began in 1975 will remain incomplete.

Notes

1. Grele, *Envelopes of Sound*, 2nd ed., xvii.
2. Ibid., 136.

3. Yow, "'Do I Like Them,'" 70. See Thompson, *Voice of the Past*, 2nd ed.; Frisch, *Shared Authority*; and Portelli, *Death of Luigi Trastulli*.

4. Frisch, "Oral History and *Hard Times*"; Friedlander, *UAW Local*; Grele, *Envelopes of Sound*, 2nd ed.; Passerini, "Italian Working Class Culture"; Portelli, "Time of My Life"; Plummer, *Documents of Life*; Dunaway and Baum, *Oral History*; Stricklin and Sharpless, *Past Meets the Present*; Frisch, *Shared Authority*; Passerini, *Fascism in Popular Memory*; Jeffrey and Edwall, *Memory and History*; Gluck and Patai, *Women's Words*; Yow, "'Do I Like Them,'"; Van Maanen, *Representation in Ethnography*.

5. Mishler, *Research Interviewing*; Briggs, *Learning How to Ask*; Jackson, *Fieldwork*; Silverman, *Interpreting Qualitative Data*; Lindlof, *Qualitative Communication*.

6. Clark, Hyde, and McMahan, "Communication" (1978), 1.

7. Clark, Hyde, and McMahan, "Communication" (1980), 30.

8. Ibid., 30–31.

9. Ibid., 31–32. See also McMahan, *Elite Oral History Discourse*.

10. Clark, Hyde, and McMahan, "Communication" (1980), 33.

11. Gadamer, *Truth and Method*, 330, quoted in Clark, Hyde, and McMahan, "Communication" (1980), 33.

12. Hyde, "Prescriptive Theory."

13. Clark, Hyde, and McMahan, "Communication" (1978), 14–15.

14. McMahan, *Elite Oral History Discourse*, xiv, 5, 25.

15. For related findings, see Greatbach, "Management of Disagreement."

16. McMahan, *Elite Oral History Discourse*, 33–34.

17. Ibid., 52.

18. Ibid., 78.

19. See Greatbach, "Management of Disagreement."

20. McMahan, *Elite Oral History Discourse*, 72–73.

21. McMahan and Rogers, *Interactive Oral History Interviewing*.

22. Ibid., vii.

23. See Fontana and Frey, "Interview," 656.

24. An extensive overview of conversation analysis can be found in Hutchby and Wooffitt, *Conversation Analysis*.

25. Zimmerman, "On Conversation," 406.

26. Ibid., 407.

27. Ibid., 408, 423.

28. Schegloff, "What Next?" 141.

29. Moerman, *Talking Culture*, xiii.

30. Hutchby and Wooffitt, *Conversation Analysis*, 1.

31. Drew and Heritage, "Talk at Work," 3.

32. Heritage and Roth, "Grammar and Institution"; Clayman, "Answers and Evasions"; Greatbach, "Management of Disagreement"; Atkinson, "Displaying Neutrality"; Button, "Answers"; Heath, "Delivery and Reception"; Bergmann, "Veiled Morality."

33. Drew and Heritage, "Talk at Work," 3–4.

34. Moerman, *Talking Culture*, 9.

35. McMahan, *Elite Oral History Discourse*, 10.

36. See Clayman, "Answers and Evasions"; Heritage and Roth, "Grammar and Institution."

37. Button, "Answers," 227.

38. McMahan, *Elite Oral History Discourse*, 55.

39. Clayman, "Displaying Neutrality," 474.

40. Clayman, "Footing."

41. See McMahan, *Elite Oral History Discourse*, 55–78, for a related discussion regarding the achievement and management of disputable assertions.

42. Clayman, "Footing," 174–79.

43. Greatbach, "Topical Organization," 443, 454–55.

44. Frankel, "Talking in Interviews," 231.

45. Greatbach, "Management of Disagreement."

46. Hutchby and Wooffitt, *Conversation Analysis*, 171.

47. Kvale, *Interviews*, 14.

48. Hutchby and Wooffitt, *Conversation Analysis*, 35.

49. Ibid., 35–36.

50. McMahan, *Elite Oral History Discourse*, 1.

51. Heritage and Roth, "Grammar and Institution," 18.

52. Bull, "Identifying Questions," 120–29.

53. Greatbach, "Supplementary Questions," 86–123.

54. Clayman, "Reformulating the Question," 161.

55. Ibid.

56. Ibid., 163, 165.

57. Ibid., 165, 166, 177.

58. Clayman, "Answers and Evasions," 404.

59. Ibid., 407, 409.

60. Ibid., 414.

61. Ibid., 416–17, 418–19, 423.

62. Clayman, "News Interview Openings," 48.

11

Women's Oral History: Is It So Special?

Sherna Berger Gluck

Is women's oral history a distinct genre, clearly differentiated from other forms of oral history? Certainly at its origin we believed that to be the case, as reflected in 1977 in one of the first methodological articles on women's oral history published in the United States.[1] Some thirteen years later, as more literature was published and women's studies had taken new turns, Susan Geiger challenged this somewhat naïve and seemingly essentialist feminist assumption, asking, "What is so feminist about doing women's oral history?"[2] In the following dozen years, writings in women's oral history proliferated even further, and the practice today has become more highly nuanced and complex, compelling us to examine more closely the very notion of women's oral history—or feminist oral history—as a distinct genre. What kind of clues can be found in the nature of the work usually referred to as women's oral history? Is it a question of content, of who is the narrator, the interviewer? Is the methodology really distinct, or is it more a matter of the perspective that marks the analysis of interviews and their presentation and use? The questions themselves have changed over time, and so, too, have the answers.

Charting the history of these developments in the U.S. reveals both continuity and change in methodologies: continuity in interviewing techniques and in commitment to feminist ethics, but change in the modes of analysis of both the interview process and its resulting narrative. It also points to the ways in which women practitioners imbued with a feminist sensibility have influenced the general field of oral history and, in turn, have been influenced by the writings of several leading male practitioners. Perhaps it is time to question if women's oral history is really so special—assuming that it ever was—and to talk instead about the feminist practice of oral history, recognizing that men and women alike might share the sensibility that produces women's oral history. By taking a historical approach to a discussion of women's oral history and drawing on selected examples to highlight issues, one can assess the various approaches taken in response to recurring questions. Some of these have evolved into current "best practices," and others have entered the pantheon of choices from which an oral historian can draw.

The Early Years

Although people came to women's oral history from different points, the origin of what might be called the U.S. women's oral history movement might be traced to the founding conference of the National Women's Studies Association in January 1977. Some ten years after the founding of the Oral History Association, which had its base in academe, grassroots feminist activists and scholars initiated an informal network of feminist oral historians. While many women had been gathering oral histories for several years as part of their involvement in community-based feminist organizations, others had been using oral history as a pedagogical tool in the burgeoning women's history and women's studies movements. Later in 1977, these practitioners and the voices of the women they were helping to bring forth were made more visible and public with the launching of the first special issue on women's oral history of *Frontiers: A Journal of Women Studies*.[3] Even at this early stage, the number of oral history projects listed in the resource section of that issue was staggering.

In the ensuing twenty-five years, two more special issues of *Frontiers* focused on women's oral history,[4] and an anthology of original essays on the topic appeared.[5] The proliferation of

English-language articles on women's oral history testified to the expansion of the dialogue on feminist research methodology, and their substance marked the increasingly sophisticated questions raised by practitioners, some of which went to the heart of the question about genre.

What characterized the work in women's oral history from the beginning was the effort to bring forth women's voices—an effort shared by the new social historians who were seeking to make visible and give voice to those who had been rendered historically invisible and voiceless. At that stage of the enterprise, women historians were mainly committed to what in the 1960s and 1970s they characterized as "recovery." Their rhetoric, and indeed practice, was rooted in the women's liberation movement, on the one hand, and in the new social history movement, on the other.

In contrast to the first generation of mainly academic historians and the archivists who ran oral history collections programs in universities, many of the early women oral historians were feminist advocates. And although much of the current discourse was yet to be adopted, there is no doubt that they were operating on the assumption that women's experiences and, consequently, their narratives, were gendered. As a result, the oral histories conducted by this first generation of feminist practitioners tended to focus on women's everyday lives, with particular emphasis on ordinary women, especially from the working class and communities of color. There was a near, though unspoken, consensus that this meant asking women about certain aspects of sexuality, reproduction, and family relationships. The commitment to pursuing such intimate subjects, based on the belief that the "personal is political," often placed feminist oral historians squarely in conflict with other women practitioners who had been conducting interviews with elite women and believed that they couldn't possibly ask the women they interviewed these kinds of personal questions. Their reluctance revealed the vast differences in perspective on both class and gender between themselves and the new feminist generation of women oral historians.

Clearly, even in its earliest formulations in the 1970s, women's oral history encompassed more than merely interviewing women. In other words, in the lexicon of the early debates about feminist research, women's oral history was not merely *about* women. It was *by* and *for* women, as well. There was an assumption that the interview process was governed by some shared gendered experiences between interviewer and narrator; the interview itself was seen by many as a feminist encounter that empowered interviewer and narrator alike. This commitment to empowerment caused one early writer, Ann Oakley, to assert that the concept of interviewing women was "a contradiction in terms." The commitment of feminist research to validating women's subjective experience led Oakley to advocate equalizing the relationship between the interviewer and narrator, to transform it from what some characterized as a "directed monologue" into an interactive dialogue designed to promote commonality and even friendship.[6]

Most feminist women oral historians also subscribed to a connection between interviewer and narrator and tended to assume that gender transcended all other differences and created a bond between the two. Furthermore, underpinning these assumptions, which were rooted largely in the women's liberation movement, was a commitment to advocacy.[7] Not only did the oral histories that were being collected help to introduce women into history, but also this very process implied advocacy; it did not merely expose women's oppression, but promoted women's agency.[8]

Methodological Prescriptions

Although there were few real differences in the methodological recommendations made by early practitioners, most did not subscribe to the kind of extreme leveling of the relationship between interviewer and narrator to which Oakley subscribed. However, no one located themselves at the opposite end of the spectrum and advocated "objectivity." The challenge to the objectivity promoted in positivist research, in fact, was one of the hallmarks of feminist methodology and the nascent field of women's studies. Nevertheless, one of the most widely circulated and reprinted early methodological articles strayed little from many of the standard prescriptions for conducting an oral history interview. Rather, what differentiated it from the earlier, nongendered advice was the emphasis both on focus and content—on exploring the "rhythm of women's lives"—and on the political base.[9] The latter was grounded in making the connection between the public and private and the emphasis on subjectivity and the intersubjectivity of interviewer and narrator, although this latter concept was only named later.

The emphasis on subjectivity, on capturing the rhythm of women's daily lives, led to a greater tolerance for a more open and fluid interview, and even for lengthy digressions. Whether or not the turn to subjectivity reflected a cultural conversational convention in which U.S. women participated is debatable.[10] The end result, however, was that in the attempt to uncover women's experiences, and particularly to give women a voice, feminist oral historians were more patient; they were hoping to find "the diamonds of the dust heap" to which Virginia Woolf alluded.[11] The task, then, was to learn how to balance the narrator's agenda with our own; to let her meander and offer up the diamonds instead of our focusing mainly on our sense of what was important—which might produce merely the pearls.

Clearly, then, the grounding of women's oral history in feminism placed it in opposition to the objectivist emphasis and the search for "facts" that was promoted by the first generations of male oral historians. For instance, instead of following prescriptions such as those advising the interviewer not to laugh, women's oral history was likened to any other human interaction with the expectation that the same kind of warm, human responses would govern it. Regardless of this attentiveness to the intersubjectivity of the narrator and interviewer, the interview was still viewed as a "quasi-monologue on the part of the narrator," which was to be "encouraged by approving nods, appreciative smiles, and enraptured listening and stimulated by understanding comments and intelligent questions."[12]

Another prescription, which the androcentric practitioners did not specifically acknowledge, centered on the question of cultural similarity. Feminist practitioners—who initially were always women—assumed a guaranteed rapport based on gender. They did acknowledge cultural differences based on race, class, ethnicity, and even regional identifications, and while the preference was for cultural likeness/similarity, there was an understanding that the role of the "outsider" was often a critical necessity. There was even a recognition that the outsider sometimes was able to do a better interview than an insider—or at least explore certain aspects of identity and experience better than the insider.[13] In those days of binary distinctions, however, attention had not yet been called to the complexity of positionality.

Going against the Grain: Focusing on Orality/Aurality

While the first generation of oral historians, men and women alike, focused on creating text/transcriptions, many of the second generation focused more on voice, recognizing that the oral history was "a unique 'document,' one which above all is oral/aural"[14]—a theme to which we will return. The politics of women's oral history, with its rhetoric of giving voice to the voiceless, coupled with limited resources and a commitment to advocacy and empowerment, led many second-generation practitioners to develop simple, alternative means of processing interviews. While anthropologists such as Dennis Tedlock were recommending creative transcription as early as 1972,[15] keeping the focus on aurality often meant creating simple means of easily locating material on the sound recording. Passages might then be used in audio and audiovisual presentations, such as the tape-slide shows on woman's suffrage and on shipyard workers, and even in performances, such as the theatrical community presentations later introduced by women in Montana and Idaho. None of this is to say that women's oral history was not used as a documentary source in scholarly articles and books, or that it was never transcribed. In fact, in addition to their use as documentary sources, an increasing number of edited oral histories were being published.

Inspired, empowered, and flush with the new knowledge imparted by the voices of formerly unknown and unrecognized women, some feminist oral historians touted the oral history narratives as a reflection of women's experience. Indeed, they uncovered many secret aspects of women's lives: how women obtained abortions or how they practiced self-abortion; their relationships with other women and with the members of their families; ways that they were crushed by patriarchy, or alternatively, subverted it. Also, they tended to accept everything they heard as a transparent view of reality. In other words, during this age of recovery, feminist oral historians were not yet ready to problematize the oral history narrative. They focused more on content than on form, and even as they acknowledged the meaning imparted by subtle communication patterns and performance, they were not yet prepared to dig deeper.

The Second Decade—The Next Step(s)?

By 1983, some six years after the launching of the first systematic discussion of women's oral history in *Frontiers: A Journal of Women's Studies*, another special issue appeared with a promise that the second decade would lead to what Susan Armitage called "the next step." As she pointed out, the recovery/discovery stage had led to publications that emphasized the uniqueness of women's stories, and she urged moving "from the single story to the whole picture," with the full recognition that it was necessary to "be systematic and critical." As others would caution over the next decade, even as calls to be critical grew louder, Armitage counseled that caring and appreciativeness still served as guideposts. In other words, the hallmark emphasis on the relationship between interviewer and narrator remained primary. But Armitage pleaded for women's oral history to move beyond discovery, urging practitioners to "step back and ask questions about meaning, about comparability, about context." Failing that, she argued, the full potential of women's oral history would be unrealized.[16] Other scholars of women's studies were likewise concerned about comparability, and several projects incorporated social science methods into their designs.[17]

Many of the articles in this second collection of U.S. women's oral history work revealed a growing emphasis on women's subculture, paralleling to a great extent the kind of analysis in which earlier women historians had engaged in the nineteenth century and early twentieth century. In other words, it was uncovering another layer of women's reality, marking a shift from the individual and unique experience to the group experience. Nevertheless, few of the articles in the volume heralding the next step, the second decade, really challenged the notion of the transparency of the account. New projects and new and creative uses of oral history were documented, most of these pointing to the continued adherence to the ethics and advocacy of women's oral history promoted earlier.

Perhaps the most significant feature of this 1983 volume was the attention paid by Sherry Thomas, editor of a collection of farm women's oral history interviews, to the question of orality, to the problems of rendering voice into text.[18] Despite the title of her article—"Digging beneath the Surface: Oral History Techniques"—which suggests something different, Thomas did not really advocate any new interviewing methods or techniques. Rather, she focused on the difficulty of rendering voice into print. She was practically the first among women oral historians to discuss the problem in any depth, pointing out how "the material can absolutely lie, depending on the sentence structure and the spelling of the words . . . even if every word is exact." Although as she edited the farm women's interview transcripts—Thomas removed her own questions and did quite a bit of cutting and pasting to render a seamless, dramatic story—she remained cognizant of the meaning derived from orality. Ultimately, she depended on her sense of the person, her sense of "what they were trying to convey about their lives."[19] The fact that the women liked the final product confirmed her belief that she had rendered the material correctly. But we have to ask if that is enough. What exactly was the product? Isn't it more like the "autobiography" that Alex Haley shaped of Malcolm X's life? In other words, who assigned the meaning to the material, the narrator or the interviewer/editor? The question of assigning meaning, as we shall see, is one that began to dominate the field of women's oral history as the end of the 1980s approached. But even in the earlier part of that decade, Thomas joined European practitioners such as Luisa Passerini in understanding the significance of silence.[20]

Opening the Door: New Question, New Challenges

Just as questions about meaning were beginning to surface, rendering the oral history narrative a bit more opaque, the empowering potential of the oral history process also came into question. The validation that women seemed to experience in recounting their life stories, a validation referred to repeatedly by feminist interviewers and documented by quotes from their narrators, came under scrutiny. The packed and attentive audience at a 1988 Oral History Association roundtable titled "Appropriation or Empowerment: Oral History, Feminist Process, and Ethics" testified to the fact that the kinds of ethical questions about which feminists ruminated regularly had much broader resonance.[21] Daphne Patai had tried several years earlier to concretize some of these concerns by surveying a range of oral historians, both men and women.[22] Although feminist practitioners did not have a monopoly on ethics, the issues that they kept raising seemed to influence the larger oral history movement. For instance, although early versions of the Oral History Association's *Evaluation Guidelines* addressed ethical considerations, their paramount concern was legal questions. Beginning with the 1989 review of the guidelines, the emphasis shifted considerably. Ultimately, a set of standards and principles were adopted that not only prescribed guidelines but also laid out a series of responsibilities. Most significantly, for the first time the relational and intersubjective nature of oral history received official recognition by the professional organization, a recognition that implicitly undermined the positivist practices long before abandoned by feminists.[23]

It is no surprise that the inspiration for some of the changes in the standards and principles for the oral history profession, as well as some of the new terminology and concerns adopted by feminist oral historians, in particular, came from anthropology. After all, the life history interview, which feminist oral historians had largely adopted in the beginning of the recovery/discovery process, was a standard methodology in anthropology and qualitative sociology. Historians, however, had no professional guideposts of their own for women's oral history. In their practice of oral history, they relied mainly on their commitments to "feminist process," a guiding principle that remained relatively unchallenged by historians until well into the 1980s.

Shifting Sands

Where the first decade of women's oral history had assumed unproblematically that "women's oral history" was naturally feminist, and that women's experience, of course, was gendered, these terms and categories came under more critical scrutiny in the 1980s. Moreover, new language was developed that both challenged some of the early assumptions and gave a name to others. *Intersubjectivity* and *reflexivity* entered the lexicon, naming some of the processes that had been understood and often followed, but that had been rooted more in women's liberation rhetoric and praxis than in anthropology. Coupled with these refinements and a logical outcome of their implications was a more highly nuanced understanding of positionality, moving away from the rather simplistic and oppositional insider/outsider distinction.

One of the major developments that undermined some of the bedrock assumptions about women's oral history was the problematizing of the category "woman." Theoreticians such as Joan Scott challenged the unitary category "woman" and shifted the focus to gender.[24] Although from the beginning feminist historians presupposed that women's experiences were gendered, there was nevertheless a tendency to treat gender as primary, and even all encompassing. As a result, in most early women's oral histories, even while acknowledging women's multiple identities, the underlying premise of women's unitary experience went unchallenged.

Indeed, the argument that there was something distinctly identified as women's oral history stemmed from the principle of women's unitary experience. In turn, this led to the implicit assumption that women's oral history was a feminist enterprise and, like other feminist research, it was *by*, *about*, and *for* women. Toward the end of the second decade of women's oral history, however, challenges arose against both this assumption and the formulaic definition of feminist research. Simultaneously, and largely as a result of the influence of post-structuralism, a very different lens was being used to analyze the oral history narrative, and the literature moved from characterizing the narrative as a transparent reproduction of real experience to discussing it as a more complex representation of that experience. As noted by the Personal Narratives Group at the close of the second decade of women's oral history: "When talking about their lives, people lie sometimes, forget a lot, exaggerate, become confused, and get things wrong. Yet they *are* revealing truths. These truths don't reveal the past 'as it actually was,' aspiring to a standard of objectivity. They give us instead the truths of our experiences. . . . The truths of personal narratives are neither open to proof nor self-evident. We come to understand them only through interpretation, paying careful attention to the contexts that shape their creation and to the world views that inform them."[25]

The issue of interpretation had slowly transformed the use and presentation of women's oral history. Grounded originally in the recovery/discovery process, feminist oral historians eagerly had grasped the new voices being heard through women's oral narratives, voices that were often presented "raw," justified by the paean that they were letting women speak for themselves. By contrast, during the second decade, there emerged a call for and expectation that feminist oral historians would engage in interpretation and contextualization. Of course, with more attention paid to the creation of text, the fact was recognized that the printed version of an oral narrative was highly mediated, but the interpretation that had shaped the written form remained hidden from view.

The *Testimonio* Tradition: Lessons from Latin America

While many North American practitioners began to question the transparency of the "raw" narrative in which women were "speaking for themselves," scholars of the Latin American *testimonio* genre were raising a different challenge.[26] The oral narratives they produced there, though presented in the voice of an individual woman, such as the Guatemalan Indian civil rights organizer Rigoberta Menchú, were emblematic of a collectivity.[27] In other words, another layer was added, making the narrative even more opaque. Not only did it have to be treated as a representation of reality rather than a transparent image, but also that representation had to be understood as standing for more than the depiction of the individual's experience. This added layer challenged many of the assumptions inherent in life history, but instead of accepting the emblematic nature of the *testimonio*, some critics questioned the authenticity of the narrative because all the "facts" didn't fit. Perhaps even more disturbing was the way that the collective voice of the Third World *testimonio* often was erased as it was prepared for publication in the First World. The most dramatic example of this erasure is found in the English version of the title of Rigoberta Menchú's book: *I, Rigoberta Menchú*. As Claudia Salazar notes in her analysis of Menchú's testimony, the English title's individualistic proclamation completely contradicts the reference to the collectivity embodied in the original Spanish-language title: *Me Llamo Rigoberta Menchú y Así Me Nació La Conciencia* (My Name Is Rigoberta Menchú and This Is How My Consciousness Was Born).[28]

Testimonio literature contributed to the ongoing evaluation of feminist oral history practice by calling attention to the collective voice in the narrative, particularly if it was an oral history of an activist. It also raised another challenge to the presentation of the "raw" narrative—the tendency to "let them speak for themselves"—without any interpretive or contextual analysis.

The Third Decade

Despite the many challenges to earlier thinking and the provocative new—and sometimes troubling—approaches that were inspired by theoretical shifts in a host of disciplines, not until the approach of the next decade did practice catch up with theory in women's oral history. Then there was an explosion of provocative publications that dramatically changed the practice of oral history in general and women's oral history in particular.

Where earlier there was an implicit assumption that feminism was the defining feature and guiding light of what had come to be known as women's oral history, Geiger, a longtime commentator on life history, called for a more explicit and precise formulation. Noting that "there is nothing inherently feminist . . . about women's oral histories or women doing women's oral histories," she posited four objectives that determined whether or not women's oral histories were indeed feminist: "They presuppose gender as a (though not the only) central analytical concept; they generate their problematic from the study of women as embodying and creating historically and situationally specific economic, social, cultural, national and racial/

ethnic realities; they serve as a corrective for androcentric notions and assumptions about what is 'normal' by establishing and contributing to a new knowledge base for understanding women's lives and the gendered elements of the broader social world; they accept women's own interpretations of their identities, their experiences, and social worlds as containing and reflecting important truths."[29]

In addition to clearly articulating what had, in fact, been the implicit feminist objectives of women's oral history from its inception, Geiger, like Michael Frisch, called attention to the question of interpretive authority. As she pointed out, the issue of authority is grounded in "the relationship between the researcher and her living 'source.'"[30] Even as she called for accepting women's own interpretations of their identities, experiences, and social worlds, Geiger did not abdicate the scholar's responsibility of interpretation. Rather, she believed that feminist oral history methodology reflects and values the practice of the researcher and the narrator—whom she designated as the oral historian[31]—alike, and that "if she is careful, the feminist historian's own interpretive product will encompass radical, respectful, newly accessible truths, and realities about women's lives."[32]

Geiger made it clear, however, that this does not necessarily mean that the researcher will have the same interpretation as the "living sources." Rather, the feminist practitioner cannot wittingly or unwittingly violate the words of the individuals that have become the "subject matter." In other words, despite her attempt to make explicit the feminist determinants of women's oral history, Geiger ultimately relied on the same subjective standards that have been embodied in the feminist ethic governing women's oral history from its inception. It goes beyond the "do no harm" advice proffered in the earliest standards of the oral history field and comes closer to the new thinking reflected in the language of the current Oral History Association *Evaluation Guidelines* that references the letter and *spirit* of the narrator's agreement.

In *Women's Words: The Feminist Practice of Oral History*, co-editor Daphne Patai and I struggled with the question of what constitutes women's or feminist oral history. We rejected the "three little words"—*by*, *for*, and *about* women—and viewed this requirement as a reflection of both feminist arrogance and essentialism.[33] It had become increasingly clear that women did not necessarily or exclusively use what might be characterized as feminist methodologies in their work, and furthermore, that they might not necessarily be studying only women, but rather might be interviewing men and women. Moreover, it had also become obvious that some men, particularly those engaged in popular history, were also employing what had come to be referred to as feminist methods, that is, they were attentive to the relationship between narrator and researcher, questioned interpretive authority, and were advocates for social change and challenging the gender system.

As a result, Patai and I chose to characterize what previously had been referred to as women's oral history as "the feminist practice of oral history." As it turned out, all the contributors to *Women's Words* were women, but the points had been made that women did not hold an exclusive franchise to the practice—in other words, just being a woman was not sufficient—and that a gendered analysis might also reflect feminist practice, even if the focus was not exclusively on women. Indeed, only one of the requisite "three little words" continued to have resonance: work *for* women. At a minimum, it was expected to serve as an alternative to the androcentric body of literature. Despite the other challenges to the defining characteristics of feminist research, and hence what had been labeled women's oral history, the adherence to advocacy remained one of its hallmarks.[34]

The Quest for Meaning

The turn to the analysis of gender, in contrast merely to a focus on and assumption of the unitary category "woman," was part of a larger theoretical shift that influenced all disciplines, particularly those that dealt with narrative. The impact of this shift is reflected in many of the essays published in *Women's Words*. Post-structuralist influence promoted problematizing of both the oral history interview itself and the sense that was made of the narrative. On the one hand, as alluded to earlier, it meant a more critical and complex analysis of the relationships of the researcher and the narrator, demanding, among other things, attention to all the implications and complexity of the positionality(ies) of the interviewer. On the other hand, this in turn led to more meaningful discussions of reflexivity, that is, the critical analysis of the researcher's positionalities, expectations, and subjectivities and how these factors affected the interview process.[35]

Problematizing the interview process itself, including the complex relationship between the interviewer and narrator, and addressing questions about performance, language, and memory gained prominence in the work of all oral historians, with feminist practitioners adding gender to the mix. Earlier recognition that oral histories revealed only a partial truth about a life was extended to an understanding that there were multiple truths, multiple stories that unfold, not only among people involved in the same events and communities, but even for one narrator. Alessandro Portelli's work probably has had the most far-reaching impact in oral history circles, in general, perhaps because it is also the most engaging and accessible.[36] The work of Portelli and others led to deeper discussions of memory. Unlike the much earlier questions about the accuracy of memory, subsequent questions focused on the social construction of memory.

Gender, Memory, and Speech

If men's and women's lived experiences are gendered, then it is only logical to assume that the way they remember their experiences and narrate them is also gendered. Nevertheless, as Selma Leydesdorff, Luisa Passerini, and Paul Thompson discovered, this idea, although noted early on in memory studies, remained long unexamined among oral historians.[37] Recent studies of women in the Western world have certainly pointed to the different emphases on how women reconstruct and communicate their memories. For example, Richard Ely and Allyssa McCabe's study of the narratives of white North American working- and middle-class children and adults found that girls and women used more reported speech and dialogue than boys and men. As the researchers explained, when telling stories, females were more likely than males to "include what someone once said."[38] Likewise, Caroline Daley's analysis of the oral histories of four sets of brothers and sisters from a small New

Zealand town revealed how they "constructed themselves and their histories within a dominant gendered ideology," a fact reflected both in the focus and emphasis of their stories/memories and in how these were communicated. The women, not unexpectedly, talked about "home and family, religion and community." By contrast, Daley noted, the men "were more forthcoming when asked about crime and disorder, alcohol and fighting" than about domestic life or familial relationship. Their style of telling differed, too: "The men, who were much more likely to talk in long bursts, saw themselves as the natural storytellers of the community, and tended to place themselves as the heroes of the tale." Daley concluded that "whether these women were home-loving or not, whether the men personally were involved in any bravado or not, this is the way they present their past. In this way memories and self-perceptions, and thus oral history, has a gendered form." Moreover, in relating incidents from their early childhoods and family life, the siblings' stories diverged so widely that it was almost as if they did not live in the same family. While a brother in a sibling pair presented an authoritative account of their father's bookmaking activities, his sister was very tentative; she "only has a feeling" that her father participated in bookmaking. While it is obvious that gender-specific experiences led to gender-specific reporting, Daley reminded us that, at another level, the differences are also part of a gendered ideology.[39]

Just as current theories challenge the early work in women's oral history that suggested an "essential" woman, feminist historians must also be careful not to essentialize gendered memory in exploring the complex interplay of experience, language, and discourse. Class and ethnicity must certainly be brought into the equation. Also, as Adriana Piscitelli noted, although "gender influences the themes, structure, shape, and expressive styles that form life narratives," how gender impacts the transmission of memory is also determined by age (generation). Like Daley's New Zealand research discussed above, Piscitelli's work among three generations of Brazilians revealed that in the narratives of older Brazilian women, in contrast to those of the men of their age group, family life was the dominant theme. By contrast, the next generation of women, those who joined the professional world, no longer used kinship group memberships as a fundamental reference point. Nevertheless, they were still more inclined than their male peers to organize their life stories around affective life.[40] It is not only generational age differences that reveal different modes of remembering and telling, but also the age at which experiences occurred. In analyzing her oral histories of African American professional women, sociolinguist Gwen Etter-Lewis noted that the women used black English to recount their childhood experiences, while they used highly nuanced standard English in recounting their professional lives.[41]

Some writers, heavily influenced by the post-structuralist turn, with its focus on the construction of meaning through language, began to subject the text produced from interviews to narrative analysis. An example of this approach is Marie-Françoise Chanfrault-Duchet's narrative analysis of the text derived from the life histories of two working-class French women. Examining the text for key phrases and patterns, she borrowed from literature to construct three narrative models: the epic, Romanesque, and picaresque. Beyond that, she delineated myths that were at play in the narratives. While Chanfrault-Duchet's emphasis on the "socio-symbolic" content of the two women's narratives yielded interesting typologies, it ultimately relied on an overdetermination of "ideological blueprints," which she assumed the women had internalized.[42]

Whatever Happened to Agency?

The ideological blueprints to which Chanfrault-Duchet referred reflected the growing influence of post-structuralism among feminist scholars and the shift in emphasis from experience to discourse. The earlier argument by Scott against using "woman" as a unitary category certainly challenged the near essentialist view of earlier work in women's oral history and promoted more nuanced and complicated work. Beyond that, however, as noted by Penny Summerfield, Scott's insistence that gender "is constantly constructed and reconstructed by powerful sources which define women and men and control the parameters of possibility in their lives" deeply upset the world of women's history. Summerfield claimed, "It sounded like a recipe for abandoning the focus on women, individually and collectively, which was so central to the 'recovery' of women from and for history in the 1970s. It appeared to recommend the study of discourses about women, produced by powerful institutions, rather than women's words and women's actions themselves."[43]

While the ensuing debates over experience, agency, and the role of discourse separated many women historians into two camps, Summerfield and others argued against the false dichotomy of experience and discourse. Instead, they subscribed to Judith Butler's argument that "construction . . . is the necessary scene of agency, the very terms in which agency is articulated and becomes culturally intelligible."[44] Following this line, Summerfield's oral history of British women's wartime experience relied heavily on discourse analysis. Even though wartime might very well produce a unified, dominant discourse, Summerfield observed that gender nevertheless differentiated the discourse, that "the war effort, national unity, and post-war reconstruction meant different things for men and women, as well as those of different social class and colonial status." She argued that the personal narratives were both "products of a relationship between discourse and subjectivity" and products of the relationship "between subjects and their audiences . . . and the performance models available to them." She used this framework to explore how the narrators understood and explained their wartime subjectivities and the reconstruction of their wartime lives. Based on their narrative forms, Summerfield categorized the women as "heroics" or "stoics" and illustrated how they drew on different wartime discourses of femininity.[45]

Other feminist oral historians, such as Canadian Joan Sangster, were more critical of post-structuralist writings but nevertheless sought to draw on insights derived from them. Sangster noted that she is attentive not only to the role of "past and current political ideology" in constructing historical memory, but also to the " ingredients of the narrative form, such as expression, intonation, and metaphors." Nevertheless, she expressed grave concern about the latter:

> While an emphasis on language and narrative form has enhanced our understanding of oral history, I worry about the

dangers of emphasising form over context, of stressing deconstruction of individual narratives over analysis of social patterns. . . . Nor do we want to totally abandon the concept of
experience, moving towards a notion of a de-politicised and
"unknowable" past. We do not want to return to a history
which either obscures power relationships or marginalises
women's voices. Without a firm grounding of oral narratives in
their material and social context, and a probing analysis of the
relation between the two, insights on narrative form and on
representation may remain unconnected to any useful critique
of oppression.[46]

Seeking to situate post-structuralist insights in a feminist ma-
terialist context, Sangster analyzed the strike stories of five
Canadian women. She made sense of the very different versions
of their strike experiences—versions that diverged considerably
from the written accounts of labor militancy—by examining not
only "the power relations of age, gender, ethnicity, and class,"
but also "the dominant gender ideals of the time." Her analysis
enabled Sangster to detect "discernible patterns" in the strikers'
very diverse stories. The women remained real live actors whose
stories reflected their lived experiences, as influenced by gender,
class, family relations, and political ideology.[47]

Problematizing Meaning

Attempts such as Sangster's to draw on the insights of post-
structuralism while retaining a solid grounding in lived experiences have proliferated, resulting in different kinds of analyses.
The oral history process and resulting oral narratives have been
problematized in a host of ways, leading both to more careful
scrutiny of how language is used and how public discourse
shapes the story. More consideration is also being given to the
way that the present shapes the telling. All of these new directions have motivated some feminist oral historians of the "first
generation" to return to their earlier work and reexamine their
assumptions and conclusions.

Emily Honig, for example, in the mid-1990s, returned to her
1977–1978 interviews with Chicana garment workers who had
participated in a two-year strike against Farah Manufacturing

Company in El Paso, Texas. At the time of the interviews, the women were still consumed by the 1972–1974 strike and still very involved with the union. Looking back with a more critical eye and with an ear attuned to the implications of the particular interview moment, Honig wondered if the language of social justice so prevalent during and immediately after the strike led the women to invoke stories of working-class heroism within family members and if accounts of their work life at Farah before the strike were more indicative of union discourse than of their lived experiences. Was the strong feeling of community that they attributed to the barrio another product of the poststrike "narrative moment"? And what sense could one make of the stories of rebellious childhood incidents, particularly since the women tended to characterize themselves as timid and passive in the past, in contrast to their self-confident poststrike present. Honig concluded that the "women are not inventing nonexistent past experiences, but they are telling them with the language, perceptions and mandates of the present." Moreover, paying greater attention to the intersubjectivity of narrator and interviewer, Honig also questioned if the women's claims of the transformative impact of the strike might have been a response to the interviewers who came to hear about their strike experience. Despite her questioning, Honig claimed, "This does not mean that oral history should be devalued or rejected. Rather, it should be problematized as one of many possible tellings of a woman's life story and not the source of her single 'true' experience."[48]

The importance of the "narrative moment" in making sense of oral history interviews was revealed to me with even more clarity in my own reexamination of oral histories of Palestinian women's movement activists. Tracking the changes in the narratives that I recorded in repeated interviews with the same women in 1989–1994, I initially pointed to an evolving feminist consciousness among women activists, contextualizing these in the shifting rhetoric on women in the Palestinian movement as a whole. However, in a study of the "memory of politics and the politics of memory," in which I drew on both my own interviews and those done by someone else in the early 1980s with some of the same women, I discovered that the discourse of 1991 reflected the very same consciousness that some of the women had revealed almost ten years earlier. Drawing on the insights of Ted Swedenburg's analysis of his interviews on the 1936–1939 revolt, I detected the same varying influence of the political environments, which alternated between pluralism and conformism. During the height of the 1987–1993 intifada, the pressure for political conformism muted expressions of feminist consciousness, whereas both before the intifada and toward its end political pluralism had prevailed, enabling the women's movement to diverge from the discourse of national unity and more openly display a feminist consciousness.[49]

Yet another model of the way that gender, memory, intersubjectivity, and political ideology can be problematized in women's oral history is provided by Daniel James in his book on the life of Argentinian political activist María Roldán. James first presented Doña María's "voice" through the transcript and then "read" her narrative. Because the central events and experiences of Roldán's life were presented primarily in class terms, gender does not seem a promising theme. Yet, as James proceeded with his "reading" of the text, which is almost a "prototypical Peronist woman's life script," he unpacked other images, roles, and themes that gave her story a different "twist." Rather than merely accepting the emblematic traditional, feminine model of Evita Perón, heroine for Peronistas such as Doña María, James worked at uncovering counter-discourses. Ultimately, he did not present a new, feminist "life script," but rather saw Doña María's story as being "told out on the borderlands" with all its "unresolved contradictions, silences, erasures and conflicting themes."[50]

The Fourth Decade

Launching the fourth decade of women's oral history—or the feminist practice of oral history—two special issues of *Frontiers: Journal of Women Studies* appeared in 1998. As indicated by the titles of the special issues, the first highlighted varieties of women's oral history, and the second, problems and perplexities in women's oral history. That second issue opened with a reflective discussion between Armitage and me, two of the first generation of women oral historians, that acknowledged the new directions in women's oral history but also expressed a certain level of uneasiness.[51] While I traced my growing appreciation of the importance of complex power relations and the difficulties of representation, Armitage expressed her concerns that "undue emphasis on complexity encourages interviewer self-absorption at the cost of enthusiasm and interest"[52]—a concern raised a decade earlier in *Women's Words*. Undoubtedly, this matter stemmed from the initial infatuation with post-structuralism and the erasure of experience in favor of disembodied textual analysis. However, as the third decade progressed, as evidenced by some of the works discussed above, feminist scholars were achieving a balance between the insights offered by post-structuralism and a respect for "lived experience." Indeed, the articles in the 1998 special issues of *Frontiers* on women's oral history, appearing some twenty-one years after the first, groundbreaking one, reflected both the more problematized approach to the narratives and the more naïve presentation of recovery narratives.

Re/Current Tensions/Contradictions

The ongoing search for meaning in/derived from oral narratives certainly has been enhanced by the new analytical directions discussed earlier. However, while these might increase the understanding of women's lives, they too often grant the historian/interpreter a new hegemonic role. In other words, they seem to be counter to the feminist commitment to advocacy and ethics.

While historians can certainly maintain feminist ethical standards in the interview process, simultaneously adopting a critical stance of self-reflexivity and sensitivity to and appreciation of the narrator, the next stage of the oral history process presents a greater challenge. What role does/should the narrator have in the search for meaning? Does the application of sophisticated interpretive models mute her voice and strip her of her authorial control? These questions go to the heart of how/for whom historians produce their work.

Can historians share authorial control with the narrator, asking for her interpretation and/or her reaction to their interpretation? The latter requires that historians use accessible language, a goal to which many feminist scholars still subscribe, but that is too often undermined by some of the language used by advocates of postmodernism. And, of course, even if historians do manage to discuss their interpretations with their narrators, what if they disagree? Who has the last word? It is still very seldom that oral historians of any stripe engage in this effort at shared authority.[53]

Presenting women's voices and writing them back into history was long considered a mode of advocacy, but has problematizing the oral history process and narrative stripped us of this pretense? Does it work to use a model where the narrator's "voice" is first presented without interpretation, followed by the scholars "reading" of the narrative? Perhaps. It must be acknowledged, however, that the "voice" has already been mediated when it is presented as written text, although new technology does facilitate presentation of the unmediated voice in its original oral form. Can we still view oral history as a medium for combining scholarship and activism in the form of advocacy? Or must we now separate our two roles and goals, presenting voice on the one hand and analysis on the other?

Another thorny set of questions persist with regard to ethics. As discussed previously, some early women oral historians, in their rejection of "objectivity," prescribed practices that attempted to remove the social distance between interviewer and narrator. However, others later began to realize that this attempt at erasure of a "professional" relationship was, instead, potentially more exploitative.[54] Over the past decade, most feminist practitioners have attempted to develop a model that is based neither on forming a "friendship" nor on adopting the stance of the remote "observer/researcher."

Clearly, a host of ethical dilemmas, in addition to issues relating to power differentials and authority and control over the meaning of the narrative, will continue to face scholars in pursuit of a feminist practice of oral history. Do we resign ourselves to the impossibility of formulating a single prescription, *a* best practice? Written more than a decade ago, the words that close the *Women's Words* anthology probably remain the best advice for dealing with the re/current questions and contradictions faced by feminist oral historians:

> There is not merely one appropriate methodology, nor one type of research project, that all scholars should rush to duplicate. No blanket prescription will help us; we need, rather, to engage in self-critical examination of our practices and to go on to develop a range of models from which to select our procedures according to the needs of specific, and often unique, research situations. It is possible to be temporarily immobilized by an awareness of serious problems in the oral history process, whether these relate to procedures, or to ethics, interpretation, or politics. . . . Alternatively, researchers can decide to ignore these problems for the sake of proceeding unimpeded. But a third path is possible . . . [that] shows us how to get on with our work even as we reflect on its procedures and its uses and take steps to change these where needed.[55]

Regardless of the decisions made about methods, the self-reflexivity engaged, and the theories employed for interpretation, feminist practice still requires that the narrator is not effaced.

Conclusion

At the opening of this chapter, I raised the question, Is women's oral history a distinct genre? What can we now conclude? Certainly, it is now clear that not only women can produce women's oral history; nor does the study of women by any woman necessarily produce women's oral history. A feminist perspective is still the basic determinant, a perspective that not only understands how women's experience is gendered, but that also understands the tension between women's oppression and resistance. Does this perspective necessarily change the conduct of oral history interviews? It does, in the sense that sensitivity to the gendered nature of women's experiences necessarily leads to an exploration of certain topics and attention to the complexity and layering of meaning in women's responses. But other prescriptions about sensitivity to pluralism, the complex nature of intersubjectivity, and balancing the narrator's and interviewer's agendas should apply equally to the conduct of any good oral history interview.

What does the future hold for the feminist practice of oral history? Most likely it will mean a continued debate about ways to best balance the insights of post-structuralism with a commitment to women's agency, to documenting women's lived experiences. In this regard, the new technology that enables presentation of the unmediated voices of narrators might provide one solution, particularly if that presentation includes the unmediated *voice* along with our analysis.[56] New online journals present a unique opportunity to do just that.[57] The ethical issues raised by the online delivery of oral history recordings will be an ongoing consideration, and *all* historians will have to be attentive to them as new practices emerge.

Perhaps one of the most exciting developments in women's oral history since its "official" inception in the U.S. twenty-five years ago is how its questions and processes have influenced the wider practice of oral history. James's gendered analysis of the oral history of Doña María is one indication of this. So, too, is the way that some of the insights and practices of women's oral history have become codified in the standards and practices of the Oral History Association.

Clearly, there is not any single answer to the increasingly complex questions raised about the practice of women's oral history. Yet, even as the debate continues, many historians would still argue about the need to recover women's voices. For one thing, as Armitage argues, women's oral history remains a powerful discovery and connective tool in the classroom.[58] Beyond that, it remains an important tool both for empowering women, by bringing forth their voices and their sometimes hidden forms of resistance, and for advocating on their behalf by documenting their experiences of discrimination and subordination.

Notes

1. Gluck, "What's So Special" (1977).
2. Geiger, "What's So Feminist."

3. *Frontiers* 2: 2 (1977). Also in 1977 the British Oral History Society published a special journal issue on the topic. See Bornat et al., "Women's History."

4. Special issues focusing on women's oral history appeared in *Frontiers* 7:1 (1983), and fifteen years later, in *Frontiers* 19:2 (1998) and 19:3 (1998). In 2002, selected articles from the various *Frontiers* issues were compiled in Armitage, Hart, and Weathermon, *Women's Oral History*.

5. Gluck and Patai, *Women's Words*.

6. Oakley, "Interviewing Women."

7. Sociologists Joan Acker and Dorothy Smith were among the early promoters of this idea. See Acker, Barry, and Essevelt, "Objectivity and Truth"; D. Smith, "Sociology for Women"; and D. Smith, *Everyday World*.

8. Bloom, "Listen! Women Speaking."

9. Gluck, "What's So Special" (1977), 3.

10. Kristina Minister referred to a different mode of conversation embraced by women in Minister, "Feminist Frame."

11. Woolf, *Writer's Diary*, 7.

12. Gluck, "What's So Special" (1977), 8.

13. Ibid., 6–7. Yvonne Tixier y Vigil and Nan Elsasser, one a New Mexico Hispanic and the other an Anglo, were among the first to compare the differential results of their interviews with the same women. See Tixier y Vigil and Elsasser, "Effects of the Ethnicity."

14. Gluck, "What's So Special" (1977), 11.

15. Tedlock, "Learning to Listen."

16. Armitage, "Next Step," 3, 4.

17. Sample projects included "Rosie the Riveter Revisited: Women and the World War II Work Experience," at California State University, Long Beach, and "Lives of Arizona Women: Past and Present," at Arizona State University, Tempe. For descriptions of these projects, see Mann, "Directory," 114.

18. Thomas, *We Didn't Have Much*; Thomas, "Digging beneath the Surface."

19. Thomas, "Digging beneath the Surface," 52, 53.

20. Ibid. See X, *Autobiography*; Passerini, "Italian Working Class," 8–9.

21. Sherna Gluck, Marcia McAdoo Greenlee, Daphne Patai, and Liz Kennedy, "Appropriation or Empowerment: Oral History, Feminist Process, and Ethics," panel presentation, Oral History Association annual conference, Baltimore, MD, October 14, 1988.

22. Patai, "Ethical Problems,"12–18.

23. See Oral History Association, "Evaluation Guidelines."

24. Scott, *Politics of History*, 25–27.

25. Personal Narratives Group, *Interpreting Women's Lives*, 261.

26. See D. Sommer, "Women's *Testimonios*."

27. See Menchú, *I, Rigoberta Menchú*.

28. Salazar, "Third World Woman's Text," 96.

29. Geiger, "What's So Feminist," 169, 170.

30. Ibid., 175. See Frisch, *Shared Authority*.

31. Geiger, "What's So Feminist," 180n6.

32. Ibid., 180.

33. Gluck and Patai, introduction to *Women's Words*, 2.

34. The persistence of advocacy as a hallmark of feminist research is evident in the host of books on feminist methodology, including Fonow and Cook, *Beyond Methodology*; DeVault, *Liberating Method*; and to some extent Reinharz and Davidman, *Feminist Methods*.

35. Hale, "Feminist Method," is a preeminent example of this kind of reflexivity. It is no coincidence that Hale is an anthropologist.

36. Portelli, *Death of Luigi Trastulli*.

37. Leydesdorff, Passerini, and Thompson, *Gender and Memory*, 2.

38. Ely and McCabe, "Gender Differences," 17.

39. Daley, "Gender and Oral History," 345, 347, 355.

40. Piscitelli, "Love and Ambition," 89, 95, 100.

41. Etter-Lewis, "Black Women's Life Stories," 50–52.

42. Chanfrault-Duchet, "Narrative Structures," 79, 80–81, 90.

43. Summerfield, *Women's Wartime Lives*, 10. See also Scott, "Useful Category."

44. Butler, *Gender Trouble*, 147, quoted in Summerfield, *Women's Wartime Lives*, 11.

45. Summerfield, *Women's Wartime Lives*, 12, 16, 82–99.

46. Sangster, "Telling Our Stories," 8–9, 22.

47. Ibid., 21.

48. Honig, "Getting to the Source," 145, 148, 154–55, 156.

49. Gluck, "Memory of Politics." See also Gluck, "Advocacy"; Gluck, *Intifada Years*; Hiltermann, *Behind the Intifada*; and Swedenburg, *Memories of Revolt*.

50. James, "Reading Doña María's Story," 217, 242.

51. Armitage and Gluck, "Reflections."

52. Armitage, "Introduction," iii.

53. One of the most engaging discussions of this effort is Borland, "'Not What I Said.'" Interestingly, Borland changed the article's original title, which was "When We Women Disagree."

54. Stacey, "Feminist Ethnography," 113.

55. Gluck and Patai, afterword to *Women's Words*, 222.

56. See, for example, California State University, Long Beach, VOAHA: Virtual Oral/Aural History Archive, http://salticid.nmc.csulb.edu/cgi-bin/WebObjects/OralAural.woa/ (accessed March 2, 2005).

57. See, for instance, *Journal for MultiMedia History*, http://www.albany.edu/jmmh/ (accessed January 26, 2005).

58. Armitage and Gluck, "Reflections," 7.

12

Narrative Theory

Mary Chamberlain

Recent years have seen what Ken Plummer refers to as the "narrative turn" in the social and behavioral sciences and the humanities.[1] It is a turn closely allied (and in many ways synonymous) with the "turn" to biographical methods or the renewal of interest in autobiography.[2] Within history, this "turn" was first noted by Lawrence Stone in his 1979 essay "The Revival of Narrative: Reflections on an Old New History" in *Past and Present*. History (at least in the Western tradition) has always prided itself on its use of narrative as a means of re-creating the past. Indeed, in some languages (French, Italian, German, Norwegian) the words for *history* and *story* are interchangeable. The linkages between history and story (and even in English the words echo each other) point to sequence as a structure, to ways of presentation (from prose to epic poem), and to the exploitation of emotions, suspense, and drama in order to sustain attention. What, therefore, was new about this old form?

While Stone noted its "new" development in history, there were parallel developments in sociology, anthropology, and psychology and a renewed interest in narrative in literary studies. That scholars in these fields "turned" to narrative as an analytical model was partly a response to the emphasis on the positivist methods that dominated the social sciences between the 1940s and 1970s. Within anthropology, for instance, the "turn" to nar-

384

rative highlighted the role of culture and the symbolic and in-
verted emphasis on structure and function that had dominated
the 1950s and 1960s. Rather than observing everyday behavior
and actions as manifestations of rational purpose, which may
produce cultural artifacts and activities that are observable, ex-
plicable, and utilitarian, such behavior and activity could be seen
as signs of the underlying imaginative and conceptual frameworks. Clifford Geertz, one of the earliest and frequently cited
exponents of this cultural "turn," for instance, based his influential argument for "thick description" on a concept of culture that
was "essentially a semiotic one." Within this, he argued, the student must engage with the "imaginative universe" within which
the acts and activities of human agents "are signs." In this interpretative perspective, culture was "not a power, something to
which social events, behaviours, institutions or processes can be
causally attributed; it is a context, something within which they
can be intelligibly—that is thickly—described."[3]

The move away from the observable and measurable into the
symbolic and the semiotic emerged as part and parcel of the
post-structural and postmodern intellectual climate, challenging
established disciplines and enabling fresh approaches to the
study of culture and new cultural phenomena such as the media.[4] It also spilled into history, that branch of the humanities
that considered itself immune to the ravages of intellectual fashion, dealing, as it did, with past activities within well established
methodological parameters. Indeed, as Paul Cobley argues,
"Narrative is absolutely crucial to an understanding of postmodernism."[5]

These phenomena appear to be connected, for the rapid advances in technology and changes in the political environment in
the latter half of the twentieth century transformed the social
and material world, reducing to hazy traces the old certainties of
an economy based on manufacture and industry, of a social
world predicated on class, of communications that predated
global connectedness, and of emancipatory political projects. In
their place, "globalization" (notably of capital and its international institutions) connected the financial and material world in
ways that challenged the traditional agendas of nation-states, reducing the citizen to the status of consumer and the worker to a

member of the army of international reserve labor, while the grand ideologies of communism and liberalism gave way to the micropolitics of identity. The collapse of constancy in the political and economic world was paralleled by an intellectual crisis in the academic world. Thomas Kuhn's *The Structure of Scientific Revolutions* was an early, and influential, indicator of this, pointing to the way in which knowledge acquisition proceeded not in a steady, cumulative fashion, but as a result of ruptures and shifts in dominant intellectual processes—paradigms—that dominated methods as much as inquiry.[6] Truth and certainty did not and could not exist, for the ultimate quest was at the mercy of the preoccupations and practices of successive generations. The immediate, knowable past seemed infinitely fragile, as the intellectual, political, and cultural emperor was revealed to be naked rather than suited; the past was nothing more than a "construction," a story, a narrative that represented, but could not consolidate, the real world. The exploration into narrative took many forms.

Whereas for Stone, and apparently for generations of historians before him, narrative was a straightforward description of what history was—a well-written unfolding of the sequence of the past—for the new historians (and the anthropologists, sociologists, and psychologists) the term *narrative* became a far more complex phenomenon. As we have seen, one of the key insights that emerged from post-structuralism related to the gap between representation and experience, for the former can only represent, not reproduce, the latter, and then only through the use of cultural symbols, of which language is the most ubiquitous. While historians may engage in telling the past as it actually was, they could at best only *represent* what they imagine to have been the case based on the historical record (i.e., the documents) as they find them. The historical record itself was, however, as Cobley indicates, "a discursive entity made up of signs [which] means that it offers a *re*-presented, thoroughly selective account of what actually happened."[7] Documents became less the substance and more the sign of the past. Once their symbolic, as well as (or rather than) actual, reading was acknowledged, then the imaginative universe of history could move into exploring other symbols as historical meat, historiography could become a more reflexive exercise in meaning, and history itself, a set of competing "fictions." It was a short move from seeing history as a record of the past (albeit subject to competing interpretations)—based on solid, empirical evidence, conforming to Leopold von Ranke's principle of showing "the past as it actually was,"[8] in which a narrative form seemed the most appropriate descriptive agent—to seeing it as an infinitely more problematical representation of human agency. In this sense, the writing of history bore close affinity with other forms of imaginative writing and engaged with the similar narrative devices.

A parallel, and related, development in history was a dissatisfaction with the broad Whiggish interpretation of history as a record of progress that—with its concomitant emphasis on the actions of great men and nations, its dependence on the written document as the historical record, and the periodization of the past into "watersheds" of historical determinism—necessarily disenfranchised those sectors of the population who neither engaged with nation building nor left written documents. The flowering of histories "from below," which began in the late 1960s and early 1970s and included feminist, working-class, black, and other minority history, demanded new sources and methods.[9] The growth of oral history was integral to this movement.[10] (The use of narrative as a descriptor of oral histories and life stories did not become commonplace, however, until the 1980s, and as a mode of analysis, not until the 1990s, by which time it was also an established subfield in other disciplines, notably psychology and anthropology.)[11]

Narrative

The challenge to the *composition* of history found articulation in notions of narrative. Paul Ricoeur's monumental three-volume *Time and Narrative* not only marked the apex of this "turn" to narrative but also located it theoretically *at* the heart of and *as* the heart of historical inquiry. Histories have, after all, always told a story. But the explanation for why history and the narrative form are such natural bedfellows lay, for Ricoeur, in the underlying quest and mystery of human existence. For him, this

mystery resided in the impossibility of understanding, accounting, and describing time. The response to this intractable problem was the creation of narrative as an allegory and metaphor
of time, a means to depict it, and humanity's relationship to and
location within it. History, dealing ineluctably with the past,
present, and future, and people, aware of their intermediate position between their predecessors and successors, have used
narrative as the only way through which the vast expanse of
time ("cosmic" time) can be reduced to human proportions and
their movement through time and their measurement of it can
be located. Ricouer explains, "The . . . calendar . . . cosmologizes
lived time and humanizes cosmic time. This is how it contributes to reinscribing the time of narrative into the time of the
world." Furthermore, he states, "Time becomes human time to
the extent that it is organized after the manner of a narrative;
narrative, in turn, is meaningful to the extent that it portrays
features of temporal existence."[12]

All notions of time involve narrative as their primary descriptor, for narrative necessarily involves tense; narratives look
not only backward but forward, locate the self in the present,
and pivot the focus through time and space. "So," Ricoeur argues, "the future seems to be representable only given the assistance of anticipatory narratives that transform a living present
into a future perfect mode—this present will have been the beginning of a history that will one day be told." But if tense was
integral to narrative, so too was language: "To have a present
. . . someone must speak. The present is then indicated by the coincidence between an event and the discourse that states it. To
rejoin lived time starting from chronicle time, therefore, we have
to pass through linguistic time, which refers to discourse."[13]

Shortly after Ricoeur published *Time and Narrative*, Hayden
White, in the United States, published *The Content of the Form*:
Narrative Discourse and Historical Representation. While concur-
ring with Ricoeur's emphasis on the importance of narrative to
human life, White refined it by charting the development of historical narrative from the primitive annals (which, he argued,
narrated but did not narrativize) through to the medieval
chronicles, to the intricate weaving of history into a recogniza-
ble narrative form. For him, the impulse to narrativity lay less

in the insoluble quest to describe time than in a far more Hegelian rationale: to legitimate power. For White, the narrativization of history was only necessary, and possible, once some rudimentary state demanded it. "Narrativity," he argues, "is . . . related to, if not a function of, the impulse to moralize reality, that is, to identify it with the social system that is the source of any morality that we can imagine." While its rationale may differ, White (like Ricoeur) saw historical narrative as having both a figurative and a symbolic function.[14] These not only described time and events, measuring and judging in the process (actions that necessarily invoked time), but they also turned those events into icons, symbols of deeper cultural meaning. Indeed, what distinguishes a historical event from a natural one is precisely that we confer on one a symbolic meaning as historical event, a meaning both compounded and repeated by its location within a historical narrative. The irony, however, was that we can confer symbolic meaning because we order our world according to a preexisting idea of what is possible as an object of knowledge.[15] In other words, in order to figure out what may have happened, we first have to prefigure it. This is as much the case with the grand "narratives" of history as with the ordinary way we order our lives and stake out our priorities. We cannot look, imagine, remember, describe, or recount without first having the imaginative structures that enable this, a point subsequently argued by the French sociologist Maurice Halbwachs in his *On Collective Memory*.

A final strand in the development of narrative as a theory of explication emerged in the same time frame: in 1984, Jean-François Lyotard published his modestly titled *The Postmodern Condition: A Report on Knowledge*. For Lyotard, narrative was the means by which knowledge was contained and conveyed. The language of the narrative, its content, its location, its narrator, and its listener provided a cumulative understanding of knowledge in which who was talking and who was listening were all implicated in presentation of the narrative and its re-presentation in terms of meaning. Thus the repetition of narratives both legitimated as well as reproduced them, making narrative central to our knowledge of the world in which we lived. Narrative, thus, "determines in a single stroke what one must say in order to be heard, what one must listen to in order to speak and what role one must play . . . to be the object of a narrative."[16] Like Ricoeur and White, Lyotard observed that the latter half of the twentieth century witnessed the collapse of what he calls the "metanarratives" or "grand narratives" on which our understanding of politics, history, and science depended, proving themselves to be no more than cultural chimera.

Narrative and the Self

Yet if everyone, and everything, could be reduced to narrative, then the term would cease to offer any new insights into contemporary, or past, human behavior. One of the earliest attempts at definition emerged from the Russian formalists working in literary theory. For them, a narrative had three components: the *fabula*, or theme (such as jealousy, love, ambition, redemption); the *sjuzet*, or discourse (effectively, the plot); and the *forma*, or genre (novel, poem, comedy, tragedy). As narrative has entered into the analytical vocabulary of other disciplines, its original formalist meaning, applied to literature, has become refined and adapted.[17] Nevertheless, most users concur that the original denominators of narrative—theme, plot, and genre—remain common to all manifestations and usages.[18]

At first glance, it may seem strange that oral historians engage with "narrative," with all that it implies of fabrication and representation. Oral histories were created as a result of a particular intervention. Oral history engaged with the "real," with past events, and offered, in the words of one of its early proponents, Oscar Lewis, a new "social realism," as informants "talk about themselves and relate their observations and experiences in an uninhibited, spontaneous and natural manner."[19] Indeed, oral history appeared to be the antithesis of narrative. Replete with the potential of *really* showing things as they were, it was neither constructed nor controlled. Documents may be imperfect renditions of the past, but to talk to a *witness* was to engage directly with the making of history, and we asked no more of a witness than that they *narrate* what they saw or experienced.

As oral historians developed their craft, however, the opaqueness and fragility of memory, its relation to the self, and the structures on which it relied for recall and recount pointed to the artifice of memory and, hence, the self. Neither were spontaneous happenings; both were constructed by the social worlds they inhabited, the moral universes they referred to, and the cultural symbols they employed. It became insufficient to trawl oral history for the information it offered, for that information was contaminated by memory and the imagination, though not in the way the early critics of oral history assumed when they pointed to the fallibility of memory, but by the ways in which the individual necessarily narrativized the past. In other words, *recounting* the past involved *accounting* for it; as Alessandro Portelli argued, "Oral testimony has been amply discussed as a source of information on the events of history. It may, however, also be viewed as an event in itself and, as such, subjected to independent analysis in order to recover not only the material surface of what happened, but also the narrator's attitude toward events, the subjectivity, imagination, and desire that each individual invests in the relationship with history."[20]

The self, in other words, was linked inextricably to the human facility to create—and be created. As such, the self became the artist, the author of his or her life. And, as psychologists such as Jerome Bruner began to argue, narrative was the way "we organize our experience and our memory of human happenings."[21] Or, as Oliver Sacks eloquently expressed it:

> We have each of us, a life story, an inner narrative—whose continuity, whose sense, *is* our lives. It might be said that each of us constructs and lives "a narrative," and that this narrative *is* our identities.
>
> If we wish to know about a man, we ask "what is his story, his real inmost story?"—for each of us *is* . . . a singular narrative, which is constructed, continually, unconsciously, by, through, and in us—through our perceptions, our feelings, our thoughts, our actions; and not least, in our discourse, our spoken narrations. Biologically, physiologically, we are not different from each other; historically, as narratives, we are each of us unique.

> To be ourselves, we must have ourselves—possess, if need be repossess, our life stories. We must "recollect" ourselves, recollect the inner drama, the narrative of ourselves. A man needs such a narrative, a continuous inner narrative to maintain his identity.[22]

Once made, the link between narrative and identity appeared immutable, as relevant for a nation as an individual. To quote Ricoeur again:

> To answer the question "Who?" as Hannah Arendt so forcefully put it, is to tell the story of a life. The story told tells about the action of the "who." And the identity of this "who" therefore itself must be a narrative identity. Without the recourse to narration, the problem of personal identity would in fact be condemned to an antinomy with no solution. . . . This narrative identity, constitutive of self-constancy, can include change, mutability, within the cohesion of one lifetime. The subject then appears both as a reader and the writer of its own life. . . . As the literary analysis of autobiography confirms, the story of a life continues to be refigured by all the truthful or fictive stories a subject tells about himself or herself. This refiguration makes this life itself a cloth woven of stories told.[23]

The problem, as Adriana Cavarero points out, is that every self-narration contains within it a lack, for the points at which we start and end the narration—birth and death—are points at which we, by definition, are incapable of recalling: "The first and fundamental chapter of the life story that our memory tells us is already incomplete. The unity of self . . . is already irremediably lost in the very moment in which that same self begins to commemorate herself."[24]

A similar argument, though from a psychological rather than a philosophical perspective, is posited by Daniel Albright, who points out that the implicit assumption in psychology is that "the self is by nature whole, adjusted and organized." Yet the self is inherently fragile: it lacks "a proper foundation. . . . The remembered self . . . begins and ends in a state of nothingness." It is also inherently plural, mutable; it edits and selects, while the act of remembering, Albright states, "alters the rememberer as well as the remembered self. . . . Our mode of remembering has been re-shaped along with the content of our memories."[25]

But as Lyotard points out, individuals did not choose one narrative through which to recount and construct their lives, but several, which varied depending on the geographic and temporal location and the perceived rationale at any one time. The plurality of narratives is a point equally addressed in the literary field, notably by Mikhail Bakhtin, who argues that narratives necessarily involve a "dialogic" element in that the narrator and the listener are equally implicated in the creation of the text.[26] This introduces a further fragility into narrative, challenging the authority of the authorial voice.

If oral historians accept that the memories they tease from their informants are episodes selected from a total narrative of life, in the Ricoeurian sense of narrative as an analogy and appraisal of time, and that a life's narrative is one that is itself under constant revision (and, therefore, the lies and lapses of memory have to be seen not as weaknesses in an oral account, but as evidence of the revisioning self), where do the elements basic to narrative—plot, theme, and genre—fit in?

Narrative, Memory, and Language

Oral historians rely on their informants' memories. Memory, that seemingly most individual of all our faculties, is, however, both personal to us *and* social. Values and priorities are often implanted in memory descriptions, revealed by the language used or by the generic structure of the recollection, and point to what Halbwachs describes as the *collective* nature of memory, particularly when they become embedded in or through the dominant culture. Not only do other peoples' memories become incorporated into our own (and nowhere is this more true than family memories), but what he calls the "frameworks" that permit and fashion recollection are not merely social, but socially and culturally specific.[27] Without such structures, recollection would not be possible. Moreover, the language, images, contours, and colors of memory are shared, and therefore social, as are the guidelines and judgments, omissions and commissions that inform the imaginative act of remembrance. All memories, therefore, share meanings and understandings, language and images, dreams and nightmares.[28] Of these shared factors, perhaps language is the most central for, as Ernst Gellner argues, "How many things would we do altogether, if the concepts of those things were not built into the language of our culture? . . . Words are a very great deal: the rules of their use is wound up with—though not in any simple or obvious way—the activities and institutions of the societies in which they are employed. They embody the norms—or, indeed, the multiplicity or rival and incompatible norms—of those societies."[29]

The relationship between language and thought, language and experience, and, necessarily, language and memory has long been recognized in ethnographic and anthropological research. Furthermore, the symbolic structures integral to a culture are both reflected and embedded in the language used. Tenses, for instance, lead us to assume, as Charlotte Linde stated, that "there really is such a thing as time . . . [which] consists of past, present and future. . . . The temporal order of clauses, or narrative order . . . is likely to be understood as a causal order as well."[30] Metaphors, rhetoric, sayings that punctuate life-story narratives all signify values and priorities, ways of looking at the world and interpreting it for, as Edward Sapir observed, "We see and hear and otherwise experience very largely as we do because the language habits of our community predispose certain choices of interpretation."[31] These linguistic turns provide a shorthand for a particular cultural worldview, which requires interpretation: the language and the thoughts are closely bound, "collaborating," in Benjamin Lee Whorf's words, with cultural practices, "where the 'fashions of speaking' are closely integrated with the whole general culture . . . and there are connections within this integration, between the kind of linguistic analyses employed and various behavioral reactions and also the shapes taken by various cultural developments."[32]

Relatedly, as language to a large extent sculpts and makes available thought and memory, and as there appears to be an impulse to narrate in order to secure a sense of self and identity, what we relate and how are necessarily prefigured by the tools at our disposal, by the frameworks for recall, by the narratives through which a society (or a nation) tells the story of itself. The mind, as Bruner reminds us, "needs cultural symbols for expression," symbols found in both language and narrative.[33] While the personal narrative may be seen as the property of the individual, intrinsic to and defining of the individual, the plot that it follows and the themes that are woven through it may reflect and conform to the cultural narratives to which any one individual is exposed at any one time. Margaret Somers suggests, for instance, that there are four kinds of narrativity: first, the ontological narrative, those stories that compose a life, that is, that make sense of it and enable the individual to act within it; second, public, cultural, and institutional narratives that exist beyond the individual and are larger than the individual, for example, "the family," "the workplace," and so on; third, the "conceptual, analytic, sociological narrativity," the intellectual narratives that we, as researchers, have available to us (and not always confined to researchers, of course);[34] and fourth, the metanarratives, or master narratives, that each society will also have (à la Lyotard).[35] As Bruner points out,

> One important way of characterizing a culture is by the narrative models it makes available for describing the course of a life. And the tool kit of any culture is replete not only with a stock of canonical life narratives (heroes, Marthas, tricksters, etc.) but with combinable formal constituents from which its members can construct their own life narratives. . . . Eventually the culturally shaped cognitive and linguistic processes that guide the self-telling of life narratives achieve the power to structure perceptual experience, to organize memory, to segment and purpose-build the very "events" of a life. In the end, we *become* the autobiographical narratives by which we "tell about" our lives.[36]

In so doing, of course, who we have become continues to select and structure our memories and experiences and the narratives through which we record them. Social class, for instance, as George Steinmetz has argued, conditions some narrative models so that "events are interpreted, emplotted and evaluated to emphasize class rather than other constructs."[37] The plots and themes we select and through which we choose to recount our lives have effectively prefigured the way we see ourselves, in much the same way that historians, in White's terms, discern the "plots 'prefigured' in historical actions and 'configure' them as stories and therefore make explicit the meaning implicit in historical events."[38] Of course, some plots and themes are not of our choosing—gender, for instance, or race. Our "gendered," "raced" selves become, as it were, our default narrative, affecting the language we use and the structure of our memories. Yet within these fundamental narratives there exist themes—the "passive" woman, for instance, or the "good mother," "the cruel stepmother," the "Uncle Tom"—through which, or against which, we choose to tell our lives. In many cases, the themes are also replicated in and drawn from popular culture and literature, as Angela McRobbie has shown in her work on girls' comics or Graham Dawson in his work on masculinities.[39] Indeed, the extent to which the narratives of self conform or fail to conform is the principal mechanism through which a sense of identity is secured, acknowledged, and recognized by others, for narrative structures and meanings are necessarily shared and therefore public. They are part of the culture. They cannot, as Molly Andrews and her co-authors argue, be understood apart from it.[40] They are also part of the way in which we understand and make sense of the world we inhabit. This is not to suggest that all and every life story or oral history account is culturally predetermined, or necessarily coherent or consistent. The narrative may follow an order that conforms to the narrative priorities, rather than one that charts a chronological life course (and "life course" itself is, of course, one example of a narrative plot). Moreover, individuals may dip and weave among their narrative choices as the life history course—time, no less—demands, or as excuses and rationales are required to explain or excuse behavior that appears to breach (in Bruner's terms above) the "canon." Thus, for instance, the narrative we tell as childless young women may be a very different narrative from the one we tell in middle age, after motherhood. Our narrative selves are necessarily multilayered and polyvocal.

Narrative Genre

In much the same way as people may relate their life stories (and the stories of their lives) to a thematic repertoire (for example, redemption, corruption, victimization, or heroism), so they also relate them to the repertoire of *genre* available to them. All stories, from the personal anecdote to the scientific theory, follow conventions of process and purpose, presentation and style, place and performance. Broadly speaking, these conventions alert us to the type or genre of story we are hearing, reading, or seeing. We distinguish a scientific text from a history, a theological treatise from a fairy story, a novel from literary criticism, a joke from a eulogy. At the same time, when we tell a story, we choose the genre appropriate to the occasion.[41] We abide by what Elizabeth Tonkin calls "the conventions of discourse."[42] It is this that provides both meaning and understanding.

While we are familiar with genre in written and oral tradition, and while we may accept that the notion of narrative can be applied to an oral history, the notion of oral histories and life stories being subject to comparable typologies is less obvious. As with narrative, it appears to run counter to common sense. The life story is, after all, a particular construction in itself. At its most basic, a life story is the result of the interaction between the interviewer and the interviewee. It is determined by the culture of the interview, the nature and form of the questions asked, the skill of the interviewer, the relationship between interviewer and interviewee, and the place where the interview occurs. In this sense, a life-story interview is essentially dialogic. It also constitutes a genre of its own, as Portelli argues.[43] Marie-Françoise Chanfrault-Duchet likewise contends: "Life story is the product of a ritualized speech act, which results from the conjunction, in the 1970s, of a genre, autobiography, with a new medium, the tape recorder, within the institutional framework of social science. Life-story is thus at first a methodological tool used to collect information from social categories (among them women) which, although social actors, do not have access to the public stage. But considered as a genre, it can be viewed as an object created by the form and the contents, which produces meaning, just like a literary form."[44]

When the oral historian or the sociologist or the anthropologist collects life stories, they collect a particular story at a particular time and in a particular location. What the historian may hear may never have been told before in that form, in that sequence, in that time frame. For the most part, even within the interview, people remember their lives in fragments, in Walter Benjamin's words, "moments and discontinuities."[45] To suggest that oral histories contain genres hints that an informant is engaged in a performance that somehow detracts from the authenticity of the memories recounted.

Yet, when collecting life stories, one is struck by the similarities between them and by recurring themes of content or intent. There are, for instance, as Portelli points out, repetitions of type—the war story, the hospital story—or of moral purpose.[46] It is not just, or always, the experience that is shared and that explains such similarity. It is also the understanding and interpretation that are shared, that give that kind of story, at that time, a priority and value, a moral and an emphasis, that explain or exonerate behavior, that reinforce a particular cultural or social code. It is these that constitute genres and that determine the form and the content of the account.[47] But, as Elizabeth Tonkin has pointed out in her work on the Jlao of Liberia, in order to understand the content and import of what is being said, it is essential to understand the genre through which the words are spoken.[48] The same story, for instance, may be given a very different treatment and gloss depending on the genre chosen to recount it. The genre, in turn, will depend on the circumstances. While Tonkin's insights emerged from her anthropological fieldwork in Liberia, the insight into genres has a wider application; every culture, including our own, has a rich set of rhetorical devices through which we recount the stories of our lives, from the anecdote of childhood to the professional report. Recognizing this necessarily breaks down the divide between an oral tradition (perceived to be the prerogative of preliterate peoples) and oral history: oral history also relies on narrative devices embedded in the culture. A particularly brilliant exposition of this was developed by Timothy Ashplant in his analysis of Angela Hewins's oral history, *The Dillen*, in which he shows how the apparently spontaneous "natural" narrative of George Hewins was a carefully crafted mosaic of performance genre gleaned from the music hall, from entertainers, from parody and irony.[49] Indeed, the genres at his disposal were carefully layered, a point also made by Portelli.[50] Similarly, how people react and make choices is governed by their enculturation, that is, by the range of stories, fables, parables, myths, and legends that offer guidance at moments of choice or dilemma.[51] How people present themselves, including the silences as well as the articulations, may reveal as much about their values as about their experiences and as much again about cultural practices. What is remembered, when, and why is molded by the culture in which they live, the language at their disposal, and the conventions and the genre appropriate to the occasion. Cultural practices, moreover, become manifest in the content, intent, and form of stories, emerging out of the traditions and genres of storytelling. Memories refer to and reflect the deep imaginative structures of the social mind. These are our cultural templates.

Cross-Cultural Narratives

We take the concept of "life story" as a given, but it relies on a very particular concept of the self, one that is rooted in Western modernity, in which, as Anthony Giddens puts it, "the self . . . [is] reflexively understood by the person in terms of her or his biography."[52] There has been, as we have seen, a considerable interest recently in the relationship between identity and biography and its development in the West.[53] This, however, presupposes the universality of what Cavarero calls the "narratable self."[54] Indeed, the quest of modernity (as reflected in the European Romantic tradition) has been to elevate the individual and to identify the self with, or in terms of, memory.[55] Cavarero, for instance, can argue that "we are all familiar with the narrative work of memory, which, in a totally involuntary way, continues to tell us our own personal story. Every human being . . . is aware of being a *narratable self*—immersed in the spontaneous auto-narration of memory. . . . The narratable self is at once the transcendental subject and the elusive object of all the autobiographical exercises of memory."[56]

This emphasis on the self may be a peculiarly European angst. Who is an individual, a self, is by no means universally understood, any more than the rhetorical devices of stories or narratives are universally recognized. "The presentation of self," as Linde argues, "may not be at all a natural discourse for the subject; indeed, the whole notion of *self* present in the subject's culture may be quite different from that of the anthropologist."[57]

Thus who is recalling may have a very different sense of self, may be remembering from a different epistemological base, through different narrative conventions and different narrative functions. They may, in other words, be fashioning themselves according to a different cultural dynamic. Interviewing, particularly cross-culturally, demands therefore a sensitivity and an awareness that the interview itself may be imposing a pattern and a practice alien to the informant's own. For instance, Yvette Kopijn, in her work on elderly Javanese–Surinamese women, found that communicating through storytelling, recalling, and recounting was primarily a collective, communal event governed by particular norms and practices (including gender) that directed the content and context of the communication. It was the antithesis of the one-to-one interview, for which that society had no cultural precedent.[58] Similarly, in my own work on the Caribbean, two features in the narratives stand out that suggest a very different epistemological base. First, the language of self conveys markedly different concepts and approaches. Despite Sidney W. Mintz's assertion that the Caribbean peoples were the first "modern" people, the sense of self conveyed in these life stories is one in which, on the one hand, descent and rebirth consistently blur the boundaries of selfhood ("I am a grandmother child," "I am from my mother") and, on the other, there exists an intrinsic existentialism, epitomized by phrases such as "when I first knew myself coming up" or "when I born and I got the sense." The concept of self and its narration and the concept of biography may have different meanings and purposes in which some identification with the group (predecessors and successors) takes precedence over the metaphysics of the self and where memories of individuals may be recounted in terms of prototypical behavior that may function as both an individual and collective biography, or where one individual stands as the embodiment of all. Many of the narratives of Caribbean women, I have argued, may conform

> to a different narrative of self, which enfolds within it an acknowledgement of lineage. . . . [It is] as much to do with origins as continuity. . . . Women, in other words, may have a plural sense of self, fashioned by . . . their positioning as intermediaries in their lineage. Indeed, a sense of self emerges precisely out of the co-operation which is integrally involved (with younger and older family members) in the act of positioning, the tensions and ambiguities of adjusting the individual within the social. They may even invoke a variety of terms to talk about the self, as Gloria Wekker notes in relation to Afro-Surinamese women, calling in the ancestors and spirits, and using their voices to mask both criticism and affirmation.[59]

Equally, if we acknowledge that the use of narrative appears to be a universal human characteristic, we need then to acknowledge that those narratives will be culturally specific. Thus Stephan Feuchtwang, for instance, in his study of a Chinese village, noted that the narrative of history through which particular events were recounted was one that prefigured not human agency, but human destiny.[60] In my study of Caribbean families and migration, what I identify as a formulaic *genre* in many of the narratives suggests its role as a prescription for the good life, conveying social principles and a social world characterized by order and respect, standing for—singing—the praises of ideal types.[61] In this, the formulaic, almost ritualistic, descriptions become mnemonics in which prescriptions are both encoded and remembered. Many reveal the values and philosophies that underpin social organization, inform cultural representation, and provide an idiom through which Caribbean peoples converse and survive in the Caribbean and beyond. Conveying meaning through metaphor is not only a practice with a long African pedigree; it was also (arguably) a way of hoodwinking the plantation and colonial world.[62] Similarly, Maureen Warner-Lewis, in her work on the Yoruba in Trinidad, for instance, suggests that many of their cultural narratives were the remnants of song and poems that suggested "not only that African culture overseas has been retained by way of ritual act and secular mores, but also that such customs had formal and systematized literary ve-hicles to sustain and articulate them."[63]

Narrative: Methodological Issues

Does this "turn" to narrative offer any new insights? In particu-lar, what value is it for the oral historian? How can these insights affect the practice and methods of oral history? The principal ap-plication of narrative theory is in interpretation of our data. The kinds of interviews we conduct are likely to be determined by the topic under investigation. It could be a particular topic (a strike, for instance) or a moment (the civil rights movement); we may choose to ask our informant questions on a particular theme or to encourage a more sustained life-story interview. The result, from whichever approach, will be at one level highly in-dividual. At a deeper level, however, it will be primarily a *social* document. History, as Raphael Samuel reminds us, is "a social form of knowledge; the work, in any given instance, of a thou-sand different hands."[64] The first application therefore of narra-tive theory is to recognize that the interview is a multilayered document. It can and does contain information, and often it is in-formation not possible to glean from more conventional histori-cal sources. It contains an individual perspective; one person is recounting in a style of their choosing. But there, immediately, we run into the first interpretative problem—or insight—that narrative theory has highlighted, if not resolved.

Oral testimony is a *narrative*, subject to the same forms and controls as more popularly acknowledged narratives. In the be-ginning it is, as Bakhtin pointed out, dialogic. That is, the inter-viewer, the historian, is engaged with the informant, the subject, in negotiating and creating a text. Within that, the questions the historian asks, the responses chosen, the omissions and commis-sions, as well as the range of paralanguage utilized (such as fa-cial expressions, body language, and vocal tones) to enhance or undermine meaning, correspond to a set of visual and aural nar-ratives that we learn to recognize and understand.[65] Thus the in-formants may recount their life story (or part of it), selecting a particular theme as a narrative principle or genre appropriate to the occasion. One outstanding example of this is Gadi BenEzer's *The Ethiopian Jewish Exodus: Narratives of the Migration Journey to Israel 1977–1985*. In a narrative tour de force, BenEzer picks apart the various themes through which the survivors of the migration described their journey. Indeed, the "journey" itself was one such narrative theme, but within that, further themes of identity, suffering, or bravery and inner strength dominated the self composition of his informants. At the same time, as he also points out, his informants had a desire to tell their story, not least to make a reluctant Israel more willing to acknowledge what they went through in order to reach Israel and therefore, perhaps, relinquish an ambivalence about their Jewish credentials.[66]

BenEzer distinguishes between what he terms "historical truth," the objective reality of what happened; "psychological truth," what the informants believe happened, which then determines response; and "narrative truth," which governs what is told or not, how content is organized, and how the nonverbal text accompanies the narrative. For BenEzer, the narrative truth "provides us . . . with an additional way of understanding the experience of the life-event and its meaning for the individual. For instance, it can give us additional clues to the person's psychological state of mind."[67]

While the notion of narrative truth was particularly important in dealing with a group as traumatized as the Ethiopian Jews (and BenEzer is a clinical psychologist who worked with this group of people), the broad principles of the insights remain.[68] Even within the confines of an interview, informants move across the terrain of their memories in what may appear a random fashion, highlighting and silencing as they travel through the journey of their lives. If, however, this journey is seen as akin to a plot, then such priorities and silences and the order of telling can convey a meaning that in turn requires attention. One informant of mine, for instance, prefaced his interview by saying he had only one thing to tell me, and he began with the words, "When I were at the age of twelve years old." He then proceeded to tell how he had been "robbed" of his education. The priority he gave to this event in the "plot" of his life in this and its subsequent unfolding provided an invaluable clue to understanding and locating his narrative historically.[69]

A further insight that narrative theory offers the oral historian is the recognition that the individual is engaged in a continuous revision of the self. Not only do individuals select—often, if not always, unconsciously—from the repertoire of narrative compositions available, but also this will change according to and alongside the life course or according to and alongside the range of contexts in which individuals find themselves, and the range of audiences engaged with, including, of course, in the interview itself. Relatedly, at any one time the individual voice contains a multiplicity of voices. This is not to say that informants perform an act of ventriloquism throughout their lives; the voice is theirs, but it also holds within it the shared meanings of languages and cultural narratives and the range of relationships, recountings, and challenges that contributed to a memory at any one time and a representation of the self at any one time. For the revisioning of self necessarily involves a revisioning of memory, which in turn influences and alters what is remembered and how.[70] Both the self and self's memory engage in a constant dialectic. The cultural sensitivity, and specificity, of narratives is one of their strengths, linking individuals integrally with their time and place and social world. Narratives of self can therefore be used to offer real insights into cultural priorities and values; conversely, to recognize a cultural narrative within a life story offers a deeper understanding of an informant's location within history.

Conclusion

The alacrity with which the concept of narrative has become adopted by disciplines in the social and behavioral sciences and in the humanities may be indicative of a fashion, but it has also meant that there has been considerable cross-fertilization of ideas and interpretations across the fields. This, in itself, is a welcome development as old disciplinary boundaries (some would say, scientific narratives) have become eroded and intellectual distances, generated as part of the Enlightenment endeavour, have been bridged. Indeed, as the editors of the *Routledge Studies in Memory and Narrative* argue in their inaugurating preface: "Disparate disciplines thus prove to be linked by common interests and preoccupations, so that historians as well as social and behavioural scientists now are concerned with searching for the narrative structures which inform the memories they seek to analyse, while literary scholars seek out the meanings of the memories which have inspired and driven their narrative texts."[71]

Clearly, the "turn" to narrative is historically and culturally located. It may even represent a Kuhnian paradigm shift. But at the moment it is an exciting theoretical development that has exposed the plasticity of the social world we inhabit and has made and added a much needed degree of sophistication to our understanding of oral history narratives. We can no longer bask in the radicalism of the oral historian, content to have democratized history. If, as Thompson wrote, "the full potential of oral history is realized, it will result not so much in a specific list of titles to be found listed in a section of historical bibliographies, as in an underlying change in the way in which history is written and learnt, in its questions and its judgements, and in its texture."[72]

Perhaps the turn to narrative—coinciding, as we have seen, with the development of oral history—has been one way in which the potential of oral history is being realized, although it may not be a way in which Professor Thompson envisaged.

Notes

1. Plummer, *Documents of Life 2*, 185–203.
2. Chamberlayne, Bornat, and Wengraf, *Biographical Methods*, 1–25; Cosslett, Lury, and Summerfield, *Feminism and Autobiography*, 1–2; Cavarero, *Relating Narratives*, 3–4, 32–45.
3. Geertz, *Interpretation of Cultures*, 5, 13, 14.
4. See, for instance, Barthes, *Image–Music–Text*; Baudrillard, *Political Economy of Signs*.
5. Cobley, *Narrative*, 183.
6. Kuhn, *Scientific Revolutions*.
7. Cobley, *Narrative*, 30.
8. Powell, introduction to *Leopold von Ranke*, xv.
9. Fukuyama, *End of History*, xi, proposes a very different thesis, that the "end" of history was posited by the collapse of the Soviet regime and with it the demise of ideology as a driving force of national and international behavior.

10. Thompson, *Voice of the Past* (1978), 8–9. Interestingly, neither the first nor second edition of *Voice of the Past* refers to "narrative."

11. McAdams, Josselson, and Lieblich, introduction to *Turns in the Road*, provides a sharp summary of the development of narrative in the social sciences and humanities. See also Sewell, "Narratives and Social Identities," 480–86.

12. Ricoeur, *Time and Narrative*, 3:109, 1:3.

13. Ibid., 3:260, 3:108–9.

14. White, *Content of the Form*, 14, 177

15. See White, *Metahistory*.

16. Lyotard, *Postmodern Condition*, 21.

17. For a brief but succinct summary of how narrative has been adapted in other disciplines, see Plummer, *Documents of Life 2*, 11, 186–87.

18. For an elaborated summary of narrative features, see Bruner, "Narrative Construction," 6–20.

19. Lewis, *Children of Sanchez*, xii.

20. Portelli, "Uchronic Dreams," 143.

21. Bruner, "Narrative Construction," 4.

22. Sacks, *Man Who Mistook*, 105–6, quoted in Plummer, *Documents of Life 2*, 185.

23. Ricoeur, *Time and Narrative*, 3:246.

24. Cavarero, *Relating Narratives*, 39.

25. Albright, "Literary and Psychological Models," 20, 22, 37.

26. Bakhtin, *Dialogic Imagination*.

27. See Halbwachs, *Collective Memory*.

28. See Alexander, *Becoming a Woman*.

29. Gellner, *Thought and Change*, 195.

30. Linde, "Explanatory Systems," 347.

31. Sapir, quoted in Whorf, "Habitual Thought," 134.

32. Ibid., 159; see also Linde, "Explanatory Systems."

33. Bruner, "Narrative Construction," 10.

34. For an interesting example of how the "anthropologized" appropriated the anthropologists' conceptual framework and narrative form, see Lopes and Alvim, "Brazilian Worker's Autobiography," 74–78.

35. Somers, "Narrative Identity," 603.

36. Bruner, "Life as Narrative," 15.

37. Steinmetz, "Social Narrative," 489.

38. White, *Content of the Form*, 174.

39. McRobbie, "Jackie"; see also Berger, *Narratives in Popular Culture*, 100–102; Dawson, *Soldier Heroes*.

40. Andrews et al., *Lines of Narrative*.

41. For a more detailed discussion, see Chamberlain and Thompson, "Genre and Narrative."

42. Tonkin, *Narrating Our Pasts*, 2.

43. Portelli, "Oral History as Genre," 23–24.

44. Chanfrault-Duchet, "Textualisation of the Self," 62.

45. Benjamin, "Berlin Chronicle," 316.

46. Portelli, "Oral History as Genre," 26–28.

47. For a fuller discussion of this, see Chamberlain and Thompson, "Genre and Narrative," 13–15.

48. Tonkin, *Narrating Our Pasts*, 2–3.

49. Ashplant, "Anecdote," 104–5, 109–110. For George Hewins's oral history, see Hewins, *Dillen*.

50. Portelli, "Oral History as Genre," 28–32.

51. Sarbin, "Narratory Principle."

52. Giddens, *Modernity and Self-Identity*, 53.

53. For an excellent discussion of this, see Chamberlayne, Bornat, and Wengraf, *Biographical Methods*.

54. Cavarero, *Relating Narratives*, 33.

55. See Steedman, "Enforced Narratives."

56. Cavarero, *Relating Narratives*, 33–34.

57. Linde, "Explanatory Systems," 345.

58. Kopijn, "Oral History Interview," 151.

59. Chamberlain, "Praise Songs," 124. See Wekker, "One Finger."

60. Feuchtwang, "Distant Homes," 136–37.

61. Chamberlain, "'Praise Songs,'" 122.

62. Austin-Broos and Smith, *Jamaica Genesis*.

63. Warner-Lewis, *Guinea's Other Suns*, 113.

64. Samuel, *Theatres of Memory*, 1:8.

65. Portelli, "Peculiarities"; Chamberlain, "Gender and Memory."

66. BenEzer, *Ethiopian Jewish Exodus*, 46.

67. Ibid., 45.

68. For discussion on the use of narrative and trauma, see Rogers, Leydesdorff, and Dawson, *Trauma and Life Stories*.

69. Chamberlain, *Exile and Return*, 58.

70. For a detailed and sophisticated discussion of this, see Hodgkin and Radstone, *Contested Pasts* and *Regimes of Memory*.

71. Chamberlain et al., "Introduction to the Series," xiv.

72. Thompson, *Voice of the Past* (1978), 65–66.

IV

APPLICATIONS

13

Publishing Oral History: Oral Exchange and Print Culture

Richard Cándida Smith

Since the earliest days of "oral history," long before the term had achieved any currency, writers and scholars kept records of conversations with historical informants and used quotes from these sources in the work they published. Books based largely, though seldom exclusively, on interviews have also long had a niche in the publishing business. Back in the sixteenth century, Giorgio Vasari based his now classic text *The Lives of the Artists* on conversations with the friends and colleagues of the leading Italian Renaissance painters, architects, and sculptors. Their insights were credible to readers, though perhaps less so to subsequent art historians. The use of conversations helped Vasari convey the human side of men whom he nonetheless wanted readers to see as geniuses. In a very different vein, Henry Mayhew's *London Labour and the London Poor: A Cyclopaedia of the Condition and Earnings of Those That Will Work, Those That Cannot* gripped English readers in 1851 by allowing them entry into the lives of the most desperate members of their society as recounted by themselves. Many early twentieth-century classics of sociological and anthropological literature relied heavily on the presentation of firsthand testimony, as in works such as Harvey Zorbaugh, *The Gold Coast and the Slum: Chicago's Near North Side*; Nels Anderson, *The Hobo: The Sociology of the Homeless Man*; Sidney Mintz, *Worker*

411

in the Cane: A Puerto Rican Life History; and Oscar Lewis, *Children of Sanchez: Autobiography of a Mexican Family.*

Studs Terkel's books, which braid together the voices of Americans sharing their experiences of economic hard times, war, social protest, and most recently, aging and mortality, have been national best-sellers.[1] Individual narratives by Chicano labor activist Bert Corona, Communist Party leader Dorothy Healey, gay rights pioneer Harry Hay, and Alabama sharecropper Ned Cobb have also found significant readership, as have books based on oral histories with both jazz and classical musicians.[2] Interviews with painters and writers remain a staple of the publishing trade, perhaps for the same reason that Vasari's volumes proved so successful. Books based largely on oral history interviews provide a tantalizing glimpse into the human side of historical change.

When authors begin working with oral sources for print publication, they must answer several key questions. The first and most important is whose voice or voices will provide the narrative spine. In books based on an interview with a single individual, it has been most common to tell the life history in the subject's own voice, but authors must then decide whether to organize the narrator's voice around a question-and-answer framework or as an autobiographical narrative. Authors of books using multiple interviews have taken quite different strategies in how to combine their sources into a unified story. Terkel weaves the multiple voices he has collected into a collage of typically contrasting perspectives. Stories wrap around each other as Terkel builds an emotional arc that helps define how larger historical processes have limited each and every one of his informants, the powerful and wealthy no less than the average working man and woman.

In *Amoskeag*, a now classic historical study of a New England mill town, authors Tamara K. Hareven and Randolph Langenbach arrange the voices into a sequence of stories grouped by thematic topics such as work, family life, and unionization. In *Like a Family: The Making of a Southern Cotton Mill World*, Jacquelyn Dowd Hall and her co-authors tell the historical narrative with a professional academic voice, interpreting the industrialization of North Carolina and its effects on a variety of social issues. Copious selections from the many oral histories they col-lected are found in quotations throughout the text to support the authors' arguments while grounding their analysis in the lived experiences of their informants.

All of these approaches have been equally effective in gain-ing both critical and popular acclaim. The choice of how to or-ganize and present interview material must follow the author's sense of what is the most effective way to communicate story and argument. Authors will need to decide whether their goal is primarily storytelling or scholarly analysis, for that will affect which segments of the interviews are most important and how to arrange them in building toward the conclusion. Authors need to decide if the goal of the book is to provide readers with information, an argumentative point of view, or human-interest stories. These are not mutually exclusive goals, but writers need nonetheless to have a sense of the hierarchy of their goals if they are to develop effective print texts. Authors must also consider how much editing will be required to translate the oral texts into effective, readable print documents, as well as how much context they need to provide readers as background to narra-tors' accounts. Context can come in the shape of end- or foot-notes, prologues and postscripts, framing sections for each chapter, or a narrative that weaves in and out of the quotations from oral history throughout the book. A decision on how much contextual information needs to be included will determine the balance of voices within the work and whether readers perceive the narrators or the researcher as the book's author. Issues of confidentiality, defamation, and invasion of privacy must also be taken into account. With the exception of historical figures with public reputations, Theodore Rosengarten in preparing Ned Cobb's life story for publication changed the names of everybody discussed. Even Cobb's name was changed, and he became "Nate Shaw."[3]

The decisions that authors of oral history books make to arrange the interview texts they have collected into effective nar-ratives usually remain hidden. Terkel has said little of his work-ing method, other than the commonplace that he listens for emotional truth.[4] Elena Poniatowska has provided a colorful im-age of herself typing away, transcribing the notes she had made from hours of conversation with Josefina Bórquez, the working-class veteran of the Mexican Revolution whose life story forms the basis of Poniatowska's first novel, *Hasta No Verte, Jesús Mío*.[5] Poniatowska in this case is not after a verbatim rendition. Through constant return to the flow of words she recorded over many sessions, she strives to connect themes and to strengthen stories by combining material from different days into a single retelling on paper. Poniatowska stresses her role as a listener, seeking to find the truth in the words and finding a way to convey that truth in language readers will understand. In this case, the text is presented as a "novel" rather than a journalistic reporting, in part because both narrative and phrasing have been reworked so heavily. The first-person narrative of the novel is based on interviews but transforms into poetry by a process of imaginative encounter that remakes Poniatowska from interviewer into author.

Poniatowska may have an unusually free approach in her handling of oral narratives as raw source material, but her account can help clarify one of the most important dynamics involved in turning interview material into books. On the simplest level, when presented with a proposal for a book based on oral history materials, publishers will inevitably ask the question, Who is the author? They want to know whose vision will guide the creation of a print product. The temptation for oral historians might be to defer to the primacy of their subjects' voices, but this is to mistake the different roles the parties involved in oral history and publication play. The author of a book is the person who pulls together the material and provides an organizing structure. The author develops a rhythm of context, anecdote, and argument within which narrators find the setting for their thoughts. Even in a book almost entirely based on oral interviews, the narrator is the creation of the author of the book, in this case the editor who transformed hours of raw conversation into a meaning-laden account, a meaning that is imaginatively produced by the editor. This may be a difficult point for many to accept, because the narrator is not simply words on paper for them, but a vibrant human being oral historians have come to know, respect, and often admire. It is that emotional response that an author must convey to readers, almost none of whom will ever personally meet the interviewee. The reader enters into a relationship with the author, who by sharing his or her response to interviewees and their stories allows a much broader public to get a glimmer of the effect the narrator can have on others.

Rosengarten, in his preface to *All God's Dangers: The Life of Nate Shaw*, describes a multilayered, multiyear process behind the book.[6] He first met Ned Cobb in 1969 when researching the history of the Alabama Sharecroppers Union. Cobb, a veteran of that organization, had just turned eighty-four years old. Over a period of two years, Rosengarten continued to visit Cobb and his wife to discuss the Sharecroppers Union. During these discussions, many aspects of Cobb's tumultuous life came out, though not in any coherent narrative. At this time, Rosengarten was not taping Cobb, but recording their conversations with handwritten notes. In 1971, Rosengarten proposed tape recording Cobb's account with the idea of preparing a book based on the recordings. The history of the organization had given way to an oral memoir that Rosengarten understood could reveal in more depth the social forces that African American sharecroppers contended with during the Jim Crow period.

Rosengarten showed up for the first taping session with a hundred pages of questions, most of which were never asked, much less answered. Cobb's life story took on its own momentum, developing in an ongoing and somewhat free-ranging conversation between the historian and the subject. Rosengarten recorded sixty hours of tape over sixteen sessions. "I hadn't asked the questions I'd come with," he notes, "and I had to choose between that and going over the same ground with a finer-toothed comb."[7] Rosengarten decided for the latter course and, working from extensive notes made while playing back the first set of tapes, recorded another sixty hours of tape in fifteen sessions, this time asking more pointed questions.

Rosengarten only briefly describes the editing process that condensed 120 hours of tape and hundreds of pages of notes into a 561-page book. He typically had multiple versions of stories to choose between for many of the most important accounts. He combined parts of one version with others in order to arrive at the most complete story. Despite the best of intentions on Rosengarten's part, his on-tape discussion with Cobb did not follow any strict chronological order. Memory and association often led to asides that leaped across the years and back. The sequence of Cobb's stories in the book had to be determined by Rosengarten, who wanted to do "justice both to their occurrence in time and [Cobb's] sequence of recollection. I tried, within the limits of a general chronology, to preserve the affinities between stories. For memory recalls kindred events and people and is not constrained by the calendar."[8] The historical goals guiding Rosengarten were quite distinct from Poniatowska's search for a new type of novel based in popular experience, but both authors felt their way to a publishable book by a slow process of continually refiltering the words of their narrators through their own emotional responses. With each pass through, the accounts became crisper and more pointed, ironically, better expressing the power of the speaker the further they moved from the original words. It is this single-minded focus on the emotional resonance of the narrator within the author that gives structure to two books that have powerful emotional impacts on readers.

A labyrinth of detailed decisions, usually hidden, lies behind this general process of responding to the emotional truth that interviews awaken within the author of a published oral history work. In his essay, "Preparing Interview Transcripts for Documentary Publication: A Line-by-Line Illustration of the Editing Process," Michael Frisch seeks to remove some of the mystery behind editing by presenting the editorial decisions he made in arranging for publication an interview with a steelworker.[9] After discussing the principles for his decisions, he presents two line-by-line versions of the interview transcript, the first as edited for publication, the second a relatively verbatim transcript of the original recording. Frisch numbers the lines so readers can trace the decisions he has made, which—as with Terkel, Rosengarten, and Poniatowska—involve isolating the emotional truth that he as listener had heard in the conversation but which could be lost when reduced to mere text.

The first step was to isolate and concentrate the sections of the interview that expressed the core of a narrator's ideas in the most concise fashion while preserving much of his patterns of speech. The most obvious change as a result of Frisch's converting conversation into edited text is the deletion of large chunks of the interview, particularly sections where the speaker speaks with less clarity. The sections Frisch preserves give the speaker a crisper, more concise feel. Frisch also pares down his own questions.

Frisch maintains that accessibility has to be the primary goal in presenting oral history materials to the public. *Accessibility* means more than opportunity to read collected interviews. The reader should come away with an understanding of the narrator's communicative intent. The immediate listening process involves ignoring irrelevancies that often enter into a discussion, as well as sidetracking or delaying speech that occurs while the speaker figures out what he or she really wants to say. Face-to-face communication includes a range of vocal and gestural cues that help listeners know when one thing said is more important than another. Words on paper, stripped of these physical cues, have a false equality that did not exist in the conversation. One task of the editor of oral transcripts is to restore hierarchy of thought within a person's expressions.

Frisch's second strategy for extracting the core communicative exchange is to combine discussions of the same topic otherwise scattered through the original conversation. Rearrangement on the simplest level is to restore the narrator's authority by allowing the printed text to convey the intent of his or her words as crisply as possible. This intent would be clearer in immediate communication, and if it were not, listeners could query the elements of the account that were confusing. That sort of negotiation is impossible in the printed text, and the editor must anticipate the confusions of the original text and answer the queries that readers might address to the speaker if they were actually in the same room. Rearrangement also heightens drama and emotion, making for a better read, but from a more purely intellectual perspective, its primary functions are to help the reader see as clearly as possible choices that narrators recall having faced in the past along with emotional and practical consequences.

Frisch's detailed presentation of his working method is a practical, valuable account of how one author made his research accessible to others, a process that remains invisible if an author succeeds in focusing attention on the narrators' stories. Readers are impressed by the emotional power of the accounts Terkel presents, but they do not see, and in most cases are not inter-ested in seeing, the lengthy editorial process that led to a well-shaped book with the power to engage them even after they have put it down.

The desire for coherence is powerful. It is typically shared by interviewer, interviewee, and subsequent readers alike. It is also a danger in that it gives priority to the conventional and the al-ready known. Combined with a commitment to a narrow defi-nition of "accessibility," the conflicts and contradictions of the spoken situation can become technical problems for erasure. The goal of making a transcript as easy to understand as possible as-sumes that everything in the original communication was open and transparent. Difficulties become interference that can be screened out much as a filter reduces the static of old sound recordings. In this case, "accessibility" may tacitly become little more than not having to think. Interviews will then contain in-formation that readers can extract, but only if authors have pre-viously erased the narrators' confusions, memory slips, or emotional struggles that lie outside the arc of the story the au-thor wants to tell.

Interviewees can often be inconsistent in different accounts of the same event, and differences in their moods may reveal depth to how they themselves responded to life's challenges. To create the text for *Everybody's Grandmother and Nobody's Fool: Frances Freeborn Pauley and the Struggle for Social Justice*, Kathryn L. Nasstrom edited a stock of existing interviews that had been recorded over a twenty-year period together with interviews that Nasstrom taped specifically for the book project. She was impressed by the consistency over time of Pauley's stories. As she worked more deeply with the material, attempting to con-struct a single, unified personal account, however, Nasstrom be-gan to see more clearly differences in emotional register in the sources she was combining. Pauley's tone typically was upbeat and energetic, but there were more than a few instances when she said things such as, "I am tired, tired, tired of giving up, giv-ing up, cutting back, cutting back. I guess that's what life is. So, it is correct to say that I am tired of life."[10] Nasstrom decided to include some of the downbeat material to underscore the com-plexity of Pauley's thought. Nonetheless, as a progressive white

Southerner who had fought for civil rights over many years, Pauley had succeeded in having an impact because of a largely positive approach. Nasstrom decided to preserve "some of this contradictory material, but the text as a whole favors the Frances who always found a way to persevere and, I think, favors the way that Frances wants to be remembered."[11] The challenge that the editor faced was not simply how to combine apparently contradictory material, but how to make sense for herself of how important these contradictions were for understanding a life. The resolution at which Nasstrom arrived gave depth to the narrator she presented to readers without sacrificing the key characteristics that had made her subject so compelling to her.

In *Oral History: From Tape to Type*, one of the most widely used manuals for oral history practice, Cullom Davis, Kathryn Back, and Kay MacLean advise: "The ideal transcript is an accurate verbatim reflection of the interview's content, preserves as much of the quality of the interview and the individualities of the speakers as possible, and is easy to read and understand. . . . If the meaning of a sentence is ambiguous to you as a reader," they continue, "it must be clarified. This is tricky business because you must *be sure* you understand the speaker's meaning."[12] The test for clarity is whether one stumbles on reading a sentence or section and returns to reread it.

The goal as articulated is basically impossible because the chief interference to the coherence, or closure, of a printed text derived from oral history materials comes from the open-ended communicative *exchange* of the original interview situation. The problem for print versions of oral history is that the relation of reader and narrator lacks the interactive negotiation found between speaker and listener, that is, between Rosengarten and Cobb, or between Nasstrom and Pauley. This is not a question that can be resolved by finding the best written translations for oral language. Nor is it even a question of how to interpret what was said, much less of style of presentation. The problem rests in the social relations constituting oral exchange, something a book cannot reproduce.[13] Alienation from the source is inevitable whenever an interview is prepared for public presentation. This alienation is augmented by the myth that the interview captures the narrator's "story," because the dialogic process is not one of exchanging discrete, reproducible narratives. There is a mental process that occurs when two people encounter each other that cannot be reproduced but might be indexed.

The complexity of the relationship between oral sources and their print referents may be clarified by considering the distinction that Roger Chartier makes between "text" and "print." Chartier works on the history of the book and print culture. Different productive processes are involved in the process of creating a text, or the content an author has created, and manufacturing print objects such as books or periodicals. In "print," the editorial decision process mediates the relation of readers and authors. Editorial motivations have little to do with the intentions of authors.[14]

In oral history that has been published, there are two distinct, though related texts: the original spoken words, which I'll designate $text_1$, which when transcribed are read in a first-level print version ($print_1$). The author of a book version works with the transcript, not with the original words, to create $text_2$, the narrative manuscript from which a book will be produced ($print_2$). Within this theoretical perspective, it is helpful to think of author, editor, and reader not as actual persons but as activities and expectations. "Readers" is a term referring to structuring conventions, providing a set of expectations against which "authors" (originators of texts) and "editors" (designers and disseminators of print objects) can measure their activities. A further distinction needs to be made between the "author" and the "narrator" in that the voice articulated in a text exists only for that communicative act and is addressed to the readers whose expectations have been imagined.

In oral history publication, there is a doubling effect that complicates the process and may help explain why converting oral history interviews into satisfactory books can often be difficult. In $text_1$, an author is the speaker who projects an interpretation of himself or herself to the listener, who is analogous to the reader but possesses the inherent capability of reminding the authors of his or her expectations at any time during the creation of the oral text. $Narrator_1$ is a product of the interaction between $author_1$ and the listener or $reader_1$. When the listener begins to prepare the interview for publication by transcribing the conversation, he or she becomes an editor preparing a print object with a relatively fixed and quotable version of the content the author has provided in an improvised, spoken text. Conversation ($text_1$) between $author_1$ and listener ($reader_1$) becomes transcript preparation ($print_1$), which transforms $reader_1$ from a listener into $editor_1$, controlling presentation of the text to $reader_2$.

As the interview is prepared for publication, the transcript ($print_1$) becomes the basis for $text_2$, the manuscript developed as a book project. The conversation, to the degree that it is maintained, is an effect of the text that is a creation of $author_2$, who is no longer the original interviewee, but the interviewer, scholar, or journalist who has decided to present the interview to a broader public than the transcript alone will allow. In order to reach that public, $author_2$ submits the text to $editor_2$, who is motivated by the expectations of $reader_2$ for an accessible narrative that conforms to genre expectations. The narrator ($narrator_2$) within the imaginary conversation presented in $text_2$ is no longer a situationally specific narrative voice deployed by the interviewee to represent himself or herself while creating $text_1$ for the listener or $reader_1$, but a character created by $author_2$ specifically for $text_2$ in order to satisfy the expectations of $reader_2$. $Narrator_1$, while not identical to $author_1$, emerges in an immediate relationship in which expectations and texts are generated simultaneously through a process of dialogic negotiation. $Narrator_2$ is the product of genre conventions predetermined by the impersonal relations of $editor_2$ and $reader_2$. $Narrator_2$ is an effect appropriate for the commodity relation that structures the interaction of $author_2$, $editor_2$, and $reader_2$.

The immediate and personal relationship of an oral history interview in which two people explore the meanings of the past becomes an increasingly impersonal transaction surrounding the creation of a commodity. The value of the resulting print product is not the creation of a relationship between $narrator_1$ and $reader_2$ but a satisfaction of expectations that the reader has formed for a class of print objects that appear regularly on the market. In the case of oral history publications, the expectations may involve a sense of participating more directly in the past through reading the perspectives of eyewitnesses and thereby gaining a deeper and livelier sense of what occurred and of the effects past events had on "real people." These expectations can be satisfied only if the author shapes the narrator of her book around her own interpretative and emotional responses, which are the only connection within the book linking the reader back to the original narrator.

If alienation from the source is inevitable whenever interview material is represented to the public, the question facing authors of books or articles based on oral history work is not one of techniques but of principles. They need first to decide what it is that they must present for the project to have intellectual validity and what they are willing to settle for as a reasonable facsimile of what began as an immediate human relationship. Any hope for direct communication between interviewees and book readers should give way to a goal of conveying to subsequent readers the spark of insight that occurred during the oral history exchange. That might mean retaining the confusions and contradictions in oral testimony as indicators of areas where further thought is needed.

Some of the most successful and emotionally powerful presentations of oral sources have occurred in projects that question the need for a coherent story, consequently making invisible the process of interpretation/narrative construction. An extreme but effective example is Claude Lanzmann's film *Shoah.* Lanzmann sought witnesses to and participants in the Nazi genocide of European Jewry.[15] Interviewees were forced to provide explanations for their actions and to assume responsibility for a past that they had tried to evade for decades. The film audience, while unable to interact directly with interviewees, observes a narrative process in which the author seeks to highlight expressions that belie the more benign words interviewees develop to conceal their personal responsibility. The meaning and intent an interviewee wishes to convey are no longer important. Indeed, they are shown as superficial to a larger process of relationality. Understanding is not the point of transforming the past into history, but positioning oneself in relation to others today.

The *testimonio* literature that emerged in Latin America during the 1960s similarly eschews the illusion that the narrators, whose spoken recollections provide the bases for a series of powerful books on the lives of the poor, necessarily are going to tell the whole truth and nothing but the truth. Why would one seek to conceal important aspects of one's life rather than invite potentially sympathetic readers into an intimate relationship?[16]

Donna Haraway has observed that facts are opposed to opinion and prejudice but not to fiction. *Fact* derives from the past participle of the Latin verb meaning "to act." A fact is done; it is action that has occurred and is no longer changeable. Fiction, by contrast, is inventive and open to possibilities.[17] This distinction is pertinent to oral history in general, for while narrators struggle to explain what has happened to them, they may not want to be defined by the mere facts of their lives, that is, the accumulation of past actions. This has been particularly true for the genre of oral testimony that emerged in Latin America in the 1960s. The facts of the narrators' lives were often so brutal that to accept them as inescapable was to accept tragedy as final and unchangeable. Testimonial literature was closely linked to the boom in the Latin American novel of the 1960s, in that the speaking out by the oppressed prefigured the transformation of society. Truth was less important than an act of speaking out. Rigoberta Menchú, in the beginning of the book based on her story, does not promise to tell the truth but instead to provide listeners with what they need to hear. She also states she will conceal, even from sympathetic readers, what is necessary for her and her community to maintain their autonomy.[18]

Menchú's assertion of a right to concealment—in a document whose appeal might be a sharing of personal experience—might seem contradictory. It underscores, however, the degree to which the relation of narrator and reader is mediated by an extensive interpretive process that must conceal aspects of the narrator that interfere with the effect the book is intended to convey. The words an interviewee speaks remain alive only to the degree that they have moved someone enough to want to pass on a rendition to another person. Authors of the print publication based on oral texts are more than conveyor belts. They actively engage the words of another person and make them their own by conveying their own responses to the person to a broader public. Keeping interpretation alive and keeping interest alive are not simple tasks, or word of mouth would suffice.

When work derived from oral sources is published, it crosses over to another universe. This is inevitable and salutary if oral history work is to effect public understanding of the past, but the price is loss of direct contact with the speakers whose accounts make oral history such a vital contribution to understanding the complexity of the past. My goal in identifying assumptions that accompany strategies for presentation is to refocus attention onto the circuits of meaning that constitute public communication. Exchange of perspectives characterizes oral speech. Publication of oral history work may involve an inevitable alienation from the source, but if such work perpetuates dialogue, if it opens up new ways of looking at social relations and retains the roots of the present in the past, it remains faithful to the inner logic of oral history.

Notes

1. Terkel, *Division Street, Hard Times, American Dreams, "Good War," Working, Race,* and *Will the Circle Be Unbroken?*

2. Garcia, *Chicano History*; Healey, *Dorothy Healey Remembers*; Hay, *Radically Gay*; Bryant et al., *Central Avenue Sounds*; Lomax, *Mister Jelly Roll.*

3. Rosengarten, *All God's Dangers.* Oral History Association, *Evaluation Guidelines,* 5, stresses the importance of interviewees' right to maintain their anonymity.

4. Terkel, *Interviews with Interviewers.*

5. Poniatowska, *Hasta No Verte*; composition discussed in Jorgensen, *Elena Poniatowska,* 60–61.

6. Rosengarten, *All God's Dangers,* xiii–xxv.

7. Ibid., xx.

8. Ibid., xxiv.

9. Frisch, *Shared Authority* (1990), 81–146.

10. Nasstrom, *Everybody's Grandmother,* 197.

11. Ibid.

12. Davis, Back, and MacLean, *Tape to Type,* 35, 53.

13. Nor can film or video, for while a visual image conveys much more of the performance dynamics of an interview, the viewer's relation to the oral history film remains passive. There is still no dialogue possible between the recipient of the oral history and the narrator.

14. Chartier, "Texts, Printing, Readings," 161.

15. Lanzmann, *Shoah, an Oral History.*

16. For an introduction to *testimonio* literature, see Gugelberger, *Real Thing.*

17. Haraway, *Primate Visions,* 4.

18. Menchú, *I, Rigoberta Menchú,* 247.

14

Biography and Oral History

Valerie Raleigh Yow

Germaine Greer said that biographers are the "equivalent of flesh-eating bacterium."[1] We live off of the carcass. And we profit and grow fat. I once asked a group of academic biographers if they had ever made a fortune; none had. Possibly biographers of current media stars or old standbys such as Thomas Jefferson make a fortune. Leon Edel, the major theorist of biography as a genre, said in *Literary Biography*, "If one were to measure the hours of work and the reward, it would be discovered that biography is the costliest of all labors on this earth."[2]

What is this pursuit that biographers undertake with so much diligence and labor? Biography can be narrowly defined as "the written record of the life of an individual."[3] Recently, "life writing" has been used to refer to the kind of writing social scientists do, a report of a case study; "life history" and "life story" refer to the account of one's life told to another.[4] Biographers, social scientists, and visual artists all study human life and can appropriately claim "life study."

"Autobiography" is an account told by the individual on her own initiative, not in response to the specific questions given by someone else.[5] The writer of an autobiography has an audience in mind, though, even if it is just herself. In *Reading Autobiography: A Guide for Interpreting Life Narratives*, Sidonie Smith and Julia Watson offer this definition: "Autobiographical or life narrative . . . [is] a historically situated practice of self-representation. Narrators selectively engage their lived experience through personal story-telling. Located in specific times and places, they are at the same time in dialogue with the personal processes and archives of memory."[6] Biographers who are oral historians record a "life history" and then use it and autobiographical writings and other personal documents such as letters, as well as artifacts such as photographs, furniture, houses, gardens, and information on the history of the time. They can, therefore, present a narrative that positions the individual life in a wide social and historical context.

Biography is considered by some as a literary genre; by others, as history. Professor of English Paul Kendall, biographer of Richard III, declares, "Biography is a genuine province of literature."[7] Historian and biographer B. L. Reid says biography is a branch of history because "its essence is fact and its shaper is time."[8] The confusion stems from the fact that it is an interdisciplinary endeavor, a blend of historical research methods and concepts, psychological insights, sociological ways of looking at the individual in the group, and anthropological ways of understanding the individual in his culture—with attention to writing style and narrative techniques appropriate to literary work. Above all, biography, as Lyndall Gordon, the biographer of Virginia Woolf and Charlotte Brontë, says, is "a searching genre; it strives for infinite complexity."[9]

There is another genre—fictional biography—that does not restrain the researcher/writer's imagination by requiring adherence to historical evidence. The author invents occasions, characters, and dialogue. An example of this type at its best is *Girl with a Pearl Earring*, which takes as its starting point a painting by the Dutch artist Vermeer and constructs a life story about the artist and his model.[10] I do not deny the truths that fiction can suggest, but fictional biography really is a different genre from biography considered here.

Biography that declares its intention to be based solely on evidence, whose biographer believes herself to be an "artist under oath" to tell the truth, is the kind of biography this essay explores. Recently, scholars have used the term "auto/biography" to indicate the postmodernist approach that biographical writing is based not only on shifting, subjective memories of the narrator but also on the intrusion of the biographer's own feelings.[11] Of course, autobiographical testimony and biographical writing are interpretive at every stage, and biography can present only an approximation of an actual life. Who can ever know completely what that life was all about? Who can say that her interpretation is the only valid one? Postmodernists are correct in reminding biographers that we must be humble enough to admit the elusive nature of accounts of human experience. Brian Roberts in *Biographical Research* explains that postmodernism recognizes that "interpretation should be attentive to inconsistency and ambiguities in stories rather than assume one story and a simple receptiveness of the audience."[12]

Nevertheless, the biographer must at least strive to get as close as possible to the lived experience. This means that we do not invent evidence, that we look at what evidence we have critically, and that we seek to discern our own biases in selecting and interpreting it. In spite of the complexities, we pursue biography because we recognize that it is a special art form whose *evidence-based* truth gives a glimpse of the "beautiful and awful mystery"[13] of a human life as it was lived.

Biography has been changing in its scope, now taking into account such influences on lives as gender, for example, and the way scholars in different disciplines regard biography has been changing. These changes, the uses of biography, the practice of oral history in researching biography, and ways that oral history and written documents complement each other in the study of biography are the chief subjects considered in this essay.

Why Research and Read Biography?

But to return to eating the carcass, why do biographers spend their lives studying and writing someone else's? Biographical research and the offering of written biography to the world does have its rewards: it enables us, although we can live only one life, to know and understand others' lives. This process compels us to establish some kind of connection to another, and this empathy enriches our own lives.

As long as the effects of a historical event—a world war, a depression, arrival in a new country—are expressed in general terms, we find it hard to understand the impact on individual lives. When we read a biography, we know how individuals experienced the historical event. Historian Barbara Tuchman calls biography "a prism of history." She believes that "it encompasses the universal in the particular."[14]

The study of a single life enables us to hold up a mirror to events we have been immersed in or touched by and see how different solutions were played out in others' lives. We can see how intricately bound up within an individual's life are outside influences—social class, material conditions, historical period, cultural assumptions. And we can glimpse in another's life the interplay of these with the individual's inner compulsions.

Human beings individually as well as collectively make decisions that change history. We want to know why they made these decisions, how they made them, and even how they got to that point. A blatant example of a powerful individual whose behavior provokes these questions is Joseph Stalin; Robert Tucker in his biography of Stalin shows a man whose psychological issues affected the decisions that resulted in the destruction of millions of lives.[15]

But underlying all these reasons is the hope that by studying other people's lives we can better understand our own. Biographer Martin Stannard sums up this compelling endeavor: "We tell stories to try to make sense of our lives. We read stories for the same reason."[16] Researching, writing biography is compelling. Richard Ellmann, biographer of James Joyce, Oscar Wilde, and William Butler Yeats, declares, "The effort to come close [to understanding the life], to make out of apparently haphazard circumstances a plotted circle, to know another person who has lived as well as we know a character in fiction and better than we know ourselves is not frivolous. It may even be, for readers as for writers, an essential part of experience."[17]

Biography, the Poor Country Cousin?

In spite of what I and other biographers think are the great rewards of biographical research, until recently the study of biography was considered by many academicians as a poor relation to real historical study or productive social science investigation or respectable literary production. Because of the predominant reliance on survey research and statistical method, many sociologists refused to see biographical research as scientifically reliable: it is subjective and deals only with the one-case study.

But these methods themselves began to look less than an objective means to truth. In 1960, Thomas S. Kuhn, in *The Structure of Scientific Revolutions*, argued that scientific findings are themselves the product of a changing culture: the very questions asked are liable to change, the research results are interpreted differently at different times, acceptance of them depends on concepts current among the dominant figures in the discipline at different times.[18] For some social scientists, this was validation for their belief that survey research is not as objective as believed. A few sociologists even wondered if such concerns as validity and reliability appropriate to statistical research can be meaningfully applied to biographical research. Research methodologist Norman K. Denzin argued that these "must be set aside in favor of a concern for meaning and interpretation."[19]

Now there is a growing interest in qualitative research and, among some sociologists, an acceptance of the usefulness of a biographical approach. To employ sociologist Brian Roberts's succinct phrasing, some sociologists and psychologists have been involved in debate that enabled them to "move from a positivist orientation to a more reflective and interpretive practice."[20] However, since the early twentieth century, sociologists at the University of Chicago had been happily using the case study as a basis for research. Especially books such as William Isaac Thomas and Florian Znaniecki's *The Polish Peasant in Europe and America* alerted scholars both in the United States and in Europe to the efficacy of this approach.[21] Their work influenced other sociologists in both Europe and America. In 1935, John Dollard published his classic, *Criteria for the Life History: With Analyses of Six Notable Documents*, arguing that "the life-history view of social facts is a fundamental perspective for the student of culture."[22] However, in America, sociological research based on individual lives remained for a time marginal. In 1960, at the University of North Carolina, Glen Elder, influenced by the Chicago school, began his work studying the life course of individuals by means of in-depth interviews. He used this qualitative data in conjunction with statistical data to discover how the individual's life is linked to the lives of others of his age and historical moment.[23]

Sociologists' new appreciation of biography was presented in such publications as *The Turn to Biographical Methods in Social Science*, a collection of essays centered on sociology in Europe.[24] In the year 2000, the editors went back to American sociologist Dennis Wrong's 1961 statement that biographical study deepens "our understanding of individual agency as *historical* means," and by this we avoid "an excessively present-centered and functionalist concept of man."[25]

In the same volume, sociologist Michael Rustin summarizes the current attitude of some social scientists: "While it may seem from a scientific point of view that social truths are established only by abstract general propositions or laws, in fact understanding of the social world has been equally accomplished through the luminosity of single cases. Ethnography and biography explore process, rather than merely structure. It is because it is through single cases that self-reflection, decision and action in human lives can best be explored and represented that the case study is essential to human understanding."[26]

Not just in sociology but also across disciplines there are different views now about biographical research. A contribution to this new acceptance of the validity of biographical research is the "rediscovery of culture." Anthropological approaches make us aware that "material policies and practices are lived out . . . through networks of relationships and shared assumptions and meanings which vary greatly with societies. . . . Formal systems are played out in interaction with informal cultures and structures and through the lives and strategies of individuals."[27]

Among physical scientists, there has been disdain for biographies of contributors to scientific discovery on the grounds that an individual's personality and living conditions have no bearing on the work. But biographies of scientists always have had a readership, and now in academe a new interest and acceptance is surfacing. An anthology, *Telling Lives in Science: Essays on Scientific Biography*, edited by Michael Shortland and Richard Yeo, explores and confirms the usefulness of biography to understanding the scientific enterprise.[28] At a conference in 1999 at Cambridge University, women who are scientists and historians of science agreed that "biography remains a genre used far too little by historians of science."[29]

As early as 1979, Thomas Hankins published an essay, "In Defence of Biography: The Use of Biography in the History of Science," in which he admits that it is difficult to bring together the personal life of a scientist and the technical aspects of his work. Nevertheless, he argues, biography at its best can "tie together the parallel currents of history at the level where the events and ideas occur." He concludes, "A fully integrated biography of a scientist which includes not only his personality, but also his scientific work and the intellectual and social context of his times, is still the best way to get at many of the problems that beset the writing of history of science."[30]

Thomas Soderqvist, biographer of the immunologist Niels K. Jerne, in his 1996 article "Existential Projects and Existential Choice in Science: Biography as an Edifying Genre," points to the scientist's need to realize his or her unique talent and passion and to make divergent judgments and unconventional choices—and to biography's function in illuminating these decisions and their consequences for science. Furthermore, he sees a didactic use for biographies of scientists: biographical studies can inspire self-scrutiny by other scientists and contribute to the communal discourse about the scientific process.[31]

Still another influence on thinking about biography comes from analytical psychology, which builds theory on the basis of individual case studies. Freud followed the lead of his contemporaries in using case studies to argue for definitions of clinical conditions. Today, this is the acceptable procedure among practicing analysts and some clinical psychologists as well. But across disciplines, humanists use psychoanalytic ideas and the case history approach in carrying out life studies. Humanist psychologists follow Carl Jung's concept that human beings continue to develop psychologically in adulthood and Erik Erikson's case studies of this development. Two studies stand out especially: George Vaillant's *Adaptation to Life* uses interviews with a limited number of men over decades to chart the different ways that men in American culture progress through life and meet the challenges of each stage. Daniel Levinson and his associates employed in-depth interviews to discover men's development in adulthood and describe the findings in *The Seasons of a Man's Life*. This book's counterpart appeared in 1996 as *The Seasons of a Woman's Life*.[32]

Among people in the arts, the findings of psychoanalytic studies have been taken seriously and portrayed in artistic work, whether poetry or fiction or painting. Rustin observes the basis for finding truth in artistic production: "'Typicality' is represented in art not in the form of abstract generalizations, but as imagined instances of particular configurations of experience. Truth is recognized by identification, by the recognition of identity or similarity."[33] This process is similar to the identification sought by readers of individual biography.

However, biographies of visual artists have been suspect because many art critics argue that the artist's state of mind or living conditions do not shed significant light on the work of art itself. In the journal *Art History* in 1988, J. R. R. Christie and Fred Orton published an article, now often quoted, "Writing on a Text of the Life," in which they argue that biography is "unavoidable." They declare, "This is because humans are irreducibly narratable, narrating beings. . . . In every historically and culturally human head is a script writer and speaker who never stops writing and speaking these historically and culturally specific stories." Such scripts inevitably are in the artist's thinking processes as she works. They go on to point out the ways that art is controlled by cultural managers (art dealers, museum directors, art historians, critics, and so forth). Biography can expose these social and institutional dynamics that influence the individual's work.[34]

Recently, oral histories have brought attention to artists who are productive in their local areas but not famous. In particular, oral histories of visual artists have shown the public that artists understand the relationship of their lives to their work. Artists see and insist on a connection in such volumes as *I Stand in the Center of the Good: Interviews with Contemporary Native American Artists*, edited by Lawrence Abbott, which features seventeen artists talking about the way their traditions affect the images in their art. Another anthology, this one concerning famous artists,

The Oral History of Modern Architecture: Interviews with the Greatest Architects of the Twentieth Century, by John Peter, describes the mutual influencing of technology, society, and art.

In literary studies, a major influence against the consideration of biography as capable of accurately presenting a life or offering significant information on the text came from structuralism and post-structuralism. The first proponent of structuralism, Ferdinand de Saussure (1857–1913), argued that every human, whether writing or reading, is a player who must play by handed-down rules—the conventions of literature, the boundaries of the genre, the special underlying meaning of each word. The focus is on the language of the text, not the author of it.[35]

Post-structuralist theory, advanced by such critics as Jacques Lacan (psychoanalyst), Michel Foucault (philosopher), Roland Barthes (semiotics), and Jacques Derrida (originator of deconstruction theory), emphasized that meaning can never be definitive. Every text has multiple interpretations, and what writers and readers think and say about it is shaped by the very language they use. Barthes, in "Death of the Author," asserts, "A text . . . is a multi-dimensional space in which a variety of writings, none of them original, blend and clash."[36] Post-structuralists agree that interpreting the meaning of a literary work by pointing to the ways an author came to write it is futile. They question whether the individual life under scrutiny by biographers had any unity or even meaning except what the biographer gave it. Instead, the focus, according to Barthes, must be on the reader: it is the reader who draws from language and culture to attribute meaning to the text. Or, as he puts it, "the birth of the reader must be at the cost of the death of the author."[37]

Since for post-structuralists what is of interest is the text—especially discussion of the literary traditions that dictated how a story can be told—and the infinite variety of meanings the reader can give it, biography is diminished in importance. Acceptance of biography in literary disciplines has been affected also by the postmodernist view that there is no stable core which is the self. Sociologists James A. Holstein and Jaber F. Gubrium confront this view in *The Self We Live By: Narrative Identity in a Postmodern World*. They present discussion of theorists in the past who assumed the existence of a self that, even though socially shaped, was a constant. They go on to discuss varieties in the postmodernist spectrum, such as Norman Denzin's view that the world is "exploding with images and representations of what we are, knocking our sense of self off center, but not totally eliminating identity as a primary category of experience." At the other end is the contention that there is nothing in the world—"no things at all in the traditional sense of a universe of objects separate and distinct from their representation."[38] In this view, there is no possibility of a self as agent, and therefore no biography can be anything more than a fictional construction. Holstein and Gubrium suggest ways that postmodernist theory of the self can be modified: they argue that there is a "distinctly social self, but one more complex than its pragmatist originators could have ever imagined."[39] For a practical solution to the problem, let us go back to 1981 to the explanations anthropologists L. L. Langness and Gelya Frank give in *Lives*: "But even though there are consequently many ways in which to see ourselves at any moment, undoubtedly there is a unity of some kind that binds together an individual's life. After all, we recognize other people not just because their name remains the same, or by their physical features, which also remain consistent to a degree, but also by their character. In time as we get to know people, they become somewhat predictable and a pattern emerges."[40]

In spite of attention to postmodernist theory in academe, biography never ceased to be an important scholarly pursuit, but it went against the grain. Now with increasing discussion of the limitations of post-structuralism and with attempts to modify postmodernist theory of the self, there is a renewed interest among literary scholars concerned with biography's possibilities. Edel's words about literary biography have current relevancy and application for biography in general: "The biographer enters into the heart of each piece of writing as if it were the only work ever written; and as he reads and studies it he relates it to the consciousness that gave it birth and to the world in which that consciousness functioned. He discovers recurrent images and recurrent modes of thought; patterns have a way of repeating themselves, for each writer has his own images and his own language and his own chain of fantasy."[41]

I have mentioned attitudes about biography among sociologists, anthropologists, visual artists, literary scholars, psychoanalysts, and humanist psychologists, but what about historians? Among historians, a major hindrance to the acceptance of the value of biographical study has been the dominance of macroanalysis of social movements or conditions. For example, scholars grouped together as the influential *Annales* School in France stressed that knowledge about society can be gained most reliably by using statistical methods to analyze social conditions. Pierre-Philippe Bugnard examines articles that appeared in three major French journals concerned with the study of human society—*Annales, Économies, Sociétés, Civilisations*; *Revue Historique*; and *Revue d'Histoire Moderne et Contemporaine*—from 1929 to 1976, and found that biography in midcentury was not a popular approach with French historians.[42] It was not until the late 1970s that biography began to be once again acceptable to French historians as a valid approach to the study of history.

British and German historians never gave up respect for biography entirely; among American historians, some individuals argued that biography should be accepted as a kind of intellectual or cultural history. As early as 1968, David Brion Davis stated that historians of culture should "examine in detail how the personality crises of a complex individual reflect tensions within the general culture and how the individual's resolutions of conflicts within himself lead ultimately to transformations within the culture." He was thinking of such individuals as Martin Luther. He argued in addition that biography can provide a "concreteness and sense of historical development that most studies of culture lack."[43]

Nevertheless, there was an eclipse in biography's reputation in the 1970s and 1980s among American historians as they pursued statistical studies and macroanalysis of social movements. Today, historians vary in their attitudes toward biography as useful research in gaining historical knowledge, but the renewed interest in cultural and intellectual history has provided a more accepting climate. Even a military historian such as Frank Vandiver can say, "Good biographies deal with the ways people faced living—tell how they met problems, how they coped with big and little crises, how they loved, competed, did the things we all do daily."[44] Tuchman, in describing her study of the Crusader Coucy in *A Distant Mirror*, expresses this idea a little differently: "I knew that there in front of me was medieval society in microcosm and . . . the many-layered elements of Western man."[45] Today, many historians see biography as a way to understand what happens when individual, cultural, and historical moments intersect.

Uses of Oral History in Biographical Research

Oral history research methods are especially useful in biographical study. Oral history can give the biographer whose subject is living a chance to understand motivation, to ascertain feelings, fears, hopes, aspirations—internal events never committed to print—and to gain a knowledge of how the subject views the life. And, of course, this is the one research method that allows the researcher to ask questions of his subject[46] and the subject to interject information not asked for or even glimpsed by the researcher, so matters of great importance as well as mundane but necessary details can be set straight. In short, individuals whose lives were lived in a period within the memory of living witnesses can be understood in richer context than is available for the biographer of subjects of the distant past, who must rely only on written records and artifacts.

In this essay, to illustrate the use of oral history in biography, I draw on my research for the biographies of two women writers, Bernice Kelly Harris (1891–1973) and Betty Smith (1896–1972). My aim in each study was to relate the individual's inner world, which produced the literary work, to the outer, objective world that both feeds the inner world and is influenced by it. Smith drew from her memories and psyche the account of growing up in a Brooklyn tenement, which she wrote in *A Tree Grows in Brooklyn*, and then millions of readers of this best-seller began to define their own personal histories in its terms. My aim was to reveal the interplay of her individual experiences with the influence of her expressions of it on the general culture. Harris chose a conventional life, marrying and carrying out all the duties of a housewife in a small North Carolina town. But in five of her seven novels, she articulated for generations of women a central question: How much of myself do I give up in order to belong to you?[47]

My two subjects were not living at the time I began research for their biographies, but I used oral history interviewing extensively with individuals who had known them. In the research on Harris, I had her collection of letters, manuscripts, and autobiographical writings available to me at the University of North Carolina, and in another collection I was permitted to read her correspondence with a close friend, contained in the friend's family archives. But these written records became more meaningful when I recorded the oral histories of people who knew her.

Harris longed for a child, but her husband Herbert Harris, intending to prevent the family wealth from being distributed, refused to have children. She wrote of her sorrow over this, but I did not know from the written sources if this feeling persisted over time. During an oral history interview, a journalist who as a young man was her friend stated that he once took his two children to visit her when she was in her seventies and that he was shocked when she blurted out angrily, "Herbert never let me have a child."[48] Bernice loved Herbert passionately and in her writings she skipped over his faults, but the townspeople who recorded their experiences of living on Harris's block said that Herbert was a "hard man."

According to the witnesses, Herbert was the richest man in town. He left no written documents, but the oral history testimony gave me glimpses of him, such as his standing late at night on the street corner talking to his partner about their cotton gin business, refusing to give up the subject to go to bed after a long day of work. This report was in accord with the written document, Bernice's account of his lying awake at night, counting his money in his head, out loud.

An unexpected bonus came when narrators told me stories that revealed the origin of some events and characters that appear in Harris's novels. I had been impressed that in one novel, *Sage Quarter*, Harris had her main character, a lame orphaned girl, figure out that she could support herself in spring by growing daffodils and selling them in the nearby town market. In an oral history interview, Harris's niece told me that her mother

(Harris's sister) had used her pennies to buy daffodil bulbs, which her father tried to uproot with his ploughshare, saying that people could not eat flowers. The blade only divided the bulbs so that a magnificent harvest of daffodils came up the next spring. In fact, the daffodils were sold in the town market and sustained the family every spring for many years. This oral history was a clear indication to me that I should seek the origin of other events in Harris's novels in her early life.

Bernice Kelly Harris would never have praised herself, but the oral histories provided insight into the ways she helped other writers, from published authors to the little boy in the neighborhood who came to her house every Saturday morning to write. And it is the oral testimony that showed me what courage and heroism she had; she was too self-effacing to have ever admitted this.

Like many southern women writers, she had a "mask" for public use; the oral histories revealed my subject in unguarded moments. Harris suffered from depression, but she maintained a cheerful countenance when she was with others. One narrator remembered that when she did not know he was looking, the sad expression he saw on her face broke his heart. Edel described the importance of such glimpses: "Certain psychological signs . . . enable us to understand what people are really saying behind the faces they put on, behind the utterances they allow themselves to make before the world . . . the pleasant joking remark that is accompanied by a hostile gesture . . . the sudden slip of the tongue that says the opposite of what has been intended."[49]

Oral history is the research method likely to give us information about the subject's impact on others. Near the end of her life, when she had had a heart attack and was in a nursing home, Harris wrote some autobiographical passages (not meant for others' eyes) in which she characterized herself as good only for the trash bin. A narrator who brought her to his family's home one evening for dinner during that time said that she was a joyous person, that when she entered the room, she made it light up.

Stories remembered in oral history interviews can also suggest motivation. A question came up about whether Betty Smith intended *A Tree Grows in Brooklyn* to be didactic. In an oral history interview, her granddaughter remembered a story that

Smith's second husband, Joe Jones, told her. Shortly after the publication of the novel, he and Betty were eating in a New York restaurant. She watched the tired, harried woman who was their waitress. She asked the waitress if she had read *A Tree Grows in Brooklyn*. The woman replied that she had not. Betty reached in her bag and pulled out the novel and gave it to her, saying, "Read this—it might help."[50]

Oral history helped me understand immediate circumstances in the individual's life. At the time Smith was writing *A Tree Grows in Brooklyn*, her Rockefeller grant to write plays ended. I knew from letters that she was seeking alternate sources of income, but I did not know how desperate the situation was. Her daughter, in her oral history, told me that one week when they had nothing in their house to eat, she found an unmarked envelope on the street with two dollars in it. Smith figured out how to use that money to feed her two daughters and herself for a week.

Later, when Smith was working on her second novel, *Tomorrow Will Be Better*, living in the house with her were Joe Jones, her daughter Mary and son-in-law Walter, with their toddler daughter and newborn son, and Smith's other daughter Nancy, who was recovering from an illness—in all, six people and a newborn. The woman who usually cooked and kept house was unavailable to work because she was grieving over a death in her family. In an oral history interview, the narrator shared a memory of Smith at the farmers' market one Saturday morning: she was wearing an old black coat even though it was a warm April day and carrying a large basket to hold the food she was buying. I realized then that *she* was doing the food shopping and cooking for her family and did not even have time to pay attention to her clothing, much less work on her second novel. Near the end of her life, Smith lost the ability to summon words. (Although no diagnosis was ever made, the symptoms suggest aphasia.) She could no longer write. I learned from oral history testimony that far from being unthinking, she communicated by acting out meanings.

I have mentioned here some other uses of oral history for writing biography—finding out motivation, ascertaining the influence of the subject or her work on others, discovering the origin of ideas, catching a glimpse of the subject in an unguarded moment, understanding the circumstances at a given time. Other biographers have talked about still other uses of oral history; but above all, oral history is especially effective in presenting remarkable lives that would have remained unknown otherwise. Theodore Rosengarten, in recording the testimony of Ned Cobb and publishing it as *All God's Dangers: The Life and Times of Nate Shaw*, makes available to us the life of an African American tenant farmer. Rosengarten said, "He was the first to convey to the book-taught world the whole life of an unlettered tenant farmer."[51] Ned Cobb, that is, Nate Shaw, this extraordinary, brave man, is one of many whose lives we would not have known except for the use of oral history in writing biography.

Agendas in the Life Study Interview

Ned Cobb knew that Rosengarten intended to help the cause of the Southern Tenant Farmers Union somehow and that Rosengarten respected him. As biographer Andrew McFadzean states, "The dynamics of an interview suggest that the outcome is often the result of a complex interplay between individual memories and personal agendas."[52] Biographical research, like family history research, is an extremely complex and delicate matter because it concerns close personal relationships. Both interviewer and narrator have a relationship with the subject (sometimes the narrator *is* the subject), and both have agendas. It is productive to be aware of these agendas.

Sometimes during the interview the narrator so obviously likes the subject that it is easy to figure out what his agenda is: he wants a positive view written of the subject. A newspaperman who had been a colleague and drinking buddy of Walter Carroll, Betty Smith's son-in-law, recorded his memories for me. It soon became clear to me that my narrator adored Walter and wanted to make sure I gave him "a good press."

At other times, the narrator so obviously hates the subject that his agenda, too, is easy to see. But this process is often complicated and subtle. I interviewed a man who had been a friend of Joe Jones. In the preliminary interview, he said he would tell me things Smith's second husband had said about her. But in the recording session, when I asked if he remembered anything Jones said about Smith after the divorce, he hedged. He said, "I do remember some remarks Joe made about Betty but these are insignificant," and passed on to another topic, declining to return to the previous one.[53] He had begun the interview by telling me he owed a lot to Joe Jones. It became clear to me that over the years since Jones's death the narrator had constructed a myth of sainthood about him that he was not going to let me destroy. He did not want me to print anything negative Jones said, even about his former wife, lest it tarnish this aura of sainthood. This narrator did not like my subject, but repeating Jones's criticism of her was contrary to his agenda. He used the interview to pay back his debt to his friend.

Another narrator had a view of himself as witty and sophisticated, and one agenda was to project that. He succeeded: his testimony was enlightening and delightful. His other agenda became apparent only at the end of the interview. He refused to sign a release form, and I realized then that privacy and control of his story were of utmost importance to him. True, he did not know me; he did not know what I would do with his testimony. When I finished writing the biography, I sent the manuscript to him, noting specifically the pages on which he was quoted. Only after he had read the manuscript was he willing to sign.

During another interview, I soon understood that I would not be able to follow my interview guide at all. The narrator's agenda was to think through things that had happened to herself some fifty years ago when she knew Betty Smith. Definitely her agenda differed from mine, but she gave me a historical context in which to see my subject.

Sometimes the narrator answers in a way that is contrary to the evidence in both written and oral sources, or a reason-why question elicits a pat answer that is not convincing. The interviewer senses that there is dissimulation, evasion, or outright lying. Jean Strouse, biographer of Alice James, declared that there are good reasons and the real reasons.[54] One of the real reasons for evasion when you are interviewing members of your subject's family is that every family has its own secrets. And every family has its own myths—some that have a basis in truth—that are believed. Interviewing members of your subject's family lands you in a minefield of secrets and myths. The narrator's agenda here is to protect the family.

Family members may view a parent or child in terms of society's expectations and find it difficult to see the individuality of the person. The editors of *The Challenge of Feminist Biography*, discussing in their introduction the problems women's biographers face, write: "Some children, we found, blanked out everything negative about their mothers, others everything favorable. Because society still expects mothers to be more responsible for domestic life than fathers, might children judge mothers more harshly than fathers?"[55]

And individuals have myths about themselves that they must put to good use: these internal representations form a central theme that is a guide in living a life.[56] Educator John McAdams asserts the value of "personal myth that integrates the reconstructed past with the perceived present and anticipated future and provides life with that sense of unity and purpose that is so characteristic of mature adult identity."[57] In oral history interviews for biography, the interviewer may find that the narrator's choice in the stories they tell may have something to do with a personal myth. It became clear to me during an interview with a close friend of Bernice Kelly Harris that this narrator saw herself—indeed, *was*—a quiet and efficient philanthropist, an aspect of the mythic dimension of her life as a Christian journey. She talked about how she found out that Harris was poverty stricken. Herbert had deposited the money from Bernice's novels in his bank account and then effectively disinherited her by refusing to make a will; after his death, the family's lawyer made sure that five-sixths of his wealth went to his family. My narrator organized a group of friends to make a monthly contribution to a fund marked "Anonymous Patron of the Arts," which arrived regularly in Bernice's post office box and sustained her in her last years. However, when I asked how Herbert managed to avoid having children, the narrator, a maiden lady, replied that they had separate bedrooms. I know that they did not. Nevertheless, in my narrator's myth (true in reality) about herself and Bernice as true ladies, she would never tell the truth about such intimate matters to a stranger.

The narrator may have a philosophy of life that she or he holds onto and that the narrator does not want the interviewer to prove groundless. When I asked Betty Smith's daughter about the possibility of sexual abuse by her mother's stepfather in Smith's teen years, the daughter was outraged. I had a letter that intimated that sexual abuse had occurred—although it was not given a name, and the perpetrator was not identified—but her mother's letter made no difference to the daughter. In her worldview, things like that do not happen.

Agnes Hankiss, in her essay, "Ontologies of the Self: Mythological Rearranging of One's Life History," shows how a narrator may create a view of the past that justifies a decision made then or explains a present condition.[58] That is an ongoing process for each of us and is bound to show up in an oral history interview.

To sum up the caveats in these examples, the narrator has to protect herself or himself; and so there inevitably will be agendas, some not readily known. After the interview, reflect on this oral document and approach it critically—a process required by any document, written or oral. Ken Plummer in his chapter, "The Doing of Life Histories" in *Documents of Life*, suggests some questions to ask of the narrator's testimony: "Is misinformation (unintended) given? Has there been evasion? Is there evidence of direct lying and deception? Is a 'front' being presented? . . . How much has been forgotten? How much may be self-deception?"[59]

For testimony that does not ring true, seek corroboration or refutation in other oral sources and in written sources. You can access a city on the Internet, find its records office, and read ways to obtain birth, marriage, and death records as well as addresses of its schools, churches, and synagogues that may have personal records. Be aware, though, that often the governmental agency or religious organization requires permission from nearest of kin to show these records to a researcher. Another Internet resource is the genealogy the family has published, but look at this critically. I have found that errors occur there, too.

The Biographer's Agenda

Biographers have their own agenda. On the most obvious level, it is to gather as much information about the subject as possible. But the process is more complicated than that, as Rosengarten

states: "To talk of objectivity then, is to talk of concealment."[60]
There has been a conceptual shift in academic disciplines allied
to the shift from an emphasis on objectivity to consideration of
subjectivity discussed in the beginning of this essay; now there
is increasing acceptance of the need to reflect on the interviewer's effects on research and the effects of the research on the
interviewer.[61]

Indeed, affinity of biographer with subject is now seen to
have advantages—for one thing, it increases the possibility of
empathy. And empathy is, according to Vandiver, "the biographer's spark of creation."[62] Without it, a biography is simply a
recounting of factual information; with it, the biographer can
achieve "a conceptual grasp" of the subject.[63] Even with the
most despicable of subjects, the biographer must have some
will to see the world for a brief time through the subject's eyes
if he is to understand—and enable the reader to accept—the
subject as a real human. If the biographer has some experience
in common—such as having a special understanding of the subject's background or religion or employment problems or type
of work—empathy may arise without effort. It is not an accident
that I keep investigating the lives of women writers outside of
academe.

Or there may be some overreaching philosophy of life or life
goal that strikes a responsive chord. Samuel Baron believes he
chose to write a biography of the Russian intellectual and politician G. V. Plekhanov because he just needed a suitable subject
for a doctoral thesis. Whenever he was asked, Do you like
Plekhanov? he was vaguely annoyed. Only years later did he realize, "I knew relatively little about Plekhanov when I made my
choice, but I was certainly aware that he devoted his life to study,
writing, and politics, with Marxism his lodestar, in an effort to
change his world for the better. It would seem that I chose
Plekhanov because I sensed a resonance between his life history
and my life plan."[64]

One evening at dinner with a friend, historian Lois Rudnick
discovered her unconscious motivation for writing a biography
of Mabel Dodge Luhan: "I realized that Luhan appealed to the
side of my imagination that likes to fantasize about being the
queen of my own universe, with the money, creative power, and

imperious will to do good and interesting things, to know adventurous people, to influence my times, and to live on the edge—psychologically and politically." As the research went on, she found that "one of its most paradoxical delights was entering worlds that helped to explain my own but that were at the same time the antithesis of my own."[65]

Richard Lebeaux, who wrote a biography of Henry David Thoreau, says that he liked Thoreau at first because he shared his subject's love of nature. Later, in college, he realized that he was attracted to Thoreau because of his "emphasis on non-materialistic values, the necessity of loving one's work, the legitimacy of noncommitment, and (with our growing entanglement in Vietnam), the need for civil disobedience."[66] He chose, partly consciously and partly unconsciously, a subject to fill his own needs. Lebeaux characterizes the complexity and intimacy of the relationship of biographer to subject with an interesting metaphor: "Yes, biography for me has been a 'joining with reservations,' a 'marriage' of my life with Thoreau's; the relationship has lasted—not without some stormy arguments, separations, and passionate reconciliations."[67]

As Lebeaux's political concerns changed, he began to draw back from Thoreau's stress on individuality; Lebeaux began to see the value of working with others to change institutions. Like Lebeaux, I believe that the reasons for pursuing a subject may not be the same as the reasons a biographer had at the beginning of the study. The biographer's life changes, and so it is inevitable that interests change; but usually by the time the biographer notes serious difference, he has begun to see the complexity of the subject's character and to appreciate the subject so that there is investment in presenting the life.

In every endeavor there are motivations and feelings not conscious until the individual determines to make them so. Becoming aware by self-reflection, the biographer can use these to understand the research process better. Halfway through the research for the biography of Bernice Kelly Harris, I realized I had begun to like her immensely. I became afraid that I wanted to see her in the best light and so it was possible that I was building a case for a plaster saint. During the oral history interviews, I insisted that the narrators tell me something she had said or done that was not ethical or kind or wise. The problem was that she actually was an extremely ethical and compassionate person, and so I did not get much information, no matter how hard I pressed. It is true that people are loathe to speak ill of the dead, but the examples of her kindness toward others and her rock-bottom honesty were so specific and consistent in the oral histories that I accepted them. I turned to the written documents—her autobiographical writing where she was self-critical—and using narrator's testimony and written documents such as letters to her, tried to figure out how realistically she had assessed her shortcomings.

In the biographical research concerning Betty Smith, I found myself having empathy and admiration for the way she managed as a single parent to sustain the lives of herself and her two daughters. I felt like pouncing on the narrators who disparaged her as a hack who would write stories for romance magazines. I wanted to say, "You don't know what it's like to raise two children with so little money. If you were in the same situation, you too might have sold stories where you could." But awareness of my own inclination to defend her (or myself?) kept me from interrupting the narrator. (I tried to maintain a neutral expression, but I now find myself wondering, Did my body stiffen?) Everybody has a point of view, and I used narrators' statements—although I was conscious that I did not like them—to describe the reluctance of her contemporaries in the academy to accept her writings as serious literature.

Dan Bar-On, a psychology professor and a Jew living in Israel, decided to interview Nazis involved directly in the Holocaust, and he also interviewed their children. At the very beginning of the interviewing process, he asked himself, "What if someone would express an opinion or feeling that I would be very much hurt by (e.g., that the Holocaust was justified or never happened)? How will I be able to go on conducting the interview?" After interviewing one perpetrator, he realized that he could not interview any more. However, he made a decision: "I felt differently about their children: They had not themselves done anything to my people. When I found out that I could feel empathy for their pain and anguish, I decided to go on and conduct more such interviews."[68]

The biographer/oral historian can profitably ask how as researcher he has affected the research process. Undertake a dialogue with the self by asking: Why did I choose this individual to study? What are my beginning assumptions about this individual's life? In reflecting on an oral history interview, consider Plummer's advice in *Documents of Life* and ask, How have my attitudes, demeanor, personality, and expectancies shaped the interview?[69]

Necessity of Interviewing a Range of Narrators

In composing a list of potential narrators, the biographer/oral historian should not throw out a single name, but rather prioritize. Of course, interview first the subject and then the oldest or most frail members of the family or colleagues or close friends. Consider also that others not so close can offer ideas about the subject's impact on the people outside the circle of her immediate associates—people such as the dressmaker, the cook, the gardener, the neighbor down the street, the student in her class, the child next door, the official at the post office, the policeman on her block, the druggist, her physician, the minister at her mother's funeral, the grocery store clerk, her child's first-grade teacher, the realtor who sold her a house. Sometimes only a glimpse is needed to provide the piece that makes other bits of information fall into place in the puzzle.

Situating the Subject in the Culture and the Times

All of the people mentioned above will give information that helps the biographer get a picture of the neighborhood, the town, and local and world concerns for the period and place. Historian Marc Raeff, in a review of biographies of Russian historical figures, says that in order to have lasting value, "biographies need to be set in their proper cultural, social, and political contexts; only then will they shed new light and afford insights into the public life."[70]

My interests have been focused on the difference that social class, gender, and culture made on the lives of the two women writers I studied, but certainly world events impinged on their lives. The social historian can see in Harris's life effects of World War II, even though she spent the war years not in Europe but seemingly safe in Seaboard, North Carolina. She learned to search for enemy airplanes and spent hours every night with her search partner, examining the skies; she rolled bandages; she cut and sewed clothes for the women of besieged Leningrad; she sat at a table, helping people with ration books. She wept over every death overseas of Seaboard men, knowing that each death "destroyed a world."[71] I do not think that it is by chance that her worst depression and resulting hospitalization occurred in 1943.

Gender

It seems unthinkable that biographers could ignore the fact that gender permeates the life course of both men and women. But in earlier centuries, most biographies were about men and written by men. Writers and readers assumed that a biography was warranted if the individual was outstanding—a famous politician, a great military leader, a renowned writer, a successful businessman. Needless to say, few women had access to these powerful positions. Rudnick concluded, "Women's lives have rarely fit the model of the normative biographical hero."[72]

In biographies of men, the writers focused on external events, especially on great deeds. Linda Wagner-Martin says that in comparing biographies of Franklin Delano Roosevelt and Eleanor Roosevelt, she found that Franklin's biographers focused on external events, political decisions, and associations with other political leaders. Eleanor's biographies were about family relationships, domesticity, and social events.[73] Somehow, in the early biographies, Franklin did not live daily in a house, or concern himself with his little children, or feel emotional loneliness, or glimpse his inadequacies, or indulge in extramarital affairs. Eleanor was not seen as an originator of ideas, an influence on political decisions, an inspiration for social change. Such a strange bifurcation!

Earlier, discussion of topics not thought important by editors—who were concerned with the public arena—were discouraged. Wagner-Martin describes how her writing about Sylvia Plath's cooking distressed her editor. Plath had limited means and limited time but she prepared the food for her family. In giving the details about Plath's cooking, Wagner-Martin wanted to show the reader Plath's choice about how to spend her time and thus reveal the real caring that was part of her personality. Her editor cut out the parts about cooking because he saw them as trivial.[74]

Biography has now changed in several important ways. First, unlike traditional biography, the new biography recognizes the indissoluble link between the private and public worlds. Because of women biographers' insistence, such topics as details of daily living, feelings about private and public events, relationships, and personal, intimate events are no longer ignored. These are the very topics that are often not found in written records but that oral history interviewing can reveal. We humans are social creatures and play a variety of roles that mutually influence each other. An interview guide that contains a range of questions about private life and daily life can best bring these to light.

Second, special conditions of women's experience, previously ignored, are being treated even though they may not have seemed important to men. In the past, for example, editors questioned the emphasis women biographers placed on friendships. Research suggests that men form friendships that are different in important ways from the friendships women have. Men's friendships are not characterized by discussion of feelings and sharing of confidences as much as by playing sports, attending games, or drinking together.[75] Women seek close friendships in which they can safely reveal their vulnerability, talk about things that trouble them, share confidences. Now research indicates that friendships are not as crucial in men's lives as they are in women's for still another reason: men in crisis may experience the "fight or flight" response, while women in crisis turn to other women in a "tend and befriend" response. Women use their close friendships to reduce stress and to get through crises.[76] Biographies of women from now on must confront this information—even if only to show that this need can be negated by some individuals. Betty Smith said she hated women; oral history testimony suggests that she helped other women and at times confided in them. Apparently, in spite of what she *thought*, she felt a need for this kind of interaction with other women.

Third, women whom society may not see as great have found biographers and readers. There are recent outstanding studies of women's lives, based on oral history. For example, Rosemary Joyce interviewed at length a seemingly ordinary woman and illuminates, in the book *A Woman's Place: The Life History of a Rural Ohio Grandmother*, a picture of a woman in rural middle America early in the twentieth century. Collections of brief biographies based on oral histories of women who would not otherwise be able to make their lives known have appeared, such as *Walking on Fire: Haitian Women's Stories of Survival and Resistance*, by Beverly Bell. Now we can know their strategies for resisting a brutal political regime as well as the ways they are changing their destiny by banding together in coalitions, cooperatives, and unions.

Fourth, the gendered construction of men's and women's lives is being seen as a reality that the biographer cannot ignore. In *The Challenge of Feminist Biography*, the editors remind readers, "Few biographies of men highlight gender issues in men's lives." Instead, they treat "a man's preparation for and fulfillment of his life course in the public arena." But a fuller, more complex biography would "explore the constraints by which society forces men into certain molds of behavior. It would not ignore, or dismiss as irrelevant, a man's private life or the nature of his family and work relations with individuals of both sexes."[77]

And in writing about women's lives, biographers are alert to the ways that gender influences their subjects; the ways are both obvious and subtle. It is obvious that women were shunted away from work that was defined as appropriate only for men and within the workplace were denied pay equal to their male coworkers' and equal access to promotion. But less obvious influences operate: Carolyn Heilbrun warns biographers of women against focusing solely on the woman's marriage, thus blinding themselves by assuming that marriage is the main goal and all other accomplishments are secondary. Furthermore, she questions Western society's view of the ideal marriage. Rather, she suggests a different question: Does this committed partnership work for these two people?[78]

The tensions within the thinking process of a woman who wants to modify traditional expectations for her gender are treated in Levinson's *Seasons of a Woman's Life*. The oral historian will find that women differ from men in their choices in moral dilemmas[79] and in the way they communicate—what they choose to talk about and how they say it.[80]

The biographer of women must also be cognizant of *gender influencing the research* of the life. We researchers also have internalized society's assumptions. For example, society's view is that women are less useful after they have completed childbearing. Heilbrun states that in the past biographers have often found "little overtly triumphant in the late years of a subject's life, once she has moved beyond the categories our available narratives have provided for women."[81] Now women's biographers note that great bursts of creativity may occur late in women's lives. Both of my subjects were in their late forties when they wrote their first novels. Joyce Antler's biography of Lucy Mitchell shows that the seventh and eighth decades of Mitchell's life were the most productive.[82] New studies on the process of aging indicate that we should throw out stereotypes both for women and men and look instead at the meanings individuals attribute to the experience of aging and to the ways they live in each decade.[83]

The biographer today must examine the effects of gender-specific prescriptions for behavior, especially on a woman's life. When Harris was married in 1926, even though she was only thirty-five, she obediently gave up her teaching job, as the norms at the time required. She remained a southern small-town housewife, doing all the expected things the position required. But behind the closed door of her substantial brick house, she used the financial and societal security of this position: she was able to hire help in the house, and as soon as Herbert left each day, she was free to write. Still, if a visiting preacher required sustenance and entertainment or the woman's Bible circle was meeting, she left her writing. I kept assuming that she was conforming to her society's expectations—often the oral history testimony reinforced this assumption—until I realized that she seemed to conform but in fact crossed the boundary for women by progressing from reading books to writing books. By that time, I could laugh when I found out that after her first novel, *Purslane*, was published, some townswomen were irked, and one said, "I don't know why she wrote a book, she already has a husband."[84]

Betty Smith rebelled. In the 1930s and '40s, a single parent supporting two children, she did not choose to marry a suitor who would provide. She was determined to make a living as a writer, to be as competitive as any man, and to demand compensation for her writing equal to any man's. Some observers of her life might conclude that she paid a price for her independence; that is one of the notions we have all learned in our culture. Asking narrators and reading her letters, I tried to find out if Smith felt this, but that was not a complaint that she ever expressed.

Rudnick, in her biography of Mabel Dodge Luhan, explores the contradictions her subject felt and acted out: "She had been brought up in the late Victorian era to believe that as a woman she needed to depend on men to achieve power and to realize her identity; she came of age during the Progressive era, in a time and place when many women of her class were seeking to define themselves and to achieve their own dreams." Luhan both flaunted societal expectations and concurred with them. Now Luhan is criticized for having needed men to make herself feel like "a real person"; she is accused of being "male-identified— a woman who defines herself in terms of her intimate relationships with men." Rudnick wants her subject to define her own dreams but accepts that Luhan was unable "to discover her own route to self-fulfillment."[85] Rudnick confronts the forceful societal message—a woman has to be in relationship to a man to be a complete person. Any woman's biographer today must at least acknowledge that this question will be on narrator's minds and her own as well.

Which brings this discussion to women's behaviors defined as "nice" or as "bad." Undoubtedly, narrators will reveal their social class and gender in articulating these attitudes. Rudnick observes, "Certainly no one has ever expected the subjects of male biographies to be 'nice.'"[86] She urges the biographer to break free of these judgments and present the subject in the full range of her personality and deeds, even though some behaviors will not be defined in our society as "nice." The biographer has to be aware, though, that narrators who like the subject may be reluctant to talk about her behaviors that they do not consider nice.

Lyndall Gordon, biographer of Virginia Woolf and Charlotte Brontë, discusses the set stories of traditional biographies that continue to influence our thinking: "We are adept at stories, the approved stories our culture has produced: the romantic doomed-genius story (for the Brontës); the quaint-spinster story (for Emily Dickinson); the child-abuse/frigidity story (for Virginia Woolf)." Gordon asks the salient question, "What story will elicit the uncategorized ferment of hidden possibilities?" She advises the biographer of a woman to consider that "what is most distinctive in women's lives is precisely what is most hidden."[87] The biographer can use questioning in oral history interviews to find the hidden, unique aspect of a subject's life.

Biographer as Psychologist

Mark Twain observes in his autobiography, "What a wee little part of a person's life are his acts and his words! His real life is led in his head, and it's known to none but himself."[88] Nevertheless, readers today expect more than a description of actions—recounting events without discussion of motivation or description of feelings is like offering a half-empty plate. Even in that fortress of "correct" historical thinking, the American Historical Association, there was heard a defense of the use of psychology in writing history. William Langer, in his presidential address to the association in 1957, described the "urgently needed deepening of our historical understanding through exploitation of the concepts and findings of modern psychology." We can only wonder if, at that moment half a century ago, his listeners spilled their after-dinner coffee. He continued, "And by this, may I add, I do not refer to classical or academic psychology which, so far as I can detect, has little bearing on historical problems, but rather to psychoanalysis and its later developments and variations as included in the terms 'dynamic' or 'depth psychology.'" He concluded, "Since psychoanalysis is concerned primarily with the emotional life of the individual, its most immediate application is in the field of biography."[89]

Langer's advice does not mean that the biographer has to enter a psychoanalytic institute to study for four years, but that there are some concepts from analytic and psychological literature that may help inform thinking about one's subject. Miles Shore, a professor of psychiatry at the Harvard Medical School, advises, "The modern biography should reflect an understanding of the central role of object loss, disappointment, and life change in precipitating emotional distress, significant changes in behavior, and clinical symptoms."[90] He writes that biographers would do well to study the work on human development, especially the writings of Erik Erikson, Daniel Levinson, and George Vaillant. Through these, the biographer can become aware of the normal crises of life stages and use this information as benchmarks for understanding the biographical subject's crises. The recent work of sociologist Glen Elder and other scholars in life-course research reveals that individuals vary in their experience of life stages, depending on personal characteristics, gender, race, class, and national origin.[91]

Carl Jung suggested that humans can gain some understanding by interpreting their actions or characteristic behaviors in terms of archetypes.[92] Film is a means of purveying archetypes in our culture. For example, several movie versions of Dracula show him as the Demon Lover who literally sucks the blood of the loved one. This view, expressed metaphorically, popped up in oral history portrayals of Herbert Harris.

If you were writing a biography of Tony Soprano (the star character of a televised serial) and your narrators told you that he was a tense and sad man, given to outbursts of anger, you would search for a theory to help you understand. You might see him as embodying the archetype Everyman—a modern American man, caught between traditional values of family and church learned in his ethnic family and the values of his contemporary culture: power, money, unrestrained sex.[93] But within this overall archetype, Tony seeks to play the archetypal roles: Husband, Father, Tyrant, Money-Lender (that is, manipulator of money/power as a Mafia boss).[94] The dissonance between the first two and last two roles causes him almost unbearable tension. As biographer, you could use this approach to understanding one reason for his unhappiness.

At different points, do we see ourselves or the biographical subject as the quintessential Martyr, Magician, Innocent, Orphan, or Wanderer?[95] It is clear to me that I began to see Betty Smith as Warrior—a real fighter—and that my narrators saw her that way, too. Jungian analyst Carol Pearson defines the characteristics of this archetype as an ability to "claim our power and to assert our identity in the world," to show a "willingness to defend ourselves," and to create "healthy boundaries."[96] But since that is not a stance expected of women, I was directed to exploring gender issues around this archetype, especially narrators' reactions to her.

All of this may seem far afield from writing biography, but biographer Alan Elms sums up a productive research strategy: "Seek out and use whatever is useful from the known universe of psychological theories."[97] Women's biographers will find, however, that often research has omitted aspects of living a life that women do not share with men. Even Levinson's *Seasons of a Woman's Life* explores developmental stages only up to age forty-nine. Nevertheless, I tried to apply findings in Levinson's works on both men and women as well as Carol Gilligan's work on moral development and her study of adolescent girls.[98] For example, reading *Seasons of a Man's Life*, I was better able to understand Harris's turn, in the last two decades of her life, to mentoring writers rather than writing novels herself. I felt sad about this until oral history interviews made me aware of her delight in mentoring other writers. Theory and oral history were mutually reinforcing.

Harris's loss of her father in her middle age and Smith's loss of her father in her adolescence affected each woman greatly, and I brought focus on the importance of loss in each woman's life. Smith's choice of the man who would become the compelling love of her life was understandable because he was so much like her father. I realized the similarities more and more as my narrators talked to me about this much-loved third husband. Oral history testimony concerning Harris's sad affect and uncharacteristic behavior following the death of her brother revealed to me the significance of this loss. I kept this in mind as I read her letters and realized that the cryptic, atypical passages that had puzzled me indicated the extent of her suffering.

Reading Jung's work on symbols, I became mindful of symbolism in my life and the lives I was studying.[99] I could see that the act of buying a house was for Betty Smith not just a materialistic acquisition but a symbol that she, the third generation in a German immigrant family, had become truly American. She immediately built a walled garden, again a powerful symbol for her. She wrote in a letter to her friend, the philosopher and playwright Paul Green, "Serene is a lovely word. It means to me, a walled garden with a gate in it and end-of-the-day sunshine and peace and sanctuary. Ever since I was a child and day-dreamed about princesses in the walled gardens of the fairy tales I read, I longed for a walled garden with a gate. And now I am having a walled garden built to my house."[100] *Serene* was the first word in *A Tree Grows in Brooklyn*—a word that held a depth of longing for her. In an oral history interview with her granddaughter, I asked whether she remembered her grandmother sitting in her walled garden. She did remember and said that was a place where Smith seemed especially happy.

Jung's autobiographical book, *Memories, Dreams, Reflections*, also alerted me to the importance of dreams.[101] Another classic study to consult about using dreams is Montague Ullman and Nan Zimmerman's *Working With Dreams*; among several recent studies, there is Jeremy Taylor's *Where People Fly and Water Runs Uphill*.[102] I asked narrators about their own dreams and whether they remembered dreams Smith had described to them. I was able to get some insights into Smith's preoccupations and family dynamics from this approach. The night before she bought her house, Smith dreamed she could not protect the children in the family from a ravenous beast. Afterward, she never recorded that dream again, and she told her husband that she felt now the children would always have a safe home to come to. A glimpse of Harris's presence in her family came in an oral history interview when a beloved niece said that, as a child, in happy dreams she would often be in Bernice's house.

In spite of Langer's endorsement of psychoanalytic applications to biography, the question of whether the biographer should indulge in explanation of this kind has been debated. I argue that when the subject's life events or introspective writings require such an explanation and oral and written documents provide sufficient evidence, the biographer can rightly be expected to provide this kind of insight. However, biographers must be wary of a simplistic application of psychoanalytic concepts or of applying them without sufficiently clear evidence. Biographer Samuel Baron writes, "One cardinal sin is to reduce a whole life to a single psychological formula."[103] Shore cautions the biographer against applying complex theoretical concepts to "explain" behavior. Rather the biographer needs to "build up a chain of events and behavior" that indicates a path to understanding the studied life—sometimes this path requires a psychological explanation.[104] The observations of narrators in oral history interviews may offer some examples of events and behavior in such a chain.

Ethical Issues in Biographical Research

In the usual oral history interviewing process, the interviewer must in a tactful way indicate that this cannot be an ongoing relationship; such a relationship is not possible when you are interviewing thirty people within a defined time frame. To insinuate that "I'm your friend" in order to get information is the danger here. In biographical research, with some narrators—casual friends, distant relatives, neighbors of your subject—contact will be limited once the interviewing process is over. But the oral historian who is a biographer accepts that studying one life does necessitate an ongoing relationship with the subject and with those closest to her.

In wanting to tell everything we consider significant, we may have to confront issues of harm to the subject and individuals close to him. Even if the subject is deceased, the biographer still has to weigh the need to tell the truth against possible harm to associates who are still living. Anthropologist James Clifford considered the matter of an illegitimate son of a biographical subject who was not aware of his paternity. Clifford suggests that perhaps in cases such as this the biographer should consider keeping the evidence for a future biographer to see. He urges, as a general rule, that biographers consider the subject's own reasons for secrecy.[105]

I have on occasion omitted from a publication personal details that proved hurtful to a narrator when they read the manuscript biography. My first guideline is: if the passage merely adds information not significant, or otherwise treated in the book, and is objectionable to a living person, omit it. When I sent the manuscript biography of Betty Smith to her daughter, she objected to another narrator's description of her mother's walking as being like the waddle of a duck. I omitted the description, but I cautioned the reader that Smith's gait was awkward. Her granddaughter objected to a line I quoted from a letter by Smith saying that her pregnant daughter's doctor warned he might have to extract the unborn baby (the granddaughter) in pieces. I took it out but indicated in general terms the seriousness of the situation.

I did not omit the account of Harris's depression, although some family members did not want it in the book. Nor did I omit a letter indicating Smith's traumatic event in adolescence that suggests sexual abuse, even though a family member wanted that section omitted. I did caution my reader that my interpretation was based only on an insinuation and on literary evidence. Both traumatic events (whatever Smith's was) reveal the emotional pain of my subjects and had a bearing on what they were writing in fiction.

My second guideline is that if harm is certain to result and yet the information is of great importance, weigh the benefit against the cost. I did not omit discussion of a letter that indicated that Smith had an abortion, although publishing this was extremely upsetting to one member of the family. I have been in agreement with biographers who vowed that we would tell the truth about women's lives. Too much that is hurtful to women has been covered up. Although Smith loved children, she made that decision when she was utterly bereft of support; this was the lowest point in her life. I agonize still; I told what I see as the truth about my subject but caused another woman anguish.

And yet, I do not want to manipulate the readers of this biography by pretending that this is the closest to the truths of the life that I have been able to come and then leave out significant experiences. So the benefit of including certain information is that I present a biography that is the closest to the truth on important topics that I can get it. But does this benefit outweigh the cost? Psychologist Thomas Cottle sums up this uneasy situation: "The dilemma of preserving privacy while publicly recording the way lives are led is unresolved and will remain unresolved."[106] For further discussions of this troubling issue of what we should and should not publish, read Judith Stacey's "Can There Be a Feminist Ethnography?" and Gesa Kirsch's *Ethical Dilemmas in Feminist Research.*[107]

An even more important ethical concern is that we who use oral history and who write biography interpret people's experiences and therefore run the risk of using our position to cause them to feel differently about their lives. Every person has a right to make meaning of his or her own life. Researchers impinge on this: we do it by the questions we ask and by what we write. The possibility of influencing—both negatively and positively—the ways the people we study see their lives is inherent in any kind of research with human subjects. We must keep constantly in mind the effects of what we do.

Of course, narrators may find the meanings we come up with interesting but not necessarily true. An incident, now widely cited, is described by Katherine Borland, who wanted to tape her grandmother Beatrice's oral history for published research. Beatrice described a summer day in 1944 when she, as a young woman, went with her father to the harness races at the local fair. The men around her studied the information on the horses' histories given on scorecards. But Beatrice liked to study both horse and driver, and using these criteria, she bet on an unknown horse. She was aware that there was an important relationship involved: both father and son (who was driving the unknown horse) were in the race, and she expected there would be some kind of collaboration, that the father would help his son. There were three heats, three times in which the same horses and drivers competed, three races in which spectators betted. Beatrice insisted on betting—women did not usually bet—and won each time, although her father was so upset that he refused to place her bet the third time and she had to ask another man to bet for her. After winning the third time, Beatrice, exhilarated, threw her pocketbook in one direction and her gloves in another and declared, "You see what know-it-all said! *That's* my father!"

Borland saw her grandmother's account as "a female struggle for autonomy within a hostile male environment." Beatrice cast off her purse and gloves, items of woman's dress, signs of her protected societal position and her lack of independence. (Later she would cast off her first husband in a divorce that shocked her community; Borland interpreted the betting behavior as proof of her grandmother's growing independence of mind.) When Borland sent Beatrice her account, however, Beatrice expressed strong objections to her granddaughter's feminism, saying that she herself was not a feminist: "So your interpretation of the story as a female struggle for autonomy within a hostile male environment is entirely YOUR interpretation. You've read into the story what you wished to—what pleases YOU. . . . The story is no longer MY story."[108]

Beatrice was a born rebel. My chief worry is about those who internalize interpretations outsiders have given to their lives, who accept that the authority is right. Bar-On reminds us, "In such a delicate kind of research, we hold the meaning of people's lives in our hands."[109]

Borland sent the manuscript to her grandmother before it was published. Even when there is a signed release form, the interviewer/writer should return the portion of the manuscript biography to the narrators to peruse if they have been quoted extensively.[110] Factual errors can be discovered. And along the lines of minimizing surprise, I want to give the narrator a chance to see personal information before the work appears in printed form for many to see. Most important, I want to know where I have deviated from their interpretation and give that knowledge consideration before the finality of printing.

Some Questions for the Interview Guide

For suggestions on topics to be included in the interview guide for biographical research, consult Catherine Parke in *Biography: Writing Lives*. She offers general questions for the biographer to consider:

How and why did a particular person do what she did, think what she thought, imagine what she imagined?

How did the person's private and public lives relate to and influence one another?

How did childhood affect the adult life?

To what degree is the subject conscious of various shaping forces?

How did cultural and historical events and context affect the person's life?

How may these elements, organized as a pattern by the biographical narrative, serve in turn to account for and explain a particular life and the forms it took?[111]

Parke considers the problem of how the biographer will find information on the inner life. Certainly, in an oral history interview, ask the narrator direct questions about this. Robert Atkinson in *The Life Story Interview* suggests asking such questions as, "What primary beliefs guide your life? Has imagination or fantasy been a part of your life? What single experience has given you the greatest joy?"[112]

If you are planning research using a series of biographical studies, see the specific questions for the life-story interview offered by Atkinson and also by Paul Thompson in the third edition of *Voice of the Past: Oral History*.[113]

This essay began with a comment on the complexity of biographical research; this is its challenge. I stubbornly pursue biography, and oral history remains an important component of this research. The results are worth the effort, but also the process is so fascinating that it is in itself a reward. I take to heart the words of psychologist David Bakan: "The most significant truths about human beings inhere in the stories of their lives."[114]

Notes

1. Germaine Greer, "Me, My Work, My Friends, and My Parasite," *Guardian* 31 (October 1994): 8.
2. Edel, *Literary Biography*, 33.
3. Winslow, *Life-Writing*, 4.

4. Roberts, *Biographical Research*, 3–4; Atkinson, *Life Story Interview*, 7; Linde, *Life Stories*, 2, 20.

5. Bjorklund, *Interpreting the Self*, xi.

6. Smith and Watson, *Reading Autobiography*, 14.

7. Kendall, "Walking the Boundaries," 33.

8. Reid, *Necessary Lives*, 4.

9. Gordon, "Women's Lives," 97.

10. Chevalier, *Pearl Earring*.

11. Stanley, *Auto/Biographical 'I'*; Stanley, "How Do We Know."

12. Roberts, *Biographical Research*, 7.

13. Reid, *Necessary Lives*, 6.

14. Tuchman, "Biography," 93.

15. Tucker, "Stalin Biographer's Memoir."

16. Stannard, "Life and Death," 36.

17. Ellmann, *Literary Biography*, 19.

18. Kuhn, *Scientific Revolutions*.

19. Denzin, *Interpretive Biography*, 25.

20. Roberts, *Biographical Research*, 100.

21. Thomas and Znaniecki, *Polish Peasant*.

22. Dollard, *Life History*, 6.

23. Giele and Elder, *Life Course Research*, 17.

24. Chamberlayne, Bornat, and Wengraf, *Biographical Methods*, 8.

25. Wrong, "Concept of Man," 8.

26. Rustin, "Reflections," 49.

27. Chamberlayne, Bornat, and Wengraf, *Biographical Methods*, 8.

28. Shortland and Yeo, introduction to *Telling Lives in Science*, 6.

29. Govoni, "Biography," 399.

30. Hankins, "Defence of Biography," 5, 14.

31. Soderqvist, "Existential Projects," 75–77.

32. Erikson, *Childhood and Society*; Vaillant, *Adaptation to Life*; Levinson et al., *Man's Life*; Levinson, *Woman's Life*.

33. Rustin, "Reflections," 42.

34. Christie and Orton, "Text of the Life," 559, 561.

35. On Saussure, see Dosse, *History of Structuralism*, vol. 1, 43–51.

36. Barthes, "Death of the Author," 148.

37. Ibid.

38. Holstein and Gubrium, *Self We Live By*, 57.

39. Ibid., 100.

40. Langness and Frank, *Lives*, 108.

41. Edel, *Literary Biography*, 52–53.

42. Bugnard, "Retrouvailles de la Biographie"; Piketty, "Biographie."

43. Davis, "Recent Directions," 704–5.

44. Vandiver, "Biography," 61.

45. Tuchman, "Biography," 136.

46. Weidman, "Biography," 50.

47. Yow, *Bernice Kelly Harris*.

48. Ibid., 41.

49. Edel, "Figure under the Carpet," 25.

50. Yow, "Betty Smith."

51. Rosengarten, *All God's Dangers*; Rosengarten, "Stepping over Cockleburs," 131.

52. McFadzean, "Robert Bowie," 37.

53. Roland Giduz, interview with author, September 5, 2000, tape in author's possession.

54. Strouse, "Real Reasons," 163.

55. Alpern et al., *Feminist Biography*, 13.

56. Feinstein, Krippner, and Granger, "Mythmaking."

57. McAdams, "Narrating the Self," 132; Stevens, *Private Myths*, 202; McAdams, *Stories We Live By*, 35.

58. Hankiss, "Ontologies of the Self."

59. Plummer, *Documents of Life* (1983), 103.

60. Rosengarten, "Stepping over Cockleburs," 113.

61. Yow, "Do I Like Them"; Watson, "Understanding a Life History."

62. Vandiver, "Biography," 50.

63. Frank, "Becoming the Other," 197.

64. Baron, "Life with Plekhanov," 197.

65. Rudnick, "Male-Identified Woman," 131.

66. Lebeaux, "Thoreau's Lives," 228–29.

67. Ibid., 225.

68. Bar-On, "Ethical Issues," 10–11.

69. Plummer, *Documents of Life* (1983), 103.

70. Raeff, "Autocracy," 1155.

71. Yow, *Bernice Kelly Harris*, 141.

72. Rudnick, "Male-Identified Women,"118.

73. Wagner-Martin, *Telling Women's Lives*, 6

74. Ibid., 7.

75. Lewis, "Emotional Intimacy," 108–9, 113.

76. Taylor et al., "Biobehavioral Responses."

77. Alpern et al., *Feminist Biography*, 8.

78. Heilbrun, *Writing a Woman's Life*, 92–95.

79. Gilligan, *Different Voice*; Gilligan and Brown, *Crossroads*.

80. Tannen, *Don't Understand*.

81. Heilbrun, *Writing a Woman's Life*, 131.

82. Antler, "Having It All, Almost."

83. Birren et al., *Aging and Biography*.

84. Yow, *Bernice Kelly Harris*, 77.

85. Rudnick, "Male-Identified Woman," 122, 125, 126.

86. Ibid., 131.

87. Gordon, "Women's Lives," 96.

88. Samuel Langhorne Clemens, quoted in Christie and Orton, "Text of the Life," 559.

89. Langer, "Next Assignment," 284–87.

90. Shore, "Biography in the 1980s," 99.

91. Giele and Elder, *Life Course Research*, 18.

92. Jung, *Man and His Symbols*.

93. Frattaroli, "Healing the Soul."

94. Linda Leonard, conversation with author, March 22, 2003, Chapel Hill, North Carolina.

95. Jung, "Relations"; Leonard, *Witness to the Fire*; Pearson, *Hero Within*; Stevens, *Private Myths*.

96. Pearson, *Hero Within*, 75.

97. Elms, *Uncovering Lives*, 10.

98. Levinson, *Woman's Life*; Gilligan, *Different Voice*; Gilligan and Brown, *Crossroads*.

99. Jung, *Man and His Symbols*.

100. Betty Smith to Paul Green, undated, Paul Green Papers, Louis Round Wilson Library, University of North Carolina, cited in Yow, "Betty Smith."

101. Jung, *Memories, Dreams, Reflections*.

102. Ullman and Zimmerman, *Working with Dreams*; Taylor, *Where People Fly*.

103. Baron, "Psychological Dimensions," 11.

104. Shore, "Biography in the 1980s," 105.

105. Clifford, *Puzzles to Portraits*, 124.

106. Cottle, *Private Lives*, 11

107. Stacey, "Feminist Ethnography"; Kirsch, *Ethical Dilemmas*.

108. Borlund, "Not What I Said," 65–70.

109. Bar-On, "Ethical Issues," 20.

110. Yow, *Recording Oral History* (1994), 108; see also Yow, "Ethics."

111. Parke, *Biography*, xiv.

112. Atkinson, *Life Story Interview*, 50–51.

113. Thompson, *Voice of the Past* (2000), 309–23.

114. Bakan, "Some Reflections," 5.

15

Fractious Action: Oral History–Based Performance

Jeff Friedman

> History begins with bodies and artifacts. . . . Oral his-
> tory does not escape that law. . . . The moment of fact
> creation is continually carried over in the bodies of the
> individuals who partake in that transmission. The
> *source* is alive.
>
> —Michel-Rolph Trouillot, *Silencing the Past*

I am a dancer–choreographer who collects oral history. During
the 1980s and 1990s, friends and colleagues in the San Francisco
dance community were dying of AIDS, and I began collecting
their personal narratives through a program I created called
LEGACY and archiving their life histories at the San Francisco
Performing Arts Library and Museum.[1] As a practicing artist, I
eventually conjured performances based on my oral history
practice, resulting in *Muscle Memory*.[2] Touring *Muscle Memory* as
a soloist throughout the United States, I began to realize the
hunger of audiences for the performance of personal narratives.
I became an avid collector of oral history–based performances
wherever I toured, whenever I encountered them in theaters,
and whenever I found documentary traces in newspaper reviews, journals, and academic texts.

Consequently, my personal trajectory as an artist transformed into a deeper investigation of the theoretical foundations

of oral history as performance. This essay expands on two existing approaches to this performance subgenre. First, I discuss broad theoretical issues concerning not only oral history *in* performance, but also oral history *as* performance. Second, to illustrate my expanded theoretical foundation, I explore several case studies exemplifying the link between oral history and theatrical or musical theater stagings, including additional genres such as choreography, instrumental and choral music, and multidisciplinary installations.

Literature Review

Existing print text literature on the intersection of performance and oral history fields is limited. In fall 1990, the Oral History Association published and then later reprinted a special thematic issue of the *Oral History Review* on theater and performance. This issue begins with an introductory essay by historian Michael Frisch, who considers the range of possibilities for converting oral history materials into performance.[3] The lead article, "Telling the Told: Performing *Like a Family*," by performance theorist Della Pollock, traces her emerging interest in enlivening print text in performance. Pollock's personal arc toward performance reenactments of oral history provides a model as we begin to address these issues: "As a reader already interested in the rhetoric of performed story, I felt charged to take up the narrative agency expressed [in *Like a Family*]. I felt I could no more remain a passive reader than the authors had remained 'master'-narrators. . . . [L]ive performance could extend the book's mission, . . . heighten . . . the 'felt significance' of the stories, engage the dynamics of change and exchange expressed in their telling, and, in general, celebrate the power of storytelling."[4]

Later in this compilation, Shaun S. Nethercott and Neil O. Leighton's essay "Memory, Process, and Performance" discusses their work with the Labor Theater Project, which emerged from the Labor History Project at the University of Michigan-Flint campus. The authors' stance is that oral history–based theater can account for unheard stories or "community anesthesia" by involving diverse groups in a theatrical recovery operation.[5] Important for both authors is avoiding a celebratory master narrative form of theater and instead recovering and promoting the specificity of multiple viewpoints, that is, "portray[ing] the struggles of the past as struggles."[6] "Precious Blood: Encountering Inter-Ethnic Issues in Oral History Research, Reconstruction, and Representation" is the final essay in *Oral History Review*'s thematic issue. Author Chris Howard Bailey addresses one of the important outcomes of Nethercott and Leighton's strategy. Once Bailey recovers a complex history, the author then questions whether it is ethical or even possible to stage conflicts that reveal deeply held community values, biases, and prejudices. Bailey's resolution is theatricalization's power to generate performance metaphors that can both embed individual testimony in context and forge a new alloy between differences.[7]

In addition to the above essay collection, two other texts appear in the oral history literature. Richard Owen Geer's essay "Out of Control in Colquitt: Swamp Gravy Makes Stone Soup," in *The Drama Review*, echoes Bailey's concerns. Geer experienced many of the same ethical problems as Bailey while working within a close-knit community that revealed many painful back texts in the process of creating oral history–based theater.[8] Also, U.S. Senate oral historian Donald Ritchie's book *Doing Oral History* includes a brief discussion, "Oral History On Stage," that is a beginning catalog of oral history–based theater.[9]

A plethora of literature published within the performance studies field over the past twenty years constructs a general theoretical framework for performance as it intersects with history. Important scholars in this area include Richard Bauman, Dwight Conquergood, Joseph Roach, and Richard Schechner. The field of performance studies occupies a large and heterogeneous field that names performance as a practice of everyday life, including staged theater, storytelling, religious ritual, and many practices in between. As a result, not all the above authors' works are directly relevant for my approach here, but they are excellent references for future reading.[10] For the purposes of this essay, I return to performance artist and theorist Pollock for her text *Exceptional Spaces: Essays in Performance and History*, a broadly conceived anthology that introduces the reader to various approaches to this rapidly expanding scholarly project. In particular, Pollock's introductory essay, "Making History Go," addresses embodiment, the most basic and important analytic tool I deploy throughout the rest of my essay.[11]

In order to frame performing history theoretically, Pollock focuses on the now well-known crisis of representation from the perspective of a performance artist who cares deeply about history. Historians are taken to task for their objectification of complex processes, which often results in deracinating the politics of production. In other words, how historians perform the making of history must be examined and accounted for. Conversely, Pollock asks artists and performers to account for their own "entailments in structures, codes and discourses of power."[12] Artists are always already inside the political, economic, and social discourses of their time and, as a result, are party to making history as well. Pollock undoes this conundrum by naming embodiment as key: "The body in action makes history answer to the contingency and particularities, or what Feldman calls the 'radical heterogeneity,' of everyday life. It performs its difference *in* and *from* history and so articulates history *as* difference."[13] The contest, or Nethercott and Leighton's "struggle" previously cited, is to keep history alive to its messy, contingent specificity, to real human lives that enact resistance to a totalizing hegemony. The ongoing concrete practices of human beings on the ground continually upset purgation through their "radical heterogeneity."

In particular, Pollock cites oral historians as celebrants of that radical heterogeneity.[14] Rather than accept facts as objective evidence in order to construct a selective master narrative, we engage human beings in the flesh, sorting out choices, rejecting alternative options, and submitting contradictory stories. Further, in the interview process, oral historians are present at the construction of historical narratives. Our recordings document the intersubjective relations through which those narratives are constructed. Our own fleshly presence coconstructs the narrator's multiple choices, options, and contradictory statements.

As a dancer and choreographer deeply invested in oral history practice, I am concerned with how the body helps create meaning within the process of making history. What corporeal practices have made a difference in supporting individual agency or decision making during historical processes? Dance study contributes a fuller understanding of the role any body plays in the practices of everyday life, including the making of history. Dance scholars generate theories about how movement contributes to cultural practice; we study practices on the ground where embodied action carries and transmits deeply held values. In support of Pollock's call for a radical heterogeneity based on bodily actions, I oppose any generalized idea of "the body" that purges our particularities. Instead, we can develop a more specific analysis of how a particular body enacts history. While the ultimate purpose of this essay is to address the subsequent staging of collected oral history materials in a variety of performance genres, I preface my investigation with a caveat: oral history, as a documentary method and as praxis on the ground, was "always already" a performance, fully embodied. My *cri de corps* is not in any way a contradiction of performance outcomes of oral history, but an extension in retrograde. Before addressing outcomes, I want to investigate how bodies are present and accounted for during the data collection stage. This and other questions interrogate ways the corporeal foundations of oral history support future staged performance outcomes in multiple genres, including music, theater, dance, installation art, and other interdisciplinary performance practices. Once established, that foundation supports a set of case studies including choral, symphonic, and experimental music; text-based plays, community theater, and the Broadway musical; dance theater and experimental concert dance; and interdisciplinary genres, such as installation and performance art.

Theoretical Foundations

Performance as a Paradigm for Life in the Twenty-First Century

Discourses that address culture may find their object of study does not easily lend itself to representations in print text formats. In *Power and Performance*, anthropologist Johannes Fabian notes, "What has not been given sufficient consideration is that about large areas and important aspects of culture no one, not even the native, has information that can simply be called up and expressed in discursive statements. This sort of knowledge can be represented—made present—only through action, enactment, or performance."[15]

This swing toward process is supported by an epistemological shift toward temporality that, in a new way, articulates how we know and how we tell about what we know. Cultural critic Barbara Adam coins this shift "the temporal turn," allowing for new ways to know and to represent knowledge. Adam describes this epistemic shift as an opportunity to represent multiple and simultaneous processes over time, one of the basic tenets of postmodernity.[16] Historian Stephen Kern's text *The Culture of Time and Space, 1880–1915* describes a rift between extant human time consciousness based on agricultural cycles in the late nineteenth century and a rationalized time consciousness rising from rapid technological development. The deepening schism made temporality in and of itself an explicit contestation, and the differences provided fuel for the shift in time consciousness. Kern points out several then-contemporary artists who made creative works out of this timely conflict, such as Oscar Wilde in *The Picture of Dorian Gray*, Marcel Proust in *Remembrance of Things Past*, the Italian Futurists, and the Impressionist painters. These works comment on a changing world for which temporality became an important trope.[17] The shift in time consciousness made possible a realignment of how we think. In a temporally inflected worldview, multiple and nonlinear perspectives could occur simultaneously. Under these new circumstances, I posit, temporally phrased embodied experiences became phenomenologically viable modes of thinking and theorizing; Einsteinian and later quantum physics are primary examples. Consequently, performance as a mode of knowing edges out onto center stage, not only in popular culture but also in the academy.

Victor Turner and Performance as Cultural Process

Anthropologist Victor Turner became an early proponent of the temporal mode. Turner's text *The Anthropology of Performance* opened up the field of social science away from static structural concerns toward the examination of cultural processes. Citing his mentor Milton Singer's fieldwork in South India, Turner refines the idea of cultural performances as set-aside events within the quotidian economic, legal, political, and domestic culture. These performances, found in rituals, festivals, dramatic readings, even films, are *experienced* from within as temporally and spatially different modes of being within the larger culture. These events also use a variety of mixed media, including movement, text, visual image, and theatrical combinations of all media. Turner is quick to note that these separate performances are not only reflective mirrors of the larger cultural container but are also transformative, effecting real change on the agents involved. When they return from the boundaried container of performance to their everyday lives, their status has changed in some significant way.[18]

I cite Turner's contribution to the literature on performance as exemplary for how the temporal turn enables us to experience our world from a different stance, one that places performance inside cultural processes as a vital and central mode of being. Theorists in other disciplines critiqued Turner, however, challenging his strict boundaries between performance and our life worlds. Instead, performance, as an emerging conceptual framework for approaching and analyzing experience, could cast the quotidian world as a performance space within which we, as subject and objects both, constantly stage ourselves.

Goffman and Everyday Life as Performance

Erving Goffman's text *The Presentation of Self in Everyday Life* advocates this notion of performance as both innate and effective in quotidian life. From a sociologist's perspective, Goffman suggests that what we present to others in a social environment is a constructed performance. There is no originary self separate from performances of self, as there is no self without the social world. We are embedded within the social structure of our culture.[19] In his text *Behavior in Public Places*, Goffman notes that messages can be verbal or nonverbal: "The information that an individual provides, whether he [or she] sends it or exudes it, may be *embodied* or *disembodied*. A frown, a spoken word, or a kick is a message that a sender conveys by means of his own *current* bodily activity, the transmission occurring only during the time that his body is present to sustain this activity."[20] Goffman provides a typology of embodied signals beyond verbals, including clothing, make-up, hair arrangement, and other decoration; limb and face discipline; and proper motor activity through space. All these signals, along with the verbal channel, are dependent on our understanding of culturally approved, appropriate signal systems used in a variety of circumstances. This knowledge does not preclude acting outside normative parameters, but we interpret any outsider action as a reaction against known existing norms. Quotidian performance norms shift according to who the actors are within a wide variety of social encounters, private or public. These signals are emergent in that they develop within specific situations as a result of mutual signals from actors involved. Included are metacommunication signals, that is, "moves about moves" or "talk about talk." Examples of metacommunication include gestures or eye contact that signal how we begin or end dialogue in a social situation. I now turn to these metacommunicative signals to link my theoretical discussion to the practice of oral history interviewing.

A major part of Goffman's theory is on the rules of talk. These rules include how we initiate talk, its length and frequency, how we indicate attention and regulate interruptions and lulls in talk, how we limit attention to externals, and how we develop and maintain an atmosphere. These rules affect both verbal and nonverbal communication channels, including embodied locomotor movements through space, limb movements, hand gestures, or facial expressions. In particular, Goffman points out that an integrated verbal and nonverbal personal line develops for each actor. We contrive our line to be consistent with our current role. We constantly evaluate the symbolic meaning of each communication event against the current self that is being presented and maintained. To illustrate, I cite Goffman from his introduction to *Forms of Talk*, where he includes corporeal embodied communication signals: "In what follows, then, I make no large literary claim that social life is but a stage, only a small technical one: that deeply *incorporated* into the nature of talk are the fundamental requirements of theatricality" (emphasis added).[21]

As we know, an oral history interview is different from conversation. Accordingly, Goffman suggests that some social situations include an additional layer of instrumentality. For oral history there is both the emergent dialogue occurring in the present moment and a more instrumental documentation process for the record. This difference is expressed in the temporal relationship to actors involved in the social situation. For Goffman, the performance of talk in face-to-face encounters includes the embodied actors only. For oral history, it is a performance that includes both the local embodied social situation and a more public and official historical posterity for whom the narrators stage their experiences. This additional layer requires a complex public performance from both the interviewer and narrator within the oral history event. More recent narrative theory offers specific commentary on oral history as a complex and multilayered performance event.

Oral History as Performance

Kristin Langellier is a narrative theorist who traces the trajectory of how oral narratives have become part of the canon of performance texts. In her essay, "Personal Narratives: Perspectives on Theory and Research," for *Text and Performance Quarterly*, Langellier shows how personal narrative falls between the cracks of "literary and social discourse, between written and oral models of communication, between public and private spheres of interaction, between ritual performance and incidental conversation."[22] The result of this unsteady positionality has been a lack of critical attention to personal narrative as a legitimate object of study, worthy of theoretical value and explication. We have seen in Goffman's discussion how oral history interviews also straddle the public and the private, the embodied and the verbal. Where Goffman attends to the microanalysis of conversational codes, Langellier provides another layer of theory that undergirds Goffman's coding of talk as performance.

Langellier carves out a new space for the personal narrative as not just important content for inquiry but also as a narrative event, in and of itself. There is story and then the storytelling event itself that provides the performance container for that story. According to the author, a variety of scholars have begun to excavate how the "story-text" is always embedded in a social context that is dynamically invested in performance.[23] In particular, Langellier contends, theorist Richard Bauman's text *Story, Performance, and Event* integrates the discursive mix in this emerging field where the blurred genre of personal narrative lives to tell its tale. Bauman's contribution clarifies how the narrated events of the story and the narrative event of the storytelling are radically interdependent.[24]

This notion helps lay the foundation for my thesis regarding the emergence of staged oral history–based performances. Not only is the content of an oral history a powerful basis for performance outcomes, but also the performative quality of the narrative container itself prefigures these stagings. I suggest that the theatricality of staged public performance reveals how oral history narratives bracket themselves as staging containers.

Goffman addresses metacommunication signals as an important set of signals for the rules of talk.[25] Translated to the theater stage, many signals remind us when performances begin: the lights dim, a curtain rises, the conductor raises his baton, a dancer gestures. All of these are conversational metacommunication writ large, so to speak, by the bodies of the performers and the concomitant lighting and architectural effects of the theater space itself. While these are all familiar theatrical conventions, not all performances are content to remain conventional, but instead manipulate those rules to clarify how the rules operate to both regulate and even control our performances, on stage and off. Bertolt Brecht is the primary exponent of this approach, naming the *gestus* of theater that maintains the theatricality of performance events as an explicit set of signals.[26] Consequently, staged performances of oral history narratives provide an opportunity to explore and clarify Bauman's "radical interdependence" between narrative and the narrative event.[27]

Performance is a phenomenon invested in the embodied copresence of actors within a contingent situation. As a result, we must include the audience as part of the copresence in our model of staged oral history. Langellier and folklorist Elizabeth C. Fine both note that textual representations of personal narratives often fail to account for both action and reception of any copresenced event.[28] As a result, the purely analytic approach still adheres to an underperforming literary model of narrative. Fine cites attempts to vivify the literary transcript of oral narratives in her introduction to *The Folklore Text: From Performance to Print.* The author shows how authors Dell Hymes and Dennis Tedlock are particularly focused on inscribing the performance and reception elements of an oral narrative into text.[29] In his essay "On the Translation of Style in Oral Narrative" from the *Journal of American Folklore,* Tedlock developed notation and text style formats that acknowledge multiple extratextual presence of vocal production, including pitch and volume among others, as well as pauses, nonsemantic vocalizations such as breathing and laughter, and gestures.[30] Hymes goes further, and Fine cites his attempts to reconstruct the performance of a Chinook text at the 1974 presidential address of the American Folklore Society. As a critique of his own performance, Hymes notes: "Short of preservation in the form of boxed storage in locked vaults, our efforts to preserve tradition through record, description, interpretation, find their natural end in *presentation,* that is, communication" (emphasis added).[31]

Summary of Theoretical Foundations

In this brief summary of performance theory as it references oral history, I have linked several discourse areas into an integrated theoretical framework that sets the stage for my presentation of case studies. The temporal turn toward processuality evokes the presence of radically heterogeneous actors in their life worlds. These actors' expressions, both verbal and nonverbal, all fully embodied, are not only content but also frame the narrative event as cued by the metacommunicative signals we use to signify our performance of self in a social context. How we perform self in the social world has been shown to inform the oral history process and the presenced coproduction of those narratives for multiple audiences. How the performance of oral history narratives is then transformed into staged performance comprises the next section of this essay.

Case Studies: Oral History–Based Performance Genres

To concretize my theoretical framework, I have developed a series of case studies in a variety of performance genres. I describe and analyze a continuum of staging approaches allied to the performance of oral history. I have grouped my examples into three themes: the laboring body, performing the aural, and performing the history in oral history. Each performance event specifically supports my theoretical framework, emphasizing how oral history can be conceptualized as performance through its corporeal foundations. At this time, a few words are necessary on the collection of data for these case studies. To enliven my already eclectic collection of oral history–based performances, I sent a survey to a wide variety of artists and community organizations who produce work in this performance subgenre. In some cases, I followed up with telephone or electronic conversations and viewed videotapes of works when possible to clarify or elaborate survey answers. Because of the limitations of this essay, the end of each section includes a note suggesting additional works within each theme for future interrogation.

Performing Oral History: The Laboring Body

It is notable that oral history interviews with individuals deeply invested in physical work have often made their way onto the stage. Nethercott and Leighton note that, during his interview, a labor activist could not resist reenacting a particularly dramatic event about his secret meetings: "We'd cut off the lights and wait in the dark [Knock on table, then whispering] Who is it? and they'd answer, 'Joe—from the stampin' plant' or some such. . . . We'd let 'em in and set 'em in the dark. They'd set there for a while and if anyone made a sound, there'd be 'Sh, sh, sh' all around. Finally, I'd light a single candle, 'Boys, we got a difficult job ahead of us.' By then they'd be ready to hear whatever I had to say."[32] As Nethercott and Leighton note, "The silence, the candle, the whispering created an aura of mystery, urgency, and heroism which drew members in."[33] They link this narrator's performance to Brecht's concept of primitive epic theater, in which the content of the performance is *about* performing. I suggest that when the content of the narrator's life work is particularly informed by a practice of physicality, there is an increased possibility of this type of performative reenactment within the oral history interview. As a result, we may see the subsequent selection of these dramatic life histories as likely texts for restaging. I address three examples of this subgenre of oral history–based performance about physicality: two musical theater productions—*A Chorus Line* and *Working*—and one physical theater production, *MSM*.

Musical Theater: Michael Bennett and A Chorus Line

Produced and directed by Michael Bennett, *A Chorus Line* represents an enormous shift in both the content and process of creating commercial musical theater. Whether or not Bennett was aware of oral history as a formal methodology, his impulse to record interviews with dancers gave them a forum to tell their stories in their own words in order to fill a missing gap in the historical record. Author Ken Mandelbaum suggests that *A Chorus Line* evolved from years of resentment about how dancers were treated in musical theater. Bennett had been a chorus dancer in several Broadway shows, personally experiencing infantilization and abuse of dancers during the creative process. According to Mandelbaum's text, *A Chorus Line and the Musicals of Michael Bennett*, Bennett's idea was "to do a show where the dancers are the stars."[34] Dancers Michon Peacock and Tony Stevens likewise had bad experiences and concluded that in musical theater "there was a point of view lacking and it was the point of view of the dancers."[35] The invisibility of the world of dancers was belied by the enormously productive dancing bodies on stage.

Original collaborators Robert Viagas, Baayork Lee, and Thommie Walsh trace the collaborative process in their text *On The Line: The Creation of A Chorus Line*. In 1974, Bennett, Peacock, and Stevens sent out a call to a preselected group of dancers to show up at a loft in downtown Manhattan after their nightly performances. As Walsh recalled, "Tony called and said, 'We're doing this workshop next week and we're going to talk about being dancers. Michael Bennett is going to be there and we're going to dance. It's going to be a marathon. We're going to try and stay up all night, talk about life, and what it's like to be a dancer.'"[36] According to the testimonies of several original narrators, that first session lasted twelve hours, and many stories from the recordings appeared in the final script of *A Chorus Line*. Main themes emerging from those recordings include childhood memories of family and early training that inform several song lyrics: Kelly Bishop's early childhood romantization of "[Everything's Beautiful] At the Ballet," Priscilla Lopez's poor training as an adolescent in "[I Felt] Nothing," Wayne Cilento's expression of self-confidence in "I Can Do That," the sexualized infantilization of female adult dancers in "Tits and Ass," and Nicholas Dante's powerful monologue of growing up gay and Puerto Rican.[37]

In Mandelbaum's text, lyricist Ed Kleban and composer Marvin Hamlisch describe how the taped and transcribed interviews became the source material for their original score. Kleban notes, "Most of it was intensely boring, the same nonsense over and over again. . . . Except that every twenty or twenty-five pages, there would be something interesting to the outsider and not just to a chorus gypsy. Suddenly you discovered something like the realization that 'I can do that,' that that young man could excel and have a special life if he danced. There was a song."[38] Kleban listened to Lopez's comment on the death of a former teacher who had mistreated her: "She said, 'Good,'" and he decided, "She was a truth-teller and I wanted to go with that story. . . . The truth is that these people's lives were full of people who did damage to them."[39] For cowriter James Kirkwood, the tapes and transcripts were at first useless. Instead, he spoke directly with the dancers, trying to get them to elaborate upon their experiences.[40]

The workshop process of creating *A Chorus Line* was Bennett's innovation and required several new ways of working. Selecting material from the original tapes and transcripts was ongoing during the creative process. I suggest this novel process is directly linked to Bennett's original impulse to work from oral history method. First, the creative collaborators, Bennett as director, Robert Avian as choreographer, Kleban and Hamlisch for the score, and Kirkwood and Dante as cowriters, went into the workshop process without finalized materials. Dante says, "We went into rehearsal with no music and no lyrics and ¾ of a script. There was no ending, and the script was mainly the material from the tapes somehow slogged down from 24 hours into monologues and chunks."[41] Consequently, the dancers, as original narrators, became creative collaborators with the usual team of director/choreographer, composer, and writer. Bennett would constantly go back to ask the dancers how and "why they started dancing; Avian would ask people what they would do if they couldn't dance anymore; and Kleban would ask for greater elaboration of phrases from the tapes that had captured his imagination."[42] The original cast members remember that late in the creative process, as they were refining a story or song, Bennett would stop the rehearsal and ask someone on stage at that moment what their experience had been. Kleban would occasionally ask for a specific dancer to come into the studio with him and talk about his or her life, "hoping to elicit a word or feeling that would lead him to a lyric."[43] (According to Mandelbaum, even after the premiere of the work, both Bennett and Avian would interview new cast members in order to use their particular qualities to find their role.)[44]

The emergent workshop method of creating *A Chorus Line* aligns with a parallel process in oral history interviewing. Given the copresence of the original oral history narrators in the creative process, Bennett and his collaborators not only encouraged but were compelled by Pollock's radical heterogeneity, by actual bodies in action, to continue that emergent process in rehearsals. It's not a coincidence that Bennett himself was a dancer as well as a frustrated director/producer. He wanted to create both a way to tell dancers' stories and a new way to make musicals; these desires were interdependent, and the result may not be surprising. In the final production, after the audition sets us up at the beginning, the line of action of *A Chorus Line* is a corporate life history of dancers. Avian notes, "It's a composite evening about the life of a dancer, which most people don't realize. The first story is about a four-year-old, the next is about an eight-year-old, the next is about an eleven-year-old, the next is about adolescence, and so on, getting older and older."[45]

I have detailed the process of creating *A Chorus Line* to clarify the links between the use of oral history methodology and not only the content but also the creative process and eventually the innovative structure of the work. I have yet to find evidence, however, that actual physical representations—movements, gestures, or facial expressions—of the oral history narrators contributed specifically to the work. It is not clear from primary

texts about the creation of *A Chorus Line* whether dance sequences in the show may have emerged from actual steps produced in an oral history situation. There seems to be a tenuous
link between the vocal production of individual narrators and
the production of lyrics. Any further investigation of this proposal regarding lyrics and composition alone would require significant research in the original tapes and transcripts.[46] My next
example examines a particular instance where physicality expressed during data collection is represented on stage in the theatrical event.

Musical Theater: Studs Terkel and Steven Schwartz's Working

The oral history–based text *Working: People Talk about What
They Do All Day and How They Feel about What They Do* provides
the foundation for the musical theater production *Working*,
which premiered on Broadway in 1978 and ran for twenty-five
performances before closing.[47] While the original production
lacked initial commercial success, *Working* has enjoyed a durable
and admirable record of continuous productions in local and regional professional, amateur, and educational theater. Studs
Terkel's original text has been a model interpretive format for
bringing oral history interviews into the public discourse. His
publications explore his interests in not only how the world
works from the perspective of the unheard, often the working
class, but also in the inside and unheard stories of the upper
class. Because of this diversity of themes, Steven Schwartz developed the musical theater production as a collaborative exercise: "When I first became interested in adapting *Working* as a
musical, I originally intended to write all the songs myself. But
as I thought about it more, it seemed to me that the breadth of
characters and ethnicities went beyond my own personal style
and that I would wind up writing pastiche or in other people's
styles a lot of the time, and because of the necessity for authenticity in a documentary-style piece such as *Working*, I didn't
want to do that."[48]

Schwartz documents his creative process as it evolved over
time. Perhaps unconsciously, he attributes his decision to collaborate with multiple musical creators from a stance that sounds fa-

miliar to practitioners of oral history. A social historical approach mandates that one doesn't presume a singular epistemological position in the research process. Instead, the researcher commits to generating multiple voices in not only the content but also the construction of historical materials. In his text *The Death of Luigi Trastulli*, Alessandro Portelli notes that the oral historian's work as interviewer derives from the inevitable difference between at least two different individual consciousnesses.[49] Someone else knows about something that the oral historian does not know, and so the research agenda presumes the collaborative process of resolving that difference. Consequently, Schwartz approached several songwriters to adapt Terkel's interviews into lyrics and movement for the stage. These collaborators worked under an agreement that the documentary style of the production mandated a close reading and respect for the original transcripts: "The songwriters tried to use as much of the words and locution of the characters they were writing about as possible. . . . The stated mission for all the songwriters was to be true to the characters. They were, after all, real people, not fictional creations."[50] Schwartz cites his own song, "It's An Art," about waitress Dolores Dante, where the composer uses much of the same text from the interview transcript in his song lyric.[51] I followed up on Schwartz's comments in a telephone interview in 2002 to explore his reference to locution as a particularly rich area for investigation and representation. I was interested in how he worked with the physicality of vocal production as it transferred from oral history interview to the songs on stage. Schwartz replied that he tried to "remain faithful—but at the same time theatricalize." He gave other examples where the vocal production in interviews provided material for that theatricalization process. Several qualities came to mind that contributed to his music composition process, including the speed and rhythm of speech, garrulousness, and also hesitancies that fragmented the text. In particular, for the housewife's song, Schwartz noted that he uses hesitancies to generate character through musical composition techniques. The previously mentioned waitress's song was noted for the speed of her original recording.[52]

As I mentioned previously, the reenactment of physical labor during the interview process lends itself to the staging of those reenactments in theatrical settings. In the newspaper boy's case, both the locutionary energy and the physicality of the situation are restaged. *The New York Times* theater reviewer Richard Eder notes that the newsboy "recounts his pleasure in throwing newspapers into the bushes. 'Boing,' they go, and he disintegrates into a 'boing' himself, to illustrate."[53] Schwartz explains that the newspapers would land in the bushes and bounce up and down before landing again; the bushes themselves would bounce up and down as a result. In Terkel's text, one of the newsboys said, "It's fun throwing papers. Sometime you get it on the roof. But I never did that. You throw the paper off your bicycle and it lands some place in the bushes. It'll hit part of the wall and it'll bounce down into the bushes and the bushes are so thick that it'll go— boongg! That's pretty fun, because I like to see it go boongg! (Laughs.) It bounces about a foot high. You never expect bushes to bounce. I always get it out of the bushes and throw it back on their porch."[54] The newsboy's song incorporates the bounciness of the newspapers into performances of both the song's locutions and choreographed movement. Schwartz commented that, in subsequent productions, choreographers have elaborated the staging by having other performers reenact bushes that bounce up and down. When the choreography works, it deepens the performance by tapping into the presence of bodies at play in their life worlds.

Where artists replicate the original vocal production of the interview in restaging the text in performance, audiences engage more fully in the embodied nonverbal energy of the original oral history narrator. This enhanced engagement serves both Terkel and Schwartz's projects well, where the original intent was to represent not only unheard voices, but the working, laboring class of bodies who contain those narratives as well. In addition, the movement of "boongg!" expresses not only the factuality of bouncing newspapers and bushes but also the exuberance of youthful newsboys, the excitement of news itself, and possibly the energy of a social period where a self-motivated kid could get somewhere with a paper route. (My observation might stretch to include a portrait of Terkel himself, who if you've ever met him, is about the size of a newsboy and still, in his nineties at this writing, excited about just about everything.)

Both *A Chorus Line* and *Working* aspire to represent, if not fully reenact, the full physical life world of their narrators. *A Chorus Line* contributes an innovative creative workshop process that emerged from the collection method for dancers' oral histories. As discussed above, however, the performance's finished form represents the structure of a life history rather than reenacting the performers' physicality as generated in the interviewing process. *Working* also mandated an emergent collaborative creative process for director and composer Steven Schwartz, allowing for more authentic representations of the original narrators from Terkel's text. The creators' attention to vocal production and other paralinguistic aspects of the interview process helped them generate a more fully realized reenactment in the musical score. In its staging, however, *Working* also aspired to transforming the physical life world of at least one of its narrators into full-bodied choreography. I now turn to a more recent dance/theater production, titled *MSM*, created by British choreographer Lloyd Newson in collaboration with his group DV8 Physical Theater. Newson's work specifically addresses the use of oral history interviews to stage a more embodied theatrical reenactment of narrators' stories.

Physical Theater: DV8's MSM

MSM premiered in 1993 at the Théâtre d'Aujourd'hui as part of Montreal's Festival International de Nouvelle Danse. The United Kingdom premiere followed immediately the same year at the Nottingham Playhouse. Choreographer Lloyd Newson collaborated with sound designer Jocelyn Pook, set designer Michael Howell, and Newson's company of performers. Newson defines his general aesthetic approach to this collaborative process in an artistic policy statement found on DV8's Web site:

> DV8 is about taking risks, aesthetically and physically, about breaking down barriers between dance, theatre and personal politics. . . . Great emphasis is placed on the process by which new work is created. The company has fought successfully for funding to cover lengthy research and development periods in order to maintain rigorous artistic integrity and quality in each

> new project . . . commission[ing] set designers and living com-
> posers to help investigate the relationship between body, ar-
> chitecture and music. DV8's work inherently questions the
> traditional aesthetics and forms . . . and attempts to push be-
> yond the values they reflect to enable discussion of wider and
> more complex issues.[55]

In specific, Newson's work *MSM* seeks to explore the three main
tenets of his artistic policy, taken in reverse order. First, *MSM* addresses a social history that contextualizes homosexual cruising
for sex, or "cottaging" in the British slang. (Cottaging refers
specifically to public privies that provide nocturnal cruising
zones for men who have sex with men. Importantly, cottages
provide transitional spatial zones in which public and private
spheres of behavior come into direct conflict.) Here, Newson directly approaches the complexity of public homosexual behavior
and the agents who engage in that behavior, ranging widely
from self-identified homosexuals to married men who identify
as heterosexual. In fact, the tension between those two polarities
provides the dramatic theatricality for the work. Second, *MSM*
restages that dramatic spatial zone in the theater by creating an
architectural and audio sound installation that both reproduces
and comments on this sexual nexus. Third, Newson commits
himself and company to a significant period of research and development that allows the work to emerge from a documentary
oral history project with over fifty men who frequent cottages.
These interviews provided material on both the motivations and
experiences of the narrators as they recounted their cottaging
practices. In an interview with dance writer David Tushingham,
Newson comments: "In *MSM* . . . one of my primary concerns—
and I only discovered this after doing the fifty interviews—was
that each man who cottaged had different reasons, and had different histories. There was no simple set rule. I try to avoid
generalising. However, there is a truth and a lie in every gener-
alisation and sometimes it's valuable to find the individual in
the stereotype and the stereotype in the individual."[56]

Newson clarifies how the interview process necessarily complicates any generalized stance, whether artistic or otherwise, toward the nexus of behavior he is investigating. Here, Newson is

addressing a primary objective of oral history, to provide primary observation from individuals on their own agentive behavior as well as a historical trend that contextualizes those actions. Newson directly addresses how oral history methods give him access to the larger social issues contextualizing an individual's behavior: "I really don't see a difference between what is personal and political, and therefore I prefer to look at the individual's actions, responsibilities, and how they reflect on the large political, sociological, psychological arena."[57] Newson insists on interviews with not only the narrators who function within that nexus of behavior, but also with the members of the cast who reenact a theatrical mediation of those behaviors on stage. Newson insists on cast members' self-identification with the issues and themes that emerge during the data collection and creative process. The company then goes into the studio and develops movement materials reenacting the narrators' body language and the interpersonal dynamics of the interview process. Newson then directs a process of embodied extrapolation and adaptation that results in a series of choreographed movement phrases that develop into a full work.

Along with generating movement based on his oral history research, Newson also uses text from transcripts to develop live performance scripts and taped audio environments. "If I can't find movement, I will also use words. I'm not a purist," said Newson.[58] He has noted that language has a level of specificity that may overdetermine the complexity and ambiguity of movement in his choreography.[59] In another interview, however, with art critic Nadine Meisner, Newson also enjoys the possibilities of text as sound, "a form of music theater where there is sound without specific words."[60]

In *MSM*, composer Jocelyn Pook's sound environment includes ambient sound of water, an original musical score, and direct but fragmentary citations from interview texts with both cottagers and performers. Rather than directly engaging the vocal production of an individual's text, Newson's (and Pook's) vision for sound is more environmental in scope. Their artistic interest is how an architectural environment (that contains and channels a human behavior nexus) can be theatrically represented on stage. According to dance writer Josephine Leask in her essay on Newson for *Ballett International*, the set for *MSM* involves a revolving space that includes all the accoutrements of the *pissoir*: toilets in stalls, urinals in cubicles, and the ubiquitous lavatories. The overall surface is a highly reflective tile that enables the generation of multiple acoustic effects.[61]

Set designer Michael Howells adapted his site-specific environment to provide performers with multiple points of entry not limited to the horizontality of doors or even windows. The performers appear on stage both whole and as fragmented body parts emerging from unexpected sources—from the ceiling above, floor hatches below, and unexpected crevices in the walls—emphasizing the fleeting encounters at the core of the work. Newson converts the theater into a machine of deliberately partial knowledge, refiguring the work's oral history research process on stage as an inevitably partial record. In *MSM*, Newson has created a theatrical metaphor for how individuals seek their sexual fulfillment in out-of-the-way places, momentarily inhabiting one sexual identity before returning to another. One character is a policeman who uses his inside knowledge as an enforcer of public sex prohibitions in an unexpected way while temporarily satisfying his own desires; a married man nips in "for a quick bout of mutual masturbation . . . leaving everything on hold, and then nipping back with (hopefully) nothing affected."[62] These fragmentary encounters reflect the partiality of all oral histories resulting from the temporary encounters between copresenced interviewer and narrator.

These three works of musical and dance theater reveal an arc of different approaches to using oral history as source material for staging oral histories from narrators that embody a particularly physical life world.[63] Bennett's use of oral history left a general trace form on the ultimate structure of *A Chorus Line's* libretto. *Working* developed more of the vocal production of narrators' text for creating musical composition and lyrics. Newson's *MSM* invests heavily in the use of oral history, using its embodied channels of communication for developing choreography in *MSM*. In addition, Newson both acknowledges and then theatricalizes the basic objectives of oral history, including linking individual agents to broader behavioral trends as well as citing the ontological partiality of oral historical records in his

Andrew Hammerson in MSM by DV8 Physical Theater; choreography and direction by Lloyd Newson; photo by Hugh Glendinning.

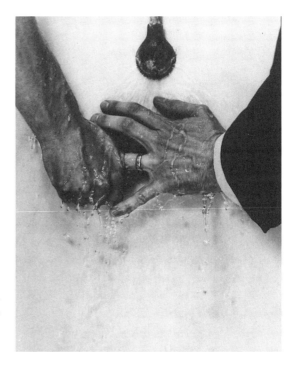

MSM by DV8 Physical Theater; choreography and direction by Lloyd Newson; photo by Gavin Evans.

performance event. Like Pollock's title essay "Telling the Told," the telling of oral history is necessarily embodied; the presence of bodies in all of their complex partiality, their radical heterogeneity, bleeds through into the theatrical productions that represent their narrative.

Performing the Aural in Oral History

Another subgenre of oral history–based performance can be called "sound performances." Sound performances transform song, speech, or other aural production collected about historical events into musical composition. Since oral history's primary format is aural, sound performances use not only semantic content but also the pitch, tempo, timbre, and rhythmicity of intersubjective oral communication to generate innovative musical forms.

Folk Music: Roadside Theater's The New Ground Revival

Roadside Theater serves audiences primarily in central Appalachia. Ron Short, a member of the Roadside Theater group, describes one work that emphasizes the use of song and instrumental music as containers for one family's oral history.[64] As the primary playwright and composer at Roadside Theater, Short initiated and implemented a project with his cousins, the Mullins family. Ron felt strongly that the Mullins family's annual ritual honoring their ancestors through song, prayer, "shouts," and food was a powerful cultural event process originating in Appalachia that could be staged for public audiences.

During this annual event, the family attends church and then meets afterward in a secular space to eat and play music. In addition, the family has a formal story circle. Ron decided that since song and instrumental music were such important ways to tell their own family history, these media would be primary during the script development stage for *The New Ground Revival*. The performance score includes music and scripted text drawn directly from the Mullins family story circles, incorporating language "so their cadence, rhythms and tone would be there for them to use when it came time to speak their lines." Short also noted body language and facial expression so that he could remind the performers (who do identify themselves not as actors but as singers) with "visual cues about their emotions . . . when the performance time came."

Performers in *The New Ground Revival* included four members of the Mullins family, as well as Ron and one other Roadside Theater member. The performance also included three other musicians and relied primarily on singing and instrumental performances with shorter sections of narrative text tying the work together. Ron terms this type of performance a "cultural landscape . . . about music, family and family music." Roadside Theater tours works such as *The New Ground Revival* outside of their indigenous areas. Venues for performances include churches, school cafetoriums, social clubs, outdoor theaters, and occasionally theatrical stages. To orient the new audiences it encounters here, the theater company includes educational outreach programs that help inform those unfamiliar with the performance genres being presented. Afterward, company members often finds themselves jamming with local musicians, singing at churches, or performing for senior citizens.

Roadside Theater's performance of *The New Ground Revival* occupies a slippery spot on the scale between folklore and oral history. While folklore and oral traditions about music and family history are valuable, even indispensable, artifactual processes about indigenous cultural practices, they do not necessarily function as oral history. The difference is where the individual's unique observations about an oral tradition or, in this case, family history and musical practices are elicited and recorded. It seems as if the story circles that Short discusses provide an important present-time reflective practice during which family members also may have the chance to pass on their own personal versions of their family's oral traditions in music or about family history. Whether a family member constructs an individually reflexive statement within that context is not clear. Oral tradition affects the construction of personal narrative, however; these forms are not wholly separate. The oral history of any one individual is embedded within the narrative oral traditions of his or her culture. When it comes to music production, both instrumental and singing, the Mullins family has a present-time practice during which the opportunity is available for personally flavoring the transmission of beloved traditions.

Western Classical Music: Arnold Schoenberg's
A Survivor from Warsaw

A second example of sound performance that emerges from oral history is *A Survivor from Warsaw*, Arnold Schoenberg's seven-minute cantata for orchestra, male chorus, and narrator. Written in August 1947, when the composer was seventy-two, *Survivor* was one of Schoenberg's last compositions. His opus 46 uses a narrative source with unclear provenance; music scholars debate how the text was constructed and whether that text is primary or secondary testimony. Music critic and scholar Nancy Van de Vate suggests that the composer used a first-person account of a survivor from the 1943 Warsaw ghetto liquidation.[65] Music critic Christopher Wintle writes that Schoenberg himself considered the account coming "first or second hand" from German Nazi's oppression of Polish Jews in the Warsaw ghetto.[66] Without more specific attribution, it is difficult to verify the final provenance of the text. With a limited number of examples of music compositions that use oral testimony, if not actual interviews, however, I provide a qualified account of the work in hopes of stimulating further dialogue on the work and its sources.

Schoenberg's cantata is a brief work that packs an emotional wallop. The effect is intense due to the particular compositional strategies that triangulate the work as a piece of music. The work includes two texts bracketed and underscored by an instrumental composition. The first text is a monologue, ostensibly drawn from the oral historical materials cited above. This monologue describes the brutal roundup of Jewish inhabitants of the ghetto for liquidation. Notably, the text names its own fallibility in the introductory statement: "I cannot remember ev'rything! I must have been unconscious [most] of the time!" A harrowing narrative follows with the sounds of German reveille signaling the population to gather. In German: "*Achtung! Stilljestanden!*" (Attention! Stand still!). Elderly men and women, sick and well individuals begin to groan and moan. The soldiers hit people with the butts of their rifles. The narrator suggests that he was also hit and was knocked unconscious. "The next thing I heard was a soldier saying, 'They're all dead!' . . . Then I heard the Sergeant shout: '*Abzählen!*'" (Count off!). Each individual then counts themselves as the next victims of the gas chambers.[67]

I cite selected excerpts of this harrowing narrative not to reinscribe images of oppression or to stimulate painful memories but to show how Schoenberg used auditory qualities of the narrative to generate musical composition. The English-language narration is musically notated by Schoenberg to dictate pitch, volume, and other vocal production. Van de Vate notes that, during the narrative, orchestral scoring incorporates the trumpet fanfare and military drumming as illustrative components. The musical score is punctuated by instruments mimicking the sergeant's Germanic guttural tones calling for order. "Unusual string effects from taps or scratching strings with bow sticks, high woodwind trills, muted brass fluttertonguing and snarls of muted horns and trumpets" represent the growing fearful outcries and protestations of the gathering crowd.[68] The oral narrative has been reconfigured into a spoken score that is neither speech nor music but *sprechstimme*, a hybrid form calling on musical qualities of vocal production as its dramatic core. The final dramatic effect of Schoenberg's work is the climactic moment of the narrative. During the rapidly increasing count-off of individuals, we hear the second text, a ritual chanting of the *Sh'ma Yisroel* (Hear, O Israel) often recited in extremis, when death draws near. This orally chanted ritual prayer is not sung to its usual traditional cantillation score, but instead is reset to what Wintle calls "a twelve-tone line supported by a fraught orchestral texture." Wintle suggests that this effect recalls Schoenberg's opera *Moses und Aaron*, where English-language text cedes to Hebrew chant and to prior orchestral works that introduced the same volatile instrumentation.[69]

A Survivor from Warsaw is a powerful work of music and theater, combining both spoken word performed in Schoenberg's own *sprechstimme* format, chanted ritual prayer text, and a brief but dramatic orchestral score that is wholly integrated with the text. The provenance of the text does not have clear attribution that identifies it as oral history narrative, a secondhand account, or apocryphal. Whichever the narrative source may be, however, the work is an example of how the musical qualities of orally given narrative can be fully integrated into Western musical composition practice.

Western Experimental Music: Steve Reich's Different Trains

My last example in the sound performance subgenre is contemporary composer Steve Reich's work *Different Trains*. Like Schoenberg, Reich is interested in the musicality of human speech. In a conversation with music critic Edward Strickland, Reich recalls: "To get to the authenticity of American speech, which had impressed me so much in the work of William Carlos Williams, I thought, why not use tape? That doesn't lie. So I began to fool around with recorded speech. Not oscillators, not weird sounds. Speech . . . richness of sound, an acoustical fact, and meaning, a psychological fact, that are imbedded in human speech."[70]

Early Reich works *It's Gonna Rain* (1964–1965) and *Come Out* (1966) use portions of recorded speech divided into what Reich calls psychoacoustic fragments. The composer transforms these fragments into rhythms articulating the vowels and consonants that surround them and uses two slightly unsynchronized tape recorders playing the same looped sound fragments to generate a series of canonic musical relationships between them.[71] Reich's early works provided a foundation for later compositions that use speech as a corporeal aural experience to stimulate audience reception. As Reich mentions in an interview with music critic Jonathan Cott, "You hear a lot of psychoacoustic fragments that you can organize in a lot of different ways. . . . I[I]t's all how you interpret that data."[72] Later works in Reich's oeuvre return to what the composer calls "documentary material," citing *Different Trains* (1988) and *The Cave* (1994), in particular.[73] *Different Trains* uses Reich's own autobiographical material among others, while *The Cave* expands Reich's focus to interviews with individuals within the Israeli-Palestinian conflict.

Premiered in London on November 2, 1988, *Different Trains* is a work commissioned by Betty Freeman for the Kronos Quartet, based in San Francisco.[74] The work includes both audiotaped text and live string-quartet performance, and it uses some of the same early building blocks of sound fragments described above. According to Reich, the impetus of the work was his response to a World War II photograph of a young Jewish boy in the Warsaw ghetto holding up his hands as he surrenders to the Nazis. As a contemporary of that photographic figure, Reich had been shuttled on trains from New York to California between his divorced parents, accompanied by his governess. He strongly felt the confluence between his own in-betweenness and the contemporaneous ambiguous status of Jewish refugees. In an interview with Robert Schwarz, Reich stated: "I was in America, very sheltered and very fortunate, but had I been across the ocean, I would have been on another train. I would have been taken to Poland and I would be dead."[75]

Reich began to collect oral history interviews that would provide the sound fragments of his new work. He recorded interviews with his former governess and with Lawrence Davis, an African American Pullman train porter in his eighties. Then Reich searched sound archives for oral history interviews with Holocaust survivors and Jews living in the United States. Last, the composer collected sound samples of both American and European train sounds during the 1930s and 1940s. Reich eventually selected approximately forty-five phrases from collected oral history materials for their melodic shape, tempo, and semantic content. Using these aural fragments, Reich developed a looping narrative from multiple voices, tracing several perspectives on the Nazi oppression of Jews, wartime, and the distance traveled between both real places and metaphysical time/space.[76]

Notably, Reich developed his music composition for the string quartet after he selected and compiled the oral history texts. In conversation with Cott, Reich notes that he worked with what he terms *trompe l'oreille*, punning to make a point regarding his composition for the string quartet. Applying his previous experience with analyzing human speech into its basic rhythm, cadence, and other paralinguistic qualities, Reich developed musical lines for the quarter instrumentation based on those sound reductions. When we hear Reich's former governess say, "From Chicago," Reich hears, "dum de *dee* dum," where the long accent is placed on the third syllable of four.[77] The composer then scored this rhythmic analysis to be played by the violist.

Consequently, when listening to *Different Trains*, one hears the musical line preceding the vocal speech fragment, but in fact, the vocal production qualities of the oral history fragments precede and structure the musical score and performance. Unlike Reich's earlier works, the speech fragments remain intelligible, generating narrative that emerges gradually over several looping phases. The composer's instrumental score is derived from human speech fragments collected in oral history interviews, revealing a powerful use of the psychoacoustics of human speech communication in musical composition.

The three sound performances cited reveal another trajectory: in contrast to the aural reenactment of song and storytelling in *The Ground Revival*, Schoenberg's *Survivor* literally incorporates the physicality of vocal production into his orchestral score. Reich then furthers this type of investigation through his inventive use of psychoacoustic sound fragments as the primary source for musical composition in *Different Trains*. This set of three examples reveals a deeper commitment to the ontology of oral/aural history. Referring back to Goffman, creative use of the physical production of sound in narrative is employed in the artistic reenactment of oral history source materials. The narrative container is defined in part by the metacommunication signals of "talk about talk" or, in this case, "sound about sound."[78] I turn now to my third set of case studies, in which the performance of historicality is embodied in additional illustrations of my theoretical framework.

Performing the History in Oral History

The final subgenre of oral history–based performance works emerges from a variety of performance artists who have developed artistic works stimulated by particular historical events. In recent years, we have seen a plethora of these types of documentary theater, including the works of Anna Deavere Smith (*Fires in the Mirror*, *Twilight*) and Moisés Kaufman and his Tectonic Theater Company (*The Laramie Project*). These works and others inform our perspective of how oral history as an embodied practice contributes to new awareness of historical identity within a larger sociopolitical frame. Finally, I investigate choreographer Mark Taylor's modern dance choreography titled *Witness*, based on the murder of four individuals at Kent State by the National Guard.

Solo Monologist: Anna Deavere Smith's Fires in the Mirror

Anna Deavere Smith has established a growing body of work that uses oral history interviews as a basis for her performances. Her most notable works include *Fires in the Mirror: Crown Heights, Brooklyn and Other Identities* and *Twilight: Los Angeles*. Smith constructed both works in direct response to major historical events in contemporary times. I address only one of these works, fully aware that different motives, approaches, and processes are relevant to other works in her repertoire.

Fires in the Mirror is a performance work that reenacts conflicts between the Hasidic Jewish and the African American communities in Crown Heights, a district of Brooklyn, New York. The conflict grew from a series of escalating events that had resulted in the death of Gavin Cato, an African American child, as a result of a Hasid's allegedly reckless driving. Retaliation in the African American community involved the subsequent alleged murder of Yankel Rosenbaum, a young Hasidic student. Smith is careful, however, to acknowledge that these events, however interpreted regarding cause-effect relations, are symptomatic representations of already existing deep tensions between communities. These tensions might be attributed to fluctuations in how political and economic power are wielded or ceded both between groups and in relation to the larger infrastructure of New York City. Importantly, these fluctuations have major effects on the ground, including but not limited to the very real effects of limited housing and job opportunities and the very real differences in cultural expression in the media and on the street.[79]

Smith takes a mosaic approach to these issues. She gains access to various members of each community, careful to allow multiple and complex perspectives to emerge during each interview process and in the corporate interview materials as a whole. In this way, Smith enables the audience to focus and refocus on both different scopes and different spheres of community interests and knowledge.

Once Smith completes the interviews, she immerses herself in what communication experts Nathan Stuckey and Robert Hopper call "Everyday Life Performance" (ELP).[80] To describe this method, I cite performances and writing by lesbian performance artist Jill Carleton, who applies these techniques toward her own objectives. Using ELP, she transmutes performer Tim Miller's solo dance/text work *My Queer Body*, a gay male performance artist's work, through her own embodied performance of that artist's work to address the theoretical issues inherent in such a transfer: "This technique involves three rehearsal cycles: 1) create a micro-analytic transcript of an audio-recording, with particular attention to details of breath, pitch, rhythm, emphasis, rate, and pause; 2) memorizing the audio-recording through repeated listening and trying to talk, laugh, and breathe along with it; and 3) replicating the audio with as much accuracy as possible, without the aid of transcript or audio recordings."[81] These techniques recall prior examples by both Schoenberg and Reich that address the musical qualities of sound in oral testimony. As Reich in his early work, *Come Out*, Smith is particularly interested in using these acoustic elements to create a space for social commentary.

Smith describes these techniques as an attempt to "travel from the self to the other."[82] Here is a core concept: Smith suggests that, if an embodied self can travel toward the other in a performance setting, then performance provides an active model for social and political rapprochement for difference in real space and time. The artist notes that "the activity of reenactment could tell us as much, if not more, about another individual than the process of learning about the other by using the self as a frame of reference."[83] In fact, Smith's skillful reenactments in *Fires in the Mirror* may provide real effects on existing tensions in at least three important ways. First, she pays deep attention to agents occupying as many positions in the conflict spectrum as possible. The intentionality of this act has two corollaries: first, some people get and feel heard, perhaps for the first time. Second, through subsequent performances in a variety of media (live theater, televised formats, and print publication), their positions access a larger than normal public audience. Third, Smith carefully constructs her mosaic to provide insightful commentary at the interstices between the agents represented. For example, in *Fires in the Mirror*, the artist performs a monologue by Al Sharpton that reveals a serious genealogy of his hairstyle. Immediately juxtaposed to this monologue is a reenactment of a Hasidic housewife discussing the religious and cultural prohibitions regarding her own hair.[84] Separately, these may seem like simple projects; Smith might disagree. While trying to accurately reenact each narrator's own Goffman-like self-performance in style and content, her own construction of the larger performance work provides canny juxtapositions that suggest common cause among increasingly polarized community values.

Finally, Smith's subtle contribution to the development of heteroglossia among difference is her own embodied presence in the performance. Chameleon-like, she seems to both occupy the spatial, temporal, and corporeal realities of an other while also maintaining her own corporeal sociopolitical positionality. In the end, one asks, If she can do it, why can't I? How can I know an other as deeply as she seems to? And can I do it while remaining myself all along? Through performance, this artist teaches us about identity and its multiplicities, including when and how to develop human connection across what seem unencroachable divides.

Experimental Theater: Tectonic Theater Company's The Laramie Project

Theater director Moisés Kaufman and his New York–based Tectonic Theater Company have produced a theatrical production titled *The Laramie Project* based on the events surrounding the October 1998 murder of a young gay man named Matthew Shepard in Laramie, Wyoming. Similar to Smith, Kaufman and his company responded to a local yet global historical event, one of the "moments in history when a particular event brings the various ideologies and beliefs prevailing in a culture into sharp focus. At these junctures, the event becomes a lightning rod of sorts, attracting and distilling the essence of these philosophies and convictions."[85]

There are primary differences between the approaches of Smith and Kaufman. First, rather than Smith's solo process,

Kaufman involved a large company of actors doing on-site interview research, collaborative dramaturgy, writing, rehearsal, and performance. Second, rather than an implicit reference to the actor's presence, *The Laramie Project* script explicitly names interviewers' personae; the actors act the role of themselves, while also taking on various roles of Laramie residents.

One effect of these differences is an increased scale in production; the full, unedited original production of *The Laramie Project* involves eight actors performing sixty-seven roles among them. Different from Smith, *The Laramie Project* explicitly performs the dialogic production of knowledge. The play uses oral history interviews as materials for scripted monologues and dialogues and also as a performative process in the script. For example, actor Greg Pierotti begins the play this way: "My first interview was with Detective Sergeant Hing of the Laramie Police Department. At the start of the interview he was sitting behind his desk, sitting something like this (he transforms into Sergeant Hing.): 'I was born and raised here. . . .'"[86]

Many additional opportunities accrue over the two to three hours' running time of *The Laramie Project*, during which juxtapositions of actor (as self) to actor (as other) become elegantly constructed commentary on issues specific to *Laramie* and Shepard, but also questions of identity and performance in general. Tectonic Theater explicitly names performance conventions to avoid lulling audiences into a sympathetic response that supplants the pedagogic aspirations of the work. As we have seen from Langellier and others, oral history uses the corporeality of copresenced bodies and embodied channels of communication to name itself as a performance container for the narrative told. Kaufman and his company use Brecht's *gestus* to keep the audience aware of both the drama and its sociopolitical effects.

Modern Dance: Mark Taylor's Witness

Witness is a multimedia performance work created by Mark Taylor and commissioned by the Kent State University as a commemoration of the murder of four individuals on campus during a Vietnam War protest on May 4, 1970, by members of the National Guard. The work premiered on April 29, 1995, on the

Kent State campus at Stump Theatre as part of a twenty-fifth year commemorative event for "May 4th," as many of the community members call it.

Mark Taylor is former artistic director and choreographer for Dance Alloy, a modern dance company based in Pittsburgh. Taylor and Dance Alloy's mission addresses questions of identity and cross-communication between individuals and cultures. Taylor was attracted to the "site-specific, event-specific and time-specific" quality of the Kent State project.[87] This approach is coherent with Pollock's interest in sustaining the specificity of history, especially through the embodied experiences of human agents. No a priori viewpoint is assumed other than any one subject's own consciousness. Taylor avoids a hegemonic approach to the construction of history by deliberately choreographic multiple narratives. At the same time, he admits his own subjectivity in his assumptions that such a project might help create healing within a community still at odds with itself over events close to twenty-five years old.

To accomplish their artistic and community-building goals, Kent State's Dance Division created a two-year residency structure for the creation of *Witness*, allowing Taylor significant access to print and photographic archives, which contributed sources for still-life tableaux in the choreography, and also to community members who were potential collaborators in the creative process. Like DV8's Newson, Taylor required this sort of commitment in order to generate a rich work: "I wanted to hear from a cross-section of the community, based on politics (attitudes towards the event) and experience (relationship to the event). . . . I visited the campus four times and . . . identified people with a range of experience to the shootings. . . . It was easy to find people whose political attitudes were critical. . . . It was more difficult to find voices of the political right who were willing to speak with us."

Taylor identified four narrators from the Kent and Kent State communities willing to be interviewed about their experiences. Among these four, only one had been an eyewitness to the riot and shootings. Another was a local newspaperman who reported on the aftermath. One was a local dance student's father, a local resident and Vietnam veteran. The fourth narrator was professor

An embodied re-enactment of the Kent State events. Kent State University dance department production of Witness, *choreographed by Mark Taylor, 4/29/95. Featuring Dance Alloy Dance Company, Kent Dance Ensemble, and members of the community. Photography by Ray Black.*

of physics at the university who had not arrived on campus until the following fall but had dealt with the aftermath ever since. As a result, Taylor took care to generate multiple viewpoints, not only politically but also in terms of their recollective stance. The construction of Taylor's work *Witness* involved the witnessing of different kinds of historical time. This approach gave the work a powerful tool for making explicit how our perspective in the present helps construct our version of the past. Multiple viewpoints in both space and time also contribute to my earlier reference to the radical heterogeneity of history making.

Taylor recorded interviews on audiotape. These documents were transcribed and edited into scripted texts read or spoken live by the narrators. To amplify the heterogeneity of the oral interviews in choreographic terms, Taylor then spent months generating movement sequences that embodied the qualities of the oral history texts. Some of the narrators interacted with the

Kent State faculty member recounts scripted interview material while dancers support and amplify her gestural vocabulary. Kent State University dance department production of Witness, *choreographed by Mark Taylor, 4/29/95. Featuring Dance Alloy Dance Company, Kent Dance Ensemble, and members of the community. Photography by Ray Black.*

dancers. In one case, a young man in the dance division danced with his father, the Vietnam veteran. In one poignant section of *Witness,* the father spoke of his willingness to volunteer for Vietnam, his experiences at war and coming home to reprobation, and his shock at the shootings. Behind and around him, his son performs a movement score complementing his father's narration but representing his own perspective. In the end, they move together in unison as a symbol of bridging their differences through the exchange of information, both textual and kinesthetic. Finally, they merge into a heartfelt hug, purposefully ambiguous.[88] Was this a part of their staged movement score or was the hug a spontaneous expression of personal rapprochement? The real/not real quality of this moment on stage is cannily presented without clear signals. As receptors, we must explicitly take on the role of interpretation in order to understand this embodied moment. Remember Pollock's injunction: "The body in

Choreographer Mark Taylor directing groups of students in complex spatial paths. Kent State University dance department production of Witness, *choreographed by Mark Taylor, 4/29/95. Featuring Dance Alloy Dance Company, Kent Dance Ensemble, and members of the community. Photography by Ray Black.*

action makes history answer to the contingency and particularities . . . of everyday life. It performs its difference *in* and *from* history and so articulates history *as* difference."[89]

Remember, too: the contest is to keep history alive to its messy, contingent specificity to real human lives that enact resistance to a totalizing hegemony. The ongoing concrete practices of human beings on the ground continually upset their possible purgation through their radical heterogeneity. Bodies force us to take on difference, preventing us from purging their ongoing performance of difference. History *as* difference. Taylor accomplished this work through his choreographic configuration of a powerful father–son duet that queried personal, political, and theatrical difference, performed literally at the same time/in the same space: an ambiguous hug.

Taylor also used other choreographic means to accomplish his goals. Like the DV8 performers, Kent State dancers watched the narrators perform their text and generated a pool of limb gestures, full-body postures, and facial expressions that reflected their delivery. For example, while presenting a poignant memoir of one of the student victims, a narrator remembers "Allison [Krause] came up to him and licked his face" as the dancers stuck out their tongues.[90] But these choreographed gestures did more than amplify existing expression. After a still-life tableau of student protesters comes to stormy, scatological life ("Fuck you! 1-2-3-4, What are we fighting for?!"), four young women in a row stick out their tongues. In this moment, they not only express a specific (humorous) moment in the oral history text, but in juxtaposition with previous theatrical moment, they also enact a puerile stance on the part of the protesters. Like Smith, Taylor has carefully juxtaposed events to generate multiple and unexpected interpretations. Life is messy; his choreography stages that radical heterogeneity. And, as with DV8's attention to staging the partiality of knowledge, we come to know that what we know is only our part of a larger dialogue.

Taylor's use of choreographic space also expresses the heterogeneity of experience. Purposefully, Taylor staged the work as much like an in-the-round theater as possible. Three sides of the stage were arranged with a row of chairs so that audience seating completed the fourth side. As a result, depending on which segment of the stage performers emerged from, the perceived "front" of the movement sequences keeps changing. At one point, to emphasize anarchy and chaos during the riot, phalanxes of students facing multiple fronts simultaneously tear through the space, passing directly through one another as they pursue their singular goals. This expert arrangement of choreographic space enacts, through bodies in action, the force of many perspectives on the events of May 4 and the resulting unmaking of order.

Taylor's final choreographic gambit is to recapitulate several previous segments of spoken and taped text in a final scene, mixed with solo and group movement sequences seen before throughout the piece. Here, the choreographer maximizes historical heterogeneity through a *coup de theatre*, recouping a mosaic of previous experience that collapses time and space into a single extended present moment. Eventually, Taylor's tour de

force is leavened by a gradual diminution of chaos. Out of max-
imized heterogeneity of stage action, lines of four performers
emerge. Each line walks upstage away from the audience,
pauses briefly, and then slowly reenacts a slow-motion version
of each of the four deaths. Walk. Pause. Impact. Crumple. Over
and over, new lines of four march upstage, while the bodies of
the previously fallen roll backward, stand, and follow them,
again and again. To the sound of Beethoven's *Moonlight Sonata*,
this inexorable sequence continues until it becomes the only action on stage. As the music subsides, the fallen remain, inert in
the now unforgettable positions we know from historical photos.
Their comrades slowly incline their torsos forward and, as the
curtain falls, place their ears to the stilled hearts of the dead.
Black out. Final chords. Silence.[91]

Witness ties together many of the issues of interest in this essay. Taylor's choreographic strategies highlight both the heterogeneity of historical action and the production of history. Where
the specificity of embodied action is foregrounded, either in the
corporeal foundations of oral history narrators or by amplifying
movement through choreography and performance, heterogeneity avoids purgation. Instead, performance celebrates the specificity of human bodies in action. Throughout this essay I have
emphasized oral history's specific narratives of personal action
and how the narrative container highlights that specificity to
provide a rich source for staged performance in multiple genres.
Each case study reveals creative work in a variety of performance genres that reflects these theoretical points. These and other
works reveal that fractious action can be recovered in the embodied staging of humans struggling to perform their lives.

Notes

1. The mission of LEGACY's Oral History Project is to record, preserve, and
make accessible the life histories of San Francisco Bay Area performing arts
community members who are at risk: elders, those facing life-threatening illnesses, and individuals whose work is invisible because it falls outside the
mainstream historical continuum.

2. Originally created in 1994 as a trio dance, the work was revised in 1995
for solo touring. Live and taped text was edited and adapted from two oral
histories—Eve Gentry, "Eve Gentry: A Kaleidoscopic History," interview by

Mercy Sidbury, 1991, and Frank Everett, "Frank Everett: 1968–1994," inter-view by Jeff Friedman, 1993—both housed at LEGACY Oral History Project, San Francisco Performing Arts Library and Museum, San Francisco. The choreographic structure of *Muscle Memory* evokes several ontological aspects of oral history practice, including the production of memory through the lens of contemporary inquiry and how qualities of embodied vocal and gestural production are innate to the production of interview "text."

3. Frisch, "Editor's Introduction," i–ii.

4. Pollock, "Telling the Told," 3–4.

5. Nethercott and Leighton, "Memory, Process, and Performance," 44. See also an adapted version of this essay in Nethercott and Leighton, "Out of the Archives."

6. Faires, "Great Flint Sit-Down Strike," 122, quoted in Nethercott and Leighton, "Memory, Process, and Performance," 45.

7. Bailey, "Precious Blood," 62.

8. Geer, "Out of Control," 106.

9. Ritchie, *Doing Oral History*, 2nd ed., 243–45.

10. Among other publications by these authors, see Bauman, *Story, Perfor-mance, and Event*; Conquergood, "Performing as a Moral Act"; Roach, *Cities of the Dead*; and the entire oeuvre of Richard Schechner, including *Performance Theory*.

11. Pollock, "Making History Go." For more information on Pollock's artis-tic work combining oral history and performance, see my media review on a presentation by Pollock's group, in Friedman, "Wave When You Pass," 131.

12. Pollock, "Making History Go," 4

13. Feldman, *Formations of Violence*, 2, quoted in Pollock, "Making History Go," 4

14. Pollock, "Making History Go," 18.

15. Fabian, *Power and Performance*, 6.

16. Adam, *Timewatch*, 159–75.

17. Kern, *Culture of Time and Space*, 16, 21–22.

18. Turner, *Anthropology of Performance*, 21–27

19. Goffman, *Presentation of Self,* 252–53.

20. Goffman, *Behavior in Public Places*, 14.

21. Goffman, *Forms of Talk*, 4.

22. Langellier, "Personal Narratives," 244.

23. Ibid., 244, 249. Langellier refers, among others, to Fine, *Folklore Text*, and Georges, "Storytelling Events."

24. Langellier, "Personal Narratives," 250. See Bauman, *Story, Performance, and Event*, 2.

25. Goffman, *Forms of Talk*, 2–3.

26. For a more detailed discussion of Brechtian *gestus* and oral history–based performance, see Friedman, "*Muscle Memory*," 164–68.

27. Bauman, *Story, Performance, and Event*, 2.

28. Langellier, "Personal Narratives," 249; Fine, *Folklore Text*, 4.

29. Fine, *Folklore Text*, 4.

30. Tedlock, "Translation of Style," 125–29.

31. Hymes, "Folklore's Nature," 356.

32. Nethercott and Leighton, "Memory, Process, and Performance," 52. See also Nethercott and Leighton's description of how their students reenacted, in performance, their original narrators' own reenactments. Ibid., 39–40. I suggest this reinterpretation is an example of Fabian's continuous recycling performance/textual representations of experience cited earlier.

33. Nethercott and Leighton, "Out of the Archives," 461.

34. Mandelbaum, *Chorus Line*, 95.

35. Ibid., 98.

36. Viagas, Lee, and Walsh, *On the Line*, 28.

37. Ibid., 72, 100, 129, 171, 194–95; Mandelbaum, *Chorus Line*, 178–80. Many but not all of the song lyrics and text monologues ended up being montages of two or more dancers' original taped narration. Dante's monologue remains nearly verbatim, however.

38. Mandelbaum, *Chorus Line*, 117.

39. Ibid., 131.

40. Ibid., 126

41. Ibid., 121.

42. Ibid., 123.

43. Viagas, Lee, and Walsh, *On the Line*, 172.

44. Mandelbaum, *Chorus Line*, 173.

45. Ibid., 159–60.

46. Tapes and transcripts available in Edward Kleban Papers, 1960–1986, Rodgers and Hammerstein Archives of Recorded Sound, New York Public Library for the Performing Arts.

47. Terkel, *Working*.

48. Stephen Schwartz, "Working: How the Songwriters Were Chosen," posted July 23, 2002, Stephen Schwartz Forum, Archives, http://www.stephen schwartz.com//ubbthreads/postlist.php?Cat=&Board=archives (accessed January 26, 2005).

49. Portelli, *Death of Luigi Trastulli*, 43–44.

50. Stephen Schwartz, "You and James Taylor: *Working* Video," posted January 15, 2003, Stephen Schwartz Forum, Archives (see note 49).

51. Ibid.

52. Stephen Schwartz, telephone interview with the author, February 8, 2002.

53. Richard Eder, "'Working' Opens at 46th Street: From Studs Terkel," *New York Times*, May 15, 1978.

54. Terkel, *Working*, xl.

55. DV8 Physical Theatre, Artistic Policy, DV8 Physical Theatre, About DV8, http://www.dv8.co.uk/about/about.policy.html (accessed January 26, 2005).

56. Lloyd Newson, "Lloyd Newson . . . Dance *About* Something," interview with David Tushingham, in *Food for the Soul: A New Generation of British Theater Makers, Live*, ed. David Tushingham (London: Metheun, 1994), DV8 Physical Theatre, Press Archive, Section One: Interviews with Lloyd Newson, index, http://www.dv8.co.uk/press/interviews/list.html (accessed January 26, 2005).

57. Ibid.; Lloyd Newson, "Lloyd Newson interviewed by Jo Butterworth: 18 August 1998," in *Dance Makers Portfolio: Conversations with Choreographers*, ed.

Jo Butterworth and Gill Clarke, 1 (Leeds: Centre for Dance and Theatre Studies at Bretton Hall, 1998), DV8 Physical Theatre, DV8 Archive, Bibliography, http://www.dv8.co.uk/press/interviews/butterworth.pdf (accessed February 6, 2005).

58. Newson, "Interviewed by Jo Butterworth," 4 (see note 57).

59. Newson, "Dance *About* Something" (see note 57).

60. Nadine Meisner, "Introduction to 'Strange Fish: Lloyd Newson Talks to *Dance and Dancers* about His New Work,'" *Dance and Dancers* (Summer 1992): 10, DV8 Physical Theatre, Press Archive, Section One: Interviews with Lloyd Newson, index (see note 57).

61. Josephine Leask, "The Silence of the Man: An Essay on Lloyd Newson's Physical Theatre," *Ballett International* (August/September 1995), 48–53, available at DV8 Physical Theatre, Press Archive, Section One: Interviews with Lloyd Newson, index (see note 57).

62. Paul Taylor, "Coming Out on the Tiles," *Independent*, November 12, 1993, available at DV8 Physical Theatre, Press Archive, Section Two: Press Notices, http://www.dv8.co.uk/press/reviews/msm/ti_12.11.93.html (accessed January 26, 2005).

63. The following additional works that also use labor as performative content maintain oral history's function of not only recollecting personal narratives but also linking those narratives to important historical trends and events. In particular, works about labor reveal a reciprocity where physical edifices created by many of the narrators continue to shape history as well. *Body of Work*, chor. Dorothy Jungels and Aaron Jungels, Everett Dance Theater, Bentley College, Waltham MA, January 28, 1997, included performances by interviewees who had worked with Bell Telephone, as a carpenter, union organizer, and longshoreman. *City Water Tunnel #3*, chor. Marty Pottenger, City Water Tunnel #3, New York, 1999, a solo performance work, used 250 interviews with laborers who helped build the largest nondefense public works project in the Western Hemisphere, an underground water aqueduct begun in 1970 and completed decades later. Pottenger's work was site-specific, returning the performance event to the original aqueduct site. *Ace*, by Isabel Maynard, chor. Amy Mueller, Talespinner's Theater, Life on the Water Theater, San Francisco, 1987, was based on Charles Kuralt's interviews with Al Zampa, a steelworker who in the 1930s fell during the construction of the Golden Gate Bridge and swung on his rigging until rescued.

64. Ron Short, e-mail message to author, 2001. All of Ron Short's citations in this section are quoted verbatim from his response to my survey of oral history–based performance sent by electronic mail to Roadside Theater, among others, in fall 2001.

65. Nancy Van de Vate, brochure notes for Arnold Schoenberg, *A Survivor from Warsaw*, orchestra and chorus cond. Szymon Kawalla, compact disc, Vienna Modern Masters VMM 3015, 1992, 1.

66. Christopher Wintle, brochure notes for Arnold Schoenberg, *Schoenberg: Ein Uberlebender aus Warschau*, orchestra and choir cond. Claudio Abbado, compact disc, Deutsche Grammophon 431774-2, 1993, 5.

67. Arnold Schoenberg, *A Survivor from Warsaw, for Narrator, Men's Chorus, and Orchestra, Op. 46*, rev. ed. by Jacques-Louis Monod (Hillsdale, NY: Boelke-Bomart, 1979): 3.

68. Van de Vate, brochure notes, 1 (see note 66).

69. Wintle, brochure notes, 5 (see note 66).

70. Strickland, *American Composers*, 39–40.

71. For more on Reich's method, see Reich, *Writings about Music*, 49–71.

72. Jonathan Cott, "Interview with Steve Reich," in booklet for *Steve Reich: Works, 1965–1995*, compact disc, Nonesuch 79451-2, 28. See Schwarz, *Minimalists*, 64, for Reich's development of *Come Out* for a music benefit to support the Harlem Six, "a group of black teenagers who had been arrested for (and subsequently convicted of) the murder of a white shop-owner." The police recorded ten hours of taped interviews, including Daniel Hamm's testimony that to prove the severity of his wounds, he had to "open the bruise up and let some of the bruise blood come out to show them." For the musical composition, Reich chose one speech fragment of five words, "Come out to show them."

73. Cott, "Interview," 30 (see note 72).

74. Members of the Kronos Quartet in 1988 were David Harrington, violin; John Sherba, violin; Hank Dutt, viola; Joan Jeanrenaud, cello. See Kronos Quartet, Kronos Quartet, http://www.kronosquartet.org (accessed January 26, 2005).

75. Schwarz, *Minimalists*, 95.

76. Ibid., 95–96. There is currently no record of attribution or archival location for the oral history interviews with Reich's governess and Lawrence Davis, former Pullman porter. Recorded speech phrases are excerpted from testimonies of Holocaust survivors used by permission of the Fortunoff Video Archive for Holocaust Testimonies, Yale University Library, and the Holocaust Collection of the American Jewish Committee's William E. Wiener Oral History Library.

77. Cott, "Interview," 30 (see note 72).

78. Additional music compositions that use oral history interviews include Steve Reich, *The Cave*, compact disc, Nonesuch 79327, 1995, a multimedia theater work for piano, sampling keyboard, and voice, based on oral history interviews with Israeli, Palestinian, and American narrators. Theater artist Mark Hall Amitin has explored oral history–based theater productions involving collaborations between Israeli and Palestinian performers. John Crigler and Jean Maria Arrigo, *Pulled through the Bush Backward*, Moments of Moral Discovery: The Military Series, compact disc, 2002, includes interviews with a Tibetan refugee, a former U.S. undercover counterintelligence officer, a World War II U.S. artillery infantryman, an academic professor, and Arrigo, who participated as a child agent for her father, an undercover intelligence officer, during the Cold War.

79. Smith, *Fires in the Mirror*, xliii-xlv.

80. Hopper, "Conversational Dramatism," 182.

81. Carleton, "Embodying Autobiography," 74.

82. Smith, *Fires in the Mirror*, xxvi.

83. Ibid., xxvii.

84. Ibid., 19–25. I am grateful to Anna Beatrice Scott for detailing this particular juxtaposition.

85. Kaufman and Fondahouski, *Laramie Project*, 11.

86. Ibid., 21.

87. Mark Taylor, e-mail message to author, 2001. All quotations of Mark Taylor are from his responses to my survey of oral history–based performance sent out by electronic mail in the fall of 2001. In the spirit of self-disclosure, Taylor's e-mail response notes that I acted as a consultant to Dance Alloy at his request to provide basic interviewing protocols prior to the creation of *Witness* in 1994.

88. Mark Taylor, *Witness*, videotape created by Darwin Prioleau and the Dance Division, Theater and Dance Department, Kent State University (Kent, OH: Kent State University, 1994). I am grateful to Darwin Prioleau and Mark Taylor for the use of this videotape to enhance my perceptions and analysis of the work

89. Pollock, "Making History Go," 4.

90. Taylor, *Witness* (see note 88).

91. Ibid. Additional examples of oral history–based theater works include *The Exonerated*, Actor's Gang, Los Angeles, 2001, based on interviews with prisoners held until DNA evidence proved their innocence; *What Happened*, by Amy Green, New York, April 2002, a spoken-word event based on oral history about the terrorist attacks on New York City, September 11, 2001; and Doug Wright and Charlotte von Mahlsdorf, *I Am My Own Wife: Studies for a Play about the Life of Charlotte von Mahlsdorf* (New York: Faber and Faber, 2004), a one-person play based on extensive interviews with a transvestite survivor of both the Nazi and Communist regimes in the former East Germany.

16

Oral History in Sound and Moving Image Documentaries

Charles Hardy III and Pamela Dean

Watch me. I might say it, shout it, celebrate the word.

—Robert Pruitt, in J. M. Smith,
Never a Man Spake Like This

The beginning is the word. And the narrator speaks the words. And the tape recorder records the words. And the transcriber transcribes the words. And the researcher reads the words. And the researcher writes a book quoting some of the words. And the reader reads the words the writer quotes in the book. And that is a long way from the beginning, which was the spoken word.

Such was the practice when oral historians first used audio recorders to collect and preserve information about the past. In those early days, they measured the technical quality of recordings by whether or not they were audible enough for transcription. Considering the transcript the primary historical document, they often reused the tapes. At the same time, radio journalists and documentary producers, focusing on the potential use of taped interviews for broadcast, seldom thought of either drawing on archived oral history recordings ("We want to ask our own questions")[1] or of preserving their own interviews. Despite occasional cooperative projects, historians, producers, and journalists lived and worked in separate worlds, failing to realize that oral historians could teach documentary producers how to ask a broader range of questions and how to think in archival terms of tape deposit and preservation and that documentary producers could teach oral historians how to use their equipment, think in sound, and share their work with expanded audiences.[2]

But in the twenty-first century, we have a new paradigm. The narrator speaks the word and the online, film, or radio audience watches and/or listens to the narrator speak the word—mediated, of course, by the interviewer, recorder, and editor/producer, but nonetheless providing a far more direct experience than when the audience is left to conjure up in the mind's ear and eye the original audio or visual performance based on the written approximation that appears on the page. Acknowledging the importance of the original recording, the Oral History Association (OHA) incorporated into its *Evaluation Guidelines* the interviewers' responsibility to "use the best recording equipment within their means to accurately reproduce the interviewee's voice and, if appropriate, other sounds and visual images."[3] The institution of an award for the best use of oral history in nonprint media and the popularity of field recording and broadcast-related workshops at the association's annual conferences also suggest oral historians' growing recognition of the value of such works. This chapter traces several significant aspects of the history of the use of oral history interviews in documentaries and analyzes some notable examples of the genre.

What Oral History Brings to the Documentary

"People have been listening to stories for millions of years," radio producer Scott Carrier asserts. "It's hard wired into our brains; people will choose a story over sex, over drugs, even over rock and roll."[4] When we record oral history interviews, we invite our informants to tell us their stories, their histories, their unique perspectives on the past. Like social history, with which oral history is often linked, such interviews "give voice to the voiceless," bringing heretofore underrepresented groups onto the historical stage, complicating the narrative with multiple perspectives shaped by region, race, age, gender, class, ethnicity, and individual experience. Moreover, in this process we do far more than just collect data. We collect passion, detachment, enthusiasm, hesitancy, accent, cadence, sarcasm, sincerity, shyness, bombast, and a dozen other nuances that rarely make it into even the most scrupulously accurate transcript.

"Radio is our most visual medium," Ira Glass, of *This American Life*, asserted in what sounds like an oxymoron.[5] What he meant is that while print tends to flatten, simplify, and standardize voices, resulting in the loss of essential information and vitality, radio and other forms of sound presentation utilize the mind's ability to create visuals that are often more compelling and engaging than the real thing. A well-recorded voice standing alone tends to draw people in and is intimate in a way that even film and video are not.

On the Radio: Early Days

All of these elements made oral history recordings a natural fit with radio documentaries. But the history of the genre is not smooth. Even as they were perfecting their new sound recording technologies, Thomas Edison and Emile Berliner recognized the importance of their inventions for preserving for posterity the voices of the great men and women of their era. As early as the 1890s, a handful of academics and phonograph companies began to record folk music and oral reminiscences, but the expense and technical limitations of the available recording technologies curtailed such research. The utopian visions of early radio pioneers for both media as mechanisms of universal public education soon withered beneath the onslaught of popular music, formulaic fiction, and advertisements.[6]

Aural reminiscences, including interviews with prominent Americans, recorded on phonograph discs and broadcast over radio reached the national airwaves by the early 1930s in a series of syndicated programs. Recognizing that recorded programming was a cost-effective way to reach local radio audiences, Chevrolet commissioned production of the *Chevrolet Chronicles*, which first aired in October 1930, as part of a national advertising campaign. Each half-hour program, hosted by World War I flyer Eddie Rickenbacker, presented the personally narrated ex-

periences of prominent American war heroes. Enormously successful, the *Chevrolet Chronicles* spawned a number of imitators.[7]
Early in the 1930s, despite the availability of equipment to make
recordings that could be broadcast within minutes of their creation, the major radio networks colluded to keep all recordings
off the air, a decision purportedly made to protect artists but implemented, in fact, to increase the networks' control of content.
The prohibition, which shaped the sound of American radio
during its golden age, ended the use of syndicated recordings
that had competed with the networks' programming, made coverage of the news especially difficult, and inhibited the development of an actuality-based audio documentary tradition.

The broadcast ban of recorded materials forced radio news,
public affairs, and documentary producers to rely upon dramatic re-creations to tell their stories. In the U.S., the radio documentary really began with the March 1931 debut on CBS radio
of *The March of Time*, which aired dramatizations, or "dramatic
documentaries," as they were called, of lead stories in *Time* magazine. Emerging during the golden age of radio and enormously
successful, *The March of Time* became the prototype of the radio
documentary formula, introducing the disembodied "voice-of-
doom" narrator who provided exposition and set the stage for
the actors' performances. American radio documentaries for
decades to come remained locked in the aesthetic conventions
associated with this program.[8]

After 1929, when *Amos and Andy* compellingly demonstrated
the potential of radio as a mass medium for advertising, the resulting corporate dominance of American broadcasting limited
the presentation of history by and large to safe, sanitized, and
celebratory visions of an Anglo-American past. Programs such
as *Cavalcade of America*, sponsored by the E. I. duPont Company
and produced by a prestigious advertising agency, tended to be
tributes to a great American hero or heroine. In the 1930s, funded
by the Rockefeller Foundation, the Library of Congress developed a number of programs dealing with social problems in
America, and a handful of documentarians, most notably John
and Alan Lomax, produced pioneer programs on the nation's
cultural heritage.[9] By and large, however, programs on African
Americans, labor history, and the roles of women outside of a

limited range of achievements were strictly taboo. As a result, the work being carried out by folklorists and historians working in sound, such as the interviews with former slaves recorded by fieldworkers in the Federal Writers' Project, never found their way onto the nation's airwaves.

In the late 1930s, the network ban on the use of recordings began to erode, paving the way for the emergence of actuality-based radio documentaries. The recording of announcer Herb Morrison's anguished description of the explosion of the German dirigible *Hindenburg*, at Lakehurst, New Jersey, in 1937 was simply too compelling to keep off the air. Orson Welles's epoch Halloween "trick" the next year, the legendary *The War of the Worlds* broadcast, led to a ban not only on the use of simulated news broadcasts in dramatic programming, but also on the use of dramatic techniques in news programs. The network proscription of the broadcast of recordings finally ended during World War II. The public desire for news from the front was met by reports from journalists in the field, who filed their reports not only live, but also on portable phono disc recorders and newly introduced optical film and magnetic wire recorders. Eric Severeid's parachuting with troops into Burma, Edward R. Murrow's broadcasts from London, and George Hick's wire-recorded reports on D-Day from the deck of a ship and then from the beaches of Normandy electrified Americans, bringing the war into people's homes and revolutionizing American broadcast journalism. Able to bring news from the front to Americans almost instantaneously, radio challenged print journalism as the nation's most important source of news and information. Sixty-one percent of those responding to a poll in 1946 indicated that radio was their primary source of daily news.[10]

Also in 1946, CBS set up its first documentary unit armed with state-of-the-art, analog, reel-to-reel tape recorders. Developed by German engineers during the war, these recorders represented the most important breakthrough in audio technology since the invention of the vacuum tube in the mid-1920s. By the late 1940s, American companies began marketing affordable reel-to-reel tape recorders, and the new technology had a profound impact not only on popular music, but also as an adjunct to the democratization of mass communications that marked the second half of the twentieth century. Although they were heavy and bulky, often the size of small suitcases and weighing thirteen to thirty pounds, the new recorders revolutionized broadcast journalism by enabling easy splicing and editing without degenerating the sound, which had occurred with the dubbing required in phono disc editing. For the first time, postwar producers could create sophisticated and multilayered sound documentaries by mixing down from two or more prerecorded tapes onto a mastering machine. Armed with the new technology, network journalists for a brief time turned their attention to domestic issues, producing documentaries that were often critical of the inequalities in American life, such as ABC's *Slums* and CBS's *The Eagles Brood*, on juvenile delinquency, both broadcast in 1947. The same year witnessed the debut of *CBS Is There*, which aired dramatic re-creations of events drawn from ancient to modern history in which CBS correspondents acted the part of on-the-spot narrators of historical events. Renamed *You Are There* in 1948, the program enjoyed a popular three-year run. *Hear It Now*, another CBS program, produced by Edward R. Murrow and Fred Friendly, made perhaps the most significant and ambitious use of the new documentary style. Using the new analog tape technology, *Hear It Now* was able to create "pictures for the ears," bringing the voices of newsmakers into American homes and covering modern history since 1932.[11]

NBC entered the documentary field in 1948 with *Living*, a series of programs dedicated to "showing America to itself" that also made extensive use of taped interviews. In *Yesterday, Today, and Tomorrow*, which ran from May through October of 1951, the NBC News and Special Events Department presented "issues out of the past, problems of the present and prospects for the future," including a three-part series on narcotics, a documentary on professional baseball, and a program titled "Country Fair," in which field engineer George Robinson brought the Bangor, Maine, state fair to life via his tape recorder. Some of the NBC programs also utilized old recordings, such as the August 5, 1951, program built on recordings of famous, deceased American poets reading their works.[12]

By the early 1950s, an actuality-based radio documentary formula had emerged in the United States, a formula that has undergone comparatively little change from that date to the present. The rise of television as the new in-home storytelling medium during the same period briefly allowed radio documentarians to delve into more controversial and "adult" issues. But network-produced public affairs programming did not last long. Documentary historian A. William Bluem's summary of its brief history is worth quoting at length.

> In the six years, then, between the end of the war and the final demise of a national radio service which had dominated the American scene for a quarter of a century, the interaction of various forces within radio, together with technological advances and a constant pressure of example from the documentary film movement, had brought the radio documentary to its most faithful expressions in the dramatic interpretation of reality. From experience gained in earlier experiments, it had evolved an authentic and dramatic form of journalistic documentary, dealing with the crises of the world as they continued to arise. It had worked forward from dramatic restatement of fact to drama made *with* fact. It had presented information in a compelling form on numberless major and minor issues and problems confronting the American people. It had evolved a special combination of drama, journalism, and education in a successful presentation of history. And as it did all these things, it gave a legacy to television which had begun, by the early 1950's to assume radio's role as the dominant mass medium of this nation.[13]

This brief era of reform-minded journalism ground to a halt during the anti-Communist hysteria of the Cold War. Commercial radio's public information programming quickly became restricted to presentation of hourly headline news reports, sandwiched between top-forty music, and a dwindling flow of special features to local affiliates and subscribers. Television, as Bluem notes, had "absorbed" the documentary role of radio. As a result, network-based producers failed to take advantage of the technological breakthroughs that have transformed audio production since World War II. The radio documentary quickly became the "forgotten art."[14]

To understand the subsequent history of the radio documentary, one must turn from the United States to Canada, Germany, and England, countries that built state-sponsored, public service broadcasting systems on the premise that a mix of serious and popular programming could lead their audiences to "higher" standards of taste and outlook. Free to broadcast prerecorded materials, Europeans pioneered development of the audio documentary. German radio producers began thinking seriously about the potentials of radio as a storytelling medium back in the 1920s. Hoping to develop an imaginative literature, or "radio art," produced expressly for the new medium that would turn the absence of visual stimuli into an aesthetic advantage, Hans Flesch, Hans Bodensteedt, Bertolt Brecht, and other young writers and intellectuals challenged radio conventions. They introduced unexpected interruptions, sound effects, and distortions to demonstrate the magical aspects of the new medium, and they experimented with "sound portraits" of cityscapes. Flesch, founding director of the Berlin Radio Hour, wrote in 1929: "We need to fashion not only a new medium, but a new content as well. Our program cannot be created at a desk." In accord with Flesch's manifesto, Bertolt Brecht began to create a series of original works for radio in which he sought to break patterns of passive, "concert" listening by insisting on the listening audience's participation in choral recitation and engagement in debate about social issues. The Germans also developed what they called "acoustical films," a plot-oriented radio literature, which grew in sophistication in the 1930s when the acoustic strip on sound films enabled the cutting and manipulating of stored sounds more precisely and predictably than ever before.[15] Viewing broadcasting as a national asset that should be used for the public good, the British Broadcasting Corporation in 1931 also began to develop a radio documentary tradition, introducing recordings of events for delayed or repeat broadcast. By the late 1940s, U.S. listeners found a refreshing alternative to American radio offerings in BBC programming picked up on short-wave radios or heard on Canadian stations whose signals carried into the northern states.[16]

Inspired by British and Canadian programming, U.S. radio documentary producers survived at small, underfunded, volunteer-staffed educational radio stations, based predominantly at the old land grant colleges and state universities of the Midwest.

Educational radio throughout the middle decades of the twentieth century remained America's "hidden medium." Despite grand expectations and predictions, educational radio never became firmly established in the U.S. Although before 1920 early radio pioneers had allocated them certain frequencies, educational stations were eventually driven to the ends of the radio dial by burgeoning commercial stations. Plagued by inadequate funding, the nation's handful of educational radio stations offered a mix of lectures, practical information, and college courses for credit.[17]

Collectors of Endangered Sounds and Information

The introduction of affordable magnetic tape after World War II not only revolutionized radio production, but also made it possible for people of moderate incomes to record endangered sounds and recollections, thereby democratizing the process of sound collection. At the same time, historians' expanding use of the new recorders to fill the growing holes in the historical record created by modern communication technologies led to the growth of the field of oral history. Folklorists used the machines to document the music, stories, and games being transformed or driven into extinction by the mass media and a nationalized mass consumer culture. Radio documentary producers used the technology to create "sound portraits," a new documentary form that abandoned the old voice-of-doom narrator in favor of stories told through sound and a growing array of voices. From the 1940s through the 1960s, these would all emerge and grow as separate, parallel worlds with little interpenetration. Not until the late 1970s would these different groups begin to recognize common interests and agendas.

Perhaps the most important of the American postwar sound documentarians was hobbyist Tony Schwartz, whose fascination with history and folk music led him to record urban folklore and soundscapes. Schwartz bought his first wire recorder in 1946, then switched to tape in 1947. In a time when many people still made their own music on the streets and in their homes, Schwartz traveled the streets of New York armed with a twelve-pound Magnemite recorder and a microphone strapped to his wrist, recording street songs, children's games, huckster cries, and other sounds he found of interest. In the mid-1950s, Schwartz began to release his recordings on the innovative Folkways label. In addition, Schwartz produced *Nueva New York*, the first documentary in the Folkways collection, on the experiences of New York's Puerto Rican immigrants, based upon stories told to Schwartz by his father about his grandparents' immigration experience.[18]

When WNYC asked Schwartz to produce a program built around the question, "What can a person living in, or visiting, New York hear?" he spent two months editing and assembling *Sounds of My City: The Stories, Music and Sounds of the People of New York*. Released in 1956, *Sounds of My City* reflected Schwartz's fascination with the sounds of everyday life and the music of ordinary people. By bringing the sounds of daily life to the foreground of awareness, Schwartz was able to make listeners appreciate sounds that by reason of their ubiquity had been previously obscure. Magnetic tape enabled Schwartz to record and repackage these sounds in such a way as to make people hear their rhythm and beauty. For drawing attention to this "universal rhythm that pulses throughout the city," Schwartz was awarded a Prix de Rome in 1956.[19]

Tony Schwartz was a collector of endangered sounds, not a journalist or oral historian. Nonetheless, his work influenced the first generation of tape-recorder–wielding oral historians in how it suggested, early on, the importance of sounds as historical artifacts and the potential of the ear as a significant sensory organ through which to engage in the study of history. In the aftermath of World War II, historians, too, were coming to recognize the potential value of the new reel-to-reel analog recorders to fill in the growing gaps in the "written" record. In a story by now familiar to most if not all oral historians, Allen Nevins recorded his first interview on a wire recorder in January 1949, and within a short time he switched over to a less cumbersome and more reliable tape recorder. Coming from a discipline in which "truth" was closely associated with the written word, Nevins used his tape recorders primarily as dictation machines until audiophile and record collector Victor Whitten—a friend of Schwartz—finally persuaded him to preserve the recordings. But with tape expensive and oral history projects, then as now, poorly funded, the reuse of previously recorded tapes remained a common practice among American oral historians for years to come.[20]

Much of the best radio documentary work produced during the 1950s and 1960s continued to come out of the government-sponsored British and Canadian broadcasting systems, which put sufficient money into radio to allow their producers to create more ambitious programs than their American counterparts could afford. Able to make a living in public radio, some of these producers worked in the medium long enough to develop a "sound" or style of production that made ambitious use of ambiances and sound effects. One of the most influential of the new radio documentary series to feature the life stories and voices of working-class people was *Radio Ballads*, a BBC series of musical radio documentaries produced between 1957 and 1964 by English folklorists Ewan McColl and Peggy Seeger with BBC producer Charles Parker. Based upon hundreds of hours of interviews, each program interwove storytelling, folk songs, and vernacular speech.[21]

The first person to seriously bridge the worlds of "oral" and "aural" history was Canadian radio producer Imbert Orchard, who continued the tradition of *Radio Ballads* with his work in "aural history" and what he called the "document in sound." In the early 1970s, Orchard began to record oral histories of rural Canadians and Native people throughout British Columbia. Interweaving recorded sounds and voices with running commentary and historical reenactments, he attempted to create evocative sound pieces that made extensive use of oral histories. Recognizing the value of his sound recordings as documents of living history worthy of archival preservation, he also helped establish the Aural History Division of the Provincial Archives in Victoria, British Columbia. Better known among oral historians than radio producers, Orchard's programs still have devoted fans, although they are somewhat conventional in voicing and approach. *Skeena, River of Clouds*, for example, which many consider one of his best pieces, follows a traditional radio documentary formula, making extensive use of a formal male narrator and a prose that reads better than it speaks. Nor does it make particularly creative use of sound to help contextualize or tell the story. Nonetheless, Orchard did bridge worlds and produce a series of ambitious "aural history" documentaries that demonstrated to many oral historians the importance of sound and the potential usefulness of radio presentation.[22]

More successful in his search for a form that better utilized the new technology—and better fit a democratizing society— was Chicago journalist Studs Terkel. After dropping out of law school in the 1930s, Terkel wrote radio scripts on great artists for the Illinois Writers Project and worked as an actor in radio dramas before embarking on his career as a Chicago journalist. By the late 1950s, he was host on Chicago's classical radio station WFMT of *Studs Terkel's Wax Museum*, a morning program that presented interviews, musical and dramatic presentations, and sound documentaries. A self-professed technophobe who never learned to drive a car, Terkel traveled the world, at first with an old Uher reel-to-reel tape recorder, recording, as one commentator put it, humanity's "deepest feelings, joys, and sorrows."[23] From these and interviews conducted live for *Wax Museum*, he produced a series of innovative radio documentaries and best-selling books based on aural reminiscences. *Hard Times: An Oral History of the Great Depression*, a 1970 best-seller, marked Terkel's arrival as a major voice in American oral history.[24]

One of Terkel's best early radio documentaries was *Born to Live*, an hour-long program that asked what one should do between the times of birth and death in a world threatened by nuclear annihilation. Bracketed in between a Japanese woman's recollections of the dropping of the bomb on her hometown of Nagasaki, Terkel allowed an illustrious multicultural and interracial cast of scientists, writers, and artists—among them, Pete Seeger, Simone de Beauvoir, James Baldwin, Miriam Makeba, William Sloan Coffin Jr., Albert Einstein, Bertrand Russell, and Sean O'Casey—to contemplate the meaning of life and the moral decisions and awesome challenges confronting humankind in the nuclear age. Focusing on their words rather than their celebrity, Terkel kept these famous speakers, singers, and musicians anonymous until the end credits, where he gave equal weight to each one's contributions, effectively conveying his own belief in the equal worth of all people. Rather than focusing on dark scenarios of gloom and destruction, *Born to Live* uplifted and inspired, resulting, wrote Terkel's biographer, in a show "celebrating life . . . [that] forcefully captures and orchestrates the joyful and sorrowful sounds that compose human experience."[25] Released by Folkways five years before publication of *Hard Times* and awarded UNESCO's Prix d'Italia in 1962, *Born to Live* demonstrated compellingly how spoken words, poetry, music, and sound effects gave people's words an immediacy and brought their meaning to life in a way that could not be duplicated on the printed page. Terkel did this making only very spare but effective use of musical bridges and beds, fade ins and fade outs, and other radio production techniques.[26]

Terkel was one among many radio producers in the 1950s and 1960s at educational and noncommercial radio stations who were experimenting with the new forms of voicing and production made possible by analog tape. Few had his skills or extraordinary range of interviewees. Broadcast only locally or distributed through a fledging educational radio system, most audio documentary productions during these years were erased or dumped in a closet and quickly forgotten. It is clear, however, that a number of radio producers were creating programs based upon extensive oral history interviews. Ralph Johnson, for example, working in 1966 at WUOM in Ann Arbor, Michigan, produced *The American Town: A Self-Portrait*, a series of seven one-hour programs "drawn entirely from the remembered past." Armed with a Nagra tape recorder, Johnson spent four to five days in seven different small towns in Ohio, Pennsylvania, Michigan, Wisconsin, and Kentucky, conducting more than one hundred extended oral history interviews with elderly residents and producing a series of audio montages, or "spoken histories," that evoked the life and history of the communities. Johnson, like most radio documentary producers at the time, was inventing the sound as he went along. (Like most radio documentary producers, too, he failed to preserve his original interviews.) Influenced by Canadian broadcasts and borrowing the technique of montage from film documentaries, Johnson chose to create these pieces without the use of a narrator. To do so, he spent days in the studio experimenting with the layering of sounds and voices using a battery of reel-to-reel playback decks. Johnson's impatience with the voice-of-doom narrator that dominated American commercial broadcasting and his fascination with the voices of "common" people place him clearly in the transatlantic Canadian Broadcasting Corporation/BBC school.[27]

Pacifica and the Resurgence of the Long-Form, Social Documentary

By the 1960s, the most extensive use of aural reminiscences on U.S. radio took place at the stations of the Pacifica network, an independently funded, socially progressive radio system with stations on the West Coast and in New York. Founded by American pacifists, Pacifica first went on the air in 1949 in Berkeley over KPFA, which received the first noncommercial license in the U.S. not to go to an educational or religious institution. Joined by KPFK in Los Angeles in 1959 and New York station WBAI in 1960, the Pacifica network became the model for a new kind of socially conscious broadcasting in the U.S. Committed to social justice and relying upon volunteers for most of its staff and producers, Pacifica provided a forum for people and views that otherwise had no broadcast outlet.[28]

Modeling the BBC, the Pacifica stations at first devoted only a small part of their programming to politics and social issues. Nonetheless, KPFA broadcast some of the most provocative programming in the U.S. during the first decade of the Cold War. Staffed by liberals and radicals who wanted to present their listeners in-depth coverage of social problems and the dawning American civil rights movement and free to plan its programming without the time constraints of commercial radio, Pacifica found its ideal formats in extended interviews and the long-form documentary, a type of programming rapidly disappearing from commercial radio. The key figure in the development of Pacifica's politically oriented long-form documentary was Public Affairs Director Elsa Knight Thompson. Following the BBC model, Thompson gave her producers a great deal of freedom in creating their programs and allowed them the air time necessary to present their stories in depth. Pacifica thus carried on the BBC tradition of treating listeners seriously and demanding a great deal from them. Under Thompson's direction, Pacifica developed a cadre of committed documentary producers who eschewed the voice-of-doom narrative style for a more personal and reportorial form of address. Laboring in relative obscurity during the 1950s, Pacifica came into its own in the 1960s, when its stations provided early and sympathetic coverage of the liberation movements either ignored or misunderstood by the mainstream media. Pacifica stations broadcast long-form interviews with drug addicts, political radicals, social activists, and others on the margins of the American social and political spectrum, some of which, such as Byron Bryant's 1958 interview with social activist Ammon Hennacy, editor of *Catholic Worker* and author of *Autobiography of a Catholic Anarchist*, delved extensively into oral history.[29] It was Pacifica that brought many white listeners their first extended exposure to the voices of the civil rights movement, in its broadcast and distribution of interviews with Rosa Parks (1956), James Farmer (1961), and Fannie Lou Hamer (1965), and in speeches by Martin Luther King (1957), Malcolm X (1964, 1965), and Eldridge Cleaver (1968).[30]

Pacifica reporters produced a series of extraordinary long-form documentaries on the civil rights and antiwar movements, from Birmingham in May 1963 and Mississippi during the summer of 1964 to the streets at the Democratic Convention in Chicago in August 1968. The Pacifica reporters recorded these events as they unfolded, then used extended actualities to transport the listener in place and time, the narrator cutting back and forth between on-the-spot narration of what was taking place and the scripted continuity. *Freedom Now*, a riveting report from Birmingham, Alabama, recorded in the summer of 1963, is an ideal example of the Pacifica long-form documentary. Covering the five-day period from Monday, May 13, when the civil rights leaders and local merchants first reached an accord, through Saturday, May 18, the day after the bombing of the Gaston Motel, producers Robert Kramer, Chris Koch, and Dale Minor built the program on extended cuts with major participants on both sides of the struggle. Listeners hear CORE organizer Mary Hamilton speaking about her incarceration just after her release from jail, Martin Luther King exhorting his followers to keep the peace,

Birmingham Mayor Haynes railing against Communists and outside agitators, and King and Abernathy speaking in the Birmingham pool halls the morning after the bombing, calling for calm. The documentarian is on the scene as participant observer, providing explanation and description. One hears the sounds of gunfire and the events as they unfold.[31]

In producing these pieces, the Pacifica documentarians practiced a form of radio that was unique in American broadcasting history. Pacifica's long-form documentaries offered distinct opportunities for reflection, allowing listeners to ruminate about what was taking place and to consider their own responses to the events. The Pacifica stations allowed their volunteers a great deal of latitude to experiment with their documentaries. Former WBAI documentary producer Chris Koch, who in the early 1980s became director of *All Things Considered*, described the situation at Pacifica in 1965: "Someone may sit up all night for weeks miking the sounds of people and things and come out with a sound montage that adds a new dimension to our experience of ourselves and each other. Someone may go out and raise the money to go to Mississippi, or Mexico, or to California's central valley and live with the people there for a while, recording their conversations and their music, and then come back and make beautiful programs out of it."[32]

Despite their importance at the time, few aural documentaries from the 1950s or 1960s held up particularly well. Far into the 1970s, most producers still worked in isolation, reinventing the form as they went along. Shoestring budgets, lack of training or knowledge of the field, inferior, bulky, and sensitive equipment, begged or borrowed—all conspired to make programs such as Terkel's *Born to Live* or Pacifica's *Freedom Now* quite rare. Most producers drawn into noncommercial radio before the arrival of National Public Radio (NPR) took their inspiration not from radio documentary productions, but from Larry Josephson at WBAI in New York, Studs Terkel in Chicago, nationally syndicated Jean Shepherd, and other radio personalities who were reinventing the sound of American radio by breaking down the walls between listener and broadcaster and who were introducing a new form of more spontaneous, experimental, unpredictable, and therefore exciting programming.

National Public Radio (NPR) and the
Renaissance of the Sound Documentary

The next major step forward in the aural documentary came with the availability of the audio cassette recorder and the establishment of NPR. The use of sound to tell a story was facilitated in the late 1960s with the introduction of inexpensive, lightweight, portable, broadcast-quality cassette field recorders that could record anywhere from thirty minutes to an hour on each side of a small, self-enclosed, and inexpensive "cassette." The cassette recorder gave producers and news gatherers unprecedented flexibility in recording in the field. Once back in the studio, they could dub their actualities and ambiances onto reel-to-reel tapes, which could then be mixed together with narration and music from different sources onto a mastering deck. Having once mastered the basic production techniques of segue, cross-fade, and layering, a producer could then skillfully edit mixed segments together into seamless sound pieces. The NPR revolution was built upon this new recording technology.

Recognizing the need for commercial-free television, Congress passed the Public Broadcasting Act of 1967. As an afterthought—and in response to heavy lobbying by Jerrold Sandler, then head of National Education Radio—Congress added a provision for the creation of a national educational radio network. Incorporated in 1970, with a mandate to provide national programming, NPR went on the air in April 1971 with live broadcasts of the Senate Foreign Relations Committee hearings to end the Vietnam War.[33] Under the direction of William Siemering, former station manager of WBFO in Buffalo, New York, NPR embraced both the social idealism of the 1960s and the premise pioneered in noncommercial radio during the previous decade: the sound should help tell the story. At WBFO during the mid-1960s, Siemering had become interested in oral history while producing *The Nation within a Nation*, a radio series on Iroquois in upstate New York. Convinced that radio could be exciting, live, and spontaneous, he began production of *This Is Radio*, the forerunner of *Fresh Air*, a public affairs program that included interviews.[34] In 1969, Siemering outlined the concept for an ambitious new approach to public affairs radio based on the programming innovations at WBFO, and within a year, as a member of the founding board of NPR, he wrote its original mission statement. Imbued with the social idealism of the era, the mission mandated that NPR "will promote personal growth rather than corporate gains . . . [and] it will encourage a sense of active constructive participation, rather than apathetic helplessness."[35]

Siemering brought these concepts to life in NPR's new flagship program, *All Things Considered* (*ATC*), which debuted in May 1971, two weeks after NPR went on the air, with live coverage of antiwar demonstrations in Washington, D.C. To help give *ATC* a new sound, Siemering replaced the impersonal *March of Time* narrative voice with a natural, conversational style of address, slowing the pace of the newscasts and allowing, as much as possible, the sound to tell the story, with enough time provided to tell the story in depth. Integrating innovations pioneered in educational radio stations in the Midwest and in the Pacifica stations, *ATC* became the first nationally syndicated program committed to telling stories and presenting news through the use of sound. In the process, NPR began to attract or hire away from its own and the Pacifica stations many of the best young producers in the country, bringing an actuality-based approach to radio broadcast journalism to a growing national audience and initiating a renaissance for the audio documentary.[36]

Unrestricted by the old radio documentary and news report formulas, young producers such as Joe Frank, Josh Darsa, and Robert Montiegal extended the *ATC* emphasis on sound. One of the first to abandon altogether any third-person narration was independent producer Keith Talbot, who in 1972 began producing a series of pieces he called *Sound Portraits*, the only outside features to which *ATC* awarded a regular time period. Talbot had been drawn to radio through listening to Pacifica's WBAI during the late 1960s. Determined to put "ordinary" people on radio and to push the emphasis on sound already present at NPR, Talbot recorded people talking about their lives right where they lived and worked, then produced a series of short, five-minute audio montages that let them speak for themselves. Talbot approached his pieces as a storyteller, attempting to give individual lives a dramatic form by fashioning audio portraits from monologues. In one early piece, Talbot used sound to help tell the story of black street vendor Mark Johnson, whose love of the bustle and activity of ballpark crowds and of rush-hour traffic and pedestrians is reflected in the traffic noise and humming of voices that fill the piece. Another example is "Mara O'Carty," which first aired in December 1972. The piece is built around O'Carty's reflections on her own upbringing and the upbringing of her children, which leads to her contemplation of suicide. Talbot's spare use of sound mirrors O'Carty's isolation, both psychologically and geographically. Each sound in the piece, from the ticking clock, heard briefly at the beginning and end, to O'Carty's own sighs and sniffles, complements and contextualizes her story, bringing her words to life, providing audio clues about her state of mind and drawing the listener into her world.[37]

Talbot's sound portraits represent the many experiments undertaken in the 1970s by documentary producers searching to discover the unique qualities and strengths of radio. What gave NPR much of its excitement and provided those rare moments that kept listeners tuning in was its audio documentaries and essays, such as *Father Cares: The Last of Jonestown*, a ninety-minute documentary on the Jonestown commune in Guyana that included riveting tapes recorded during the final few months before the mass suicide.[38] NPR's original mission statement included a mandate to open the airwaves to groups underrepresented in the commercial media, especially minorities, women, and people residing in regions outside of the major metropolitan areas.[39] Diversity helped give NPR its wonderful and unique sound: hard news mixed with feature pieces that democratized the airwaves and gave voice to a broad cross-section of Americans who would otherwise have remained unheard. In this, one can recognize NPR as an expression of the same forces that were fueling the new social history, the new community history, and the expanding mission of oral history as a tool for documenting the worlds of those previously excluded from the historical record.

ATC and NPR's special programs series became the forum for producers who were breaking away from the traditional continuity/actuality/sound bridge formula and experimenting with new forms. Independent producers carried the sound portrait forward, some of them making sophisticated and sensitive use of oral histories and archival recordings. One of the most successful of the new generation of sound pieces utilizing oral histories was *War and Separation*, produced by Davia Nelson and Nikki Silva, who work together as the Kitchen Sisters. Broadcast in May 1982 as an audio remembrance on life at home during World War II, *War and Separation* made superb use of oral histories combined with popular music, new reports, and movie clips of the time. What really brings it all to life is the incorporation of recorded letters from the 1940s made by wives and girlfriends to their loved ones overseas, and by GIs to loved ones back home. Moving back and forth between past and present, between private, first-person experiences and the romanticized vision of the war presented in motion pictures and the popular music of the day, the Kitchen Sisters were able to fashion a powerful commentary on the dynamics of public propaganda and private existence. Produced without narration, a technique that continues to characterize the producers' work, the piece is absolutely gripping, truly a story better told in sound than any other medium.[40]

During the 1970s, the number of noncommercial, community-based radio stations grew dramatically. More than two hundred of these stations affiliated under the National Federation of Community Broadcasters (NFCB), thus creating a third noncommercial radio system and expanding the market for producers. In 1980, the Public Radio Satellite System gave producers the first inexpensive, simple, and efficient means of program distribution, replacing the archaic system of the mail to deliver taped programming. To encourage independent producers and bring new people into the system, the Corporation for Public Broadcasting set up a special Satellite Program Development Fund (SPDF) to support new programming to fill the new channels, including work by and about women and minorities, many of which utilized oral histories.[41] One of the best of the SPDF-funded programs was Judi Moore Smith's *Never a Man Spake Like This*, a superb, one-hour, stereo documentary on the art of traditional black preaching. For programs devoted to women and minorities, the old, authoritative voice-of-doom narrator was particularly inappropriate. To avoid imposing upon the program a narrative voice from another culture, Smith fashioned what she called a "docu-sermon." Using a preacher, Dr. Robert Pruitt, as narrator, Smith designed the piece in such a way as to match the pattern of a traditional black sermon. Painting pictures with words, Pruitt leads the listener through segments on call-and-response, motivation, storytelling—using the "ordinary" to get to the "extraordinary," as he puts it—timing and movement, musicality, and poetry, concluding with an extended five-preacher montage of sermonizing that recapitulates these basic characteristics of the traditional black preaching style. Smith's program makes clear that radio was the perfect medium in which to present this story. Documenting a tradition of aural performance clearly works better in sound than on the printed page, as the absence of potentially distracting visual information focuses the audiences' attention squarely on Pruitt's "words of God."[42]

The opening of the airwaves in the 1970s to groups traditionally excluded from the mass media coincided with the revolution in historical studies already sweeping American higher education. Public radio and the new social history were made for each other. The late 1970s and early 1980s witnessed the broadcast of a series of oral history documentaries produced collaboratively by historians and radio producers. Historian Ann Banks teamed with WGBH in Boston to produce *First Person America*, a six-part series based on dramatic readings of life histories collected by the 1930s Federal Writers' Project. Historians with the Oral History of the American Left program at New York University's Tamiment Institute Library teamed with radio documentarians Charles Potter and Beth Friend to produce *Grandma Was an Activist: A Radio Series on Radical Women in the 1930s*, six half-hour documentaries produced for Pacifica station WBAI. Producer Louise Cleveland worked with a team of historians in producing *The Golden Cradle*, a series, funded by the National Endowment for the Humanities (NEH), of thirteen half-hour oral history documentaries on immigrant women in America since the 1840s.[43]

At the same time, a small number of young academics also began to produce their own programs. David Dunaway, working at KPFA while in graduate school at the University of California at Berkeley, produced in 1978 an award-winning documentary, *The Weavers*, based on interviews with folk musician Pete Seeger.[44] Also in the mid-1970s, University of Buffalo graduate student Jo Blatti received an assistantship at the university-affiliated radio station WBFO. Attracted to radio as a forum for the presentation of the new social history, Blatti received a National Endowment for the Humanities grant to produce the *Buffalo Social History Project.* Over the next year, she produced twelve three-hour magazine-format programs that combined live interviews with highly produced feature pieces, many of them utilizing oral histories. This she followed with *American Dreams*, a spin-off of twelve one-hour historical documentaries that also utilized oral histories, and *Live Long Day.*[45] Debra Bernhardt, oral history project planner at the Wagner Labor Archives in New York, in 1981 produced *New Yorkers at Work: Oral Histories of Life, Labor and Industry*, eight half-hour programs on New York City's labor history, from more than two hundred interviews.[46] Two years later in Philadelphia, Temple University graduate student Charles Hardy produced *I Remember When: Times Gone But Not Forgotten*, a series of thirteen half-hour oral history documentaries on the lives of working-class Philadelphians. This he followed with *Goin' North: Tales of the Great Migration*, five half-hour oral history documentaries aired by Philadelphia's WHHY-FM in 1985 highlighting black migration to that city during the early decades of the twentieth century. Part of a broader-based public history project administered by Philadelphia's Atwater Kent Museum, which became the archives for the interviews, the series was correlated with an educational supplement that included full transcriptions of the programs, historical photographs, photos of interviewees, and "how to" sections on collecting old photos and conducting oral histories.[47]

Perhaps the most ambitious and successful of the new oral history radio series in this period was *Living Atlanta*, a series of fifty NEH-funded oral history documentaries produced at Atlanta community radio station WRFG. *Living Atlanta* was the brainchild of sociologist Harlon Joye, who hired historians Cliff Kuhn and Bernard West to conduct interviews for the project. Using local historians to help develop outlines, suggest areas of study, and identify informants, the producers recorded nearly two hundred separate interviews. The series debuted locally in

November 1979. NPR picked up six of the programs, distributed by tape through the National Federation of Community Broadcasters. Its producers later converted the radio programs into a book, *Living Atlanta: An Oral History of the City, 1914–1948*.[48] Subsequently, Joye, West, and Kuhn produced or coproduced a succession of oral history radio documentaries.

The 1980s brought NPR serious financial disappointments well documented elsewhere. From the perspective of the history of the audio documentary, NPR and the public radio system was drying up as a market for independently produced radio documentary series. Even during the boom years of the 1970s, public radio was too small to support more than a handful of producers, and the turnover rate among them was extremely high; radio documentary production tended to be a step on the road to other, more lucrative careers or avocations. Unable to make a living as radio documentary producers, the few oral historians working in public and community radio—including Blatti, Kuhn, and Hardy—sought employment elsewhere. Some of the more talented independent producers also left the field, and the remainder confronted the difficulty of getting funding and the contraction of markets. NPR's weekend programs continued telling stories through sound, but the feeling was widespread among many public radio veterans that an era had ended, just as new breakthroughs in audio technology promised once again to revolutionize audio production.[49]

Soundprint: The Audio Equivalent of Photojournalism

By the mid-1980s, the established independent producers were feeling the crunch of budget cutbacks and NPR's movement toward hard news. Paying more attention to "market share" and the bottom line, stations were becoming more conservative and set in their ways, not just politically but also aesthetically. The use of sound that had helped give public radio its distinctive character in the 1970s was increasingly out of place in the news/interview/music formats of the 1980s.

Fearing that the audio documentary was becoming an endangered species, independent producers Jay Allison and Larry

Masett and WJHU general manager David Creagh conceived the idea of creating a weekly, half-hour, nonfiction series for the distribution of independently produced sound documentaries. Committed to the belief that the radio documentary is a unique medium for the expression of ideas, the series provided a vehicle by which to continue advancing the American documentary tradition by encouraging the creative and inventive use of sound. Funded by the CPB, National Endowment for the Arts, and the American Radio Program Fund, *Soundprint* went on the air in January 1988 and continues to provide an important forum for interesting and skillfully produced radio documentaries, many of them utilizing oral reminiscences. *ATC* originator William Siemering, as the series' first executive producer, modeled *Soundprint* on *Life Magazine*, creating "the aural equivalent of photojournalism," as he put it. Siemering envisioned the series as a showcase for the finest works of radio journalism that told their stories through sound, set new standards, and stretched the limits of the medium.[50]

One early (1989) *Soundprint* documentary of interest to oral historians is independent radio producer Dmae Roberts's *Mei Mei: A Daughter's Story*, the account of Roberts's attempt to understand herself by making peace with her Chinese mother (her father was American), a story told through a sophisticated and engaging use of recurring motifs and storytelling techniques, including oral history, interior monologues, and mise-en-scène actualities. Ten years later, Roberts said of *Mei Mei,* "The piece was ahead of its time and ahead of me. . . . It's not news, it's not a regular doc with actualities. It's radio literature, it's theatre, it's audio art and it's me ripping out my heart."[51] The story is fraught with dramatic possibilities: a daughter ashamed of her Old World mother and a mother disappointed in her American daughter, each carrying the psychological scars and burdens of a lifetime. Its historical sweep touched upon family history, modern Chinese history, the American immigrant experience, the conflict between Old World parents and their Americanized children, and the universal story of the relationship between a mother and a daughter.

Oral history was Roberts's primary source of information about her mother's past, but she worked with a reluctant informant. When interviewed, the mother spoke without feeling of her own early life, giving information only reluctantly and in small bits and pieces. (As a child in war-torn China in the 1930s and 1940s, she was sold—twice—by her parents.) In addition, a language barrier inhibited the effort: the mother's limited grasp of English and Roberts's own weak grasp of Chinese. What this meant for the documentary was that Roberts could not rely on oral history actualities to carry the program and needed to be creative in presenting her mother's story. With only brief oral history segments as referents and starting points, a spare use that made those segments all the more powerful and meaningful, Roberts used her own first-person narration to fill in the biographical details, to contextualize and frame her mother's story, and to explain the significance of these autobiographical fragments to her own search for an understanding of her mother and herself. Roberts solved the problem of how to present her mother's voice by dramatizing her oral testimony in the voice of a young Chinese American woman. At times the listener is drawn into the past through the dramatization of some critical moment in the mother's life, and at other times, one hears the mother's actual retrospective narration. This mixed voicing, a very effective documentary technique, uproots the story from its time-boundedness and shifts it from the historical to the universal.

Roberts's split focus on her mother and growing up with her mother also makes explicit the dual focus and relationship between interviewer and interviewee. Clearly, Roberts's relationship to her mother is much more intimate than that of the typical oral historian or journalist and interviewee. By foregrounding the double focus, however, she achieves the self-reflexivity so valued by many contemporary scholars: not just to acknowledge the interviewer's role in the process, but also to incorporate oneself into the interpretation as a cosubject, if not of the history, then of the creation of the historical document. Again, Roberts's motives are clear and compelling. Her objective is to find out who she is and why her mother is the way she is. And as shared traits appear in the course of the story, she notes those continuities and inheritances from her mother. In the process, Roberts provides a valuable model of how this dual focus can bring the shared creation of oral history into the mix in a manner that may be more honest, more personal, and therefore more interesting.[52]

Glenn Gould and "Contrapuntal Radio"

The pieces by Talbot, J. M. Smith, and Roberts discussed above represent the broad range of authors' efforts to communicate effectively in sound. Most oral history-based radio documentaries, however, were less creative. Armed with open-reel and then audiocassette recorders, radio producers quickly learned how to take advantage of the multidimensionality of sound, recording the sound environment of the interviewee, be it a workplace, home, club, or street corner, and then using those sounds to carry the listener to different times, places, and moods. By the mid-twentieth century, however, a documentary formula had taken hold that was structured by a linear storyline and a sonically elementary production style that made more sense on the printed page than to the human ear. Basic rules taught to almost all radio journalists and producers—those who received any instruction at all—were that only one person should be heard at a time; that each person heard should be identified; that musical beds, preferably instrumental, should be kept low so as not to "compete" or interfere with the listener's ability to hear the featured speaker. The formula assumed that the listener should comprehend everything in a single listening. To support the illusion of objectivity, most sound documentarians also adopted the linguistic and stylistic conventions of journalists and historians. Too often, the coupling of a pseudo-objective writing style with the "news" or journalistic aesthetic proved a deadly combination, turning listeners away from content.

Few have challenged the radio documentary formula or attempted to find alternative aural forms of presentation more seriously than Canadian pianist Glenn Gould. Commissioned by the Canadian Broadcasting Corporation's Public Affairs Radio to produce a sound piece for the 1976 Canadian Centennial, Gould built an hour-long "oral tone poem," or documentary "which thinks of itself as a drama," on five interviews. The outcome, *The Idea of North*, explored the meaning of the North as both dream and reality and the role that the vast untamed land had played in the imaginative lives of Canadians. The piece became the first of three sound documentaries published on compact discs in 1992 under the title *Glenn Gould's Solitude Trilogy*.[53]

All audio documentary producers face the challenge of how to condense into short segments essential information that is excessively time consuming or dull. Building *Idea of the North* on a musical, symphonic model, Gould solved the issue by layering and overlapping voices in a fashion he called "contrapuntal radio." He used the sound of a railroad train speeding north to form a constant sound bed that also served as his basso continuo. The piece begins with an extended multivocal montage. He used this prologue—Gould called it a "trio-sonata"—not only to present potentially dull contextual information in an aesthetically pleasing manner, but also to open up the listener's ears and mind. Teasing, foreshadowing, and intimating, it serves as a hearing exercise that prepares the listener for that which follows. He devoted a second multivoice montage, placed a bit more than halfway through the piece, to the subject of the Eskimo. Gould again used his contrapuntal technique to convey a great deal of information in a short amount of time, drawing in and leading the listener through the scan with skill and sensitivity. Here, at last, was an audio documentary that integrated a musical, auditory aesthetic.

In the third and final *Solitude Trilogy* piece, *The Quiet in the Land*, the use of stereo enabled Gould to push his contrapuntal radio to new heights. Fascinated by the move of a small group of Canadian Mennonites from the country to the city, Gould focused on their unique relationship to the world: being "in the world, but not of it." In an extended, ten-minute multivoice montage that begins about three-fifths of the way through the piece, Gould explored this dynamic tension by orchestrating a succession of overlapping voices. Soon it becomes impossible to follow any individual voice, and one begins to follow the rhythm of spoken words and music of the voices, the variation of impressions, rather than the completed thoughts. Once the listener lets go of the monovocal narrative thread and becomes an observer of the passing ebb and flow of voices and stories, hears the rhythms, and experiences the polyphony of thought, a feeling of great calm and knowing takes over, a retreat into the self that enables a much more dispassionate and perhaps "objective" relationship to the history—being *in this world but not of it!*

Here, then, is how contrapuntal radio may have relevance to the practice and presentation of oral history. Oral history is a dialogue and joint creation. Biographies and other histories based on oral history interviews in certain ways create the illusion of sequentiality and a single point of view. In musical terms, traditional historical writing breaks down the symphonic composition of one's life into single instrumental lines to be examined one voice at a time. The segmentation, division, compartmentalization, and dissection necessary for historical analysis is essential to understanding the past, but synthesis is required to bring the history back to life. The articulation of thought and memory is first an aural, not visual, process. It would seem logical, then, that at some point aural historians must learn to think and create aurally. To do so, traditional oral historians must overcome a lifetime of print-based education that has closed their ears as much as it has opened their eyes. Those who would author in sound must learn to "think" in sound. It took a musician to break out of the print-based paradigm. To date, few have taken up Gould's challenge to cross over the perceptual threshold from monotony to polyphony, and his documentary pieces remain little known outside a handful of audio artists and older radio producers.

Sound Documentaries at the Turn of the Century

The ongoing digital revolution of the late twentieth century inaugurated a second renaissance of the sound documentary. The introduction of portable digital audio tape (DAT) recorders in 1989, soon supplemented and then outmoded by minidisc and compact disc recorders and, in the early 2000s, by affordable solid-state field recorders, enabled aural historians, sound ecologists, and documentary producers to record high-fidelity interviews and other sound documents that one could previously capture only with the most expensive open-reel recorders. The development of computer software for audio editing and of affordable digital audio workstations (DAWs) revolutionized sound documentary and music production, enabling authors to produce sophisticated, high-fidelity, stereo programming on a personal computer with easily learned software downloaded free from the World Wide Web. While it remained difficult for sound documentary producers to find funding for their work—and to convince stations to broadcast it—compact disc (CD) offered an affordable medium upon which to distribute work either separately or in tandem with print publications. Two well-received examples of this are *Remembering Slavery: African Americans Talk about Their Personal Experiences of Slavery and Emancipation* (1998) and *Remembering Jim Crow: African Americans Tell about Life in the Segregated South* (2001), both of which packaged oral history–based radio documentaries previously aired on National Public Radio with annotated collections of oral testimonies. While the former used both archival recordings and actors to bring to life transcriptions of Works Progress Administration (WPA) interviews with former slaves, the latter drew upon interviews conducted by graduate students in the early 1990s that were part of the larger *Behind the Veil* collection from Duke University's Center for Documentary Studies.[54]

During the past decade, the Kitchen Sisters, David Isay, Steve Rowland, Jay Allison, Joe Richman, Ira Glass, and others have brought a wealth of new oral history–based documentaries to the air. Transom.org, an online site for discussion of radio documentaries; Radio College, a more general radio-focused site; and the training programs at the Duke University Center for Documentary Studies and the Salt Institute for Documentary Studies, among others, have also contributed to this trend.[55] The Third Coast International Audio Festival, sponsored by Chicago Public Radio, is "a celebration of the best feature and documentary work . . . designed to bring extraordinary and format-breaking radio to broader audiences, drawing listeners to radio's powerful ability to document the world we live in," and its success is another mark of the growing sophistication and popularity of the genre.[56]

"Dave Isay and his collaborators," Jay Allison asserts, "have made a singular mark on the public radio documentary, not just by their excellent work and steadfast idealism, but by building national awareness that there even is such a thing as radio documentary. Chances are, if you know the actual title of a radio piece, it's probably one of Dave's: *Ghetto Life 101, The Sunshine Hotel, Witness to an Execution*."[57] Isay began his career in 1983 with *Remembering Stonewall: A Radio Documentary of the Birth of a Movement*, a half-hour documentary based upon oral histories that retells the story of the 1969 riot that sparked the gay rights movement and of the impact it had upon the lives of gay men and women.[58] It was while working on this project that Isay began to perfect one aspect of his signature style, the rejection of the "formula of 'acts and trax'—slang for alternating sections of the ambient sound called actualities and vocal tracks—in favor of using editing and overdubbing to create a dense aural tapestry."[59]

A decade later, Isay armed two eighth graders—LeAlan Jones and Lloyd Newman—with tape recorders and microphones to document what it was like to grow up near the Ida B. Wells Housing Development on the South Side of Chicago. The result, *Ghetto Life 101*, which aired on NPR in June 1993, was one of the most heralded and controversial radio documentaries of its time. The program included interviews with the boys' principal, Lloyd's alcoholic father, and LeAlan's sister, a high school dropout and unwed mother who acknowledges on tape that she knows the names of the murderers of some of her friends. These candid interviews helped *Ghetto Life 101* win a bevy of awards and generated concern among critics who not only found the program exploitative but also feared that it endangered LeAlan's sister. Overlooked in much of this controversy was the remarkably collaborative nature of the project. Recognizing that what many of his programs do is allow NPR listeners, an audience that despite NPR disclaimers is predominantly white and middle class, to hear the human side of people whom the mass media usually portray with stereotypes, Isay involves members of the community he is documenting as collaborators and corecipients of proceeds. For *Ghetto Life 101*, Isay, who produced the program in New York, involved LeAlan and Lloyd in each stage of production, playing sections over the phone for the boys to hear and approve. They also wrote and recorded their own narration. In 1996, Isay and the boys produced a second documentary on the 1994 murder of five-year-old Eric Morse by two minors in the Ida. B. Wells apartments. Broadcast of *Remorse: The*

Fourteen Stories of Eric Morse on NPR in March of 1996 yielded sales of more than one thousand cassettes and CDs, an indication of the growing ancillary markets for sound works that are broadcast. A book version, *Our America*, followed in 1997.[60]

As with *Ghetto Life 101*, Isay's *Witness to an Execution* began with many hours of interviews, in this case with the warden and staff of the Walls Unit in Huntsville, Texas, where one-third of the executions in the U.S. have taken place since the 1977 reinstatement of the death penalty. These interviews were boiled down into a script, again with the collaboration and approval of the participants. They then recorded the script, which takes listeners step by step through the execution process from a variety of perspectives, including that of the warden, chaplain, tie-down crew, and witnesses.[61] This redaction may not fit exactly the definition of oral history or the immediacy touted at the beginning of this essay, but it in no way diminishes the authenticity and emotion in the narrators' voices or the impact on listeners. When guard Fred Allen tearfully recalls his breakdown brought on by the stress of participating in 120 executions and speaks of seeing the faces of those 120 men as if watching a slide show, he is not just reading a script, he is seeing those men again, reliving the experience as if he speaks it for the first time. Without ever directly addressing the legitimacy or morality of the death penalty, *Witness* is a chilling evocation of the gravity of the practice, from an unexpected perspective.[62]

Isay's use of community members as interviewers, shared authority in project design and interpretation, and equitable division of proceeds demonstrate some of the synchronicities between the audio documentary and community oral history movements. *Ghetto Life 101* also demonstrated the democratizing potential of new technologies. The ability of thirteen- and fourteen-year-old kids from the South Side of Chicago to record compelling broadcast-quality interviews and to help produce a fascinating, award-winning sound documentary has inspired others to place tape recorders and microphones into the hands of their subjects.

Joe Richman's *Radio Diaries* is a particularly effective example of the format that collapses the interviewer/interviewee dichotomy. For *Teenage Diaries*, *Prison Diaries*, and a number of other series, Richman gave his narrators tape recorders and asked them to keep an audio journal. Their voices are moving and eloquent, but it is Richman's skill at finding the telling moment from the many hours of tape that opens up the stories. For a gay teenager, it is a conversation with her parents, who insist her sexual preference is unnatural and a passing phase; for twenty-year-old Laura Rothenberg, who has cystic fibrosis, it is her father recalling their conversation when she was eleven and he first told her that she might not have long to live. "There is tape in there that is just so intimate you couldn't get it with a reporter there," Richman asserts. Recent work at *Radio Diaries* has focused on South Africa. Their five-part series, *Mandela: An Audio History*, broadcast in April 2004, won the Alfred I. duPont Award, one of the genre's highest accolades.[63]

One of the few documentary projects to rely extensively on archival tape is the Southern Regional Council's *Will the Circle Be Unbroken?* (1997), a series of twenty-six half-hour radio programs documenting the civil rights movement in five southern towns. Produced and written by George King, civil rights leader Julian Bond, and NPR commentator Vertamae Grovsner, the series won OHA's 1998 Nonprint Media Award, among many other honors. The producers scoured regional archives for speeches, news reports, and interviews with movement participants and wove them together with recent interviews and the powerfully evocative music of the period. This is a masterful use of oral history, relying on only the sparest narration to set the context and introduce the speakers, and serves well the series' main thesis, that the movement was essentially a local, grassroots phenomenon.[64]

A much different tone is set by what is probably public radio's most popular and acclaimed series, *This American Life*. Since its 1995 debut, the program has offered an important venue for writers, raconteurs, and documentary makers of a certain kind. Hosted by Ira Glass, each program consists of several segments or "acts" loosely focused on a common theme. Tone and structure vary widely—some are fiction, others, humorous essays, still others, more conventional documentaries with ambient sound, interviews, and narration. *This American Life* has broadcast thought-provoking, creative, and compelling oral-reminiscence–based pieces, many of which demonstrate the interest in memory, narrative, and the construction of identity that so fascinates oral historians and scholars. In the 1996 Father's Day program, to cite but one example, radio producer Jay Allison and writer Dan Robb collaborated on an audio montage on events that happened on the day that Robb's parents divorced when he was a child. First, Robb tells his recollection, then his mother and father separately recount what took place, each one offering different and distinctive memories. This and all other pieces must meet Glass's high standards: "I . . . feel like my job is to document these real moments that surprise me and that amuse me, and that just gesture at some bigger truth." He looks for characters, scenes, and transformation. "We reject a lot of stuff," Glass says, citing a "beautiful" essay that didn't make the cut: "There just wasn't enough of a narrative arc."[65]

One of the most notable and ambitious series of recent years was *Lost and Found Sound*, the millennium documentary project produced by the Kitchen Sisters along with Jay Allison. Echoing Glass's emphasis of the visuality of audio productions, Davia Nelson describes the working methods of the "sisters":

> I don't think we set out consciously in the beginning to make cinematic radio, but it seems to be one of the main ways we work. History with a theatrical twist. Archival artifacts merging with stories from people whose voices don't often make the airwaves merging with music. Ricky Leacock, D.A. Pennebaker, the Maysles all have a place in the inspirational pantheon, as does the Grand Canyon. Layer upon layer of rock that is layer upon layer of time. Bright angel shale into fluted schist, into the Tapeats formation. Sounds stacked and stretched, individual stories building into a bigger story, human stories so minute, detailed and particular, that when layered they become the universal story.[66]

This rich layering of sound and story is the essence of *Lost and Found Sound*. With its take-off point the importance of recorded sound in the last century, the subjects for this eclectic series included sound collector Tony Schwartz, the 1900 Galveston hurricane, the rediscovery of recordings of the last singer of the creation-song cycle of the Mojave Indians, recorded letters sent home from the battlefronts of World War II and the Vietnam War, the seminal blues and rock records of Sam Phillips and Sun Records, an all-women radio station, and the sounds of home and assimilation recalled by Vietnamese manicurists, among others. Many of these programs draw on interviews to one degree or another, but one episode takes oral history as its explicit subject. "A Man Tapes His Town: The Unrelenting Oral Histories of Eddie McCoy" features a North Carolina man who has been recording the history of his town since 1979, when laid up from an accident, he came across a discarded tape recorder. One hundred and forty interviews later, McCoy was still excited about the stories he heard. His enthusiasm, the intrinsic interest of his informants, and skillful framing of the interview segments overcome the sometimes imperfect audio quality of his tapes.[67] With the destruction of the World Trade Center on September 11, 2001, the *Lost and Found Sound* team shifted focus to a new series, the *Sonic Memorial Project*. The last calls made by many victims of the attack provided inspiration, and of the process Silva said, "We really mined the depths. . . . We spent two years listening to those last words over and over and over, getting to know survivors. We just felt this tremendous sense of responsibility."[68]

Leonard Bernstein: An American Life, an eleven-hour opus on the life and times of Leonard Bernstein, produced by Steve Rowland, narrated by Susan Sarandon, and broadcast beginning in October 2004, is another ambitious production. Based on more than one hundred interviews, rare recordings, access to Bernstein family members, and letters from the Bernstein Collection at the Library of Congress, the program plays back and forth between events as experienced and as remembered and provides at times spellbinding glimpses into the worlds of twentieth-century American conducting, classical and popular music, and the broader social and cultural environments in which Bernstein lived and worked.[69]

Oral history interviews have become central to many radio documentaries being produced today. Much of the best work, such as *Will the Circle be Unbroken?* and that of the Kitchen Sisters, uses little if any narration, relying instead on the voices of the subjects to carry the story. Layered with ambient sound and music, the voices reach out to us, pulling us into their world. As

Sam Phillips put it, "There's somethin' about your voice-comin' out of the night, out of the light, out of the sky, out of the ground—over the airwaves comes your voice, out of a little Atwater Kent radio."[70]

Oral History in Film and Video Documentaries

Long the poor stepchild of feature films, of interest only to art house audiences and academics, documentary films and videos have gained popularity in recent years. The phenomenal critical and commercial success of Michael Moore's *Fahrenheit 9/11* in 2004 is but the most recent example of this trend. Ken Burns is another name many viewers doubtlessly think synonymous with documentary filmmaking, and along with Moore, Burns certainly deserves much of the credit for the upswing in interest in the genre. Burns's dynamic use of still photos and dramatic readings of primary documents in *The Civil War* brought a new standard of vitality to historical documentaries. His use of interviews or oral history in films is not, however, always an exemplary model. Too often, Burns does not trust his interviewees to tell the story, allowing them only a few seconds for comments that seem to be included merely to vary the rhythm or reinforce a point already made by his omniscient voice-over narrator. In *Jazz*, for example, Burns relies on Winton Marsalis to carry much of the story.[71] Marsalis, without question informed and insightful, often speaks as a scholar, not as a witness to or participant in the events he discusses. Thus Burns denies his audience the full richness of first-person testimony, an unfortunate outcome for a series on such a deeply personal and individualistic art form.

In the late twentieth century, as historians turned to social history and oral historians moved from the elite interviews of the pioneering Columbia University program to a more populist focus, filmmakers likewise became interested in the use of interviews to tell more complex and nuanced stories. Marcel Ophüls's 1970 *The Sorrow and the Pity* was perhaps the most influential example of the new appreciation for personal testimony. Focusing on wartime France under the Nazis, Ophüls uses both interviews and archival film footage. "The results," media historian Erik Barnouw observes, "were unexpected and explosive, largely because of the skillful work by Ophüls as interviewer and provocateur. The war years were veiled in myth—the heroic saga of the resistance, as built up over a quarter of a century. With patient prodding and questioning, Ophüls reached a more complex reality behind it, a mixture of courage, cowardice, venality, dedication."[72]

In 1981, Warren Beatty's inclusion of oral testimony from actual "witnesses" in his epic historical romance *Reds* (1981) gave oral history some brief mainstream visibility. The film tells the story of John Reed—leftist journalist and author of the best-selling account of the Russian revolution, *Ten Days That Shook the World* (1919)—and his romance with fellow journalist Louise Bryant. Throughout the film, Beatty intersperses footage of interviews with over two dozen of Reed and Bryant's contemporaries, a technique Jay S. Steinberg calls "an intriguing device to effectively lend his narrative a sense of time and place."[73]

Claude Lanzmann's *Shoah* (1986) provides a brilliant and powerful demonstration of how interviews can push beyond the surface to deeper truths and emotions. Lanzmann tracked down not only Holocaust survivors but also camp guards, indifferent neighbors, and bureaucratic facilitators of the final solution. In addition, he chose to include himself in the film. Viewers hear him cajoling, badgering, even lying to his Nazi informants in order to get them to talk on camera. Asked whether he hated the Nazis he interviewed, Lanzmann responded, "Hate! I was beyond hate. The point was not to kill them, but to kill them with the camera, which was much more important." Nine-and-a-half hours long, *Shoah* is in its own right and without question an essential document on the Holocaust.[74]

Skillful interviewing also characterizes the work of Erroll Morris, winner of a recent Academy Award for *Fog of War*. When Morris's *The Thin Blue Line* appeared in 1988, it was highly controversial for its use of dramatic re-creations as well as multiple perspectives. The story of the murder of a policeman and the subsequent conviction of an innocent man, *The Thin Blue Line* features long sections of interviews. As one reviewer said, "It is a masterful film that slowly reveals a hidden universe by simply allowing everyone involved—criminals, judges, police officers, and witnesses—to talk and then talk some more." Morris's use of silence as a prompt is a model of the technique. The lack of a voice-over narrator speaking directly for the filmmaker in no way reduces the clarity of Morris's message: the accused was innocent. If anything, it strengthens the impact as Morris lets his audience follow him through the process of uncovering the "truth."[75]

While Morris, like Lanzmann, allows his subjects to damn themselves with their own words, he uses another technique as controversial as the contents of his films. Unlike most oral historians—and other documentary producers, for that matter—he conducts most of his interviews in the studio and adds another layer of artificiality to the process through the use of what he calls the Interrotron. While the interviewee sits in one room in front of the camera, Morris is in another room with a similar setup. The Interrotron is a monitor mounted atop the camera, letting the interviewee see Morris and vice versa. In a review of Morris's *Fog of War*, one critic stated, "The filmed result [of the Interrotron] is the subject speaking directly to the camera, and in effect to the audience. Morris has said that he believes this results in true first-person cinema. Well, that's nonsense."[76] Most likely, experienced oral history interviewers would concur with the critic's conviction that one cannot achieve the desired degree of trust and rapport in such a situation. Morris vehemently disagrees, and his response merits full quotation. Asked if the Interrotron isn't "essentially dehumanizing," he replied, "No. . . . We think of technology working counter to human intimacy. But in fact, that is not true. It's a simplification, and perhaps, just wrong." Morris continued:

> There's that one scene where McNamara (in *Fog of War*) is talking about war crimes in connection to the firebombing of Japan. He stops talking . . . but he's looking right into the lens. . . . He asks that question, "Why is it a war crime if you lose and not if you win?" In a case like that, where there's an important relationship with the subject, people know I'm there, but it's also very important that there be a direct connection with McNamara and I believe there is. It goes back to this whole question of eye contact. When a person is talking to you in a room, you're very much aware of eye contact. A person

makes eye contact, he looks away, he disconnects, he recon-
nects and makes eye contact again, and that has enormous dramatic value. And the Interrotron duplicates that. . . .

I would go back to the other style of interviewing people, if
there was a reason for it. If you were trying to create that distance, if you were trying to pull people away from the individual being interviewed and to show the interviewing
process. I believe all interviews without the Interrotron are basically vérité interviews, because you are that fly on the wall,
looking at two people talking. . . . I could imagine myself not
using the Interrotron, but for most of what I do, I can't.[77]

Along with the popularity of investigative journalism, the
1970s and 1980s witnessed a growing interest in compilation
films that drew on the rich resources of recently opened news-
reel, television news, and government film archives, which
yielded new evidence and fresh perspectives on important
events. In contrast to earlier compilation films, which were often
dominated by a single narrator, these films also featured interviews with participants. *Vietnam: A Television History* (1983) laid
the groundwork, and *Eyes on the Prize* (1987) became probably
the definitive example of the genre. Focusing on the civil rights
movement, the series, like *Will the Circle be Unbroken?* discussed
above, eschewed the great men–great events emphasis of traditional history to focus on the hundreds of men and women
whose individual decisions to stand and resist created and sustained the movement. There was, as Barnouw puts it, "irony,
drama, tragedy, comedy, all fusing into a staggering panorama,
likely to remain a key document of the era."[78] The ability of these
films to juxtapose period artifacts, such as television news reports, with the later recollections and reflections of historic actors was a powerful tool for debunking propaganda and
mythology and challenging ideological shibboleths.

The Life and Times of Rosie the Riveter (1980), produced by
Connie Fields, brought this technique to the fields of women's
history and labor history. *Rosie* highlights the stories of the
women who went to work in traditionally male jobs during
World War II. The testimony of five women is "interwoven with
rare archival recruitment films, stills, posters, ads, and music
from the period, which contrast their personal stories with the

popular legend and mythology of Rosie the Riveter."[79] *Rosie* is especially affecting as the women recall the satisfaction their jobs gave them and their concomitant frustration when, after the war, they were forced out of well-paying manufacturing jobs and back to pink-collar work and domesticity. The Library of Congress cited *Rosie* as "culturally significant," and the U.S. National Film Registry selected the film for preservation.[80]

A more recent labor history film uses personal testimony to reveal not only a forgotten and suppressed episode in the past but also the processes by which history and memory are made. Winner of the 1995 Oral History Association Award for Nonprint Media, *The Uprising of '34*, a film by George Stoney and Judith Helfand, tells the story of the General Textile Strike of 1934, a massive but little-known walkout by hundreds of southern mill workers. The strike was a challenge to the mill owners' dominance of the region and was ruthlessly suppressed. Strikers were "fired, blacklisted, evicted from their homes, and ostracized from their communities."[81] Today, little knowledge of this event remains, and for those who do recall it, the memories are of danger, violence, and defeat. Presenting the event from the varying viewpoints of eyewitnesses, *The Uprising of '34* raises critical questions about the role of history in individual lives, the relationship between history and memory, and how history is written and taught.[82]

Another type of documentary film, in which the director turns his camera on his own life and that of his family, might be called "autobiographical." But in the hands of top documentarians, such films are a far cry from home movies. Alan Berliner is a master of this genre. Starting with his award-winning 1986 feature *The Family Album*, based on home movies and audio recollections of some sixty families, Berliner went on to make two films about his own family. In *Intimate Stranger* (1991), he focuses on his maternal grandfather and the impact of his prolonged absences on his wife and children. Interviews become therapy as some of his subjects end the sessions literally stretched out on the couch. *Nobody's Business* (1996) is about Berliner's father, Oscar, "a man who has lived an ordinary, unexamined life," and who insists that Berliner is wasting his time trying to find significance in it. But the story is in the process not in the facts that Berliner is trying to pull from his reluctant subject. As critic Tom Keogh observes, "It is, in fact, this tension between father and son . . . that becomes the powerful, and funny, thrust of *Nobody's Business*. . . . The net result is a poignant, occasionally stinging portrait of conflict and ambivalence between men and their fathers."[83]

In recent years, the digital revolution has revolutionized the field of video documentary production and distribution. The coming of age of videotape in the 1980s gave rise to a multibillion-dollar nonbroadcast market for films and television programs and provided documentarians an increasingly affordable means to distribute their work to educational and consumer markets. Cable television networks led by the History Channel and A&E Television created new outlets for historical programming and placed unprecedented demands on oral history archives. Requests from new researchers more interested in sound and moving-image documents than written transcripts forced archives to address the unpleasant and perplexing questions about the duplication, conservation, and preservation of analog and digital media, to retool their research rooms, purchase new equipment, and grapple with the serious legal and ethical questions about uses unforeseen by earlier oral historians, archivists, and interviewees. The introduction of affordable video cameras with which a single operator could capture broadcast-quality images enabled a new generation of low-budget documentarians to span the globe. Computer-based software democratized video production, giving anyone with first a desktop and then a laptop computer production tools that previously cost tens of thousands of dollars. Broad-band Internet connections enabled the streaming first of low resolution video modules and then the downloading of DVD-quality feature-length films. And the introduction of DVD provided an off-line digital platform of unprecedented and still growing capacity that could include produced video and audio features, outtakes, images, documents, and more.

Convergence and Collaboration

At the heart of the digital revolution has been the introduction and development of the World Wide Web, which at first supplemented and then replaced broadcast radio and "books on tape"—most of which have already migrated to CD—as the major venue for sound and multiple media publications. Noncommercial radio and television never lived up to their early promise as educational media. Few people ever made a living by producing broadcast documentaries. Funding was always difficult to obtain, convincing stations to pick up a program or series was time consuming and difficult, and the marketing and promotion for independently produced programming was often negligible. Programs requiring years of work typically appeared as only one or two broadcasts and were then rarely heard or seen again. Video and film documentaries fared better than sound documentaries through distribution on videotape to educational and consumer markets. In the late 1990s, the World Wide Web began to offer a permanent home and potentially vast new audiences for these works. The past decade also has witnessed the appearance of a growing number of sites that feature and archive sound and video documentaries and oral history interviews.

One of the pioneering Web sites for the archiving and distribution of aural history programming was Talking History, based at the University at Albany, State University of New York. In the mid-1990s, U Albany historian Gerald Zahavi began broadcasting sound documentaries and interviews with historians on WRPI public radio in Troy, New York. In 1996, Zahavi set up a Web page to make his broadcast materials permanently available to educators and the lay public. Since then, Talking History has grown into an impressive online library of interviews and aural history documentaries free and accessible to teachers and other browsers. In the late 1990s, Zahavi also added "Contributing Producers" pages, providing Dan Collison, David Isay, and other sound documentary producers server space to archive their materials and link to their own Web sites. More recently, Zahavi added a "From the Archives" segment, based on audio documents solicited from sound archives around the country. Zahavi also began to teach a radio documentary production course and placed its syllabus online. This syllabus, updated on a regular basis, is a unique and outstanding resource for anyone interested in aural history.[84] Zahavi, along with U Albany historian Julian Zelizer, was the guiding spirit behind the creation of the *Journal for MultiMedia History* (*JMMH*), "the first peer-reviewed electronic journal that presents, evaluates, and disseminates multimedia historical scholarship." Through *JMMH*, the founding editors sought "to utilize the promise of digital technologies to expand history's boundaries, merge its forms, and promote and legitimate innovations in teaching and research that we saw emerging all around us."[85]

JMMH 2 (1999) featured "I Can Almost See the Lights of Home: A Field Trip to Harlan County, Kentucky," an experimental aural history "essay in sound" created specifically for Web publication rather than radio broadcast. A collaborative work scripted by oral historians Charles Hardy and Alessandro Portelli during a Columbia University Oral History Research Office's Summer Institute, "Lights of Home" includes a full transcription of the sound essay and articles by Portelli on his fieldwork in Harlan County and by Hardy on the "authoring" of the "essay in sound." An index, organized by "chapter" and "movement," enables browsers to navigate through the heart of the publication: a two-and-a-half hour stereo audio essay. Hardy's essay also includes excerpts from early radio documentaries and rejected mixes for "Lights of Home" that enable browsers to hear the audio productions he discusses in his written essay. Winner of the 1999 Oral History Association Nonprint Media Award, "Lights of Home" offers, according to the editors' introduction,

> a new mode of thinking about and presenting oral history. . . . It is an attempt by two oral historians, one from Pennsylvania, USA, and the other from Rome, Italy, to create a new aural history genre that counterpoises the voices of subject and scholar in dialogue—not merely the dialogue that takes place in the real time of an oral interview, but the one that occurs as interpretations are created and scholarship is generated. . . . It challenges oral historians to truly explore the full dimension of the sources they create and utilize in scholarship—to engage the "orality" of oral sources. It challenges all historians to consider alternative modes of presenting interpretations, modes that render the very act of interpretation more visible while preserving and respecting the integrity of primary sources.[86]

How well "Lights of Home" achieves its goal remains open to debate, of course, but the essay does represent an ambitious attempt to use sound media rather than the printed word as a platform for aural history scholarship.

JMMH 3 (2000) included an oral history interview with the Kitchen Sisters that may be both read or heard in its entirety, accompanied by video excerpts of the interview, photographs, and Web links. The issue also featured the article, "Miner's Son, Miners' Photographer: The Life and Work of George Harvan," by Thomas Dublin and Melissa Doak. Here *JMMH* clearly demonstrated the use of multiple media in a complementary fashion. "Miner's Son" includes an extensive photo exhibition, oral history interview—both transcription and audio files—and a historical essay, each of which, say the editors, "offers multiple entry points into the array of visual, oral, and textual resources presented in this electronic retrospective."[87]

In addition to sound recordings and the spoken word, the World Wide Web has played a major role in stimulating oral historians' interest in moving images by providing a platform for their presentation that has a global span. Before the advent of digital technology, comparatively few oral historians utilized videotape because of the expense, the difficulty of use, and the widespread belief that the presence of cameras, light kits, cables, and equipment operators inhibits the rapport and trust upon which oral historians depend. The conservation and preservation of moving image documents was also a serious concern. As mentioned above, the recent introduction of affordable, easily operated digital video cameras made video a viable option for oral history interviewing. For example, the Survivors of the Shoah Visual History Foundation's Online Testimony Viewer includes extensive videotape excerpts from its close to fifty-two thousand interviews with survivors and witnesses of the Holocaust.[88]

The impact of digital media on oral history practice is further evident in multimedia, oral history–based Web sites, and online library/databases of audio and video oral history interview files. The Virtual Oral/Aural History Archive at the California State University, Long Beach, created by Sherna Berger Gluck and Kaye Briegel, is an expanding online library of audio files, photographs, and biographies from the university's audio tape collections on women's history, Asian American history, and other topics. The Civil Rights Movement in Kentucky Oral History Project, launched in 2005 by the Kentucky Oral History Commission, is an interactive, online, digital media database of audio and video interviews and more than ten thousand pages of electronic transcripts. In a collaboration with Northwestern University, the National Archives and Records Administration, Glasgow Caledonian University, and the BBC Information and Archives, Michigan State University's Center for Humane Arts, Letters, and Social Sciences Online (MATRIX) launched HistoricalVoices.org. Designed "to create a significant, fully searchable online database of spoken word collections spanning the 20th century," the site proposes to include public galleries on a broad variety of topics. On a smaller scale, with increasing frequency, excerpts from oral history–based sound and visual recordings are being archived online, often with supplemental documents and educational materials. For example, History Matters: The U.S. Survey Course on the Web, a popular site for teachers of American history produced by the American Social History Project and the Center for Media and Learning at the City University of New York Graduate Center and the Center for History and New Media at George Mason University, features oral history interview audio files as well as descriptions and reviews of Web sites featuring aural history interviews of particular interest to teachers.[89]

For most of the twentieth century, documentary producers, journalists, and oral historians worked in separate professional worlds, knowing little about the others' skills and expertise even when it was clear that they had much to gain from each other. Increasing collaboration and a recognition of mutual interests is accompanying media convergence. Oral historians are more attentive to the hardware required to capture and present in various media high-quality sound and moving image documents. Documentary producers are more aware of the importance of depositing their interviews in an appropriate archive and of preserving the complete interview—traditionally dismissed as the outtakes. One project that typifies the growing convergence of media and interests—and that demonstrates the democratizing potential of digital media—is StoryCorps. Inspired by the 1930s Works Progress Administration interview projects and by his commitment "to tell the stories of ordinary Americans with dignity, celebrating the power and poetry in their words," David

Isay and his Sound Portraits production company in October 2003 opened their first StoryBooth in New York's Grand Central Station. Here, for just ten dollars, people can conduct forty-minute oral history interviews with the help of a trained facilitator and, if they like, a "question generator" from which they can draw specific questions or inspiration for the interview. Afterward, participants receive a CD copy of the interview. Isay and his team then use the interviews to produce pieces aired on public radio. Some of the interviews, along with a photograph of the interviewer and interviewee, appear on the StoryCorps Web site. There are also plans for creation of "Best of StoryCorps" CDs. Eventually, the interviews are placed on permanent deposit in the StoryCorps Archive at the American Folklife Center of the Library of Congress, where they are also made accessible on the library's Web site. The Grand Central StoryBooth was a pilot for a project now going national through portable story booths that travel throughout the country.[90]

Today the ongoing digital revolution offers unprecedented opportunities and challenges for all who record, archive, and author with aural history interviews. New technologies on the horizon include four- and five-channel sound systems, already standard on DVD, and virtual reality, in which aural history documents and programming will be placed in virtual universes and museum spaces that mimic the three dimensions of the real world. Even now, in the horse-and-buggy stage of this revolution, existing technologies and projects hint at how aural history practice will change. In *Born to Live*, Studs Terkel's 1962 radio sound portrait of life under the threat of nuclear annihilation, writer Arthur C. Clarke turned on its head the old Chinese proverb about the curse of living in interesting times, insisting that rather than a curse it is a great "privilege."[91] One might do well to take this attitude to heart as technology continues to move from type and tape to hard drive and multiple-media digital domains.

Notes

1. Joe Richman, telephone conversation with Pamela Dean, May 3, 2003, in response to the question, "Have you ever thought of using already recorded interviews?"

2. Classic articles on oral history in sound and moving image documentaries are Dunaway, "Radio" and Sipe, "Media."

3. Oral History Association, *Evaluation Guidelines*, 5. Hardy, "Prodigal Sons," illustrates recent concepts on oral history and media. On the complex editorial process required for using oral history interviews in media presentations, see Frisch, "Preparing Interview Transcripts."

4. Scott Carrier, "Getting Good Tape," Radio College project, Association of Independents in Radio, http://www.radiocollege.org/readingroom/articles/craft/good_tape.php (accessed February 1, 2005).

5. Ira Glass, "Mo' Better Radio," lecture, Minnesota Public Radio's broadcast journalists' lecture series, Macalester College, St. Paul, MN, February 11, 1998; complete transcript available from *Current*, http://www.current.org/people/p809i2.html (accessed February 22, 2005).

6. On utopian visions for the educational power of radio, see Biocca, "Pursuit of Sound," and Koppes, "Social Destiny of Radio."

7. On the *Chevrolet Chronicles* and other early radio broadcasts of oral reminiscences, see Biel, "Broadcast before 1936," 435–38.

8. Lichty and Bohn, "Radio's 'March of Time'"; Barnouw, *Tower in Babel*, 277–78. On the early history of the radio documentary, see Bluem, "Forgotten Art"; Barnouw, *Sponsor*, 28–37; and MacDonald, "Broadcast Journalism."

9. Barnouw, *Sponsor*, 34; Bluem, "Forgotten Art," 63. On the commercial takeover of American broadcasting, see McChesney, *Telecommunications, Mass Media*.

10. Bluem, "Forgotten Art," 63–66; Biel, "Broadcast before 1936," 1030–45. On Murrow's popularity, see Sperber, *Murrow*, 174, and on his influence on future radio documentarians, see Collins, *National Public Radio*, 18.

11. Bluem, "Forgotten Art," 66–72. For a brief history of tape recorders, see Dearling and Dearling, "Tape Recording." On the early use of the tape recorder in radio broadcasting, see "Radio 'Newspaper'"; Barnouw, *Golden Web*, 237–38. On *Hear It Now*, see Leab, "*See It Now*," 5–7, and on *You Are There*, see Horowitz, "History Comes to Life."

12. NBC program cards, central file, "Yesterday, Today and Tomorrow" (May 20–October 21, 1951), Museum of Television and Radio, New York.

13. Bluem, "Forgotten Art," 71.

14. Ibid., 71–72. On the impact of the Cold War on radio journalism and documentaries, see MacDonald, "Broadcast Journalism," 315–25. For a brief popular history of radio after the arrival of television, see Fornatale and Mills, *Radio in the Television Age*.

15. Hans Flesch, quoted in Cory, "Soundplay," 339. For more on Brecht and other German innovators, see Cory, "Soundplay." On the relationship between sound and radio, see Truax, *Acoustic Communication*, and Kahn and Whitehead, *Wireless Imagination*.

16. See Siepmann, "British, Canadian, and Other Systems," Blakely, *To Serve the Public Interest*, 127.

17. See the discussion of Herman W. Land Associates' 1967 *Hidden Medium: A Status Report on Educational Radio in the United States* in Blakely, *To Serve the*

Public Interest, 149–51. For more on the history of U.S. educational radio, see Blakely, *To Serve the Public Interest*, as well as Greenwood, "Radio's Part."

18. Schwartz, *1, 2, and 3*; Schwartz, *Nueva York*.

19. Schwartz, *Sounds of My City*. Information on Schwartz comes from Jeanne Lowe, "Tony Schwartz: Master Tape Recordist," biographical notes accompanying Schwartz, *Sounds of My City*. Schwartz remains one of the most insightful writers on the impact of radio and the new mass media on American culture. See Schwartz, *Responsive Chord*; Schwartz, *Media*.

20. Schwartz, *Media*, 168–69.

21. Truax, *Acoustic Communication*, 190–92.

22. Ibid., 192–93. An introduction to Orchard's thoughts is available in Langlois, "Soundscapes."

23. Baker, *Studs Terkel*, 37.

24. On Terkel as oral historian, see Frisch, "Oral History and *Hard Times*"; Baker, *Studs Terkel*, 36–43; and de Graaf and Stein, "Guerrilla Journalist." Terkel published his own oral memoirs in *Talking to Myself*.

25. Baker, *Studs Terkel*, 44–45.

26. Terkel's album, *Born to Live*, includes brief liner notes and a complete transcription of the program. Terkel, *Hard Times*, is basically a series of interview excerpts, one following the other. For recordings of these works available online, see Chicago Historical Society, "Studs Terkel: Conversations with America," http://www.studsterkel.org/galleries.php (accessed February 22, 2005).

27. Ralph Johnson, telephone interview with Charles Hardy, October 27, 1993. Promotional flyer for *American Town: A Self-Portrait* (Ann Arbor: University of Michigan Broadcasting Service for National Education Radio, 1966).

28. For a brief history of Pacifica, see the booklet, "Pacifica: Radio with Vision Since 1949" (Berkeley, CA: Pacific Radio Foundation, 1989); Blakely, *To Serve the Public Interest*, 125–26; and McKinney, *Exacting Ear*. See also Pacifica Radio Foundation, Pacifica Radio, http:// (accessed February 16, 2005).

29. Ammon Hennacy, *Catholic Worker Movement*, interview by Byron Bryant, recording of broadcast on KPFA, October 6, 1958 (Los Angeles: Pacifica Radio Archive, no. BB0146, 1958), 1 reel. Transcript available in Bryant, "Interview with Ammon Hennacy."

30. Chris Koch, telephone interview with Charles Hardy, January 20, 1994. Tapes of the interviews aired on Pacifica are available through the Pacifica Foundation National Office or from Pacifica Radio Archive, http://www.pacificaradioarchives.org (accessed February 16, 2005).

31. Robert Kramer, Chris Koch, and Dale Minor, producers, *Freedom Now*, recording of broadcast on WBAI, 1963 (Los Angeles: Pacifica Radio Archive, no. BB0385, 1963), 2 reels. Transcript available in Minor, "Freedom Now!"

32. Koch, "Working at Pacifica," 38. On Pacifica in the 1980s, see Marc Fisher, "Pacifica's Next Wave," *Mother Jones* (May 1989): 50–51.

33. On the early history of NPR, see Witherspoon and Kovitz, *Public Broadcasting*, and Barnouw, *Sponsor*, 57–68.

34. William Siemering, telephone interview with Charles Hardy, October 25, 1993; Bill Siemering, "Bill Siemering's Manifesto: My First Fifty Years in Radio

and What I Learned," *Transom Review* 3, No. 1 (2003), http://www.transom.org/guests/review/200303.review.siemering.html (accessed February 28, 2005).

35. Siemering, "Manifesto" (see note 34).

36. Keith Talbot, telephone interview with Charles Hardy, October 5, 1993.

37. Ibid.

38. Adams et al., *Father Cares*.

39. See Witherspoon and Kovitz, *Public Broadcasting*, 69–70.

40. National Public Radio, Kitchen Sisters: Davia Nelson and Nikki Silva, *War and Separation*, 1982, http://www.npr.org/programs/lnfsound/collaborators/kitchensisters.html (accessed March 7, 2005).

41. NFCB's quarterly program listing, *Soundchoice*, included annotated listings of documentaries as well as radio dramas and special features. For more on these developments, see National Federation of Community Broadcasters, "About NFCB: History," http://nfcb.org/about/history.jsp; Public Radio Satellite System, "What Is the PRSS?" http://www.prss.org/about (both accessed February 25, 2005). Satellite Program Development Fund, Application (Washington, DC: Satellite Program Development Fund, 1985). For an annotated list of programs funded by SPDF between 1980 and 1986, see "SPDF Program Catalogue" (Washington, DC: SPDF, National Public Radio, Spring 1986).

42. J. M. Smith, *Never a Man Spake Like This*; Judi Moore Latta, telephone interview with Charles Hardy, October 26, 1993.

43. Banks, *First Person America*; Beth Friend and Charles Potter for Radio Arts, *Grandma Was an Activist*, recording of six broadcasts by WBAI, 1983 (Los Angeles: Pacifica Radio Archive, nos. SZ0162-SZ0167, 1983), 21 reels; National Public Radio, *Golden Cradle Series*.

44. Tapes and transcripts are available at the Library of Congress, American Folklife Center, Guides to Special Collections in the Archive of Folk Culture, David Dunaway/Pete Seeger Interviews Collection, AFC2000/019, http://www.loc.gov/folklike/guides/DunawaySeeger.html (accessed February 25, 2005).

45. Jo Blatti, telephone interview with Charles Hardy, August 29, 1994. Blatti's interviews are deposited in the Buffalo Social History Project and American Dream Series Collection, 1976–1978, University Archives, University of Buffalo, Buffalo, New York.

46. Audio cassettes of the original broadcasts plus teaching materials are available in Bernhardt, *New Yorkers at Work*. See also Skotnes, review of *New Yorkers at Work*.

47. See Blatti's review of *Goin' North* in Blatti, "Complex Sense of Reality," 124–28. Some of Hardy's programs are accessible through Talking History: Aural History Productions, "Contributing Producers: Charles Hardy III," http://www.talkinghistory.org/hardy.html (accessed February 22, 2005).

48. Cliff Kuhn, telephone conversation with Charles Hardy, November 6, 1993; Kuhn, Joye, and West, *Living Atlanta*, xiii–xix.

49. On NPR in the mid-1980s, see Laurence Zuckerman, "Has Success Spoiled NPR?" *Mother Jones* (June–July 1987): 32–45; Porter, "Has Success Spoiled NPR?"; Marc Fisher, "NPR Considered: From Radical Radio to Washington

Institution," *Washington Post Magazine* (October 22, 1989): 16–23, 37–42; and Fox, "NPR Grows Up."

50. See Soundprint Media Center, "Producers Guidelines: Soundprint Style," http://www.soundprint.org/radio/produce.php (accessed March 1, 2005). William Siemering, interview with Charles Hardy, August 7, 1994.

51. Dmae Roberts, "An Interview with Dmae Roberts," Third Coast International Audio Festival, Chicago Public Radio, http://www.thirdcoastfestival .org/pages/extras/interviews/2002/roberts.html (accessed February 1, 2005).

52. Dmae Roberts's current work is available at Stories1st.org, http://www.stories1st.org, which also presents her two-part essay, "How to Produce a Doc" (accessed February 17, 2005).

53. Gould, *Solitude Trilogy*. The extended discussion on Gould follows information from the booklet accompanying the three compact discs.

54. Berlin, Favreau, and Miller, *Remembering Slavery*; also available at Smithsonian Productions Presents *Remembering Slavery*, Smithsonian Institution, http://rememberingslavery.si.edu/welcome.html (accessed February 23, 2005). Chafe, Gavins, and Korstad, *Remembering Jim Crow*, and the accompanying compact discs by S. Smith and Amos; also available at Minnesota Public Radio, American RadioWorks, *Remembering Jim Crow*, http://americanradioworks .publicradio.org/features/remembering/ (accessed February 23, 2005). The *Behind the Veil* collection contains thirteen hundred oral history interviews; see Duke University, Center for Documentary Studies, *Behind the Veil*, http://cds .aas.duke.edu/btv/btvindex.html (accessed February 23, 2005).

55. These producers and programs are accessible through Web sites: Kitchen Sisters, Davia Nelson, and Nikki Silva, http://kitchensisters.org/; David Isay, Sound Portraits.org: About Sound Portraits, http://sound portraits.org/about/; Steve Rowland, Action on the Web, http://www .steverowland-action.com/; Jay Allison, About Jay Allison, http://www.jay allison.com/; Joe Richman, Radio Diaries: People Documenting Their Lives on National Public Radio, http://www.radiodiaries.org/staff.html; Steven Barclay Agency, "Lectures and Readings: Ira Glass," http://www.barclay agency.com/glass.html; Atlantic Public Media, Transom.org, A Showcase and Workshop for New Public Radio, http://www.transom.org/index.html; Association of Independents in Radio, Radio College, http://www.radiocollege .org; Duke University, Center for Documentary Studies, "Radio: Documentary Audio Programs," http://cds.aas.duke.edu/radio/index.html; Salt Institute for Documentary Studies: Telling Stories in Images, Sound, and the Written Word, "Radio at Salt," http://www.salt.edu/radio.html (all the above sites accessed on February 24, 2005).

56. Chicago Public Radio, Third Coast International Audio Festival, "What Is the Third Coast Festival?" http://www.thirdcoastfestival.org/pages/ whatis.html (accessed February 23, 2005).

57. Jay Allison, introduction to "David Isay and Sound Portraits," *Transom Review* 3, no. 4 (July 2003): 1, http://www.transom.org/guests/review/200307 .review.isay.html (accessed February 1, 2004).

58. For *Remembering Stonewall* and other Isay documentary projects, see Sound Portraits Productions, "On-Air: An Archive of Sound Portraits Radio

Documentaries," http://www.soundportraits.org/on-air (accessed February 1, 2005).

59. Samuel G. Freedman, "David Isay: A Microphone on the Margins," *New York Times* (August 11, 1998): A30.

60. Jones, Newman, and Isay, *Ghetto Life 101*; Jones, Newman, and Isay, *Our America*.

61. David Isay, e-mail message to Pamela Dean, July 25, 2003.

62. The transcript, including Allen's testimony, is available from Sound Portraits Productions, *Witness to an Execution*, http://www.soundportraits.org/on-air/witness_to_an_execution/transcript.php3 (accessed February 1, 2005).

63. From Richman, *Radio Diaries* (see note 55), access audio files and transcripts of *Prison Diaries*, http://www.radiodiaries.org/prisondiaries.html; *Teenage Diaries*, http://www.radiodiaries.org/teenagediaries.html; Rothenberg's "My So-Called Lungs," http://www.radiodiaries.org/transcripts/Other Docs/laura.html; and *Mandela*, http://www.radiodiaries.org/mandela/index.html. Richman quote from Dinitia Smith, "Battling Failing Health, in Her Own Words," *New York Times on the Web* (August 5, 2002), available at http://www.radiodiaries.org/lauranyt.pdf (all accessed February 24, 2005).

64. Southern Regional Council, *Will the Circle Be Unbroken?* http://unbrokencircle.org/home.htm (accessed February 24, 2005). See also Bolton, review of *Will the Circle be Unbroken?*

65. Hear the Robb family's story at *This American Life* from WBEZ Chicago, 1996 Archive, Episode 26, "Father's Day," June 14, 1996, http://www.thislife.org. Glass quotes from Jacqueline Conciatore, "If You Love This Show, You Really Love It," *Current.org*, June 2, 1997, http://www.current.org/rad/rad710t.html; and Julia Barton, "The Thief Who Wiped His Butt on Fudge-Colored Towels, and Other Tales from 'This American Life,'" *Salon.com*, July 23, 1997, http://www.salon.com/july97/media/media2970723.html (all accessed February 25, 2005).

66. Davia Nelson, "Notes from the Kitchen," *Transom Review* 1, no. 4, http://www.transom.org/guests/review/200105.review.ksisters.html (accessed March 7, 2005).

67. Eddie McCoy, "A Man Tapes His Town: The Unrelenting Oral Histories of Eddie McCoy," National Public Radio, http://www.npr.org/programs/lnfsound/stories/001005.stories.html (accessed February 1, 2005).

68. Sonic Memorial Project, "Stories," http://www.sonicmemorial.org/sonic/public/stories.html (accessed February 24, 2005). Silva quote from Samuel G. Freedman, "Finding History (and Wild Rice and George Foreman Grills) Under a Rock," *New York Times* (November 27, 2004), B9.

69. More on *Bernstein* and Rowland's other series is available at Rowland's Web site, Artistowned.com, http://www.artistowned.com/index.html (accessed February 24, 2005).

70. Sam Phillips, quoted on Kitchen Sisters, "The Stories," *Lost and Found Sound*, National Public Radio, http://www.npr.org/programs/lnfsound/stories/index.html (accessed February 24, 2005).

71. See MichaelMoore.com, *Farenheit 9/11*, "About the Movie," http://www.fahrenheit911.com/; *Jazz:* A Film by Ken Burns, "About the Show:

How We Made It Happen," Public Broadcasting System, http://www.pbs
.org/jazz/about (both accessed February 24, 2005).

72. Barnouw, *Documentary*, 260–61.

73. Jay S. Steinberg, *Reds*, Turner Classic Movies, TCM This Month, Featured
Films, http://www.turnerclassicmovies.com/ThisMonth/Article/0,,90474,00
.html (accessed March 7, 2005).

74. Lanzmann, *Shoah*, DVD. Fred Camper, "Shoah's Absence," *Motion Picture* 4 (Winter/Spring 1987), with revisions by the author, available at Fred
Camper's Web site, http://www.fredcamper.com/Film/Lanzmann.html (accessed March 7, 2005).

75. Ronnie D. Lankford Jr., review of *The Thin Blue Line*, Documentary
Films.net, http://www.documentaryfilms.net/Reviews/ThinBlueLine/; Tom
Snyder, "Stage of Justice," *Columbia Chronicle Online* 33, no. 15 (February 14,
2000), http://www.ccchronicle.com/back/00feb14/ae4.html (accessed February 24, 1005).

76. Charles Taylor, review of *Fog of War*, *Salon.com* (December 19, 2003),
http://archive.salon.com/ent/movies/review/2003/12/19/fog_of_war/ (accessed February 1, 2005).

77. Andy Kaufman, "War! What Is It Good For? Errol Morris Finds Out with
'Fog of War,'" *indieWIRE* (December 29, 2003), http://www.indiewire.com/
people/people_031229morris.html (accessed February 1, 2005).

78. Barnouw, *Documentary*, 319–20.

79. Clarity Educational Films, "*Life and Times of Rosie the Riveter*: The Story,"
http://www.clarityfilms.org/Rosie/story.html (accessed February 1, 2005).

80. Wikipedia, s.v., "Life and Times of Rosie the Riveter," http://www
.4reference.net/encyclopedias/wikipedia/The_Life_and_Times_of_Rosie_
the_Riveter.html (accessed February 24, 2005).

81. First Run/Icarus Films, *Uprising of '34*, http://www.frif.com/cat97/
t-z/the_upri.html (accessed February 25, 2005).

82. For a review of the film from the viewpoint of oral history, see Benson,
"Screening Labor Militancy."

83. Berliner, *Family Album*; Berliner, *Intimate Stranger*; Berliner and Berliner,
Nobody's Business. Tom Keogh, editorial review of Berliner and Berliner, *Nobody's Business*, Amazon.com, http://www.amazon.com (accessed February
25, 2005).

84. Gerald Zahavi, Talking History: Aural History Productions, University
at Albany, State University of New York, http://www.talkinghistory.org; Gerald Zahavi, "Producing Historical Documentaries and Features for Radio,"
University at Albany, State University of New York, http://www.albany.edu/
faculty/gz580/documentaryproduction/index.html (both accessed February
25, 2005). Zahavi's extensive syllabus includes the unpublished manuscript
Hardy, "Authoring in Sound."

85. Gerald Zahavi and Julian Zelizer, "About the *Journal for MultiMedia History*," *Journal for Multimedia History* 3 (2000), http://www.albany.edu/jmmh
(accessed February 25, 2005).

86. Charles Hardy III and Alessandro Portelli, "I Can Almost See the Lights
of Home: A Field Trip to Harlan County, Kentucky," *Journal for Multimedia His-*

tory 2, no. 1 (1999), http://www.albany.edu/jmmh/vol2no1/lights.html (accessed February 25, 2005).

87. Nikki Silva and Davia Nelson, with Charles Hardy III, "Turning the Tables: An Oral History of the Kitchen Sisters," *Journal for MultiMedia History* 3 (2000), http://www.albany.edu/jmmh (accessed February 25, 2005); Thomas Dublin and Melissa Doak, "Miner's Son, Miner's Photographer: The Life and Work of George Harvan," *Journal for MultiMedia History* 3 (2000), http://www.albany.edu/jmmh (addressed February 25, 2005). Due to a dearth of quality submissions, *JMMH* has not published a new issue since 2000.

88. Shoah Foundation, Survivors of the Shoah Visual History Foundation, http://www.vhf.org (accessed February 25, 2005).

89. California State University, Long Beach, VOAHA: Virtual Oral/Aural History Archive, http://salticid.nmc.csulb.edu/cgi-bin/WebObjects/OralAural.woa/; Kentucky Historical Society, Kentucky Oral History Commission, Civil Rights Movement in Kentucky Oral History Project, http://history.ky.gov/civilrights.htm; Michigan State University, MATRIX, HistoricalVoices.org, http//www.historicalvoices.org/; American Social History Productions, George Mason University, History Matters: The U.S. Survey Course on the Web, http://historymatters.gmu.edu (all sites accessed February 25, 2005).

90. "National Oral-History-of-America Project Kicks Off at Grand Central Terminal," press release, StoryCorps, September 29, 2003, http://storycorps.net/about/pressroom/press_releases/pr20030929. Listen to the interviews at StoryCorps, http://storycorps.net (accessed February 25, 2005).

91. Terkel, *Born to Live*.

References

Abbott, Lawrence. *I Stand in the Center of the Good: Interviews with Contemporary Native American Artists*. Lincoln: University of Nebraska Press, 1994.

Abercrombie, Thomas A. *Pathways of Memory and Power: Ethnography and History among an Andean People*. Madison: University of Wisconsin Press, 1998.

Acker, Joan, Kate Barry, and Joke Essevelt. "Objectivity and Truth: Problems in Doing Feminist Research." *Women's Studies International Forum* 6 (1983): 423–35.

Adam, Barbara. *Timewatch: The Social Analysis of Time*. Cambridge: Polity, 1995.

Adams, Noah, Bill D. Moyers, Robert Jay Lifton, Philip G. Zimbardo, Ishmael Reed, James Reston, and Deborah Amos. *Father Cares: The Last of Jonestown*. Washington, DC: National Public Radio, 1981. 2 audiocassettes.

Adler, Glen. "The Politics of Research during a Liberation Struggle: Interviewing Black Workers in South Africa." In Grele, ed., *International Annual 1990*, 229–45.

Agar, Michael. "Transcript Handling: An Ethnographic Strategy." *Oral History Review* 15 (Spring 1987): 209–19.

Albright, Daniel. "Literary and Psychological Models of the Self." In Neisser and Fivush, eds., *Remembering Self*, 19–40.

Alexander, Sally. *Becoming a Woman: And Other Essays in 19th and 20th Century Feminist History*. London: Verso, 1995.

———. "Women, Class, and Sexual Difference." *History Workshop* 17 (Spring 1984): 125–49.

Allen, Barbara, and William Lynwood Montell. *From Memory to History: Using Oral Sources in Local Historical Research*. Nashville, TN: American Association for State and Local History, 1981.

Allen, Susan Emily. "Resisting the Editorial Ego: Editing Oral History." *Oral History Review* 10 (1982): 33–45.

Alpern, Sara, Joyce Antler, Elisabeth Israels Perry, and Ingrid Winther Scobie, eds. *The Challenge of Feminist Biography.* Chicago: University of Illinois Press, 1992.

Althusser, Louis. *For Marx.* Translated by Ben Brewster. London: New Left, 1969.

——. "On Ideology." In *Lenin and Philosophy, and Other Essays*, 158–86. New York: Verso, 1971.

American Association of University Professors. "Protecting Human Beings: Institutional Review Boards and Social Science Research." *Academe* 87, no. 3 (May–June 2001): 55–67.

Anderson, Kathryn, and Dana C. Jack. "Learning to Listen: Interview Techniques and Analysis." In Perks and Thomson, eds., *Oral History Reader*, 157–71.

Anderson, Nels. *The Hobo: The Sociology of the Homeless Man.* Chicago: University of Chicago Press, 1923.

Andrade, Eva Salgado. "Epilogue: One Year Later." *Oral History Review* 16, no. 1 (Spring 1988): 21–31.

——. "Oral History in Mexico." *International Journal of Oral History* 9, no. 3 (November 1988): 215–20.

Andrews, Molly, Shelley Day Sclater, Corinne Squire, and Amal Treacher, eds. *Lines of Narrative: Psychosocial Perspectives.* London: Routledge, 2000.

Antler, Joyce. "Having It all, Almost: Confronting the Legacy of Lucy Sprague Mitchell." In Alpern et al., eds., *The Challenge of Feminist Biography*, 97–115.

Applebaum, David. *Voice.* Albany: State University of New York Press, 1990.

Araújo, Paulo Cesar de. *Eu Não Sou Cachorro, Não: Música Popular Cafona e Ditadura Militar.* Rio de Janeiro: Editoria Record, 2002.

Armitage, Susan H. "Introduction." *Frontiers: Journal of Women Studies* 19, no. 3 (1993): iii–iv.

——. "The Next Step." *Frontiers: Journal of Women Studies* 7, no. 1 (1983): 3–8.

Armitage, Susan H., and Sherna Berger Gluck. "Reflections on Women's Oral History: An Exchange." *Frontiers: Journal of Women Studies* 19, no. 3 (1998): 1–11.

Armitage, Susan H., Patricia Hart, and Karen Weathermon, eds. *Women's Oral History: The Frontiers Reader.* Lincoln: University of Nebraska Press, 2002.

Ashplant, Timothy G. "Anecdote as Narrative Resource in Working-Class Life Stories: Parody, Dramatization, and Sequence." In Chamberlain and Thompson, eds., *Narrative and Genre*, 99–113.

Atkinson, J. Maxwell. "Displaying Neutrality: Formal Aspects of Informal Court Proceedings." In Drew and Heritage, eds., *Talk at Work*, 199–211.

Atkinson, R. *The Life Story Interview.* London: Sage, 1998.

Austin-Broos, Diane, and Raymond T. Smith. *Jamaica Genesis.* Chicago: University of Chicago Press, 1997.

Baddeley, Alan D. *Your Memory: A User's Guide.* New York: Macmillan, 1982.

Bailey, Chris Howard. "*Precious Blood*: Encountering Inter-Ethnic Issues in Oral History Research, Reconstruction, and Representation." *Oral History Review* 18, no. 2 (Fall 1990): 61–108.

Bakan, David. "Some Reflections about Narrative Research and Hurt and Harm." In Josselson, ed., *Ethics and Process in the Narrative Study of Lives*, 1–8.

Baker, James T. *Studs Terkel*. New York: Twayne, 1992.

Bakhtin, Mikhail M. *The Dialogic Imagination: Four Essays*. Edited by M. Holquist. Translated by C. Emerson and M. Holquist. Austin: University of Texas Press, 1981.

———. *Speech Genres and Other Late Essays*. Translated by Vern W. McGee. Austin: University of Texas Press, 1986.

Banks, Ann, ed. *First Person America*. New York: Random House, 1980.

———. *First Person America: Voices from the Thirties*. Washington, DC: National Public Radio, 1980. 3 audiocassettes.

Barber, Karin. "Interpreting *Oriki* as History and as Literature." In *Discourse and Its Disguises: The Interpretation of African Oral Texts*, edited by Karin Barber and P. F. de Moraes Farias, 13–23. Birmingham: University of Birmingham Centre of West African Studies, 1989.

Barnouw, Erik. *Documentary: A History of the Non-fiction Film*. 2nd rev. ed. Oxford: Oxford University Press, 1993.

———. *The Golden Web*. Vol. 2, *A History of Broadcasting in the United States*. New York: Oxford University Press, 1968.

———. *The Sponsor: Notes on a Modern Potentate*. New York: Oxford University Press, 1978.

———. *A Tower in Babel*. Vol. 1, *A History of Broadcasting in the United States*. New York: Oxford University Press, 1966.

Bar-On, Dan. "Ethical Issues in Biographical Interviews and Analysis." In Josselson, ed., *Ethics and Process in the Narrative Study of Lives*, 9–21.

Baron, Samuel. "My Life with Plekhanov." In Baron and Pletsch, eds. *Introspection in Biography*, 191–208.

———. "Psychological Dimensions of the Biographical Process." In Baron and Pletsch, eds., *Introspection in Biography*, 1–32.

Baron, Samuel, and Carl Pletsch, eds. *Introspection in Biography: The Biographer's Quest for Self-Awareness*. Hillsdale, NJ: Erlbaum, 1985.

Barthes, Roland. "The Death of the Author." In *Image–Music–Text*, 42–48. Translated by Stephen Heath. New York: Hill and Wang, 1977.

Bartlett, Frederic C. *Remembering: A Study in Experimental and Social Psychology*. 1932. Reprint; Cambridge: Cambridge University Press, 1967.

Baudrillard, Jean. *For a Critique of the Political Economy of Signs*. Translated by C. Levin. St. Louis: Telos, 1981.

Baum, Willa. *Oral History for the Local Historical Society*. Stockton: Conference of California Historical Societies, 1969.

———. *Oral History for the Local Historical Society*. 3rd ed. American Association of State and Local History Book Series. Walnut Creek, CA: AltaMira, 1995.

———. *Transcribing and Editing Oral History*. Walnut Creek, CA: AltaMira, 1991.

Bauman, Richard. *Story, Performance, and Event: Contextual Studies of Oral Narrative*. Cambridge: Cambridge University Press, 1986.

Bell, Beverly. *Walking on Fire: Haitian Women's Stories of Survival and Resistance*. Ithaca, NY: Cornell University Press, 2001.

BenEzer, Gadi. *The Ethiopian Jewish Exodus: Narratives of the Migration Journey to Israel 1977–1985*. London: Routledge, 2002.

Benison, Saul. "Reflections on Oral History." *American Archivist* 28, no. 1 (January 1965): 71–77.

Benjamin, Walter. "A Berlin Chronicle." In *One-Way Street and Other Writings*. London: Verso, 1997.

Benmayor, Rina, Ana Juarbe, Blanca Vazquez Erazo, and Celia Alvarez. "Stories to Live By: Continuity and Change in Three Generations of Puerto Rican Women." *Oral History Review* 16, no. 2 (Fall 1988): 1–46.

Bennett, Olivia. "The Real Costs of Forced Settlement." *Oral History: Journal of the Oral History Society* 27, no. 1 (Spring 1999): 35–46.

Benson, Susan Porter. "Screening Labor Militancy." *Oral History Review* 24, no. 2 (Winter 1997): 95–100.

Berger, Arthur Asa. *Narratives in Popular Culture: Media and Everyday Life*. London: Sage, 1997.

Bergmann, Jorg R. "Veiled Morality: Notes on Discretion in Psychiatry." In Drew and Heritage, eds., *Talk at Work*, 137–62.

Berlin, Ira, Marc Favreau, and Steven F. Miller. *Remembering Slavery: African Americans Talk about Their Personal Experiences of Slavery and Freedom*. New York: New Press, 1998. Book and 2 audiocassettes.

Berliner, Alan. *The Family Album: A Film*. New York: Milestone Films, 1986. Videocassette.

———. *Intimate Stranger*. New York: Milestone Film and Video, 1991. Videocassette.

Berliner, Alan, and Oscar Berliner. *Nobody's Business*. New York: Milestone Film and Video, 1996. Videocassette.

Berman, Morris. *The Twilight of American Culture*. New York: Norton, 2002.

Bernhardt, Debra. *New Yorkers at Work: Oral Histories of Life, Labor, and Industry*. New York: Robert F. Wagner Archives, New York University, 1981. Audiocassette.

Berube, Allan. *Coming Out under Fire: The History of Gay Men and Women in World War Two*. New York: Free Press, 1990.

Bidney, David. "Myth, Symbolism, and Truth." In *Myth: A Symposium*, edited by Thomas A. Seboeck, 3–24. Bloomington: Indiana University Press, 1988.

Biel, Michael J. "The Making and Use of Recordings in Broadcast before 1936." Ph.D. diss., Northwestern University, 1977.

Biernacki, Richard. "Method and Metaphor after the New Cultural History." In Bonnell and Hunt, eds., *Beyond the Cultural Turn*, 62–94.

Biocca, Frank. "The Pursuit of Sound: Radio, Perception, and Utopia in the Early Twentieth Century." *Media, Culture, and Society* 10 (1988): 61–79.

Birren, James E., Gary M. Kenyon, Jan-Erik Ruth, Johannes J. F. Schroots, and Torbjorn Svenson, eds. *Aging and Biography: Explorations in Adult Development*. New York: Springer, 1996.

Bjorklund, Diane. *Interpreting the Self: Two Hundred Years of American Autobiography*. Chicago: University of Chicago Press, 1998.

Blackman, Margaret. *During My Time: Florence Edenshaw Davidson, a Haida Woman*. Seattle: University of Washington Press, 1982.

Blakely, Robert J. *To Serve the Public Interest: Educational Broadcasting in the United States*. Syracuse, NY: Syracuse University Press, 1979.

Blatti, Jo. "Toward a Complex Sense of Reality." *Oral History Review* 13 (1985): 123–29.

Blee, Kathleen M. "Evidence, Empathy, and Ethics: Lessons from Oral Histories of the Klan." *Journal of American History* 80 (1993): 596–606.

Bloom, Lynne Z. "Listen! Women Speaking." *Frontiers: Journal of Women Studies* 2, no. 2 (Summer 1977): 1–3.

Bluem, A. William. "Radio: The Forgotten Art." In *Documentary in American Television: Form, Function, Method*, chap. 3. New York: Hastings House, 1965.

Boatright, Mody C., and William A. Owens. *Tales from the Derrick Floor: A People's History of the Oil Industry*. Garden City, NY: Doubleday, 1970.

Bodnar, John. "Pierre Nora, National Memory, and Democracy: A Review." *Journal of American History* 87, no. 3 (December 2000): 951–63.

———. "Power and Memory in Oral History: Workers and Managers at Studebaker." *Journal of American History* 75, no. 4 (March 1989): 1201–21.

———. *Remaking America: Public Memory, Commemoration, and Patriotism in the Twentieth Century*. Princeton, NJ: Princeton University Press, 1992.

Bolter, Jay David. "Hypertext and the Question of Visual Literacy." In *Handbook of Literacy and Technology: Transformations in a Post-Typographic World*, edited by David Reinking, Michael C. McKenna, Linda D. Labbo, and Ronald D. Kieffer, 3–14. Mahwah, NJ: Erlbaum, 1998.

Bolton, Charles C. Review of *Will the Circle Be Unbroken?* by George King (Atlanta: Southern Regional Council, 1997). *Oral History Review* 27, no. 2 (Summer–Fall 2000): 183–85.

Bonfield, Lynn A. "Conversation with Arthur M. Schlesinger, Jr.: The Use of Oral History." *American Archivist* 43, no. 4 (Fall 1980): 461–72.

Bonnell, Victoria E., and Lynn Hunt, eds. *Beyond the Cultural Turn: New Directions in the Study of Society and Culture*. Berkeley: University of California Press, 1999.

———. Introduction. In *Beyond the Cultural Turn*, 1–32.

Borland, Katherine. "'That's Not What I Said': Interpretive Conflict in Oral Narrative Research." In Gluck and Patai, eds., *Women's Words*, 63–75.

Bornat, Joanna. "Two Oral Histories: Valuing Our Differences." *Oral History Review* 21, no. 1 (Spring 1993): 78–95.

Bornat, Joanna, Eve Hostettler, Jill Liddington, Paul Thompson, and Thea Vigne. "Women's History." Special issue, *Oral History: Journal of the Oral History Society* 5, no. 2 (Autumn 1977).

Botkin, B. A. *Lay My Burden Down: A Folk History of Slavery*. Chicago: University of Chicago Press, 1945.

Botz, Gerhard. "Oral History in Austria." In Hartewig and Halbach, eds., "History of Oral History," 97–106.

Boudon, Raymond. *The Analysis of Ideology*. Translated by Malcolm Slater. Chicago: University of Chicago Press, 1989.

Bozzoli, Belinda. "Interviewing the Women of Phokeng." In Perks and Thomson, eds., *Oral History Reader*, 145–56.

Bozzoli, Belinda, and Peter Delius. "Radical History and South African Society." *Radical History Review* 46/47 (January 1990): 13–46.

Bravo, Anna. "Solidarity and Loneliness: Piedmontese Peasant Women at the Turn of the Century." *International Journal of Oral History* 3, no. 2 (June 1982): 76–91.

Brecher, Jeremy. Review of *Brothers: Male Dominance and Technological Change*, by Cynthia Cockburn. *International Journal of Oral History* 5, no. 3 (November 1984): 194–97.

Brecher, Jeremy, Jerry Lombardi, and Jan Stackhouse, eds. *Brass Valley: The Story of Working People's Lives and Struggles in an American Industrial Region*. Philadelphia: Temple University Press, 1982.

Briggs, Charles L. *Learning How to Ask: A Sociolinguistic Appraisal of the Role of the Interview in Social Science Research*. Cambridge: Cambridge University Press, 1986.

Brooks, Michael. "'Long, Long Ago': Recipe for a Middle School Oral History Program." *OHA Magazine of History* 11, no. 3 (Spring 1997): 32–35.

Browne, George P. "Oral History in Brazil off to an Encouraging Start." *Oral History Review* 4 (1976): 53–55.

Browne, Vincent J. "Oral History and the Civil Rights Documentation Project." In *Selections from the Fifth and Sixth National Colloquia on Oral History*, compiled by Peter D. Olch and Forrest C. Pogue, 90–95. New York: Oral History Association, 1972.

Bruemmer, Bruce H. "Access to Oral History: A National Agenda." *American Archivist* 54, no. 4 (Fall 1991): 494–501.

Bruner, Jerome. *Actual Minds, Possible Worlds*. Cambridge, MA: Harvard University Press, 1986.

———. "Life as Narrative." *Social Research* 54, no. 1 (1987): 11–32.

———. "Myth and Identity." In *On Knowing: Essays for the Left Hand*, 127–86. Cambridge, MA: Harvard University Press, 1971.

———. "The Narrative Construction of Reality." *Critical Inquiry* 18, no. 1 (Autumn 1991): 1–21.

Bryant, Byron. "Interview with Ammon Hennacy." In McKinney, ed., *Exacting Ear*, 43–61.

Bryant, Clora, Buddy Collette, William Green, Steve Isoardi, Jack Kelson, Horace Tapscott, Gerald Wilson, and Marl Young, eds. *Central Avenue Sounds: Jazz in Los Angeles*. Berkeley: University of California Press, 1998.

Bugnard, Pierre-Philippe. "Les Retrouvailles de la Biographie et de la Nouvelle Histoire." *Schweizerische Zeitschrift fur Geschichte, Revue suisse d'Histoire* 45, no. 2 (1995): 236–54.

Bull, Peter. "On Identifying Questions, Replies, and Non-replies in Political Interviews." *Journal of Language and Social Psychology* 13, no. 2 (1994): 115–31.

Burger, Peter L., and Thomas Luckman. *The Social Construction of Reality: A Treatise in the Sociology of Knowledge*. New York: Anchor, 1966.

Butler, Judith. *Gender Trouble: Feminism and the Subversion of Identity*. London: Routledge, 1990.

Button, Graham. "Answers as Interactional Products: Two Sequential Practices Used in Job Interviews." In Drew and Heritage, eds., *Talk at Work*, 212–31.

Campbell, Joan. "Developments in Oral History in Australia." *Oral History Review* 4 (1976): 49–52.

Capussotti, Enrica. "Memory: A Complex Battlefield." In Losi, Passerini, and Silvia, eds., "Archives of Memory," 194–218.

Carleton, Jill. "Embodying Autobiography: A Lesbian Performance of Gay Male Performance Arts." *Women and Performance: A Journal of Feminist Theory* 10, nos. 19–20 (1999): 73–83.

Carr, David. *Time, Narrative, and History*. Bloomington: University of Indiana Press, 1986.

Carr, Edward Hallett. *What Is History?* London: Macmillan, 1961.

Carroll, John B. *Language, Thought, and Reality: Selected Writings of Benjamin Lee Whorf*. Cambridge: Technology Press of Massachusetts Institute of Technology, 1956.

Cash, Joseph H., and Herbert T. Hoover. *To Be an Indian: An Oral History*. New York: Holt, Rinehart and Winston, 1971.

Cavarero, Adriana. *Relating Narratives: Storytelling and Selfhood*. Translated by Paul A. Kottman. London: Routledge, 2000.

Chafe, William Henry, Raymond Gavins, and Robert Rogers Korstad. *Remembering Jim Crow: African Americans Tell about Life in the Segregated South*. New York: New Press, 2001.

Chamberlain, Mary. "Gender and Memory: Oral History and Women's History." In *Engendering History: Caribbean Women in Historical Perspective*, edited by Verene Shepherd, Bridget Brereton, and Barbara Bailey, 94–110. New York: St. Martin's, 1995.

——. *Narratives of Exile and Return*. New York: St. Martin's, 1997.

——. "'Praise Songs' of the Family: Lineage and Kinship in the Caribbean Diaspora." *History Workshop Journal* 50 (Autumn 2000): 114–28.

Chamberlain, Mary, and Paul Thompson. "Genre and Narrative in Life Stories." In Chamberlain and Thompson, eds., *Narrative and Genre*, 1–22.

——, eds. *Narrative and Genre*. Routledge Studies in Memory and Narrative. London: Routledge, 1998.

Chamberlain, Mary, Paul Thompson, Selma Leydesdorff, and Kim Lacy Rogers, eds. "Introduction to the Series." In Chamberlain and Thompson, eds., *Narrative and Genre*, xiii–xv.

Chamberlayne, Prue, Joanna Bornat, and Tom Wengraf, eds. *The Turn to Biographical Methods in Social Science: Comparative Issues and Examples*. London: Routledge, 2000.

Chanfrault-Duchet, Marie-Françoise. "Narrative Structures, Social Models, and Symbolic Representation in the Life Story." In Gluck and Patai, eds., *Women's Words*, 77–92.

——. "Textualisation of the Self and Gender Identity in the Life Story." In Cosslett, Lury, and Summerfield, eds., *Feminism and Autobiography*, 61–75.

Charlton, Thomas L. *Oral History for Texans.* Austin: Texas Historical Commission, 1981.

———. *Oral History for Texans.* 2nd ed. Austin: Texas Historical Commission, 1985.

———. "Videotaped Oral Histories: Problems and Prospects." *American Archivist* 47, no. 3 (Summer 1984): 228–36.

Chartier, Roger. "Texts, Printing, Readings." In *The New Cultural History*, edited by Lynn Hunt, 154–75. Berkeley: University of California Press, 1989.

Chase, Susan E., and Colleen S. Bell. "Interpreting the Complexity of Women's Subjectivity." In McMahan and Rogers, eds., *Interactive Oral History Interviewing*, 63–81.

Chatterley, Cedric N., Alicia J. Rouverol, and Stephen A. Cole. *"I Was Content and Not Content": The Story of Linda Lord and the Closing of Penobscot Poultry.* Carbondale: Southern Illinois University Press, 2000.

Chevalier, Tracy. *Girl with a Pearl Earring.* New York: Dutton, 1999.

Child, Margaret S., comp. *Directory of Information Sources on Scientific Research Related to the Preservation of Sound Recordings, Still and Moving Images, and Magnetic Tape.* Washington, DC: Commission on Preservation and Access, 1993.

Christie, J. R. R., and Fred Orton. "Writing on a Text of the Life." *Art History* 11, no. 4 (December 1988): 545–62.

Church, Jonathan T., Linda Shopes, and Margaret A. Blanchard. "Should All Disciplines Be Subject to the Common Rule?" *Academe* 88, no. 3 (May–June 2002): 62–69.

Clark, E. Culpepper, Michael J. Hyde, and Eva M. McMahan. "Communication in the Oral History Interview: Investigating Problems of Interpreting Oral Data." Paper presented at the annual meeting of the Speech Communication Association, Minneapolis, November 5, 1978.

———. "Communication in the Oral History Interview: Investigating Problems of Interpreting Oral Data." *International Journal of Oral History* 1 (February 1980): 28–40.

Clayman, Steven E. "Answers and Evasions." *Language in Society* 30 (2001): 403–42.

———. "Displaying Neutrality in Television News Interviews." *Social Problems* 35, no. 4 (1988): 474–92.

———. "Footing in the Achievement of Neutrality: The Case of News-Interview Discourse." In Drew and Heritage, eds., *Talk at Work*, 163–98.

———. "News Interview Openings: Aspects of Sequential Organization." In *Broadcast Talk*, edited by Paddy Scannell, 48–75. London: Sage, 1991.

———. "Reformulating the Question: A Device for Answering/Not Answering Questions in News Interviews and Press Conferences." *Text* 13, no. 2 (1993): 159–88.

Clifford, James. *From Puzzles to Portraits: Problems of a Literary Biographer.* Chapel Hill: University of North Carolina Press, 1970.

Clifford, James, and George E. Marcus, eds. *Writing Culture: The Poetics and Politics of Ethnography.* Berkeley: University of California Press, 1986.

Cobb, James C. *"The Most Southern Place on Earth": The Mississippi Delta and the Roots of Regional Identity.* New York: Oxford University Press, 1992.

Cobley, Paul. *Narrative.* London: Routledge, 2001.

Cohen, Gillian. "The Effects of Aging on Autobiographical Memory." In Thompson, ed., *Autobiographical Memory,* 105–24.

Coles, Robert. *Doing Documentary Work.* New York: New York Public Library/ Oxford University Press, 1997.

Collins, Mary. *National Public Radio: The Cast of Characters.* Washington, DC: Seven Locks, 1993.

Colman, Gould P., ed. *The Fourth National Colloquium on Oral History.* New York: Oral History Association, 1970.

———. "Oral History—An Appeal for More Systematic Procedures." *American Archivist* 28, no. 1 (January 1965): 79–83.

———. "Where to Now?" In Colman, ed., *Fourth National Colloquium,* 1–3.

Conaway, Charles William. "Lyman Copeland Draper, Father of American Oral History." *Journal of Library History* 1, no. 4 (1966): 234–41.

Conkin, Paul. Review of *Black Mountain,* by Martin Duberman. *Journal of American History* 60, no. 3 (September 1973): 512.

Connerton, Paul. *How Societies Remember.* Cambridge: Cambridge University Press, 1989.

Conquergood, Dwight. "Performing as a Moral Act: Ethical Dimensions of the Ethnography of Performance." *Literature in Performance* 5, no. 2 (April 1985): 1–13.

Contini, Giovanni. *La Memoria Divisa.* Milano: Rizzoli, 1997.

———. "Toward a Story of Oral History in Italy." In Hartewig and Halbach, eds., "History of Oral History," 57–69.

Cory, Mark E. "Soundplay: The Polyphonous Tradition of German Radio Art." In Kahn and Whitehead, eds., *Wireless Imagination,* 331–72.

Cosslett, Tess, Celia Lury, and Penny Summerfield, eds. *Feminism and Autobiography: Texts, Theories, Methods.* London: Routledge, 2000.

Cottle, Thomas J. *Private Lives and Public Accounts.* Amherst: University of Massachusetts Press, 1977.

Couch, William Terry. Preface to *These Are Our Lives.* Chapel Hill: University of North Carolina Press, 1939.

Crane, Susan A. "Writing the Individual Back into Collective Memory." *American Historical Review* 102, no. 5 (December 1997): 1372–85.

Crawford, Charles W. "Oral History—The State of the Profession." *Oral History Review* 2 (1974): 1–9.

Curry, Constance. *Silver Rights.* Chapel Hill, NC: Algonquin, 1999.

Cutler, William, III. "Accuracy in Oral History Interviewing." In Dunaway and Baum, eds., *Oral History,* 2nd ed., 99–106.

Daley, Caroline. "'He Would Know, But I Just Have a Feeling': Gender and Oral History." *Women's History Review* 7, no. 3 (1998): 343–59.

Davis, Cullom, Kathryn Back, and Kay MacLean. *Oral History: From Tape to Type.* Chicago: American Library Association, 1977.

Davis, David Brion. "Recent Directions in American Cultural History." *American Historical Review* 73, no. 3 (February 1968): 696–707.

Dawson, Graham. *Soldier Heroes: British Adventure, Empire, and the Imagining of Masculinities.* London: Routledge, 1994.

Dearling, Robert, and Celia Dearling. "Tape Recording." Section 5 in *The Guinness Book of Recorded Sound.* London: Guinness, 1984.

Deering, Mary Jo, and Barbara Pomeroy. *Transcribing without Tears: A Guide to Transcribing and Editing Oral History Interviews.* Washington, DC: George Washington University, 1976.

de Graaf, John, and Alan Harris Stein. "The Guerrilla Journalist as Oral Historian: An Interview with Louis 'Studs' Terkel." *Oral History Review* 29, no. 1 (Winter/Spring 2002): 87–107.

Denning, Michael. *Culture in the Age of Three Worlds.* New York: Verso, 2004.

Denzin, Norman K. *Interpretive Biography.* Thousand Oaks, CA: Sage, 1989.

DeVault, Marjorie. *Liberating Method: Feminism and Social Research.* Philadelphia: Temple University Press, 1999.

Dexter, Lewis Anthony. *Elite and Specialized Interviewing.* Evanston, IL: Northwestern University Press, 1970.

Dhupelia-Mesthrie, Uma. "Dispossession and Memory: The Black River Community in Cape Town." *Oral History: Journal of the Oral History Society* 28, no. 2 (Autumn 2000): 35–43.

Dickins, Dorothy. "Nutrition Investigation of Negro Tenants in the Yazoo Mississippi Delta." *Mississippi Agricultural Experiment Station Bulletin* 254: 30–33, 47.

Diaz, Rose T., and Andrew B. Russell. "Oral Historians: Community Oral History and the Cooperative Ideal." In *Public History: Essays from the Field*, edited by James B. Gardner and Peter S. LaPaglia, 203–16. Malabar, FL: Kreiger, 1999.

Dittmer, John. *Local People: The Struggle for Civil Rights in Mississippi.* Urbana: University of Illinois Press, 1994.

Dixon, Elizabeth I. "Definitions of Oral History." In Dixon and Mink, eds., *Oral History at Arrowhead*, 4–24.

Dixon, Elizabeth I., and Gould P. Colman. "Objectives and Standards." In Dixon and Mink, eds., *Oral History at Arrowhead*, 69–89.

Dixon, Elizabeth I., and James V. Mink, eds. *Oral History at Arrowhead: The Proceedings of the First National Colloquium on Oral History.* Los Angeles: Oral History Association, 1967.

Dollard, John. *Criteria for the Life History.* New Haven: Yale University Press, 1935.

Dosse, François. *History of Structuralism. Vol. 1. The Rising Sign, 1945–1966.* Translated by Deborah Glassman. Minneapolis: University of Minnesota Press, 1977.

Drew, Paul, and John Heritage. "Analyzing Talk at Work: An Introduction." In Drew and Heritage, eds., *Talk at Work*, 3–65.

———, eds. *Talk at Work: Interaction in Institutional Settings.* Cambridge: Cambridge University Press, 1992.

Duberman, Martin. *Black Mountain: An Exploration in Community*. New York: E. P. Dutton, 1972.

Dudley, Kathryn Marie. "In the Archive, in the Field: What Kind of Document Is an 'Oral History'?" In Chamberlain and Thompson, eds., *Narrative and Genre*, 160–66.

Dunaway, David King. "Field Recording Oral History." *Oral History Review* 15, no. 1 (Spring 1987): 21–42.

———. "The Interdisciplinarity of Oral History." In Dunaway and Baum, eds., *Oral History*, 2nd ed., 7–22.

———. "The Oral Biography." *Biography* 4, no. 3 (1991): 256–66.

———. "Radio and the Public Use of Oral History." In Dunaway and Baum, eds., *Oral History* (1984), 333–46.

———. "Radio and the Public Use of Oral History." In Dunaway and Baum, eds., *Oral History*, 2nd ed., 306–20.

———. "Transcription: Shadow or Reality?" *Oral History Review* 12 (1984): 113–17.

Dunaway, David K., and Willa K. Baum, eds. *Oral History: An Interdisciplinary Anthology*. Nashville, TN: American Association for State and Local History, 1984.

———. *Oral History: An Interdisciplinary Anthology*. 2nd ed. American Association for State and Local History Book Series. Walnut Creek, CA: AltaMira, 1996.

Dundes, Alan, ed. *Sacred Narrative: Readings in the Theory of Myth*. Berkeley: University of California Press, 1984.

———. "Texture, Text, and Context." *Southern Folklore Quarterly* 28 (1964): 251–65.

Eagleton, Terry. *Ideology: An Introduction*. London: Verso, 1991.

Ebbinghaus, Hermann. *Memory: A Contribution to Experimental Psychology*. Translated by Henry A. Ruger and Clara E. Bussenius. 1913. Reprint; New York: Dover, 1987.

Edel, Leon. "Figure under the Carpet." In *Telling Lives*, 16–34.

———. *Literary Biography*. London: R. Hart Davis, 1957.

———. *Telling Lives: The Biographer's Art*. Edited by Marc Pachter. Washington, DC: New Republic Books, 1979.

Edwards, Jane A., and Marin D. Lampert, eds. *Talking Data: Transcription and Coding in Discourse Research*. Hillsdale, NJ: Erlbaum, 1993.

Elder, Glen H., Jr. *Children of the Great Depression: Social Change in Life Experience*. Chicago: University of Chicago Press, 1974.

———. *Children of the Great Depression: Social Change in Life Experience*. 25th Anniversary ed. Boulder, CO: Westview, 1999.

———. "The Life Course and Human Development." In *Handbook of Child Psychology*, edited by William Damon, 5th ed., Vol. 1, *Theoretical Models of Human Development*, edited by Richard M. Lerner, 939–91. New York: Wiley, 1998.

———, ed. *Life Course Dynamics: Trajectories and Transitions, 1968–1980*. Ithaca, NY: Cornell University Press, 1985.

———. "Time, Human Agency, and Perspectives on the Life Course." *Social Psychology Quarterly* 57 (1994): 4–15.

Eley, Geoff. "Is All the World a Text? From Social History of Society to the History of Society Two Decades Later." In *The Historic Turn in the Social Sciences*, edited by Terrence McDonald, 193–244. Ann Arbor: University of Michigan Press, 1996.

Elias, Norbert. "On Human Beings and Their Emotions: A Process Sociological Essay." In *The Body: Social Process and Cultural Theory*, edited by Mike Featherstone, Mike Hepworth, and Bryan S. Turner, 103–25. London: Sage, 1991.

Ellmann, Richard. *Literary Biography.* Oxford: Clarendon, 1971.

Elms, Alan C. *Uncovering Lives: The Uneasy Alliance of Biography and Psychology.* New York: Oxford University Press, 1994.

Ely, Richard, and Allyssa McCabe. "Gender Differences in Memories for Speech." In Leydesdorff, Passerini, and Thompson, eds., *Gender and Memory*, 17–30.

Erikson, Erik. *Childhood and Society.* New York: Norton, 1950.

Erofeyev, Victor. "Dirty Words." *New Yorker*, September 15, 2003, 42–48.

Etter-Lewis, Gwendolyn. "Black Women's Life Stories: Reclaiming Self in Narrative Texts." In Gluck and Patai, eds., *Women's Words*, 43–58.

Eustis, Truman W., III. "Get It in Writing: Oral History and the Law." *Oral History Review* 4 (1976): 6–18.

Evans, George Ewart. *Where Beards Wag All: The Relevance of Oral Tradition.* London: Faber, 1970.

Everett, Stephen E. *Oral History Techniques and Procedures.* Washington, DC: Center of Military History, U.S. Army, 1992.

Eynon, Bret. "Oral History and the New Century," *Oral History Review* 26, no. 2 (Summer/Fall 1999): 16–27.

Fabian, Johannes. *Power and Performance: Ethnographic Exploration through Proverbial Wisdom and Theater in Shaba, Zaire.* Madison: University of Wisconsin Press, 1990.

Faderman, Lillian. *Odd Girls and Twilight Lovers: A History of Lesbian Life in Twentieth-Century America.* New York: Columbia University Press, 1991.

Faires, Nora. "The Great Flint Sit-Down Strike as Theater." *Radical History Review* 43 (1989): 121–35.

Faris, David E. "Narrative Form and Oral History: Some Problems and Possibilities." *International Journal of Oral History* 1, no. 3 (November 1980): 159–80.

Farmer, Paul. "On Suffering and Structural Violence: A View from Below." In *Social Suffering*, edited by Arthur Kleinman, Veena Das, and Margaret Lock, 261–84. Berkeley: University of California Press, 1997.

Farquhar, Peter, and Marjorie Bridge Farquhar. *MBF Marjory B. Farquhar: A Family History.* Berkeley: University of California, Berkeley, Regional Oral History Office, 1996. CD-ROM.

Faseke, Modupeola M. "Oral History in Nigeria: Issues, Problems, and Prospects." *Oral History Review* 18, no. 1 (Spring 1990): 77–91.

Fee, Elizabeth, Linda Shopes, and Linda Zeidman, eds. *The Baltimore Book: New Views of Local History.* Philadelphia: Temple University Press, 1991.

Feierman, Steven. "Colonizers, Scholars, and the Creation of Invisible Histories." In Bonnell and Hunt, eds., *Beyond the Cultural Turn*, 182–216.

Feinstein, David, Stanley Krippner, and Dennis Granger. "Mythmaking and Human Development." *Journal of Humanistic Psychology* 28, no. 3 (1988): 23–50.

Feldman, Allen. *Formations of Violence: The Narrative of the Body and Political Terror in Northern Ireland.* Chicago: University of Chicago Press, 1991.

Feldstein, Mark. "Kissing Cousins: Journalism and Oral History." *Oral History Review* 31, no. 1 (Winter/Spring 2004): 1–22.

Fentress, James, and Chris Wickham. *Social Memory.* Oxford: Blackwell, 1992.

Fetner, Gerald L. *Immersed in Great Affairs: Allan Nevins and the Heroic Age of American History.* Albany: State University of New York Press, 2004.

Feuchtwang, Stephan. "Distant Homes, Our Genre: Recognizing Chinese Lives as an Anthropologist." In Chamberlain and Thompson, eds., *Narrative and Genre*, 126–41.

Feynman, Richard P. *What Do You Care What Other People Think? Further Adventures of a Curious Character.* New York: Norton, 1988.

Fields, Karen E. "What One Cannot Remember Mistakenly." In Jeffrey and Edwall, eds., *Memory and History*, 89–104.

Fields, Mamie Garvin, with Karen Fields. *Lemon Swamp and Other Places: A Carolina Memoir.* New York: Free Press, 1983.

Fine, Elizabeth C. *The Folklore Text: From Performance to Print.* Bloomington: Indiana University Press, 1984.

Finnegan, Ruth. *Oral Literature in Africa.* Nairobi: Oxford University Press, 1970.

Fisher, H. A. L. *A History of Europe.* Complete edition in one volume. 1936. Reprint; London: Edward Arnold, 1941.

Fogerty, James E. "Filling the Gap: Oral History in the Archives." *American Archivist* 46, no. 2 (Spring 1983): 148–57.

———. "Oral History as a Tool in Archival Development." *Comma: International Journal on Archives* 1–2 (2002): 207–10.

Fonow, Mary Margaret, and Judith A. Cook. *Beyond Methodology: Feminist Scholarship as Lived Research.* Bloomington: Indiana University Press, 1991.

Fontana, Andrea, and James H. Frey. "The Interview: From Structured Questions to Negotiated Text." In *Handbook of Qualitative Research*, 2nd ed., edited by N. K. Denzin and Y. S. Lincoln, 645–72. Thousand Oaks, CA: Sage, 2000.

Fornatale, Peter, and Joshua E. Mills. *Radio in the Television Age.* Woodstock, NY: Overlook, 1980.

Foronda, Marcelino A., Jr. *Kaysaysayan: Studies on Local and Oral History.* Manila: De La Salle University Press, 1991.

———. "Oral History in the Philippines." *International Journal of Oral History* 2, no. 1 (February 1981): 13–25.

Fosl, Catherine. "When Subjects Talk Back: Writing Anne Braden's Life-in-Progress." Paper presented at the annual meeting of the Oral History Association, Bethesda, MD, October 10, 2003.

Foucault, Michel. "What Is an Author?" In *Textual Strategies: Perspectives in Post-Structuralist Criticism*, edited by Josué V. Harari, 141–60. Ithaca, NY: Cornell University Press, 1979.

Fox, Nicols. "NPR Grows Up." *Washington Journalism Review* 13, no. 7 (September 1991): 30–37.

Franco, Barbara. "Doing History in Public: Balancing Historical Fact with Public Meaning." *AHA Perspectives* 33, no. 5 (May–June 1995): 5–8.

———. "Raising the Issues." Paper presented at Raising Our Sites conference, Pennsylvania Humanities Council, Philadelphia, February 2000.

Frank, Gelya. "'Becoming the Other': Empathy and Biographical Interpretation." *Biography* 8, no. 3 (1985): 189–210.

Frankel, Richard. "Talking in Interviews: A Dispreference for Patient-Initiated Questions in Physician-Patient Encounters." In *Everyday Language Studies in Ethnomethodology*, edited by G. Psathas, 231–62. Lanham, MD: University Press of America, 1979.

Frantz, Joe. "Video-Taping Notable U.S. Historians." In *Third National Colloquium on Oral History*, edited by Gould P. Colman. New York: Oral History Association, 1969.

Frattaroli, Elio. "Healing the Soul: Why Medication for Anxiety and Depression Is Not Enough." Paper presented to the North Carolina Psychoanalytic Foundation, Research Triangle Park, March 1, 2003.

Friedlander, Peter. *The Emergence of a UAW Local, 1936–1939: A Study in Class and Culture.* Pittsburgh, PA: University of Pittsburgh Press, 1975.

Friedman, Jeff. "Muscle Memory: Performing Embodied Knowledge." In *The Art and Performance of Memory: Sounds and Gestures of Recollection*, edited by Richard Cándida Smith, 156–80. London: Routledge, 2003.

———. "'Wave When You Pass': Presented by the StreetSigns Center for Literature and Performance." *Oral History Review* 28, no. 1 (Winter–Spring 2001): 127–32.

Friedman, W. J., and P. A. deWinstanley, "Changes in the Subjective Properties of Autobiographical Memories with the Passage of Time." *Memory* 6 (1998): 367–81.

Frisch, Michael. "Commentary, Sharing Authority: Oral History and the Collaborative Process." *Oral History Review* 30, no. 1 (Winter–Spring 2003): 111–14.

———. "Editor's Introduction." *Oral History Review* 18, no. 2 (Fall 1990).

———. "Oral History and *Hard Times*: A Review Essay." *Oral History Review* (1979): 70–79.

———. "Oral History and *Hard Times*: A Review Essay." In *Shared Authority* (1990), 5–13.

———. "Oral History and *Hard Times*: A Review Essay." In Perks and Thomson, eds., *Oral History Reader* (1998), 29–37.

———. "Preparing Interview Transcripts for Documentary Publication: A Line-by-Line Illustration of the Editing Process." In *Shared Authority*, 81–146.

———. *A Shared Authority: Essays on the Craft and Meaning of Oral and Public History.* Albany: State University of New York Press, 1990.

Frisch, Michael, and Linda Shopes. "Introduction." *Journal of American History* 81 (1994): 592–93.

Frontiers: A Journal of Women Studies 2, no. 2 (Summer 1977).

Frontiers: A Journal of Women Studies 7, no. 1 (1983).

Frontiers: A Journal of Women Studies 19, no. 2 (1998).

Frontiers: A Journal of Women Studies 19, no. 3 (1998).

Fry, Amelia R. "Reflections on Ethics." *Oral History Review* 3 (1975): 17–28.

Fukuyama, Francis. *The End of History and the Last Man*. Harmondsworth: Penguin, 1992.

Futrell, Allan W., and Charles A. Willard. "Intersubjectivity and Interviewing." In McMahan and Rogers, eds., *Interactive Oral History Interviewing*, 83–105.

Gadamer, Hans-Georg. *Truth and Method*. Edited by Garrett Barden and John Cumming. New York: Seabury, 1975.

Gaines, Kevin. *Uplifting the Race: Black Leadership, Politics, and Culture in the Twentieth Century*. Chapel Hill: University of North Carolina Press, 1996.

Gallacher, Cathryn A., and Dale Treleven. "Developing an Online Database and Printed Directory and Subject Guide to Oral History Collections." *Oral History Review* 16 (1988): 33–68.

Garcia, Mario T. *Memories of Chicano History: The Life and Narrative of Bert Corona*. Berkeley: University of California Press, 1994.

Garner, Lori Ann. "Representations of Speech in the WPA Slave Narratives of Florida and the Writings of Zora Neale Hurston." *Western Folklore* 59, no. 3/4 (Summer/Fall 2000): 215–31.

Gay, Peter. *Freud: A Life for Our Time*. New York: Norton, 1988.

Geer, Richard Owen. "Out of Control in Colquitt: Swamp Gravy Makes Stone Soup." *Drama Review* 40, no. 2 (Summer 1996): 103–30.

Geertz, Clifford. "Ideology as a Cultural System." In *Interpretation of Cultures*, 193–233.

———. *The Interpretation of Cultures*. New York: Basic, 1973.

Geiger, Susan. "What's So Feminist about Women's Oral History?" *Journal of Women's History* 2, no. 1 (1990): 169–82.

Gellner, Ernst. *Thought and Change*. London: Weidenfeld and Nicolson, 1964.

Georges, Robert A. "Toward an Understanding of Storytelling Events." *Journal of American Folklore* 82 (1969): 313–28.

Giddens, D. John Anthony. *Modernity and Self-Identity: Self and Society in the Late Modern Age*. Cambridge: Polity, 1991.

Giele, Janet Z., and Glen H. Elder Jr., eds. *Methods of Life Course Research: Qualitative and Quantitative Approaches*. Thousand Oaks, CA: Sage, 1998.

Gilb, Corrine L. "Tape Recorded Interviewing: Some Thoughts from California." *American Archivist* 20 (October 1957): 335–44.

Gilligan, Carol. *In a Different Voice*. Cambridge, MA: Harvard University Press, 1982.

Gilligan, Carol, and Lyn Mikel Brown. *Meeting at the Crossroads: Women's Psychology and Girls' Development*. Cambridge, MA: Harvard University Press, 1992.

Gilyard, Keith. *Let's Flip the Script: An African American Discourse on Language, Literature, and Learning*. Detroit: Wayne State University Press, 1996.

Glaser, Barney, and Anselm Strauss. *The Discovery of Grounded Theory: Strategies for Qualitative Research*. Chicago: Aldine, 1967.

Glassie, Henry. *Passing the Time in Ballymenone: Culture and History of an Ulster Community*. Philadelphia: University of Pennsylvania Press, 1982.

Gluck, Carol. *Japan's Modern Myths: Ideology in the Late Meiji Period*. Princeton, NJ: Princeton University Press, 1989.

Gluck, Sherna Berger. "Advocacy Oral History: Palestinian Women in Resistance." In Gluck and Patai, eds., *Women's Words*, 205–19.

———. *An American Feminist in Palestine: The Intifada Years*. Philadelphia: Temple University Press, 1994.

———. "From First Generation Oral Historian to Fourth and Beyond." *Oral History Review* 26, no. 2 (Summer–Fall 1999): 1–9.

———, ed. *From Parlor to Prison: Five American Suffragists Talk about Their Lives*. New York: Random House, 1977.

———. "'We Will Not Be Another Algeria'; Women's Mass Organizations, Changing Consciousness, and the Potential for Women's Liberation in a Future Palestine State." In Grele, ed., *International Annual 1990*, 211–28.

———. "What's So Special about Women? Women's Oral History." *Frontiers: Journal of Women Studies* 2, no. 1 (Summer 1977): 3–13.

———. "What's So Special about Women? Women's Oral History." In Dunaway and Baum, eds., *Oral History* (1984), 221–37.

———. "What's So Special about Women? Women's Oral History." In Dunaway and Baum, eds., *Oral History*, 2nd ed. (1996), 215–30.

Gluck, Sherna Berger, and Daphne Patai. Afterword. In *Women's Words*, 221–23.

———. Introduction. In *Women's Words*, 1–5.

———. "The Memory of Politics and the Politics of Memory: Palestinian Women's Narratives." Paper presented for Middle East Studies Association, San Francisco, 1997.

———, eds. *Women's Words: The Feminist Practice of Oral History*. London: Routledge, 1991.

Gluck, Sherna Berger, Donald A. Ritchie, and Bret Eynon. "Reflections on Oral History in the New Millennium: Roundtable Comments." *Oral History Review* 26 (Summer–Fall 1999): 1–28.

Goffman, Erving. *Behavior in Public Places: Notes on the Social Organization of Gatherings*. New York: Free Press of Glencoe, 1963.

———. *Forms of Talk*. Philadelphia: University of Pennsylvania Press, 1981.

———. *The Presentation of Self in Everyday Life*. Garden City, NY: Doubleday Anchor, 1959.

Goldberg, Stanley. "The Manhattan Project Series." In Schorzman, ed., *Introduction to Videohistory*, 83–100.

Good, Francis. "Voice, Ear and Text: Words & Meaning." *Oral History Association of Australia Journal* 22 (2000): 104.

Gordon, Lyndall. "Women's Lives: The Unmapped Country." In *The Art of Literary Biography*, edited by John Batchelor, 87–98. Oxford: Clarendon, 1995.

Gorfein, David S., and Robert R. Hoffman. *Memory and Learning: The Ebbinghaus Centennial Conference 1985*. Hillsdale, NJ: Erlbaum, 1987.

Gould, Glenn. *Glenn Gould's Solitude Triology: Three Sound Documentaries*. Toronto: CBC Records, 1992. 3 compact discs.

Govoni, Paolo. "Biography: A Critical Tool to Bridge the History of Science and the History of Women in Science." *Nuncius* 15, no. 1 (2000): 399–409.

Greatbach, David. "Aspects of Topical Organization in News Interviews: The Use of Agenda-Shifting Procedures by Interviewees." *Media, Culture, and Society* 8 (1986): 441–55.

———. "On the Management of Disagreement between News Interviewees." In Drew and Heritage, eds., *Talk at Work*, 268–301.

———. "Some Standard Uses of Supplementary Questions in News Interviews." In *Belfast Working Papers in Language and Linguistics*, edited by J. Wilson and B. W. Crow, 86–123. Belfast: University of Ulster, 1986.

Green, Anna. "Returning History to the Community: Oral History in a Museum Setting." *Oral History Review* 24, no. 2 (Winter 1997): 53–72.

Green, Jim. Review of *Rank and File: Personal Histories of Working Class Organizers*, edited by Alice Lynd and Staughton Lynd. *History Workshop* 4 (Autumn 1977): 223–25.

Greenspan, Miriam. *Healing through the Dark Emotions: The Wisdom of Grief, Fear, and Despair*. Boston: Shambhala, 2003.

Greenwood, Dorothy F. "Radio's Part in Adult Education." In Marx, ed., *Television and Radio*, 147–52.

Grele, Ronald J. "Can Anyone over Thirty Be Trusted?: A Friendly Critique of Oral History." *Oral History Review* (1978): 36–44.

———. "Concluding Comment." *International Journal of Oral History* 6, no. 1 (February 1985): 42–46.

———. "The Development, Cultural Peculiarities and State of Oral History in the United States." In Hartewig and Halbach, eds., "History of Oral History," 3–15.

———. "Editorial." *International Journal of Oral History* 1, no. 1 (February 1980): 2–3.

———, ed. *Envelopes of Sound: Six Practitioners Discuss the Method, Theory, and Practice of Oral History and Oral Testimony*. Chicago: Precedent, 1975.

———, ed. *Envelopes of Sound: The Art of Oral History*. 2nd ed. New York: Praeger, 1991.

———. "History and the Languages of History in the Oral History Interview: Who Answers Whose Questions and Why?" In McMahan and Rogers, eds., *Interactive Oral History Interviewing*, 1–18.

———, ed. *International Annual of Oral History 1990: Subjectivity and Multiculturalism in Oral History*. London: Greenwood, 1992.

———. Introduction. *The UCLA Oral History Program: Catalog of the Collection*, compiled by Constance S. Bullock with the assistance of Saundra Taylor. Los Angeles: University of California, 1982.

———. "Listen to Their Voices: Two Case Studies in the Interpretation of Oral History Interviews." In *Envelopes of Sound*, 2nd ed., 212–36.

———. "Movement without Aim: Methodological and Theoretical Problems in Oral History." In *Envelopes of Sound*, 2nd ed., 126–54.

———. "Oral History." In *Encyclopedia of Historians and Historical Writing*, edited by Kelly Boyd. 2 vols. Chicago: Fitzroy Dearborn, 1999.

———. "Riffs and Improvisations: An Interview with Studs Terkel." In *Envelopes of Sound*, 2nd ed., 10–49.

———. "A Surmisable Variety: Interdisciplinarity and Oral Testimony." In *Envelopes of Sound*, 2nd ed., 156–95.

———. "Why Call It Oral History: Some Ruminations from the Field." *Pennsylvania History* 60, no. 4 (October 1993): 506–9.

Greven, Philip. *Four Generations: Population, Land, and Family in Colonial Andover, Massachusetts*. Ithaca, NY: Cornell University Press, 1970.

Gugelberger, George M., ed. *The Real Thing: Testimonial Discourse and Latin America*. Durham, NC: Duke University Press, 1996.

Hagestad, Gunhild O. "Social Perspectives on the Life Course." In *Handbook of Aging and the Social Sciences*, 3rd ed., edited by Robert H. Binstock and Linda K. George, 151–68. San Diego: Academic, 1990.

Halbwachs, Maurice. *On Collective Memory*. New York: Harper and Row, 1980.

Hale, Sondra. "Feminist Method, Process, and Self-Criticism: Interviewing Sudanese Women." In Gluck and Patai, eds., *Women's Words*, 121–36.

Haley, Alex. "Black History, Oral History, and Genealogy." *Oral History Review* 1 (1973): 1–25.

———. *Roots: The Saga of an American Family*. Garden City, NY: Doubleday, 1976.

Hall, Jacquelyn Dowd. "'You Must Remember This': Autobiography as Social Critique." *Journal of American History* 85, no. 2 (September 1998): 439–65.

Hall, Jacquelyn Dowd, James Leloudis, Robert Korstad, Mary Murphy, Lu Ann Jones, and Christopher B. Daly. Foreword by Michael Frisch. *Like a Family: The Making of a Southern Cotton Mill World*. 2nd ed. Chapel Hill: University of North Carolina Press, 2000.

Hall, Lesley. "Confidentially Speaking: Ethics in an Interview Situation." *Oral History in New Zealand* 11 (1999): 19–22.

Halttunen, Karen. "Cultural History and the Challenge of Narrativity." In Bonnell and Hunt, eds., *Beyond the Cultural Turn*, 165–81.

Hamilton, E. Douglas. "Oral History and the Law of Libel." In Starr, *Second National Colloquium on Oral History*, 41–56.

Hanke, Lewis. "American Historians and the World Today: Responsibilities and Opportunities." *American Historical Review* 80 (1975): 1–20.

Hankins, Thomas L. "In Defence of Biography: The Use of Biography in the History of Science." *History of Science* 17 (1979): 1–16.

Hankiss, Agnes. "Ontologies of the Self: On the Mythological Rearranging of One's Own Life History." In *Biology and Society: The Life History Approach in the Social Sciences*, edited by Daniel Bertaux, 203–9. Beverly Hills, CA: Sage, 1981.

Hansen, Arthur. "A Riot of Voices: Racial and Ethnic Variables in Interactive Oral History Interviewing." In McMahan and Rogers, *Interactive Oral History Interviewing*, 107–39.

Haraway, Donna. *Primate Visions*. London: Routledge, 1989.

Hardy, Charles, III. "Authoring in Sound: An Eccentric Essay on Aural History, Radio, and Media Convergence." Unpublished manuscript.

———. "An Interview with Alice Hoffman." *Oral History Review* 28, no. 2 (Summer–Fall 2001): 101–35.

———. "Prodigal Sons, Trap Doors, and Painted Women: Reflections on Life Stories, Urban Legends, and Aural History." *Oral History: Journal of the Oral History Society* 29, no. 1 (Spring 2001): 98–105.

Hareven, Tamara K. *Aging and Generational Relations: Life-Course and Cross-Cultural Perspectives*. New York: Aldine de Gruyter, 1996.

———. "The Search for Generational Memory." In Dunaway and Baum, eds., *Oral History*, 2nd ed., 241–56.

Hareven, Tamara K., and Randolph Langenbach. *Amoskeag: Life and Work in an American Factory-City*. New York: Pantheon, 1978.

Hareven, Tamara, and Andrejs Plakans. *Family History at the Crossroads*. Princeton, NJ: Princeton University Press, 1987.

Harris, J. William. *Deep Souths: Delta, Piedmont, and Sea Island Society in the Age of Segregation*. Baltimore, MD: Johns Hopkins University Press, 2001.

Harris, Ramon, Joseph Cash, Herbert Hoover, and Stephen Ward. *The Practice of Oral History: A Handbook*. Glen Rock, NJ: Microfilming Corporation of America, 1975.

Hart, James D. Foreword. *Catalogue of the Regional Oral History Office 1954–1979*, edited by Suzanne B. Riess and Willa K. Baum. Berkeley: Bancroft Library, University of California, 1980.

Hartewig, Karin, and Wulf R. Halbach, eds. "The History of Oral History: Development, Present State, and Future Prospects." Special issue, *BIOS: Zeitschrift für Biographieforschung und Oral History*, 1990.

Hay, Harry. *Radically Gay: Gay Liberation in the Words of Its Founder*. Edited by Will Roscoe. Boston: Beacon, 1996.

Healey, Dorothy. *Dorothy Healey Remembers: A Life in the American Communist Party*. Edited by Maurice Isserman. New York: Oxford University Press, 1990.

Heath, Christian. "The Delivery and Reception of Diagnosis in the General Practice Consultation." In Drew and Heritage, eds., *Talk at Work*, 235–67.

Hebrew University of Jerusalem, Institute of Contemporary Jewry, Oral History Division. *Catalogue* 1. Jerusalem: The Division, 1963.

Heilbrun, Carolyn G. *Writing a Woman's Life*. New York: Ballantine, 1989.

Henige, David. *Oral Historiography*. New York: Longman, 1988.

Heritage, John, and Andrew Roth. "Grammar and Institution: Questions and Questioning in the Broadcast News Interview." *Research in Language and Social Interaction* 28, no. 1 (1995): 1–60.

Hewins, Angela. *The Dillen: Memories of a Man of Stratford-upon-Avon*. Oxford: Oxford University Press, 1981.

Hill, Jonathan D. "Myth and History." In *Rethinking History and Myth: Indigenous South American Perspectives on the Past*, 1–18. Chicago: University of Illinois Press, 1988.

Hill, Ruth Edmonds, ed. *Women of Courage: An Exhibition of Photographs by Judith Sedwick*. Cambridge, MA: Radcliffe College, 1984.

Hiltermann, Joost R. *Behind the Intifada: Labor and Women's Movements in the Occupied Territories.* Princeton, NJ: Princeton University Press, 1991.

Hinsdale, Mary Ann, Helen M. Lewis, and S. Maxine Waller. *It Comes from the People: Community Development and Local Theology.* Philadelphia: Temple University Press, 1995.

Hirsch, Jerrold. *Portrait of America: A Cultural History of the Federal Writers' Project.* Chapel Hill: University of North Carolina Press, 2003.

History Workshop Journal. "Editorial: Oral History." *History Workshop Journal* 8 (Autumn 1979): i–iii.

Hodgkin, Katherine, and Susannah Radstone, eds. *Contested Pasts: The Politics of Memory.* London: Routledge, 2003.

———. *Regimes of Memory.* London: Routledge, 2003.

Hoffman, Alice. "Reliability and Validity in Oral History." In Dunaway and Baum, eds., *Oral History* (1984), 67–73.

———. "Reliability and Validity in Oral History." In Dunaway and Baum, eds., *Oral History*, 2nd ed. (1996), 87–93.

———. "Who Are the Elite, and What Is a Non-Elitist?" *Oral History Review* 4 (1976): 1–5.

Hoffman, Alice M., and Howard S. Hoffman. *Archives of Memory: A Soldier Recalls World War II.* Lexington: University Press of Kentucky, 1990.

———. "Reliability and Validity in Oral History: The Case for Memory." In Jeffrey and Edwall, eds., *Memory and History*, 107–30.

Hofmeyr, Isabel. "Jonah and the Swallowing Monster: Orality and Literacy on a Berlin Mission Station in the Transvaal." *Journal of Southern African Studies* 17, no. 4 (December 1991): 633–53.

———. "'Nterata'/'The Wire': Fences, Boundaries, Orality, Literacy." In Grele, ed., *International Annual 1990*, 69–92.

Holman, Barbara D. *Oral History Collection of the Forest History Society: An Annotated Guide.* Guides to Forest and Conservation History of North American, no. 1. Santa Cruz, CA: Forest History Society, 1976.

Holstein, James A., and Jaber F. Gubrium. *The Self We Live By: Narrative Identity in a Postmodern World.* New York: Oxford University Press, 2000.

Honig, Emily. "Getting to the Source: Striking Lives, Oral History, and the Politics of Memory." *Journal of Women's History* 9, no. 1 (1997): 139–57.

Hoopes, James. *Oral History: An Introduction for Students.* Chapel Hill: University of North Carolina Press, 1979.

Hopper, Robert. "Conversational Dramatism and Everyday Life Performance." *Text and Performance Quarterly* 13, no. 2 (April 1993): 181–83.

Horowitz, Robert F. "History Comes to Life and *You Are There*." In O'Connor, ed., *American History, American Television*, 79–94.

Howe, Michael A. *Introduction to Human Memory: A Psychological Approach.* New York: Harper and Row, 1970.

Hutchby, Ian, and Robin Wooffitt. *Conversation Analysis.* Cambridge: Polity, 1998.

Hutton, Patrick. *History as an Art of Memory.* Hanover, NH: University Press of New England, 1993.

Hyde, Michael J. "Paradox: Toward a Prescriptive Theory of Communication." Ph.D. diss., Purdue University, 1977.

Hymes, Dell. "Folklore's Nature and the Sun's Myths." *Journal of American Folklore* 84 (1975): 345–69.

Ihde, Don. *Listening and Voice: A Phenomenology of Sound*. Athens: University of Ohio Press, 1976.

Ives, Edward D. *The Tape-Recorded Interview: A Manual for Field Workers in Folklore and Oral History*. Rev. and enl. ed. Knoxville: University of Tennessee Press, 1980.

———. *The Tape-Recorded Interview: A Manual for Field Workers in Folklore and Oral History*. 2nd ed. Knoxville: University of Tennessee Press, 1995.

Jaarsma, Sjoerd R., ed. *Handle with Care: Ownership and Control of Ethnographic Materials*. Pittsburgh, PA: University of Pittsburgh Press, 2002.

Jackson, Bruce. *Fieldwork*. Urbana: University of Illinois Press, 1987.

Jacobs, Wilbur R. *On Turner's Trail: 100 Years of Writing Western History*. Lawrence: University Press of Kansas, 1994.

James, Daniel. "'The Case of María Roldán and the Señora with Money Is Very Clear, It's a Fable': Stories, Anecdotes, and Other Performances in Doña María's Testimony." In *Doña María's Story*, 120–56.

———. *Doña María's Story: Life History, Memory, and Political Identity*. Durham, NC: Duke University Press, 2000.

———. "Meatpackers, Peronists, and Collective Memory: A View from the South." *American Historical Review* 102, no. 5 (December 1997): 1404–12.

———. "'Tales Told Out on the Borderlands': Reading Doña María's Story for Gender." In *Doña María's Story*, 213–43.

James, William. *Psychology*. Cleveland: World Publishing, 1948.

Jamieson, Ronda. "Some Aspects of Oral History in New Zealand, the United States of America and the United Kingdom." *Report for the Winston Churchill Memorial Trust of Australia*. Melbourne: Oral History Association of Australia, 1992.

Jay, Martin. "Should Intellectual History Take a Linguistic Turn? Reflections on the Habermas-Gadamer Debate." In LaCapra and Kaplan, eds., *Modern European Intellectual History*, 86–110.

Jefferson, Alphine. "Echoes from the South: The History and Methodology of the Duke University Oral History Program, 1972–1982." *Oral History Review* 12 (1984): 43–62.

Jeffrey, Jaclyn, and Glenace Edwall, eds. *Memory and History: Essays on Recalling and Interpreting Experience*. Lanham, MD: University Press of America, 1994.

Jelin, Elizabeth, and Susana C. Kaufman. "Layers of Memory: Twenty Years after in Argentina." In *The Politics of War: Memory and Commemoration*, edited by T. G. Ashplant, Graham Dawson, and Michael Roper, 87–110. London: Routledge, 2000.

Jensen, Richard. "Oral History, Quantification, and the New Social History." *Oral History Review* 9 (1981): 13–25.

Johnson, Richard. "Edward Thompson and Eugene Genovese and Socialist Humanist History." *History Workshop* 6 (Autumn 1978): 79–100.

Jones, LeAlan, Lloyd Newman, and David Isay. *Ghetto Life 101; Remorse: The Fourteen Stories of Eric Morse.* New York: Sound Portraits Productions, 1997. Compact disc.

———. *Our America: Life and Death on the South Side of Chicago.* New York: Scribner, 1997.

Jones, Rebecca. "*Blended Voices*: Crafting a Narrative from Oral History Interviews." *Oral History Review* 31, no. 1 (Winter/Spring 2004): 23–42.

Jorgensen, Beth Ellen. *The Writing of Elena Poniatowska: Engaging Dialogues.* Austin: University of Texas Press, 1994.

Josselson, Ruthellen, ed. *Ethics and Process in the Narrative Study of Lives.* Thousand Oaks, CA: Sage, 1996.

Joutard, Phillipe. *La Legende des Camisards: une Sensibilite au Passé.* Paris: Gallimard, 1977.

Joyce, Rosemary O. *A Woman's Place: The Life History of a Rural Ohio Grandmother.* Columbus: Ohio State University Press, 1983.

Jung, Carl. *Man and His Symbols.* Garden City, NY: Doubleday, 1964.

———. *Memories, Dreams, Reflections.* Edited by Aniela Jaffe. Translated by Richard and Clara Winston. New York: Random House, 1961.

———. "The Relations between the Ego and the Unconscious. Part Two: Individuation." In *The Basic Writings of C. G. Jung,* edited by Violet Staub de Laszlo, 181–229. New York: Modern Library, 1993.

Kahn, Douglas, and Gregory Whitehead, eds. *Wireless Imagination: Sound, Radio, and the Avant-Garde.* Cambridge, MA: MIT Press, 1992.

Kahn, Robert L., and Toni C. Antonucci. "Convoys of Social Support: A Life-Course Approach." In *Aging: Social Change,* edited by Sara B. Kiesler, James N. Morgan, and Valerie Kincade Oppenheimer, 383–405. New York: Academic, 1981.

Kammen, Michael. *Mystic Chords of Memory: The Transformation of Tradition in American Culture.* New York: Knopf, 1991.

Kamp, Marianne R. "Theme Articles: Restructuring Our Lives: National Unification and German Biographies." *Oral History Review* 21, no. 2 (Winter 1993): 1–81.

———. "Three Lives of Saodat: Communist, Uzbek, Survivor." *Oral History Review* 28, no. 2 (Summer–Fall 2001): 21–58.

Kaufman, Moisés, and Leigh Fondahouski. *The Laramie Project.* New York: Dramatists Play Service, 2001.

Kay, H. "Learning and Retaining Verbal Material." *British Journal of Psychology* 46 (1955): 81–100.

Kayser, John A., and Charles T. Morrissey. "Historically Significant Memories in Social Work: Two Perspectives on Oral History Research and the Helping Professions." *Reflections: Narratives of Professional Helping* 4, no. 4 (Fall 1998): 61–66.

Kendall, Paul Murray. "Walking the Boundaries." In Oates, ed., *Biography as High Adventure,* 32–49.

Kennedy, Elizabeth Lapovsky, and Madeline D. Davis. *Boots of Leather, Slippers of Gold: The History of a Lesbian Community.* New York: Routledge, 1993.

Kern, Stephen. *The Culture of Time and Space, 1880–1918*. Cambridge, MA: Harvard University Press, 1983.

Kerr, Daniel. "'We Know What the Problem Is': Using Oral History to Develop a Collaborate Analysis of Homelessness from the Bottom Up." *Oral History Review* 30, no. 1 (Winter–Spring 2003): 27–46.

Kessler-Harris, Alice. Introduction. In Grele, *Envelopes of Sound* (1975), 1–9.

———. "Social History." In *The New American History, Revised and Expanded Edition*, edited by Eric Foner, 231–55. Philadelphia: Temple University Press, 1997.

Kikumura, Akemi. "Family Life Histories: A Collaborative Venture." *Oral History Review* 14 (1986): 1–7.

Kirk, G. S. *Myth: Its Meaning and Functions in Ancient and Other Cultures*. Cambridge: Cambridge University Press, 1970.

Kirsch, Gesa E. *Ethical Dilemmas in Feminist Research: The Politics of Location, Interpretation, and Publication*. Albany: State University of New York Press, 1999.

Kleinman, Arthur. "The Violences of Everyday Life: The Multiple Forms and Dynamics of Social Violence." In *Violence and Subjectivity*, edited by Veena Das, Arthur Kleinman, Mamphela Ramphele, and Pamela Reynolds, 226–41. Berkeley: University of California Press, 2000.

K'Meyer, Tracy E. "An Interview with Willa K. Baum: A Career at the Regional Oral History Office." *Oral History Review* 24, no. 1 (Summer 1997): 91–112.

Koch, Chris. "On Working at Pacifica." In McKinney, ed., *Exacting Ear*, 35–39.

Kohli, Martin. "The World We Forgot: A Historical Review of the Life Course." In Marshall, ed., *Later Life*, 271–303.

Kopijn, Yvette. "The Oral History Interview in a Cross-Cultural Setting: An Analysis of Its Linguistic, Social and Ideological Structures." In Chamberlain and Thompson, eds., *Narrative and Genre*, 142–59.

Koppes, Clayton R. "The Social Destiny of Radio: Hope and Disillusionment in the 1920s." *South Atlantic Quarterly* 68 (1969): 363–76.

Krieger, Leonard. *Ranke: The Meaning of History*. Chicago: University of Chicago Press, 1977.

Kuhn, Clifford M., Harlon E. Joye, and E. Bernard West. *Living Atlanta: An Oral History of the City, 1914–1948*. Athens: University of Georgia Press, 1990.

Kuhn, Thomas. *The Structure of Scientific Revolutions*. Chicago: University of Chicago Press, 1970.

Kvale, Steiner. *Interviews: An Introduction to Qualitative Research Interviewing*. Thousand Oaks, CA: Sage, 1996.

Kwang, Luke S. K. "Oral History in China: A Preliminary Review." *Oral History Review* 20, no. 1–2 (Spring–Fall 1992): 23–50.

LaCapra, Dominick. *History and Memory after Auschwitz*. Ithaca, NY: Cornell University Press, 1998.

———. "Holocaust Testimonies: Attending to the Victim's Voice." In *Catastrophe and Meaning: The Holocaust and the Twentieth Century*, edited by Moishe Postone and Eric Santer, 209–31. Chicago: University of Chicago Press, 2003.

———. "Rethinking Intellectual History and Reading Texts." In LaCapra and Kaplan, eds., *Modern European Intellectual History*, 47–85.

LaCapra, Dominick, and Steven L. Kaplan, eds. *Modern European Intellectual History: Reappraisals and New Perspectives.* Ithaca, NY: Cornell University Press, 1982.

La Hausse, Paul. "Oral History and South African Historians." *Radical History Review* 46/47 (January 1990): 346–56.

Lance, David. *An Archive Approach to Oral History.* London: Imperial War Museum, 1978.

———. "Oral History in Britain." *Oral History Review* 2 (1974): 64–76.

———. "Oral History Project Design." In Dunaway and Baum, eds., *Oral History*, 2nd ed., 135–42.

———. "An Update from Great Britain." *Oral History Review* 4 (1976): 62–64.

Langellier, Kristin. "Personal Narratives: Perspectives on Theory and Research." *Text and Performance Quarterly* 9, no. 4 (October 1989): 243–76.

Langer, William. "The Next Assignment." *American Historical Review* 63 (1958): 283–304.

Langlois, W. J., ed. *Guide to Aural Research.* Victoria: Provincial Archives of British Columbia, 1976.

———. "Soundscapes: Interview with Imbert Orchard." In Dunaway and Baum, eds., *Oral History* (1984): 407–14.

Langness, Lewis L., and Gelya Frank. *Lives: An Anthropological Approach to Biography.* Novato, CA: Chandler and Sharp, 1981.

Lanzmann, Claude. *Shoah.* New York: New Yorker Films Video, 2003. DVD.

———. *Shoah, an Oral History of the Holocaust: The Complete Text of the Film.* New York: Pantheon, 1985.

Larson, Mary Ann. "Keeping Our Words as Keepers of Words." Paper presented at the annual meeting of the Society of American Archivists, Orlando, FL, September 1998.

Larson, Mary Ann. "Potential, Potential, Potential: The Marriage of Oral History and the World Wide Web." *Journal of American History* 88, no. 2 (September 2001): 596–607.

Lasch, Christopher. *The Culture of Narcissism: American Life in an Age of Diminishing Expectations.* New York: Norton, 1979.

Laslett, Peter. "Necessary Knowledge: Age and Aging in the Societies of the Past." In *Aging in the Past: Demography, Society, and Old Age*, edited by David I. Kertzer and Peter Laslett, 3–77. Berkeley: University of California Press, 1995.

———. *The World We Have Lost.* New York: Scribners, 1966.

Lazarus, Richard S. "Hope: An Emotion and a Vital Coping Resource against Despair." *Social Research* 66, no. 2 (Summer 1999): 653–79.

Leab, Daniel J. "*See It Now*: A Legend Reassessed." In O'Connor, ed., *American History, American Television*: 1–32.

Lebeaux, Richard. "Thoreau's Lives, Lebeaux's Lives." In Baron and Pletsch, eds., *Introspection in Biography*, 225–48.

Lee, Chana Kai. *For Freedom's Sake: The Life of Fannie Lou Hamer.* Urbana: University of Illinois Press, 1999.

Leonard, Linda. *Witness to the Fire: Creativity and the Veil of Addiction.* Boston: Shambhala, 1989.

Levin, David Michael. *The Listening Self: Personal Growth, Social Change and the Closure of Metaphysics*. London: Routledge, 1989.

Levinson, Daniel. *The Seasons of a Woman's Life*. In collaboration with Judy Levinson. New York: Knopf, 1996.

Levinson, Daniel, Charlotte N. Darrow, Edward B. Klein, Maria H. Levinson, and Braxton McKee, eds. *The Seasons of a Man's Life*. New York: Knopf, 1978.

Lewin, Rhoda. *Witnesses to the Holocaust: An Oral History*. Boston: Twayne, 1990.

Lewis, Oscar. *The Children of Sanchez: Autobiography of a Mexican Family*. London: Penguin, 1970.

Lewis, Robert A. "Emotional Intimacy among Men." *Journal of Social Issues* 34, no. 1 (1978): 108–21.

Leydesdorff, Selma. "The Screen of Nostalgia: Oral History and the Ordeal of Working Class Jews in Amsterdam." *International Journal of Oral History* 7, no. 2 (June 1986): 109–15.

Leydesdorff, Selma, Luisa Passerini, and Paul Thompson, eds. *Gender and Memory*. New York: Oxford University Press, 1996.

Lichty, Lawrence, and Thomas Bohn. "Radio's 'March of Time': Dramatized News." *Journalism Quarterly* 51, no. 3 (Autumn 1974): 458–62.

Linde, Charlotte. "Explanatory Systems in Oral Life Stories." In *Cultural Models in Language and Thought*, edited by Dorothy Holland and Naomi Quinn, 343–66. Cambridge: Cambridge University Press, 1987.

———. *Life Stories: The Creation of Coherence*. Oxford: Oxford University Press, 1993.

Lindlof, Thomas R. *Qualitative Communication Research Methods*. Thousand Oaks, CA: Sage, 1995.

Lindqvist, Sven. "Dig Where You Stand." *Oral History: Journal of the Oral History Society* 7, no. 2 (Autumn 1979): 24–30.

Linton, Marigold. "Transformations of Memory in Everyday Life." In Neisser, ed., *Memory Observed*, 77–91.

Lochead, Richard. "Directions in Oral History in Canada." *Canadian Oral History Association Journal* 6 (1983): 5.

Loftus, Elizabeth F., and John C. Palmer. "Reconstruction of Automobile Destruction." In Neisser, ed., *Memory Observed*, 109–15.

Lomax, Alan. *Mister Jelly Roll: The Fortunes of Jelly Roll Morton, New Orleans Creole and "Inventor of Jazz."* Berkeley : University of California Press, 2001.

Lomax, James W., and Charles T. Morrissey. "The Interview as Inquiry for Psychiatrists and Oral Historians: Convergence and Divergence in Skills and Goals." *Public Historian* 11, no. 1 (Winter 1989): 17–24.

Lopes, José Sérgio Leite, and Rosilene Alvim. "A Brazilian Worker's Autobiography in an Unexpected Form." In Chamberlain and Thompson, eds., *Narrative and Genre*, 63–80.

Losi, Natale. "Beyond the Archives of Memory." In Losi, Passerini, and Salvatici, eds., "Archives of Memory," 5–14.

Losi, Natale, Luisa Passerini, and Silvia Salvatici, eds. "Archives of Memory: Supporting Traumatized Communities through Narration and Remembrance." *Psychosocial Notebook* 2 (October 2001).

Lowenstein, Wendy. *Weevils in the Flour: An Oral Record of the 1930s Depression in Australia*. Melbourne: Hyland House, 1978.

Lummis, Trevor. "Structure and Validity in Oral Evidence." *International Journal of Oral History* 2, no. 2 (June 1983): 109–20.

Lutz, Helma, Ann Phoenix, and Nira Yuva-Davis, eds. *Crossfires: Nationalism, Racism and Gender in Europe*. London: Pluto, 1993.

Lynd, Alice, and Staughton Lynd. *Rank and File: Personal Histories by Working-Class Organizers*. Boston: Beacon, 1973.

Lynd, Staughton. "Guerrilla History in Gary." *Liberation* 14 (October 1969): 17–20.

———. "Oral History from Below." *Oral History Review* 21, no. 1 (Spring 1993): 1–8.

———. "Personal Histories of the Early CIO." *Radical America* 5, no. 3 (May–June 1971): 50–51.

Lyotard, Jean-François. *The Postmodern Condition: A Report on Knowledge*. Translated by Geoff Bennington and Brian Massumi. Manchester, England: Manchester University Press, 1984.

MacDonald, J. Fred. "The Development of Broadcast Journalism." In *Don't Touch That Dial: Radio Programming in American Life from 1920 to 1960*, chap. 6. Chicago: Nelson-Hall, 1979.

Mader, Wilhelm. "Emotionality and Continuity in Biographical Contexts." In Birren et al., eds., *Aging and Biography*, 39–60.

Maguire, Peter. *Facing Death*. New York: Columbia University Press, 2005.

Maier, Charles. "A Surfeit of Memory? Reflections on History, Melancholy and Denial." *History and Memory* 5 (1993): 136–51.

Manchester, William. *The Death of a President, November 22–November 25, 1963*. New York: Harper and Row, 1967.

Mandelbaum, Ken. *A Chorus Line and the Musicals of Michael Bennett*. New York: St. Martin's, 1989.

Mann, Nancy D., comp. "Directory of Women's Oral History Projects and Collections." *Frontiers: Journal of Women Studies* 7, no 1 (1983): 114–21.

Marshall, Victor W., ed. *Later Life: The Social Psychology of Aging*. Beverly Hills, CA: Sage, 1986.

———. "A Sociological Perspective on Aging and Dying." In Marshall, ed., *Later Life*, 125–46.

Martin, Wallace. *Recent Theories of Narrative*. Ithaca, NY: Cornell University Press, 1986.

Marx, Herbert L., Jr., ed. *Television and Radio in American Life*. New York: H. W. Wilson, 1953.

Massey, Ellen Gray, ed. *Bittersweet Country*. Garden City, NY: Doubleday, 1978.

Matters, Marion. *Oral History Cataloging Manual*. Chicago: Society of American Archivists, 1995.

Mayer, Arno. *Why the Heavens Did Not Darken?: The "Final Solution" in History*. New York: Pantheon, 1988.

Mayhew, Henry. *London Labour and the London Poor: A Cyclopaedia of the Condition and Earnings of Those That Will Work, Those That Cannot*. London: G. Woodfall, 1851.

McAdams, Dan P. "Narrating the Self in Adulthood." In Birren et al., eds., *Aging and Biography*, 131–48.

———. *The Stories We Live By: Personal Myths and the Making of the Self.* New York: William Morrow, 1993.

McAdams, Dan, Ruthellen Josselson, and Amia Lieblich, eds. Introduction. In *Turns in the Road: Narrative Studies of Lives in Transition.* Washington DC: American Psychological Association, 2001.

McChesney, Robert W. *Telecommunications, Mass Media, and Democracy: The Battle for the Control of U.S. Broadcasting, 1928–1935.* New York: Oxford University Press, 1993.

McFadzean, Andrew. "Interviews with Robert Bowie: The Use of Oral Testimony." *Oral History Review* 26, no. 2 (Summer–Fall 1999): 29–46.

McGuire, Susan Allen. "Expanding Information Sets by Means of 'Existential' Interviewing." *Oral History Review* 15, no. 1 (1987): 55–70.

McKinney, Eleanor, ed. *The Exacting Ear: The Story of Listener-Sponsored Radio, and an Anthology of Programs from KPFA, KPFK, and WBAI.* New York: Pantheon, 1966.

McMahan, Eva M. *Elite Oral History Discourse: A Study of Cooperation and Coherence.* Tuscaloosa: University of Alabama Press, 1989.

McMahan, Eva M., and Kim Lacy Rogers, eds. *Interactive Oral History Interviewing.* Hillsdale, NJ: Erlbaum, 1994.

McMillen, Neil R. *Dark Journey: Black Mississippians and the Age of Segregation.* Urbana: University of Illinois Press, 1989.

McRobbie, Angela. "Jackie: An Ideology of Adolescent Femininity." In *Popular Culture: Past and Present: A Reader*, edited by Bernard Waites, Tony Bennett, and Graham Martin, 263–83. London: Taylor and Francis, 1982.

Menand, Louis. "Bad Comma: Lynne Truss's Strange Grammar." *New Yorker*, June 28, 2004.

Meihy, José Carlos Sebe Bom. "The Radicalization of Oral History." *Words and Silences* New Series 2, no. 1 (June 2003): 31–41.

Menchú, Rigoberta. *I, Rigoberta Menchú: An Indian Woman in Guatemala.* Edited and introduced by Elisabeth Burgos-Debray. London: Verso, 1984.

Mercier, Laurie, and Madeline Buckendorf. *Using Oral History in Community History Projects.* Los Angeles: Oral History Association, 1992.

Merton, Robert K., Marjorie Fiske, and Patricia L. Kendall. *The Focused Interview: A Manual of Problems and Procedures.* 2nd ed. New York: Free Press, 1956.

Meyer, Eugenia. "Elena Poniatowska, Task and Commitment." *Oral History Review* 16, no. 1 (1988): 1–5.

———. "Oral History in Mexico and Latin America." *Oral History Review* 4 (1976): 56–61.

———. "Recovering, Remembering, Denouncing: Keeping Memory of the Past Updated: Oral History in Latin American and the Caribbean." In Hartewig and Halbach, eds., "History of Oral History," 17–25.

Miller, Donald, and Lorna Touryan Miller. "Armenian Survivors: A Typological Analysis of Victim Response." *Oral History Review* 10 (1982): 47–72.

Millwood, Elizabeth. "How Oral History Offices Deal with Legal Challenges." Plenary panel presentation, annual meeting of the Oral History Association. Bethesda, MD, October 12, 2003.

Minister, Kristina. "A Feminist Frame for the Oral History Interview." In Gluck and Patai, eds., *Women's Words*, 27–42.

Minor, Dale. "Freedom Now!" In McKinney, ed., *Exacting Ear*, 163–85.

Mintz, Sidney. *Worker in the Cane: A Puerto Rican Life History*. New Haven, CT: Yale University Press, 1960.

Mishler, Eliot G. *Research Interviewing: Context and Narrative*. Cambridge, MA: Harvard University Press, 1986.

Modell, John. *Into One's Own: From Youth to Adulthood in the United States, 1920–1975*. Berkeley: University of California Press, 1989.

Moerman, Michael. *Talking Culture: Ethnography and Conversation Analysis*. Philadelphia: University of Pennsylvania Press, 1988.

Montell, Lynwood. *The Saga of Coe Ridge: A Study in Oral History*. Knoxville: University of Tennessee Press, 1970.

Montenegro, Antonio Torres, ed. *História Oral e Memória: Cultura Popular Revisitada*. Sao Paulo: Contexto, 1994.

Morrissey, Charles T. Foreword. In Hoffman and Hoffman, *Archives of Memory*, xii–xv.

———. "On Oral History Interviewing." In Dexter, *Elite and Specialized Interviewing*, 109–18.

———. "Oral History and the Mythmakers." *Historic Preservation* 16 (November–December 1964): 232–37.

———. "Stories of Memory, Myth, and Contrivance: The Oral Historian as Skeptic." *Sound Historian: Journal of the Texas Oral History Association* 6, no. 1 (2000): 1–8.

———. "Truman and the Presidency: Records and Oral Recollections." *American Archivist* 28, no. 1 (January 1965): 53–61.

———. "The Two-Sentence Format as an Interviewing Technique in Oral History Fieldwork." *Oral History Review* 15, no. 1 (Spring 1987): 43–54.

Morrow, Phyllis, and William Schneider, eds. *When Our Words Return: Writing, Hearing, and Remembering Oral Traditions of Alaska and the Yukon*. Logan: Utah State University Press, 1995.

Moss, William. "The Future of Oral History." *Oral History Review* 3 (1975): 5–15.

———. "Oral History: An Appreciation." In Dunaway and Baum, *Oral History*, 2nd ed., 107–20.

———. *Oral History Program Manual*. New York: Praeger, 1974.

———. "Oral History: What Is It and Where Did It Come From?" In Stricklin and Sharpless, eds., *Past Meets the Present*, 5–14.

Moye, Joseph Todd. "'Sick and Tired of Being Sick and Tired': Social Origins and Consequences of the Black Freedom Struggle in Sunflower County, Mississippi, 1954–1986." Ph.D. diss., University of Texas, 1999.

Mpe, Phaswane. "Orality and Literacy in an Electronic Era." *South African Archives Journal* 40 (1998): 80–86.

Murphy, John. "The Voice of Memory: History, Autobiography and Oral History." *Historical Studies* 22 (1986): 157–75.

Musto, David F., and Saul Benison. "Studies in the Accuracy of Oral Interviews." In Colman, ed., *Fourth National Colloquium*, 167–81.

Nash, Christopher. *Narrative in Culture: The Uses of Story Telling in the Sciences, Philosophy and Literature*. London: Routledge, 1990.

Nasstrom, Kathryn L. *Everybody's Grandmother and Nobody's Fool: Frances Freeborn Pauley and the Struggle for Social Justice*. Ithaca, NY: Cornell University Press, 2000.

Nathan, Harriet. *Critical Choices in Interviews: Conduct, Use, and Research Role*. Berkeley: University of California Institute of Governmental Studies, 1986.

National Archives (Singapore). *Kampong Days: Village Life and Times in Singapore Revisited*. Singapore: National Archives, 1993.

National Public Radio. *The Golden Cradle Series: Immigrant Women in the United States*. Washington, DC: National Public Radio, 1984. 5 audiocassettes.

Nesse, Rudolph M. "The Evolution of Hope and Despair." *Social Research* 66, no. 2 (Summer 1999): 429–70.

Neisser, Ulric, ed. *Memory Observed: Remembering in Natural Contexts*. San Francisco: Freeman, 1982.

———. "Memory: What Are the Important Questions?" In Neisser, ed., *Memory Observed*, 3–19.

———. "Self-Narratives: True and False." In Neisser and Fivush, eds., *Remembering Self*, 1–18.

Neisser, Ulric, and Robyn Fivush, eds. *The Remembering Self: Construction and Accuracy in the Self-Narrative*. Cambridge: Cambridge University Press, 1994.

Neithammer, Lutz. "Oral History in the United States: *Zur Entwicklung und Problematic Daichroner Befragungen*." *Archive für Sozialgeschichte* 18 (1978): 457–501.

Neithammer, Lutz, and Alexander von Plato, eds. *Lebensgeschichte und Sozialkultur im Ruhrgebiet 1930–1960*. 3 vols. Bonn: Dietz, 1989.

Nelson, Cary. "Can E. T. Phone Home? The Brave New World of University Surveillance." *Academe* 89 (September–October 2003): 30–35.

Nelson, Cary, and Laurence Grossberg, eds. *Marxism and the Interpretation of Culture*. Urbana: University of Illinois Press, 1988.

Nesmith, Tom. "Hugh Taylor's Contextual Idea for Archives and the Foundation of Graduate Education in Archival Studies." In *The Archival Imagination: Essays in Honour of Hugh A. Taylor*, edited by Barbara Lazenby Craig, 13–37. Ottawa: Association of Canadian Archivists, 1992.

Nethercott, Shaun S., and Neil O. Leighton. "Memory, Process, and Performance." *Oral History Review* 18, no. 2 (Fall 1990): 37–60.

———. "Out of the Archives and onto the Stage." In Perks and Thomson, eds., *Oral History Reader*, 457–64.

Neuenschwander, John A. *Oral History and the Law*. 3rd ed. Carlisle, PA: Oral History Association, 2002.

———. "Remembrance of Things Past: Oral Historians and Long Term Memory." *Oral History Review* 6 (1978): 45–53.

Nevins, Allan. *The Gateway to History*. New York: D. Appleton-Century, 1938.

———. "Oral History: How and Why It Was Born." In Dunaway and Baum, eds., *Oral History* (1984), 31–32.

———. "The Uses of Oral History." In Dixon and Mink, eds., *Oral History at Arrowhead*, 25–37.

Nora, Pierre. "Between Memory and History." In *Realms of Memory: Rethinking the French Past*. Vol. 1. *Conflicts and Divisions*, 1–20. Translated by Arthur Goldhammer. New York: Columbia University Press, 1996.

Oakley, Ann. "Interviewing Women: A Contradiction in Terms." In *Doing Feminist Research*, edited by Helen Roberts, 30–61. London: Routledge, Kegan and Paul, 1981.

Oates, Stephen B., ed. *Biography as High Adventure: Life-Writers Speak on Their Art*. Amherst: University of Massachusetts Press, 1986.

O'Connor, John E., ed. *American History, American Television: Interpreting the Video Past*. New York: Frederick Ungar, 1983.

Odom, Howard. *Southern Regions of the United States*. Chapel Hill: University of North Carolina Press, 1936.

O'Farrell, Patrick. "Oral History: Facts and Fiction." *Quadrant* (November 1979): 3–9.

Okihiro, Gary. "Oral History and the Writing of Ethnic History: A Reconnaissance into Method and Theory." *Oral History Review* 9 (1981): 27–46.

Okpewho, Isidore. *African Oral Literature: Backgrounds, Character, and Continuity*. Bloomington: Indiana University Press, 1992.

Olson, David R. *The World on Paper: The Conceptual and Cognitive Implications of Writing and Reading*. Cambridge: Cambridge University Press, 1994.

Ong, Walter J. "Grammar Today: 'Structure' in a Vocal World." *Quarterly Journal of Speech* 43, no. 4 (December 1957): 399–407.

———. *Orality and Literacy: The Technologizing of the Word*. New York: Routledge, 2002.

Oral History Association. *Oral History Evaluation Guidelines*. Adopted 1989. Revised 2000. Carlisle, PA: Oral History Association, 2001. Also available online at http://www.dickinson.edu/oha/pub_eg.html (accessed February 1, 2005).

———. "Oral History: Evaluation Guidelines: The Wingspread Conference." *Oral History Review* 8 (1980): 6–19.

Oral History Association of Australia. "Local History, Family History, and Oral History." Special issue, *Oral History Association of Australia Journal*, 4 (1981–1982).

Oral History in the United States: A Report from the Oral History Research Office of Columbia University. New York: Columbia University Oral History Research Office, 1965.

Oral History Index: An International Directory of Oral History Interviews. Westport, CT: Meckler, 1990.

Oral History Society (UK). "The Interview in Social History." Special issue, *Oral History: Journal of the Oral History Society* 1, no. 4 (1972).

———. "News from Abroad: Australasia." *Oral History: Journal of the Oral History Society* 8, no. 1 (Spring 1980): 12–13.

———. "News from Abroad: Europe." *Oral History, Journal of the Oral History Society* 13, no. 1 (Spring 1985): 17–18.

———. "News from Abroad: Finland." *Oral History, Journal of the Oral History Society* 25, no. 2 (Autumn 1997): 19.

Osterud, Nancy Grey, and Lu Ann Jones. "'If I Must Say So Myself': Oral Histories of Rural Women." *Oral History Review* 17, no. 2 (Fall 1989): 1–23.

Parke, Catherine N. *Biography: Writing Lives*. New York: Twayne, 1996.

Passerini, Luisa. "An Afterthought on a Work in Progress and a Forethought towards Its Future." In Losi, Passerini, and Salvatici, eds., "Archives of Memory," 219–26.

———. *Autobiography of a Generation: Italy 1968*. Hanover, NH: Wesleyan University Press, 1996.

———. *Fascism in Popular Memory: The Cultural Experience of the Turin Working Class*. Translated by Robert Lumley and Jude Bloomfield. Cambridge: Cambridge University Press, 1987.

———. "Italian Working Class Culture between the Wars: Consensus to Fascism and Work Ideology." *International Journal of Oral History* 1 (1980): 1–27.

———, ed. *Memory and Totalitarianism*. Oxford: Oxford University Press, 1992.

———. "Memory: Resume of the Final Session of the International Conference on Oral History in Aix-en-Provence." *History Workshop* 15 (Spring 1983): 195–96.

———. "Mythbiography in Oral History." In Samuel and Thompson, eds., *Myths We Live By*, 49–69.

———. "Oral History in Italy after the Second World War: From Populism to Subjectivity." *International Journal of Oral History* 9, no. 2 (June 1988): 114–24.

———. "Work Ideology and Consensus under Italian Fascism." *History Workshop Journal* 8 (Autumn 1979): 82–108.

Patai, Daphne. "Ethical Problems of Personal Narratives, or, Who Should Eat the Last Piece of Cake?" *International Journal of Oral History* 8, no. 1 (1987): 5–27.

———. "U.S. Academics and Third World Women: Is Ethical Research Possible?" In Gluck and Patai, eds., *Women's Words*, 137–53.

Pearson, Carol S. *The Hero Within: Six Archetypes We Live By*. New York: Harper, 1989.

Perdue, Theda. *Nations Remembered: An Oral History of the Cherokee, Chickasaws, Choctaws, Creeks, and Seminoles*. Norman: University of Oklahoma Press, 1993.

Perks, Robert, and Alistair Thomson. "Critical Developments." In Perks and Thomson, eds., *Oral History Reader*, 1–8.

———. Introduction to Part III, "Advocacy and Empowerment." In Perks and Thomson, eds., *Oral History Reader*, 183–88.

———, eds. *The Oral History Reader*. London: Routledge, 1998.

Personal Narratives Group, eds. *Interpreting Women's Lives: Feminist Theory and Personal Narrative*. Bloomington: Indiana University Press, 1989.

Peter, John. *The Oral History of Modern Architecture: Interviews with the Greatest Architects of the Twentieth Century*. New York: Abrams, 1994.

Peterson, Eric E., and Kristin M. Langellier. "The Politics of Personal Narrative Methodology." *Text and Performance Quarterly* 17, no. 2 (April 1997): 135–52.

Piketty, Guillaume. "La Biographie Comme Genre Historique." *Vingtieme Siecle* 63 (1999): 119–26.

Pillemer, David B. *Momentous Events, Vivid Memories*. Cambridge, MA: Harvard University Press, 2000.

Pillemer, David B., A. B. Desrochers, and C. M. Ebanks. "Remembering the Past in the Present: Verb Tense Shifts in Autobiographical Memory Narratives." In Thompson, ed., *Autobiographical Memory*, 145–62.

Piscitelli, Adriana. "Love and Ambition: Gender, Memory, and Stories from Brazilian Coffee Plantation Families." In Leydesdorff, Passerini, and Thompson, eds., *Gender and Memory*, 89–103.

Plummer, Ken. *Documents of Life: An Introduction to the Problems and Literature of a Humanistic Method*. London: George Allen and Unwin, 1983.

———. *Documents of Life 2*. London: Sage, 2001.

Pogue, Forrest C. *George C. Marshall*. New York: Viking, 1963.

———. *Pogue's War: Diaries of a WWII Combat Historian*. Lexington: University Press of Kentucky, 2001.

Polishuk, Sandy. *Sticking to the Union: An Oral History of the Life and Times of Julia Ruuttila*. New York: Palgrave Macmillan, 2003.

Polkinghorne, Donald E. *Narrative Knowing and the Human Sciences*. Albany: State University of New York Press, 1988.

Pollock, Della. "Making History Go." In *Exceptional Spaces: Essays in Performance and History*, edited by Della Pollock, 1–45. Chapel Hill: University of North Carolina Press, 1998.

———. "Telling the Told: Performing Like a Family." *Oral History Review* 18, no. 2 (Fall 1990): 1–36.

Polsky, Richard. "An Interview with Elizabeth Mason." *Oral History Review* 27, no. 2 (Summer–Fall 2000): 157–79.

Poniatowska, Elena. "The Earthquake." *Oral History Review* 16, no. 1 (Spring 1988): 7–20.

———. *Hasta No Verte, Jesús Mío*. México: Editiones Era, 1969.

———. *Nothing, Nobody: The Voices of the Mexico City Earthquake*. Translated by Aurora Camacho de Schmidt and Arthur Schmidt. Philadelphia: Temple University Press, 1995.

Popular Memory Group. "Popular Memory: Theory, Politics, Memory." In *Making Histories: Studies in History-Writing and Politics*, edited by Richard Johnson, Gregor McLennan, Bill Schwarz, and David Sutton, 205–52. London: Hutchinson, 1982.

Portelli, Alessandro. "*Absalom, Absalom!*: Oral History and Literature." In *Death of Luigi Trastulli*, 270–82.

———. *The Battle of Valle Giulia: Oral History and the Art of Dialogue*. Madison: University of Wisconsin Press, 1997.

———. *The Death of Luigi Trastulli and Other Stories: Form and Meaning in Oral History*. Albany: State University of New York Press, 1991.

———. "The Death of Luigi Trastulli: Memory and the Event." In *Death of Luigi Trastulli*, 1–26.

———. "Oral History as Genre." In Chamberlain and Thompson, eds., *Narrative and Genre*, 23–45.

———. *The Order Has Been Carried Out: History, Memory, and Meaning of a Nazi Massacre in Rome*. New York: Palgrave Macmillan, 2003.

———. "The Peculiarities of Oral History." *History Workshop Journal* 12 (Autumn 1981): 96–107.

———. "Philosophy and the Facts: Subjectivity and Narrative Form in Autobiography and Oral History." In *Battle of Valle Giulia*, 79–90.

———. "The Time of My Life: Functions of Time in Oral History." *International Journal of Oral History* 2 (1981): 162–80.

———. "Tryin' to Gather a Little Knowledge: Some Thoughts on the Ethics of Oral History." In *Battle of Valle Giulia*, 55–71.

———. "Uchronic Dreams: Working-Class Memory and Possible Worlds." In Samuel and Thompson, eds., *Myths We Live By*, 143–60.

———. "What Makes Oral History Different." In *Death of Luigi Trastulli*, 45–58.

Porter, Bruce. "Has Success Spoiled NPR?" *Columbia Journalism Review* 29, no. 3 (September–October 1990): 26–32.

Powell, James M. Introduction. In *Leopold von Ranke and the Shaping of the Historical Discipline*, edited by Georg G. Iggers and James M. Powell, xiii–xxii. Syracuse, NY: Syracuse University Press, 1990.

Preston, Samuel H., and Michael R. Haines. *Fatal Years: Child Mortality in Late Nineteenth-Century America*. Princeton, NJ: Princeton University Press, 1991.

Pym, Anthony. Review of Olson, *World on Paper*. *European Legacy* 3, no. 1 (February 1998): 134–35.

Quadrango, Jill. *The Color of Welfare: How Racism Undermined the War on Poverty*. New York: Oxford University Press, 1994.

"A Radio 'Newspaper.'" In Marx, ed., *Television and Radio*, 85–88.

Raeff, Marc. "Autocracy Tempered by Reform or by Regicide." *American Historical Review* 98, no. 4 (1993): 1143–55.

Raphaël, Freddy, and Roswitha Breckner. "The German Working Class and National Socialism: Two Reviews." In *Between Generations: Family Models, Myths, and Memories*, edited by Daniel Bertaux and Paul Thompson, 201–6. Oxford: Oxford University Press, 1993.

Rapport, Leonard. "How Valid Are the Federal Writers' Project Life Stories?: An Iconoclast among the True Believers." *Oral History Review* 7 (1979): 6–17.

Read, Peter. "Presenting Voices in Different Media: Print, Radio and CD-ROM." In Perks and Thomson, eds., *Oral History Reader*, 414–20.

Reich, Steve. *Writings about Music*. Halifax: Press of the Nova Scotia College of Art and Design, 1974.

Reid, Benjamin Lawrence. *Necessary Lives: Biographical Reflections*. Columbia: University of Missouri Press, 1990.

Reingold, Nathan. "A Critic Looks at Oral History." In Colman, ed., *Fourth National Colloquium*, 213–27.

Reinharz, Shulamit, and Lynn Davidman. *Feminist Methods in Social Research*. New York: Oxford University Press, 1992.

Rickard, Wendy. "Collaborating with Sex Workers in Oral History." *Oral History Review* 30, no. 1 (Winter–Spring 2003): 47–60.

Ricoeur, Paul. *Interpretation Theory: Discourse and the Surplus of Meaning*. Fort Worth: Texas Christian University Press, 1976.

———. *Time and Narrative*. Translated by Kathleen Blamey, David Pellauer, and Paul Rico. 3 vols. Chicago: University of Chicago Press, 1984–85.

Riley, Matilda White. "Age Stratification." *Encyclopedia of Gerontology: Age, Aging, and the Aged*. New York: Academic, 1996.

Riley, Matilda White, and Ann Foner. *Aging and Society*. New York: Russell Sage, 1968.

Ritchie, Donald A. *Doing Oral History*. New York: Twayne, 1995.

———. *Doing Oral History: A Practical Guide*. 2nd ed. New York: Oxford University Press, 2003.

Roach, Joseph R. *Cities of the Dead: Circum-Atlantic Performance*. New York: Columbia University Press, 1996.

Roberts, Brian. *Biographical Research*. Buckingham: Open University Press, 2002.

Rocha Lima, Valentina da. "Women in Exile: Becoming Feminist." *International Journal of Oral History* 5, no. 2 (June 1984): 81–99.

Rogers, Kim Lacy. "A Crisis of Opportunity: The Movement and Head Start." *Life and Death*, chap. 5. Forthcoming.

———. *Life and Death in the Delta: African American Narratives of Violence, Resilience, and Social Change*. New York: Palgrave, forthcoming.

———. *Righteous Lives: Narratives of the New Orleans Civil Rights Movement*. New York: New York University Press, 1993.

———. "Trauma Redeemed: The Narrative Construction of Social Violence." In McMahan and Rogers, eds., *Interactive Oral History Interviewing*, 31–46.

Rogers, Kim Lacy, Selma Leydesdorff, and Graham Dawson, eds. *Trauma and Life Stories: International Perspectives*. London: Routledge, 1999.

Romney, Joseph. "Legal Considerations in Oral History." *Oral History Review* 1 (1973): 66–76.

Roper, Michael. "Analysing the Analysed: Transference and Counter-Transference in the Oral History Interview." *Oral History: Journal of the Oral History Society* 31, no. 2 (Autumn 2003): 20–32.

Rosaldo, Renato. "Doing Oral History." *Social Analysis* 4 (September 1980): 89–99.

Rosen, Dale, and Theodore Rosengarten. "Shoot-Out at Reeltown: The Narrative of Jess Hull." *Radical America* 6 (November–December 1972): 65–85.

Rosengarten, Theodore. *All God's Dangers: The Life of Nate Shaw*. New York: Knopf, 1974.

———. "Stepping over Cockleburs: Conversations with Ned Cobb." In Edel, *Telling Lives*, 104–31.

Rosenwald, George C., and Richard L. Ochberg, eds. *Storied Lives: The Cultural Politics of Self-Understanding*. New Haven, CT: Yale University Press, 1992.

Rouverol, Alicia J. "Collaborative Oral History in a Correctional Setting: Promise and Pitfalls." *Oral History Review* 30, no. 1 (Winter–Spring 2003): 61–86.

Rubin, David C. "Beginnings of a Theory of Autobiographical Remembering." In Thompson, ed., *Autobiographical Memory*, 47–68.

Rudnick, Lois. "The Male-Identified Woman and Other Anxieties: The Life of Mabel Dodge Luhan." In Alpern et al., eds., *Challenge of Feminist Biography*, 116–38.

Rustin, Michael. "Reflections on the Biographical Turn in Social Science." In Chamberlayne, Bornat, and Wengraf, eds., *Biographical Methods*, 33–52.

Sacks, Oliver. *The Man Who Mistook His Wife for a Hat*. London: Picador, 1986.

Salazar, Claudia. "A Third World Woman's Text: Between the Politics of Criticism and Cultural Politics." In Gluck and Patai, eds., *Women's Words*, 93–106.

Samuel, Raphael. *East End Underworld: The Life of Arthur Harding*. London: Routledge, 1981.

———. "Local History and Oral History." *History Workshop Journal* 1 (Spring 1976): 191–208.

———. "People's History." In *People's History and Socialistic Theory*, xv–xxxix.

———, ed. *People's History and Socialistic Theory*. London: Routledge, 1981.

———. "Perils of the Transcript." *Oral History: Journal of the Oral History Society* 1, no. 2 (1971): 19–22.

———. "Perils of the Transcript." In Perks and Thomson, eds., *Oral History Reader* (1998), 389–92.

———. *Theatres of Memory*. Vol. 1, *Past and Present in Contemporary Culture*. London: Verso, 1994.

———. "Unofficial Knowledge." In *Theatres of Memory* 1: 3–51.

Samuel, Raphael, Alison Light, Sally Alexander, and Gareth Stedman Jones, eds. *Island Stories: Unraveling Britain*. Vol. 2, *Theatres of Memory*. London: Verso, 1998.

Samuel, Raphael, and Paul Thompson. Introduction. In *Myths We Live By*, 1–22.

———, eds. *The Myths We Live By*. London: Routledge, 1990.

Sangster, Joan. "Telling Our Stories: Feminist Debates and the Use of Oral History." *Women's History Review* 3, no. 1 (1994): 5–28.

Sarbin, Theodore R. "Steps to the Narratory Principle: An Autobiographical Essay." In *Life and Story: Autobiographies for a Narrative Psychology*, edited by D. John Lee, 7–38. Westport, CT: Praeger, 1994.

Sarris, Greg. "'The Woman Who Loved a Snake' and 'What People of Elem Saw': Orality in Mabel McKay's Stories." *American Indian Quarterly* 15, no. 2 (Spring 1991): 171–85.

Schacter, Daniel L. *The Seven Sins of Memory: How the Mind Forgets and Remembers*. Boston: Houghton Mifflin Company, 2001.

Schafer, R. Murray. *The Tuning of the World: Toward a Theory of Soundscape*. Philadelphia: University of Pennsylvania Press, 1980.

Schechner, Richard. *Performance Theory*. London: Routledge, 2003.

Schegloff, Emmanuel A. "What Next?: Language and Social Interaction Study at the Century's Turn." *Research on Language and Social Interaction* 32, no. 1/2 (1999): 141–49.

Schendler, Revan. "'They Made the Freedom Themselves': Popular Interpretations of Post-Communist Discourse in the Czech Republic." *Oral History: Journal of the Oral History Society* 29, no. 2 (Autumn 2001): 73–82.

Schiffrin, Deborah. "Linguistics and History: Oral History as Discourse." In *Linguistics, Language, and the Real World: Discourse and Beyond,* edited by Deborah Tannen and James E. Alatis, 84–113. Washington, DC: Georgetown University Press, 2003.

Schiffrin, Deborah, Deborah Tannen, and Heidi E. Hamilton, eds. *The Handbook of Discourse Analysis.* Malden, MA: Blackwell, 2001.

Schippers, Donald J. "Techniques of Oral History Interviewing." In Dixon and Mink, eds., *Oral History at Arrowhead,* 47–68.

Schlesinger, Arthur M., Jr. *The Disuniting of America: Reflections on a Multicultural Society.* New York: Norton, 1992.

———. *Robert Kennedy and His Times.* Vol. 1. Boston: Houghton Mifflin, 1978.

Schneider, William. "Lessons from Alaska Natives about Oral Tradition and Recordings." In *When Our Words Return: Writing, Hearing, and Remembering Oral Traditions of Alaska and the Yukon,* edited by Phyllis Morrow and William Schneider, 185–204. Logan: Utah State University Press, 1995.

———. *So They Understand: Cultural Issues in Oral History.* Logan: Utah State University Press, 2002.

Schorzman, Terri A., ed. *A Practical Introduction to Videohistory: The Smithsonian Institution and Alfred P. Sloan Foundation Experiment.* Malabar, FL: Krieger Publishing, 1993.

Schrager, Samuel. "What Is Social in Oral History?" *International Journal of Oral History* 4, no. 2 (June 1983): 76–98.

Schutz, Alfred. "Common-Sense and Scientific Interpretation of Human Action." In *Collected Papers I: The Problem of Social Reality,* 3–47. The Hague: Martinus Nijhoff, 1962.

Schwartz, Tony. *1, 2, and 3, and a Zing, Zing, Zing: Street Songs and Games of the Children of New York City.* Folkway Records FP 703, 1953. Microgroove.

———. *Media: The Second God.* New York: Random House, 1981.

———. *Nueva York: A Tape Documentary of Puerto Rican New Yorkers.* Folkways Records FP 58-2, 1956. Microgroove.

———. *Sounds of My City: The Stories, Music, and Sounds of the People of New York.* Folkways Records FC741, 1956. Microgroove.

———. *The Responsive Chord.* Garden City, NY: Anchor Press, 1973.

Schwarz, K. Robert. *Minimalists.* London: Phaidon, 1996.

Scott, Joan Wallach. "Gender: A Useful Category of Historical Analysis." In *Feminism and History,* edited by Joan Wallach Scott, 152–80. Oxford: Oxford University Press, 1996.

———. *Gender and the Politics of History.* Rev. ed. New York: Columbia University Press, 1999.

Scully, James. "In Defense of Ideology." In *Line Break: Poetry as Social Practice,* 9–22. Seattle: Bay Press, 1988.

Sewell, William H., Jr. "The Concept(s) of Culture." In Bonnell and Hunt, eds., *Beyond the Cultural Turn,* 35–61.

———. "Narratives and Social Identities." *Social Science History* 16, no. 3 (1992): 479–88.

Shariff, Shamsi. "Narrating History through Oral History Technique in Malaysia." *International Journal of Oral History* 9, no. 1 (February 1988): 40–42.

Sherbakova, Irena. "The Gulag in Memory." In Perks and Thomson, eds., *Oral History Reader*, 235–45.

Shircliffe, Barbara. "'We Got the Best of That World': A Case Study of Nostalgia in the Oral History of School Segregation." *Oral History Review* 28, no. 2 (Summer–Fall 2001): 59–84.

Shopes, Linda. "Commentary: Sharing Authority." *Oral History Review* 30, no. 1 (Winter–Spring 2003): 103–10.

———. "Developing a Critical Dialogue about Oral History: Some Notes Based on an Analysis of Book Reviews." *Oral History Review* 14 (1986): 9–25.

———. "Using Oral History for a Family History Project." In Dunaway and Baum, eds., *Oral History*, 2nd ed., 231–40.

Shore, Miles F. "Biography in the 1980s." *Journal of Interdisciplinary History* 12, no. 1 (Summer 1981): 89–113.

Shores, Louis. "Directions for Oral History." In Dixon and Mink, eds., *Oral History at Arrowhead*, 38–46.

Shortland, Michael, and Richard Yeo. Introduction. In *Telling Lives in Science*, 1–44.

———, eds. *Telling Lives in Science: Essays on Scientific Biography*. Cambridge: Cambridge University Press, 1996.

Siepmann, Charles A. "British, Canadian, and Other Systems." In *Radio, Television, and Society*, chap. 7. New York: Oxford University Press, 1950.

Silverman, David. *Interpreting Qualitative Data: Methods for Analysing Talk, Text, and Interaction*. Thousand Oaks, CA: Sage, 1993.

Sipe, Dan. "Media and Public History: The Future of Oral History and Moving Images." *Oral History Review* 19, nos. 1–2 (Spring–Fall 1991): 75–87.

Sitton, Thad. "The Descendants of *Foxfire*." *Oral History Review* 6 (1978): 20–35.

———, ed. *The Loblolly Book*. Austin: Texas Monthly Press, 1983.

Sitton, Thad, George L. Mehaffy, and O. L. Davis Jr. *Oral History: A Guide for Teachers (and Others)*. Austin: University of Texas Press, 1983.

Sitzia, Lorraine. "Shared Authority: An Impossible Goal?" *Oral History Review* 30, no. 1 (Winter–Spring 2003): 87–102.

Skotnes, Andor. Review of Bernhardt, *New Yorkers at Work*. *Oral History Review* 16, no. 1 (Spring 1989): 203–5.

Slim, Hugo, Paul Thompson, Olivia Bennett, and Nigel Cross. "Ways of Listening." In Perks and Thomson, eds., *Oral History Reader*, 114–25.

Smith, Anna Deavere. *Fires in the Mirror: Crown Heights, Brooklyn and Other Identities*. New York: Anchor/Doubleday, 1993.

Smith, Anthony. *Myths and Memories of the Nation*. Oxford: Oxford University Press, 1999.

Smith, Betty. *A Tree Grows in Brooklyn*. New York: Harper, 1943.

Smith, Bruce R. *The Acoustic World of Early Modern England: Attending to the O-Factor*. Chicago: University of Chicago Press, 1999.

Smith, Dorothy. *The Everyday World as Problematic: A Feminist Sociology*. Boston: Northeastern University Press, 1987.

———. "Some Implications of a Sociology for Women." In *Woman in a Man-made World: A Socioeconomic Handbook*, 2nd ed., edited by Nona Glazer and Helen Y. Washrer, 15–39. Chicago: Rand McNally, 1977.

Smith, Judi Moore. *Never a Man Spake Like This*. Washington, DC: National Federation of Community Broadcasters, 1982. Audiocassette.

Smith, Richard Cándida. "Popular Memory and Oral Narratives: Luisa Passerini's Reading of Oral History Interviews." *Oral History Review* 16, no. 2 (Fall 1988): 95–107.

Smith, S. A. "The Social Meanings of Swearing: Workers and Bad Language in Late Imperial and Early Soviet Russia." *Past & Present* 160 (August 1998): 167–202.

Smith, Sidonie, and Julia Watson. *Reading Autobiography: A Guide for Interpreting Life Narratives*. Minneapolis: University of Minnesota Press, 2001.

Smith, Stephen, and Deborah Amos. *Remembering Jim Crow: African Americans Tell about Life in the Segregated South*. St. Paul: Minnesota Public Radio, 2001. Compact disc.

Smith, Steven B. *Reading Althusser: An Essay on Structural Marxism*. Ithaca, NY: Cornell University Press, 1984.

Soapes, Thomas F. "The Federal Writers' Project Slave Interviews: Useful Data or Misleading Source." *Oral History Review* 5 (1977): 33–38.

Soderqvist, Thomas. "Existential Projects and Existential Choice in Science: Science Biography as an Edifying Genre." In Shortland and Yeo, eds., *Telling Lives in Science*, 45–84.

Somers, Margaret. "Narrativity, Narrative Identity and Social Action: Rethinking English Working Class Formation." *Social Science History* 16, no. 4 (Winter 1992): 591–630.

Sommer, Barbara W., and Mary Kay Quinlan. *The Oral History Manual*. Walnut Creek, CA: AltaMira, 2002.

Sommer, Doris. "'Not Just a Personal Story': Women's *Testimonios* and the Plural Self." In *Life/Lines: Theoretical Essays on Women's Autobiography*, edited by Bella Brodzki and Celeste Schenck, 107–30. Ithaca, NY: Cornell University Press, 1988.

Spence, Donald P. *Narrative Truth and Historical Truth: Meaning and Interpretation in Psychoanalysis*. New York: Norton, 1982.

Sperber, A. M. *Murrow: His Life and Times*. New York: Freundlich, 1986.

Spivak, Gayatri Chakravorty. "The Politics of Interpretation." In *The Politics of Interpretation*, edited by W. J. T. Mitchell, 347–66. Chicago: University of Chicago Press, 1983.

Stacey, Judith. "Can There Be a Feminist Ethnography?" In Gluck and Patai, eds., *Women's Words*, 111–19.

Stanley, Liz. *The Auto/Biographical 'I': Theory and Practice of Feminist Auto/Biography*. Manchester, England: Manchester University Press, 1992.

———. "How Do We Know About Past Lives? Methodological and Epistemological Matters Involving Prince Philip, the Russian Revolution, Emily Wilding Davison, My Mum and the Absent Sue." In *Women's Lives into Print: The Theory, Practice and Writing of Feminist Auto/Biography*, edited by Pauline Polkey, 3–21. London: Macmillan, 1999.

Stannard, David E. "Death and the Puritan Child." In *Death in America*, 9–29. Philadelphia: University of Pennsylvania Press, 1975.

Stannard, Martin. "A Matter of Life and Death." In *Writing the Lives of Writers*, edited by Warwick Gould and Thomas F. Staley, 1–17. New York: St. Martin's, 1998.

Starr, Louis. "Oral History." In Dunaway and Baum, eds., *Oral History* (1984), 3–26.

———. Review of *The Voice of the Past*, by Paul Thompson. *Oral History Review* 6 (1978): 67–68.

———. *The Second National Colloquium on Oral History*. New York: Oral History Association, 1968.

Steedman, Carolyn. "Enforced Narratives: Stories of Another Self." In Cosslett, Lury, and Summerfield, eds., *Feminism and Autobiography*, 25–39.

Stein, Jean. *American Journey: The Times of Robert Kennedy*. Edited by George Plimpton. New York: Harcourt, Brace, Jovanovich, 1970.

Steinmetz, George. "Reflections on the Role of Social Narrative in Working Class Formation: Narrative Theory in the Social Sciences." *Social Science History* 16, no. 3 (1992): 489–516.

Stephens, Carlene. "Videohistory at Waltham Clock Company: An Assessment." In Schorzman, ed., *Introduction to Videohistory*, 101–13.

Stevens, Anthony. *Private Myths: Dreams and Dreaming*. Cambridge, MA: Harvard University Press, 1995.

Stone, Lawrence. "The Revival of Narrative: Reflections on an Old New History." *Past and Present* 85 (1979): 3–24.

Storm-Clark, Christopher. "The Miners: The Relevance of Oral Evidence." *Oral History: Journal of the Oral History Society* 1, no. 4 (1970): 72–92.

Strassler, Robert B., ed. *The Landmark Thucydides: A Comprehensive Guide to the Peloponnesian War*. New York: Free Press, 1996.

Strauss, Anselm, and Juliet Corbin. *Basis of Qualitative Research: Grounded Theory Procedures and Techniques*. Thousand Oaks, CA: Sage, 1998.

Strouse, Jean. "The Real Reasons." In *Extraordinary Lives: The Art and Craft of American Biography*, edited by William Zinsser, 161–95. New York: American Heritage, 1986.

Strickland, Edward. *American Composers: Dialogues on Contemporary Music*. Bloomington: Indiana University Press, 1991.

Stricklin, David, and Rebecca Sharpless, eds. *The Past Meets the Present: Essays on Oral History*. Lanham, MD: University Press of America, 1988.

Summerfield, Penny. *Reconstructing Women's Wartime Lives: Discourse and Subjectivity in Oral Histories of the Second World War*. Manchester, England: Manchester University Press, 1998.

Susman, Warren I. "History and the American Intellectual: Uses of a Usable Past." *American Quarterly* 16, Part 2 (Summer 1964): 243–63.

Swedenburg, Ted. *Memories of Revolt*. Minneapolis: University of Minnesota Press, 1995.

Talsma, Jaap, and Selma Leydesdorff. "Oral History in the Netherlands." In Hartewig and Halbach, eds., "History of Oral History," 65–75.

Tannen, Deborah. "The Commingling of Orality and Literacy in Giving a Paper at a Scholarly Conference." *American Speech* 63, no. 1 (1988): 34–43.

———, ed. *Spoken and Written Language: Exploring Orality and Literacy*. Norwood, NJ: Ablex, 1982.

———. *You Just Don't Understand: Women and Men in Conversation*. New York: Ballantine, 1990.

Taylor, Jeremy. *Where People Fly and Water Runs Uphill*. New York: Warner, 1993.

Taylor, Shelley E., Laura Cousino Klein, Brian P. Lewis, Tara L. Gruenewald, Regan A. R. Gurung, and John A. Updegraff. "Biobehavioral Responses to Stress in Females: Tend-and-Befriend, Not Fight-or-Flight." *Psychological Review* 107, no. 3 (2000): 411–29.

Tedlock, Dennis. *Finding the Center: Narrative Poetry of the Zuni Indians*. New York: Dial, 1972.

———. "Learning to Listen: Oral Poetry as History." In Grele, *Envelopes of Sound*, 2nd ed., 106–25.

———. "On the Translation of Style in Oral Narrative." *Journal of American Folklore* 84 (1971): 114–33.

Terkel, Studs. *American Dreams: Lost and Found*. New York: Pantheon, 1980.

———. *Born to Live: Hiroshima, with Documentary Recordings*. Folkways Records FD5525, 1965. Microgroove.

———. *Division Street: America*. New York: Pantheon, 1967.

———. *"The Good War": An Oral History of World War Two*. New York: Pantheon, 1984.

———. *Hard Times: An Oral History of the Great Depression*. New York: Pantheon, 1970.

———. *Hard Times: The Story of the Depression in the Voices of Those Who Lived It. The Original Tapes on Which the Book Was Based*. Caedmon, 1971. Microgroove and audiocassette.

———. *Interviews with Interviewers—About Interviewing*. New York: In Motion Productions, 1985. Videorecording.

———. *Race: How Blacks and Whites Think and Feel about the American Obsession*. New York: Pantheon, 1992.

———. *Talking to Myself: A Memoir of My Times*. New York: Pantheon, 1973.

———. *Will the Circle Be Unbroken?: Reflections on Death, Rebirth, and Hunger for a Faith*. New York: Pantheon, 2001.

———. *Working: People Talk about What They Do All Day and How They Feel about What They Do*. New York: Pantheon, 1974.

Terrill, Tom E., and Jerrold Hirsch. "Replies to Leonard Rapport's 'How Valid Are the Federal Writers' Project Life Stories, An Iconoclast among the True Believers.'" *Oral History Review* 8 (1980): 81–92.

Thelen, David. "Memory and American History." *Journal of American History* 75, no. 4 (March 1989): 1117–29.

Therborn, Goran. *The Power of Ideology and The Ideology of Power*. London: Verso, 1980.

Thomas, Sherry. "Digging Beneath the Surface: Oral History Techniques." *Frontiers: Journal of Women Studies* 7, no. 1 (1983): 50–55.

———. *We Didn't Have Much, But We Sure Had Plenty: Stories of Rural Women*. Garden City, NY: Anchor, 1981.

Thomas, William Isaac, and Florian Znaniecki. *The Polish Peasant in Europe and America: Monograph of an Immigrant Group.* 5 vols. Chicago: University of Chicago Press, 1918–1920.

Thompson, Charles P., ed. *Autobiographical Memory: Theoretical and Applied Perspectives.* Mahwah, NJ: Erlbaum, 1998.

Thompson, Paul. "The Achievement of Oral History." In *Voice of the Past* (1978), 65–90.

———. "Believe It or Not: Rethinking the Historical Interpretation of Memory." In Jeffrey and Edwall, eds., *Memory and History,* 1–16.

———. *The Edwardians: The Remaking of British Society.* Bloomington: Indiana University Press, 1975.

———. "Evidence." In *Voice of the Past* (1978), 91–137.

———. "Oral History in North America." *Oral History: Journal of the Oral History Society* 3, no. 1 (1975): 26–40.

———. "Problems of Method in Oral History." *Oral History: Journal of the Oral History Society* 1, no. 4 (1971): 1–47.

———. "Projects." In *Voice of the Past,* 2nd ed., 166–95.

———. "Sharing and Reshaping Life Stories: Problems and Potential in Archiving Research Narratives." In Chamberlain and Thompson, eds., *Narrative and Genre,* 167–81.

———. *The Voice of the Past: Oral History.* Oxford: Oxford University Press, 1978.

———. *The Voice of the Past: Oral History.* 2nd ed. New York: Oxford University Press, 1988.

———. *The Voice of the Past: Oral History.* 3rd ed. Oxford: Oxford University Press, 2000.

Thompson, Paul, and Natasha Burchart, eds. *Our Common History: The Transformation of Europe.* Atlantic Highlands, NJ: Humanities Press, 1982.

Thompson, Paul, Luisa Passerini, Isabelle Bertaux-Wiame, and Alessandro Portelli. "Between Social Scientists: Responses to Louise A. Tilly." *International Journal of Oral History* 6, no. 1 (February 1985): 19–39.

Thomson, Alistair. "The Anzac Legend: Exploring National Myth and Memory in Australia." In Samuel and Thompson, eds., *Myths We Live By,* 73–82.

———. *Anzac Memories: Living with the Legend.* Oxford: Oxford University Press, 1994.

———. "Anzac Memories: Putting Popular Memory Theory into Practice in Australia." *Oral History: Journal of the Oral History Society* 18, no. 2 (1990): 25–31.

———. "Sharing Authority: Oral History and the Collaborative Process." *Oral History Review* 30, no. 1 (Winter–Spring 2003): 23–26.

Tilly, Louise. "Louise Tilly's Response to Thompson, Passerini, Bertaux-Wiame, and Portelli." *International Journal of Oral History* 6, no. 1 (February 1985): 40–42.

———. "People's History and Social History." *International Journal of Oral History* 6, no. 1 (February 1985): 5–18.

Tixier y Vigil, Yvonne, and Nan Elsasser. "The Effects of the Ethnicity of the Interviewer on Conversation: A Study of Chicana Women." In *Proceedings of the Conference on the Sociology of the Languages of American Women,* 2nd ed., edited by Betty DuBois and Isabel Crouch, 161–70. San Antonio, TX: Trinity University Press, 1983.

Tolnay, Stewart. *The Bottom Rung: African American Family Life on Southern Farms.* Urbana: University of Illinois Press, 1999.

Tonkin, Elizabeth. "The Boundaries of History in Oral Performance." *History in Africa* 9 (1982): 273–84.

————. "Implications of Oracy: An Anthropological View." *Oral History: Journal of the Oral History Society* 3, no. 1 (Spring 1975): 41–49.

————. *Narrating Our Pasts: The Social Construction of Oral History.* Cambridge: Cambridge University Press, 1992.

————. "Subjective or Objective? Debates on the Nature of Oral History." In *Narrating Our Pasts,* 83–96.

Torpey, John, ed. *Politics and the Past: On Repairing Historical Injustices.* New York: Rowman and Littlefield, 2003.

Treleven, Dale E. "An Interview with Jim Mink." *Oral History Review* 27, no. 1 (Winter–Spring 2000): 117–42.

————. "Oral History Audio Technology and the TAPE System." *International Journal of Oral History* 2, no. 1 (February 1981): 26–47.

Trouillot, Michel-Rolph. *Silencing the Past: Power and the Production of History.* Boston: Beacon, 1995.

Truax, Barry. *Acoustic Communication.* Norwood, NJ: Ablax, 1984.

Tuchman, Barbara. "Biography as a Prism of History." In Edel, *Telling Lives,* 132–47.

————. "Distinguishing the Significant from the Insignificant." In Dunaway and Baum, eds., *Oral History* (1984), 74–78.

————. "Distinguishing the Significant from the Insignificant." In Dunaway and Baum, eds., *Oral History,* 2nd ed. (1996), 94–98.

Tucker, Robert. "A Stalin Biographer's Memoir." In Baron and Pletsch, eds., *Introspection in Biography,* 249–71.

Turner, Victor Witter. *The Anthropology of Performance.* New York: PAJ, 1988.

Ullman, Maurice, and Nan Zimmerman. *Working with Dreams.* Los Angeles: Tarcher, 1985.

Vaillant, George E. *Adaptation to Life.* Boston: Little, Brown, 1977.

Van Bogart, John W. C. *Magnetic Tape Storage and Handling: A Guide for Libraries and Archives.* Washington, DC: Commission on Preservation and Access, 1995.

Van den Hoonaard, Will C., ed. *Walking the Tightrope: Ethical Issues for Qualitative Researchers.* Toronto: University of Toronto Press, 2002.

Vandiver, Frank E. "Biography as an Agent of Humanism." In Oates, ed., *Biography as High Adventure,* 50–64.

Van Maanen, John. *Representation in Ethnography.* Thousand Oaks, CA: Sage, 1995.

Vansina, Jan. *Oral Tradition.* Harmondsworth: Penguin, 1961.

————. *Oral Tradition: A Study in Historical Methodology.* Chicago: Aldine, 1965.

————. *Oral Tradition as History.* Madison: University of Wisconsin Press, 1985.

Vasari, Giorgio. *The Lives of the Artists.* New York : Oxford University Press, 1998.

Viagas, Robert, Baayork Lee, and Thommie Walsh. *On the Line: The Creation of a Chorus Line*. New York: William Morrow, 1990.

Vigne, Thea, ed. "Family History." Special issue, *Oral History: Journal of the Oral History Society* 3, no. 2 (Autumn 1975).

Vilanova, Mercedes. "The Struggle for a History without Adjectives: A Note on Using Oral History Sources in Spain." *Oral History Review* 24, no. 1 (Summer 1994): 81–90.

Wallot, Jean-Pierre, and Normand Fortier. "Archival Science and Oral Sources." In Perks and Thomson, eds., *Oral History Reader*, 365–78.

Wagner-Martin, Linda. *Telling Women's Lives: The New Biography*. New Brunswick, NJ: Rutgers University Press, 1994.

Ward, Alan. *A Manual of Sound Archive Administration*. Brookfield, VT: Gower, 1990.

Warner-Lewis, Maureen. *Guinea's Other Suns: The African Dynamic in Trinidad Culture*. Dover, MA: Majority, 1991.

Waserman, Manfred, comp. *Bibliography on Oral History*. New York: Oral History Association, 1971.

———. *Bibliography on Oral History*. Rev. ed. New York: Oral History Association, 1975.

Watson, Lawrence. "Understanding a Life History as a Subjective Document: Hermeneutical and Phenomenological Perspectives." *Ethos* 4, no. 1 (Spring 1976): 95–131.

Webb, Walter Prescott. "History as High Adventure." In *An Honest Preface and Other Essays*, 194–216. Boston: Houghton Mifflin, 1959.

Weidman, Bette S. "Oral History in Biography: A Shaping Source." *International Journal of Oral History* 8 (February 1987): 41–55.

Wekker, Gloria. "One Finger Does Not Drink Okra Soup: Afro-Surinamese Women and Critical Agency." In *Feminist Genealogies, Colonial Legacies, Democratic Futures*, edited by M. Jacqui Alexander and Chandra Talpade Mohanty, 330–52. London: Routledge, 1997.

Welch, H. Mason. "A Lawyer Looks at Oral History." In Colman, ed., *Fourth National Colloquium*, 182–95.

White, Hayden. *The Content of the Form: Narrative Discourse and Historical Representation*. Baltimore, MD: Johns Hopkins University Press, 1987.

———. "Foucault Decoded: Notes from Underground." *History and Theory* 12, no. 1 (1973): 23–54.

———. *Metahistory: The Historical Imagination in Nineteenth Century Europe*. Baltimore, MD: Johns Hopkins University Press, 1973.

White, Naomi Rosh. "Marking Absences: Holocaust Testimony and History." In Perks and Thomson, eds., *Oral History Reader*, 172–82.

Whorf, Benjamin. "Language, Mind, and Reality." In Carroll, *Language, Thought, and Reality*, 246–70.

———. "The Relation of Habitual Thought and Behavior to Language." In Carroll, *Language, Thought and Reality*, 134–59.

Wigginton, Eliot, ed. *The Foxfire Book*. Garden City, NY: Doubleday, 1972.

———. *Sometimes a Shining Moment: The Foxfire Experience, Twenty Years Teaching in a High School Classroom*. Garden City, NY: Anchor Books/Doubleday, 1985.

Williams, Brien. "Recording Videohistory: A Perspective." In Schorzman, ed., *Introduction to Videohistory*, 138–54.

Williams, T. Harry. *Huey Long*. New York: Knopf, 1969.

Wilmsen, Carl. "For the Record: Editing and the Production of Meaning in Oral History." *Oral History Review* 28, no. 1 (Winter/Spring 2001): 65–85.

Winograd, Eugene. "The Authenticity and Utility of Memories." In Neisser and Fivush, eds., *Remembering Self*, 243–51.

Winslow, Donald J. *Life-Writing: A Glossary of Terms*. Honolulu: University Press of Hawaii, 1980.

Winter, J. M., and Emmanuel Sivan. "Setting the Framework." In *War and Remembrance in the Twentieth Century*, 6–39. Cambridge: Cambridge University Press, 1999.

Witherspoon, John, and Roselle Kovitz. *The History of Public Broadcasting*. Washington, DC: Current, 1987.

Wood, Linda P. *Oral History Projects in Your Classroom*. Dickinson, PA: Oral History Association, 2001.

Woodruff, Nan Elizabeth. *American Congo: The African American Freedom Struggle in the Delta*. Cambridge, MA: Harvard University Press, 2003.

Woods, Clyde. *Development Arrested: The Blues and Plantation Power in the Mississippi Delta*. London: Verso, 1999.

Woolf, Virginia. *A Writer's Diary: Being Extracts from the Diary of Virginia Woolf*. Edited by Leonard Woolf. New York: Harcourt, Brace, 1954.

Wrong, Dennis. "The Over-socialized Concept of Man in Modern Sociology." *American Journal of Sociology* 26, no. 2 (1961): 183–93.

X, Malcolm. *The Autobiography of Malcolm X*. With Alex Haley. New York: Grove, 1965.

Yans-McLaughlin, Virginia. "Metaphors of Self in History: Subjectivity, Oral Narrative, and Immigration Studies." In *Immigration Reconsidered: History, Sociology, and Politics*, 254–92. New York: Oxford University Press, 1990.

Yeo, Stephen. "The Politics of Community Publications." In Samuel, *People's History and Socialist Theory*, 44–46.

Yow, Valerie Raleigh. *Bernice Kelly Harris: A Good Life Was Writing*. Baton Rouge: Louisiana State University Press, 1999.

———. "Betty Smith and *A Tree Grows in Brooklyn*." Unpublished manuscript.

———. "'Do I Like Them Too Much?': Effects of the Oral History Interview on the Interviewer and Vice-Versa." *Oral History Review* 24 (Summer 1997): 55–79.

———. "Ethics and Interpersonal Relationships in Oral History Research." *Oral History Review* 22, no. 1 (Summer 1995): 51–66.

———. *Recording Oral History: A Guide for the Humanities and Social Sciences*. 2nd ed. New York: Rowman and Littlefield, 2005.

———. *Recording Oral History: A Practical Guide for Social Scientists*. Thousand Oaks, CA: Sage, 1994.

Zimmerman, Don H. "On Conversation: The Conversation Analytic Perspective." In *Communication Yearbook* 11, edited by J. A. Anderson, 406–32. Newbury Park, CA: Sage, 1988.

Zorbaugh, Harvey. *The Gold Coast and the Slum: A Sociological Study of Chicago's Near North Side*. Chicago: University of Chicago Press, 1929.

Index

About the Editors
and Contributors

Mary Chamberlain is professor of modern social history at Oxford Brookes University. She was one of the pioneers of oral history and life story methods and has published widely on these and, most recently, on the Caribbean and Caribbean families. Her books include *Fenwomen* (1975; trans. 1976; 1983), *Old Wives Tales* (1981; trans. 1983), *Writing Lives* (ed. 1988), *Growing Up in Lambeth* (1989), *Narratives of Exile and Return* (1997, 2004) and *Family Love in the Diaspora: Migration and the Anglo-Caribbean Experience* (2005). In addition, she is editor of *Caribbean Migration: Globalised Identities* (1998); co-editor, with Paul Thompson, of *Narrative and Genre* (1998, 2004); and co-editor, with Harry Goulbourne, of *Caribbean Families in Britain and the Transatlantic World* (2001). She is a fellow of the Royal Historical Society, a principal editor of the book series Studies in Memory and Narrative, and has served on a number of editorial, academic, and governmental advisory boards.

An Arkansas native and naturalized Texan, **Thomas L. Charlton** holds degrees in history from Baylor University (B.A.) and the University of Texas at Austin (M.A. and Ph.D.). He has been on the Baylor faculty since 1970, specializing in the history of Texas and the Southwest, the American South, public history/historic preservation, and oral history. He has been an active member of the Department of History, directed the Institute for Oral History (1970–1993), and served as vice provost in three capacities (1992–2003), and has served as director of the Texas Collection library/archival center since 2003. He has been active in oral history research and teaching at both the state level (cofounder of the Texas Oral History Association, TOHA) and the national level (active in the Oral History Association, OHA president in 1990–1991). TOHA honored him with its first lifetime achievement award in 1999. He is the author of *Oral History for Texans* (1981, 1985).

Pamela Dean received her B.A. and M.A. in history from the University of Maine and her Ph.D. in history from the University of North Carolina at Chapel Hill. She was the founding director of the T. Harry Williams Center for Oral History at Louisiana State University, where she wrote and produced *You've Got to Hear This Story* (1998), a how-to video on oral history interviewing. She is now the archivist for the Maine Folklife Center at the University of Maine and host and producer of the radio program *Maine Roots: Traditional Music and Stories from the Archives of the Maine Folklife Center.*

James E. Fogerty is head of the Acquisitions and Curatorial Department of the Minnesota Historical Society, which includes the society's Oral History Office. He has directed oral history projects with a number of immigrant communities and for individual corporations, on issues relating to agriculture, the environment, the recreation industry, and the medical device industry. He teaches workshops on the use of oral history and videohistory in archives, corporations, and cultural organizations. Fogerty is a fellow of the Society of American Archivists and served on its governing council and on the council of the Oral History Association. He chaired the Oral Sources Committee of the International Council on Archives and is currently a member of its Business Archives Section. He has authored numerous articles, especially on the development of oral history and archives in business.

Dancer and choreographer **Jeff Friedman** was based in San Francisco from 1979 to 1997. After completing his Ph.D. research at the University of California, Riverside, focusing on embodied aspects of oral history, Friedman was appointed to the dance faculty of Mason Gross School of the Arts at Rutgers, the State University of New Jersey, in 2003. Jeff's most recent publications are "Performing Embodied Memory" in *Sounds and Gestures of Recollection: Art and the Performance of Memory* (2003), based on his solo performance work *Muscle Memory*, and a forthcoming article for the *Journal of the British Oral History Society*. He is founding director of LEGACY Oral History Project, which has documented life histories of performing artists since 1988.

Sherna Berger Gluck directs the oral history program at California State University, Long Beach, where she formerly taught women's studies. She is considered a pioneer in women's oral history and published the first methodological article in the field in the U.S. In 1991, with Daphne Patai, she co-edited *Women's Words: The Feminist Practice of Oral History*. Her own publications include *From Parlor to Prison* (1976); *Rosie the Riveter Revisited* (1987); and *An American Feminist in Palestine* (1994). She recently launched the Virtual Oral/Aural History Archive project, which presents complete oral history (audio) recordings at the World Wide Web: http://salticid.nmc.csulb.edu/cgi-bin/WebObjects/OralAural.woa.

Ronald J. Grele is the former director of the Columbia University Oral History Research Office in New York City and a former president of the Oral History Association. He is the author of *Envelopes of Sound: The Art of Oral History* (1975, 1985) and editor of *Subjectivity and Multiculturalism in Oral History* (1992). For many years, he was editor of the *International Journal of Oral History* and taught a graduate seminar in oral history with the Columbia University Department of History. His essay in this volume is part of a larger project on the state of the art of oral history.

A member since 1990 of the Department of History of West Chester University, in Pennsylvania, **Charles Hardy III** is an award-winning producer of radio, video, and Web-based documentaries. His two-and-a-half hour essay-in-sound, "I Can Almost See the Lights of Home: A Field Trip to Harlan County,

Kentucky," which appears online in *Journal of Multimedia History* 2 (1999), co-authored with Alessandro Portelli, won the 1999 Oral History Association's biennial Nonprint Media Award. Currently, he is supervising historian for ExplorePAHistory.com, a collaborative state history Web site, at http://www.explorePA history.com, that builds historical content and lesson plans around Pennsylvania's historical markers.

Alice M. Hoffman taught labor history and founded the Labor Archives and Oral History Project at the Pennsylvania State University. She subsequently taught oral history methodology at Bryn Mawr College. She has been active in the Oral History Association from its inception and has held the office of both secretary and president. She has served as the president of the Pennsylvania Labor History Society. With Howard Hoffman, she is author of *Archives of Memory: A Soldier Recalls World War II* (1990).

Howard S. Hoffman taught experimental psychology, first at the Pennsylvania State University and later, for more than twenty years, at Bryn Mawr College, where he is now professor emeritus. He served for eight years as a member and then chairman of a National Institute of Mental Health Committee to peer review applications for research grants. Throughout his career, his research was focused on the areas of social attachment, perception, and memory. With Alice Hoffman, he is author of *Archives of Memory: A Soldier Recalls World War II* (1990).

Mary A. Larson, who earned her Ph.D. from Brown University, came to oral history from a background in anthropology. She is the assistant director at the University of Nevada Oral History Program, having worked previously with the oral history office at the University of Alaska, Fairbanks. From service as media review editor for the *Oral History Review* and on many committees of the Oral History Association, she has moved to elected membership on the OHA Council. She is also editor for the H-Oral-hist discussion list. On the regional level, Mary served six years on the board of the Southwest Oral History Association. Her research interests include the geographical areas of the Inter-mountain West and the Arctic as well as issues pertaining to the methods and ethics of digitizing oral histories and increasing their accessibility.

Elinor A. Mazé is a member of the faculty of Baylor University and serves as senior editor at the university's Institute for Oral History. She holds an M.L.S. degree from Texas Woman's University and M.A. and B.A. degrees from the University of Texas at Austin. She has taught English in Japan and served as a technical reference librarian in Saudi Arabia before joining Baylor in 2001.

Eva M. McMahan, professor and director, School of Communication Studies, James Madison University, received her Ph.D. in interpersonal communication from the University of Illinois, Urbana-Champaign. She is the author of numerous scholarly papers and publications in the areas of oral history, interpersonal communication, and medical communication. She is the author of *Elite Oral History Discourse: A Study of Cooperation and Coherence* (1989) and co-editor of *Interactive Oral History Interviewing* (1994). McMahan's teaching experience includes classes in interpersonal communication, persuasion, and media studies. As a consultant to medical teams, education administrators, and management personnel, McMahan specializes in leadership, teamwork, and diversity.

A past president of the Oral History Association, **Charles T. Morrissey** began his career in 1962 by interviewing former members of the White House staff during the Truman administration for the Truman Library, and he subsequently directed the John F. Kennedy Library Oral History Project. He has also directed projects for and about the Ford Foundation, the Pew Charitable Trusts, the Howard Hughes Medical Institute, the Bush Foundation of Minnesota, Baylor College of Medicine in Houston, and a Washington group, Former Members of Congress. He frequently teaches oral history workshops and has published more than fifty articles about oral history skills and applications.

Lois E. Myers is associate director of the Baylor University Institute for Oral History, in Waco, Texas, where since 1986 she has participated in all the steps of creating oral history, from planning to publication. Secretary/treasurer of the Texas Oral History Association since 1987, she consults with a wide variety of people involved in recording the histories of their communities, occupations, families, and businesses. She has conducted numerous workshops on oral history methodology and is active in the national Oral History Association. She is author of *Letters by Lamplight: A Woman's View of Everyday Life in South Texas 1873-1883* (1991) and co-author, with historian Rebecca Sharpless and photographer Clark Baker, of *Rock beneath the Sand: Country Churches in Texas* (2003).

Kim Lacy Rogers, professor of history and American studies at Dickinson College in Carlisle, Pennsylvania, is the author of *Righteous Lives: Narratives of the New Orleans Civil Rights Movement* (1993). She is also co-editor, with Eva M. McMahan, of *Interactive Oral History Interviewing* (1994) and co-editor, with Selma Leydesdorff and Graham Dawson, of *Trauma and Life-Stories: International Perspectives* (1999). Her most recent work is *Life and Death in the Delta: African American Narratives of Violence, Resilience, and Social Change* (forthcoming). She lives in Carlisle with several genteel boxer dogs.

Rebecca Sharpless began her work in oral history in 1977, transcribing interviews on an electric typewriter with lots of Liquid Paper. After receiving her bachelor's and master's degrees from Baylor University, she completed her Ph.D. degree at Emory University and returned to Baylor in 1993 as director of the Institute for Oral History, where she conducts interviews on a wide variety of topics. She is the author of *Fertile Ground, Narrow Choices: Women on Texas Cotton Farms, 1900–1940* (1999) and co-author of *Rock beneath the Sand: Country Churches in Texas* (2003). She is former executive council member and executive secretary of the Oral History Association and is the 2005–2006 president. She teaches courses on U.S. history and oral history at Baylor.

A historian at the Pennsylvania Historical and Museum Commission, **Linda Shopes** has participated in and consulted on dozens of oral history projects. She has written widely on both oral and public history, including, most recently, "Making Sense of Oral History" for the Historymatters Web site, available at http://historymatters.gmu.edu/sme/oral. She is a past president of the Oral History Association, for whom she also cochaired the committee that drafted the legal and ethical guidelines in the *Oral History Evaluation Guidelines*. She currently co-edits the Palgrave Studies in Oral History Series. Also, She has been active in efforts throughout the U.S. to exclude oral history from regulations governing research on what are termed human subjects.

Richard Cándida Smith is professor of history at the University of California at Berkeley, where he also directs the Regional Oral History Office. He is the author of *Utopia and Dissent: Art, Poetry, and Politics in California* (1995) and *Mallarmé's Children: Symbolism and the Renewal of Experience* (1999), and the editor of *Art and the Performance of Memory: Sounds and Gestures of Recollection* (2003).

Valerie Raleigh Yow, book review editor for the *Oral History Review*, received a Ph.D. in history from the University of Wisconsin. Her first oral history project (1974–1975) involved interviewing three generations of women mill workers in Carrboro, North Carolina. A member of the Oral History Association, the Organization of American Historians, and Cheiron, the International Society for the History of the Behavioral and Social Sciences, Yow teaches workshops on oral history and is a consultant on oral history projects. Her textbook on the in-depth interview, *Recording Oral History: A Guide for the Social Sciences and Humanities* (1994), was published in its second edition by AltaMira Press in 2005. Her first published biography was *Bernice Kelly Harris: A Good Life Was Writing* (1999), and her most recently researched biography has been submitted for publication with the title *Betty Smith and A Tree Grows in Brooklyn*. In addition to her oral history scholarship, Yow is a community activist, working on issues of peace, social justice, and protection of the natural environment. A member of the C. G. Jung Society of the Research Triangle and the North Carolina Psychoanalytic Association, she maintains a private psychotherapy practice in Chapel Hill, North Carolina.